COWBOYS FULL

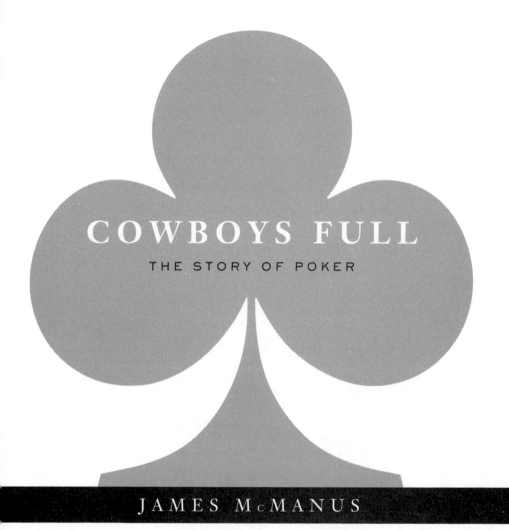

COWBOYS FULL

THE STORY OF POKER

JAMES McMANUS

FARRAR, STRAUS AND GIROUX

NEW YORK

Farrar, Straus and Giroux
18 West 18th Street, New York 10011

Library of Congress Cataloging-in-Publication Data
McManus, James.
    Cowboys full : the story of poker / James McManus.
        p.   cm.
    Includes bibliographical references and index.
    ISBN 978-0-374-29924-8 (hardcover)
    1. Poker—History.   2. Poker—Social aspects.   I. Title.

GV1251.M398 2009
795.412—dc22
                                                    2009029533

Designed by Debbie Glasserman

www.fsgbooks.com

1   3   5   7   9   10   8   6   4   2

JAA

The Kid laid down a full-house—three kings and a pair of treys—which made Fallon's aces look small. As The Kid hauled in the mountain of chips he'd won, he announced, "That's the last poker-hand I'll play! I'm cured!"

—Kenneth Gilbert, *Alaskan Poker Stories*

With bluffs so much easier to make and threats so much more portentous than any previous time in history, it is essential not only for our own State Department but for the entire world to understand what bluffs and threats mean; when they are appropriate; whether they should be avoided at all cost; in short, what is the sanest way to play this deadly, real-life version of poker.

—Oskar Morgenstern, on the subject of nuclear diplomacy

CONTENTS

COWBOYS FULL

POKERTICIANS

The game is the same, it's just up on another level.
— BOB DYLAN, "PO' BOY"

Poker skill didn't vault Barack Obama into the presidency. No cool-eyed read of a Hillary Clinton tell made it obvious he should reraise her claims to be an agent of change. Nor did he shrewdly calculate the pot odds necessary to call John McCain on his commitment to the Bush economic policies or extending the war in Iraq. At least not literally, he didn't. But when Senator Obama was asked by the Associated Press in 2007 to list a hidden talent, he said, "I'm a pretty good poker player." He seemed to be talking about the tabletop card game, but the evidence also suggests he was right in the much larger sense.

As a writer, law professor, and community organizer, Obama was greeted coolly by some of his fellow legislators when, in 1998, he arrived in Springfield to take a seat in the Illinois Senate. Springfield had long been the province of cynical, corrupt backroom operators, hidebound Republicans and Democrats addicted to partisan gridlock. So how was this ink-stained, highly educated greenhorn supposed to get along with Chicago ward heelers and conservative downstate farmers? By playing poker with them, of course.

"When it turned out that I could sit down at [a bar] and have a beer and watch a game or go out for a round of golf or get a poker game going," Obama recalled, "I probably confounded some of their expectations." He was referring to the regular Wednesday night game that he and his fellow freshman senator, Terry Link, a Democrat from suburban Lake County, got going in the basement of Link's Springfield house. Called the Committee Meeting, its initial core was four players, but it quickly grew to eight regulars, including Republicans and lobbyists, and developed a waiting list. But whatever your affiliation, Link says, "You hung up your guns at the door. Nobody talked about their jobs or politics, and certainly no 'influence' was bartered or even discussed. It was boys' night out—a release from our legislative responsibilities." The banking lobbyist David Manning recalls, "We all became buddies in the card games, but there never were any favors granted." Another regular was a lobbyist for the Illinois Manufacturers' Association, and the game eventually moved to the association's office—which didn't keep Senator Obama from voting to raise taxes and fees for manufacturers. He says the games were simply "a fun way for people to relax and share stories and give each other a hard time over friendly competition," adding that they provided "an easy way to get to know other senators—including Republicans."

Most Committee Meetings began at seven o'clock and ran until two in the morning, with the players sustained by pizza, chips, beer, cigars, and good fellowship. Obama wore workout clothes and a baseball cap, but his approach to the cards wasn't casual. He wanted to win. His analytical background—president of the *Harvard Law Review*, University of Chicago law professor—helped him hold his own at stud and hold'em, though it did him less good in the sillier, luck-based variants other players chose, such as baseball and 7-33.

Link, who probably played more hands with Obama than anyone else in Springfield, observed that his lanky table-mate played "calculated" poker, avoiding long-shot draws in favor of patiently waiting for strong starting hands. "Barack wasn't one of those foolish gamblers who just thought all of a sudden that card in the middle [of the deck] was going to show up mysteriously." He relied on his brain, in other words, instead of his gut or the seat of his pants. "When Barack stayed in, you pretty much figured he's got a good hand," recalls Larry Walsh, a conservative corn farmer representing Joliet, who neglected to note that such a rock-solid image made it easier for Obama to bluff. "He had the stone face," Link recalled.

Yet even as one of the boys—bluffing, drinking, bumming smokes, laughing at off-color yarns—there were lines he wouldn't cross. When a married lobbyist arrived at a Springfield office game with someone described as "an inebriated woman companion who did not acquit herself in a particularly wholesome fashion," Obama made it clear he wasn't pleased, though he managed to do it without offending his poker buddies. Link says they all were displeased, and that the lobbyist and his girlfriend were "quickly whisked out of the place."

Obama also made sure he never played for stakes he couldn't easily afford. Only on a very bad night could one drop a hundred bucks in these games, typical wins and losses being closer to twenty-five. Among the regulars, the consensus was that "Obama usually left a winner." The bottom line politically was that poker helped Obama break the ice with people he needed to work with in the legislature.

"Barry," as he was called before college, had learned the game from his maternal grandfather, Stanley Dunham, a World War II army veteran whose black friends played poker as well. Barry also played with classmates at Punahou High School in Honolulu. His best game, however, was basketball. He wore a Dr. J 'fro, and his teammates respectfully called him "Barry O'Bomber." They won the state championship in 1979, and Obama later told HBO's Bryant Gumbel that, despite the O'Bomber nickname, "My actual talent was in my first step. I could get to the rim on anybody." His problem as an in-shape, thirty-six-year-old legislator was that very few pols who'd been around long enough to run things in Springfield could still make it up and down a hard court. His solution was the game in Link's basement. To connect with those who didn't play basketball or poker, he also took up golf, a game at which Link says "he wasn't a natural." But he counted every stroke. "When he'd shoot an 11 on a hole, I'd say, 'Boss, what did you shoot?' and he'd say, 'I had an 11.' And that's what he'd write on his scorecard. I always respected that." Determined to write down fewer 11s, Obama took enough lessons to be able to shoot in the low nineties, and he eventually beat Link a few times.

But the freshman legislator seems to have understood that, as a networking tool, poker is the most efficient pastime of all. Its tables often serve as less genteel clubs for students, workers, businessmen, and politicians of every rank and persuasion. Instead of walking down fairways forty yards apart from each other, throwing elbows in the paint, or quietly hunting pheasant or muskie, poker buddies are elbow to elbow all night, competing and drinking and talking. The experience can tell them a lot about the other fellows' ability to make sound decisions, whether electoral or parliamentary, tactical or strategic. As Abner Mikva, one of the deans of Chicago's legal and political worlds and a longtime Obama adviser, put it simply, "He understands how you network." The networking paid off when, against all expectations, Obama hammered out a compromise bill called "the first significant campaign reform law in Illinois in 25 years" and other bills mandating tax credits for the working poor, the videotaping of police interrogations, and reform of the state's antiquated campaign-finance system.

After being "spanked"—his word for losing by 31 percent to the incumbent, Bobby Rush, in a run for Illinois's first congressional district in 2000—Obama returned to Springfield and set to work even harder. He also began speaking publicly about national issues. After September 11, 2001, he said, "Even as I hope for some measure of peace and comfort to the bereaved families, I must also hope that we as a nation draw some measure of wisdom from this tragedy," and called for a better understanding of "the sources of such madness." After President Bush called for the invasion of Iraq, Obama chose an antiwar rally to say, "I stand before you as someone who is not opposed to war in all circumstances." He cited his grandfather's service and praised the sacrifices made during the Civil War and World War II, before saying, "I know that even a successful war against Iraq will require a U.S. occupation of undetermined length, at undetermined cost, with undetermined consequences. I know that an invasion of Iraq without a clear rationale and without strong international support will only fan the flames of the Middle East, and encourage the worst, rather than best, impulses of the Arab world, and strengthen the recruitment arm of Al Qaeda. I am not opposed to all wars. I'm opposed to dumb wars."

After his keynote speech at the Democratic Convention in July 2004 made him an even brighter political star, Obama easily won election to the United States Senate in November. John Kerry's loss at the top of the ticket, however, prompted David Mamet to write an unconventional postmortem for the *Los Angeles Times*. "The Republicans, like the perpetual raiser at the poker table, became increasingly bold as the Democrats signaled their absolute reluctance to seize the initiative," he said, arguing that Kerry had lost in part because of his timid response to the distortion of his service in Vietnam. "A decorated war hero muddled himself in merely 'calling' the attacks of a man with, curiously, a vanishing record of military attendance." Mamet went on to say, "Control of the initiative is control of the battle. In the alley, at the poker table or in politics, one must raise. . . . How, the undecided electorate rightly wondered, could one believe that Kerry would stand up for America when he could not stand up to Bush?" Mamet made his poker parallel even more specific by suggesting that a better "response to the Swift boat veterans would have been, 'I served. He didn't. I didn't bring up the subject, but, if all George Bush has to show for his time in the Guard is a scrap of paper with some doodling on it, I say the man was a deserter.' This would have been a raise. Here the initiative has been seized, and the opponent must now fume and bluster and scream unfair. In combat, in politics, in poker, there is no certainty; there is only likelihood, and the likelihood is that aggression will prevail." Anticipating future elections, Mamet chided the Democrats for "anteing away their time at the table. They may be bold and risk defeat, or be passive and ensure it."

The playwright's point was uncannily in sync with advice Admiral John S. McCain Jr. once gave his children. "Life is run by poker players, not the systems analysts," he told them, referring to poker players' cunning and toughness, and their tendency to have a bold strategic vision, not fussy myopia. His son John III, while certainly cunning and tough, turned out to prefer craps, a loud, mindless game in which the player never has a strategic advantage and must make impulsive decisions and then rely on blind luck. His selection of Sarah Palin for the vice presidential slot and his unsteady response to the economic crisis were two of the better examples of a dice-rolling mind-set.

By contrast, the Obama campaign's preparation of a separate website featuring a fifteen-minute documentary video about McCain's role in the savings-and-loan scandal of 1989 was but one piece of evidence that the candidate understood Mamet's point about raising. "We don't throw the first punch," he said, "but we'll throw the last." In other words, if the McCain campaign or its surrogates wanted to raise the specter of Bill Ayers or Jeremiah Wright, Obama was going to reraise. As he'd told his fledgling staff back in January 2007, "Let's put our chips in the middle of the table and see how we do."

Mamet's and Obama's analogies appear more traditional when we learn that as early as 1875, a *New York Times* editorial declared that "the national game is not base-ball, but poker," noting that the newspapers of the day were already in the "daily" habit of using "the technical terms of poker to illustrate the manner in which political questions strike the Thoughtful Patriot." This book will offer cases in point from nearly every decade since.

Where Mamet made clear why a politician must raise, especially with a stronger hand, Andy Bloch, a poker pro with degrees from Harvard and MIT, explained how bluffs might be read in military and diplomatic arenas. "In poker you have to put yourself in the shoes of your opponents, get inside their heads and figure out what they're thinking, what their actions mean, what they would think *your* actions mean." Contrasting Obama with his predecessor, Bloch said, "One thing that got us into the Iraq War was that George Bush didn't realize that Saddam Hussein was basically bluffing, trying to look like a big man, when he really had no weapons of mass destruction."

Back in 2002, Obama read that bluff correctly. He also understood that the most pressing threats to American security were the bin Laden strongholds in Afghanistan and Pakistan. President Bush, Vice President Cheney, Secretary of State Colin Powell, John McCain, and seventy-six other senators misread (or allowed themselves to be misled about) Saddam's bluff. The Bush administration then proceeded to squander tall stacks of military and diplomatic chips it should have deployed against Al Qaeda.

In April 2003, the Iraqi Most Wanted poker deck, with Saddam as the ace of spades and fifty-one other Baathists beneath him in the hierarchy, was officially designated the "personality identification playing cards" by Brigadier General Vincent Brooks of the U.S. Central Command. The pattern on their backs was the desert camouflage worn by our troops. Cards with a similar purpose had been deployed by both sides during the Civil War and in every important American military campaign since. So it seemed rather telling that no deck depicting members of Al Qaeda was requisitioned by President Bush.

Although he was more likely to be seen on the campaign trail playing Uno with his daughters, or a pickup game of basketball, than poker, Obama has already extended the long tradition of presidents who have used the card game to relax with friends, extend their network of colleagues, or even deploy its tactics and psychology in their role as commander in chief. His tendency to finish poker sessions in the black puts him in the company of Chester Arthur, Dwight Eisenhower, and Richard Nixon. But by limiting his play to small, friendly games, Obama is more like Franklin Roosevelt and Harry Truman. He has also played the national card game, as Theodore Roosevelt and Lyndon

Johnson did, at least in part because of the entrée it gave him to political circles he would not have had otherwise.

George Washington (1732–1799) and Andrew Jackson (1767–1845) both loved to play cards and gamble, and would no doubt have taken up poker had the game been around in their heydays. As a young officer, Washington received a rebuke "for wasting so much of his time at the gaming table," and Jackson was one of the most notorious gamblers of the early nineteenth century. But it wasn't until Jackson's old age that the French game of *poque* evolved in New Orleans—the city he'd saved from the British in 1815—and began moving north on Mississippi steamboats as poker. By the 1850s, however, it was the card game of choice among savvy risk takers in nearly every state and territory, and most politicians were playing it.

In November 1861, with Union armies generally stymied and the capital threatened by rebel armies under Beauregard and Johnston, Abraham Lincoln used a poker analogy to explain a difficult wartime decision to an anxious Northern public. The British mail steamer *Trent*, bearing two Confederate envoys to London, was intercepted by the Yankee captain Charles Wilkes. When Wilkes decided to take the envoys prisoner, he created an incident that threatened to bring Britain into the war on the side of the South. The British delivered a stern ultimatum: release the ambassadors and apologize, or else. "One war at a time" was Lincoln's rationale as he "cheerfully" freed them. Yet reporters and politicians on both sides of the Atlantic wanted to know whether the president would also apologize, as the British had insisted. Said Lincoln to one of them: "Your question reminds me of an incident which occurred out west. Two roughs were playing cards for high stakes, when one of them, suspecting his adversary of foul play, straightway drew his bowie-knife from his belt and pinned the hand of the other player upon the table, exclaiming: 'If you haven't got the ace of spades under your palm, I'll apologize.'" As the great Civil War historian Shelby Foote would write of the *Trent* Affair: "Poker was not the national game for nothing; the people understood that their leaders had bowed, not to the British, but to expediency."

Theodore Roosevelt gained access to the middle echelons of New York's Republican Party in the early 1880s by showing up at their informal gatherings in a smoky room above a saloon on East Fifty-ninth Street. To overcome the mostly Irish bosses' impression that he was a "mornin' glory," a well-to-do poseur who "looked lovely in the mornin' and withered up" quickly, he insisted on taking part in every profanity-laced "bull session," in spite of his loathing for vulgarity and tobacco. "Some of them sneered at my black coat and tall hat. But I made them understand I should come dressed as I chose," he recalled. "Then after the discussions I used to play poker and smoke with them." His intention, writes David McCullough, was "to get inside the machine."

And it worked. These and other masculine gambits helped the formerly frail young man shimmy up the political totem pole with astonishing speed: assistant secretary of the navy by thirty-eight, governor of New York by forty, president of the United States by forty-two. What our youngest chief executive called the Square Deal was inspired by a set of silver scales presented to him by the black citizens of Butte, Montana, in 1903. Roosevelt used the term to promote a sweeping series of policies designed to ensure that all Americans could earn a living wage and that the scales of justice would be put into balance for black and white, rich and poor citizens. "When I say I believe in a square deal," he explained, "I do not mean to give every man the best hand. If the cards do not come to any man, or if they do come, and he has not got the power to play them, that is his affair. All I mean is that there shall not be any crookedness in the dealing."

When the dark-horse candidate Warren Harding was asked by reporters how he'd managed to win the Republican Party's nomination in 1920, he said, "We drew to a pair of deuces, and filled." (That is, he made a full house.) After soundly defeating James M. Cox in the first national election in which women could vote, he continued playing poker at least once a week. Harding's games while in office were for fun and relaxation, not profit or political advantage, and the rumor that he lost the White House china in one of them is merely a bit of embroidery. The more significant charges are that Harding took poker, alcohol, and his affairs with at least two women more seriously than his responsibilities as president, and that he fostered a spirit of corruption. One of the regulars in his game, Interior Secretary Albert B. Fall, went to prison in the Teapot Dome scandal for accepting bribes for leasing oil-rich fields in Wyoming without competitive bids. Other regulars included Speaker of the House Nicholas Longworth and his wife, Alice, a daughter of Teddy Roosevelt, along with other members of Harding's administration, who came to be known as the Poker Cabinet. "Forget that I'm President of the United States. I'm Warren Harding, playing poker with friends," he would say, "and I'm going to beat hell out of them." Alice Longworth described the Prohibition-era gatherings this way: "No rumor could have exceeded the reality; the study was filled with cronies . . . the air heavy with tobacco smoke, trays with bottles containing every imaginable brand of whiskey stood about, cards and poker chips ready at hand—a general atmosphere of waistcoat unbuttoned, feet on desk, and spittoons alongside."

It was to promote policies designed to lift the United States out of the Depression in 1933 that Franklin D. Roosevelt, following the example of his fifth cousin, Theodore, chose a term from the game he knew millions of ordinary Americans loved: the New Deal. Throughout his three terms (and the few weeks he served of his fourth), FDR played relatively sober nickel-ante stud games in the White House to unwind after his grueling days managing the Depression and then the Second World War. Beginning only eight days after his first inauguration, he steadied and soothed anxious Americans with a series of popular evening radio broadcasts from his second-floor study, where the poker games also took place. "Good evening, friends," he'd begin. As he delivered at least one of these Fireside Chats, he kept hold of some of his chips, fingering them the way others might use worry beads or a rosary. His friends gathered around their boxy wooden radios could hear them clicking together in his hand.

FDR's final vice president, Harry Truman, had played poker as a doughboy in France and kept up with war buddies at small, friendly games in Missouri. In *Truman*, David McCullough teased out poker's role in our most mainstream president's careers as an artillery officer, haberdasher, judge, and politician. "He never learned to play golf or tennis, never belonged to a country club. Poker was his game, not bridge or mah-jongg." Truman's Monday-night sessions with old army buddies "had a 10-cent limit. A little beer or bourbon was consumed, Prohibition notwithstanding, and the conversation usually turned to politics. Such was the social life of Judge Harry Truman in the early 1930s, the worst of the Depression." During his years in the White House, he played with chips embossed with the presidential seal, though only once did he allow himself to be photographed doing so.

Eisenhower and Nixon, both of whom came from working-class backgrounds, played for significant stakes during their military service. At West Point in 1915, Ike attended cadet dances "only now and then, preferring to devote my time to poker." During the First World War he paid for his dress uniform and courted the wealthy Mamie Doud with his winnings. As supreme allied commander in 1944, he outfoxed the Germans on D-day with a series of bluffing maneuvers before taking Normandy Beach.

As a navy lieutenant in the Pacific theater, Nixon won enough in five-card draw and stud games to finance his first congressional campaign in 1946. That same year, an up-and-coming Texas congressman named Lyndon Johnson tried to get himself invited to President Truman's poker sessions aboard the yacht *Williamsburg*—not to win money, of course, but because a seat in that game would have been a precious political asset. When those efforts failed, Johnson started his own game with more junior politicians, though he did play with Truman a couple of times at the home of Treasury Secretary Fred Vinson. And while John Kennedy didn't play much poker with cards and chips, his ability to call Khrushchev's bluff without triggering a nuclear war during the Cuban missile crisis in October 1962 may be the best example we have of how the tactic at the heart of our national card game helped alter the course of our history. Even so, Aaron Brown, the hedge fund manager who wrote *The Poker Face of Wall Street*, credits Khrushchev as "the one who made a wise fold. He had a strong hand but not an unbeatable one, and he sensed the other guy was going to call everything to the river. Good laydown."

As we'll see in Chapter 29, bluffs, counterbluffs, and strong laydowns throughout the cold war, from Khrushchev's threats to nuke Britain during the Suez crisis to Ronald Reagan's Star Wars initiative, gradually made it more apparent how important poker's most basic maneuver was to modern military and diplomatic strategy. It is hardly an exaggeration to say that the survival of Western civilization depended on bluffing effectively. One of the most inventive scientists of the nuclear age, John von Neumann, began his monumental *Theory of Games and Economic Behavior*, cowritten with the economist Oskar Morgenstern, as a mathematical expression of bluffing. "As in poker," wrote Morgenstern after serving as an adviser to Eisenhower, "both we and the Russians must realize the importance of making threats commensurate with the value of the position to be defended, and not bluff so grossly that the raise is sure to be called."

Chapter 34 tells the story of the Massachusetts congressman Tip O'Neill's tide-turning change of heart about Lyndon Johnson's Vietnam strategy. During a poker game at the Army and Navy Club, General David Shoup told the hawkish O'Neill that the conflict was a civil war between Vietnamese factions and wasn't winnable by U.S. forces, at least not the way LBJ was fighting it. The president later admitted to O'Neill that he had severely limited his military options against Hanoi for fear of triggering a nuclear response from China or the Soviet Union. More recent nuclear bluffs by Iran (the subject of Chapter 42) and North Korea have driven home how vital to our national interest poker logic, and in particular the ability to bluff and read bluffs, continues to be.

The book will also show how naturally poker thinking extends into such arenas as law, business, education, the Internet, and artificial intelligence—all this in spite of the fact that more than a few politicians, historians, biographers, and editors have tried to minimize poker's importance. The latest edition of *The New Oxford American Dictionary*, for example, fails to include flop (as a poker term), hold'em, Omaha (as a game), and World Series of Poker. (Terms deemed fit to appear there include floptical, holdall, Pokemon, and World Heritage Site.) Similar omissions occur in the Merriam-Webster, thefreedictionary.com, encarta.msn.com, and other online dictionaries. Such cultural blind spots persist in the face of poker's expanding global popularity, as well as abundant evidence that the game has helped not only presidents and prime ministers and Supreme Court justices but countless other movers and shakers make their way in the world—that it was essential to the development of their character, education, bankroll, military and business practices, as well as to their networks of contacts and friends.

"He played poker and Boston [a form of whist] all through his Presidential career for money." Here we have William Tecumseh Sherman writing privately in 1889 to the president of Harvard about Ulysses S. Grant, who had died four years earlier. Sherman well knew of his comrade in arms's penchant for bluffing at Vicksburg, Chattanooga, and other key battles, and of his keen feel for poker. Yet Grant's majestic two-volume *Personal Memoirs* made no mention of poker; nor would the 880 pages of Sherman's own *Memoirs*, even though he had used the Confederate general John Bell Hood's poker tendencies against him to destroy Hood's army outside Atlanta.

A similar whitewash occurs in even the best works of Civil War history. Chapters 13–15 tell how Southern generals such as Lee, William Mahone, and Nathan Bedford Forrest deployed poker tactics in battle at least as effectively as their blue-coated counterparts. Even so, Bruce Catton's three-volume *The Civil War* and James M. McPherson's *The Battle Cry of Freedom* each have a single fleeting reference to poker; James Ford Rhodes's *History of the Civil War*, Stephen Sears's *Gettysburg*, and Jeff and Michael Shaara's bestselling *Civil War Trilogy* of novels have zero. Generations of history buffs were therefore unable to appreciate the extent to which officers and enlisted men on both sides of the slavery divide played the game avidly, and that the supplest minds among them, including seven future presidents, learned to apply its tactics in diplomatic and military contexts alike. As Albert Upton, Nixon's lit professor at Whittier College, would observe: "A man who couldn't hold a hand in a first-class poker game isn't fit to be President of the United States."

However one feels about Nixon, it's hard to disagree with Professor Upton. One reason so many voters have disagreed in the past is what the historian Garry Wills calls the "cult of the common man," which makes people "think of their heroes as rising almost by magic, rather than by ambition, hard effort, and shrewd calculation." Ever since our earliest presidents aristocratically refused to campaign for the job, many citizens came to believe that the shrewd calculations of a frankly ambitious candidate were traits to be counted against him.

Moral crusaders in the nineteenth century also tried to censor or downplay poker's growing appeal, mainly because the game wasn't virtuous. It involved gambling, for one thing, often in combination with hard liquor, foul cigars, painted harlots, and concealed weapons. You either lost money or took other people's—not by hard, honest toil but by cunning and ruthlessness. Perhaps their most legitimate reason was that during its first several decades, poker was a cheater's paradise, the villainous details of which are explored in Chapters 7–12. President Grant's gambling at poker and in the stock market is forever linked, fairly or not, with the corruption and other failures of his two terms in office.

In the twentieth century we saw presidents Franklin Roosevelt, Truman, Eisenhower, Johnson, and Nixon—every regular player but Harding, it seems—downplay or even deny their affection for the game. Poker's reputation as a backroom cheating fest helped make it a political minus, even though by the time Eisenhower first ran in 1952 it was usually played on the square—and even though malfeasance occurred in every game Americans loved, baseball most certainly included. The Brooklyn Dodgers, after all, had just been cheated out of the '51 National League pennant when the Giants used a telescope and buzzer wire to tip Bobby Thomson that Ralph Branca's next pitch would be a fastball. Meanwhile even friendly little White House poker games during the FDR and Truman administrations had to be kept from the public, despite the fact that poker went hand in hand with the military weapons and tactics that had won World War II and bolstered our cold war diplomacy (subjects covered in Chapters 25–29).

Politicians and biographers have numerous motives, of course, but there's no doubt quite a few of them have seen poker as either a dirty secret or, at best, "just a game," never as a key to achievement. Whereas if a president split a rail, shot a buffalo, played football, or simply played a character who did, we got to read a chapter or hear a speech about it, with more than a few Gipper or White Hunter moments sprinkled in thereafter. Even today, "Governator" Arnold Schwarzenegger is evidently more proud of his steroid-fueled pecs and flamboyantly homicidal film roles, as Bob Dole was of his comedic talent, John Kerry of his grouse hunting, and George W. Bush of his exercise regimens, than of whatever poker skills he might possess—skills much more relevant to the job they aspired to, including shrewdness, psychological acuity, risk and resource management, and the ability to leverage uncertainty.

The habit of sweeping presidential poker under a carpet of virtue was first exposed in 1970, when Wills published *Nixon Agonistes*, which used wartime poker sessions to illuminate the character of one of our most accomplished but least popular leaders. "Nick," as he was called in the Navy, had taken home $8,000—a genuinely whopping haul in the forties—from games in the Pacific. Once, while holding the ace of diamonds, he drew four cards to make a royal flush, about a 250,000–1 shot. "I was naturally excited," he would write in his autobiography. "But I played it with a true poker face, and won a substantial pot."

Wills zeroes in on the Quaker lieutenant's "iron butt" and the fact that he "got to know his fellows, not in foxholes but across the tables, in endless wartime poker games." Since most American fighting men played, Nixon's participation could have been seen simply as part of his lifelong campaign to be a regular guy, but Wills shows how much more to it there was. The presidential biographer Bela Kornitzer agrees: "Out there Nixon passed over the traditional Quaker objections to gambling. Why? He needed money. He learned poker and mastered it to such a degree that he won a sizable amount, and it became the sole financial foundation of his career."

"Nick, as always, did his homework," writes Wills. "He found poker's local theoreticians, men willing to play and discuss, replay and debate, out of sheer analytic zeal." He persuaded one expert, Jim Stewart, to spend a few days coaching him on five-card-draw strategy. Nixon's term for such preparations was war-gaming. He reveled in risk-averse tactics and began to make serious money playing tight, rocky poker. His Quaker mother may not have approved of fighting or gambling, but he had "eased his way into the military past her scruples. The war became a moral hiatus. Besides, motive is what matters, and Nick's motive was pure, was puritan. He was not playing games; with him it was a business." Wills continues: "Show him the rules, and he will play your game, no matter what, and beat you at it. Because with him it is not a game." Looking ahead to his subject's checkered political career, Wills adds, "It helps, watching Nixon's 'ruthless' singlemindedness when bigger pots have been played, to remember those poker days." Sometimes, in other words, the game is much more than just a game.

Wills also shows that while Nixon played ruthlessly, Eisenhower was even better at poker, perhaps because he was more of a natural—and played with a greater sense of virtue to boot. "Like Nixon, he made large sums of money in the long games at military bases," writes Wills. "Unlike Nixon, he was so good he had to stop playing with enlisted men; he was leaving too many of them broke." Even so, when he chose Nixon as his running mate in 1952, both men stopped playing or even mentioning poker, fearing voters would think it unsavory.

A more partisan Republican than Eisenhower, who was considered to be "above" political parties, Nixon was "a hot political property" after helping to convict Alger Hiss of perjury during an investigation into whether Hiss was a Soviet spy. But neither Ike nor Dick ever mentioned the game while campaigning, even though both of them had played for life-changing stakes while serving in their country's armed forces.

Nixon, for his part, was raised in East Whittier, a working-class Quaker community twelve miles southeast of Los Angeles, where any kind of gambling, he said, was "anathema." His family's modest means forced him to turn down a full-tuition scholarship to Harvard in 1930 because it didn't include living expenses and would have kept him from helping out at his family's gas station and grocery store. Instead he attended Whittier, the small Quaker college not far from his home. A star debater as an undergraduate, he did accept a scholarship to the Duke School of Law, then returned home to practice in Whittier, where he married Pat Ryan, a schoolteacher and aspiring actress, in June 1940. After the Japanese attacked Pearl Harbor, he volunteered for sea combat duty, but because of his age (thirty) and advanced education, the navy assigned him to the South Pacific Combat Air Transport at Guadalcanal and later on Green Island. He spent the war preparing manifests and flight plans for C-47 Skytrains, prosaic but necessary duty that helped make American forces more mobile than their Japanese adversaries. Promoted to lieutenant, he served from May 1943 until December 1944.

Even though his austere Quaker upbringing prohibited poker, he later admitted that "the pressures of wartime, and the even more oppressive monotony, made it an irresistible diversion. I found playing poker instructive as well as entertaining and profitable. I learned that the people who have the cards are usually the ones who talk the least and the softest; those who are bluffing tend to talk loudly and give themselves away."

Nixon was "as good a poker player as, if not better than, anyone we had ever seen," one of his navy buddies testified. "I once saw him bluff a lieutenant commander out of $1,500 with a pair of deuces." While serving on Green Island, Nixon was invited to a small dinner party for the celebrity pilot Charles Lindbergh, who was testing prototype planes for the air force. Having earlier agreed to host a poker game that night, Nixon RSVP'd in the negative. As he explains in *RN*, "In the intense loneliness and boredom of the South Pacific our poker games were more than idle pastimes, and the etiquette surrounding them was taken very seriously." He continues: "With my pay, Pat's salary, and my poker winnings, we had managed to save $10,000 during the war." Upon discharge, he used those impressive profits to bankroll his first congressional campaign. In November 1946, he defeated the popular incumbent Jerry Voorhis in part by accusing the forty-five-year-old FDR Democrat of being a draft-dodging Communist—though he did refrain from calling him "a jerry." In 1950, Nixon used the Communist smear and other dirty tricks to swiftboat Helen Gahagan Douglas, a three-term congresswoman once called "ten of the twelve most beautiful women in America," for a seat in the U.S. Senate. After Nixon called her "the Pink Lady" and claimed the attractive New Dealer was "pink right down to her underwear," she retorted with a nickname that stuck: "Tricky Dick."

Presidents have been useful in writing the story of poker because at least one biography and thousands of articles have been written about each of them. While the habits of ordinary Americans go unrecorded for the most part, we can reasonably infer that if as profound a communicator as Lincoln quoted the lore about poker cheats to explain a diplomatic decision in 1861, most citizens knew enough of that lore to understand what he was telling them. If Truman, the Model Son of the Middle Border, as David McCullough calls him, played pot-limit five-card stud aboard the *Williamsburg* in the late 1940s, a fair number of average Americans must also have been playing that variant then. And if most news reports today about nuclear standoffs with Iran or North Korea include the word "bluff," we can be sure the world's citizens understand what this tactic involves.

But it's not just the game's wartime applications that this book is concerned with. As we'll read in Chapter 6, decades before New Yorkers like Alexander Cartwright began tinkering with the English game of rounders, our other national pastime was being cooked up in the polyglot gumbo of New Orleans during its turbulent first years after the Louisiana Purchase, which President Jefferson had announced to the nation on July 4, 1803. Baseball and poker emerged as dueling national pastimes well before the Civil War and have been among the brightest, most durable threads in our social fabric ever since.

My goal is to show how the story of poker helps to explain who we are. The game has gone hand in hand with pivotal aspects of our national experience for a couple of centuries now. As our language adopts more and more poker terms, the ways we've done battle and business have echoed, and been echoed *by*, poker's definitive tactics: cheating and thwarting cheaters, leveraging uncertainty, bluffing and sussing out bluffers, managing risk and reward. I rely on the memoirs of ordinary citizens, interviews with poker stars and everyday players, newspaper and magazine articles, popular and scholarly histories, as well as presidential biographies (especially those written after *Nixon Agonistes*), all of which help to reveal poker's distinctive double helix in our evolving DNA.

Questions this book seeks to answer include: Why would *poque*, an eighteenth-century parlor game played by a few French and Persian aristocrats, take hold and flourish in kingless, democratic America? Why did *poque* evolve into our national card game, some say our national pastime, instead of piquet or cribbage or whist? How much has poker's popularity had to do with bluffing and risk management, or with the fact that money is its language, its leverage, its means of keeping score?

American DNA is a notoriously complex recipe for creating a body politic, but two strands in particular have always stood out in high contrast: the risk-averse Puritan work ethic and the entrepreneur's urge to seize the main chance. Proponents of neither MO like to credit the other with anything positive. Huggers of the shore tend not to praise explorers, while gamblers remain unimpressed by those who husband savings accounts. Yet blended in much the same way that parents' genes are in their children, the two ways of operating have made us who we are as a country.

Ever since the *Mayflower* carried separatist Puritans to Plymouth in 1620, what is often called the American Experiment has lavishly rewarded and punished those who take risks. From Washington's attack on Trenton after crossing the Delaware in a Christmas night hailstorm, Alexander Hamilton's revolutionary banking and credit systems, to the nine-figure compensation packages for CEOs and hedge fund managers, our military, political, and economic systems have all been tipped in favor of people who bet big and won—as opposed to Old Europe, where nearly every advantage went to those who were lucky enough to be born aristocrats.

Geneticists have now learned there is literally such a thing as American DNA, not surprising given that nearly all of us are descended from immigrants. We therefore carry an immigrant-specific genotype, a genetic marker that expresses itself—in some environments, at least—as energetic risk taking, restless curiosity, and competitive self-promotion. Even when famine, warfare, or another calamity strikes, most people stay in their homeland. The self-selecting group that migrates, seldom more than 2 percent, is disproportionately inclined to take chances; they also have above-average intelligence and are quicker decision makers. There's something about their dopamine-receptor systems, the neural pathway associated with a taste for novelty and risk, that sets them apart from those who stay put. While the factors involved are numerous and complex, the migratory syndrome has been deftly summarized by the journalist Emily Bazelon: "It's not about where you come from, it's that you came at all."

The migratory gene was probably even more dominant among those Americans who first moved west across the Appalachians, up and down the Ohio and Mississippi rivers, then out to Nevada and California during the Gold Rush. Their urge to strike it rich made poker much more appealing to them than point-based trick-taking games like whist, bridge, and cribbage.

Today, the U.S. population teems with exuberant, curious, energetic risk takers, a combination of traits called "hypomania" by Peter C.

Whybrow, a behavioral scientist at UCLA. Why aren't Canada, Central and South America, and Australia, where so many immigrants and their descendants also live, as hypomanic as the United States? Whybrow argues that human behavior is always a function of genetics and environment—of nature plus nurture. In America, "You have the genes and the completely unrestricted marketplace," he says. "That's what gives us our peculiar edge."

Our national card game still combines Puritan values—self-control, diligence, the steady accumulation of savings insured by the FDIC—with what might be called the open-market cowboy's desire to get very rich very quickly. The latter is the mind-set of the gold rush, the hedge fund, the lottery ticket of ordinary wage earners. Yet whenever the big-bet cowboy folds a weak hand, he submits to his puritan side.

Sometimes outsiders can see our traits even more clearly than we see them ourselves. The Budapest-born historian John Lukacs calls poker "the game closest to the Western conception of life . . . where men are considered moral agents, and where—at least in the short run—the important thing is not what happens but what people think happens." Another keen foreign observer, Alexis de Tocqueville, wrote in *Democracy in America*: "Those living in the instability of a democracy have the constant image of chance before them, and, in the end, they come to like all those projects in which chance plays a part." This was true, he deduced, "not only because of the promise of profit but because they like the emotions evoked."

It remains unclear which chancing games Tocqueville witnessed, but the perceptive Frenchman came to appreciate our allegiance to risk, initiative, and democratic opportunity while traveling in 1831 aboard the steamboat *Louisville* along Mark Twain's Mississippi, the original American mainstream, at the very moment poker was coming of age. Twain himself would become a highly paid steamboat pilot just before the Civil War closed the river to commercial traffic. Forced to make his way as a writer instead, he produced numerous reports and "yarns" about the game, the most famous of which appeared in *Life on the Mississippi*. Echoing both Tocqueville and Twain, a headline in the April 23, 2003, *New York Times* declared: "Whoever wants to know the heart and mind of America had better learn poker."

Cowboys Full does not always proceed chronologically. I explore a few subjects (luck in poker, poker in literature, no-limit hold'em tournaments, the emergence of women players) independently of the historical time line. But since time lines are crucial to any story, this one begins with prehistoric gambling, the invention of playing cards, and the Renaissance vying games that eventually gave rise to twenty-card *poque* in New Orleans during the Jefferson administration. By Lincoln's election, Americans of every variety were using fifty-two cards to play the new riverboat bluffing game. After the army split into blue and gray factions when Fort Sumter was fired upon in April 1861, just about every soldier became familiar with poker's cunning and expedient stratagems. The game also provided them with an upgrade from such entertainments as bare-knuckle boxing, chuck-a-luck, or betting on the outcome of a race between lice. Given an acre or two in warm sunshine, most Yankees preferred baseball, which they often played with a walnut wound with twine for the ball and just about any length of wood as a bat. But when cramped terrain, weather, or darkness kept everyone close to his tent, poker helped both Confederate and Federal troops pass the time between marches and field drills and bloodbaths. The lucky survivors then took the game home with them to every state and territory and introduced it to the next generation.

After peace was secured at Appomattox, the story moves west with the prospectors and railroad workers, with outsize characters as different as Twain, Doc Holliday, Alice Ivers, Wild Bill Hickok, and George Armstrong Custer taking the stage in their turn. After 1890, it follows a few of the cowboys and Rough Riders back east, where poker's popularity spread among soldiers in the Great War to end all wars and all our other wars that followed.

The huge cast of characters includes the cryptographer and spy Herbert Yardley; Arnold "the Brain" Rothstein, who fixed the 1919 baseball World Series and lost $350,000 in a single weekend stud game; "Texas Dolly" Brunson, who bridges the span between the dangerous road games of the 1950s and the safely legitimate mountains of loot in the twenty-first century; the crack addict and hold'em genius Stuey Ungar, often called the best player ever; Phil Ivey, the "Tiger Woods of Poker," and his friend Barry Greenstein, the "Robin Hood of Poker," who donates all of his tournament winnings to charity; the ninety-five-pound Jennifer Harman, winner of two World Series bracelets, who took on a billionaire heads-up while awaiting her second kidney transplant; the witty and charismatic Canadian pro Daniel Negreanu; the Texas banker Andy Beal, who invited the best in the world to compete as a tag team against him and still almost busted them in the biggest poker game ever played; and scores of other pros, amateurs, studs, ballas, donkeys, and fish.

Chapters 35 and 37–42 cover the World Series of Poker, which after being dominated by Texans for most of its first decade (1970–1979) has now crowned champions from the Bronx, the Lower East Side, Los Angeles, Madison, Grand Rapids, Boston, China, Ireland, Vietnam, Spain, Laos, Norway, Indonesia, Sweden, and Iran. Foreign-born players like Men "the Master" Nguyen, John Juanda, Gus Hansen, Humberto Brenes, Carlos Mortensen, Joe Hachem, and Peter Eastgate have won hundreds of millions of dollars in American tournaments. In 2004, the European Poker Tour began to challenge the American circuit in prestige and the size of its purses. Lucrative events are also being played in southern Africa, South America, Australia, and eastern Asia. And despite the Unlawful Internet Gambling Enforcement Act (the subject of Chapter 49), scarcely a minute goes by without a tournament beginning on the Internet, with buy-ins ranging from zero to $25,000. The biggest winners online go by names like durrrr, Ziigmund, SNoOoWMAN, OMGClayAiken, Annette_15, AJKHoosier1, and Gus Hansen.

Above all, I trace poker's development from what was accurately called the Cheating Game, a cutthroat enterprise that for much of its first century was dominated by cardsharps, to what is today a mostly honest contest of cunning, mathematic precision, and luck that is open to everyone. The quarter of a billion dollars at stake during the World Series every summer in Las Vegas is merely the tip of the iceberg. America has been a melting pot since New Orleans was defended in 1815 by Andrew Jackson's regulars and sizable contingents of French pirates, Choctaw warriors, and freed Haitian slaves. But it wasn't until about thirty years ago that our national card game began to welcome a few hundred million contenders on every inhabited continent, including a young Hawaiian hoopster called Barry Obama.

LOADED KNUCKLEBONES TO DONKEYS IN CYBERSPACE

Games of chance require a wager to have meaning at all.
—JUDGE HOLDEN IN *BLOOD MERIDIAN*

Nothing is more natural, or more essential to human achievement, than gambling—than risking something, taking a chance. It's not just a matter of "nothing ventured, nothing gained," though that is certainly part of it. The need to take risks is deeply embedded in our cells and emotions. For two million years, our brains have evolved by genetic chance amid environmental uncertainty. In the twenty-first century, risk haunts and invigorates nearly every decision we make—whether or when to have children, fight or negotiate, invest in real estate or the stock market, cross the street or board a 787, enroll in an MBA program or go on the poker circuit. Those who accept risk and learn how to leverage or "play" it continue to have big advantages over those who do not.

Not only humans, of course. Every organism needs to manage a series of life-or-death risks. Ants and beetles, hyenas and monkeys all must maintain their physical safety while competing for nourishment and opportunities to copulate. When either of these pursuits could be lethal, especially to our earliest ancestors, the human nervous system made success all the more satisfying with the release of dopamine by the hypothalamus gland. Failure caused the anterior lobe of the pituitary gland to release more prolactin, too much of which causes impotence. Today, when we take a "sick" beat at the poker table, what we're actually experiencing is too much prolactin, the product of both our genetic heritage and the coolly vicious laws of randomness. We somehow got lost in the shuffle.

In *The Selfish Gene*, Richard Dawkins makes it wonderfully clear that as mammals compete, often to the death, for scarce resources, they "should give no inkling of when they are going to give up. Anybody who betrayed, by the merest flicker of a whisker, that he was beginning to think of throwing in the sponge, would be at an instant disadvantage. . . . Natural selection would instantly penalize whisker-flickering and any analogous betrayals of future behaviour. The poker face would evolve." And so it has, even if today it is often artificially enhanced by sunglasses, hoodies, and baseball caps.

The Harvard neurobiologist Steven Pinker explains the instinctual poker face by saying what it isn't: namely, the countenance of a bald-faced liar. "Just as a poker player actively tries to hide his reactions," he writes, "natural selection may select against features of an organism that would otherwise divulge its internal state. And just as it would do no good for the poker player to lie about his hand (because other players would learn to ignore the lie), selection would not favor an animal giving a false signal about its intentions (because its adversaries would evolve to ignore the signal)." Pinker concludes that "just as an adversary in poker will develop increasingly sensitive radar for any twitch or body language that leaks through—the 'tell'—animals may evolve increasingly sensitive radar for any tells in their rivals." Attention, poker loudmouths: the game naturally favors the expression of a sphinx, not the babbling of a congenital liar.

Our urge to compete and take chances developed along the following lines. Pleistocene hunters risked life and limb for the best opportunities to slaughter ferocious but protein-rich animals. The closer they got with a chipped-stone spearhead to a scared, angry buffalo, the more likely they were to be trampled or gored, but the better chance they had of actually killing the beast. Courage and aggressiveness counted. Hanging back from the fray may have helped a risk-averse male survive the day's hunt, but it wouldn't have served him well otherwise. Hunters who took down fresh meat were lionized within the tribe. They received larger portions of protein and more opportunities to mate with nubile females. Meanwhile, the females were competing among themselves—painting their faces, displaying their breasts and genitalia—for the chance to mate with the best food providers. Once copulation took place, protection became even more vital to the females who might become pregnant, so the sexual bounty was even more lavish for the hunters-turned-warriors who killed the most enemy tribesmen. By this means and others, a taste for bold risk taking was efficiently bred into our species. Perhaps the most obvious example today occurs when the prettiest cheerleader dates the star of the varsity team.

We may no longer hunt or fight with spears, but in every tribe and country today physical sports represent, and often attach whopping monetary value to, hunter and warrior skills. Since our ancestors depended for survival on the ability of elite males to run fast and wield lethal projectiles, it shouldn't be surprising that modern male (and, lately, female) athletes mimic those feats in symbolic rituals, sometimes called games. The penetrative power of a golfer or fullback or pitcher, or the home-protecting prowess of a center or goalie or catcher evokes the life-and-death urgency felt on hunting grounds and battlefields a thousand generations ago. This is why so many of us have, without even placing a bet, such intense emotional interest in the outcomes of sporting events.

But at the higher symbolic level on which most modern humans also operate, cerebral games like chess, bridge, poker, Scrabble, and what we call trading or handicapping—betting on the performance of horses, humans, corporations, or currencies—mimic what scouts, hunting-party leaders, and tribal chiefs used to do and, nowadays, what captains, coaches, CEOs, generals, and presidents do. While our physical and mental skill sets are both still evolving, our competitive urge probably feels much the same as it did twelve thousand years ago on the Colorado plateau or Kenyan savanna.

While basic survival was the goal of ordinary cavemen and -women, our most thoughtful ancestors also wanted to understand the *nature* of their perilous world, if only to divine the will of their war god or decide in which direction to send the hunting party. Lacking even rudimentary science, tribal visionaries looked for meaningful portents in the patterns of thrown sticks and bones, or by studying the entrails of eviscerated animals. Patterns in splashes of urine and piles of feces were also believed to be telling, if sometimes overwhelmingly pungent. It was high time, more than one feces decoder must have thought, to come up with a better system for divining what the gods held in store.

As humans evolved, their systems for reading portents grew more intricate. Archaeologists tell us that astragali, the roughly cubic hucklebones (also called knucklebones) above the heels of goats and sheep, began to be widely used several thousand years ago as tools of augury. The bones were cleaned and dried, then marked with crosshatching or drilled with holes that were either left empty or, ominously, filled with lead. With different values ascribed to each side, they were tossed across a flat surface, then tallied. Whichever sides landed faceup were believed to indicate, for example, where a herd of antelope would be grazing the next morning. In other words, it was assumed by some tribesmen that the hunting god spoke through those bones. But for others, such tosses amounted to wagers—to determine, for example, that the lowbrow guy grunting the Neanderthal version of *don't come* owed the shooter a couple of flank steaks by sundown. Those who were best at guessing, or fixing, which side landed up the most often could wolf down extra protein and have some to share with a woman. Among those with a dominant risk-taking gene, the step from divination to wagering contests was probably a short one.

Long before they had words for such concepts, some of these early bonesmen imagined hucklebones to be conduits of chance or fate, while others believed them to be oracles of one god or another. Still others must have thought they were both. David G. Schwartz surmises in *Roll the Bones: The History of Gambling* that one hunter might have said to another, "If the bones land short side up, we will search for game to the south; if not, we look north." In another scenario, after the hunt, they might have "cast bones to determine who went home with the most desirable cuts. If ascribing the roll of the bones to the will of a divine presence, that would be divination; if the hunters simply rolled and hoped for the best, they were gambling." Whether the gods or the odds were believed to be speaking, very few things were more intimately connected to one's fate than the emotions stirred by tossing those primitive dice. Indeed, it's easy to imagine one of humankind's very first prayers being hopefully uttered as a couple of hucklebones tumbled across a flat patch of earth.

Yet because of variations, inadvertent or otherwise, in their shape or lead content, astragali were inevitably "loaded," which must have led to some hairy exchanges among people with inch-high foreheads to go with their spears, clubs, and questionable hygiene. Grinding down irregular edges would have been one obvious improvement. An even better one would be carving artificial astragali that yielded more random results. Eventually, four-sided dice shaped like pyramids were sculpted from nuts, wood, bone, and soft stone. Such advances occurred earlier in some places, later—or never—in others, depending on myriad factors. What is certain is that thousands of years before Roman numerals, before numbers were introduced by Arabs and Hindus, an arrow, a trio of dots, or a four-pointed antler on the surface of a die indicated to our ancestors what the future might hold—or, less grandly, who had won a bet.

As agriculture developed and early civilizations emerged, brainpower began to take precedence over muscle, and the appeal of ever more intricate games began to assert itself, at least among the urban elite. The more possible moves, the more elaborate the rules and scoring, the better they liked it. By 3500 BCE, Sumerians and Egyptians were tossing pairs of dice to determine how many spaces a piece should advance in complex, warlike board games. Such games became so important that the gods were believed to play, too. Thoth, the great god of science and writing, was believed to have defeated the moon god, Sin, in a game much like checkers. Thoth's prize was 1/72nd of each day, which he combined into five full days and added to the 360-day lunar year to create the first solar calendar.

When casting four-sided dice, the range of possible outcomes could be squared by rolling two at a time. To satisfy the craving for even greater complexity, the next stage of gaming R & D yielded six-sided dice. Precisely carved from ivory and wood, cubic dice appeared in Mesopotamia around 3000 BCE, along with painted wood objects resembling backgammon boards.

A game much like backgammon is under way on a famous Greek amphora painted by Exekias around 530 BCE but depicting an earlier epoch. Holding two spears in one hand, fingering markers or dice in the other, the black figures of Achilles and Ajax compete across the surface of a low, legless table during a break in the ten-year Trojan War, which occurred sometime between 1230 and 1180 BCE. Their shields are leaning close by, at the ready. Achilles, on the left, in his tall plumed helmet, calls out, "Four!" while Ajax pleads, "Three!"

Homer's *Iliad* tells us that Patroclus, when young, in a wrathful act worthy of his future lover (or close friend) Achilles, had once killed a boy with the eyebrow-raising name of Clitonymus while "quarreling over a dice game." Forced into exile by this murder, Patroclus sought refuge in the house of Peleus. It was there that he met Achilles, the demigod whose rage and lethality would soon doom the Trojans, his friend, and himself.

Romans upped the ante by betting on gladiatorial contests on the floor of their Coliseum, the oval design of which both concentrated the butchery and allowed bloodthirsty spectators to view it up close—and may have inspired the shape of modern poker tables. Roman artisans also made tesserae, dice exquisitely carved from ivory or bone. These led to games in which four dice were rolled across a board. The worst possible throw, in which all four sides came up 1, was called *canis*, the dog; the best throw, *venus*, which meant charm or beauty, showed four different values.

Dice figure prominently in the works of Tacitus, Dante, Chaucer, Cervantes, Goethe, Molière, and other European authors. Shakespeare's King Richard III was speaking for a long line of existential risk takers when he said

> *Slave! I have set my life upon a cast,*
> *And I will stand the hazard of the die.*

Yet two thousand years before Shakespeare wrote these lines, the great Hindu epic *Mahabharata* told of dice carved from nuts being used for both divination and gambling. Sanskrit poems even more ancient tell of the god Shiva throwing dice with his wife, Parvati, and their sons. The thirty-fourth hymn of the tenth mandala of the Rig Veda, a collection of religious hymns dating back to 4000 BCE, is known as the gambler's hymn.

> *These dice nuts, born of a lofty tree in a windy spot, which dance on this gambling ground, make me almost mad. These nervous dice intoxicate me like a draught of soma from Mount Mujavant.*
>
> *Without any fault of hers I have driven my devoted wife away because of a die exceeding by one. My mother-in-law hates me. My wife pushes me away.*

In his defeat the gambler finds no one to pity him. No one has use for a
gambler. He's like an aged horse put up for sale.

Whether or not a losing gambler is like an old horse, or his mother-in-law and wife are both nags, modern Indians who fail to place at least a small wager during Diwali, the Festival of Lights celebrating Shiva and his family, are believed to be reincarnated as donkeys. Today's on-line poker players may also thank Shiva that making such wagers became dramatically easier in August 2001, when the Bengali software whiz Anurag Dikshit (pronounced Dixit) launched the platform he wrote for PartyPoker.com. That site quickly became the world's busiest by enabling tens of thousands of players in twenty-four time zones to compete for pennies or serious money at thousands of virtual tables. The religious dimension of wagering also seems weirdly confirmed by the fact that playing pitifully at one of these tables, whatever the stakes, is to risk being labeled a donkey.

A SHIVERING SHAMAN AND THE
CONCUBINES OF INVENTION

As if beyond will or fate [man] and his beasts and his trap-
pings moved both in card and in substance under consign-
ment to some third and other destiny.

— *BLOOD MERIDIAN*

The anthropologist Stewart Culin traced the lineage of playing cards back to Korean divinatory arrows. Fired into the air by a shaman, these shafts of bamboo fletched with cock feathers literally and theologically pointed the way—to where game would be grazing or an enemy would attack from, or to reveal the best young soldier to receive the hand of the warlord's daughter in marriage. Archery must also have been considered more manly and regal than squatting on the ground with some bones. Even so, sometime during the sixth century divinatory arrows were miniaturized into strips of oiled silk unattached to any shaft. What, we might ask, was the tipping point?

One possibility is that it gradually dawned on a shaman that the random fall of sacred arrows—arrows unguided, that is, by human will— could be achieved more efficiently by mixing up pieces of silk marked with the same insignia the arrows bore, then turning over the silks one by one. This first act of shuffling would save him the steps of going outside, launching arrows skyward, and scurrying around to read and interpret which one had landed where, at what divine angle, and so forth. One frigid January morning our shivering but imaginative soothsayer must have returned to the hearth of his cozy shelter, set down his quiver and bow, shuffled some previously marked pieces of silk, and dealt them out on a table. "Stay inside, fool," he might have interpreted them to advise. "Transfer fletching design onto silk. Convince warlord new prognostications will be even more accurate . . ."

Like fletching, the Korean silk cards were about eight inches long and half an inch wide. To further emphasize where they came from, their backs were etched with featherlike patterns. Eventually they were standardized into packs of eight suits—men, fish, crows, pheasants, antelopes, stars, rabbits, horses—of ten cards each, numbered 1 through 9. The tenth and highest-ranking card was a general, not surprising in a martial society that had recently launched arrows to learn what its gods had in mind, and whose word for cards, "htou-tjyen," means "fighting tablets." Modern military R & D continues to generate both useful and lethal inventions, from ambulances and radar to supersonic aircraft and nuclear fusion. Replacing three-foot arrows with eight-inch strips of silk was one of the first instances of what we call nanotechnology.

Around 700, just to the west of the Korean peninsula, cards of an altogether different provenance began to appear. David Schwartz tells us that in the T'ang dynasty capital of Chang'an, imperial courtesans were said to be the creators of dotted cards, a thinner, cheaper version of dominoes, a progression that seems confirmed by the Chinese word "p'ai," which means both "dice" and "playing cards." Having descended from six-sided dice, dominoes were fashioned from ivory and ebony, neatly fitted for storage in lacquered sandalwood boxes, and probably kept under lock and key until the emperor wanted to play. With roughly three thousand members in his household and harem— including the empress and her handmaidens, along with hundreds of his consorts, concubines, and even assistant concubines—a busy emperor could hardly find the time, let alone summon the energy, to keep them all entertained. What were the underemployed beauties to do once they'd developed a taste for dominoes but couldn't afford them? Boredom and affordability thus become the mothers, or perhaps the concubines, of invention.

One avid domino-card player was Wu Zhao, China's only empress, who began her fifteen-year reign in 690, eight and a half centuries before Elizabeth I succeeded to the throne of England. In 750, Emperor Ming Huang played cards with his "precious consort" Yang Kuei-fei, the Jade Beauty who had been his son's wife; the young woman was so stunning, in fact, that she distracted the emperor from affairs of state and led to his downfall. And on New Year's Eve 969, the official chronicle of the Liao dynasty records a game of cards played by the more uxorious Emperor Mu-tsung and his wife.

The historian Ou-yang Siu believed his nation's cards evolved from dominoes near the middle of the T'ang dynasty (618–907). The northeastern border of the T'ang empire extended well beyond the Great Wall to abut the Korean peninsula, so it's reasonable to assume that a variety of dominoes and cards migrated back and forth across the border. Whether East Asian playing cards were originally inspired by arrows or dominoes, divination or boredom, by the eighth century the most advanced peoples on earth had progressed well beyond rolling dice across flattened dirt for their pleasure or edification.

What made Korea and China such fertile territory for the gaming revolution? The ground had been prepared by their high degree of civilization. It was under T'ang rule, for example, that the first precise tax and legal codes were written, the first organized cavalry deployed, the first reliable censuses taken. Bows and arrows were used to fell enemies or prey at a safer remove than spears could afford. Singer-poets such as Wang Wei and Li Po had begun performing in distant cities, a cultural expansion leading to both opera and popular music. The tools and craftsmanship of their artisans had reached a level of sophistication capable of producing functional and elegant cards.

As David Parlett notes in *The Oxford Guide to Card Games*, the most salient characteristic of cards is their two-sided nature. One side is marked uniformly, the other individually. Once a deck has been adequately shuffled, the order of the individual sides is random, and after they're dealt the uniform sides keep the values of the facedown sides a secret. In addition to the greater complexity a hand of cards can generate, it's the combination of randomness and mystery that elevates a card game over one played with dice.

The human brain has a fondness for categories, hierarchies, and intricacy, so people of advanced intelligence and learning tend to find card games more satisfying than those played with dice. Psychological acuity, educated guesswork, and a lively imagination are required to play card games well. A civilization equipped with fine inks and brushes, with a productive economy spinning off leisure time, with precise legal codes on the books and intricate poems in their hearts were likelier to fall for a card game than were primitive nomads drifting across bone-strewn landscapes.

The Chinese historical dictionary *Ching-tsze-tung* described a variety of card games being played by 1120. Most decks by then had been streamlined into three suits or categories: money, strings, and men. Cards used in the imperial court were still painted by hand, a labor-intensive process only royalty could afford. By 1131, however, functional decks were being mass produced by woodblock printing on cardboard. Their faces were primarily red and black. Red represented fire, good fortune, and joy; black was considered the king of colors, representing water, heaven, and yin to white's yang. On a more practical level, the corners of the cards were rounded to keep them from fraying. And because the Chinese fanned them from the top, the lower right quadrant was left blank so a player could spread his hand without losing sight of the numbers and suits, which were printed on both ends to be readable without having to flip the cards over.

Playing cards spread along trade routes, particularly to cultural centers in which literacy rates were higher. Once priests, scribes, and warriors took up cards, they were further disseminated via military conquest. A parallel development was the invention of paper by the artisan Ts'ai Lun of the Eastern Han dynasty in 104 CE. This had triggered a cultural shift as momentous as those brought about by Gutenberg's printing press in the fifteenth century or by the Internet at the dawn of the twenty-first. Along with portable money and materials for drawing and record keeping, numbers and images printed on thicker "card board" became fundamental by-products of the paper revolution. Unfortunately, the fact that cards were usually made of paper means that fewer of them have survived the millennia intact.

In *Guns, Germs, and Steel*, Jared Diamond writes that the transfer of Chinese papermaking techniques to the Islamic world was "made possible when an Arab army defeated a Chinese army at the battle of the Talas River in Central Asia in A.D. 751." Two papermakers among the prisoners were brought to Samarkand, the Persian capital on the ancient Silk Road between China and Europe, where they were encouraged to share their secrets. As the prisoners began their nervous demonstration, the arrival of cards in the Christian and Islamic worlds became a foregone conclusion, though it would be another six centuries before Middle Eastern decks made their way to Europe.

The first Islamic cards were oblong, with decks divided into ten suits, in keeping with the Arab decimal system. Sharia frowned on re-productions of the human form, so Islamic decks had no court figures, only symbols to indicate rank. The highest cards were the *malik* (sultan), *na'ib malik* (viceroy), and *thani na'ib* (vice-viceroy). And because Islamic women took no part in civic life, the decks had no queens. The dancing girls at the bottom of the Persian sultan's hierarchy were chastened to Arabic tens.

Indian cards, called *ganjifeh*, were derived from Persian decks that had been introduced some time before the Mughal conquest of the subcontinent in the sixteenth century. Schwartz tells us the Mughals "were Islamic, though not strict adherents to the letter of Koranic law. In addition to allowing Hindus latitude in the practice of their religion, they apparently tolerated cardplaying." The Mughal emperor Babur (1483–1530) loved to play cards with his daughter and often gave hand-painted decks as gifts to his subjects. The exquisite, almost perfectly round cards were called *kridapatram*, "painted rags for playing." A typical ninety-six-card set had eight suits ranked in descending order—slaves, crowns, swords, gold coins, harps, documents, silver coins, and supplies—which made it a revealing guide to the social strata and morality of the subcontinent. Musicians were valued more highly than clerks, for example, but outranked by soldiers and kings, while the most prized possession of all was a slave. And then there was Vali's wife, Tara, who greeted her brother-in-law Laxman with her breasts exposed, as featured in another *ganjifeh* deck.

Throughout their history, the faces of cards have provided small canvases for artistic embellishment. The themes have ranged from military and social rank to the religious and frankly erotic. And as human cultures continued to develop and spread across the globe, Persian decks found their way to a remote continent where people were still rolling dice but where civilization was poised on the brink of a Renaissance.

JEANNE D'ARC AND LA HIRE TO THE NAKED SINGULARITY OF SPADES

The woman with five hearts saw him
As a man with clubs, one fewer than he needed.
A man without enough clubs can be a pathetic thing.
Each of her bets demanded he come clean.

—STEPHEN DUNN,
"THE WOMAN WITH FIVE HEARTS"

During the second half of the fourteenth century, Christian crusaders and Venetian merchants brought what were called Saracen cards back to Medieval Europe. The poverty and superstition of what's known as the Dark Ages (roughly 500–1100) had lifted, as markets and guilds and universities began to sprout in the more fertile cultural soil. After the ravages of the bubonic plague (1347–1351), which caused nearly half of the continent's population to suffer a hideous death, many survivors migrated from the forests and farms back into the cities. Working as merchants and craftsmen, they gradually formed a new urban mercantile class. Life was getting better for most people: they lived longer, they knew more, and their standard of living was higher. They also had more time to play.

In the earliest years of the Renaissance, books, cards, and pictures were all produced by artists, not printing presses. The burgeoning arts and university communities of Siena, Bologna, and Venice all became hotbeds of cardplaying. By 1379, numerous drawings of and written references to cards had appeared in Basle, Barcelona, Brussels, Paris, and Viterbo, a center of learning forty miles north of Rome. As itinerant scholars and artists moved from school to school, the popularity of card games began to grow exponentially. In 1414 a single *briefmaler* (card painter) was enough to supply the entire demand of Nuremberg, but within two generations playing cards had become so fashionable that the city employed at least thirty-seven full-time specialists.

Not everyone was persuaded of either the appeal or the morality of card games. During the Protestant Reformation (c. 1517–1648), cards were scorned as "the devil's picture book" because of the infernal wagering they facilitated. Then as now, it was considered a sin by many people to waste time, risk losing money, or have an excessive interest in the outcome of a pleasurable contest. Gamblers were often excommunicated or even put to death by the church.

Even so, the popularity of cardplaying steadily expanded. Spanish players favored forty-card decks, while Germans made do with thirty-six. Most cards used in northern Italy were based on fifty-two-card Persian decks, which were divided into four suits: coins, cups, scimitars, and polo sticks, emblematic of the officers providing a sultan's court with money, food and drink, military protection, and sporting entertainment. In Venice and other cities, the polo sticks became scepters or cudgels—clubs used for fighting, that is, not yet the three-leaf clovers farmers fed to their livestock. A small number of artisans even experimented with the idea of replacing the viceroy with, of all things, a queen.

While card games continued to be the province mainly of male aristocrats, some women and farmers and tradesmen gradually figured out ways to get in on the action. A group's social ranking system was often reflected in the deck it used to play. Ever since the Korean silk packs placed generals atop the hierarchy, cards' faces had represented cultural strata. A report from 1377 has many Swiss decks with the sun at the top, followed in descending order by the king, queen, knight, lady, valet, and maid. In other decks, the order was snarling lions, haughty kings and their ravishing ladies, soldiers in breastplates and helmets, then bare-breasted dancing girls. On Florentine decks, the ladies and dancers were naked.

When the major religious wars subsided for a while, cardplaying became wildly popular among the French nobility in the late sixteenth century, and in England around 1650. But almost a century before that, Mary, Queen of Scots, had gambled for high stakes, shocking her husband by violating the Sabbath for a card game. Henry VIII played cards "compulsively," usually with men, but often with his wives and mistresses. His daughter Elizabeth played with the men of her court in the late sixteenth century. By 1674, when many more common folk played, Charles Cotton had published *The Compleat Gamester*, which standardized the rules and explained basic strategy for more than a dozen card games.

In the wealthy Catholic city-state of Venice, aristocrats kept separate apartments, called *casini*, just to play cards and consort with *cortigiani onesti*, those well-educated, "honest" courtesans feted as symbols of Venetian splendor and liberal values. One such courtesan, Veronica Franco, became famous as a poet, ambassador, philanthropist, and player of *giochi proibiti* (prohibited card games), and as one of the first European women to compete on equal terms with courtiers. Another pleasure-loving Venetian, Giacomo Casanova, loved to play whist and *primiera* to help fund his erotic adventures. Venice was not only the birthplace of lotteries and casinos (its first one opened in 1638) but also was an early breeding ground for *primiera*, the vying game that took Renaissance Europe by storm and eventually evolved into poker. It is the subject of the following chapter.

For the first century after the arrival of playing cards, every hamlet and city produced its own idiosyncratic design, featuring suits such as monkeys, flowers, acorns, peacocks, and parrots. But it was the economical decks produced in northern France that were adopted most widely. By the middle of the fifteenth century, these decks, printed with cheaply stenciled patterns, were being sold in large quantities to Scandinavia, England, and what were called the Low Countries. As early as 1470, card makers in Rouen had settled on the four suits and two colors we're familiar with today. *Coeurs* (hearts) represented the church, *carreaux* (diamond-shaped tiles) the merchant class, both in the form of simple red icons. In black were the stylized *piques* (pikes or spearheads) signifying the state and *trèfles* (three-leafed clovers) the farmers. A more general way to understand the four suits is as representations of spirituality, money, war, and agriculture.

One of the French designers was Étienne de Vignoles, called *La Hire* (the Hero) because of his bravery during the Hundred Years War against England. Not that he saw duty every minute of it, but in the critical Siege of Orléans (1428–1429) he fought under the numinous seventeen-year-old warrior Jeanne d'Arc, who was wounded in the breast but remained on the battlefield encouraging her pikemen and archers until the siege was lifted. Legend has it that when, two years later in Rouen, the English burned Jeanne at the stake, her unflinching valor inspired Étienne to replace the soldier in French decks with *la dame*.

Unlike their Muslim counterparts, French Catholic theologians didn't object to depictions of humans; indeed, their churches positively bristled with paintings, sculptures, mosaics, and stained-glass images of apostles, saints, archangels, Mary, and Jesus. So the Rouennais designers were free to adorn their court cards with historical figures and embellish them with Judeo-Christian iconography. They drew the king of spades to resemble David, king of the Hebrews, and modeled his sword on the weapon he took from Goliath upon slaying the giant with a leather slingshot, which was shown lower down on his card. They depicted the club king as a stylized Charlemagne, the king of diamonds as Julius Caesar, and the heart king as Alexander the Great. The four kings thus represented the Jewish world, the Holy Roman Empire, and pre-Christian Rome and Greece, the four main wellsprings of Western civilization.

The queens and jacks aligned much less neatly. The queen of spades was based on Pallas Athena, the goddess whose warlike spirit called to mind Jeanne's. The queen of diamonds was modeled on Rachel, the beauty whom Jacob had to wait fourteen years to marry. The queen of hearts was inspired by Judith, the Jewish heroine who got the Assyrian general Holofernes drunk on false pretenses and then cut off his head, saving Israel in the process and rating the valiant widow her own book in the Old Testament. The club queen paid homage to "Argine," apparently an anagram of "*regina*," the Latin word for "queen," though the designer probably had Jeanne in mind too, since the king of clubs was Charlemagne, the other great French Catholic leader.

In one deck, the jack of spades was based on Ogier, a knight in Charlemagne's court; the jack of diamonds on Hector of Troy; of hearts on the proto-feminist Étienne de Vignoles; of clubs on Judas Maccabeus, who led Israel's revolt against the Syrians. In another deck, the four jacks featured full-length depictions of famous knights, whose names were printed next to their pictures: Lancelot, Ogier, Roland, and Valery. Each of these long-haired, beardless young warriors brandished a battle-ax, and all but Valery (the knight who designed these cards) were attended by a hound.

Ranked below the jacks were the cards 10 through 2, whose values corresponded to the counting scheme and were indicated by the number of pips stenciled in the shape of their suit. Just below the deuce, however, the math became fuzzier and more metaphysical. The English word *ace* meant "one," "unit," or "particle," more or less exactly what was meant by the French and Spanish *as*, the Italian *asso*, the Dutch *aas*, the German *ass*, and so on. Yet the medieval Catholic church argued strenuously that, since God was "the One," any game or scheme that assigned his number the lowest value was ipso facto the work of the devil. The lowly deuce, from the Latin word for "two," was thereafter known as the devil's card.

These days the ace can stand for whichever entity—such as alpha, Allah, God, 1, A, the sun, a minaret, a steeple, a cathedral, the hinge of a woman's legs, or what physicists call a naked singularity—outranks the most dominant human. Yet how can a single card, the plainest one in the deck, for that matter, represent so many things? And which must take precedence, the physical or spiritual world?

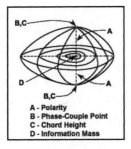

A - Polarity
B - Phase-Couple Point
C - Chord Height
D - Information Mass

Naked Singularity

Rouennais Ace of Spades: "By God, Not by Chance"

Neither, says Edward O. Wilson. The eminent biologist has shown that in complex societies, religious and earthly values have always combined to determine status. "Power belonged to kings by divine right," he reminds us, "but high priests often ruled over kings by virtue of the higher ranks of the gods." In the general absence of kings nowadays, the theocratic presidents of Iran and other countries still serve as prominent examples of this principle.

Totemic ladders organize every society, though we're never quite sure how to read all the faces and symbols. Our own ace of spades has represented Saddam Hussein and the Vietnamese goddess of death, along with numerous leaders we view much more favorably. American idiom says that this innocent scrap of cellulose acetate is as black or as bad as things get—or as good, in the sense that Batman or Catwoman, Rhett Butler or John Shaft are good. The ace of spades also is real, the most real, in that our willingness to "call a spade a spade" shows us to be forthright, clear-eyed, realistic.

Wilson goes on to suggest that rituals such as poker "celebrate the creation myths, propitiate the gods, and resanctify the tribal moral codes." In other words, when we abide by its rules, surrendering a mountainous pot to a fragile great-grandmother showing down jacks to our tens or bluffing us out with four diamonds, we participate in and "resanctify" antediluvian pecking orders. All poker players must accept that, weirdly enough, a deuce is the smallest a thing can get, smaller even than a one—unless the one completes the bottom end of a straight; that two deuces beat any ace, any face card; but that even three deuces must lose to a straight or a flush—unless, of course, another pair materializes, in which case we have a full house.

However we view any card as a symbol, poker's hierarchy of aces, kings, queens, jacks, and the nine lower numbers permutate and combine into 2,598,960 possible five-card hands. From straight flushes at the top to no-pair at the bottom, the game's recombinant totem pole is based on mathematical scarcity, the Arab counting scheme, and our status-hungry social order. As a measure of our collective values, it makes just about perfect sense. Order is maintained because each hand has a clear value relative to the others.

RANKING OF POKER HANDS

Straight flush: Five consecutive cards of the same suit. The highest possible hand is an ace-high straight flush, called a royal flush.

Four of a kind: Four cards of the same rank, called quads.

Full house: Three cards of one rank and two of another, such as three kings and two 4s, called kings full of fours or, sometimes, cowboys full.

Flush: Five cards of the same suit. The higher the top card, the more valuable the flush.

Straight: Five consecutive cards of mixed suits. An ace can be used as either the high or low card, but not in the middle. Q-K-A-2–3 is not a legitimate straight.

Three of a Kind: Three cards of the same rank.

Two Pairs: Two cards of the same rank and two cards of another rank.

Pair: Two cards of the same rank. If two players both have the same pair, the highest other card in their hand, called a kicker, determines the winner.

No Pair: The highest-ranking cards take the pot. A-Q-5-3-2 beats A-J-10-8-6, for example.

Yet every experienced player knows that these relative values are clear only until someone starts betting and raising. If you have three jacks, your opponent (who holds no facedown diamond) bets all the money you have left, and there are a number of reasons to believe (based on his previous bets, the look on his face, and the four diamonds showing) that he has a flush, how valuable are your jacks at that point? The ways such a question might be answered is a subject we'll return to again and again in this book.

5

DR. JEROME CARDPLAYER
AND THE VYING GAMES THAT
GAVE RISE TO POKER

Had [Cardano] played poker, he wouldn't have been found
drawing to an inside straight.

— LEONARD MLODINOW, *THE DRUNKARD'S WALK*

Whether cards were the work of yawning courtesans, frostbitten
prognosticators, or the devil himself, wood-block printing of standardized decks gradually made them affordable to the common folk of
nearly every country and religious persuasion. By the early fifteenth
century, much of Judeo-Christian Europe had enthusiastically taken up
card games.

The game of basset, for example, "became a craze of scandalous proportions" in the French and English courts, particularly among the numerous mistresses of Charles II, who tended to play for stakes well
beyond what they could afford. Richard Seymour opined in *Court
Gamester* that more than any other card game, basset was "the most
courtly, being properly, by the understanders of it, thought only fit for
Kings and Queens, great Princes, Noblemen, &c. to play it, by reason
of such great losses, or advantages, as may possibly be on one side or
another." Basset resembled craps or roulette played with cards. After
thirteen were dealt faceup on the table, players made wagers on one or

more of them. With a complex variety of options for escalating the stakes in later rounds, aggressive players could lose or win up to sixty times the sum they'd originally bet on a card.

The Venetian game of *trappola* became popular in Bohemia, Moravia, and much of Central Europe. It was played with a deck from which the threes, fours, fives, and sixes had been removed. The object was to take as many tricks as possible, so while its name might sound to our ears like a contest for check-raising specialists, *trappola* was actually more similar to hearts and contract bridge than to poker.

The Spanish vying game of *mus*, on the other hand, can be seen as a forerunner of both draw and the high-low poker variants. *Mus* (which means "draw") originated among the Basques before spreading throughout Spain and South America. Players competed in teams and were allowed to use their fingers to signal information about their cards. The goals were to score exactly forty (or sometimes a hundred) points, and to make high and low hands. Most cards counted at face value, with the ace worth one point and the king, *caballo* (horse), and *sota* (jack) all worth ten. But since threes counted as kings and deuces as aces, there were effectively eight kings and eight aces. Four cards were dealt to each player, followed by an optional replacement *mus* to improve one's hand. After that came another four rounds of drawing and betting. As in all vying games, the timing and size of a wager could win the pot for the player, or in this case the team, with the second-best hand.

So too with English brag, which is still played in Britain, Nepal, and India. Brag players compete only as individuals. The value of three-card brag hands climbs a pokerlike ladder: pair, flush, run (straight), flush-run, and three of a kind, called a prial, an abbreviation of "pair royal." In keeping with the spirit of three, that number is treated as a special case, so that even a prial of aces loses to a prial of treys. Yet as the game's name implies, bragging is at least as important as hand strength—even more so, perhaps, given that it isn't uncommon to brag without even looking at one's cards. The essence of the game was ornately but accurately defined by Seymour in 1720: "The endeavor to impose on the judgment of the rest who play, and particularly on the person who chiefly offers to oppose you, by boasting or bragging of the cards in your hand. Those who by fashioning their looks and gestures, can give a proper air to their actions, as will so deceive an unskillful antagonist, that sometimes a pair of fives, trays or deuces, in such a hand, with the advantage of his composed countenance, and subtle manner of over-awing the other, shall out-brag a much greater hand." That is, shall outbluff it. Cool Hand Luke (played by Paul Newman) put it more simply in 1967 after winning a hand of five-card stud with absolutely nothing. "Yeah, well, sometimes nothin' can be a real cool hand."

The German game *poch* (also called *pochen* or *pochspielen;* in Icelandic, *pukk*) originated in the early fifteenth century. More technically complicated than most other games, *poch* required a circular board with eight distinct compartments labeled Ace, King, Queen, Jack, Ten, Marriage, Sequence, and Poch. During the first round of action, players "dressed the board" by placing chips into seven of the eight compartments before being dealt five cards apiece. The next card turned over determined the trump suit. The player holding, for example, the king and queen of that suit was sure to win the Marriage compartment. In the next round, players vied to have—or to plausibly represent—the best combination of cards. Quartets were the highest-ranked grouping, followed by triplets, then pairs, with ties broken by the highest side card. But a player with no pair at all could still win the second round by betting enough to chase away all opponents. "*Ich poche,*" he would mutter (meaning "I bash" or "I pulverize"), followed by the amount he was betting. His opponents could match his bet, raise it, or pass. If one or more opponents matched him, the first bettor had the option of raising.

Not long after the *Niña, Pinta,* and *Santa María* crossed the Atlantic and a new world came slowly into focus, another close relative of poker became the rage of Renaissance Europe. Called *prime* in France, *primera* in Spain, *primiera* in Italy, and primero in England, this complex bidding and vying game was ardently contested by commoners and courtiers, playwrights and poets. In *The Merry Wives of Windsor,* Sir John Falstaff grumbles, "I never prospered since I forswore myself at primero." The final act of *King Henry VIII* finds the much-married sovereign in a game with the Duke of Suffolk on the evening of September 7, 1533, as his second wife, Anne Boleyn, is painfully giving birth to Elizabeth. We should also note that Henry's haughty bearing, parted chin whiskers, elaborately embroidered vest, and ermine stole were said to inspire the image of the modern king of hearts.

In Italy, where the game was invented, *primiera* was played with a deck stripped of eights, nines, and tens. After putting up an ante, the players (ideally four to six of them) received two cards facedown. Starting from the dealer's left, their options were to bid, stake, or pass. Those who didn't pass received two more cards, and a second round of bidding ensued. *Primiera* anticipates bridge in that the bids involved point total, hand type, and number. The hand type had to be higher than those previously bid or, if it was the same, the point total had to be greater. The hierarchy of hands naturally placed a quartet at the top. Other strong hands included a *fluxus* (four-card flush), a *supremus* (highest possible three-card flush), a *prime* (one card from each suit, and which gave the game its name), all the way down to the lowly *numerus* (two or three suited cards).

Again we turn to Parlett for context: "Primiera is often described as 'the' ancestor of Poker. This oversimplification is correct at least to the extent that the game embodies the hierarchical principle whereby several different types of combination compete against one another in a single series of relative values." The family resemblance is also expressed when poker players vie with each other by betting amounts not necessarily related to the value of their hand.

As the stratagems for solving these "prime" games became more sophisticated, and skill therefore more decisive, Renaissance card players naturally developed a keener appetite for tactical guidance. One of the first to provide a few general pointers was the Tuscan poet Francesco Berni, whose rhyming hymn of praise for the game, *Capitolo del gioco della Primiera* (Poem About Playing Primero), was published in Venice in 1526. The city was Europe's leading cultural, commercial, and military power, a place where the Muslim East and Christian West vibrantly intersected, not least in its architecture, ornament, advanced surgical techniques, and devotion to sensual pleasure. It was also the place where private *casini* and mask-wearing card players were coming into vogue. All of this made for a demographic sweet spot in which lotteries, games of chance, and other monetary instruments were likely to flourish.

But it wasn't until 1564 that the Milanese physician and math wizard Girolamo Cardano produced *Liber de Ludo Aleae* (*Book on Games of Chance*), in which he explained how to make logic and probability work in a gambler's favor. A brilliant if cantankerous fellow, Dr. Jerome Cardplayer—as his name might be translated—offered advice on several card games but deemed *primiero* "the noblest," devoting more pages to it than to all other games combined. Much more radically, he provided evidence that his tactics were sound by inventing a way to combine probabilities. In doing so, he prepared the ground not only for modern algebra, probability theory, and financial analysis—at least two risk-management firms have been named after him—but also for the scores of hold'em primers flying off the shelves of twenty-first-century bookstores.

Cardano's pioneering manuscript marked an ethical departure as well. In his day, most pamphlets and sermons harshly condemned gamblers for immorality and mathematics as the work of the devil. As a doctor and an ethicist, Cardano humanely demurred: "Even if gambling were an evil, still, on account of the very large number of people who play, it would seem to be a necessary evil. For that very reason it ought to be discussed by a medical doctor like one of the incurable diseases."

This was all well and good, but various inquisitions were in full swing as he wrote. The mere accusation that Cardano (1501–1576) was born illegitimate had barred him from the College of Physicians in Milan. He was thus forced to practice his healing art sub rosa, supplementing his income with lectures and books on mathematics, ethics, music, medicine, and gambling. The epitome of what we call a Renaissance man, Cardano was also notorious for his *mala fortuna*. He was prone to being struck by falling masonry and attacked by mad dogs. His bad luck at cards landed him briefly in Milan's debtors' prison, making the peculiar suitability of his name best appreciated by imagining a crash-prone stock car driver baptized Ford Nascaretti.

Yet despite his ill fortune, Cardano's medical and scientific expertise made him a trusted adviser to princes and popes. He was even commissioned to cast the horoscope of fifteen-year-old King Edward VI, the sickly only son of Henry VIII and half brother to Elizabeth. In a highly fraught milieu in which errant advisers and daughter-bearing wives were often beheaded, Cardano forecast that Edward would soon marry, bear sons, and continue his reign as he lived out a normal span of years. The only problem with the star-crossed horoscope was that it first appeared in print a few days after Edward passed away, probably of tuberculosis contracted during a bout with measles. Cardano somehow managed to keep his head on his shoulders, though he was imprisoned for a while by agents of the Bolognese Inquisition, this time for casting the horoscope of Jesus.

Cardano's autobiography, written shortly before his death at age seventy-five, recounts a particularly long day of *primiero* in Venice. It begins in the home of a senator who turns out to be a cheat. "When I observed that the cards were marked," writes Cardano, "I impetuously slashed his face with my poniard, though not deeply." He managed to escape the senator's palazzo with his life and most of his money, at which point things became strange. "On that same day about eight o'clock in the evening, while I was doing my best to escape from the clutches of the police because I had offered violence to a Senator, and keeping meanwhile my weapons beneath my cloak, I suddenly slipped, deceived in the dark, and fell into a canal. I kept my presence of mind even as I plunged, threw out my right arm, and, grasping the gunwale of a passing boat, was rescued by the passengers. When I scrambled aboard the skiff, I discovered in it, to my surprise, the Senator with whom I had just gambled. He had the wounds on his face bound up with a dressing; yet he willingly brought me out a suit of garments such as sailors wear. Dressed in these clothes, I traveled with him as far as Padua." In Venice's watery hotbed of knife-wielding cardsharps, all was well that ended well, apparently.

Cardano's results at the tables must have improved after he invented his method for combining probabilities, a brainstorm that allowed him to calculate the exact odds of drawing certain hands at primero. (Had he experienced better luck beforehand, of course, he would have had less incentive to come up with his radiant discovery and put his ideas onto paper.) The thirty-two short chapters of *Liber de Ludo Aleae* cover the history of dice and backgammon, how to recognize and thwart cheaters, the psychology of gambling, and the critical difference between a card and a dice game: "The latter is open, whereas play with cards takes place from ambush."

In the algebraic heart of the book, Cardano walks his reader through the math and logic of typical primero head-scratchers. If a player has three clubs, for example, he needs to know his chances of completing a *fluxus*. With seven clubs among the thirty-six unseen cards (remember, the deck has been stripped of eights, nines, and tens), Cardano's combinative method shows the odds against drawing at least one club in two tries to be $29/36 \times 28/35 = .6444$. The player thus has barely a 35 percent chance of hitting his *fluxus*. Even so, knowing he isn't quite a two-to-one underdog will help him determine how big a bet he can rationally call to continue with his draw.

Basic as this might seem to modern poker players, combining probabilities had evidently never been done before. Yet Cardano's work remained unknown for 145 years. His well-founded fear of the Inquisition had probably caused him to hide his manuscript. Finally published in 1663, it would rewrite mathematical history. Yet it wasn't until 1953 that Oystein Øre of Yale, in *Cardano: The Gambling Scholar* (which includes a translation of Cardano's Latin text), dated probability theory to the 1564 manuscript, written at least a century before the work of Blaise Pascal and Pierre Fermat, the pair who'd been credited with launching the theory. More recently, Caltech's Leonard Mlodinow called Cardano's book "a beachhead, the first success in the human quest to understand the nature of uncertainty."

Book on Games of Chance also blazed a wonky trail for such bestselling pokeraticians (in this case, poker + mathematicians) as Herbert O. Yardley, Frank R. Wallace, David Sklansky, Mason Malmuth, Dan Harrington, Gus Hansen, Daniel Negreanu, and even a few of Doyle Brunson's coauthors in *Super System* and *SS 2*, all of whom have enjoyed the advantage of working with quantitative tools designed by Cardano. Nor is it very surprising that each of them has chosen to ignore the unfortunate doctor's ultimate counsel: "The greatest advantage in gambling lies in not playing at all."

POQUE TO POKUH TO POKER

> It is incumbent on those who accept great changes to risk
> themselves on great occasions.
>
> —THOMAS JEFFERSON

As the rage for primero gradually subsided over the course of the eighteenth century, the most pokerlike pastimes in Europe were English brag, Spanish *mus*, German *poch*, and their French cousin, *poque*. An updated, simpler version of primero, *poque* was limited to four players, each of whom was dealt five cards from a twenty-card deck before vying for the antes and other bets. After a single round of betting, raising, calling, or folding, whichever players hadn't folded showed down their cards. The hand ranks were quartet, full, triplet, and pair, the same as poker's eventual hierarchy, but without straights and flushes. *Poque* was fashionable among the upper classes prior to the 1789 Revolution, and the traders, diplomats, and administrators who happened to be serving abroad were the likeliest to avoid the guillotine during the Jacobin Reign of Terror that followed. The card games they played in Persia and Louisiana survived along with them.

It was uncertain for a while whether *poque* imitated the Persian game of *as nas* (my beloved ace) or vice versa. Ever since 1673, when the

French East India Company obtained from the shah the right to trade freely in Persia, commerce between the two countries had flourished. The most commonly exchanged items were Persian textiles, carpets, and opium for French wine, indigo and cochineal dyes, and perfume, but card games and decks changed hands too.

In the 1897 edition of *Foster's Complete Hoyle*, R. F. Foster declared: "The game of poker, as first played in the United States, five cards to each player from a twenty-card pack, is undoubtedly the Persian game of *as nas*." This confident view was echoed in 1968 by Wallace Ward, a du Pont chemist whose pen name was Frank R. Wallace. In a hasty appendix to his self-published and disingenuously titled *Poker: A Guaranteed Income for Life*, he wrote: "Sailors from Persia taught the French settlers in New Orleans the gambling game As, which was derived from the ancient Persian game of As Nas." This and other speculations were probably influenced by the claim in 1950 by Louis Coffin, treasurer of the United States Playing Card Company, that poker originated in New Orleans among "French inhabitants who had been in the French Service in Persia *circa* 1800–20."

In 1990, however, Parlett's more authoritative *Oxford Guide to Card Games* noted that "*as*" isn't a card-related word in Persian but is the French word for "ace," as well as the lack of evidence that *as nas* had been played before 1790 or so. Two years later Lynn Loomis and Mason Malmuth, in *The Fundamentals of Poker*, also delinked *poque* from *as nas*, at least as far as poker's pedigree was concerned: "When French colonists arrived to settle the Louisiana Territory in the 1700s, they brought *poque* with them." No Persian sailors were necessary.

In 2002, the English writer Al Alvarez, one of poker's most judicious observers, concluded that the game's closest ancestor was first played in the late eighteenth century by French merchants and diplomats in Persia, who "adapted their own game of *poque* or *bouillotte* [its three-card cousin] to the local As-Nas deck, then taught it to their Persian hosts."

Everyone seems to agree that *as nas* involved a special deck with either twenty or twenty-five cards, depending on whether four or five people were playing. The aces depicted the *shir va khurshid* (lion and sun) atop the hierarchy, followed by the shah or *pisha* (king), *bibi* (lady), *sarbas* (soldier), and *lakat* (something of little value), usually represented by a dancing girl. The dancer always had a green background and was often sparsely clad in a flagrantly sexual pose.

Both *poque* and *as nas* players were dealt five-card hands, with the lowest card being either a ten or a dancer. No draws to better hands took place, and only quads, fulls, triplets, and pairs were recognized. Once they'd evaluated their cards, *poque* players vied for the pot by announcing, "*Je poque de dix*," or however much they wanted to bet. Four aces or four kings with an ace were the only unbeatable hands, and—ignoring mathematical scarcity as the measure of value—a measly pair of tens beat what we would recognize as a royal flush. But even if you held no pair at all, you could bluff, a tactic requiring a knack for seizing the initiative and the ability to leverage uncertainty—in other words, to take advantage of the fact that your opponent doesn't know what you have and you know that he probably doesn't have an unbeatable hand. In this, *poque* players were relying on what David Sklansky, the great modern pokeratician, would set down in 1994 as the Fundamental Theorem of Poker: "Every time you play a hand differently from the way you would have played it if you could see all your opponents' cards, they gain; and every time you play your hand the same way you would if you could see all their cards, they lose. Conversely, every time opponents play their hand differently from the way they would have if they could see all your cards, you gain; and every time they play their hands the same way they would have played if they could see all your cards, you lose." The best *poque* players intuitively understood and were able to take advantage of this, even if no one would commit it to paper for another couple of centuries.

That *poque* was pronounced with two syllables (in French mouths, more like one and a half) makes its relation to poker all the more obvious. It wasn't a very big step from playing and saying *poque* to the Southern pronunciation, *pokuh*. Later, when the action moved north of the Mason-Dixon Line, the second syllable would pick up an *r*. Even in the heart of old Dixie, though, it would be written as *poker*.

Just as no date can be fixed for the first baseball game or session of jazz, an exact time and place for poker's first hand can never be established. But we can say with confidence that the United States had just begun to expand into the ethnic and geographical contours we recognize today when poker was injected into the portal of its main artery: New Orleans. Deck types and game names (*poque, pokuh,* poker, *as nas,* and no doubt a few others) must have varied from saloon to saloon along its bustling waterfront, but players had little reason to write them down or date them; in any case, no such document has been discovered. What's clear is that poker emerged from the womb of a French vying game inflected with Persian characteristics as the flags above New Orleans were changing from Spain's to France's to the Stars and Stripes around the start of the nineteenth century and in the tumultuous decade that followed. But if we're looking for a symbolic birth date, July 4, 1803, could serve as well as any.

To understand why, we must backtrack to 1718, when a trading post along the Indian portage to Lake Pontchartrain was founded by Jean-Baptiste Le Moyne de Bienville of the French Mississippi Company, who named the place Nouvelle-Orléans to honor his sponsor, the duke of Orléans. As always in real estate, location was crucial. Instead of a winding, weeklong trip down the rest of the Mississippi to the Gulf of Mexico, a ship could cut north and east through the lake from here and be at the gulf in two days. The site was at the nexus of transatlantic commerce: for upriver traders exporting furs, grain, and produce by barge, and for Caribbean, European, and African goods—and, yes, slaves—moving in the other direction. The city that grew up around it served as the main port and customhouse for a rapidly expanding network of traders.

To its north and west, the vast territory drained by the Missouri and Mississippi rivers was named Louisiana after Louis XIV, the Sun King who reigned at Versailles for an astonishing seventy-two years. When the territory was designated a French crown colony in 1731, French settlers began to arrive, and Acadians were encouraged to migrate there from Canada. After losing the French and Indian War to the British, however, France ceded Louisiana to Spain as part of the almost hilariously complex Treaty of Paris signed in 1763 by Europe's three major colonial powers. Thousands of Acadians had already been driven by British troops from their homes in Nova Scotia, and most of them resettled along the lower Mississippi. It also seems likely that, as Loomis and Malmuth suggest, at least a few "Cajuns" brought the game of *poque* with them.

As parts of Spain proper came under pressure from Napoleon, Spain ceded control of Louisiana back to France in 1800. But no matter which European power held sway in the New World, polyglot New Orleans had become one of the planet's most savory melting pots. Its population of ten thousand or so was an unruly gumbo of Spaniards, Portuguese, French administrators and citizens, Germans from the Upper Rhine region, Anglos from Canada and the original thirteen colonies, Native Americans (mainly from the Choctaw and Acolapissa tribes), sailors and merchants from several fleets, plus a steady stream of nationless pirates and slavers. Yet even while the slave trade ignominiously thrived there until 1808, the city was home to hundreds of what were called "free persons of color." All took their place in a vibrant if contentious Creole society like no other on earth, one that was uniquely receptive to hybrid forms of music, food, language, commerce, and card games.

When Thomas Jefferson was inaugurated on March 4, 1801, the population he presided over was 5,308,483, including well over a million slaves. Nine tenths of these persons lived within a hundred miles of the Atlantic Ocean. The District of Columbia had been the seat of American government for less than ten months. Older Northern cities had become overcrowded, and two hundred years of tobacco cultivation had severely depleted the Chesapeake soil. Farmers and land-hungry city dwellers were migrating across the Appalachians, many through the Cumberland Gap. But just about the only "roads" connecting them to one another were the rivers flowing into the Mississippi, which made the port of New Orleans by far the most important place west of the Atlantic seaboard.

Jefferson immediately dispatched Robert Livingston to Paris on a mission to purchase the city. Despite his affection for France, our third president believed control of that port was crucial to American prospects. "There is on the globe one single spot, the possessor of which is our natural and habitual enemy," he wrote to Livingston in May 1802. "It is New Orleans." Why would Napoleon even consider selling such a vital piece of real estate? Because, as Livingston and Jefferson had shrewdly deduced, the emperor was desperate for capital to finance his doomed war with Britain. It was Jefferson's good fortune as well that Napoleon was stretched too thin to defend even the colony of San Domingue (Haiti), where the enslaved population would soon rise up to annihilate a massive French expeditionary force under Charles Leclerc, let alone the entire 828,000 square miles of Louisiana. The next stop for Leclerq's army was to have been New Orleans.

On July 4, 1803, Jefferson announced that Napoleon had agreed to sell all of Louisiana for $15 million, which came to about four cents an acre. Though the territory's borders were mapped imprecisely, the president had already dispatched Lewis and Clark to determine whether a river passage extended through it; none did, unfortunately, but that didn't keep their expedition from reaching the Pacific. It turned out that the territory comprised roughly the area drained by the Missouri and Mississippi rivers and their western tributaries (including most or all of thirteen current states) and was anchored by the flourishing ports of St. Louis and New Orleans. Compared to this fire sale, Peter Minuit had grossly overpaid the Conarsee Delawares in 1626 when he traded sixty guilders' worth of glass wampum beads for Manhattan.

After two and a half centuries of halting colonial expansion along the Atlantic seaboard and a seven-year war of independence, the United States had peacefully doubled in size overnight. In Jefferson's visionary imagination, if not yet in fact, the country now reached all the way to the Pacific. The entire length of the continent, he believed, would now be settled by one people "speaking the same language, governed in similar forms, and by similar laws." What he did not say was how natural it would be for such a people to share a taste for a new kind of card game, one whose rules favored a frontiersman's initiative and cunning, an entrepreneur's creative sense of risk, and a democratic openness to every class of player.

Under his successor, James Madison, Louisiana became the eighteenth state on April 12, 1812, just in time to be threatened by the redcoats in the latest installment of what seemed to be Britain's never-ending war in North America. Allied with several Indian tribes, British troops captured Detroit, wreaked commercial havoc, and even burned down the White House before heading south. A peace treaty was signed in Ghent on December 24, 1814, but word of it didn't cross the Atlantic in time to prevent the Battle of New Orleans fifteen days later. It was just as well, perhaps, because the city was triumphantly defended by General Andrew Jackson, the piratical slave-trader Jean Lafite, and sizable contingents of Haitian refugees, Creole aristocrats, and Choctaw warriors under Pushmataha. Outnumbered by better than two to one, the well-deployed American forces inflicted 2,037 casualties while suffering only 71. Jackson's reputation was made, and New Orleans soon became the second-wealthiest and fourth-most-populous city in the United States, and by far the most culturally diverse.

The propensity to gamble was an extension of daily life in New Orleans and along the new western frontier. In *People of Chance*, the Penn State historian John Findlay writes of this period: "The mixture of chance and competition, in a sphere set apart from the working world, appealed to this generation of egalitarians." Equal under the law, in the voting booth, and at the poker table, most of them also wanted to set themselves apart from their fellow citizens. "A man displayed his equality by sitting down to play in the first place," Findlay continues, "but hoped that the game's outcome would make him more equal." It was in this sense, among many others, that poker and the United States grew up together, and one reason why the game is often said to epitomize American values. As the actor Walter Matthau drily put it a century and a half later, "Poker exemplifies the worst aspects of capitalism that have made our country so great."

Meanwhile, now that New Orleans had become an American city, more English-speakers arrived, trying to make a go of it in the warmer, more open environment. Their own taste for bluff-based card games had developed while playing brag farther north or in Britain. But as they sat down and learned the rules of this not so strange Creole pastime, it must have intrigued them that what they called bragging turned out to be the ultimate tactic in pokuh as well. That game is what we now call Old Poker: five cards per player, no discards or draws, one round of betting. But Old Poker players had plenty to learn from the brag players too, besides how to bluff more effectively. The most flexible among them adopted the flushes, straights, and draws (called "taking in" by brag players), along with the fifty-two-card deck that made the draws possible and the higher-value combinations more likely. The full deck also allowed for more players per hand, which made the pots larger, as did the extra round of betting after the draw. The bigger the pots, the more players wanting in on the action. This popular new hybrid was more complex than either *poque* or brag, though it wasn't so complicated that lucky beginners had no chance to win. But what should its name be, given that Franco-American pokuh could fairly be called five-card brag?

It was poker.

Although there were fewer of them in America, Spanish *mus* players must have also found it natural to spice up the local pokuh games with fifty-two cards and a replacement draw to a wider range of hands. Like their French and Anglo counterparts, they would have mixed and matched rules in much the same way that New Orleans chefs combined ingredients from Acadian, French, Spanish, and Caribbean cooking.

As the game surged north, its new rules would gradually be standardized. According to Hoyle, by 1850 or so nearly everyone agreed that after being dealt five cards each from an unstripped deck, players determined whether their hand was worth betting or "seeing" a bet with; if not, they would "throw up" their hand, or as we would say, fold it. Each remaining player then exercised his option either to stand pat—that is, keep all five original cards—or turn in to the dealer facedown between one and four of them and receive an equal number, also facedown, from the top of the deck, followed by a second round of betting. If one player made a bet or a raise the others were unwilling to see, the bettor won the "pool" without having to show his hand—though he could choose to show it if he wanted to prove that he had, or hadn't, been bluffing. If two or more players remained when the betting was over, they turned over their cards for a "show of hands," and the same hierarchy we're familiar with today determined the winner.

With more players drawing to an expanded range of hands, pools became larger and tactical skill more decisive. Holding the red kings and three other diamonds, for instance, which cards should be replaced against a raiser in early position if the raiser drew three? (In other words, were you more likely to beat a pair of aces by hitting a third king or second pair, or by giving up the king of hearts and drawing to a fifth diamond?) How often, and against which opponents, could one get away with a bluff after standing pat with "nary pair"? It was no longer simply a matter of getting lucky, or not, on the deal, then betting for value or bluffing. Draws provided hope to players dealt weak starting hands, which in turn triggered the development of tactics to deploy against overly hopeful opponents. With fifty-two cards in play, five contenders for the pool might remain after the draw, even more if the discards were shuffled back into the stub of the deck. Assuming the game was on the square, winning money depended on memory—How, and how much, did each opponent bet on the first round? How many cards did each draw?—as well as a knack for deducing the range of hands each opponent might be holding from the number of discards and the size of the second-round bet or raise, all this in light of mathematical probabilities, previous betting patterns, facial expressions, and so on.

A new wrinkle called the *jackpot* began to appear just before the Civil War. It required a player to hold at least a pair of jacks to open the betting. If no player saw the opening bet, the bettor won the small pot and was compelled to show a pair of jacks or some higher hand. If his opening bet was called, he usually drew three to his pair, though the rules permitted him to discard one paired card and draw to a straight or flush; in this case, he discarded to the side of the pile so that after the showdown he could prove he'd held at least jacks when he opened. Failure to do so would require him to contribute twice the amount of his original bet to the pot. Another key rule of jackpots was that if no one was able to open, everyone anted again, the deal rotated clockwise, and the process was repeated until one player was able and willing to "break the pot" and the hand played out as usual. In a variant known as the *progressive jackpot*, the second round required queens or better to open, the third round kings or better, the fourth round aces, then kings, queens, jacks, and so on.

Progressive or not, jackpots were intended to build larger pots while thwarting reckless players with a habit of making huge opening bets with weak hands. Yet such players could still call or raise the opening bet, stand pat with virtually nothing, then win the pot with a bluff.

Larger pots, more diverse reckoning skills. The former would attract more cardsharps, the latter more ancestors of today's poker maestros. For the most talented players, draw's extra round of betting provided new chances to leverage probabilities or pick up a tell. But it also gave cheaters more opportunities to deal seconds, see replacement cards in a mirror, or gain other illicit advantages—opportunities they exploited with a vengeance aboard newfangled floating casinos perfectly designed to carry cardsharps and poker up into the American mainstream.

7

MISSISSIPPI STEAMBOATS, THE INTERNET CARD ROOMS OF 1814

My own conclusion is that history is simply social development along the lines of weakest resistance, and that in most cases the line of weakest resistance is found as unconsciously by society as by water.

— HENRY ADAMS

Steamboats may strike us as quaint curiosities, things only children or unadventurous nostalgia buffs can get much of a charge from. But when ships with no sails first appeared, decked out instead with smokestacks and paddle wheels, not to mention promenades, cattle pens, and three-story hotel-casinos, the bellowing steam-powered extravaganzas were as strange to the ears and eyes of antebellum America as any Spielbergian starship.

Steam power had arrived in the United States in August 1787, when the inventor John Fitch's trial run of a forty-six-foot craft on the Delaware River was witnessed by delegates to the Constitutional Convention. This boat and others designed by Fitch were mechanically sound but proved neither seaworthy nor cost-effective. It was left to Robert Fulton, an engineer and inventor, and the financier Robert Livingston, who would negotiate the Louisiana Purchase, to improve Fitch's designs, building vessels that profitably moved cargo and passengers along Eastern rivers. Henry Adams called August 17, 1807, when Fulton's

Clermont began her maiden voyage up the Hudson, "the beginning of a new era in America,—a date which separated the colonial from the independent stage of growth." No other country had produced such a vessel, and Adams noted that "for the first time America could consider herself mistress of her vast resources."

The *New Orleans*, Fulton's first craft designed for the swifter, more treacherous currents of the Mississippi, capsized because it was top-heavy. After tweaking the design, he gave the same name to another boat, and this one succeeded with colors flying. One hundred and forty feet long and twenty-eight wide, the second *New Orleans* could haul one hundred tons of freight and fifty passengers ten miles per hour downstream, four while paddling against the current. Female passengers slept in a cabin belowdecks, men in more elegant quarters in the roundhouse, with views of the river and the landscapes beyond it. Besides keeping women sequestered from ruffians, the arrangement shielded them from the midnight card games it was assumed they'd be scandalized to witness, let alone participate in.

When Fulton and his partners began providing reliable service along the 250-mile route between New Orleans and Natchez, Mississippi, in 1814, using boats twice as fast as the *New Orleans*, they changed the nature of commerce in America. Purchasing Louisiana had been one thing, integrating it with the rest of the world quite another. Fulton's boats made it inevitable that river ports would thrive, inland towns wither, by connecting the new American frontier to the rest of civilization. With virtually no roads west of the Appalachians, exploiting the vast network of rivers proved the most practical way to move people, opinions, newspapers, books, mail, furs, lumber, clothing, agricultural products, rum, whiskey, and card games from point A to point B. Steamboats and the waters they plied thus amounted to the information superhighway of 1814 and beyond.

When Fulton died the next year, the loss of his innovative genius was considered a national calamity. The best measure of his invention's importance is that in the twenty years after the *New Orleans* first steamed up the Mississippi, more people were drawn to America's interior—about two and a half million—than the original thirteen colonies had attracted in two hundred years.

Steamboats changed the nature of warfare as well. In December 1814, Captain Henry M. Shreve deployed the sidewheeler *Enterprise* to deliver a vital cache of supplies from Pittsburgh to General Andrew Jackson outside New Orleans. Not needing favorable currents or winds, Shreve's boat was even able to run the gauntlet of British guns below the city to bring more supplies to Fort St. Philip, clinching the defense of the city.

By 1820, at least four hundred gaming dens were open for business in New Orleans, most of them saloons in the district known as the Swamp. Proprietors used any means necessary to tempt the hundreds of passengers, traders, and boatmen coming ashore every day. The fluid population of twenty thousand denizens probably did as much dancing, feasting, music making, carousing, and cardplaying as the rest of the country combined. In a place far removed both morally and geographically from cultural centers like Philadelphia and Boston, visitors and even many residents thought of the Crescent City as a temporary address, both a decadent resort and the anteroom to unexplored parts of the continent where they hoped to make their fortune.

Nor were they unaware that Jackson, Old Hickory himself, gambled heavily on cockfights, thoroughbred races, and card games; that twice in his life he had staked all he owned on a bet; that he had even killed a man, Charles Dickinson, and almost died himself, in a duel over a racing wager and a perceived insult to his wife, Rachel. (After allowing Dickinson, a crack shot, to fire first from eight paces and hit him in the chest, Jackson steadied himself and intentionally shot Dickinson in the groin to cause him a slower, more excruciating death. For the last forty years of his life he carried Dickinson's lead ball an inch above his heart.) In 1828 he would be elected the seventh president of the United States, and reelected in a landslide in 1832, bringing his rough frontier values directly into the White House for two full terms. From there they emanated back across the nation again, stoking an atmosphere that favored taking outsize chances. One emphatic piece of advice the president gave his nephew about a horse race is now thought to capture the spirit of Jacksonian America: "You must *risque* to win."

Jackson's comrade-in-arms, Captain Shreve, had broken Fulton's monopoly on the river by launching commercial steamboats that extended service to Louisville by 1823. Before Fulton and Shreve, moving bulky products by ox-drawn cart between Louisville and New Orleans took two or three months. A steamboat made the trip in six days. Not surprisingly, the number of steamers on Western rivers rose from twenty in 1818 to more than two hundred just twelve years later. By 1833, more than twelve hundred boats were docking as far north as Fort Snelling, Minnesota, extending the transportation network from the continent's heart to Caribbean ports and beyond.

They also helped move America's demographic center well to the west. In 1846, Harry Truman's ancestors traveled by steamboat down the Ohio River from Louisville, north on the Mississippi from Cairo to St. Louis, then against the swift current of the Missouri 457 miles to the end of the line, settling in what was then America's westernmost town, Independence. Given all the hazards of overland travel, it seems doubtful they would have moved quite that far if not for the steamboat.

For nearly every American living outside an Eastern city, the boats provided the only regular connection with the rest of the world. To those used to getting family or national "news" several months after it happened, if ever, regularly scheduled steamers were even more life changing than e-mail would be to a person used to sending urgent letters through the post office.

The change was no less seismic for gamblers. Steamboats connected the faro and poker professionals to their flocks of new customers, the affluent traveling public. With New Orleans, Natchez, St. Louis, and Cincinnati all home to an expanding fleet of floating card rooms, a tempting little piece of those risqué ports could steam into the sleepy provinces a thousand miles away, right on schedule. This world-shrinking development was similar to one in the middle of the twentieth century, when cheap airline travel made Las Vegas accessible, and to the creation of virtual card rooms at the dawn of the twenty-first, which enabled poker players to compete internationally while staying home in their pajamas.

The prototype luxury steamer was Captain Shreve's *George Washington*, a lavish double-decker launched in 1825 with twin smokestacks, twenty-four staterooms (each named for one of the states), three saloons, and a card parlor. Shreve and his competitors soon began to outdo themselves, offering hand-carved staircases, cut-glass chandeliers, bone china, and the cuisine of famous chefs to attract a well-heeled clientele to their $200,000 showboats. Folks along the inland frontier had never seen anything like them.

The crews of these waterborne Bellagios were the envy of just about every young man who set eyes on them. When eight-year-old Sam Clemens glimpsed his first steamboat in 1844 from the dock at Hannibal, Missouri, he resolved to get a job working on one. The impending arrival of a "gaudy packet"—a high-end steamer hauling both passengers and cargo—made the day "glorious with expectancy," he wrote later. He described one packet as "long and sharp and trim and pretty" with "two tall, fancy-topped chimneys." The pilothouse, "all glass and 'gingerbread,' perched on the top of the 'texas' deck behind them; the paddleboxes are gorgeous with a picture or with gilded rays above the boat's name; the boiler deck, the hurricane deck, and the texas deck are fenced and ornamented with clean white railings; there is a flag gallantly flying from the jackstaff; the furnace doors are open and the fires glaring bravely." To further impress the locals, great volumes of black smoke came "rolling and tumbling out of the chimneys—a husbanded grandeur created with a bit of pitch pine just before arriving at a town." But as soon as the boat was reloaded with new freight and passengers and had steamed off around the next bend, "the day was a dead and empty thing." Even a lowly striker, whose main job was shoveling coal into a hellacious furnace sixteen hours a day, impressed young Sam as "notoriously worldly, and I just the reverse." A striker "had money, too, and hair oil. . . . No girl could withstand his charms."

The most envied man was the pilot, who earned $300 a month when a kid from a small town would be lucky to make $1 or $2. Pilots were represented by their mighty Benevolent Association, through which they shared information about the ever-shifting mud bars and currents. This in turn discouraged underwriters from insuring boats not piloted by a member, so pilots could more or less dictate their contracts with the owners.

Their grandeur and charm notwithstanding, steamboats had their own perils. Their primitive boilers, for example, could explode any second. About fourteen hundred people would be killed in such accidents, and Clemens lost his brother Henry in one of them. Even that couldn't quell his desire. By the time he was twenty-seven, Clemens managed to become a pilot himself, though his career was cut short when the Civil War closed the Mississippi to commercial traffic. Forced to write for a living instead, he chose as his pen name the pilot's cry signaling a safe depth of two fathoms: *Mark twain!* "The Professor's Yarn," his tale of an elaborate poker con in *Life on the Mississippi*, is a classic of American literature. "There are few things that are so unpardonably neglected in our country as poker," he observes. "Why, I have known clergymen, good men, kindhearted, liberal, sincere, and all that, who did not know the meaning of a 'flush.' It is enough to make one ashamed of one's species."

So was poker a crooked, sinful, righteous, or even legal pastime? Something that should be legal on land or only on water? No widely acceptable answer to such questions has ever been given. As early as 1823, the

Louisiana legislature sanctioned most forms of gambling, poker included. But in an effort to counterbalance the social impact of the six new "temples of chance" licensed in New Orleans, each license required an annual "contribution" of $5,000 to the Charity Hospital and the College of Orleans. Most of these "temples" were little more than tarted-up saloons, but in 1827 an émigré from Haiti named John Davis introduced a more ambitious version of the casino to America's Venice-on-the-Mississippi. His complex of buildings along Orleans Street between Bourbon and Royal included the Davis Hotel, the Orleans Ballroom, and the Théâtre d'Orléans. The hotel and gaming parlors provided free rooms, fine wine, and French cuisine for as long as a wealthy customer was willing to gamble, mostly at faro, 21, and roulette, but also brag and poker; and the higher the stakes he played for, the more luxurious his accommodations would be. Anticipating hoteliers from Bugsy Siegel to Steve Wynn, it was said that "John Davis could lodge you, feed you, amuse you, and fleece you, all in one city block." In John Findlay's judgment, "Davis had arrived at the popular American formula that combined aristocratic appearance with democratic participation in casino play."

By 1835, however, growing concern over the adverse social effects of gambling persuaded the legislature to repeal its licensing act and pass laws subjecting the keepers of gambling dens to $10,000 fines or imprisonment. Such laws could never stamp out wagering, of course, but they did encourage any number of card players and saloonkeepers to move their operations upriver, or to make the steamboats a fleet of branch offices.

Then as now, onboard gambling was relatively free of legal or moral censure, even as the sidewheeling casinos wound their way through the Bible Belt. Ticket prices varied according to season and demand, but the average cabin fare to St. Louis and back was about $25, which came to several months' pay for most Americans. But for anyone who wanted to play poker for high stakes, the biggest games were likely to be found on an opulent packet.

The biggest games but not the fairest. Nothing could have been more inevitable than that a new breed of cardsharp would quickly evolve to take advantage of these riverine venues. Moving on and off the packets in well-oiled teams, they deployed a variety of ruses and tools to fleece—not by expert play and good luck but by cheating and threats of violence—any passenger foolish enough to gamble with them. But recognizing the sharps wasn't always easy for inexperienced travelers.

David Schwartz points out that "the anonymity of the riverboat gave the professional gambler a cloak of respectability. With his handsome clothes and genteel affectations, he might be anyone: a plantation owner, a merchant, a salesman—even a minister." Sharps were usually identified only after it was too late to make a difference. When the boiler of the *Constitution* exploded in 1817, scalding eleven passengers to death, the professional gambler among them was buried separately.

By the 1830s, at least six hundred sharps were working the riverboats, with one estimate putting their number as high as fifteen hundred. In the Jacksonian spirit of gambling, gunplay, and bold speculation, many folks west of the Appalachians considered poker professionals bona fide businessmen, at least as legitimate as the stuffy Federalist bankers charging interest in far-off Manhattan. Their victims, says Findlay, were often "portrayed as members of groups out of social favor—Jews, foreigners, slave holders, immigrants, or the spoiled sons of wealthy families." And whatever the sharps' moral or social standing, they soon became so much a part of riverboat life that many captains believed it was bad luck to leave port without one aboard.

The target of the sharps, of course, was the steady supply of passengers with money to lose—not a few coppers, either, but enough to make the risk of deadly reprisals worth the sharps' while. For one thing, the expensive novelty of a packet cruise was an irresistible temptation to affluent gentry and businessmen eager to prove their worldliness and poker acumen. For another, the South was never more prosperous than during the four decades preceding the Civil War. Immense fortunes in land, sugar, cotton, tobacco, and slaves were generated by the booming plantation system. And just as the titans of e-commerce get about in Sikorsky S-92s and Learjet 60XRs today, the planters' preferred mode of transport was the poshest suites on the texas decks of luxury packets. With little else to do for a week—no cell phones or laptops, no spa gyms or ESPN—after-dinner poker was what a sporting Southern gentleman *did*. "All the things father wanted me to do and be were such boring things," Rhett Butler grouses in *Gone With the Wind*. "And finally he threw me out into the world without a cent and no training whatsoever to be anything but a Charleston gentleman, a good pistol shot and an excellent poker player." Then there is Scarlett's father's low opinion of the upright Wilkes men: "And there they sit reading and dreaming the dear God knows what," says Gerald O'Hara, "when they'd be better off spending their time hunting and playing poker as a proper man should."

Without credit cards or electronic bank transfers, businessmen and sporting gents all carried gold and/or cash. Plantation owners often traveled with slaves and property deeds and wagered them as part of a pot. As the gambler Tom Ellison recalled, "It wasn't at all uncommon to hear an old planter betting off his Negroes on a good hand. Every man who ever ran on the river knows that these old planters used to play in their lady servants, valuing them all the way from $300 to $1,500. I saw a little colored boy stand up to $300 to back his master's faith in a little flush that wasn't any good on earth."

Henry Hill recalled a game with "some planters from the lower Mississippi. They wanted a game of poker and I agreed to sit in. We played from three Saturday night until four Monday morning and when I cashed in, I had won $350,000"—this in the days when a far-as-the-eye-can-see spread might go for a tenth of that. This was how Gerald O'Hara had made his fortune in the 1830s: "The hand of Fate and a hand of poker"—four deuces—"combined to give him the plantation which he afterwards called Tara."

Yet planters were hardly the only flush passengers. In Melville's *The Confidence-Man*, the "pilgrims" aboard a New Orleans–bound steamboat include "Sante Fe traders in striped blankets, and Broadway bucks in cravats of cloth of gold; fine-looking Kentucky boatmen, and Japanese-looking Mississippi cotton-planters; Quakers in full drab and United States soldiers in full regimentals; slaves, black, mulatto, quadroon; modish young Spanish Creoles, and old-fashioned French Jews; Mormons and Papists . . . jesters and mourners, teetotalers and convivialists, deacons and blacklegs." Thomas Thorpe, a reporter for *Harper's New Monthly Magazine*, wrote of "immigrants from every nationality in Europe [who] mingled in every phase of social life— the aristocratic English lord is intruded upon by the ultra-socialist; the conservative bishop accepts a favor from the graceless gambler . . . the farmer from about the arctic regions of Lake Superior exchanges ideas . . . with a man from the Everglades." In other words, precisely the sort of diverse humanity we rub elbows with at both live and online poker tables today.

Thorpe completed his picture by sketching a few more incongruous pairings: "an old black trunk, soiled with the mud of the Lower Nile, and a new carpetbag direct from Upper California . . . an elaborate dress, direct from Paris, is in contact with a trapper's Rocky Mountain costume . . . a large box of playing cards supports a very small package of Bibles." That the decks in this box were probably marked—to be sold with seals intact by the barman to passengers looking for assurance that the poker was fair and square—puts the package of Bibles in even more interesting light. But crooked or straight, poker became so closely associated with steamboats that many manufacturers branded their decks "Steamboat Playing Cards." Unfortunately, the national card game in those days was even more closely associated with black-legs and confidence men.

8

THE CHEATING GAME

I mean, Fletcher. He plays *cards*.
— DON IN *AMERICAN BUFFALO*

The first time the word "poker" appeared in print was an account of a cold deck in James Hildreth's memoir, *Dragoon Campaigns to the Rocky Mountains; Being a History of the Enlistment, Organization, and First Campaigns of the Regiment of United States Dragoons*, published in 1836. The regiment had visited Fort Gibson in the Arkansas Territory in 1833 and the Pawnee villages of Nebraska the following year. Hildreth describes a late-night game between two officers not far from their barracks. He reports that his company's major "lost some cool hundreds last night at poker" to his captain, then pauses to vaguely define this new term in a footnote: "A favorite game of cards at the south and west."

Since it was played alongside a bayou in the early 1830s, the game was almost certainly twenty-card *poque* or Old Poker. That it had already traveled far enough north to be called poker and had been around long enough to have become a "favorite" both suggest that it had been played for a decade or two. The hand described also suggests that poker had already degenerated into the Cheating Game. Hildreth doesn't comment on the overwhelming likelihood that a cold deck was deployed—poker and its odds are foreign to him, after all—even while reporting that after half a dozen raises the major, who throws down four kings, lost his cool hundreds to the captain's four aces. "D—m—n!" roars the major, "at the same time splitting the pine table with a blow of his fist." But instead of the more ominous implications of a captain cold-decking a major, Hildreth's concern is that "we shall probably have an hour's extra drill in the morning to make up for" the major's losses.

Aaron Brown and other modern poker authorities remind us that the standards of nonfiction reliability in antebellum America were quite a bit lower than they are today, when memoir writers loose with the facts are aggressively taken to task. In the early nineteenth century, writes Brown, "Few people were literate enough to write a book, so publishers relied on professional hacks to supply popular literature." From Hildreth to Mark Twain to whatever happened at the big game last Thursday, we must always bear in mind that the entertainment value of poker lore sometimes takes precedence over hard, documentable facts.

Even so, the publications that survive from those years make clear that well before the straight flush moved to the top of the hand rankings around 1850, four kings losing to four aces had become a cliché in the yarns about cheating. When in 1845 a riverboat captain holding quad kings lost his two-thirds stake in his vessel to a cardsharp showing down the inevitable hand, the captain went to his quarters and shot himself through the heart. The note found beside his body bemoaned the cold fact, learned moments too late, that "a man who would bet his last dollar on four kings doesn't deserve standing room on earth." Unless his fifth card was an ace.

On a "foggy, wretched night" in December 1829, the English actor Joe Cowell wrote in his diary (which wasn't published until eight years after Hildreth's book) about a session of poker aboard the steamboat *Helen M'Gregor* during a trip from Louisville to New Orleans. The game he describes is Old Poker with a one-dollar ante but no limits on the bets after that. Cowell calls it "a high-gambling western game, founded on brag" but erroneously claims it was invented by Speaker of the House Henry Clay, who hailed from Kentucky. Yet the Englishman makes accurate note of its guarded rituals: "Players pack [the cards] in their hands, and peep at them as if they were afraid to trust even themselves to look." The four men are clearly enjoying themselves, and Cowell recognizes that such gambling excursions provided an opportu-

THE CHEATING GAME ♣ 69

nity for Americans to slip free of everyday constraints and mix it up with "blacklegs" and vagabonds. ("Blackleg" was probably related to "blackguard" as well as to the dark, narrow trousers professional gamblers favored.) Once on the river, he observes, "All moral and social restraint was placed in the shade."

The poker game is suddenly interrupted when the boat experiences "a most tremendous concussion" from running aground on a sandbar, causing all the players to get up and huddle near the exit. All but one player, that is: "a gentleman in green spectacles, a gold guard chain, long and thick enough to moor a dog, and a brilliant diamond breast-pin" who remains at the table "quietly shuffling and cutting the poker deck." Ominously, it is his turn to deal when the action resumes. After pitching out five cards apiece, Green Spectacles "sat quietly watching the countenances of the others." A $10 bet and call is followed by a whopping raise to $500. A young lawyer then reraises to $1,000, and two players call the huge raise. Having risked but a dollar to see their hand, with no chance to draw to a better one, what could they possibly have? The lawyer shows down four kings with an ace, an unbeatable hand. His opponents have four queens and four jacks, respectively.

"Did you ever see the like on't?" asks the dealer while pushing the $3,033 pot to the lawyer. What excellent timing for him! Quads over quads over quads, paid off in two places by well-heeled, unlucky opponents.

"The truth," Cowell deduces, was that "the cards had been put up, or stocked, as it is called." In other words, they had been presequenced to give a couple of suckers hands strong enough to call a huge bet but not quite strong enough to win. As we would say, the losing players have been *cold-decked*. Cowell also concludes that the excitement after the concussion caused Green Spectacles "to make a slight mistake in the distribution of the hand," dealing the four kings to the lawyer instead of to himself. Cowell calls the dealer a "black-leg," though not a very skillful one, failing to consider the possibility that he and the "lawyer" had set up the two suckers and would split the profits later on.

Yet given the long odds against three "quartets" being dealt from a squarely shuffled deck, and given how many cold-deck artists were at work on the Western rivers by 1829, not to mention the outfit the dealer was wearing, flawless teamwork was almost certainly how those thousands of dollars changed hands. So who were these cardsharps, and how did they learn to execute such a wicked little swindle as that?

. . .

Football coaches videotape their opponents' hand signals, and baseball scouts use binoculars to steal signs from the other team's dugout. Pitchers throw greaseballs. Cyclists, swimmers, baseball and football players, track-and-field athletes, and weight lifters inject banned body-building steroids to make themselves faster and stronger. From angles they hope the ref cannot see, boxers head-butt opponents and hit them below the belt, in much the same way that basketball players grab jerseys, throw elbows, and set moving picks. Golfers improve their lie in sand traps and rough. Tennis pros and sumo wrestlers rig tournament matches. Even solitaire players draw two instead of three when it suits them. Indeed, there is no game or sport in which every—perhaps *any*— participant always plays according to Hoyle.

"Hoyle," of course, refers to the series of authoritative books about games written and later inspired by Edmond Hoyle (1672–1769), an English expert on whist and other eighteenth-century pastimes. After his death, the series continued under his name, put together by teams of editors who codified new games as they emerged in English-speaking countries. *Hoyles* published in the United States were widely accepted as the standard arbiters of rules and opinion about "all games common or fashionable with the American people." The 1864 edition stated: "The modern game of Draw-Poker" was "Originally Brag, then passing through the successive modifications of Straight-Poker, Draw-Poker with dealer's Ante . . . and lastly Jack-Pots both simple and progressive, all combining to pace the game on a widely different footing from its original prototype." "According to Hoyle" continues to mean both "fair and square" and "by highest authority."

Yet the earliest editions of *Hoyle* that mention poker suggested that most of its players were up to no good. The *Hoyle* of 1845 spelled it "Poke," while the 1857 edition warned that "20-card poker" was "one of the most dangerous pitfalls to be found in the city [New York]." (The fifty-two-card version played along the Western rivers had yet to take hold in the East.) The 1864 *Hoyle* stated flatly: "Success in playing the game of Poker (or Bluff, as it is sometimes called) depends rather upon luck and energy than skill. It is emphatically a game of chance, and there are easier ways of cheating, or playing with marked cards, than in any other game." From reading these books, as well as from what they could gather by word of mouth, most nineteenth-century Americans probably considered poker to be more about opportunities to swindle than to fairly outplay one's opponents. And at least as far as the higher-stakes games were concerned, they were right.

It's also revealing to compare the eleven pages spent on poker in that 1864 *Hoyle* to the twenty-eight accorded to euchre, twenty-seven to cribbage, ten to faro, two to brag, and one half to a bit of silliness called Snip-Snap-Snorem, a variant of war in which the goal was to match, not beat, the card played by your adversary. The page counts imply that poker was about as widespread as faro, another game dominated by charlatans. Whist's fifty pages confirmed it was still the most popular card game, though poker's rapid proliferation in Civil War camps wasn't fully accounted for in this edition.

From colonial times until the War of Secession, whist had been the game of choice among the smart set of the Northeastern establishment. Benjamin Franklin, Paul Revere, and Abigail Adams, not to mention Tsar Alexander, Napoleon Bonaparte, Queen Victoria, and the first six American presidents—Andrew Jackson being the seventh—had all been devoted whist players. A cerebral trick-taking game encouraging honesty, partnership, sobriety, silence (for which "whist" was a synonym), and courteous manners, this precursor of bridge was seldom played for sums large enough to encourage cheating. Competing mostly for bragging rights, whist players had little cause to hoodwink each other. Between 1772 and 1775, George Washington kept detailed records of his whist results. For one of the wealthiest men in Virginia, the biggest loss was £6; his biggest win, £13, came in a game at Annapolis. In the capital, Philadelphia, Franklin noted that whist was played "not for money but for honour . . . the pleasure of beating one another." Besides, if some knave wanted to cheat, he would have to account for as many as thirty cards to gain a decisive advantage.

Once they had been introduced to poker, though, talented cardsharps immediately understood that it offered superb opportunities to fix a game profitably. Whoever could mark—or control who was dealt—only three or four high cards would have a decisive edge over his tablemates. If the game lasted long enough, even a single marked ace would be sufficient to secure all the money. While whist players toted up tricks on a pad and paid pennies per point to the winners, dollars were the scoring units of poker, the only way to measure and leverage the value of one's hand. And the higher the stakes, the more acumen and courage were required to pull off or suss out a bluff. Poker was the most natural game of the emerging market economy for a number of reasons, none more important than the fact that not playing for cash simply didn't make sense. Money was this game's very language.

Seasoned and aspiring cheats flocked to New Orleans and then onto the steamboats that called farther up the Mississippi. The first wave consisted mainly of crude, violent toughs who worked the dockside saloons, preying on sailors and bargemen, who were energetic brawlers in their own right; anyone fixing to take their money was advised to be heavily armed. A card game was merely the pretext, what Alfred Hitchcock would call the MacGuffin—a red herring to get the plot rolling or, in this case, get the money on the table. The real drama involved taking it either by cheating or at gunpoint.

More urbane and lucrative targets were the sporting gentry, wealthy Southerners who played cards as recreation. Many a planter's heir and cotton mill scion could afford to lose enough on one hand to support the average family for years. Some were quite proud of their profligacy, one-upping each other to demonstrate how blithely they wagered away massive sums. The devil may care who lost $5,000 on a horse race or the turn of a card, but a sporting gentleman most assuredly did not. Robert Bailey, a lowborn Virginia rake who gambled with such men for a living, defined a sportsman in 1822 as a "high minded liberal gentleman, attached to amusements regardless of loss or gain." Professional sharps, on the other hand, cared only about "the business of general gaming, destitute of all honor and integrity."

Professionals may have looked like gamblers, and were certainly called that by preachers and editorialists, but in fact they were businessmen working in a cutthroat enterprise, as closely related to the burglars in David Mamet's *American Buffalo* as to his real estate salesmen in *Glengarry Glen Ross*. Their nine-to-five job—p.m. to a.m., that is—was to fleece wealthy suckers. Any poker game they sat in was actually a burglary staged to look like a test of luck and skill.

Since their sole interest was the bottom line, they preferred to run "bank" games that gave the dealer advantages as steep as 50 percent. Mexican three-card monte and French roulette, faro, and vingt-et-un were fast-paced swindles appealing primarily to intoxicated, low-income rubes. But as more and more "liberal gentlemen" shunned these obvious cons in favor of American poker, a game requiring tactical skill when played on the square, many sharps decided they had little choice but to switch games themselves.

By practicing sound poker tactics, the very rare honest professional could outplay all but the craftiest amateurs. Yet the element of luck still kept him from winning often enough when the games were played straight. Instead of boom-or-bust swings, most professionals wanted their income stream to be a smoothly ascending diagonal. To guarantee this, they needed to cheat.

Rigorous training was required of every new poker sharp, as well as for monte and faro cheats looking to make the switch. Many were self-taught, while others apprenticed themselves to a master and paid handsomely for the privilege. Poker's best cons required a magician's sleight of hand and mastery of precision technology. Tiny mirrors had to be positioned *just so* to remain unnoticed while reflecting the faces of cards being dealt. Needle tips were delicately soldered to rings, then used to punch holes in well-camouflaged spots in the aces. The backs of certain cards were deftly marked or stained in precise locations—difficult enough to begin with, but especially so when the marks had to be accurately applied, read, and remembered amid the kaleidoscope of badly lit, fast-moving action.

As the steamboat era matured, simply getting a seat at the table in the suite of an overconfident millionaire called for a subtly cunning MO. You couldn't just bludgeon your victim, snatch a few dollars, and make a run for it. Working the texas deck of a luxury steamer required courtly manners, superior acting skills, slicker methods for "ringing in" a marked deck, and foolproof getaway plans. A sharp had to be convincing as a gentleman—well-spoken, recently bathed, perhaps even giving the impression that he didn't want to gamble at all. He would also require several well-tailored suits, to go with a tall black hat and below-the-knee broadcloth coat. Beneath the coat he'd sport the regalia of big-spending Southerners: ruffled white shirt, silk tie with diamond stickpin, vest with hand-painted foxhunting scenes. One sharp, George Devol, even hired black men to carry his bags aboard the steamer, enhancing the impression that he owned a plantation or two and had plenty of money to risk in a poker game—provided it was played on the square!

When the big money was finally on the table and the cards were in the air, no sharp could count on the luck of the draw or fortuitous timing—four kings with an ace, for example, when his quarry happened to hold aces full or four queens. Thousands of steps would have led up to that fatal clash of hands, and the last few steps would play out under the vigilant eyes of adversaries packing bowie knives and .41-caliber double-barrel Derringers. Rigging a six-figure poker game and getting away with it called for genuine artistry and considerable grace under pressure.

9

STYLES AND TECHNOLOGIES
OF CHEATING

Four jacks. You owe me fifteen grand, pal.
— HENRY GONDORFF IN *THE STING*

Artists or thugs, flawless mechanics or conspicuous fumblefingers, by 1835 several hundred sharps were making predatory excursions from Pittsburgh to the Nebraska Territory, from the Gulf to St. Paul, with the number reaching two thousand or so by 1850. Usually working in small, proficient teams, they often boarded a steamboat at different ports, pretending not to know one another. Assembling in the saloon after dinner, they ordered a cognac, a bourbon and branch, lit up their Cuban cigars. The most polished would make refined conversation with well-to-do passengers—about the spot price of cotton in Liverpool, say, or Frémont's latest expedition to California. Sooner or later one of the marks would suggest a game of poker, if only to pass the long evening.

Savvy sharps let the suckers win for a while, hoping to build their confidence to a level where they'd be willing, even eager, to raise the stakes; a well-hooked sucker might even call for them to be raised a second or third time. As the betting got more furious, the team's "mechanic"—a nimble-fingered sharp capable of sequencing the deck in his favor while appearing to give it an honest shuffle and cut—would take over.

Teams without a reliable mechanic figured out ways to get a marked or cold deck into the game. Failing that, partners stationed behind the sucker employed a technique known as "iteming" to reveal what cards he held. Signals could involve smoke rings, fingers held against a cheek or lapel, scratching an ear, or turning a cane like the minute hand of a clock. The sharps at the table would then raise against hands they could beat, fold against those they could not. "It was dead easy money," one retired con man admitted. Suckers, he and his colleagues believed, had no business with money anyway.

When no high-rolling gentry were available, a flexible sharp might present himself as one of the rough-hewn hicks he hoped to fleece, donning sheep's clothing and accents to win the trust of actual sheep. Others took the opposite tack, showing up the hicks and even the sporting gentlemen with dandyish extravagance: sleek English suits, ruffled Parisian shirts, thousand-dollar Swiss watches, enormous diamond pins known as "headlights." The notorious James Ashby sported a pair of gold-topped canes and often kept a diamond-studded gold pencil clenched between his teeth. But the biggest dandy of all may have been Jimmy Fitzgerald, who attached his oversize timepiece to his vest by means of a twenty-foot gold chain looped several times around his neck.

Who in his right mind would play high-stakes poker with someone ostentatiously strutting the proceeds of previous conquests? Lots of people, as it turned out. Headstrong young swells, for example, with pouches of double eagles or wads of legal tender burning holes in their pockets. Farmers or trappers who resented bigwigs and show-offs. Poker studs who hadn't lost yet. Any lawyer or planter or real estate magnate who'd convinced himself he was invincible. Sharps like Ashby and Fitzgerald were serenely aware that their gaudy costumes served as a goad to such folks: *come and get it.*

Just as Muhammad Ali inspired millions of young black men to punctuate athletic performance with loud, often rhymed, braggadocio, nineteenth-century cardsharps gave rise to rivers of gold chain and validated stylish cheating above plain, honest poker. Flamboyantly dressed con artists understood that the main difference between a common criminal and a romantic outlaw was that an outlaw had a following—or a customer base. Modern casinos have an unlimited variety of electronic bells and whistles, not to mention the exposed flesh of cocktail waitresses, to attract and stimulate customers. A cardsharp had only his persona. And much like the gangsta rappers of today—Ali's godsons— riverboat gamblers helped set the social and sartorial standards for much of antebellum America. European gaming called for understated elegance, the de rigueur tuxes and gowns of Baden-Baden, Paris, and Monte Carlo, where only wellborn aristocrats were welcome in the ritzy casinos to test their fortune at skill-free games like baccarat, 21, and roulette. The new American style emerging on steamboats emphasized gamesmanship, bejeweled extravagance, hucksterism, and skill— or at least the illusion that skill was a factor.

To create as many customers as possible, professional gamblers ignored all restrictions based on social rank. Buffalo hunters, printer's assistants, sharecroppers, freemen of color—just about everyone's money was good in their wide-open poker games. By making their business as democratically appealing and audience-friendly as possible, the sharps both glamorized poker and extended its popularity into the upper Midwest and eventually out to San Francisco in one direction, Maine in the other. And because of the monetary nature of the game, status among this new breed of players had to do with how many chips you cashed in around dawn, not who your daddy was.

At the same time, the outlaw cachet of men like Ashby, Devol, and Fitzgerald added a darkly beguiling edge to a steamboat excursion. In the days before metal detectors, few men—and no gamblers—left home without a large knife or small sidearm. Yet most other passengers realized that if they didn't sit at the faro or monte or poker table themselves, there was little danger in watching the action.

Since a sharp couldn't call the police—unless he'd bribed them beforehand—if threatened by angry victims, he usually had to serve as his own bodyguard. Physical toughness and proficiency with weapons were basic prerequisites of his trade. Most sharps relied on their partners for mutual protection, and many teams chipped in to pay off members of the boat's crew and staff, both as backups in brawls and as poker confederates—accomplices, that is, not necessarily men with a zeal for secession. A bartender could sell marked decks repackaged with official-looking stamps and seals. A waiter with 20/20 vision could linger behind a careless victim, sending prearranged signals to indicate the strength of his hand. Even the captain, after dining with affluent passengers, might steer one or two toward the poker game, assuring them that the well-dressed man awkwardly riffling the cards was a Pittsburgh attorney who lost on a regular basis.

Once at the table together, teammates carefully disguised the fact that they knew one another while signaling back and forth what cards they held or had folded. One might distract their victims with small talk while his partner dealt from the bottom of the deck or studied the backs of marked cards. Mechanics spent months perfecting their ability to control which players received the best and the second-best hands. When "dealing seconds," for example, he used the thumb of the hand holding the deck to pull back the top card, dealing the second card to another player while dealing his partner the top card, which would improve his hand to the winner. Partners also raised and reraised in tandem to drive a victim out of a pot, ideally after he'd put a fair amount into it. Over the course of several hands, one sharp might collect three or four kings and slide them into the bottom of the deck. His mechanic would "shuffle" without disturbing the sequence, crimping a card so his partner would know where to cut, then bottom-deal the kings to him. Teammates also made a habit of dealing six or seven cards to each other. Keeping the best five, they would let the extra cards drop into their laps. Once the deal had passed to them in turn, they would sneak the extras back into the deck. Other means of rigging the outcome included "belly slippers," decks with slightly wider aces and kings, making it easier to deal those cards to oneself or one's partner. Less dexterous cheats could still hold out a key card, hiding it somewhere on their person until it was time to slip it back into their two-paired hand, say, to complete a full house.

By these means and others, a team of patient blacklegs could gradually siphon up just about every chip on the table. Cold decks might get the job done more quickly, but they also risked triggering violent reprisals. More often than not, the best protection policy was to acquire the chips as inconspicuously as possible.

As cheating became more commonplace and lucrative, manufacturers began openly selling holdout devices capable of snatching a card from one's hand and tugging it up that sleeve until the time was right to push it back down again. The instructions for one device promised: "Holding out one card will beat any square game in the world." Overstated salesmanship? Hardly. John Scarne (1903–1985) was the author of twenty-eight books about magic and gambling, worked as the double for Paul Newman's hands in *The Sting*, and was hired by the army to teach GIs how to avoid being cheated. It was his opinion that not only could an expert "take all the chumps in the game simply by knowing the location of a very few cards. If he knows the exact position of only one of the 52 cards, he will eventually win all the money in sight."

P. J. Kepplinger, a San Francisco sharp known as "the Lucky Dutchman," designed what may have been the most sophisticated holdout device of all. It featured a metal slide attached to a rod retracting into a pair of steel clamps. Concealed beneath an extrawide sleeve, the device was triggered by a wire running through a series of pulleys and flexible tubes. One length of tubing guided the cable from a seam near the knee of Kepplinger's pants through a pulley system ending at his shoulder. Getting dressed before a game, he pressed a small clip that opened the seam through which the wire was threaded, letting the end of the wire hang loose in his hand. Once he'd been seated at the table, he set the tension in the circuitous rig by attaching the wire to an identical clip near his other knee. By spreading or pushing together his knees, Kepplinger, as both puppet and puppeteer, could make a clamped card snap cleanly into or out of his poker hand.

For less patient and creative cheats, gaming supply companies made a variety of gadgets designed to bust a victim in a single hand. H. C. Evans & Co. offered the Improved Cooler, for example, a "simple and noiseless" machine for switching a cold deck into the game via the waistband of one's trousers. The sharp simply waited until a strategically dropped glass or head-turning woman distracted the other players for a moment. Evans customers were encouraged to send in a pair of loose-fitting pants "so we can have the machine fitted into them by our experienced tailors. There is no extra charge for this." Charge or no charge, what sharp would want a badly fitted metal contraption malfunctioning in his pants, especially when he was trying to cold-deck a well-funded sucker?

For those who chose to work with marked decks, cards marked ahead of time were by far the easiest to use, though the work required was extensive. Steady-handed artists peered through magnifying glasses to etch tiny variations in the scrolls and arabesques of clean decks. "Line workers" might add a faint extra flower petal or hatch mark to indicate the card's value. "Edge workers" did so by thickening the lines around the back's border, while "shaders" used diluted ink to faintly tint one spot or another. (Cards marked with phosphorescent ink required the user to wear blue-tinted spectacles, which became a dead giveaway once the pool of suckers wised up.) After they'd been marked, the cards were replaced in their original package and resealed with a counterfeit tax stamp.

But suspicious opponents calling for fresh decks every other hand often forced the sharp to mark a clean deck at the table. As the action proceeded around him, he had to unobtrusively mark or nick the aces and kings that passed through his hands, using a thumbnail, file edge, or a needle point welded onto his ring. Once this was accomplished, he could read the minuscule holes and abrasions as a kind of pasteboard Braille, though this was possible only when it was his turn to deal. Fresh marks or smudges could be read during any hand—when they appeared on the facedown cards of a victim or on the top of the deck, ready to be dealt by someone else. Very few sharps were suited for these rigors. Producing and reading such a deck required almost superhuman dexterity and eyesight, together with months of practice both making and spotting the marks without staring at card backs in an obvious way.

Another approach involved "shiners," the reflective surfaces on rings, snuff boxes, or cigarette cases angled to reveal the faces of cards as the "mirror man" dealt them. Gambling supply catalogs, operating in much the same spirit that later promoted Fuzzbusters and muscle-building steroids, sold thumbnail-size reflectors designed to jut from the table bottom just above the sharp's lap. Assuming he had superb peripheral vision and a flawless short-term memory, a mirror man could reconstruct fleeting glimpses of the cards as he dealt them into an accurate picture of each opponent's hand. But because opponents losing money would become wary of a dealer glancing toward his lap as he pitched the cards around the table, the best reflectors were designed to snap out of sight at the touch of a button. Once he had won a huge pot, the mirror man—if he had any sense, that is, which in turn depended on his greed and self-confidence—could dislodge the reflector, excuse himself to visit the WC, and toss the incriminating evidence into the dark Mississippi.

As the state of the cheater's art developed over the decades, both card-sharps and honest players got smarter. Sometimes the cheats gained the upper hand along one stretch of river; other times the square players barred or intimidated them. Port authorities and steamboat companies cracked down, state legislatures wrote laws and sheriffs enforced them—or they didn't. Local magistrates got tough, while others were bribed not to.

Honest players got into the habit of watching any opponent who dressed like a blackleg, handled his cards with above-average dexterity, shoved his discards into the pile in a way that left their number unclear, paid scrupulous attention to the backs of the cards as he shuffled them, or didn't seem to shuffle them all. A cautious player might fold a big full house dealt to him by the suspected sharp, then watch for a reaction. He might ignore his own cards for a while, concentrating solely on the sharp's hands and face. He could also try to confuse the sharp by adding random scratches or watermarks of his own. Once he felt his suspicions had been confirmed, he could regularly call for new decks from a barman he trusted. He could excuse himself to play at another table, call for the crew to intervene (assuming he trusted them), or meekly head off to his bunk. But if he was especially tough or well armed, or had comrades who were, he could stand up and accuse the cheat, at the risk of one or both of their lives. As one sharp put it, "I knew that if [my victim] detected any cheating my life would be exacted as a forfeit." In Vicksburg in 1835, five suspected cardsharps were lynched by vigilantes. Being hung, shot, stabbed, tarred and feathered, or thrown overboard were not uncommon fates for a blackleg.

Hoping to do their part to keep poker square, honest printing companies offered inexpensive decks with blank backs. The theory behind these "club cards" was that any marks would be so instantly noticeable as to defeat their own purpose, because once a single card was marked, inadvertently or not, all fifty-two could be economically replaced with a virgin deck. The bottom line, however, was that thin, flimsy cards with ghostly pale backs never caught on among high-stakes players, and those who stuck to small, friendly games didn't have much use for them, either. Meanwhile, other trustworthy printers moved in the opposite direction, designing ever more elaborate backs: plaids, geometric and arabesque patterns, crosshatching, all with the purpose of foiling card markers. Yet this only challenged some edge and line artists to come up with more precise, better-camouflaged ways to mark them.

Sharps known as "smudgy movers" hid homemade dyes made from olive oil, aniline, and stearine camphor in miniature shading boxes sewn into their clothes. The best of them could wet a fingertip with the dye and transfer it to a precise point on a card's back. A few seconds later they would wipe the card clean, removing all evidence of foul play—in much the same way that grease on Gaylord Perry's or Kenny Rogers's hand used to appear and disappear from inning to inning.

As the arms race escalated among cardsharps, square players, and card makers, it was crucial to keep every card opaque under the strongest of lights. Legitimate printers glued two pieces of card stock together with a thick dark paste called "gook." Precision dies then cut them to uniform dimensions, producing a knifelike edge that prevented fraying and made them easier to shuffle. Special glazes were applied to leave them smudge- and stain-resistant. While most of these decks admirably served their purpose, innovative sharps learned to transfer a tiny smear of moisture from a mint julep, say, to imbue significant cards with watermarks visible only from certain angles to someone trained to pick them out. Because suit and rank were revealed by the stain's exact location, the watermarks had to be applied with painterly precision. Not only that, the more cards marked in this way, the better the visual and numerical memory required to keep them all straight.

As the spiraling numbers of marked decks threatened to overwhelm even the possibility of a fair game, the makers of Hart's Red Angel decks offered a guarantee that their cards were both unmarked and unstainable. But in due course a dye purveyor offered a counterguarantee that its product could stain any deck. Still another company developed a line of unglazed "Steamboat" decks, pricing them low enough to be replaced every hour or so.

Larcenous printers jumped into the arms race around 1850, producing premarked facsimiles of the most popular decks. Called "readers" or "paper," they featured slight variations in their back designs to reveal each card's rank. Suit markings raised the cost by about fifteen cents per deck, a laughably small price to pay once flushes were accepted in the hierarchy of hands. Openly advertised in catalogs and mainstream magazines as being "easy to read" or (for the cognoscenti) having "fast blockout work," readers drove home the point that confident familiarity with marked decks far outweighed any aspect of what we would call poker skill. Some sharps even worked as middlemen for crooked printers, delivering readers to unsuspecting dockside cigar stores, newsstands, or—in the best of all possible worlds for them—to the buyer in charge of a steamboat line's authorized supply. Sold by the dozen or gross in the standard colors of blue and red, readers became so widespread that it was all but impossible to know if even the smallest poker game was played on the square anymore.

Recalling the endless cheating and gimmickry that prevailed for so long over poker skill, the Mississippi cardsharp Tom Ellison rationalized his chosen career: "That's what went as gambling in those times." Ellison admitted to working with mechanics who could shuffle cards "one for one all through from top to bottom, so that they were in the same position after a dozen shuffles as they were in at first. They'd just flutter them up like a flock of quail and get the aces, kings, queens, jacks and tens all together as easy as pie. A sucker had no more chance against those fellows than a snowball in a red-hot oven."

Even against run-of-the-mill sharps, an honest player had to summon prodigious amounts of concentration and courage simply to limit the sums he was cheated out of, which didn't leave much left for playing good poker—calculating pot odds and value bets, picking up tells while disguising his own, figuring out whom to bluff and when. A poker world in which those skills were paramount wouldn't fully evolve until late in the twentieth century. In the meantime, *not* playing in the biggest game in town—or on the river, or in the mining camp—would very often be the best option. Pure poker skill withered in such an environment. Gold chains and cold decks were what drew ambitious young talent to the table, where the main kinds of skills getting sharpened were the facility to angle a mirror or bottom-deal the second-best hand.

SHARPS REFORMED AND
UNRECONSTRUCTED

As Mr. John Oakhurst, gambler, stepped into the main street of Poker Flat on the morning of the twenty-third of November, 1850, he was conscious of a change in its moral atmosphere since the preceding night.

—BRET HARTE, "THE OUTCASTS OF POKER FLAT"

Despite the popularity of rambunctious risk takers like President Jackson and the cachet of diamond-studded blacklegs, there was widespread resistance to gambling across antebellum America, especially as it moved out of upper-class staterooms and racetracks and was taken up by ordinary citizens. A variety of moral crusades against public wagering had been under way since the 1820s, many of them intertwined with temperance, abolition, and suffrage movements. New Harmony, founded in Illinois by the Socialist Robert Owen, banned currency altogether. Brook Farm, a utopian community near Boston launched by George and Sophia Ripley, Nathaniel Hawthorne, and other Transcendentalists, shunned any behavior geared to individual profit. Even in the entrepreneurial wilds of California, the gold lust and gambling fever of the 1840s would be tempered in the early '50s by legislation prohibiting most public bets. As Daniel Walker Howe notes in *What God Hath Wrought*, it wasn't at all surprising that wagering flourished "with prospecting for gold such a big gamble itself." The California argo-nauts "hoped to get rich quick and return home, not stay and build for the future." Such motives, of course, "did not foster prudence or pub-lic responsibility." Instead, "mob law" tended to be the order of the day.

Antigambling statutes written in Sacramento and other capitals were probably more honored in the breach than in the observance, if only because they tended not to discriminate between skill-based contests like poker and suckers' games with a house edge no amount of luck could overcome. Throughout the country, efforts to prosecute—or summarily execute—faro cheats too often failed to distinguish them from legitimate poker players, though the two games had little in com-mon besides cards and money. While some ports like Natchez were blighted by prostitutes, cheaters, and thieves, in other towns vigilantes wreaked more havoc than a sharp with an ace up his sleeve ever could. The lynching of five blacklegs in Vicksburg led to even more polariza-tion across the South between antigambling forces and those who wanted to play honest poker.

One man who played both sides of this divide was Jonathan Harring-ton Green. Born in 1813, Green served time at a young age in a Cin-cinnati prison for petty theft and vagrancy. Older inmates taught him to cheat at faro and monte, and upon his release in 1829 he headed straight for the steamboats, where most high-stakes gambling took place. But the most popular game on the rivers wasn't one he'd learned back in prison. The new game was *poque*, and its action was dominated by sharps using mirrors, cold and marked decks, and elaborate signal-ing systems. Green observed that the suckers who preferred *poque* to monte and faro apparently believed it offered them better odds, which made it both more challenging to play and harder to cheat at. It did and it didn't, of course.

During his twelve-year sharping career on the riverboats, Green said he learned to read a marked deck as easily as the average man reads his newspaper. He also noticed that *poque* wasn't listed in *Hoyle*, or for that matter in any publication he'd come across, so he took it upon himself to put its rules and tactics onto paper. What Edmond Hoyle had been to whist, Green would be to *poque*, though first he would post a few danger signs. In light of the cunning of his fellow blacklegs, he believed it was only fair to identify poque as "the Cheating Game."

Green's warning was also a by-product of his conversion to Chris-tianity. At some point in his late twenties, he suddenly declared himself a reformed gambler and made it his business—literally—to inform the

American public about crooked card games. In 1843, he published *An Exposure of the Arts and Miseries of Gambling, Designed Especially as a Warning to the Youthful and Inexperienced Against the Evils of That Odious and Destructive Vice.* If this bestseller's twenty-eight-word title somehow failed to make its message clear, the message was repeated in the melodramatic lectures Green began giving to sold-out auditoriums across the country. He spoke of being raised motherless and lured by older criminals into life as a swindler before he was finally saved by a newfound devotion to Jesus. And now here he stood, admonishing the good people of his audience to avoid games of chance with a vengeance.

Feeling his preacherly oats, he published a series of repetitive sequels—*Gambling Unmasked, The Gambler's Mirror, A Report on Gambling, Gambling Exposed, The Reformed Gambler, The Gambler's Life, Gambler's Tricks with Cards Exposed and Explained*—all designed to capitalize on the success of *An Exposure.* Abridged editions were sold at his lectures for $4 per dozen to those wishing to carry the crusade even wider.

Not one for half measures, Green proclaimed from the podium that *all* decks of playing cards were marked by the manufacturers. To prove it, he offered money to a randomly chosen volunteer from the audience to leave the theater and purchase a deck from any nearby shop. When the man or woman returned with a deck, Green would break the seal, shuffle, spread the cards facedown on a table, and begin declaring the rank and suit before turning each one faceup. He was right every time.

More than a few people, especially the gamblers in the audience, accused Green of choosing confederates guaranteed to return with marked decks. When that proved not to be the case, skeptics began watching the performances more closely. It turned out that Green was using a tiny mirror at the edge of the stage table to peek at the face of each card just before he pretended to scour its back for a telltale mark. In other words, he was making himself rich and famously righteous by fixing the evidence that all card games were fixed. The larger irony was that his claim was essentially true as far as high-stakes poker was concerned, though his need for a mirror tended to prove that most decks *weren't* marked. So what was a sucker to think?

Undeterred by the disclosure, confident he could ride the crest of the reformist wave, Green upped the ante, speaking and writing of ever more grandiose conspiracies foisted upon honest citizens. His book *The Secret Band of Brothers* purported to expose what he called "a widespread organization—pledged to gambling, theft and villainy of all kinds." The band was founded, he wrote, on July 12, 1798, and soon included two hundred grand masters, each with six vice–grand masters and assorted other villains: pickpockets, horse race and cockfight fixers, strong-arm enforcers, and cold-blooded murderers, all of whom communicated with coded messages left under bridges, in caves, in tree hollows, and so on. Making the band even more insidious, its masters were highly respected pillars of the community, "men of wealth and influence in almost every town," Green darkly warned. "They are sometimes lawyers, and jurors, and even judges."

Green was making these allegations in the 1840s and '50s, as the pendulum continued to swing wildly between fanatical reformers and unbudging special interests. To take the most fraught example, the question of whether territories west of the Mississippi should become slave or free states was being intensely debated by, among countless others, senators Thomas Hart Benton, John C. Calhoun, and Stephen A. Douglas, and Congressman Abraham Lincoln. As the republic was slowly torn apart by social and constitutional crises, God's approval was claimed by both sides of almost every issue. As Lincoln would soon remark while drafting the Emancipation Proclamation: "I am approached with the most opposite opinions and advice, and that by religious men, who are equally certain that they represent the divine will. . . . These are not, however, the days of miracles, and I suppose it will be granted that I am not to expect a direct revelation. I must study the plain, physical facts of the case, ascertain what is possible, and learn what appears to be wise and right." And he did.

As far as poker was concerned, God-fearing politicians in the Know Nothing Party supported Green's calls to ban all games of chance. Yet even the liberal Republican Horace Greeley editorialized in the *New York Tribune* that "not less than five millions of dollars are annually won from fools and shallow knaves, by blacklegs, in this city alone; and not less than a thousand young men are annually ruined by them." Other reformers, including the editors of the influential Whig broadsheet *The Commercial Advertiser*, were less willing to throw out the baby with the bathwater. It must have seemed wise and right to them that gambling be restricted, but that a square game of poker for affordable stakes should be legal. And whatever the editorialists and lawmakers decreed, it was abundantly clear that a critical mass of Americans felt free to play poker, anyway.

. . .

However much he may have overstated his case against card games, Green had introduced poker to the general public and contributed inadvertently to its outlaw cachet. He helped to expose and quash cheaters, mainly by alerting potential suckers to the hazards of gambling with the likes of Tom Ellison, James Ashby, Jimmy Fitzgerald, and George Devol.

While not much is known about the first three, Devol's raucous and relentlessly self-justifying 1887 memoir, *Forty Years a Gambler on the Mississippi*, made him notorious in his day and ours. Born in 1829 near the steamboat docks of Marietta, Ohio, Devol left home at age ten to work as a cabin boy, beating Sam Clemens to the punch by a good dozen years. Clemens was eight when he vowed to find work on a packet, but he didn't land a job on one until he was twenty-two. Then again, Clemens remained an honest practitioner throughout his life, whether as a typesetter, prospector, steamboat pilot, or writer. The same can't be said for Devol.

Young George's apprenticeship as a blackleg included stints dealing faro, craps, 21, and monte before moving on to brag and then poker. While working his schemes aboard a Rio Grande steamer in 1846—on his way, so he claimed, to fight in the Mexican War—Devol decided the world would be a better place if, instead of enlisting, he remained behind in camp and cheated American troops, which he did to the tune of $2,700.

While Devol was making his bones in Mexico, Second Lieutenant Ulysses S. "Uncle Sam" Grant was serving there as a regimental quartermaster, though he would eventually win a pair of medals for bravery in daring frontline action. Between battles, however, Grant indulged his tastes for alcohol and brag, a game he'd learned as a West Point plebe in 1839, before poker had reached the Hudson River. Despite his successes in the Mexican campaign, Grant was forced to resign from the army in 1854. His commanding officer alleged he was intoxicated while paying the troops, and he forced Grant to make a hard choice: resign or face a court-martial. Grant chose the former option. He went on, as we know, to fail as potato farmer and shopkeeper before returning to the army and emerging as the Union's military savior, but the less mature Grant was exactly the kind of soldier Devol would have targeted in Mexico.

The vast military expenditures of the Civil War only quickened Devol's blackleg heart. "Paymasters in the army were among the best suckers we had," he explained, particularly when they were drunk. He admitted to cheating them out of so much cash that in 1862, General Benjamin Franklin Butler, the military governor of New Orleans, was forced to find a provost judge willing to sentence Devol to a year in prison. But Devol simply fleeced the wealthy Southerners locked up with him, using their money to bribe his jailer into chaperoning him around the local red-light district. And he almost certainly bribed Louisiana governor George Shepley to pardon him, with the proviso that he not play cards with any member of the Union Army. Devol broke this promise almost immediately, bilking another paymaster out of $19,000. Yet because General Butler's command had been transferred to Virginia, Devol remained in business another two years—until General Stephen Hurlburt protected the payroll by closing Southern gambling houses.

"After cheating all the soldiers I could at cards," Devol returned his focus to civilians. One especially devious ruse was accepting backers in a high-stakes head-to-head poker match. Believing Devol's talent as a cardsharp guaranteed he would win, the backers enthusiastically put up five-figure sums. Devol then proceeded to lose on purpose to a partner, and the two split the money in secret.

Who better than Devol himself to describe his MO while cheating without the help of a partner:

> I was on board the *Sultana*, bound for Louisville, and got into a five-handed game of poker. When we landed at the mouth of the Cumberland, two of our party got off to take the boat for Nashville; that left our game three-handed. For fear that another would get away, I thought that I must get in my work without further delay; so I excused myself for a few moments and went to the bar. I got a deck just like the one we were using, and "run up" three hands, giving one three aces, one three kings, and myself four treys. We played a short time after my return, and on my deal I called their attention to something, and at the same time came up with the "cold deck." The betting was lively. I let them do the raising, and I did the calling until it came to the draw. They each took two cards, and I took one, saying, "If I fill this flush, I will make you squeal." I knew they both had "full hands," and they just slashed their money on the table until there was over $4,000 up. Then I made "raise" of $1,200, and they both "called." "Gentlemen," I said, "I suppose you have me beat; I only have two pair."

"Oh!" says one, "I have a king-full;" and the other one said, "I have an ace-full." "Well, boys, I can down both hands, for I have two pairs of treys." The game came to a close, for there was no more money on the other side.

How he avoided being accused or attacked in this case, Devol doesn't say. But he was a muscular man with a particularly thick skull who also packed a revolver he called "Betsy Jane," and he would literally butt heads with any unarmed victim who crossed him. Said one former tough guy, "The first lick he hit me, I thought my neck was disjointed; and when he ran that head into me, I thought it was a cannon ball." When challenged by the circus performer William Carroll, billed as "the Great Butter" because he smashed through heavy doors and claimed he could kill any man or beast with his forehead, Devol knocked him unconscious. When Carroll came to, he declared, "Gentlemen, at last I have found my papa." Or so Devol reported.

The thick-skulled blackleg went out of his way to befriend slaves, gentry, poor whites, and freemen of color. He bragged that he could impersonate a white deckhand or even a black musician—anything to avoid gun-toting passengers he'd bilked. After one hasty disembarkation at the wharf of a sugar plantation, Devol's guise as a planter was clinched, he wrote, when "all the niggers came to shake hands and say 'Glad youse back, Massa George.'" Yet when Massa George won a slave or two in a poker game, instead of freeing them, he cashed them in for $1,000 apiece when the boat reached New Orleans.

Before he retired, Devol claimed he'd won more than $2 million (about $50 million in today's dollars) but had lost nearly all of it back to even more crooked faro dealers. "It is said of me that I have won more money than any sporting man in this country," he wrote in 1886. "I will say that I hadn't sense enough to keep it."

Despite decades of cheating, Devol maintained that he always adhered to a code of "honor among thieves." He even insisted that the MO of most sharps was more ethical than the ways of the bourgeois, religious, and commercial worlds. "A gambler's word is as good as his bond, and that is more than I can say of many business men who stand very high in the community," he wrote. "The Board of Trade is just as much a gambling house as a faro bank. Do not the members put up their (and sometimes other people's) money on puts, calls, margins, and futures?" Not only that: "The gambler will pay when he has money, which many good church members will not." He also claimed never to have taken money from a friend and, even more dubiously, always to have checked with a riverboat's clerk to make sure his victim had sufficient funds to get home, plus a comfortable cushion besides. When he castigated a "hook-nosed son of Abraham" who, "like all the rest of his class, loved money as a duck does water," it's hard to imagine a blacker pot making such a scurrilous charge.

Devol was compared in his day to the hero of an 1844 novel by Johnson Jones Hooper called *Some Adventures of Captain Simon Suggs*, which appeared forty-one years before *The Adventures of Huckleberry Finn*. The son of a devout Christian preacher, Simon is determined to make his living as a riverboat gambler. "Simon! Simon!" his father yells, "you poor unlettered fool. Don't you know that all card-players, and chicken-fighters, and horse-racers go to hell? And don't you know that them that plays cards always loses their money, and—" At which point Simon interrupts him to ask, "Who wins it all then, Daddy?"

A born hustler, Simon understands in his bones what his father does not—that poker is a zero-sum game. And surely George Devol would agree that for every sucker getting up from the table with his pockets turned inside out, there was a skillful player or, much more likely in those days, a con artist sitting behind a righteous heap of swag. And that it was better to be him than the sucker.

II

DECKS COLD AND COLDER

Graciela Imago Portales, dark hair parted in the middle
and drawn back from her forehead, wearing a long black
riding skirt and black boots, sits shuffling cards, stacking
herself flushes, full houses, four of a kind, just for her own
amusement.

— *GRAVITY'S RAINBOW*

As Bret Harte made his name with "The Outcasts of Poker Flat"
and other morality tales about card players, Mark Twain made his with
"The Notorious Jumping Frog of Calaveras County," a story about a
cheating gambler during the 1849 gold rush. Because of his intimate familiarity with riverboats and mining camps, Twain was mighty particular about whom he played poker with, refusing to sit down with
professional gamblers. His Huckleberry Finn is no sharp, but he
crosses paths with plenty of them as he and Jim float down the Mississippi on a raft in the early 1850s. Besides Twain's, Harte's, and Jones
Hooper's fiction and the exposés of authors like Green, scores of
nineteenth-century books, many of them bestsellers, detailed the practices of one blackleg or another.

The poker game in Twain's "The Professor's Yarn" takes place on a
steamer headed from Acapulco to San Francisco. Since the gold rush
preceded transcontinental railroads and the Panama Canal, most forty-
niners took one ship to Mexico or Central America, crossed overland,

then picked up another ship for the rest of the journey, which lasted three or four weeks altogether. Risky, expensive, and time-consuming as such itineraries might be, they were usually quite a bit faster and safer than the overland route, a two-thousand-mile stretch of mountains, deserts, wild animals, and unwelcoming Native Americans.

The gentleman telling the yarn—a professor looking back on his days as a surveyor—is able to catch only glimpses of the poker action as he passes a posh stateroom on the texas deck, the door of which has been left "a little ajar to let out the surplus tobacco smoke and profanity." But he and the other passengers correctly assume the game has been rigged by professionals.

The young surveyor is soon befriended by John Backus, an Ohio cattleman of "countrified simplicity" and "beaming good nature." Bending his new friend's ear, Backus goes on—and on and *on*—in minute deal about the cattle business; he even shows him his life savings hidden in a trunk in his stateroom. "She's all there—a round ten thousand dollars in yellow-boys." Why this weird disclosure? Because he'd like to propose that the surveyor "survey in such a way" that the best grazing land in California winds up in their hands. The narrator's response is unequivocal: "I am not that kind of surveyor." Yet they change the subject pleasantly enough, with no damage done to their friendship.

Meanwhile the blacklegs press Backus, a well-funded rube, to play in their draw game. He turns them down half a dozen times, but just before the ship reaches the Bay, he agrees to play a few hands. The blacklegs ply him with glass after glass of champagne, throwing theirs over their shoulders. Pretty soon Backus's eyes are bloodshot as he blearily agrees to let the stakes be raised yet again just before the last hand is dealt. "How many cards?" asks one of the sharps. "None!" replies Backus. The sharp named Hank Wiley discards one, the others three each. A round of $20 bets and raises ensues, forcing everyone but Backus and Wiley to fold. "I see that," says Wiley, "and go you a *hundred* better!" Backus reraises a hundred. "Oh, that's your little game, is it?" says Wiley. "I see your raise, and raise it five hundred!" "Five hundred *better*!" cries Backus.

After another pair of raises, the pot has reached $10,000. At this point Wiley tosses a large bag of coins on the table. "Five thousand dollars better, my friend from the rural districts—what do you say *now*?"

"I *call* you!" shouts Backus drunkenly, putting the last of his yellow-boys on the table. "What have you got?"

"Four kings, you damned fool!" replies Wiley, turning over his hand.

"Four *aces*, you ass!" thunders Backus, suddenly covering Wiley with a cocked revolver. *"I'm a professional gambler myself, and I've been laying for you duffers all this voyage!"* At this precise moment—as if the story weren't melodramatic enough—the anchor smashes into the rocks below the wharf in San Francisco.

When Backus and the narrator bump into each other the following week, Backus admits that the sharp who dealt the last hand was his "pal." The other sharps believed he was going to deal Backus four queens. "I don't really know anything about cattle," he adds, "except what I was able to pick up in a week's apprenticeship over in Jersey just before we sailed."

Once again, it was acting, conniving, and teamwork that yielded the gold; what we would call poker skill was never an issue. Instead of studying his opponents' faces and betting patterns, Backus had countrified his wardrobe and smile, boned up on animal husbandry, and negotiated a division of spoils with his partner. Instead of the pot odds while drawing to an up-and-down straight, he'd calculated the maximal bribe-to-profit ratio.

What Twain's professor doesn't tell us is what happened to Backus's pal, though it's easy to imagine his former teammates being rather displeased. And if Backus had planned all along to use the threat of a revolver, why bother to bribe the dealer in the first place? Why not just stick up the biggest game on the steamer? What both "The Professor's Yarn" and the story that follows suggest is that out-and-out robbery would have been gauche. The most elegant plan was to beat the sharps at their own game, using revolvers only as backup. For there was always the slight possibility that the victims would fail to appreciate the elegance and irony of what you'd accomplished.

As poker stings got more elaborate and the rights of women became an issue in American life, it was inevitable that at least a few ladies would enter the workforce as blacklegs. "It was on a trip from Memphis to Natchez that I first saw a woman gamble in public," recalls a gentleman interviewed by the *New York Sun*. "The boat wasn't crowded, but there were perhaps fifty passengers on board, and among them were six or eight ladies and this woman. That she was a social outlaw was evident enough at a glance. Not only were her clothes of a fashion too pronounced for respectability and her jewelry too ostentatious for daylight wear, but there was a frank devilry in her eyes, and a defiant swing—almost a swagger—in her carriage." Traveling alone, she refuses to speak to the female passengers and talks to the men with a pronounced French accent. Just who is this she-devil? Our witness discovers that "she was a notorious character in New Orleans, where she was known as 'Flash Kate.'"

Though several poker games are in progress on this packet, the spectators focus on the biggest one, in which "each man had a wad of greenbacks lying alongside his chips [and] bets of ten or twenty at once were common." Altogether "several thousand dollars" are in play, and it's clear to our witness that two of the players, Alcott and Keene, are professionals. (Sharps in such stories often have names like Wiley or Keene, which underscores the era's more relaxed standards of nonfiction reliability. Certainly Twain was a truth teller whose work was based on precise eyewitness reporting, though many names he used were fictitious and he wasn't averse to goosing some details to make his articles more entertaining. Newspaper readers and editors encouraged this practice by Twain and other feature writers, especially when their material was humorous, while holding hard news reporters to a much higher standard of factualness. The *Sun* had been a first-class newspaper of record since 1833, predating *The New York Times* by eighteen years. We can therefore assume that its writer interviewed at least one witness to this riverboat chicanery, that the gist of the story was true, but that reporter or witness may have changed details to heighten the drama and irony.)

The sharps' targets in the *Sun* article are a cotton factor (a trader, that is) from New Orleans, with a reputation as a bold speculator; a military man the others address as "Major"; and a "nondescript" cattle dealer named Downing. Action on the first night proceeds without any huge pots won or lost, and no violence. But our witness understands that the sharps "were laying the foundations for the second night's play."

By the time it begins, anticipation has reached fever pitch. Even a few women have come to watch, though they cling tightly to their husbands' arms. It's the first time our witness "ever saw ladies look on at public gambling." But the wives find it too much to bear when Flash Kate enters the card room *alone*, and they all leave the room in a huff.

Now that the ante has been raised to $10, $50 is the most common bet. Flash Kate takes a position directly behind the cotton factor. The spectators watch in awe—one of them audibly gasps—as Keene holds out an ace. "It was cleverly done, and yet I marveled at his nerve in trying such a trick under so many watching eyes. He relied, of course, on his skill, which was really marvelous." When our witness exchanges a look with the fellow who'd gasped, "I saw that he was equally certain. Neither of us was fool enough to say anything, for interference meant fight." Indeed, everyone seems to accept a riverboat ethos in which professionals openly cheat but will injure you if you accuse them.

The deal now rotates to Downing, who has apparently spotted the holdout as well, because he tosses the rest of the cards on the floor, saying, "Bring us a fresh deck, Mr. Clerk, of another color." This cattleman is nobody's fool: "He shuffled and dealt the cards as if nothing out of the way had happened. Neither could I see any trace of chagrin or disappointment on Keene's face as he was thus cleverly checkmated."

A few hands later, Alcott opens for $100. Everyone calls. Alcott draws three and bets $100. The Major draws one card and folds without further ado. Downing draws two and calls the $100 without even looking to see whether his hand has improved. Keene, who drew two as well, studies his hand intently before calling the bet, at which point the cotton factor, having drawn three, raises $100. "I could not see his cards," our witness reports, "but I learned afterward that he had a queen full."

Alcott, who has three of a kind, raises back. After finally peeking at his hand, Downing reraises $200. Keene folds. The factor raises $500 more, trying to win the pot right there, but Alcott "without a quiver" raises $1,000 more. Downing tosses his hand in the muck. The factor studies his hand while fingering his bankroll. "I haven't as much money here as I'd like to have, but I'll see your thousand and—"

"If Monsieur cares to back his hand and will allow me, I will put up any amount he likes." This bold interruption has been made by Flash Kate. "No man would have ventured to do so," our witness observes. "I was looking at Alcott, and I was sure I saw a gleam of satisfaction, totally unmixed with surprise, on his face. The situation was getting complicated."

Red faced, the factor says, "Thank you, but I never play with borrowed money, and I never borrow from a woman." He later tells our witness that "when the woman spoke it flashed upon him that there was a conspiracy somewhere, and that he didn't care to play against it." He only pretended to study a moment longer before throwing down his cards.

As Alcott rakes the huge pot, Keene invites Kate to take a seat in the game. She accepts. Although he doesn't object, the Major seems uncomfortable playing with a woman. Our witness, for his part, feels "morally certain that it was a case of three against one, for the Major was not much in evidence." And indeed the three sharps "stacked the cards, not once, but half a dozen times, giving [Downing] excellent cards." Each time, however, the cattleman pretends to have a weak hand or to have lost his nerve, but other hands he plays with rash aggression. Within twenty minutes, he has the sharps thoroughly rattled.

Now comes a hand that our witness calls "the boldest and neatest thing I ever saw at a card table." It is Keene's turn to deal and Downing's to cut, but instead of cutting, in the blink of an eye Downing slips in a cold deck. "It sounds like an impossibility," our witness admits, "but wonderful things are possible to a sleight-of-hand performer, and he was the best I ever saw."

Much betting and raising ensues before the draw. All three blacklegs then make four of a kind, but since their partner Keene is dealing, they remain unsuspicious. After a round of even wilder betting and raising, the pot contains more than $20,000. At the showdown, Keene turns over his jacks, Alcott his queens, Flash Kate her kings, Downing the inevitable aces. Alcott and Keene lunge forward to grab the money, but a revolver appears in Downing's right hand as he suavely rakes the pot with his left.

"That was no square deal!" Alcott shouts.

"Think not?" Downing drawls. "Well, you ought to know. Your pal dealt the cards." Grinning behind the revolver, he adds, "As for me, I reckon this'll do me, unless some of you want to play any more."

The blacklegs decline, with Kate adding, "Monsieur is a most excellent player." Downing orders champagne for the spectators, and Kate is later seen with Alcott leaving the boat at Vicksburg, having learned a hard lesson.

The Twain and *Sun* stories epitomize how the long money changed hands among blacklegs: not always by marked or held-out aces, but sometimes by outsharping the sharps—recruiting the perfect "pal," for example, to fix a few decks cold and colder, then "ringing" one in via swift sleight of hand. Both stories anticipate the doubly cold deck that Henry Gondorff, pretending to be drunk, has his partner substitute for the cold deck Doyle Lonnegan had prepared for him in *The Sting* (released in 1973 but set in the '30s). "Four jacks," says Gondorff, suddenly sober. "You owe me fifteen grand, pal." In each of these cases, acting was required not to sandbag or bluff—as honest players would use it—but to build victims' confidence, the better to catch them off guard while the fatal deck was being rung into the dealer's left hand.

. . .

Another ingenious poker sharp—if he is, in fact, a sharp at all—is a guy named Fletcher, a shadowy hustler who never even makes an appearance in *American Buffalo*, David Mamet's 1976 play set in a Chicago pawnshop. Yet Fletcher's poker talent (or is it cheating skill?) makes such an impression on the play's talkative would-be burglars, Don and Teach, that their offstage games with him come vividly alive for the audience.

In the previous evening's game of five-card draw, Fletcher was once again the big winner. During a key hand, Don was dealt a pat straight but lost the night's richest pot to Fletcher, who drew two cards to complete a flush in hearts. And now, as they wait for Fletcher to arrive to spearhead a dangerous midnight burglary of a wealthy coin collector's apartment, Teach (who wants to do the break-in solo) says to Don, "He takes two on your standing pat, you kicked him thirty bucks? He draws two, comes out with a flush?"

While Don ponders the unlikelihood that a player of Fletcher's intelligence would draw two to a flush, Teach adds a kicker: "And spills his fucking Fresca?"

Don, forced to remember, says, "Yeah."

"And we look down?"

"Yeah."

"When we look back, he has come up with a king-high flush." Teach pauses to let this sink in. "After he has drawed two." Pause. "You're better than that, Don. You *knew* you had him beat, and you were right."

When Don, who prefers to see the good in his friends, stubbornly insists, "It could happen," Teach tells him he'd folded the same king of hearts that completed the flush. Fletcher, that is, must have snatched it out of the discard pile while they were glancing down at the spill. But instead of denouncing Fletcher, Don demands to know why Teach didn't say anything *then*—a fair enough question, and one to which Teach has a variety of self-serving answers. The bottom line is that so much depends on whether Fletcher cheated or won fair and square that the hand against Don becomes a hilarious Rorschach test of whether Fletcher *or* Teach should be trusted to break into the apartment and return to share the spoils. What better means than a poker game, after all, to establish who is the more trustworthy burglar?

Even more so than Twain's or Harte's tales, more than *Rounders, The Sting, The Cincinnati Kid, A Streetcar Named Desire*, or even Mamet's own film *House of Games*, his 1976 masterpiece perfectly dramatized poker's deceptive logic and honor-among-thieves morality.

THE MARY SITUATION

> You got to appreciate what an explosive element this Bonnie situation is.
>
> —JULES IN *PULP FICTION*

The Minnesota Territory became the thirty-eighth state on May 11, 1858, just in time to help elect Abraham Lincoln and provide him with twenty-two thousand troops for the initial Union war effort. Dr. William Worrall Mayo was appointed examining surgeon of draftees and volunteers in the southern half of the state, whose draft board was headquartered in Rochester. Mayo soon moved his family there and set up a practice with his sons that eventually became known as the Mayos' clinic. Meanwhile, thousands of Swedes and Norwegians kept arriving to farm the vast wheat fields and work in the forests and sawmills up north. With St. Paul and Minneapolis growing astride the headwaters of the Mississippi, and Duluth at the westernmost point of the waterway connecting Lake Superior to the Atlantic, Minnesota was emerging as a great North American crossroads.

Statehood required a slew of freshman representatives and senators to be elected in a hurry, along with a brand-new state legislature. With so many campaigns under way at once, corruption of Bunyanesque proportions would not have been surprising. Most campaigns may have operated with integrity, but a story published in the *New York Sun* told of a pokerticious exception in a close race for one of the Senate seats. The reporter withholds the candidates' names but discloses that both were Republicans. We know from other sources that the winner of one of these races was Morton Smith Wilkinson, a Republican attorney who served in Washington from 1859 to 1865. We don't know whether Wilkinson played poker, but we do know that one of his chief campaigners did—quite effectively, too.

The *Sun* writer tells us that the lumber industry was allied with the business interests in Minneapolis, and that their chief political operative was a man called Doc Martin, a high-spirited sawmill owner who spent most of the winter in the northern forests with his men. The opposing candidate was represented by a logger named Gilmartin.

Two months before the election, Doc Martin invites the correspondent along with a group of ward men to a roadhouse on the Fort Snelling Road near Minnehaha Falls for drinks, dinner, and perhaps a friendly game of cards. Martin and three others liked to play for high stakes, but they also accommodated their less affluent chums with a smaller game. As the convivial evening progresses, the pots in both games become larger.

Suddenly, and to everyone's surprise, Gilmartin appears at the door. "I don't want to 'rough in,' boys," he says, "but I stopped here to get supper on the way home, and the landlord told me you were here, so I thought I'd ask you to drink with me." A popular fellow all around, Gilmartin is invited in, though the strange coincidence of his arrival does not go unnoticed. Invited to play poker as well, he chooses to sit in the higher-stakes game. Doc Martin eyes him suspiciously. "Been out to St. Paul tonight, Gil?"

"Yes, I have," says Gilmartin with a trace of a defiance. He also begins to target his raises at Martin, seeking to isolate him in as many hands as possible. As the friendly ring game turns into more of a heads-up duel, a jackpot develops in which Martin opens, stands pat, and keeps raising after the draw until Gilmartin is his only opponent. Gilmartin turns over a jack-high flush and is about to rake in the $400 pot when Martin shows him an ace-high flush. A few hands later, Martin takes a $200 pot from his adversary. According to the *Sun* correspondent, "Gilmartin became angry, though he controlled himself tolerably well." As another big jackpot keeps building, Gilmartin finally opens for a raise and is called by everyone except the reporter, who had aces but failed to improve on the draw. Martin has drawn three. Having drawn two, Gilmartin bets the $10 limit. Once again, after a series of raises, only the two opposing canvassers remain, and both raise the limit at each opportunity.

"Ten better than you," says Gilmartin fiercely. "You won't get away from me this time."

"If you think so," Martin tells him evenly, raising, "what do you say to taking off the limit?"

"That will suit me exactly," says Gilmartin, producing a thick roll and peeling off several bills. It turns out that he's carrying $5,000 in cash, almost certainly drawn from the war chest of his candidate. "I'll see that and go you five hundred better."

"Does my check go?" asks Martin. "I haven't so much money with me."

"It's good for fifty thousand, and you know it."

Everyone now understands that both men are using identical campaign budgets as their poker bankrolls. Yet after a heated series of $1,000 raises, Gilmartin hesitates; the gravity of the situation finally seems to have dawned on him. "I have to call you," he says, "for I've only got twelve hundred left."

Apparently Martin now has him where he wants him. "I'll put up five thousand more, if you want to play for it."

"But how can I? I tell you I haven't any more money."

"If you will give me your promise to go as far south as St. Louis for sixty days, and tell nobody that you are going, I'll take that as an equivalent for five thousand." In other words, he's proposing that Gilmartin sell out his candidate, not only stealing from his war chest but leaving him in the dark about his lack of a canvasser in the state's northern districts.

Gilmartin is "deathly pale" as he peeks at his cards again, but Martin speaks so coolly that even the seen-it-all correspondent can't help shuddering. "I need not say anything to impress on the minds of all the gentlemen present that this is a private party, and that nothing which happens here can be told outside while it can by any possibility work injury to anyone concerned."

When Gilmartin looks around the room, he can see that everyone, including the reporter, agrees—if he loses the bet and leaves Minnesota till after the election, they will not turn him in to either his employer or the police. "I'll take that bet," he says finally. "But God help you, Martin, if you win it. I don't believe you can, for I've got almost a sure hand."

"If you lose," replies Martin, "you have no cause of quarrel with me. I am not forcing you to play. But if you mean enmity, all right. I'll gamble your friendship, too, along with the rest, if you like."

"So be it. It's a call, then. If you lose you pay me five thousand. If I lose I leave."

But when Martin turns over the proverbial four kings, Gilmartin shockingly fails to show him the inevitable hand. All he has is four queens, having drawn the case lady and trapped himself for his honor, his influence, and the rest of his candidate's money. "His face as he left the room was such a picture as I hope never to see again," writes the reporter, "but he kept to his bargain. At least, I imagine he did, for he was not seen again in that part of the country while I was there. I never spoke to Martin again, but his friend was elected Senator. . . . Both men are dead, or I would not have told the story."

Though we may have our suspicions, the reporter gives no hint of even the possibility of a cold deck. Gilmartin's unexpected appearance also tends to suggest that the cards were squarely shuffled, since Martin is unlikely to have prepared a cold deck for his political comrades. Then again, the odds against quads over quads fairly dealt are longer than January in International Falls.

A note on the game's open stakes is also in order. Because the rules permit players to bet not only what they have on the table and in their pockets but also any sum they might be able to promise or borrow, the *Sun* article presents a North Woods version of what might be called *A Big Hand for the Little Lady* scenario. That 1966 Western is set in roughly the same period as the Minnesota pols' game, and open stakes are crucial to its climactic hand as well.

The movie begins with the five richest men in cattle country gathering at Sam's Saloon in Laredo for their annual poker showdown, an event so important to them that the ranch owner Henry Drummond (Jason Robards) skips his daughter's wedding to play, and a lawyer abandons his client in a capital case. We next meet a family of settlers—Meredith (Henry Fonda), Mary (Joanne Woodward), and their young son, Jackie—who were on their way to buy a farm near San Antonio when a broken wagon wheel forced them to wait at Sam's until a blacksmith got around to repairing their wheel. When Meredith, a recovering gambler, learns of the poker game, he begs to go sit in the back room "just to watch," but Mary puritanically refuses to permit even that. While she's over encouraging the blacksmith, however, Meredith buys into the game, staking the nest egg it took them twelve years to accumulate.

Soon enough the title's big hand develops, with players reraising until there's more than $20,000 in the pot. Though it's clear that Meredith has drawn a monster, he's unable to call the latest raise. "That's four hundred dollars to you," Drummond tells him coldly. "And you know something, mister? You ain't got enough left to stay in this pot." The cattleman is referring to the house rules allowing players to buy or borrow any amount of chips *during the hand*, but also saying that if anyone fails to match the latest raise he must fold, no matter how much he's already contributed. *There are no side pots.*

While Andrew Carnegie would do rather well by these rules, the stress they cause the farmer Meredith, who has wagered his last earthly nickel on what he thinks is an unbeatable hand, literally gives him a heart attack. Doc Scully (Burgess Meredith) is called to the saloon, and his prognosis is less than encouraging. Barely conscious, Meredith hands his cards to his wife as he's carried away. His intention is clear: Mary should play out the hand at all costs.

Overcome with anxiety about her husband and the fix he has put her in, Mary takes his place at the table. "Gentlemen," she asks, wide-eyed, "how do you play this game?" Their first response is a series of loud objections to playing poker with a woman at all, particularly one ignorant of the rules; they conveniently ignore their vested interest in seeing her hand in the muck. Eventually, though, they give in. What choice do they have, after all, besides shamefully taking the money of a dying farmer and his vulnerable—not to mention rather attractive—wife? They gallantly explain the dire straits the little lady finds herself in: if she can't match the last raise, *along with any others that might follow*, she must fold her hand and forfeit everything that Meredith recklessly put in the pot.

The next thing we know, poor Mary is sliding her five cards into an envelope, crossing the street, and buttonholing C. P. Ballinger (Paul Ford), owner of the Cattle and Merchants' Bank. At first Ballinger assumes she's playing a practical joke, but once she shows him the hand he agrees to lend her $20,000. Mary returns to Sam's table and reraises all-in. One by one her stunned opponents reconsider their hands and then fold. Mary rakes the huge pot, pays Ballinger back with interest, smiles, and walks out.

Cut to: Black Creek, the movie's version of Abilene or Dodge, where Mary, her husband, and son are all revealed to be master sharps. Led by

Ballinger and with the collusion of Scully, they have scammed the six cattlemen—who had it coming anyway for swindling Ballinger in a land deal a few years earlier. Prim little "Mary" is actually the saucy moll Ruby.

Many real games of this period were played with open stakes, but too many scams, kited checks, deeds to twice-mortgaged farms, and other dubious IOUs eventually led to the near-universal adoption of table stakes. Each player today starts every hand with a verifiable stake on the table, and at no point during the hand may she remove money or chips from her stack or add any more from her purse, let alone from a banker across the street. But once she goes all-in, she retains full equity in the main pot as whatever side pots among better-funded players keep building.

The most obvious reason not to play for open stakes is that it would be impossible for the wealthiest person at the table—or the one with the healthiest line of credit—to lose. The open stakes in that Minnesota roadhouse let Gilmartin not only borrow $5,000 midhand but also barter his secret abstention from the Senate campaign, causing his candidate to lose a close race. His disgraceful behavior may be the ultimate example of what we would now call "going light."

LOOK AWAY, DIXIE LAND

Oh, I wish I was in the Land of Cotton
Old times there are not forgotten . . .
—DANIEL DECATUR EMMETT, 1859

By the middle of the nineteenth century, draw poker with jackpots had become the card game of choice not only for planters and settlers, but for bootblacks, cobblers, bartenders, and congressmen, too. Kentucky's Henry Clay, who served as Speaker of the House almost continuously from 1811 through 1825, played so well (often with future president Martin van Buren, Secretary of State Daniel Webster, and Vice President John Calhoun) that he was thought to have invented the game. Perhaps the best player in the district was Representative Thaddeus Stevens, a Pennsylvania Republican who served from 1853 to 1868 and was a member of Lincoln's team planning Reconstruction. The first rulebook for playing draw poker was written by the Ohio representative (and former Union general) Robert Schenck, who used it to introduce the game to Queen Victoria's court in London.

Writing in 1900, Eugene Edwards claimed that "practically all of the congressmen before the [Civil] war played poker, and did not try to conceal it as they do now." The District of Columbia, he wrote, was "the great poker center of the United States," and he offered several reasons. Among them: "The man who goes to Washington in an official capacity feels that he will be there today and home tomorrow." Senators were wealthy to begin with, and many congressmen elected biennially felt rather flush with their salaries. Foreign diplomats tended to be aristocrats with family money, whose motto might be "Easy come, easy go." Since Washington offered fewer cultural attractions than Boston, New York, or most foreign capitals, the diplomatic corps had "nothing to do with their salaries but to spend them in good living, and that includes card playing."

Not only in Washington, though. From sawdust saloons in Bleeding Kansas, where thousands of pro- and antislavery partisans fought a violent prelude to the Civil War, to sophisticated parlors in Gramercy Park, where Theodore Roosevelt was born in 1858 to parents on opposite sides of the slavery question, Americans of every station were taking up the riverboat bluffing game. Though many officers and chaplains actively discouraged it, a growing number of Mexican War veterans and younger recruits carried a deck in their knapsacks. When the army split into blue and gray factions after Fort Sumter was fired upon in April 1861, just about every soldier, from raw privates to commanders in chief, soon became conversant with poker's cunning and expedient stratagems.

For the hundreds of thousands of troops in Civil War camps, the game provided an upgrade from such entertainments as drinking, bareknuckle boxing, chuck-a-luck (a three-dice game similar to craps), or betting on the outcome of a race between lice. "There is some of the onerest men here that I ever saw," one soldier wrote to his family, "and the most swearing and card playing and fitin and drunkenness that I ever saw at any place."

Who were these young men, and where did they hail from? Stephen Vincent Benét provides a sense of their variety in his epic poem *John Brown's Body*:

> *Alloy of a dozen disparate, alien states,*
> *City-boy, farm-hand, bounty-man, first volunteer,*
> *Old regular, drafted recruit, paid substitute,*
> *Men who fought through the war from First Bull Run . . .*
> *Rocks from New England and hickory-chunks from the West,*

Bowery boy and clogging Irish adventurer,
Germans who learnt their English under the shells
Or didn't have time to learn it before they died.

As the poker players among them gradually became inured to the blistering firepower of both armies, some continued to shuffle and deal as the minié balls of snipers whistled by overhead. But most games were somewhat less tense. One glass-plate photograph shows four officers of the 114th Pennsylvania Infantry, the famous Zouaves, casually posed in a small clearing of a pine forest in front of their Sibley tents. Attended by a pair of black servants, three of the officers relax at a rickety table, playing five-card draw in the twilight.

Inevitably, some soldiers played more than was good for them, losing everything they owned and going into hock for still more. The historian Stephen Hyslop tells us that "between supper at 6:30 and lights out at 9:00, men not on picket duty had only time to kill, and gambling and drinking often did the trick." According to one Texas soldier, men "who never threw a card before the war [would] lose the last Confederate dollar they had." Playing too much could even have lethal consequences. *John Brown's Body* describes a soldier on watch who has fallen asleep:

He was tired.
Dog-tired, stone-tired, body and mind burnt up
With too much poker last night . . .

Using a blanket for a table, rank-and-file soldiers knelt or sat cross-legged on the ground, squinting through dusk or candlelight at whatever grimy cards were available. Since inadvertent marks were unavoidable in even the squarest of games, recognizing the creases or smudges on the backs of particular cards gave a substantial advantage to those with a cheating heart to go with above-average eyesight.

Decks of that era had single-ended court cards, and the lower cards were printed without index numbers. A player had to fan his hand wide, upend the face cards, and meticulously count pips to determine whether he in fact had triplet boxcars to go with his pair of red johnnies (sixes full of jacks). The backs of the cards usually featured patriotic imagery—generals, admirals, Lady Liberty, Jeff Davis, Abe Lincoln. Some decks had suits of eagles, shields, stars, and flags, with the court cards picturing colonels instead of kings, goddesses of liberty as queens, majors as jacks. Among the most widely distributed were the Highlander decks produced by the L. I. Cohn Company of New York. But whoever manufactured them, the designs on the backs of most cards were predominantly red, white, and blue. After the battle between the USS *Monitor* and the CSS *Merrimack* in March 1862, the Andrew Dougherty Company issued an "Army and Navy" deck whose ace of spades neutrally stated: "To Commemorate the Greatest Event in Naval History—the Substitution of Iron for Wood."

Although stud poker (the subject of Chapter 18) was beginning to gain a foothold in the Ohio River Valley, where Grant's Army of the Tennessee had been in control since capturing Fort Donelson in February 1862, draw was by far the most popular variant. Graycoats from the Mississippi Delta preferred a fifty-three-card version called mistigris (French for joker) in which that card was wild—that is, could be used as a fourth deuce, for example, in a hand already containing three of them. In the case of tied mistigris hands, a pair of kings lost to a king with the joker. Including the joker boosted the probability that draws to big hands would succeed, which added yet another level of reckoning and tactical prowess.

Those preferring an even more wide-open game could agree that all four deuces were wild. Four aces might then lose to five treys, though the house or camp rules would have to determine whether a straight flush outranked a quintet. Other variations in hand rank recognized mostly in the South included a Blaze, any five picture cards, which beat two pairs but lost to three of a kind; a Tiger, a seven-high hand without any pair, straight, or flush, which beat a straight but lost to a flush; a Dutch or Skipping Straight, such as 2-4-6-8-10, which beat two pairs and a Blaze; and a Round-the-Corner Straight, such as Q-K-A-2-3, which beat three of a kind but lost to a regular straight.

While such variations must have led to some testy confusion, a more serious problem for Southern players was that by 1862 decks had become fairly scarce. As the federal navy tightened its blockade, London card makers loaded their wares onto ships tasked with trying to run it. Some trading vessels passed through, but the law of supply and demand soon made cards so valuable that a Union colonel was caught smuggling some four thousand decks into Warrenton, Virginia, where he expected to turn a profit of $5,000 by selling them to a Confederate sutler. Before that deal could go down, however, the colonel was arrested by the Union detective Lafayette Baker and locked up in the Old Capitol Prison. (Baker later helped track down and kill John Wilkes

Booth.) After Grant captured Vicksburg on July 4, 1863, riverboat gamblers whose venues were drydocked by Union control of the Mississippi moved their operations back down to New Orleans or north to Chicago. In these and other cities occupied by the Union, decks cost about three cents apiece.

While Yankee soldiers had a steady supply of decks, Confederates were forced to make do with increasingly raggedy cards, sometimes playing with as few as forty-five, which made calculating the odds of drawing to certain hands even more of a challenge. For chips, working-class soldiers on both sides used buttons, pebbles, beans, or grains of rice or corn. Those who played well and got lucky in smaller games were sometimes invited to test their skill against the officers, who used proper chips, paper currency, or gold coins to bet with. An aristocratic major in a Louisiana regiment, for example, might raise a newly flush sergeant a thick wad of dixies, after the French word for ten. Dixie was the nickname not only of his home state's $10 banknote but of those used throughout the Confederacy.

"Dixie" was also a popular song by Daniel Decatur Emmett. Lincoln was so fond of it that he had chosen it to be played at his 1861 inauguration, despite winning zero electoral votes in what would soon become the Confederate States of America. Not much of a poker player himself, Lincoln as a "long-shanked young man" had wrestled and performed feats of strength for money and almost certainly tried his luck in penny-ante games while piloting flatboats along the Mississippi and its tributaries. His two-thousand-mile round-trip from Springfield to New Orleans in the spring of 1831, by far the longest of his life, included a monthlong stay in the capital of poker and a steamboat excursion back home. But he apparently gave up all forms of wagering when he became an attorney and a congressman, especially during his momentous debates in 1858 with Senator Stephen A. Douglas about whether slavery should be extended into the Western territories. Lincoln may well have believed there was too much at stake to allow any listener or potential voter to call his personal morality into question. Even so, he clearly understood poker's lore and that its ruthlessly expedient logic was essential to the American character, whether Northern or Western or Southern.

With his background as a riverman, Lincoln had witnessed cardsharps and roughnecks in action. He had also heard plenty of tales about them, one of which he fine-tuned and told to great effect during the first international crisis of his presidency. In November 1861, with

Union armies generally in retreat from Joseph Johnston, Robert E. Lee, and their feisty lieutenants, the British mail steamer *Trent*, bearing two Confederate envoys to London, was intercepted by the Yankee captain Charles Wilkes. When Wilkes decided to take the envoys prisoner, he created an incident that threatened to bring Great Britain into the war on the side of the South. The British assumed that orders to board the *Trent* had come from on high, when in fact Captain Wilkes had been acting on his own initiative. In any case, they delivered a stern ultimatum: release the envoys and apologize, or else. To back it up, an army of eleven thousand regulars set sail for Canada, and the Royal Navy began fitting out its fleet of warships. Four score years after waving the white flag at Yorktown and forty-six after Old Hickory licked them at New Orleans, the most powerful military machine on earth was bristling for a rematch. For those who thought Britain was bluffing, Lincoln had a yarn concerning a dangerous bulldog in his hometown. "I know the bulldog will not bite. You know he will not bite, but does the bulldog know he will not bite?"

Secretary of State William Seward initially favored an aggressive response to the bulldog's growling threat. Seward, after all, had publicly stated on several occasions his belief that a war with Great Britain would reunite North and South against their former antagonist. Lincoln described Seward arriving at a tense cabinet meeting "loaded to the muzzle" with reasons to defy the British. Navy Secretary Gideon Welles's congratulatory telegram to Captain Wilkes had also been made public. "Your conduct in seizing these public enemies," Welles declared, "was marked by intelligence, ability, decision, and firmness, and has the emphatic approval of this Department." A typical editorial declared, "The country would never forgive any man who should propose such a surrender." With few exceptions, Union citizens heartily agreed. Attorney General Edward Bates confided in his diary that the president and his cabinet had ample reason to fear "the displeasure of our own people—lest they should accuse us of truckling to the power of England."

As the crisis came to a head, Lincoln refused to let any such fears force his hand. "One war at a time" was his stated rationale as he "cheerfully" freed the ambassadors. To anyone feeling less cheerful about it, he and Seward cited American and international law. "We must stick to American principles concerning the rights of neutrals," said Lincoln. "We fought Great Britain [in the War of 1812] for insisting, by theory and practice, on the right to do precisely what Wilkes has done."

Reporters and politicians wanted to know whether the president would also apologize to Queen Victoria, as the British had demanded. Lincoln responded with the yarn about the poker-playing, knife-wielding roughs, one of whom had pinned the other's hand to the table with his bowie knife: "If you haven't got the ace of spades under your palm, I'll apologize."

If our most articulate president could explain his position during a wartime diplomatic crisis with such a parable, there can be little doubt that poker tactics were deeply ingrained in the American way of thinking by now, though it also lent credence to Jonathan Green's claims about the prevalence of cheating and thuggery in the national card game.

Freeing the rebel envoys had been "downright gall and wormwood" to many Northerners, including most members of the cabinet. Lincoln later admitted to Grant that it was "a pretty bitter pill to swallow." But if it was a tactical defeat in one early battle, it confidently prepared the ground for a larger strategic victory. Before that could happen, however, Lincoln and his generals had to overcome opponents as wily and aggressive as Lee, Thomas "Stonewall" Jackson, "Little Billy" Mahone, and Nathan Bedford Forrest, whose bluff-heavy tactics allowed them to defeat, escape, or fight to a gruesome draw Union armies much larger and better supplied than the ragtag ones they commanded.

THE WIZARD

If you ever try to interfere with me or cross my path again
You do so at the peril of your own life.
— BOB DYLAN, "FLOATER (TOO MUCH TO ASK)"

Just outside Rome, Georgia, in the damp spring of 1863, 450 Confederate cavalrymen under Brigadier General Nathan Bedford Forrest were about to engage a federal force about three times their size led by Colonel Abel D. Streight. Veteran Hoosiers mounted mostly on mules, Streight's bluecoats were known as "the Lightning Mule Brigade." Their black-bearded colonel, with a shaved upper lip like his president's, had been ordered by Sherman to cut the Western and Atlantic Railroad line supplying Braxton Bragg's Army of Tennessee, and Bragg deployed Forrest to make sure Streight didn't succeed. For the last two weeks of April, Forrest had been harassing his flanks and rear in daily skirmishes among the mountains of eastern Alabama. But the flatter Georgia terrain seemed to call for a more fully pitched confrontation.

Forrest, known as the "Wizard of the Saddle," had earned a reputation for elusiveness and savagery while "deviling" Sherman's lieutenants. "So fierce did his passion become," recalled one of his men, "that he was almost equally dangerous to friend or foe, and, as it seemed to some of us, he was too wildly excitable to be capable of judicious command. Later we became aware that excitement neither paralyzed nor misled his magnificent military genius." He was able to fight with hot blood and cold cunning. "War means fighting and fighting means killing," he said. In four years of fighting he killed thirty-one bluecoats in hand-to-hand combat alone—one of them with a penknife after the trooper had shot him. "No damned man kills me and lives," Forrest told him. Whenever his troops gained a real or perceived advantage, Forrest would demand that his counterpart surrender, with the same ultimatum each time: "Should my demand be refused, I cannot be responsible for the fate of your command," often adding that every Union soldier and officer would be "put to the sword." While it was impossible to tell whether he was bluffing, the consequences of being wrong could be gruesome, especially if the soldiers were black. On May 2, 1863, he put the same proposition to Streight.

"Keepin' the skeer on 'em" was how Forrest himself liked to describe it. At six two, 210 pounds, he was quite a large man by the standards of the day and even more imposing on horseback. With a bushy goatee and brown hair swept back under a wide-brimmed beaver hat, he was often compared to the devil. This was just fine with Forrest, who'd guessed that Colonel Streight was aware of his take-no-prisoners approach. He also knew Streight was operating in hostile territory and couldn't be confident of his intelligence sources. To make the "skeer" more intimidating, Forrest had marched his troops in a racetrack-shaped oval, only the home stretch of which could be seen by Streight's lookouts, creating the illusion they numbered well into the thousands.

At a prebattle parley the next morning, Forrest cordially requested that Colonel Streight surrender, if only "to stop the further and useless effusion of blood." Streight maintained that although he was willing to talk, he was by no means ready to give up the fight. As the parley continued, Forrest made sure his officers kept moving their only two howitzers across a distant rise plainly visible to Streight, then back along a lower path the colonel couldn't see, and over the rise once again. "Name of God!" Streight finally exclaimed. "How many guns have you got? There's fifteen I've counted already."

"I reckon that's all that has kept up," the poker-faced Forrest responded. Like a fellow reraising all-in with a measly pair, Forrest was blending menace, nonchalance, and deception, leveraging Streight's fear of sending his men on a suicide mission. It worked. After Streight

returned to confer with his lieutenants, the consensus was overwhelming: surrender.

As what now might be called the Donkey Brigade was marched off to
a makeshift prison camp, the size of Forrest's regiment quickly became
apparent. Streight was enraged and humiliated, but there was nothing
he could do now that his men were disarmed. Once the Yankees had
been generously fed by the relieved citizens of Rome, a rebel captain
named Charles Anderson took the opportunity to tell Streight, "Cheer
up, Colonel. This is not the first time a bluff has beat a straight."

Lee later called Forrest the best soldier who fought for either the
North or the South, and no less an intimidator than Sherman deemed
him "the most remarkable man our Civil War produced on either side.
He had a genius which was to me incomprehensible." Sherman showed
Forrest enough respect to issue orders that he be "hunted down and
killed if it cost ten thousand lives and bankrupts the Federal treasury."
Never one to make idle threats, Sherman dispatched fourteen thousand
troops to execute the order. They finally lured Forrest into battle near
Tupelo, where they managed to wound their quarry but not kill or capture him.

"He was the only Confederate cavalryman of whom Grant stood in
much dread," said a friend of the Union commander. Forrest "was
amenable to no known rules of procedure, was a law unto himself for all
military acts, and was constantly doing the unexpected at all times and
places." Like a no-limit hold'em artist running amok at a table of ABC
players, Forrest fought "by ear," he said, demoralizing opponents by
anticipating their moves, identifying the most strategic positions, and
"gittin' thar fust with the most men."

Without formal military training, this planter and slave trader had
an innate sense of hit-and-run tactics. Most cavalry officers led recon-
naissance missions for infantry generals, but Forrest deployed his
troops as a mounted infantry, more apt to attack the enemy than merely
to spy on him. In a typical raid, Forrest's horsemen would surprise a
Union outpost, destroy the railhead it was guarding along with any
bridges nearby, then escape into the mountains before a counterattack
could be mustered. While Forrest went off on his next raid, Union engineers would repair the damage of the previous one, at which point
Forrest would swoop back in to wreck things again.

Cavalrymen were thrilled to serve under him, though his lightning
dynamics often kept them sleepless and hungry and forced them to stay
ready on a moment's notice. "We were all lying in camp playing poker

and writing love-letters, when suddenly 'boots and saddles' rang out on the quiet air," Private Charles W. Button remembered. "The sick recovered instantly."

Charging too fast for even these men to keep up at Shiloh in April 1862, Colonel Forrest found himself in the midst of the enemy without a single graycoat around him. After emptying both pistols, he drew out his saber and began slashing his way through the Yankees, one of whom managed to hit him from close range with a shot that lifted him up from his saddle. The ball went through his pelvis and lodged near his spine. Using one arm, Forrest grabbed another infantryman by the collar and used him briefly as a shield as he galloped back toward his men. After a two-month convalescence and promotion to brigadier general, he was back leading troops from the saddle.

When the beautiful Union spy Pauline Cushman was brought to his camp, he "barely glanced up from the cards he was shuffling. One look from him told [her that] he was only interested in her as a prisoner." Cushman had made drawings of Confederate positions and even pilfered a battle map from the desk of General Bragg, concealing them between the inner and outer sole of her boot. Caught with these items, the former actress had already escaped once but was recaptured and taken to Forrest.

"I'm really glad to see you," he told her. "I've been looking for you for a long time; but I've got this last shuffle. . . ." After dealing the cards, he peeked at his own hand and folded, then finally glared up at Cushman. "You've been here before, I take it—know all the roads, don't you? And all the bridle paths, and even the hog paths—don't you?"

"Sir, every word you utter is as false as your own traitorous heart!" Cushman had the nerve to reply. "I've never been here before, and I should like to send a bullet through the man who is mean enough to make the charge."

"Yes," drawled Forrest, "and I'd send one through you, if I could." Other Confederate officers had fallen for her dark-haired Creole charms, but not Forrest. "I have no time now," he informed her, "to investigate your case. It is a complicated and difficult one. I will, therefore, send you to General Bragg's headquarters, and if you should be so fortunate as to prove your loyalty to the South, you may always depend upon General Forrest for protection. But this, I am sorry to say, I do not believe possible, and therefore say, prepare for the worst, for hanging is not pleasant."

But three days before this unpleasantness was set to occur, Bragg fell into retreat before William Rosecrans's Army of the Cumberland, and Cushman was rescued by bluecoats near Shelbyville, Tennessee. With her cover blown, her spying days were over. The army chief of staff (and later president) James Garfield awarded her the honorary rank of major, and Lincoln himself bestowed upon her the nickname "Little Major."

In spite of letting its guard down with Cushman, Bragg's Army of Tennessee won a crucial victory at Chickamauga over Rosecrans in September 1863. Stunned into inertia by his own losses, however, Bragg ignored the pleading of Forrest and others to pursue the routed Yankees before they could reorganize in Chattanooga. Bragg did manage to surround the city and cut most supply lines, but after being reinforced by Sherman, the larger Union force, now led by Grant, launched a ferocious counterattack. The Confederate siege line collapsed and Bragg's troops fled chaotically into Georgia. Grant's opinion was that Bragg had made "several grave mistakes: first, in sending away his ablest corps commander with over twenty thousand troops; second, in sending away a division of troops on the eve of battle; third, in placing so much of a force on the plain in front of his impregnable position."

"What does he fight battles *for*?" Forrest asked in a rage, then let it be known that he refused to serve any longer under Bragg's authority. Even before the Chattanooga fiasco, Bragg's men had considered him both imperious and incompetent. Unlike poker-playing regular fellows like Forrest, John Bell Hood, and James Longstreet, Bragg was a finicky stickler for military protocol. He not only made a habit of clashing with subordinates over trivial issues but had once engaged in a notorious written dispute with *himself* while serving as both a company's commander and quartermaster.

Now generals Forrest, Longstreet, Leonidas Polk, and William J. Hardee all told President Jefferson Davis that Bragg must be replaced. Davis reluctantly agreed, but only, he said, after a suitable replacement could be found. Before that could happen, Bragg vengefully ordered Forrest to give up command of his cavalry. His reply, made to Bragg's face, was a blistering summary of the general's tactical blunders and acts of personal spite. After calling his commanding officer "a coward," Forrest told him, "You have threatened to arrest me for not obeying your orders promptly. I dare you to do it, and I say that if you ever try to interfere with me or cross my path again, you do so at the peril of your life." Bragg apparently failed to report this threat to Davis because he understood Forrest was too valuable to be jailed for insubordination. Or perhaps he was simply afraid.

In any case, Forrest kept the "skeer" on the bluecoats, sometimes by means well outside the accepted conventions of warfare. Though Forrest and the Confederate press denied it, the belief was widespread among Union officers and newspaper editors that he participated in or at least countenanced a massacre—at Fort Pillow, on a Tennessee bluff above the Mississippi, on April 12, 1864—of unarmed black troops trying to surrender. Some reports claimed Forrest's men used sabers to hack their victims to death, others that former slaves were crucified on tent frames or set on fire while still alive. Though Southern newspapers reported that "not the first sign of surrender was ever given," the evidence continues to mount that a massacre of unarmed, defenseless troops took place under Forrest's command. One of his own men, Achilles Clark, wrote a letter to his sisters immediately after the battle: "The slaughter was awful," he wrote. "The poor deluded negroes would run up to our men[,] fall upon their knees and with uplifted hands scream for mercy but they were ordered to their feet and then shot down. I with several others tried to stop the butchery and at one time had partially succeeded[,] but Gen. Forrest ordered them shot down like dogs and the carnage continued. Finally our men became sick of blood and the firing ceased." Forrest remained unrepentant. "The river was dyed with the blood of the slaughtered for two hundred yards," he declared. "It is hoped that these facts will demonstrate to the Northern people that negro soldiers cannot cope with Southerners."

Almost a month after Grant's generous terms of surrender were accepted by Lee, Deep South governors were pleading with Forrest and others to continue the war. Still recovering from his fourth combat wound, Forrest seriously considered launching a guerrilla campaign based in Mexico. "If one road led to hell and the other to Mexico," he told an adjutant, "I would be indifferent which to take." But on May 9, 1865—three and a half weeks after Lincoln was assassinated and the day before Davis was captured in Georgia—Forrest decided he and his men could best restore Southern pride by laying down their arms and going home. "You have been good soldiers," he told them. "You can be good citizens. Obey the laws, preserve your honor, and the government to which you have surrendered can afford to be and will be magnanimous."

A tale that is almost certainly apocryphal has Forrest returning to his wife, Mary Ann, who'd been living in a log cabin on their former estate. "I went into the army worth a million and a half dollars and came out a beggar," he said. But with a single $10 bill Mary Ann had put aside, he planned to use poker to rebuild their fortune.

Mary Ann was a woman of devout Christian virtue, and Bedford, as she called him, had to persuade her that risking their last Yankee sawbuck in a card game was the best chance he had to keep them from the poorhouse. "Won't you consent to my going out tonight and hunting up a game of draw?" he begged her. "And won't you pray that I may win while I am out?" Mary Ann said that while she wouldn't try to stop him, his plan was a sin in the sight of God, and "sin cannot finally prosper." Forrest went out and played anyway, winning enough to fill his famous beaver hat. Returning home around 2:00 a.m., he turned over the hat and poured $1,500 into her lap.

While his military record suggests he was a poker natural, the God-fearing Forrest chose to understand his last-ditch parlay as follows: "Mary, in spite of her objections, really prayed for me while I was gone. At any rate, I found her still sitting up when I got back, and I know her prayers have many a time served me a good turn." It was the Almighty, not his humble servant's bluffing panache, who won all those pots for the Wizard. Or so the lore has it.

Wherever it came from, Forrest's genius as an underdog tactician is what he is remembered for, at least in places where the Confederate battle flag still ripples in the breeze. With the exception of Lee, Stonewall Jackson, and possibly Jeb Stuart, no graycoat leader is more widely honored. In 1937, five German generals, including Field Marshal Erwin Rommel, visited several Forrest battle sites, and the Wizard's use of surprise, intimidation, bluffing, and other poker-inflected stratagems continues to be studied in war colleges around the world.

But perhaps the main thing we remember Forrest for is his contempt for and slaughter of blacks. After the war, he became a prominent member of the Ku Klux Klan, which was devoted to keeping former slaves disenfranchised and reestablishing white conservative rule. When he first heard of the Klan, Forrest remarked, "That's a good thing; that's a damn good thing. We can use that to keep the niggers in their place."

Those who defend Forrest say he was told the Klan would primarily defend impoverished Confederate widows, and his gallantry in this regard is the only reason he agreed to serve as its first Grand Wizard, a title derived from his reputation as Wizard of the Saddle. They maintain that the original Klansmen did not see former slaves as the enemy so much as the carpetbaggers, Northerners who took advantage of defeated Southerners, and scalawags, white Republican Southerners. Forrest's critics insist that "carpetbagger" and "scalawag" were pro-slaver terms for people who worked to allow black people to vote, move freely, own property, defend themselves, and serve in the government. To Forrest's credit, in 1869, as the Klan became more racially violent, he resigned his membership and ordered it to disband. (It did not.) Near the end of his life he also gave speeches trying to heal the wounds of the war. On July 5, 1875, speaking to a mostly black audience, he said, "We have but one flag, one country; let us stand together. We may differ in color, but not in sentiment." But coming from a former slave trader and Grand Wizard, it may have seemed too thorn-studded an olive branch to take a firm hold of.

A much less unsavory graycoat was William Mahone. Five four and weighing less than a hundred pounds, he was nicknamed "Little Billy." His chestnut beard reached the middle button on his gray uniform jacket. Before he entered the military, his Norfolk and Petersburg Railroad was critical to moving troops and ordnance. In April 1861, federal troops occupied the Gosport Shipyard in Portsmouth, Virginia. With the Confederate garrison handily outnumbered, Mahone ran a troop transport train into Norfolk with as much noise and whistle-blowing as possible, then snuck it quietly out of town before running it back into Norfolk, creating the illusion of a much larger force. Without a shot being fired, the Union forces retreated across Hampton Roads to Fort Monroe. For saving the shipyard, Davis offered Mahone a commission as a lieutenant colonel. Despite his lack of military training, he was quickly promoted to brigadier general and decorated for valor after leading his brigade in Seven Pines and Malvern Hill, Chancellorsville, Gettysburg, and the Wilderness.

In 1864, Mahone's quick thinking in chaotic circumstances helped seal a rebel victory in the infamous Battle of the Crater. During the Union siege of Petersburg (a city crucial to the supply of Lee's army and of the capital, Richmond), coal miners from Colonel Henry Pleasants's Forty-eighth Pennsylvania infantry dug a 511-foot tunnel and placed eight thousand pounds of explosives directly under the main Confederate fort. The explosives were detonated on July 30, creating a pit two hundred feet wide and thirty feet deep, destroying the fort and breaching the defensive line around Petersburg. "Bedlam in flames," Shelby Foote called it. Instead of panicking, however, Mahone led two of his brigades in a counterattack. Their effectiveness was enhanced by the fact that Union troops had marched forward *into* the crater instead of circling around its rim. Trapped in the muck and gore, they made easy targets for Mahone's marksmen, whose "rapid-fire volleys" and bayonet charge down the side of the crater "shattered what little remained of blue resistance." (The explosion and subsequent bloodbath are the opening scenes of Anthony Minghella's film version of Charles Frazier's novel *Cold Mountain*.) The Union suffered more than five thousand casualties and failed to defend against the Confederate counterattack, though it wouldn't be long before the vastly outnumbered and undersupplied Confederates were forced to abandon Richmond and retreat toward Appomattox.

After the war, Mahone oversaw the reconstruction of Virginia's roads and railways, founded a teacher's college in Petersburg to educate former slaves (which evolved into Virginia State University), and was elected to the United States Senate in 1881. Eugene Edwards picks up his story at Chamberlain's restaurant near Capitol Hill. "When General Mahone held Virginia in his vest pocket he was a figure in Washington poker circles. He was cool and nervy, and withal played poker like a gentleman." His regular tablemates included Senator Matthew "Boss" Quay, the journalist Henry Watterson, and Walter Gresham, who served as secretary of state and the treasury. In one session, Mahone had already anted when he was called from the table on Senate business, and the other players decided it would be amusing to fix a friendly cold deck for him. When Mahone returned to the table, he found three queens and an ace in his hand. He drew one card, the case queen. Another player also drew one card, completing a straight flush. After betting the maximum, he watched along with his tablemates to see how much Little Billy would raise. Without hesitation or a word of comment, Mahone tossed his hand in the muck. As his opponent pulled in the small pot, Mahone picked up the deck and calmly began to shuffle. Unable to contain themselves any longer, the other players gave back his ante from the previous hand, and all but Mahone burst out laughing.

"Why didn't you bet your four queens?" one of them asked. "Did you suspect a joke or think someone was trying to rob you?"

"No, sir," said Mahone. "I have the utmost confidence in the honesty of every gentleman present, and I haven't the remotest idea that any one of you would ever rob me, but I make an inflexible rule to never bet a high hand when I have been absent from the deal. To be out of the room and then to return and pick up three queens and get a fourth on a one-card draw is to me very alarming. So, of course, I threw my hand in the discard."

"Well, General," replied the man who had fixed the cold deck, "it was a joke, and I must compliment you on the manner in which you received it. It showed, sir, that you are a Southern gentleman, and was complimentary alike to yourself and to us."

NARY A PAIR

There's somewhat prouder, over there—
The Trumpets tell it to the Air—
How different Victory
To Him who has it—and the One
Who to have had it, would have been
Contenteder—to die—

—EMILY DICKINSON,
"MY PORTION IS DEFEAT—TODAY"

As Garry Wills's *Nixon Agonistes* was the first presidential biography to emphasize poker ethics, Shelby Foote's *The Civil War*, published in three magnificent volumes between 1958 and 1974, was the first work of history to explore how the game's lore and logic fit into the overall scheme of America's most definitive conflict. While Wills used Nixon's poker playing as a colonoscope into the bowels of a politician he felt little sympathy for, Foote had great reserves of empathy for the game and its players. Poker had come of age in his beloved Mississippi Delta, and his ancestors avidly played it throughout the nineteenth century, along with quite a few of his favorite Civil War officers.

In the early years of the twentieth, however, Foote's paternal grandfather, Hugh, lost nearly all of the family's considerable fortune playing stud—often while drunk—in Memphis card rooms and later at the Elks Club of Greenville, Mississippi, just two doors down from the Methodist church he attended on Sundays. Raised amid servants and plantation money, the author's father "had every reason to expect," as his son later put it, "that everything was going to run smoothly for the rest of his life. He could have done what he wanted to do: play cards, go hunting, all that kind of thing." But it wasn't to be. Perhaps the only upside of the squandered inheritance was that Shelby Foote III learned early in life how profoundly the game could impact both the person who played it and the people who depended on him.

Foote's 2,836-page narrative makes vividly clear how integral the national game was to both war efforts, from penny-ante contests of draw and mistigris played by enlisted men through the do-or-die showdowns of generals and presidents—how the feints, bluffs, and general poker mind-set of Grant, Lee, Hood, Longstreet, Forrest, and others often determined how critical battles played out.

In a typical passage, Foote quotes a friend of "Fighting Joe" Hooker on the gumption of that charismatic Union commander. "He could play the best game of poker I ever saw, until it came to the point where he should go a thousand better, and then he would flunk." Not surprisingly, this shortage of intestinal fortitude turned out to have enormous military consequences as well. Having been placed by Lincoln at the head of the Army of the Potomac in January 1863, the hard-drinking Hooker quickly brought much needed discipline to an army that had been humiliated under George McClellan and other generals. Hooker even quit drinking in order to remain clearheaded as he faced off with Lee—though a belt of good moonshine might have bolstered him when the chips were down at Fredericksburg. After outflanking Lee and crossing the Rapidan River with a two-to-one troop advantage, Hooker was on the verge of crushing the rebellion with a single decisive blow. "All was *couleur de rose!*" wrote one of his generals. Another, Darius Couch, found "hilarity pervading the camps; the soldiers, while chopping wood and lighting fires, were singing merry songs and indulging in peppery jokes." It seemed to Couch that Hooker "had ninety chances in his favor to ten against him." He held overwhelming advantages in men and artillery, a commanding position on high ground from which to annihilate Lee's infantry, with an open path to Richmond after that. The war would be over in days.

But when Lee's pinned-down veterans suddenly took the initiative, Hooker lost his nerve—"flunked," as his friend might have put it. When Hooker ordered a retreat instead of a counterattack, his generals refused to believe it. When the order reached Major General Henry Slocum, commander of the Union's right wing, he called the messenger "a damned liar! Nobody but a crazy man would give such an order when we have victory in sight! I shall go and see General Hooker myself, and if I find out that you have spoken falsely, you shall be shot on my return." And yet it was true. Even more bizarrely, Hooker then ordered his main force to take a vulnerable position in the Wilderness, a place called Fairview, where he soon suffered a devastating defeat by Lee and Stonewall Jackson.

The consensus among historians is that Lee, in the words of John Steele Gordon, had "played Joseph Hooker like a fiddle, bluffing him into a defensive posture when he had overwhelming superiority." Not only Hooker, of course. Lee made a habit of performing such tricks on a series of Union commanders. In the early months of the war, as he desperately searched for reinforcements, he successfully bluffed George Meade into thinking the Army of Northern Virginia was back at full strength; Meade's failure to attack him bought Lee valuable time. When the battles were finally joined, Lee's ability to mislead, intimidate, and outmaneuver much larger armies was often enough to carry the day, though his miscalculations at Gettysburg spelled the end of his invasion of the North. Yet Gordon is certainly not the only historian who believes the war would have probably been "a lot shorter and a lot less bloody than it was" if Lee, who was opposed to secession, hadn't allowed his loyalty to Virginia to override his feelings toward the United States.

Lincoln, meanwhile, while replacing these bluffable generals, also had to deal with his brilliant but overly ambitious treasury secretary, Salmon P. Chase, who made little secret of his conviction that he, not Lincoln, deserved to be president. Having barely lost the 1860 nomination, Chase used his position in Lincoln's cabinet to campaign for himself behind Lincoln's back in '64; and in order to gain leverage for positions he favored, he regularly threatened to resign, knowing how much the president valued his management of the Union economy. After Chase submitted his fourth letter of resignation, however, Lincoln shocked him by calling his bluff and accepting it.

After so many Union defeats at the hands of Lee and Jackson that it looked as though the South would win the war, on March 12, 1864, Lincoln finally put the whiskey-loving poker player Ulysses S. Grant in command of all federal armies. Unlike his dithering predecessors Winfield Scott, McClellan, Ambrose Burnside, Meade, and Hooker—but very much like Lee, the first man Lincoln had wanted for the job—"Uncle Sam" Grant preferred forcing the action with poker-inflected aplomb. He'd proved to be especially good at misrepresenting his own position and strength and at divining his opponents' intentions, which he usually countered with devastating effectiveness. Chattanooga was surrounded? Vicksburg refortified? Raise!

Negotiating with John Pemberton for the surrender of Vicksburg, Grant's initials had picked up a new connotation when he insisted upon the "unconditional surrender" of the Confederate garrison. "Then, sir," replied Pemberton—"rather snappishly" in Grant's recollection— "it is unnecessary that you and I should hold any further discussion. We will go to fighting again at once. . . . I can assure you, sir, you will bury many more of your men before you will enter Vicksburg."

Grant remained silent in the face of this threat; "nor did he change his position or expression," according to Foote. "The contest was like poker, and he played it straight-faced while his opponent continued to sputter. . . . If the Confederate played a different style of game, that did not necessarily mean that he was any less skillful." Indeed, Pemberton's counterbluff helped persuade Grant to allow the graycoats defending the city to be paroled—with their horses, no less—instead of being taken captive, though another factor was certainly Grant's desire not to have to feed thirty thousand starving prisoners. As far as this "side pot" was concerned, Foote declared that Pemberton "won; for in the end it was the quiet man who gave way and the sputterer who stood firm." It was Grant's troops, however, who marched into Vicksburg on July 4, 1863, and Pemberton's who abandoned the city's high fortress above the river, ceding control of the Mississippi to the Union and effectively cutting the Confederacy in two.

Like any good poker player, Grant had a knack for capitalizing on the overly passive or aggressive tendencies of rebel generals, as well as of those who served under him. As he wrote in his *Memoirs*, he'd been a student at West Point "at about the right time to meet most of the graduates who were of a suitable age at the breaking out of the rebellion to be trusted with large commands." Having graduated in 1843, "I was at the military academy from one to four years with all the cadets who graduated from 1840 to 1846—seven classes. These classes embraced more than fifty officers who afterwards became generals on one side or the other in the rebellion, many of them holding high commands. All the older generals, who became conspicuous in the rebellion, I had served with and known in Mexico: Lee, J. E. Johnston, A. S. Johnston, Holmes, Hebert, and a number of others on the Confederate side."

He goes on to say that "what I learned of the characters of those to whom I was afterwards opposed" was of "immense service" to him during the war. Smart poker players like Grant prefer not to sit down in an ultrahigh-stakes game against aggressive new faces. He also pointed out that the "natural disposition of most people is to clothe the commander of a large army whom they do not know, with almost superhuman abilities. A large part of the National army, for instance, and most of the press in the country, clothed General Lee with just such qualities, but I had known him personally, and knew that he was mortal; and it was just as well that I felt this."

Remaining uncowed by his adversary helped Grant chop Lee and his fearsome Army of Northern Virginia down to size. Information about its location and troop strength gathered through spies, telescopes, balloons, and telegraph messages was not unlike knowing the predraw action, the size of the pot, and how many chips his opponent had left. What such information couldn't predict was how the opponent was likely to play the rest of the hand. To take the full measure of his adversary, Grant needed to know his tendencies. And he certainly needed to be unafraid of him.

Grant had a similar gift for telling bluster and bluff from real courage. "I have known a few men who were always aching for a fight when there was no enemy near, who were as good as their word when the battle did come. But the number of such men is small." With less dry humor, he writes that Jefferson Davis had "an exalted opinion of his own military genius," and that on many occasions "he came to the relief of the Union army by means of his *superior military genius.*"

Certainly Grant had military geniuses below him in the federal chain of command, Winfield Scott Hancock, Philip Sheridan, and William Tecumseh Sherman foremost among them. North of Atlanta in the summer of 1864, with Lincoln's presidency and the chances for reunion teetering in the balance, it was Sherman who severely outplayed the Confederate general John Bell Hood. Always courageous in battle, the Kentuckian's uncompromising recklessness became a more serious drawback as he was given command of larger forces. Lee's opinion, expressed to Davis, was that Hood was "all lion, none of the fox." But after Joseph Johnston's failures to check Sherman's advance into Georgia, a desperate Davis made Hood, at thirty-three, the youngest man on either side to be given command of an army.

Because Hood was an eleventh-hour replacement for Johnston, Sherman had little chance to pick up on his tendencies before the make-or-break battle was joined. He therefore summoned every federal officer who'd known Hood at West Point or elsewhere. One pro-Union Kentuckian informed Sherman that, before secession, "I seed Hood bet $2500 with nary a pair in his hand," though he didn't say who won the pot. Even so, bluffing such a sum in antebellum dollars confirmed Sherman's read of Hood as brave but impetuous, so he reconfigured his troops into a defensive posture and put them on highest alert. As if on cue, Hood proceeded to shatter his Army of Tennessee with four near-suicidal attacks on Sherman's well-dug-in positions.

With Atlanta now defenseless, Mayor James Calhoun wrote a letter dated September 11, 1864, imploring Sherman to spare the city. Sherman wrote back to establish his ruthless but ultimately compassionate intentions:

> We must have peace, not only at Atlanta but in all America. . . . War is cruelty and you cannot refine it, and those who brought war into our country deserve all the curses and maledictions a people can pour out. I know I had no hand in making this war, and I know I will make more sacrifices today than any of you to secure peace. But you cannot have peace and a division of our country. . . . But, my dear sirs, when that peace does come, you may call on me for anything. Then will I share with you the last cracker, and watch with you to shield your homes and families against danger from every quarter. Now you must go, and take with you the old and feeble, feed and nurse them and build for them in more quiet places proper habitations to shield them against the weather until the mad passions of men cool down and allow the Union and peace once more to settle over your old homes at Atlanta. Yours, in haste, W. T. SHERMAN

Taking Atlanta suddenly reversed the overwhelming likelihood that Lincoln would lose the November election to George McClellan, whose party's platform called for an immediate cease-fire and a negotiated settlement, which would have meant a continuation of slavery in the South. It also gave Lincoln the confidence to accept Chase's resignation. On election morning, November 8, *The New York Times* declared that before the sun set, "the destinies of this republic, so far as depends on human agency, are to be settled." Lincoln wound up winning 212 electoral votes to 21 for McClellan, including 70 percent from the Army of the Potomac, McClellan's former command. Sherman's victory in Georgia may therefore have done as much to end slavery and preserve the Union as any other single campaign.

As "Uncle Billy's bummers" ransacked the Georgia Statehouse, some of them fueled their cooking fires with Confederate currency; others used bushels of $1,000 CSA war bonds to play poker for astronomically high—though ultimately meaningless—stakes. Private U. H. Parr of the Seventieth Indiana reported watching hundreds of his fellow soldiers playing draw along the slope of a railroad embankment. They would soon heat the rails and bend them around tree trunks "until they were as crooked as a ram's horn." Known as "Sherman's neckties," they remained unusable even after the bummers moved on and Confederate crews attempted to repair the damage.

Sherman then led his men on the notoriously destructive march through Georgia to Savannah, twisting rails and making off with anything edible, before heading north through the Carolinas. After three years of rebel momentum since the First Battle of Bull Run on July 21, 1861, the tide of the war had now turned, though it would take another several months of horrific fighting before Lee finally sat down with Grant in Wilmer McLean's parlor three miles east of Appomattox, Virginia.

In the meantime their respective commanders in chief were maneuvering to achieve the best peace terms possible. Even though Davis was prepared to spill a lot more blood if he thought it might infuse his stillborn Confederacy with life, die-hard Southern journalists accused him of treason for even speaking to Union negotiators. The charge in the North was that Lincoln planned to keep Yankee troops from exacting the vengeance many now saw as their due. "With malice toward none, with charity for all," the stance Lincoln proposed in his second inaugural address on March 4, 1865, was deemed far too generous by more radical Republicans, who believed the South should be punished for starting the war. On the opposite end of the spectrum, emancipating the slaves made Lincoln the target of plenty of would-be assassins besides John Wilkes Booth. "Each of the two Presidents," writes Foote, "thus had much to fret about while playing their game of high-stakes international poker." It was endlessly fortunate for the United States that when all of their chips were finally pushed to the center of the table, it was Lincoln—thanks mainly to the efforts of Sherman and Grant and their men—who held the mortal nuts in his hand, while Davis held nary a pair.

. . .

At a meeting with Lincoln not long before Lee surrendered, Grant asked, "Mr. President, did you at any time doubt the final success of the cause?"

"Never for a moment," said Lincoln. An exaggeration, no doubt, but when Grant then asked him about the *Trent* Affair, he explained, "I contented myself with believing that England's triumph in the matter would be short-lived, and that after ending our war successfully we would be so powerful that we could call her to account for all the embarrassments she had inflicted upon us."

While refusing to apologize, that is, the president and his cabinet had decided in the dark hours of December 1861 to wait for a better hand before committing too many Union chips to a single pot against a pair of aggressive opponents. As Shelby Foote writes of his decision, "Poker was not the national game for nothing." By April 9, 1865, Lincoln, Grant, and Sherman had "busted" the Confederacy, and the re-United States was too strong to ever again be challenged by Britain.

On the morning of April 10, throngs of ecstatic citizens surrounded the White House, calling for a speech from their president on the occasion of Lee's defeat. Lincoln appeared in a second-story window and waved. As a man who liked to carefully plan and revise any public remarks, he wasn't quite ready to make a full-scale speech about the country's future, but he mollified the adoring crowd with a few impromptu words of praise for Grant and his men. He then directed everyone's attention to one of the bands. "I have always thought 'Dixie' one of the best tunes I have ever heard," he began. As the surprised musicians made ready to play it, he quipped, "Our adversaries over the way attempted to appropriate it, but I insisted yesterday that we fairly captured it. I presented the question to the Attorney General and he gave it as his opinion that it is now our lawful prize." As the crowd laughed and cheered, the doomed president—he would attend Ford's Theatre four evenings hence—smiled and said, "I now request the band to favor me with its performance."

ACES AND EIGHTS

I have fallen in love with American names,
The sharp, gaunt names that never get fat,
The snakeskin-titles of mining-claims,
The plumed war-bonnet of Medicine Hat,
Tucson and Deadwood and Lost Mule Flat . . .

I shall not rest quiet at Montparnasse.
I shall not lie easy at Winchelsea.
You may bury my body in Sussex grass,
You may bury my tongue at Champmédy.
I shall not be there. I shall rise and pass.
Bury my heart at Wounded Knee.

— STEPHEN VINCENT BENÉT,
"AMERICAN NAMES"

When the war ended in 1865, the industrialized North was flour-
ishing, while graycoats trudged home to a shattered economy. Food was
so scarce that Northerners had to organize charity drives to keep some
of their defeated countrymen from starving to death. Two-thirds of the
value of Confederate assets had been destroyed, including most of the
railroads and factories. The slave-labor force had been emancipated, and
much of the white population was demoralized and angry. In Alabama,
the *Montgomery Advertiser* noted that a "spirit of lawlessness seems to
pervade the town. Men seem the prey of reckless despair, and, forgetting
the laws of God and man, to give way to the phrensy of wild beasts."

Better news trickled in from the West. Recent discoveries of gold
and silver had spawned a more human, if no less wild, phrensy. Along
with freed blacks and other Union veterans, tens of thousands of
Southerners lit out for the territories. Many wound up in the mining
camps of Nevada and California, while others didn't make it that far.
Virtually all of them were battle-hardened gamblers armed with six-

shooters and a furious determination to strike it rich overnight. As their stampede impinged further on Native American hunting grounds, the tribes naturally took fierce exception, and the U.S. Army set about "pacifying" vast tracts of land.

Although George Armstrong Custer had graduated at the very bottom of the West Point class of '61, he turned out to be a talented cavalry officer at Gettysburg, Five Forks, and other battles. Having bestowed the nickname "Wolverines" on his Michigan Brigade and married the beautiful Elizabeth Bacon, the flamboyant Custer was promoted to general when he was only twenty-three. After the war he led cavalry raids against the Arapaho, Sioux, and Cheyenne, including at least one—the Battle of Washita River—that ended in a massacre of women and children.

In 1874, Custer's Seventh Cavalry was dispatched to the Lakota Sioux reservation in the Black Hills of Dakota. The 1868 Treaty of Fort Laramie had awarded the Sioux "absolute and undisturbed occupation" of the territory, but Custer had orders from General Sheridan to establish an outpost and investigate rumors of gold. Though his party found only modest traces of the metal, the glory-mongering Custer reported that "paying quantities" were gathered "at an expense of but little time and labor," implying that hardworking miners could probably dig up a lot more. His report helped to launch another gold rush, with one Eastern paper's headline declaring, THE NATIONAL DEBT TO BE PAID WHEN CUSTER RETURNS. A mighty horde of prospectors, gamblers, and other optimists thundered out to "them thar" Black Hills, making tiny Deadwood a boomtown, complete with painted ladies and gambling tables in the ornate saloons, though most of its housing consisted of tents. About five thousand white men staked claims, trespassing on Sioux burial grounds and disrupting their seasonal hunts. Led by Sitting Bull and Crazy Horse, the Sioux finally took their revenge on Custer's cavalry on June 25, 1876, near the Little Big Horn River. Custer's naked but unscalped body was found alongside the mutilated corpses of his men. His wife, Libbie, was one of the few who defended his tactical decisions in fighting the tribes, and she spent the rest of her long life defending his reputation as a husband and military leader.

A fortnight after Custer died, a long-haired gunman (who once may have been Libbie's lover) rode a tall horse into Deadwood. James Butler Hickok had been born on a farm near Troy Grove, Illinois, in 1837. His parents operated a station of the Underground Railroad and instilled in their children a strong abolitionist spirit. After learning to hunt wolves for bounty and deer for the family table, James headed for the Rockies at eighteen and spent the next six years as a hunter and trapper, with a brief stint as the bodyguard of a St. Louis abolitionist. When the war broke out, he volunteered as a Union marksman, performing effectively at Wilson's Creek and other Western battles. Dispatched by General Samuel R. Curtis to infiltrate Sterling Price's army, Hickok spent five months pretending to be a rebel cavalryman. "I never let on that I was good shot," he told a reporter after the war. "I kept that back for big occasions; but ef you'd heard me swear and cuss the blue-bellies, you'd a-thought me one of the wickedest of the whole crew." After sussing out crucial aspects of Price's troop dispositions, Hickok escaped back to Union lines, where Curtis heartily thanked him, said Hickok, "before a heap of generals."

In 1867, Hickok scouted for the Seventh Cavalry in Kansas, impressing both George and Libbie Custer. "Whether on foot or on horseback he was one of the most perfect types of physical manhood I ever saw," gushed the equally long-haired officer. "His skill in the use of the rifle and pistol was unerring." Hickok's perfect manhood made him irresistible to women, of course, and gossips insinuated an affair soon commenced between the scout and Mrs. Custer. Whether or not this was true, even the least salacious mind is likely to find the rumor believable when reading Libbie's description of Hickok: "He was a delight to look upon. Tall, lithe, and free in every motion, he rode and walked as if every muscle was perfection. . . . I do not recall anything finer in the way of physical perfection than Wild Bill when he swung himself lightly from his saddle . . ." and so on.

When Mrs. Custer first laid eyes on him, Hickok had just been lionized in a long, vividly illustrated profile by Colonel George Ward Nichols in *Harper's New Monthly Magazine*. Nichols met Hickok in the late summer of 1865 near Springfield, Missouri, where embers of the war were still crackling, and the merest remnant of a blue or gray uniform was enough to spark a gunfight. Nichols reported that Hickok stood "six foot and an inch in his bright yellow moccasins" and had "the handsomest *physique*" he had ever seen. "His small, round waist was girthed by a belt which held two of Colt's navy revolvers," with which Hickok claimed to have killed "hundreds of men." But when virtually all veterans went about armed with similar weapons, how had Wild Bill—a nickname based on his reckless courage—won every gunfight? "I allers shot well," he told Nichols, "but I come to be perfect by shootin at a dime for a mark, at bets of half a dollar a shot."

His latest victim was Davis Tutt, a gunfighter and professional gambler who had impugned Bill's honor over a poker debt. Nor had Tutt's status as a die-hard Confederate boosted his actuarial odds, though others claimed the two men had been friends but had a gradual falling out over women and poker. The night before the shootout, July 20, 1865, Hickok allegedly won about two hundred dollars (twice what his monthly salary would be as a cavalry scout) in a game at the Old Southern Hotel with Tutt and several other men. Annoyed by his losses, Tutt reminded Hickok of a forty-dollar debt from a horse trade. When Hickok paid the sum, Tutt said Hickok owed him an additional thirty-five dollars from a previous poker game. "I think you are wrong, Dave," said Hickok. "It's only twenty-five dollars. I have a memorandum in my pocket." The anecdote doesn't explain why, after admitting the smaller debt, Hickok didn't pay up from his winnings, though forking over a total of sixty-five dollars must have been too much to ask in the face of Tutt's attitude. It's also intriguing that in none of the many accounts of this game does either man accuse the other of cheating. In any case, the story goes that Tutt grabbed Hickok's gold watch from the table. "Fine, I'll just keep your watch 'til you pay me that thirty-five dollars!" Because the room was crowded with Tutt's allies, Hickok was unable to retaliate then and there, but he warned Tutt not to wear the watch in public.

"I intend on wearing it first thing in the morning!" Tutt sneered.

"If you do, I'll shoot you," said Hickok. "I'm warning you here and now not to come across that town square with it on."

The next day around 10:00 a.m., Tutt appeared in the Springfield square with the watch. Hickok arrived at noon with his .36-caliber Navy Colt revolver holstered on his right hip. "Dave, here I am," he called from a distance of about seventy yards. "Don't you come across here with that watch." The two men both drew and fired a single shot each. Tutt missed. Hickok's ball struck Tutt in the heart. While we don't know the fate of the watch, Hickok was acquitted of murder by a jury on the grounds that "he acted in self-defense."

"Do you not regret killing Tutt?" Nichols asked him. "You surely do not like to kill men?"

"As ter killing men, I never thought much about it," Hickok responded evasively. "The most of the men I have killed it was one or t'other of us, and at sich times you don't stop to think. As for Tutt, I had rather not have killed him, for I want to settle down quiet here now." Settling down quiet remained Hickok's goal all his days, though it's difficult to imagine how a gunfighting poker player and Indian scout ever could hope to accomplish it.

After he was appointed marshal of Abilene in April 1871, Hickok's salary came to $150 a month plus a percentage of the fines he invoked and fifty cents for every unlicensed dog he shot. Though the dogs couldn't read, the marshal posted fair warning to Abilene's mangier humans: "Leave town on the eastbound train, the westbound train, or go north in the morning." By north he meant up to Boot Hill. Mayor Joseph McCoy described him as "the squarest man I ever saw. He broke up all unfair gambling, made professional gamblers move their tables into the light, and when they became drunk stopped the game." On June 8, the *Abilene Chronicle* expressed its approval: "The Chief of Police (Bill Hickok) has posted up printed notices, informing all persons that the ordinance against carrying fire arms or other weapons in Abilene, will be enforced. That's right. There's no bravery in carrying revolvers in a civilized community. Such a practice is well enough and perhaps necessary when among Indians or other barbarians, but among white people it ought to be discountenanced."

Other sources tell us that Hickok was mainly discountenanced by interruptions to his cardplaying, and that his headquarters was a well-lighted poker table in the Alamo Saloon. Even so, the *Chronicle* of October 7 rated his performance quite highly. "The Marshal has, with his assistants, maintained quietness and good order—and this in face of the fact that at one time during the season there was a larger number of cut-throats and desperadoes in Abilene than in any other town of its size on the continent." Yet later that month, after Hickok had gunned down more men, including—by accident—one of his deputies, the city council decided to fire him.

By this point the thirty-four-year-old marksman was developing eye trouble, probably either glaucoma from all the time he had spent in the sun, or gonorrheal ophthalmalia from one of the prostitutes he slept with. While doing his best to keep his vision problems a secret, he set about making poker his main source of income. He bunked for six or eight weeks at his friend Charley Utter's rooming house in Colorado, where another boarder said Bill "put in most of his time playing poker. He was very pleasant and agreeable, and never had any trouble while there." But a few months later he went broke in a Kansas City game, which by all accounts was neither the first nor last time this would happen. Nor can his eye problem have helped in spotting creases and marks on the pasteboards, especially in poorly lit saloons whose decks were seldom replaced with new ones. It was almost certainly the reason he'd mistaken his deputy for an outlaw.

Unlucky in poker and marshaling but suddenly lucky in love, Bill married Agnes Lake on March 5, 1876, in Cheyenne. Recently widowed—though not by Bill's hand—Agnes was famous in her own right as a tightrope walker, lion tamer, and equestrienne. She now owned a lucrative circus, so neither of them would have to work anymore. After a two-week honeymoon in the bride's hometown of Cincinnati, however, Bill took a train by himself back out west to try to make some serious money, feeling it would be unmanly to live off his wife's income. He was headed for the boomtown of Deadwood because he believed a few good months in its gold-infused poker games might yield enough to support Agnes in the style to which she had become accustomed.

A bartender at Nuttal and Mann's Saloon No. 10 recalls it was "the middle of July [when] my old friend Wild Bill arrived in Deadwood. A more picturesque sight than Hickok on horseback could not be imagined. He had never been north of Cheyenne before this, although many in Deadwood knew him, some only by reputation. A good many gunmen of note were in town and his arrival caused quite a commotion." Carl Mann greeted Bill with enthusiasm "and asked him to make the saloon his headquarters. This meant money for Mann, as Hickok was a great drawing card. Hickok agreed."

Resident cardsharps and gunfighters were unsurprisingly irked that Hickok might make trouble for them, and the crew associated with Johnny Varnes plotted to murder him before that could happen. Part of Varnes's motivation stemmed from a poker game at a place called the Senate in Denver, where he'd lost all his money to Hickok. Varnes was afraid of Wild Bill, so he offered the job to seasoned quick-draw artists, all of whom remained unaware of Bill's eye trouble and so turned down the offer.

Finally convinced that no one in Deadwood would risk a showdown with Hickok, Varnes decided a sneak attack was the only alternative. "Crooked Nose" Jack McCall, an unimposing local who did odd jobs for Mann, was put upon to do the big deed. Besides money, McCall was given to believe that Hickok had killed his loudmouth brother Lew back in Abilene, so he also had revenge as a motive. There is evidence, too, that McCall acted on his own—to avenge his brother and/or out of spite for what he took to be a condescending offer from Hickok on August 1 to give him back enough money for breakfast after McCall had lost $110 playing poker the night before. Perhaps McCall also resented Bill's general handsomeness and charisma, since one reporter described McCall this way: "His head, which is covered by a thick crop of chestnut hair, is very narrow as to the parts occupied by the intellectual portion of the brain, while the animal development is exceedingly large. . . . The nose is what is commonly called 'snub,' cross eyes, and a florid complexion, and the picture is finished."

Meanwhile his physical specimen of a target was being courted by a variety of Deadwood molls, including one "Calamity Jane" Cannary. The new groom stayed true to his bride, though, at least if his letters to her can be trusted. On July 17, he wrote, "I know my Agnes and only live to love her. Never mind, pet, we will have a happy home yet, then we will be happy." And again, on August 1, as he sensed death closing in: "Agnes Darling, if such should be we never meet again, while firing my last shot I will gently breathe the name of my wife—Agnes—and with wishes even for my enemies I will make the plunge and try to swim for the other shore." He signed it, "Wild Bill."

On August 2, at around 3:00 p.m., Hickok put on his Prince Albert frock coat and went as usual to play some high draw at Saloon No. 10. The other players were Mann, the gunman Charles Rich, the Irish-born wrestler (and future marshal of Deadwood) Con Stapleton, and Captain Willie Massie, a Missouri steamboat pilot. A brief conversation at the bar with a man named Harry Young caused Hickok to be the last player seated. Since the only chair left had its back to the door, he politely asked Rich to change places. Rich "only laughed and told him not to worry—no one was going to attack him."

No one paid McCall much attention when he entered the saloon. He soon began moseying toward the back of Hickok's chair, ostensibly to watch a few hands or converse with his boss. Some say Captain Massie was indulging his habit of sneaking peaks at the discards and that Bill, in a friendly tone, was encouraging him to knock it off. Meanwhile, a sizable pot had developed involving Hickok and two other players. They were fingering coins or taking second peeks at the cards held against their chests when a Colt .45 appeared at the end of McCall's raised right arm. When it boomed, Hickok's upper body, preceded by splinters of bone and enamel and pink shreds of brain, pitched forward across the table, scattering cards and gold coins as the report ricocheted off the room's varnished walls. Part of the bullet lodged in Massie's left wrist, though he didn't notice it right away because of the commotion. When Doc Peirce, a barber who had served as a Union medic, was asked to help, he saw that Bill was obviously dead and that "his fingers were still crimped up from holding his poker hand."

The coroner's findings appeared on the front page of the August 3 *Deadwood Traveler*: "A pistol had been fired close to the back of the head, the bullet entering the base of the brain, a little to the right of the center, passing through in a straight line, making its exit through the right cheek between the upper and lower jaw bones, loosening several of the molar teeth in its passage, and carrying a portion of the cerebellum through the wound. From the nature of the wound, death must have been instantaneous."

While several men chased down McCall, someone picked up the cards from the floor near Bill's fingers. Every witness agrees they included two pairs, aces and eights, and some say the fifth card was the nine of diamonds. Whatever the kicker was, aces and eights have been known ever since as the Dead Man's Hand. No real or fictional hand of poker—not Yancey Howard's unlikely straight flush to bust the Cincinnati Kid, not Henry Gondorff's double cold deck that gave him four jacks to Doyle Lonnegan's four nines, or even Doyle Brunson's immortal 10–2, with which he won consecutive World Series championships—is anywhere near as notorious. As a piece of Americana it can only be compared to, and probably surpasses, the Giants' Bobby Thomson's pennant-clinching home run off the Dodgers' Ralph Branca in 1951.

McCall escaped justice for several months but was eventually convicted of the murder and put to death by hanging on March 1, 1877. He was buried with the noose around his neck.

Along with Jim Bowie and Davy Crockett, Hickok figured prominently in several dime novels after his death, along with a wide variety of later works, including dozens of novels, biographies, and the late, great HBO series *Deadwood*. The 1940 film *My Little Chickadee* gave us this immortal exchange: "Poker—isn't that a game of chance?" asks Mae West, and W. C. Fields tells her, "No, my dear, not the way I play it." Set in the Dakota town of "Greasewood" around the time Hickok was murdered, the farce broadly satirizes cardsharps and their sexually unrestrained molls. Cuthbert J. Twillie, played by Fields, is a con man who wouldn't think of playing poker on the square. After being appointed sheriff, he spends most of his time cheating at five-card draw and drinking. "During one of my treks through Afghanistannn," he deadpans at the table, "we lost our corkscrewww. Compelled to live on food and waterrr." West, who cowrote the screenplay with Fields, plays

Flower Belle Lee, a horny schoolteacher ("Oh, arithmetic," she cracks voluptuously, "I was always pretty good at *figures* myself") who comes on to the town's younger studs but ultimately straps on a pistol and gallops to Sheriff Twillie's rescue.

Bob Dylan calls Hickok "Rambling, Gambling Willie" in a song of that title. Hickok appears under his own name in excellent novels by Richard Matheson, Pete Dexter, and Thomas Berger. However historically accurate these portraits may be, this much is certainly true: whether he was played by Fields, Gary Cooper, Roy Rogers, Lloyd Bridges, Charles Bronson, Josh Brolin, Sam Elliott, Jeff Bridges, or Keith Carradine, it was Wild Bill Hickok who forged the strongest links in the popular imagination between gunfighting, poker, and manliness—all this despite being known as a losing player who was shot from behind by a cowardly punk at the table.

It may be argued that after his honeymoon with Agnes, Hickok should have "settled down quiet" with his well-to-do bride in Cincinnati, where as the years went by he always could have found enough poker action to keep body and soul together. But that would have made him Mild Bill.

EARLY DRAW PRIMERS

After you *master* the concepts of this section, you will be ready to step into any Draw Poker arena in the world favored to leave with a profit! You will be able to read the hands of weak opponents with "magical" precision! *You will begin to apply the* **most accurate** *statistics ever published on the game!*

— "CRAZY MIKE" CARO

By the time of Hickok's death, as the rest of the country recovered from the bloodiest conflict in human history, genuine and self-proclaimed experts began publishing books of advice about how to play poker. Among the most lucid was the math professor Henry T. Winterblossom's *The Game of Draw Poker* (1875). The seventy-two-page primer begins with a brief history of cards, followed by caveats about the morality of playing for money: "Poker, unfortunately, is one of the few games that cannot be played so as to afford any pleasure, without the interchange of money. Indeed one might as well go on a gunning expedition with blank cartridges, as to play poker for 'fun.'" Winterblossom (a pseudonym for a member of the Lotos Club, according to the February 12, 1875, *New York Times*) puts the corruptive potential of poker on a par with faro and betting on horse races, even warning prospective readers: "If they have never indulged in the game, they are earnestly exhorted at this point to seek no further information, but to remain happy in their innocence"—which sounds like a quaintly Victorian selling point, like warning viewers of the "strong sexual content" of an HBO series. "It is unnecessary to say that the game should never be permitted to enter the family circle, no matter how trifling the stake proposed may be," he tut-tuts, all part of his wobbly balancing act. "Those who have winked at [the morality of poker], and those who have denounced it, may both be in the wrong. It must be admitted, however, by its most bitter enemy that, as a source of recreation, when moderately indulged in, and stripped of its objectionable features, it presents advantages not to be obtained in any other amusement." Who, after all, could object to a game with zero objectionable features?

Once the nervous Mr. Winterblossom finally gets down to the business of showing how mathematics can make draw poker profitable, he does a fine job all around. Employing basic algebra, he stresses "the question of percentage, believing beyond doubt that the player who will avail himself of the advantage which certain combinations give, will . . . have it in his favor, and must, in the long run, win." He must also recall the number of replacement cards each opponent took and "endeavor to study his style of drawing," including the kinds of draws he favors, his betting patterns, facial expressions, and so on.

In the spirit of Girolamo Cardano, Winterblossom asks the reader to suppose he's been dealt four hearts and a card of another suit. "You discard the odd suit and draw a fresh card from the pack. Now, before seeing the fresh card, you wish to determine what your chance of making a flush is. You know of course that you hold four hearts in your hand, and that there are nine others among the 47 cards which remain in the pack. It is clear then that your chance is as 9 to 47, which would be 5⅔ to 1 against your making it."

Yet what about when our opponents are holding many of those unseen cards—wouldn't that alter the odds? By walking his reader through some slightly more complex algebra, Winterblossom proves it would not. "It may then be set down as an axiom that the *number of players* is a neutral element which determines nothing, and that the reasoning must be based on the five cards which you receive and the 47 which are unknown."

Such facts aren't news to most modern players, but to those who'd learned poker in the age of cold decks and mirror men, or who mainly relied on gut feelings and "nary pair" bluffs, Winterblossom offered what must have been eye-opening revelations. Seat-of-the-pants amateurs could suddenly calculate odds to determine the correct play in a variety of situations. If the pot offered them less than 11:2 money odds on an opponent's bet to draw to that fifth heart, for example, it was clearly a blunder to call.

What about bluffing, a more instinctual and thespian tactic? "In former days," he writes, "when the betting was unlimited, this was frequently the determining feature of a hand, no matter what the cards were; and to bluff an opponent, while holding yourself 'nary pair,' was the pinnacle of ambition at which all players aimed." In an era of limited bet sizes, however, he advises his readers to "keep steadily in view the principle of conservatism." He admits that while this strategy "may perhaps to a limited degree be open to the charge of timidity, no one will regret in the end having pursued it. The most brilliant play is rarely satisfactory when it terminates in a loss."

One of the first poker writers to focus on psychology, Winterblossom notes that "a thorough exhibition of each individual character is revealed at every step of the game." More than that, "even the most casual observer cannot help perceiving that the commodity known as selfishness predominates to an unlimited degree, notwithstanding the various contrivances the players adopt to conceal its presence." In keeping with Adam Smith's and Alexander Hamilton's insights about capitalism, he makes clear that poker is "not only a selfish game, but one that every subterfuge that can be brought to bear is introduced; every artifice that the laws of the game will permit, is pressed into service; and all directed at one object, viz: —to win your money." In other words, playing poker well involves cunning and duplicity but no outright cheating—it requires dishonesty, that is, while honestly abiding by an accepted set of rules.

Winterblossom also worries about the development of a poker credit system allowing players to compete with checks or IOUs instead of cash. "It is perfectly clear that, as the players cannot avail themselves of the national prerogative to laugh at their creditors, they must pay up or be disgraced. Hence no one should play who is not prepared to settle up his losses at the end of the game, or within a reasonable time thereafter; and that a stringent rule, tacitly acknowledged by all, making a player with outstanding poker indebtedness ineligible to play with the party, should be adopted and enforced."

The Game of Draw Poker was preceded by Robert Schenck's *Rules of Poker* (published in London in 1872) and followed by *Laws and Practice of the Game of Euchre and of Draw Poker* by "Professor" (1877), *The Rules for Playing Draw Poker* by C.H.W. Meehan (1877), and Alfred Percy's *Poker: Its Laws and Practice* (1879). Over the next two decades, the number of primers continued to rise, with an increasing emphasis on keeping the odds in one's favor. One of the most influential was *The Complete Poker-Player: A Practical Guide Book to the American National Game: Containing Mathematical and Experimental Analyses of the Probabilities at Draw Poker* by John Blackbridge (1880). "So many cultivated men love this game that it is impossible for me to do otherwise than respect it," writes the New York attorney. To those who attack it on moral grounds, he provides a compelling analogy: "The child, who tries to win a prize at school by diligent mental culture, is a fair example of the honorable cardplayer who tries to win agreed-upon stakes, from associate players, by superior calculation of chances, or superior mental force." After warning his reader about the "undetected roguery" of "the Poker-sharp" and telling some colorful stories about East Coast draw games, he gets down to mathematical cases. When holding a pair and drawing three new cards, for instance, the odds against making a "triplet" or two pairs are both 8 to 1, a full house $61\frac{1}{4}$ to one, and four of a kind 364 to 1. When holding a triplet and drawing two, it's 23 to 1 against making four of a kind, but only 23 to 2 against making a full house. Drawing to flushes and straights "are usually dearly purchased," he writes, "always so at a small table. Their value increases directly as the number of players" increases. "The chance of drawing successfully to an inside straight is $11\frac{3}{4}$ to 1. To have a fair chance, therefore, there would be required 12 players in the game, which is absurd." Finally, he recommends avoiding high-stakes, no-limit games altogether. "Nearly all Poker-players that eventually abandon the game do so because they have suffered by large play, of which some 'sharp' has reaped the benefit. No one ever abandons Poker that plays it on small limited stakes. Sharps will not play such a game, and as it never leads to ill results it prospers forever by its own merits, like the simple, healthy and unforced growth of a plant that is nourished by Nature."

Blackwell's popular guide, along with such titles as *Poker Principles and Chance Laws* by Richard Anthony Proctor (1883), *Traite Mathematique de Jeu de Poker* by J. J. Foster (1889), *Le Code du Poker: Règles, Principes et Décisions,* by Lionel Dansereau (1894), David Curtis's *The Science of Draw Poker: A Treatise Comprising the Analysis of Principles, Calculation of Chances, Codification of Rules, Study of Situations, Glossary of Poker Terms Necessary to Gain a Complete Understanding of the Great American Game* (1901), and *Poker Ein Spieler* by Edmund Edel (1912), indicates that more and more people were interested in playing honest, intelligent poker in both the United States and Europe. Other books, however—*Sharps and Flats* by John Neville Maskelyne (London 1894), *How to Spot Card Sharps and their Methods* by Sidney Radner (1957)—provide further evidence that sharping, especially in higher-stakes games, continued well into the twentieth century.

Flash forward to 1978, when Doyle Brunson's *Super System*, the bible of the post-cheating era, was published by its author, who thought he could do a better job of it than New York trade publishers. Five-card draw was already on its way out by then, the biggest loser in a popularity contest with hold'em, seven-card stud, and Omaha, the last two of which were played both high-only and as high-low, split-pot games. Since no cards were exposed until the showdown, if ever, five-card draw provided less information than these newer games did. Worst of all, it allowed only two rounds of betting, compared with four in hold'em and Omaha and five in the stud games.

Even so, Brunson had asked "Crazy Mike" Caro, arguably the best living draw player, to write a chapter of *Super System* on his specialty. "This young, wild-looking and crazy-acting hippie," according to Brunson, was performing "an act to throw his opponents off-guard," though many people were convinced that it wasn't an act. "Of course," Caro said, "it helps if everyone thinks I'm a little touched." And crazy or not, he did himself proud as a teacher. In seventy-six manically brilliant pages, he broke down the minimum opening requirements; analyzed starting hands in terms of position; broke new ground on bluffing strategy, tell reading, and gauging opponents' hands by how many cards they drew; and provided no fewer than fifty statistical tables showing the odds of improving one's hand.

Caro's analysis was so comprehensive that it seemed to "solve" five-card draw once and for all. The only problem was that hardly anyone wanted to play it anymore. "High draw has not been solved," according to the New York–based pro Steve Zolotow, "but it lends itself to conservative strategies that favor good, tight play—with not enough luck or action to keep the live ones happy." In 1983, the organizers of Binion's World Series delivered what may have been the coup de grace by dropping five-card draw from their schedule. When California legalized hold'em and other forms of poker in 1987, the exodus from draw tables accelerated to the point where, except in a few long-standing home games, five-card draw, poker's most popular variant for well over a century, went the way of the dodo.

STUD POKER

I'm goin' down the river,
Down to New Orleans
They tell me everything gonna be all right
But I don't know what "all right" even means
— BOB DYLAN,
"TRYIN' TO GET TO HEAVEN"

In Bruce Olds's historical novel *Bucking the Tiger*, Doc Holliday opines with conviction, "Five Card Stud—one down, four up—is the cleanest, the clearest, and the only true game. It requires more instinct, more judgment, and more raw nerve than any other form. The rest is for amateurs and with extreme prejudice to be scrupulously avoided." Holliday would have reached this conclusion around 1880, the height of what Twain called the Gilded Age, the time of the market-cornering robber barons, of using false claims, strong-arm tactics, and any other means necessary to seize a personal fortune. Even President Grant got caught up and bankrupted in the flood of corruption. But the rapacious national mind-set fit Doc and stud like a glove.

John Henry Holliday (1851–1888) began his professional life as a doctor of dental surgery in humid Atlanta. At twenty he was diagnosed with tuberculosis and told he had a few months to live, longer if he moved to a drier climate. Taking this bull by the horns, Holliday headed for Dallas, where his career in dentistry was cut short when he coughed too often into the faces of his patients. Seeing no alternative, he became a faro dealer and, later, a stud artist. And because playing cards professionally was a hazardous business, he also trained himself as a gunfighter. His weapons of choice were a ten-gauge double-barrel sawed-off shotgun, a wood-handled Colt .45, and, when he ran out of bullets, a long, heavy double-edged knife he affectionately called "the Hell Bitch."

According to one friend, U.S. Marshal Wyatt Earp, Holliday didn't take long to become "the most skillful gambler, and the nerviest, fastest, deadliest man with a six-gun I ever saw." Since Holliday knew the TB would kill him slowly and gruesomely, a bullet to the heart would be almost welcome, which went a long way toward making him fearless in a shootout. And as those who played stud with him learned at some cost, fearlessness also confers big advantages at the poker table.

But the more sore losers the volatile Holliday outplayed, and more suspected cheaters he killed, the farther west he had to skedaddle, scrupulously avoiding the latest posse trying to track him down with extreme prejudice. For almost fourteen years he managed to stay ahead of both TB and the noose. In October 1881, he won $40,000 in a Dodge City stud game before once again lighting out—this time with the Budapest-born madam "Big Nose" Kate Horony riding beside him—for Tombstone, where he backed up the Earp brothers in a show-down with Ike Clanton's gang at a place called the O.K. Corral. Holli-day and two of the Earps were wounded, but every one of the Clanton boys who didn't run away was shot dead.

Doc and the Earps, along with other gunslinging poker players like Billy the Kid, Jesse James, and Bill Hickok, became icons of the Wild West, no matter how immoral or trigger-happy they may have been. These days their card sense and killer instinct are celebrated in tourna-ments called the Deadwood Shootout and Texas Hold'em Showdown, in monikers like Kid Poker and Texas Dolly, even in cerebral advice books featuring a Colt .45 on the covers—since a sawed-off shotgun might trigger less nostalgia for our sepia-toned cowboy past.

Five-card stud first cropped up in the 1864 *American Hoyle*. The name came from studhorse, usually the most prized possession of a rancher or breeder, which reflects poker's westward push with a decidedly mas-culine ring. According to George Henry Fisher's *Stud Poker Blue Book*, stud originated in a backwoods saloon in Ohio during "that reckless pe-riod which followed the Civil War." Fisher goes on:

The game began as Draw, and there finally came a pot which one of the players opened with three kings. The dealer and one other man stayed, and there was much raising both before and after the Draw. At length, all his money having been staked, the opener flung his hand down and rushed excitedly outside to the hitching post. He reappeared in a moment leading a spirited stallion, which he tied to the back of his chair. Then he realized that during his absence the other players had probably seen his three kings. So he made a proposition:

"You fellows know damned well what I'm betting on," he said, "and I've got all my money up on it. Now I propose that to make it fair all around each man turns three of his cards face up—discards two—and draws two more faced down. I'll gamble this here thoroughbred stud-horse on my chances."

David Parlett seems to accept the kernel of this legend, calling stud "a cowboy invention said to have been introduced around Ohio, Indiana, and Illinois." Whatever its exact provenance, stud called for one card facedown and another faceup, followed by a round of betting, then additional rounds after the third, fourth, and fifth cards were turned. With twice as many betting opportunities as draw, stud produced larger pots—though not twice as large, since both variants were usually played either pot-limit or table stakes.

Stud's main appeal was that its four "open" cards gave players a lot more information as they weighed each decision. In draw, a player knew whether his opponent either had jacks or better or was willing to call or raise the opening bet, and then how many cards he replaced. Stud players knew fully half of every opponent's hand before deciding how to proceed; they also knew that no cards could be replaced with potentially better ones. Then, before each new round of betting, they saw an ever larger fraction of the hands, allowing smart players to narrow down their opponents' likeliest hole cards. In stud games, deductive reasoning and bet-to-pot ratios were at least as important as bluffing.

In *Sucker's Progress*, Herbert Asbury says that stud was the most popular variant in San Francisco by 1880, so popular, in fact, that the California legislature "specifically prohibited it under penalty of fine and imprisonment" in 1884.

When the seven-card version appeared later in the century, it tempted thousands—eventually tens of millions—of players to switch from draw and "short" stud. The new sequence began with two cards facedown and one faceup, followed by a round of betting; then a fourth card ("fourth street") faceup, followed by another round; and the same after fifth, sixth, and seventh street. That the seventh card was dealt facedown gave rise to the nickname "Down-the-River," with its echo of "sold down the river," which we now understand to mean cruelly betrayed. (The phrase originally referred to the fate of troublesome slaves in border states punitively sold to planters in the Deep South, where working conditions were even harsher.) Down-the-River was duly shortened to "the river," which eventually stuck as a synonym for the final community card in hold'em and Omaha, even though that card is always dealt faceup.

With five rounds of betting, seven-stud plays best with limited bet sizes, which double on the final three streets. The river card being dealt "down and dirty" makes for a more balanced 4:3 ratio between exposed and hidden cards, giving this variant a larger sweet spot—more overlap between reading and bluffing and quant skills. That seven-stud hands develop so gradually further tips the balance in favor of reckoning talent and against wild aggression.

According to James Wickstead's *How to Win at Stud Poker* (1938), there is also "a philosophical side" to the game, though most of his insights can be applied to other variants. Wickstead, a psychologist and mathematician, was writing for short-stud players looking for convivial entertainment in the waning years of the Depression; if their evening was modestly profitable, so much the better. But the goal was never to clean out their tablemates, most of whom were their friends. Cheating them would be unimaginable.

Instead of playing what we call scared money, Wickstead recommends "games in which the personal equation of finances is nearly even. This should not be difficult and, furthermore, should be the aim of those to whom poker is merely a pastime rather than a means of existence." He also recommends that, whatever the stakes, players not whine after losing a pot; instead, they should face up to the fact that the best hand will "oftentimes" be outdrawn. "Any player who objects to some opponent's trying to win any particular pot by legitimate methods has no business playing stud." But it is unlimited betting, he writes, "that ultimately ruins most players, robbing the game of that zestful pleasure without which it becomes merely an expression of gambling." Though Wickstead doesn't mention it, unrestrained gambling on the stock market had helped to trigger the Depression in the first place.

As far as stud tactics are concerned, Wickstead recommends what today is called a tight-aggressive approach. First and foremost: "Unless your hole card, paired will beat any 'up' card in an opponent's hand if that 'up' card were paired, throw your hand in the discard." Never slow-play a high pair, a tactic he calls "lying and lying in wait." Instead, he recommends aggressively betting high pairs, because "a quick quarter is better than a slow dollar." Win a sure thing early, rather than trying to build a bigger pot while increasing the odds one of your opponents will complete a long-shot draw. "If the boys show an inclination to outdraw you when you have a good pair, charge them for the privilege." To do otherwise "is presumption of the cards' mercy, as it were. You have to treat the cards properly; if you want them to win for you, 'sitting on them,' inviting disaster, is the eighth 'deadly sin.'"

Its democratic flavor notwithstanding, poker is for Wickstead a game for rugged—and noncolluding—individuals. "Every contestant should play his own hand, and two persons should never have identical interests in the same pot." We should also resist raising the stakes near the end of the evening, usually at the insistence of friends with a double-or-nothing complex. They've already lost enough by playing badly, getting unlucky, or both, and there's no reason to think either problem will be solved by playing higher.

Finally, Wickstead discourages each player from thinking the others have ganged up on him: "It certainly is no particularly pleasant satisfaction to Bill Smith to know that Izzy Cohen outdrew Mike McCarthy one time in a stud game. 'It buttered no parsnips' of Bill's, especially when Mr. Smith was in the game at the same time, and leveling, too!"

Compare Wickstead's melting-pot esprit de corps at the stud table to Holliday's Rule 20: "Play to win, or don't bother. Check friendship at the door. A 'friendly' game is a misnomer. If what you are looking for is recreation or entertainment, there is the theater. If what you want is camaraderie, there is the bar. If it is companionship you seek, there are any number of likely whores." Or to this, from Rule 21: "Played properly, poker is hard work." Granted, Holliday's rules were what Bruce Olds imagined them to be, but they have about them the ring of historical truth. In Holliday's time and for many decades afterward, friendly and cutthroat poker were by and large mutually exclusive.

Meanwhile, as both five- and seven-card stud continued to be played, several high-low variants, all designed to give more players an interest in the pot, began to appear around the turn of the century. In Low Chicago, the player with the lowest spade—the ace counting as 1—received half the pot. Games with an eight-or-better "qualifier" stipulated that all five low cards be lower than nine. In Kansas City Lowball, aces, straights, and flushes were high, so the best possible hand was 7-5-4-3-2 unsuited.

Five-card stud high was the main variant played in 1949 by Johnny Moss and Nick "the Greek" Dandalos in their winner-take-all match hosted by Benny Binion in downtown Las Vegas. (As we'll see in Chapters 31 and 35, the event garnered so much publicity that Binion was apparently inspired—after serving a stretch in Leavenworth for tax evasion—to launch the World Series of Poker twenty-one years later.) Truman, Eisenhower, Nixon, and Johnson all played five-card stud. It was also the variant that determined who was the Man in the showdown between Eric Stoner and Lancey Howard in *The Cincinnati Kid*, released in 1963 but set in Depression-era New Orleans.

In our time, the short game Parlett called "the simplest and, by general consent, dullest variety" has given way to seven-card "long" stud. That game is spread most often in Northeastern home games and card rooms, though there's plenty of action in California, Nevada, Europe, and cyberspace. Even so, none of the more than twenty annual championships on the World Poker Tour calls for stud; each is solely a no-limit hold'em affair, as is nearly every WSOP event selected for broadcast on ESPN. Stud requires too much memory of folded cards, is too hard to film compared with hold'em's five neatly centered board cards, and lacks the relentless all-in action so beloved by television's demographic. In race after race, the hold'em dealer's anonymous right hand takes the place of an arbitrary Caesar tantalizing the Colosseum's bloodthirsty mob: thumbs-up or thumbs-down on the river?

Another measure of stud's relative prestige is the WSOP schedule, which has favored Texas hold'em since the tournament was created—by Texans—in 1970. Five-card stud was dropped in 1975, and by 2007 only seven of the fifty-five events were seven-card stud high or high-low, though another five were mixed games involving either half or three-fifths stud. But while the $10,000 finale remains a no-limit hold'em contest, the tournament viewed by most professionals as poker's true championship is the $50,000 H.O.R.S.E. event, three-fifths of which calls for stud. (H.O.R.S.E. stands for *H*old'em; *O*maha high-low; *R*azz, which is stud played for low; *S*tud high; and stud high-low *E*ight-or-better.) With two smaller "equine" events on the schedule and more high-stakes action online, it's clear that this challenging mixed game has been spurring a "studhorse" revival.

HIGH PLAINS DRIFTERS

Took hold of my sweetheart and away we did drive,
Straight for the hills, the black hills of Dakota . . .
— BOB DYLAN, "DAY OF THE LOCUSTS"

While the overwhelming majority of nineteenth-century players were men, a tiny number of smart, determined women, including Kitty LeRoy, Lottie Deno, Belle Siddons, and especially Alice Ivers, made names for themselves on the Western frontier dealing vingt-et-un, faro, and poker.

Ivers was born on February 17, 1853, in Devonshire, England. The only daughter of a schoolmaster, she received quite a bit more education than the average girl of that time and was raised to become a respectable member of Victorian society. But the sedate garden path of her life took a slight detour when her family moved to the wilds of Colorado in search of precious metal when Alice was in her late teens. She was described as a "petite 5'4" beauty with blue eyes and long, lush brown hair." Having attracted several suitors, she decided to marry Frank Duffield, a handsome mining engineer and poker aficionado who was by all accounts the love of her life. The couple set up their household in Leadville, a silver-mining boomtown in the heart of the Rockies. In an act of surprising open-mindedness for 1873, Frank taught Alice to play poker too, not long before a dynamite charge he was setting tragically left her a widow.

In the days before unions and life insurance, the beautiful Mrs. Duffield now had to fend for herself in a place about as far removed from Devonshire as possible. With a population topping forty thousand, Leadville was the largest town in the Colorado Territory and, according to the crime historian Herbert Asbury, "the most lawless." During Oscar Wilde's lecture tour of the West in those years, he noticed above the piano in a Leadville casino a sign that said, "Please do not shoot the pianist; he is doing his best." After sharing a meal with miners at the bottom of a shaft, Wilde wrote, "The first course is whiskey, the second whiskey, the third whiskey, all the courses were whiskey, but still they called it supper." As to their above-ground behavior, he noted, "The revolver is their book of etiquette. This teaches lessons that are not forgotten."

Women of Alice Duffield's breeding were unaccustomed to physical labor, especially 10,350 feet above sea level. Once she'd ruled out prostitution, a job in a casino may have seemed the only career path. Her preference was to deal and play poker, but she also learned to buck the faro tiger and deal 21. Her distracting English Rose complexion, firm control of the facial muscles beneath it, and who knows what other devices all helped to maximize her yield at the tables. Few if any games in these boomtowns were strictly on the square, and while it's impossible to know the extent to which Alice cheated, most professionals took every advantage they could get away with. Alice's motto was "Praise the Lord and place your bets, I'll take your money with no regrets," though because of her Anglican upbringing, she refused to gamble on Sundays. On her best nights, she could take $3,000 or $4,000 from a game, and it's been estimated that she netted about $225,000 in her poker career. Whatever the tally was, she made enough to fund shopping trips to places as far away as New York for the latest Gibson girl fashions—high necks, puffy sleeves, fitted waistlines. Indulging her less girlish side, she also developed a taste for fat stogies. But whatever she was wearing or smoking, the nickname "Poker Alice" became her.

As a dexterous, good-looking woman, Alice was wooed by casino proprietors to deal in a string of estrogen-starved towns and mining camps. In Creede, Colorado, she was hired by Robert Ford—the man who killed Jesse James for a $10,000 bounty in 1882—to lure miners into his big-tent saloon. After drifting down to New Mexico, Alice won

$6,000 in a single night as a faro banker for the Gold Dust in Silver City. The owners hired her as a regular attraction, much as Hickok was paid to play in Saloon No. 10, but when summer came she headed back north.

While dealing in the Dakota Territory, she met and fell in love with Warren G. Tubbs, a fellow dealer who became her second husband. Tubbs changed Alice's life even more than Duffield had, not only because they produced three daughters and four sons together but because Alice gave up gambling to raise them. To make their more modest ends meet, she and Warren started a chicken farm on a homestead near Sturgis along the south fork of the Moreau River, and Warren supplemented the farm's proceeds as a housepainter. Mrs. Tubbs loved the tranquility of their spread, claiming she never once missed the card tables. During the winter of 1910, however, the already tubercular Warren came down with pneumonia and died in her arms. Leaving their oldest children in charge of the younger ones, she loaded his body onto a wagon and drove the team forty-eight miles through a blizzard to Deadwood, where she pawned her wedding ring to pay for his burial. She left herself just enough cash to begin playing poker again.

Soon enough she was hosting three or four games in the parlor of a brothel on Bear Butte Creek in Sturgis. Called Poker's Palace to rhyme with her nickname—and not, alas, the Bear Butte Bordello—the majority of its clientele was from the Fourth Cavalry Regiment stationed three miles away in Fort Meade. Demand for the action upstairs quickly outstripped the supply. As Alice tells the story, "I went to the bank for a $2,000 loan to build on an addition and go to Kansas City to recruit some fresh girls. When I told the banker I'd repay the loan in two years, he scratched his head for a minute then let me have the money." Within a year, Alice "was back in his office paying off the loan. He asked how I was able to come up with the money so fast. I took a couple chaws on the end of my cigar and told him, 'Well, it's this way. I knew the Grand Army of the Republic was having an encampment here in Sturgis. And I knew that the state Elks convention would be here, too. But I plumb forgot about all those Methodist preachers coming to town for a conference.'"

The next salvo she fired, in 1913, was less funny. A group of soldiers got so out of hand that Alice felt compelled to discharge her rifle to get their attention. Unfortunately, the bullet passed through two of the revelers, killing one of them. The police closed the Palace and took Alice into custody. At her trial, the shooting was ruled accidental, and

Alice was released. But she had earned the enmity of both the Sturgis police and the officers at Fort Meade, which spelled the swift demise of the Palace.

When Prohibition was enacted in 1920, she supplemented her income as a madam and gambler by selling whiskey and beer. Other arrests, for bootlegging and "keeping a bawdy house," followed. She paid the fines and tried to stay in business, but in 1928 she was sentenced to a term in the South Dakota State Penitentiary for selling liquor again. Being seventy-five and a woman, she was pardoned by Governor Bill Bulow, but her days running brothels were over.

The governor's reasons for the pardon are revealing about the letter and spirit of the law as the Western frontier came under territorial and then state jurisdiction. In Bulow's unpublished autobiography, he notes that although she was well past seventy, Alice was "a well preserved and remarkable old lady [who] had come to the Dakota Territory when a young girl [and] established her home in the Black Hills long before there was any law, or order or civil government there. She had been a pioneer in every sense of the word. She had lived in a day and age when everyone made their own law and did the best they could to establish a home and bring law and order to the wilderness. . . . No one had ever told her that it was wrong to take a drink of whiskey. No one had ever told her that it was wrong to give a friend a drink of whiskey." He went on: "If all the people of South Dakota who violated the liquor law were to be sent to the pen it would bankrupt the state to provide enough prison accommodations." In 1928 and today, in South Dakota and the rest of the United States, an equally persuasive argument could be made about laws banning poker.

By the time of her release, the old Gibson girl had taken to wearing men's hats and work shirts to go with a lit robusto clamped between her teeth. "At my age I suppose I should be knitting," she said, "but I would rather play poker with five or six 'experts' than eat." She was often seen playing in Deadwood until just before she died, at seventy-seven, after a gallbladder operation. She was buried in St. Aloysius Cemetery in the Black Hills, just down the road from the partially sculpted face of Mount Rushmore.

A less famous Dakotan than Alice, the attorney and Freemason Richard F. Pettigrew served as a Republican delegate to the Forty-seventh U.S. Congress from 1881 to 1883. It was during this session that Petti-

grew acquired his reputation as a maniacally fortunate draw player—
and perhaps the least skillful anyone had ever heard of.

The most damning evidence emerged during a private game in a
Washington, D.C., hotel room. Toward the end of the evening, one
player raised the pot $50, and Pettigrew raised him $50 more. When
his opponent raised $50 back, Pettigrew raised him again. Once the ini-
tial round of raises was over, his opponent stood pat and was startled to
see Pettigrew discard *four*. Pettigrew looked at his new hand, paused for
a couple of seconds, then bet $50. His opponent raised him with his last
$100. When Pettigrew called and showed him a royal flush in clubs, the
loser, who had kings full of sixes, became apoplectic. "What in thunder
did you draw to?"

"That typewriter," said Pettigrew cryptically while pointing to the
queen of clubs. Commercial typewriters had only begun to be manufactured—by the Remington Arms Company—in 1873, and it's possible the queen of clubs had picked up a secretarial nickname. Or perhaps
he meant, "None of your business."

When South Dakota became a state in 1889, Pettigrew was elected
as one of its first two U.S. senators. Rumors of how the poker gods rewarded his incorrigible play spread through the district, and his colleagues refused to invite him to what was known as the Statesmen's
Game, having deemed his blind-pig reliance on luck to be altogether
unstatesmanlike.

Another Dakota legend, a drifter who insisted on being called Poker
Jim, was less fortunate. Most reports have him working as an itinerant
ranch hand, though he was also described as an outlaw and a gentleman. We know he had an inordinate fondness for both whiskey and the
card game he took as his moniker, but like many frontier cowboys he
was happiest while enjoying the booze and the poker together. While
modern psychologists would diagnose him as a gambling addict, the
pathological by-product of a genetic predisposition, Jim's contemporaries simply said, "It was almost impossible to drag him away from a
poker table. Winning or losing, the game had a fascination for him."

He arrived in the Dakotas around 1890 as part of a cattle drive and
was later hired by Pierre Wibaux to work on his vast W Bar Ranch.
(Unlike the spreads of wellborn amateur cattlemen like the Marquis de
Mores and Theodore Roosevelt, the W Bar was a highly profitable operation.) During the ferocious winter of 1894, Poker Jim and his friend

Cash Lantis were assigned to Wibaux's Hay Draw camp on the Little Missouri River. By February their food supply was so short that Jim volunteered to ride to Glendive, Montana, sixty-five miles away, for provisions. After fitting out a packhorse, he set off into the drifting white landscape with beans, bread, tobacco, coffee, kerosene, matches, and whiskey on his shopping list and another staple much on his mind. According to the Minot historian Kim Fundingsland, Jim most likely volunteered for the hazardous trip because of "the chance to find a poker game in Glendive."

The distance between line shacks was fifteen to twenty miles, and it would have taken Jim about three days to reach Glendive. After bunking overnight at Smith Creek, he began the second leg of his frigid little run to the store. But the Smith Creek camp foreman, Harlowe "Tough" Bentley, reported that Jim appeared seriously hungover when he set out that morning. When he failed to show up at the next camp in a timely fashion, Bentley rode out with a search team. They eventually found Jim's body nine miles from camp; it was sitting against a scoria rock, "frozen solid." Burned matches near the corpse indicated that Jim had been desperately trying to build a fire. His horse, still tied to a tree, was pitifully gnawing the bark.

Because the ground was too hard to dig a grave until spring, the ranch hands wrapped Jim's body in a blanket and placed it in cold storage across the rafters of one of their unheated shacks. A few weeks later another group of cowboys gathered there for a stud game, unaware of the body above them. Their wood fire warmed up the shack well enough that Jim's body started to thaw. Before it began to reek, some of its weight shifted and its balance on the ceiling beams tipped. It finally crashed onto the rickety table below, sending chairs, cards, and cowboys ricocheting off the four walls. Only one other game in the history of poker ever broke up with as much utter shock and finality.

After his unscheduled wake in the line shack, Jim was interred in the W Bar burial plot, now called the Poker Jim Cemetery. In place of a headstone, his grave is marked by what is said to be the very rock his body was found leaning against. The cemetery's vistas take in the wetlands and ridges of McKenzie County, North Dakota, not far from Theodore Roosevelt National Park. There is also a dime novel or two bearing Jim's name, to go with the Poker Jim Oilfield, the Poker Jim Ridge Research Natural Area, and Poker Jim Butte, all this to commemorate a player whose last earthly act was—just like Bill Hickok—to gruesomely smash up a poker game.

COWBOYS PLAY POKER

Since things had been so quiet lately, they were not thinking of any trouble even though Fletcher and the new man, Stark Wilson, were in the poker game at the big table.

—JACK SCHAEFER, *SHANE*

George W. Bush was born in upper-crust Connecticut, raised in the white-collar cities of Midland and Houston, and spent most of his summers in Maine, yet he routinely appears in public wearing cowboy hats, belt buckles, denim, and boots. In June 2007, he defended the troop surge in Iraq while standing beneath a portrait of Colonel Theodore Roosevelt on horseback in full Rough Rider regalia, including a cowboy hat.

To better understand this piece of stagecraft, let's return to the affluent-cowboy phase of Roosevelt's life. After graduating magna cum laude from Harvard in 1880, the blue-blooded New Yorker married the "extraordinarily attractive, slender, graceful" Alice Lee. At twenty-three, he was elected as the youngest member of the New York State Assembly, where he worked as a progressive reformer of Tammany machine politics and the monopolistic practices of the Gilded Age, while also making time to hunt big game with his brother, Elliott. During the summer recess of 1883, he headed to the Dakota Territory, hoping to add a buffalo to his trophy case before the animal became extinct from overhunting. He finally gunned one down in the Badlands and, while he was at it, bought a pair of ranches nearby before heading home to his pregnant wife in New York. But on the following Valentine's Day, the two women he loved most were taken from him. His mother, Mittie, died of typhoid fever, and Alice of Bright's disease (nephritis of the kidneys) two days after giving birth to their daughter, named Alice in her memory.

Shattered, Roosevelt returned to Albany after the funerals, throwing himself into his legislative duties. "It was a grim and evil fate," he wrote, "but I have never believed it did any good to flinch or yield for any blow, nor does it lighten the blow to cease from working." He worked nearly around the clock for weeks at a stretch, amending bills, giving speeches, leading inspection tours of the squalid and dangerous Ludlow Street Jail. (Three decades later he would deliver a ninety-minute speech before seeking medical help after being shot in the chest by a would-be assassin.)

Once the '84 legislative session was over, he left Alice in the care of his sister Bamie and headed back west to his ranches, seeking solitude in a more vigorous outdoor environment. Physical exercise, especially on horseback, became his religion, and he recommended "the strenuous life" as the cure for a variety of physical and spiritual ailments. He wound up writing several popular books, including *Hunting Trips of a Ranchman* and a four-volume history of the West, promoting its beauty and virtues—self-reliance, honor, determination—all of which made it, he said, a proving ground of American character.

As Edmund Morris marvelously recounted in *The Rise of Theodore Roosevelt* (1979) and David McCullough did with no less authority in *Mornings on Horseback* two years later, Roosevelt's books prompted thousands of Easterners to head to Dakota and other points west. And to accommodate the wealthier Ivy League cowboys, cattlemen happily accepted money in exchange for letting them work alongside men like Poker Jim on what came to be called dude ranches—labor negotiations with a decidedly promanagement twist. The catch was that aristocratic ranchmen, in Roosevelt's opinion, need not "undergo the monotonous drudgery attendant upon the tasks of the cowboy," at least not full-time. Besides the chores of branding and herding, serious dudes needed time for reading and writing and hunting—or, in the case of Yale's Frederic Remington, for making sketches of bona fide cowboys to bring back to his New York studio. Many of Roosevelt's articles and books about the West were illustrated by Remington, whose mature work is thought to depict cowboy life with more eloquence than any other artist's.

Midwifed by the paintings, sculptures, and factual accounts of these two aristocratic New Yorkers, as well as by the fiction of the Harvard-educated Philadelphian Owen Wister, the romantic myth of the Cowboy was born. Cowboys, wrote Roosevelt, were "quiet, rather self-contained men, perfectly frank and simple, and on their own ground treat a stranger with the most whole-souled hospitality." Except, that is, when they went on their "sprees," during which they played too much poker, drank too much whiskey, and got into shootouts. Wister's 1904 best-seller, *The Virginian*, the first "Western" novel, was dedicated to Roosevelt, and it shows deep respect for poker players' creative intelligence. "If a man is built like that Prince boy was built," Wister wrote, imagining Shakespeare's resourceful Prince Hal as a cowboy, "(and it's away down deep beyond brains), he'll play winnin' poker with whatever hand he's holdin' when the trouble begins. Maybe it will be a mean, triflin' army, or an empty six-shooter, or a lame hawss, or maybe just nothin' but his natural countenance." Remington focused more on the cheating and violence associated with the game. His 1897 painting *A Misdeal* shows four dead or wounded cowboys lying prostrate around a poker table, the air above it marbled with gun smoke.

Roosevelt, as we've seen, had used poker and other manly ploys to raise himself up in the Republican Party. By 1897, at age thirty-eight, he'd been appointed assistant secretary of the navy by President William McKinley. Spain was then reasserting control over its former Caribbean colonies, and many Americans, particularly those in the merchant class looking to broaden their markets, viewed this as an incursion into what had become "our" hemisphere. Roosevelt became one of their most aggressive, articulate spokesmen. When war was declared in '98, he resigned his desk job to help recruit, equip, and train the First U.S. Volunteer Cavalry, which he nicknamed the Rough Riders. The regiment has been called "an American mosaic of cowboys, Indians, and aristocratic easterners, all of whom could ride and shoot well." Colonel Roosevelt never used a Spanish Most-Wanted poker deck to galvanize martial resolve, but he did say, "We had quite a number of professional gamblers, who, I am bound to say, usually made good soldiers." On July 1, 1898, he led them in the famous charges up Kettle and San Juan Hill during the war's climactic battle in Cuba. This is the rough-riding spirit that President Bush—neither horseman nor soldier—was hoping to summon when he defended the surge in Iraq beneath the portrait of Roosevelt. And it is the romance of the Wild West, which ceased to be very wild around 1900, that most folks in cowboy hats are hoping to recapture today.

Roosevelt returned from what was called "a splendid little war" a national hero. In stunningly short order, he became governor of New York, McKinley's vice president, and, after McKinley was assassinated in September 1901, America's youngest president. He was elected on his own in a landslide in 1904. The hallmarks of his two terms were a progressive reliance on science and technology to solve national problems, "busting" the trusts of corporate monopolies, establishing game preserves and national parks, negotiating an end to the Russo-Japanese War—for which he received the 1906 Nobel Peace Prize—and promoting, above all, a Square Deal, promising that all Americans could earn a living wage and that the scales of justice would be put into balance for every citizen. Everyone might not succeed under his policies, he said, but at least "there shall be no crookedness in the dealing."

His famous essay "The Strenuous Life" celebrated risk taking as a way to regenerate manhood and encouraged the expansion of America's empire. According to the Rutgers historian Jackson Lears, our most vigorous president fervently believed the "value of empire was not just economic; it was psychological, social, and moral. Imperial struggle demanded a resurrection of martial virtue, which would serve as a powerful antidote to the corrupting effects of commerce while at the same time securing new sources of national wealth." This assertive worldview resonated especially well, argues Lears, among deskbound men whose "opportunities for risk-taking were limited. These were the sort of people who developed a new appreciation for the gambling spirit and its military manifestations, who recognized that some agonistic games of chance required the same sort of coolness under fire that we prized in our fighting men." The ideal game for such frustrated American warriors could not have been more obvious. As Lears writes, "Real men took risks with a poker face."

Mastery of poker and of guns were widely viewed as twin gauges of masculine know-how. Along with the examples of Holliday, Hickok, and numerous military heroes, there was Roosevelt's 1901 interview with Pat Garrett, the former buffalo hunter and sheriff who twenty years earlier had personally gunned down the outlaw Henry McCarty, better known as Billy the Kid. Garrett was now seeking the hazardous position of customs collector of El Paso.

"How many men have you killed?" the president asked him.

"Three," replied Garrett.

"How did you come to do it?"

"In the discharge of my duty as a public officer."

Roosevelt seemed satisfied by this answer, though he wanted to further probe the candidate's ability to assess risk under pressure. "Have you ever played poker?" he asked.

Garrett said that he had, which was by all accounts quite an understatement, though he would later misleadingly testify before the Senate that he didn't know the difference between a straight flush and four of a kind. Meanwhile, since poker wasn't legal in Texas, the president felt bound to ask, "Are you going to do it when you are in office?"

"No," replied Garrett.

"All right," said the president, satisfied that the right words, if not the whole truth, had been uttered by the candidate, "I am going to appoint you."

While Remington, Wister, and the young TR were capturing the beauty and customs of the West, poker was emerging from grimy saloons and other dens of iniquity into well-upholstered clubs in their hometowns and other big cities. The transition didn't always go smoothly, of course; nor did players always get a square deal. In September 1880, *The New York Times* ran the following story:

A charge of gambling was preferred yesterday, in the Jefferson Market Police Court, against William Edwards, a showman, of Toledo, Ohio, by Eugene V. Davis, of No. 246 East Broadway, a foreman in a cigar factory. Davis was recently introduced at the Brunswick Club, a social organization at No. 48 West Twenty-seventh-street, where draw poker is played. When Mr. Davis played there the game was limited, so that his losses were not great, but he remarked that he had very bad luck and had won only nominal amounts. On one occasion he had lost all his money, and staked and lost a diamond ring worth $75. . . . [He] remarked that the manager of the club, of whom he (Davis) speaks unkindly, stood behind him where he could have seen his cards. The game was disastrous to Davis, as he lost $50 in money and staked and lost a gold watch and chain and a diamond stud worth $200. Davis noticed that whenever he had good cards in his hand Edwards threw up his cards, and that whenever he had bad cards Edwards

challenged him. Davis complained to Capt. Berghold, of the
Twenty-ninth Precinct, who visited the Brunswick Club on Tuesday night and arrested Edwards, who gave up Davis's watch and
chain and diamond pin and $85. In court Edwards characterized
the action of Davis as ungentlemanly, as he had won on several occasions at draw poker, and took the money of those he played
with. Justice Wandell decided to hold Edwards for trial on $1,000
bail, and to commit Davis as a witness to the House of Detention
in default of $300 bail.

Judge Wandell didn't like cheating poker players but was apparently
no fan of those who allowed themselves to be cheated, either.

As more and more social clubs like the Brunswick banned the game,
dedicated card clubs met the demand for safe poker venues. On May 9,
1886, the *Times* reported:

It is not to play faro or roulette or any of the games of the regular
gambling houses that these private card clubs are organized, but
for the purpose of indulging in the popular American game of
poker, which is prohibited in the majority of the social clubs as a
source of trouble and scandal. High play is permitted in the
Union, the Manhattan, the Knickerbocker, and the Blossom Club,
but in all other clubs poker is prohibited, particularly heavy play.
There is, indeed, a "card" annex to nearly all the clubs, where
those who wish to indulge in poker and heavy play do so outside
the club, so that any trouble at the card table cannot involve the
club or become a scandal within its walls. . . . Many of the professional "games" obtain immunity from the police by being dealt
in so-called "clubs," but such are not to be confounded with
these private card clubs organized for the purpose of privacy and
security.

In 1887, the *Times* shook its finger at the trend: "Poker-playing is
found to be a source of trouble in any club that permits it. One after another all the social clubs have adopted ordinances prohibiting poker-
playing in the cardrooms. The last to do this is the Manhattan Athletic.
The only clubs that now permit poker-playing are the Union, the Manhattan, the Blossom, and the New-Amsterdam."

In the face of such bans, arrests, and editorial reprimands, poker still thrived in New York and spread to *old* Amsterdam, too, as well as to London, Vienna, Paris, and Berlin. London's *Telegraph* reported:

> Nothing that the Americans have introduced to Vienna has met with such an enthusiastic reception there as the game of poker. The four kings have more admirers than the four sisters Barrison [a risqué Vaudeville act], and the enterprising courage of the Americans meets with less notice than their ability to astound an adversary with an empty card [a weak hand, presumably]. The passion for the game of poker has spread with such amazing rapidity that it recalls the hazard [an early version of craps] epoch. . . . The difference now is that everybody plays. In the cafés the jeunesse dorée join eagerly with merchants, lawyers, and clerks in the fascinating game. In private circles poker is played in the best houses by people in excellent positions, and what increases the evil is that it has been taken up with enthusiasm by ladies. In Winter on the *jours* and in Summer at the fashionable baths and watering places, groups of ladies engage in the favorite game with all the ardor of those half-pay officers who, after the disbanding of Napoleon's armies, spent their days and nights at faro. . . . The rage for poker spread amazingly; in fact, there are cafés whose proprietors exist only upon the proceeds of poker playing, as the charge for cards to each player is about 5s [shillings].

As comparable rages developed in other cities, the game was already popular enough in San Francisco to be banned—unsuccessfully—by the California penal code. Back in New York City, poker flourished even in prison. In 1895, it was reported that Ludlow Street Jail officials not only "permitted the prisoners, criminal and civil, to play among themselves, but that the officials at times took a friendly hand, much to their own satisfaction and emolument."

In March 1900, a high-stakes game began in a private railroad car en route from Chicago to New York. Once the train arrived at Grand Central Station, "play was resumed and it continued uninterruptedly in a room in the Waldorf-Astoria for a week. During this time the players went practically without sleep and their meals were served to them by a special corps of servants." ("The Hyphen," as the hotel was known, was the largest in the world at the time, located at Thirty-fourth Street and Fifth Avenue, where the Empire State Building now stands.) The players included John W. Gates, president of American Steel and Wire; the Chicago grain trader Joseph Leiter; L. L. Smith and John Gilbert, also of Chicago; and a Major Dougherty and another gentleman from New York. The *Times* reported that six-figure amounts were won or lost by most of them, though the only one willing to talk to the press refused to give his name but said he won a mere $80,000. He also said that Leiter lost $300,000 on the train but won most of it back at the Waldorf.

Asked by a *Times* reporter on March 18 for a comment about the game at the Waldorf, Leiter claimed he never played poker during Lent. Since Lent began on Ash Wednesday, March 7, and Easter fell on April 15, it seems that the sarcastic young trader was being economical with the truth. There are no surviving photographs, however, to determine whether he was wearing a cowboy hat.

John Wayne, an actor often thought to be quintessentially American, played draw and stud with real cowboys in an effort to pick up their mannerisms, and he developed a lifelong affection for their games. "I liked being with them," he said, "and really respected them. I listened to their stories and kind of absorbed their culture. In the evenings, I spent my time with them playing poker. There was always somebody who'd bring along a guitar or a banjo, and we'd all sit around the fire singing with the stars shining bright above us. Great times."

Wayne and the director John Ford formed the Young Men's Purity, Abstinence and Snooker Pool Association, composed of actors, writers, directors, and producers devoted to drinking too much and related manly vices. Members included the stuntman Yakima Canutt, the writer Dudley Nichols, and the actors Ward Bond and Johnny Weissmuller, any of whom could be summarily tossed out of the club for an act of sobriety. Yet drunken debauchery, too, had its limits. According to Ford, "the westerns were especially fun" when out on location, what with "the stars in the desert sky, good beef on the grill, and some music. We didn't talk film at night. It was off limits. We played poker or dominoes."

While filming *Hondo* in 1952, Wayne won the dogs that played Lassie from Rudd Weatherwax, the canine stars' owner. Seeing how devastated Weatherwax was the next morning, Wayne returned the dogs. In 1963, he bought a 136-foot navy minesweeper for $110,000. Christening it the *Wild Goose*, he hired a crew of eight and equipped it with a screening room, wet bar, and poker table. He spent as much time aboard it as possible, cruising up and down the West Coast between Canada and southern Mexico with his family and gambling buddies.

In Wayne's final movie, *The Shootist* (1976), he plays the white-hatted gunfighter J. B. Books, who has terminal prostate cancer and wants to die in the line of "duty," as he puts it. (Wayne himself had lost his left lung to cancer a decade earlier, and would die of stomach cancer within three years.) As in the case of Doc Holliday, Books's terminal condition makes him even more fearless, and therefore more deadly, in gunfights, though he succeeds in getting himself righteously killed in the final shootout. Set in 1901 in an old Nevada town beset by clanging streetcars, newfangled automobiles, and other insults to the cowboy way of life, *The Shootist* may be viewed as a eulogy for Wayne and his career, as well as for the Wild West itself.

21

DOGS PLAYING POKER

Ante up! Openers? Openers! Get y'r ass off the table, Mitch. Nothing belongs on a poker table but cards, chips and whiskey.

— STANLEY KOWALSKI IN *A STREETCAR NAMED DESIRE*

Cassius Marcellus Coolidge, the wry commercial artist who gave the world a famous series of paintings of dogs playing poker, was born in upstate New York in 1844 to abolitionist Quaker farmers. They named him after one of the most eloquent antislavery politicians of the antebellum South, the Kentucky senator Cassius Marcellus Clay. The young Quaker draftsman, known to friends and family as Cash, received no formal art education but was placing sketches in his local newspaper by the time he was twenty. He published a drawing in *Harper's Weekly* in 1878, composed an opera about the New Jersey mosquito epidemic of 1881, and invented what he called "comic foregrounds," those placards of headless musclemen and bathing beauties that tourists like to prop their own heads above, to be photographed. Coolidge accomplished all this while holding down a startling variety of day jobs in banking, education, and journalism.

In 1903, he was commissioned to produce a series of humorous paintings for the Brown & Bigelow Co. of St. Paul, a purveyor of advertising calendars. (The company also bought work from Charles Russell, Max-field Parrish, and Norman Rockwell.) In nine of the sixteen pictures Coolidge made, his mastiffs, collies, Great Danes, and St. Bernards drink bootleg whiskey and beer, smoke cigars or fusty meerschaum pipes, and avidly play five-card draw. A typical scene has them sitting in a comfortable den around the green felt top of a card table. A shaded lamp hanging above them casts the scene's only light. According to the grandfather clock in one of the dens, it's ten after one in the morning.

As Italian Renaissance masters relied almost exclusively on the New Testament for their images, American figurative painters in the early twentieth century—from the austere modernist Edward Hopper to commercial illustrators like Rockwell and Coolidge—drew on ordinary life for their subjects. At the same time, Coolidge must have also been inspired by human card players in high-art canvases by Caravaggio, de La Tour, and Cézanne.

The art historian Moira Harris tells us that humanized dogs weren't unusual in the art of Coolidge's formative years, "either at the Royal Academy level or in more popular forms of culture such as postcards, magazine illustrations, ceramic figures, children's books, or sheet-music covers. Advertisers have long found that either fierce or cuddly canines, clothed or not, are appealing logos or symbols for their products." Harris adds that nineteenth-century artists, "especially those in England, were being commissioned by pet owners to paint portraits of the family whippet, Newfoundland, or setter. The English painter Sir Edwin Landseer is credited with having transformed the study of these pedigreed and cherished pets into anecdotal genre scenes where the canine characters revealed their emotional ties to the human members of the household. Landseer's dogs already had human sensibilities. It was an easy step up to give dogs . . . human attributes and clothing as well."

Coolidge's dogs are upper-middle-class judges and lawyers and businessmen. The only females in the series are a pair of beagles who use their unfurled umbrellas to shrewishly break up a poker game in *Sitting Up with a Sick Friend* and a sexy black poodle delivering a tray of drinks in an unpublished variation on *A Bold Bluff*. The paintings depict much the same poker and sexual politics that Tennessee Williams would dramatize more darkly in *A Streetcar Named Desire*, first produced in 1947. Set in a New Orleans tenement to the strains of a tinny blues piano, the play is a world in which men drink, bellow, smoke, and play poker. (*The Poker Night*, in fact, was Williams's working title.) Except for one gentleman, Mitch, they all behave like dogs—as in, "You dog, you." The main female characters are the bitchily insecure temptress Blanche DuBois and her pregnant younger sister, Stella Kowalski. In either case, their game is to tame the bad dogs.

But unlike Stanley Kowalski (twenty-three-year-old Marlon Brando in the Broadway premier) throwing his muscular weight around in the original wife-beater T-shirt, Coolidge's dogs are cut from the same cloth as Harry Truman, the uxoriously buttoned-up Kansas City haberdasher who went on to become a judge and, by the time *Streetcar* opened, the president. Coolidge dogs wear conservative flannel suits or decorous leather collars. Like Truman, they are upstanding gents, neither prudish nor overly macho. Their games are low-key male rituals, not make-or-break showdowns. While Coolidge was painting them, Truman's Monday-night poker sessions with World War I army buddies had a ten-cent limit, with the action lubricated by bootleg hooch and bawdy anecdotes. A vulnerably attractive sister-in-law like Blanche might have been ogled as she watched them play a few hands but certainly not raped later on. Whereas the last line of *Streetcar*, "This game is seven-card stud," emphasizes the brutally seminal nature of manhood, once again equating poker prowess with forceful male potency.

Coolidge's paintings mirror the decades (roughly 1890–1930) during which poker, while never deserting the back rooms of roadhouse saloons and other outlaw haunts, finally migrated to genteel suburbia. Played weekly on "poker night" for friendlier stakes than the nightly backroom action of professionals, the game was now part of ordinary American manhood. For the vast majority of men it was a pastime instead of a way to earn a living, though winning a few bucks always beat the hell out of losing. Even the blatant cheating of Coolidge's *A Friend in Need*, in which a bulldog passes the ace of clubs under the table to a boxer holding the three other aces, seems more of an ironic reference to the riverboat sharping of old than to anything these hounds would regularly resort to while playing against one another.

As early as 1875, the *Times* had concluded that poker was the national pastime and that "poker literature is assuming formidable proportions." The popularity of primers, of course, implies a wider interest in winning fair and square. And not only had the game been exported to Europe, but in America it was no longer "confined to the rough South-West and to those far-off regions where *The Outcasts of Poker Flat* are real personages." Poker nights were now circled on the calendars of law-abiding, taxpaying citizens. In 1882, *The Saturday Review* declared, "Poker, yachting, hunting, camping out, base-ball, and limitless flirtation are recognized American institutions." By the 1890s, at least one monthly magazine, *Poker Chips*, was devoted entirely to the game, and most periodicals ran features about it. By the turn of the century, the U.S. Printing Company, a purveyor of playing cards, had compiled the first set of uniform rules and sent them to card clubs and newspapers around the country. On May 22, 1904, the *New York Sun* printed a summary of the game's rules and history, and three years later it was translated into Chinese.

As Colonel Roosevelt, Admiral George Dewey, and General John Pershing understood from experience, gambling for money in the barracks and for survival on the seas or battlefields were natural aspects of soldiering, just as showdowns in dusty streets and across piles of chips had long been part of sheriffing on the Western frontier. If you needed a man's man to do a tough job, poker skill was increasingly seen as a necessary, if not quite sufficient, condition.

When Truman and two million other doughboys arrived "over there" in March 1918, poker was their most popular form of entertainment. Having learned to play cards from his aunt Ida and uncle Harry on their Missouri farm back in the 1890s, Truman honed his draw and stud skills as an artillery officer in Alsace. Waiting to sail home after the armistice was signed in November, he and his comrades from Battery C passed that autumn in the mud near Verdun in "an almost continuous poker game," which in many cases went on for decades after they returned to civilian life.

Coolidge, who remained stateside because of his age, was busy noting the cut of the suits and hats of suburban commuters, the styles of their cards and chips and valises, the furnishing of their basements and dens. He angled these details through the prism of anthropomorphic humor to give us nine telling glimpses of middle-class men at their leisure as poker's second century was getting under way.

In the left panel of the series's only diptych, a St. Bernard holds a measly pair of deuces but has bet a large number of chips. As he peers out through a pince-nez like those worn by Truman, Woodrow Wilson, and both Roosevelts, his tablemates stare back at him hard, scrutinizing his muzzle for tells. In the right panel, the same St. Bernard rakes in a huge pot of chips, having shown the weak hand to the dismay of his opponents. Coolidge originally dubbed these two *Judge St. Bernard Stands Pat on Nothing* and *Judge St. Bernard Wins on a Bluff*, awkward mouthfuls retitled *A Bold Bluff* and *Waterloo* by Brown & Bigelow.

In *His Station and Four Aces*, the canine conductor on a commuter train informs Judge St. Bernard that his stop is approaching, so he may not be able to realize the profits from his nearly unbeatable hand. Yet perhaps it's just as well that he folds and gets up, given that in *Poker Sympathy*, a brown boxer with four aces goes broke against a white boxer showing down a straight flush, much to the leering delight of their tablemates.

Compared to the work of contemporaries like Hopper, Mary Cassatt, and John Singer Sargent (whose 1903 portrait of Theodore Roosevelt still hangs in the White House), Coolidge's technical skill is amateurish, his ideas rather schmaltzy. So who really likes his "bad" paintings? Sam Malone, the bartending ladies' man on *Cheers*, was nuts about Coolidge's pooches; Diane Chambers, the pretentious cocktail waitress drawn to the finer arts, predictably loathed them. These days they're considered to be either calendar kitsch, a stale nine-slice pack of pasteurized American cheese on a par with black-velvet Elvises, or a pithily accurate gloss on poker camaraderie—or both. Critics have ranked them as icons alongside Rockwell's Thanksgiving feasters, Grant Wood's *American Gothic*, James Montgomery Flagg's Uncle Sam (who wants YOU for the U.S. Army), Andy Warhol's cans of Campbell's soup, and even *The Scream* and *Mona Lisa*.

Whatever we think of Coolidge's paintings, the poker boom seems to have made them quite haute. In 2005, *A Bold Bluff* and *Waterloo* went on the auction block in Manhattan with an estimated value between $30,000 and $50,000 for the pair. When the gavel came down, the price—paid by a private, anonymous collector—was $590,400.

Coolidge's pasteboard hounds have also given rise to numerous parodies, from an ESPN commercial to a CD by Big Lou's Polka Casserole called *Dogs Playing Polka*. The cover, by the Los Angeles artist Laura Hazlett, features a wolfhound on saxophone, a collie on trombone, and an accordion-squeezing St. Bernard, all jamming away around a poker table beneath a picture of a slinky poodle in lacy pink lingerie. Oompah!

22

THE MIRROR, THE RIFFLE,
THE SHIFT, AND THE SHARK

Stud poker is not a very difficult game after you see your
opponent's hole card.

— HERBERT O. YARDLEY

By the turn of the game's second century, poker was fairly well established as the national pastime. More people *watched* baseball, but many millions more *played* the card game. And unlike baseball in the early twentieth century, poker was also played in many other corners of the globe. Americans and Europeans loved poker despite the latest accounts of cheating, which confirmed the square players' worst fears about the teamwork, technology, and chutzpah of the new breed of blacklegs. "Card sharping has been reduced to a science," the British magician John Nevil Maskelyne maintained in his book *Sharps and Flats*. "It is no longer a haphazard affair, involving merely primitive manipulations, but it has developed into a profession in which there is as much to learn as in most of the everyday occupations of ordinary mortals." As always, the higher the stakes, the more likely such professionals were to have infiltrated the action.

On the front page of the September 19, 1906, *New York Times* we find the following article:

PITTSBURG, Sept. 18—One of the members of the Americus Club was literally dragged from the clubhouse last night to a police station on a charge of swindling, and in court this morning was forced to return money which he was accused of winning at crooked cards. He did not deny the charge.

The Americus Club is one of the best-known Republican clubs in the country. It has about 1,000 members, many of them prominent and influential. The scandal, which was made public this morning by the arrest of W. Joseph Johnston, has been brewing for several weeks, many members of the club asserting that they had been cheated at the card tables. Several members, friends of Johnston, had been caught cheating, but had been simply thrown out of the club.

Frank Sauers of Allegheny last night lost first a big roll of money to Johnston at stud poker; then lost his diamond stud, and finally his diamond ring, valued at $750. Then he began to look closely, and when he saw that Johnston was wearing a "mirror ring," he asked no questions, but jumped upon the recent member, beat him, and later had him arrested on a charge of obtaining money under false pretenses.

With others Sauers appeared against Johnston in the police court this morning.

It is alleged that Johnston is but one of a dozen gamblers who set out to make their fortunes from the young club men of Pittsburg, and the police reports indicate that they have been very successful. Johnston came from some point in the West about a year ago and has been passing as a broker. He had money, and had little trouble getting into the famous old Americus Club as a member. His skill with cards is said to have done the rest.

The story went on to report that a single jackpot played by a judge and a bank president at the club contained almost $50,000. It described Johnston's mirror as being the size of a ten-cent piece. His ring, said the reporter, was designed to be worn on the third finger of the right hand, with the mirror being kept inside the hand. While dealing, Johnston positioned the mirror precisely under the upper left corner of each card as it slid off the top of the deck.

At the hearing, Johnston frankly admitted using the mirror at the club. The magistrate ordered him to return all the money he took from Sauers, as well as the man's ring and stud, and was fined $50 plus court costs, "all of which sneeringly he paid." But when the magistrate told him to leave Pittsburgh at his earliest convenience, Johnston said he would "take his own time about that, and would certainly not go before he told some of the Americus Club people what he thought about their 'squealing.'"

"I'm not the only one who has been getting some easy money off you Pittsburgh suckers," he added. "No, there's a whole lot of fellows down there, and are not there for their health. You fellows who have yelled at your losses have always been looking for the best of it at cards, yet when someone better than yourself at the game beats you you yell." When he offered to testify against the Americus Club and asked for his mirror ring and other sharping devices back, the magistrate threatened to have him arrested again.

Johnston in effect had maintained that such devices were a natural part of poker, things his accusers had themselves deployed while "looking for the best of it"—they just failed to do it as artfully. And when everyone knew that poker was a cheating game, it was unmanly to "squeal" when someone got the better of you. And besides, his victims were spoiled "suckers," born to squander whatever allowance their daddies doled out. By virtue of superior sharping skills, Johnston and his cronies had earned the right to take it from them.

The article also made clear why five-card stud, with its single hole card to detect and remember, would be the favorite game of the mirror men. And it raises our eyebrows even higher when Johnston, instead of lawyering up, stands cockily before the court and dishes out his withering sarcasm about the sore losers. That Sauers's assault on him seems to faze neither Johnston nor the magistrate suggests that getting caught cheating and fighting over the spoils are equally natural parts of the game. And while the magistrate is not persuaded by Johnston's defense, he does let him off rather easily.

Judicial discretion tends to emanate down from the top, of course, and the Justice Department under Theodore Roosevelt was much more devoted to prosecuting antitrust violations of blue-chip players on Wall Street than to policing short-stud games in the hinterlands. Secretary of State Elihu Root was known to play stud with a group including Henry Stimson, the U.S. attorney in charge of antitrust prosecutions; Senator Charles Curtis, a Native American from Kansas who later played in White House games hosted by Warren Harding; and the influential Rhode Island senator Nelson Aldrich, known as "the General Manager of the Nation."

In 1914, as honest players continued to face off with cheats, Theodore Hardison published an exposé in the tradition of Maskelyne and Jonathan Green that also played to the Belle Epoch's taste for grandiose titles: *Poker, A Work Exposing the Various Methods of Shuffling Up Hands, as Well as Other Ways of Cheating That Are Resorted to by Professional Gamblers, Also Embracing the Cardinal Principles by Which Every Sleight-of-Hand Trick Known with Cards May Be Played.* Anticipating the sticker shock caused by the $3 price of his 120-page booklet—a quart of milk cost nine cents in those days, and most full-length books retailed for about a dollar—Hardison declares on the title page: "The price of this book is based on the information it contains, which is worth its cost a hundred times over (in protection) to anyone who ever expects to play cards for money." By protection he means that his primer will explain how to spot poker sharps and thereby defend yourself from their sly machinations. But what will prevent would-be mechanics from boning up on his lessons in how to fix poker games, most of which are accompanied by precise illustrations? To sharps like Joseph Johnston, for example, wouldn't the book be worth its cost ten thousand times over?

Hardison hems, then he haws, before going on rhetorical tilt. He claims at one point that "it is the inclination of most all poker players to be 'on the square' (especially so in the beginning), but as the novice begins his career in the game, and is fortunate enough to enjoy a few good winnings, his natural ambition, as it is with all 'Young America,' is to go higher, (and he is not to blame), for it has been instilled into his very nature by his forefathers for generations. In fact, ever since the landing of the Pilgrims from that noted ship Mayflower, has the air which Americans breathe been contaminated with that arduous love for chance and adventure which lures the young beginner on and on, into games that are higher, and higher, and while bravely and manfully shouldering his losses he is led up into the unknown realms of space in his wandering fancy of a lucky day to come when . . ." What reputable publisher, we ask, would offer for sale such a spaced-out sermon, especially one coyly doubling as an instruction manual for sharps? Why, it is none other than the Hardison Publishing Co. of St. Louis, Missouri.

Hardison insists that his book is "solely for the protection of lovers of card games . . . in no case ever to be used for the purpose of giving an unfair advantage." Yet he seems to believe the very nature of poker makes cheating, and even a hellish death and afterlife, unavoidable. Claiming distress at this prospect, Hardison solemnly swears: "Were it within my power to do so, I would deliver in this volume the most scathing denunciation of poker playing that has ever been conceived in the mind of mortal man, and I want to say in the very beginning, if you are not a poker player, never start it." In the meantime, whether from aspiring mechanics or square players hoping to thwart them, he's happy to accept the three bucks.

Hardison goes on to cover the marking of cards and other ways of manipulating a deck, including the shift, the riffle, the slip, laying brick, and the haymow shuffle. The shift, for example, is a false cut designed to undo the real one made by the player to the dealer's right; that is, to put a cold deck's fatal sequence back into play. Just before making the shift, Hardison warns (or instructs), "The performer generally makes some pretense of straightening himself up, or seeking a more comfortable position in his chair, and at the same time, his hands, with the deck, drop slightly below the level of the table and the shift is made in the twinkling of an eye." After weeks or months of practice, a deck can be made to disappear from view so briefly that "it never creates suspicion, and will pass in any company, except among those posted in the art," a group that now includes Hardison's readers.

Where did good Mr. Hardison learn such techniques? Anticipating that his reader might wonder about this, he slips—or is it shifts?—into a disingenuous third-person voice, claiming to have innocently mastered these nimble-fingered arts "when quite a young boy." His friends were astonished by them, "and, boy-like, he delighted in pulling off his sleight-of-hand stunts" for their amusement only, never for profit. Soon he is looked upon as "something on the wizard order." Suddenly, though, "to his great surprise and regret, he noticed that he was no longer invited to their gatherings, and when he chanced to meet some of the girls, he noticed a *marked coolness*," this despite never being "other than a gentleman in their presence." It turned out that "he had been cast aside because they had learned that he was a '*professional card shark*'"—that is, an even more ravenous variety of cardsharp. Yet why would the girls shun the young Theodore, when he "had never even so much as seen a game of poker played in his life"? His denials and protestations fall on deaf ears, and the shark reputation "clings to him until this day."

An even more obvious tell that Mr. Hardison has been a shark all along is his claim that his false accusers are motivated by "envy rather than of founded suspicion, and generally voiced for an ulterior motive, which usually has its origin in a mealy-mouthed excuse to refuse payment of their losses. And these people are held in such bitter contempt by the writer of this little book that he would really like an opportunity to marry them off to his office dog in a futile attempt to improve its breed."

Whatever Cash Coolidge would have to say about such bitchiness, Mr. Hardison clearly has what we would call "issues" of "misrepresentation," though what poker player does not? His self-published booklet seems to be a well-illustrated 120-page bluff. Yet none of its weird obfuscations keep it from being a rich source of insight into how men like Johnston, Devol, and Green—and probably Hardison, too—managed, in their day, to dominate the tabletop landscape.

23

THE EDUCATION OF A
POKER PLAYER, PART I

Just imagine how little your understanding of the world on the eve of the events of 1914 would have helped you guess what was to happen next.

—NASSIM NICHOLAS TALEB, *THE BLACK SWAN*

As more and better information about cheaters became available, honest players with bluffing and reckoning skill began to outnumber the cold-deck artists and mirror men. Talented square players profited not by outsharping the sharps but by steering clear of them. Their fiercely competitive action welcomed as many suckers as possible, of course, but unlike the shark attacks still under way all around them, these were games in which today's barracudas and devilfish would be happy to play. Why? Because competence and luck, not violence or con jobs, were allowed to determine who left at dawn with the money.

The most intriguing example of this new breed of player is Herbert O. Yardley, a well-traveled Hoosier who combined Quaker discipline, studiously acquired card sense, and high-level training as a cryptanalyst into the kind of skill set we still associate with poker mastery—or, if not mastery, then with rock-solid play. The tactics he recommended in *The Education of a Poker Player*, an autobiographical primer connecting Cardano's 1564 work on primero to twenty-first-century handbooks, could not have been much more conservative.

Like most philosophical bents, Yardley's emerged from the soil of its birthplace. He was born on April 13, 1889, in Worthington, a grain terminal sixty miles southwest of Indianapolis. Surrounded by endlessly flat corn- and wheat fields, its 1,450 residents were at the demographic center of America: the same number of people lived north and east of them as lived south and west. Worthingtonians were earthy and plain folk who had settled along the Eel River in the heart of the heart of the country, with perhaps a bit more than their fair share of slipperiness. That all seven of their saloons hosted draw and stud games and allowed minors to play seemed to confirm this. It certainly demonstrated poker's mainstream appeal fourscore years after *poque* steamed up from New Orleans.

Yardley's father was a railroad station agent and telegrapher who taught his son Samuel Morse's dot-and-dash signaling system, planting the seed of a lifelong fascination with codes. Herb also rounded into an impressive student-athlete. At five foot five and 120 pounds, he was captain of the football team, playing both safety and quarterback. When he was thirteen, however, his mother suddenly died of a heart attack. Angry and despondent, Herb's own health declined, and he became a troublemaker around town and in school. He spent most of his time playing poker, a game he had learned from his grandfather, who had played it while serving in the Union Army. Determined to improve his results against classmates, Herb became more disciplined at the table as well as in the rest of his life. Once football practice was over and his homework completed, he dealt out hands on his bedspread and calculated the best ways to play them.

With $200 his mother had left him, he began, at sixteen, to compete against local adults. Scouting the games in each saloon, he decided that Monty's Place offered the most challenging action—usually the worst way to choose where to start playing. "Big-league stuff," he called it, adding, "It is one thing to face eleven football opponents when you have ten men with you, but to face six hungry wolves alone is something else indeed." The better to avoid being eaten alive, he persuaded Monty to give him regular tutorials. "I figure the odds for every card I draw," began Monty's first lesson, "and if the odds are not favorable, I fold. This doesn't sound very friendly, but what's friendly about poker? It's a cutthroat game at best." Yet if playing strictly by the odds didn't give opponents many chances to take your money, it was quite a bit friendlier than cheating them.

The chapters of *The Education* set in Monty's Place provide a well-lit diorama of where and how honest poker was played circa 1905. The card room in back was "about twenty feet square, with two barred windows high above the ground and an iron wood stove at the end," Yardley tells us. "The windows had dark drawn curtains. The walls were unplastered brick, the woodwork painted white, and the floor scrubbed. In the center was a large round table covered with a green billiard cloth and surrounded by seven cane chairs. Others, for loafers and kibitzers, were scattered here and there or were grouped around the stove when the weather was cold. The table was lighted by a single bulb, extended to the center by a cord from the ceiling and shaded against the eyes of the players. At the side of each chair was a spittoon." He went on: "When the game was in progress, the door was barred with the usual sliding window and guarded by Runt, the bouncer, so named because of his size. Strangers were welcome after being frisked for weapons." The walls of Monty's office were hung with autographed photos of the tiger hunter Jim Corbett, the gourmand and philanthropist Diamond Jim Brady, and President Theodore Roosevelt.

Because too many players, like Captain Willie Massie in Hickok's final game, were still in the habit of peeking at discards, Monty posted a warning: "Please don't FRIG with the Discards, Penalty $20," with a sign underneath adding wittily, "Vulgar Language Forbidden." Monty was nonetheless "a man's man," good with his fists and attractive to women, though Herb understands "it might have been that they attached a certain glamour to him because he was a successful gambler who had killed a man." As it was on steamboats and in the Wild West, so it would be in civilized Worthington: poker prowess just seemed to go hand in hand with an aptitude for ladies and gunplay. All three provided ample opportunities to get yourself killed. Yardley reports that, after a disagreement a few years earlier, "My own uncle, a giant of a man with a Jesse James beard, was cut down by a consumptive half his size. Uncle Bill walked a block, sat down on the corner drugstore steps, and bled to death."

To help maintain order and peace, Monty sanctions only three games: five-card stud, draw, and "deuces," draw in which the joker and all four deuces are wild. In stud, instead of seven players anteing a quarter each, the dealer antes $2, which must have been a huge disincentive to call stud in dealer's choice. In straight draw and deuces, each player antes fifty cents. Monty rakes half a buck from each pot and plays in the game when it suits him. The competition consists of strong players, not-bad players, and the "seventy-five percent" Monty deems to be either first- or second-degree "simpletons."

The usual "take-out" (buy-in) was $20, but as in antebellum Minnesota, a man is allowed to play "open; that is, he can play with the twenty dollars in chips plus whatever he had in his pocket. Aside from cash in the pockets, many play open by backing their hand with real property—cattle, farms, grain and the like." A bill of sale is written up and placed in the pot. Making it even harder to evaluate a hand, a player "was never asked how much he played open, but if he had bet more than the chips he had in front of him, he was required to put up the difference in acceptable IOUs." Unlike the farmer Meredith in Laredo, a player at Monty's couldn't be raised out of his equity in the main pot. Once he ran out of cash and collateral, a side pot was established for subsequent bets. There were no Little Lady scenarios. Pots averaged about $15, though they sometimes approached $20,000.

Most important of all, the games at Monty's were "on the level." Cheaters were identified and dealt with firmly though without violence, presumably to keep the police from becoming involved. When One-Eye Jones, a stud player from Indy, rang in a marked deck, Monty quickly spotted it. He held the cards under the light, "bent half of the deck toward him, and released the cards one at a time. When he did this fast you could see the marks. They stood out like a motion picture film turned slowly." Caught red-handed, One-Eye grinned sheepishly. Monty glared at him. "How did you switch decks?"

"I dropped a chip on the floor and made the switch when I picked it up."

"I put a sign on the wall only last week warning crooks I'd throw them out on their ass and they'd forfeit their take-out and all winnings if caught. Got anything to say for yourself?"

"No," said One-Eye, "except if I have to be thrown out I'd rather Runt did it than you." He apparently thought that flattering Monty's tough-guy reputation would soften him up. And it worked. "All right, Runt," Monty said. "Throw him out the back way but don't be too rough."

We should also note that, like Johnston at the Americus Club, One-Eye dealt short stud, in which the marked back of only one card was enough to know each opponent's entire hand. Another cheat, caught dealing seconds, had the nerve to challenge Monty's tight but honest principles. "My method is painless," the mechanic rationalized. "I give them the ax. You bleed them to death slowly." Monty, that is, wins "on superior experience and finesse; I win because I am a card manipulator." Like a magnesium flare illuminating the no-man's-land between sharp and square trenches, the cheater sincerely believes that "essentially we are no different. In the end we both bleed the sucker."

Herb rejects this moral equivalence and chooses to play as a wolf, not a shark. But instead of quitting school to play poker full-time, he treats it as a lucrative hobby. Even as a teenager, he understands that the natural swings of honest poker rule out the kind of steady income a man will need to support his family. He buckles down again, becomes editor of the school paper, and generally impresses folks as being "the smartest boy in the county," with a mind "on a different level than anyone in town." Even more to his credit, Worthingtonians said they'd never known him to lie or cheat. He was always a wolf in wolf's clothing.

After graduating in 1907 and learning more telegraphy, Yardley took a job for the Indianapolis & Vincennes Railroad. He spent most of his salary on tuition for correspondence courses offered by the University of Chicago, which he hoped to attend as an English major before entering law school. But in 1912, his plans veered dramatically when he scored the highest number on a civil service exam and was hired as a clerk at the State Department. The annual salary of $900 was enough for him to propose to Hazel Milam, a librarian. The couple moved to Washington and were married there on May 20, 1914. Five weeks later, the Bosnian Serb Gavrilo Princip assassinated Archduke Franz Ferdinand, heir to the Austro-Hungarian throne, setting the stage for "the war to end all wars."

According to Yardley's biographer, David Kahn, a respected historian of cryptology, American intelligence gathering was fairly primitive when the newlywed began work at the State Department. In part because the Union had won the Civil War with a few tethered balloons and haphazardly trained spies, the postbellum army failed to develop much of an intelligence capability; it simply "went back to subduing the Indians." Meanwhile, European technology advanced exponentially. Even in the era of dum-dum bullets, machine guns, aeroplanes, and tanks, it was radio that launched the biggest leaps forward in military strategy. Radio signals helped Germany overcome the Royal Navy's ability to cut its overseas cables. Because transmissions could be heard just as easily by the enemy, every message had to be encrypted. Kahn reminds us that once such encryptions were decoded, they would consist of "the very words of the enemy," as opposed to the often garbled or misleading data spies produced. It would be as if a draw player, instead of relying on body language while contemplating a bluff, could hear his opponent thinking, "With aces full, I'm going to reraise." Suddenly it was possible for a single cryptographer—Oswald T. Hitchings, for example, a music teacher from Pembrokeshire—to be "worth four divisions to the British Army."

Decoded messages led to stunning intelligence coups. The most decisive was the discovery by British cryptographers that in January 1917, the German foreign minister Arthur Zimmermann offered to help Mexico "reconquer the lost territory in New Mexico, Texas, and Arizona" if Mexico would ally herself with Germany. Though Mexico rejected the offer, when the Brits made it public, writes Kahn, it "helped push the United States into war [against Germany] and into world power."

As Woodrow Wilson prepared to send the doughboys Over There, Yardley was startled to learn that the president was relying on a decade-old cipher system, in which one letter of the alphabet stood for another. Having easily solved it, Yardley persuaded senior officers that the United States needed more complex codes as well as two new code-breaking services—at home to intercept diplomatic messages and along the western front for military communiqués. After drafting a hundred-page "Solution of American Diplomatic Codes," he was commissioned as a second lieutenant in the Signal Corps. The newly formed eighth section of military intelligence, MI-8, came to be known as the American Black Chamber. By July of 1917, Yardley was running it.

He was given a desk in the code room of the State-Navy-War Building, directly across from the White House. "By lifting my eyes from my work," he said, "I could see a tennis game in progress where a few years earlier President Roosevelt and his tennis Cabinet had played every day." He went on to describe the bulky codebooks and thick stacks of telegrams "from and to consular and diplomatic posts throughout the world" being thumbed by chain-smoking staffers. "The pounding of typewriters specially constructed to make fifteen copies of a telegram mingled with the muffled click of the telegraph instruments"—the sights, sounds, and smoke-marbled humidity of one of the most high-tech rooms in the world.

Since few in the military were trained as cryptanalysts, Yardley turned to civilians to staff MI-8. His chief assistant, John Manley, taught English at the University of Chicago, where he'd cut his own code-breaking teeth by debunking a cipher system that allegedly proved Francis Bacon had written the works of Shakespeare. Above all, Manley possessed what Yardley called "the rare gift of originality of mind—in cryptology called 'cipher brains.'"

Other gifted or trainable cryptanalysts included the Chaucer scholar Edith Rickert; the professor of medieval Latin Charles Beeson; Edgar Sturtevant, an expert on Hittite; the Yale professor of Spanish Frederick Bliss Luquiens; and the precocious Yale undergraduate Stephen Vincent Benét, who went on to write the Civil War epic *John Brown's Body*. Yardley's training and supervision of such literate women and men put them all in the vanguard of a revolution in code breaking. "Overnight," writes Kahn, "cryptology outgrew the form of cryptanalysis that had dominated the field for four hundred years: chamber analysis, in which an individual wrestled with a single cryptogram in an isolated room. This shift from artisanal piece work to mass production expanded the functions of the chief cryptologist. No longer was he simply first among equals, solving along with his colleagues and occasionally assigning intercepts to them for solution. Now he managed them."

Yardley proved to be an effective manager in part because he understood that the power to decode or translate literature was a key aspect of "cipher brains." Like the ability to read an intentionally misleading cipher (or bluffer), a keen eye for intricate narrative language had surprisingly useful code-breaking applications. The result was that book-learned pencilnecks in Harris tweed jackets were suddenly able to help turn the tide on the battlefield.

Promoted to captain, Yardley was dispatched by John "Black Jack" Pershing (1860–1948), commanding general of the American Expeditionary Force, to work with the more advanced British and French cipher bureaus. America's only six-star general, Pershing had learned to play poker in 1886 while stationed with the Sixth Cavalry in New Mexico. He became so obsessed that he bet hands of draw in his sleep, though he later stopped playing as an exercise in self-discipline. Even so, a sizable fraction of his officers—including Harry Truman and Dwight Eisenhower—as well as the Prince of Wales, the English medic George Wear, and countless other Allied servicemen played poker in France. A photograph shows four French and British soldiers using an ammunition crate as a table. John Dos Passos's documentary novel *1919* tells of sailors playing while on leave in Glasgow. Captain Roger

Sermon, who served with Truman in the mud near Verdun, said, "To keep from going crazy we had an almost continuous poker game." In a game played in an American trench just before a German mustard-gas attack, William Gill bet his gold watch in a pot won by Carl Grothaus. Gill died in a VA hospital in 1962 of the lingering effects of the gas. Grothaus lived until 1991, when his son Dewey inherited the watch and tried to look up the name engraved on its back: "W. B. Gill, Sioux City, IA, U.S.A." But it was only after Dewey enlisted the help of genealogists that Gill was tracked down and his survivors identified. The watch, complete with its brown leather band, was returned to his grandsons Lloyd and Bill on June 6, 2007, at an American Legion hall in Sioux City.

Yardley's assignment was cushier. Entertaining his opposite numbers at the Ritz and the Crillon, he learned what he could while deferring to those who'd been surveilling the Germans since 1914. Though tactically cooperative, his British counterparts decided that Captain Yardley had an unfortunate tendency to drop names and exaggerate, and that he wasn't sufficiently discreet to be trusted with their most strategic methods.

When the Armistice was signed on November 11, 1918, most of Europe rejoiced. With Hazel waiting for him back in Washington, Yardley's orders kept him in Paris monitoring German press reports for another four months. This left him plenty of time to play poker, sample French cuisine, and revel in the company of a beautiful black-haired dancer named Jacqueline. They rented an apartment in Passy and spent New Year's Eve at the Mumm family mansion with fifteen hundred other delirious, war-weary celebrants. More than three thousand bottles of champagne were uncorked, enough to require several ambulances to take overserved guests to the hospital—or, in the case of the British, to hospital. When Yardley departed Paris the following March, he left a briefcase full of highly confidential documents on a counter at the Gare de Lyon. Although it was recovered by an MI-8 colleague, losing it seemed to confirm British skepticism about his ability keep vital secrets.

The most notable single achievement of MI-8 had been decoding messages that identified a German secret agent who was subsequently executed for espionage. Its larger accomplishment was, in Yardley's words, "the large and constant stream of information it has provided in regard to the attitudes, purposes, and plans of our neighbors," friendly or otherwise. He had helped his country get up to speed in an area of national defense that continues to be of vital importance. Yet while no one would dispute that he was one of the best code breakers of his generation, it was how he used what he found out that became the main sticking point during the next fifteen years of his life.

Yardley and his MI-8 staff were moved to plush New York offices at 52 Vanderbilt Avenue, at the corner of Forty-seventh Street, just as the twenties began to roar. After the deprivations of war, and despite Prohibition, what Gertrude Stein called the Lost Generation was bent on enjoying itself. With *The Great Gatsby* in 1922 and *The Sun Also Rises* in 1926, F. Scott Fitzgerald and Ernest Hemingway became the toasts of Manhattan. Flappers lopped off their Edwardian tresses, kicked up their heels in short frocks, and spoke easy. New York City alone had thirty-two thousand speakeasies, many of which were attached to card rooms and brothels. George H. Fisher put it this way in the *Stud Poker Blue Book*: "As the doughboy said when his grandmother sent him cherries preserved in brandy, the important thing is the *spirit* in which an article is offered."

Because the cables Yardley's agents intercepted were thought to be confidential by those who sent and received them, MI-8 had to operate on both sides of the law, which kept it morally in sync with speakeasy culture. In 1920, the whiskey-drinking poker player Warren Harding defeated James Cox in a landslide. In 1927, Babe Ruth, fueled by "hot dogs, beer, and women," hit sixty home runs, more than any other *team* in the league, though his fellow Yankee Lou Gehrig was named MVP. Gehrig's future wife, Eleanor Twitchell, was living in Chicago then. "I was young and rather innocent," she recalled, "but I smoked, played poker, drank bathtub gin along with everyone else." Chicago was every ballplayer's favorite town to visit because of the blues and jazz thriving there; the speakeasies of Dion O'Banion, "Hymie" Weiss, and Alphonse Capone; and the abundant supply of free-spirited "circuit girls" like Twitchell. Capone's most notorious club, the Four Deuces, was a brothel named after a poker hand. The city Carl Sandburg called "crooked" and "brutal" probably had a lower percentage of legit poker games than anyplace else in the country.

Meanwhile, a threatening red sun was rising across the Pacific. After defeating Russia in 1903 and dominating the eastern hemisphere during the First World War, Japan had continued to build up its army and navy. This forced the United States to spend enormous amounts of peacetime dollars to maintain its tied-for-first ratio of 10:10:7 in naval tonnage with respect to Britain and Japan. In October 1921, President Harding convened a conference in Washington in hopes of curtailing the arms race.

Because of the serene composure he maintained during international crises, Tomosaburō Katō was called "the poker-face premier" by diplomats and journalists. His ambassador to Washington, Kijuro Shidehara, had a similarly cool disposition. A page-one headline in the November 7, 1921, *New York Times* declared, BARON SHIDEHARA COMPARES NATIONS TO POKER PLAYERS AND SAYS MR. NIPPON HAS A GOOD HAND. The article reported that the ambassador "speaks this way because he has a very good hand and knows it, reports to the contrary having been circulated for betting purposes. There are sometimes fortunes to be made by interested persons in judicious deception. Mr. Nippon, being only human, like other gentlemen, has made other errors in playing the old game of bluff, but the game was one that had been forced upon him."

Since the likeliest theater of hostile operations was the Philippines, the United States and Britain demanded extra tonnage to compensate for how far their ships would have to travel to engage the Japanese. Secretary of State Charles Evans Hughes proposed to limit the United States and Britain to 500,000 tons each and Japan to 300,000, for a 10:10:6 ratio. Shidehara insisted on 350,000 tons, or 10:10:7.

Given his poker-faced adversaries across the table, it would be enormously useful for Hughes to know what they were saying in private. Yardley told him. Working seven days a week, including Thanksgiving, in twelve-hour shifts, MI-8 had cracked the Japanese code. The November 28 cable from the negotiating team to Katō began, "Koshi, Washington URGENT 0073 vrxpm dozoorupuh uteletamme fuinfridy . . ." Decoded and translated, it said, "We are of your opinion that it is necessary to avoid any clash with Great Britain and America, particularly America, in regard to the armament limitation question. . . . In case of inevitable necessity you will work to establish your second proposal of 10:6.5." Another message revealed that Shidehara believed "many of our own people . . . desire the reaching of an immediate agreement through some compromise." Such cables confirmed Hughes's impression that Tokyo's position had softened, allowing him to negotiate more confidently. Even a skeptical member of his staff could tell that the decoded cables had "stiffened Mr. Hughes' attitude."

When the poker-faced premier signed off on 10:10:6, Yardley's apt comment was, "Stud poker is not a very difficult game after you see your opponent's hole card." For his role in a major diplomatic victory that lowered international tensions and saved his country hundreds of millions of dollars, he received a bonus of one week's salary, $184. Awarded the Distinguished Service Medal, the nation's highest honor for a noncombatant, he was cited for developing, "out of a practically unknown field of mystery and doubt, a science by which he was able to translate the most secret messages and obtain information of vital importance." Is there a better description of what pokeraticians like Yardley, Sklansky, Harrington, Hansen, and Negreanu have done for their millions of readers?

Pershing praised Yardley's "exceptionally meritorious and distinguished services in a position of great responsibility." Hughes said MI-8 under Yardley, having "developed its facilities to a very high degree, is of the utmost value to the Department of State." Then they cut Yardley's budget by 30 percent. It was peacetime, after all, and the army's new cryptographic systems had superseded MI-8's work.

It was naïveté and moral righteousness, however, that finally doomed the Black Chamber. When Henry Stimson, appointed secretary of state by Herbert Hoover in 1929, found out about it, he was neither impressed nor grateful. Furious, he quashed its funding on the grounds that "gentlemen do not read each other's mail." Much as the poker world was torn between sharp and square principles, Stimson's view reflected the ambivalence of America's diplomatic corps between the world wars about the new frontiers of intelligence gathering. Despite what Yardley had accomplished under Wilson and Harding, it was now apparently ethical to mow down the enemy with airplanes, tanks, and machine guns but not to decode an encrypted letter between "gentlemen," which might head off warfare.

MI-8 had highly placed supporters within the State Department and military, but Secretary Stimson prevailed. The Black Chamber was shut down for good on Halloween 1929, forty-eight hours after Black Tuesday, when many blue-chip stocks became suddenly worthless. The Roaring Twenties were over, America's steepest Depression was well under way, and Herb Yardley, medal and all, was officially out of a job.

24

HUMP GUNS DOWN BRAIN
OVER STUD DEBT!

"I hate pinochle," Memo said. "Let's play poker but not the open kind."

— BERNARD MALAMUD, *THE NATURAL*

Almost exactly a decade before the Depression took hold, back in October of 1919, eight members of the Chicago White Sox had thrown five games in the best-of-nine World Series to the Cincinnati Reds. The players implicated in the conspiracy—including Eddie Cicotte and Shoeless Joe Jackson—were banned from baseball for life by Commissioner Kenesaw Mountain Landis, though a movement is now under way to have Jackson posthumously inducted into the Hall of Fame at Cooperstown. Arnold Rothstein, the syndicate boss who bribed the players with $10,000 apiece, got off scot-free, as did the dozens of his associates who were also involved. Nine years later, Rothstein was gunned down for not paying up after losing $322,000 in a three-day stud marathon. That game may well have been fixed by a team of sharps led by the dapper Joe Bernstein, who would go on to win a gold bracelet in the 1973 World Series and be inducted ten years later into the Poker Hall of Fame at Binion's Horseshoe.

Before Rothstein's couriers would hand over the eighty grand in

1919, their boss demanded a clear signal that the fix was in. Cicotte provided it by hitting Cincinnati leadoff man Morrie Rath in the back with the second pitch of the series. The left fielder Jackson eventually misplayed three singles into triples, which normally result, of course, from balls hit to right or right-center. Cicotte made three fielding errors in the fifth inning of game four alone. Having confidently bet on the Reds, Rothstein and his partners made millions.

Baseball salaries in 1919 were minuscule compared with the nine-figure contracts of today. Back then, nearly all major league revenue remained in the owners' vest pockets. The Sox players, whose average salary was about $3,000, were motivated by both greed and resentment of the team's tightwad owner, Charles Comiskey; by fixing the series, they continued the decades-long pattern of collusion between underworld fixers and underpaid athletes. In 1877, the year after the National League was founded, four Louisville Grays had been expelled from baseball for throwing games. Such banishments were the exception, however. "The men who ran professional baseball at the time generally chose to ignore such malfeasance," writes Daniel A. Nathan, "allowing game fixing to continue." Nathan says many major leaguers "felt that the team owners exploited them, thanks in large part to the reserve clause, which was first implemented in 1879 and effectively bound players to their teams indefinitely." Such a system all but guaranteed that some of them would throw games for money that tripled their salaries.

When the "Black Sox" conspiracy began to unravel, Rothstein testified before a Cook County grand jury that he was an innocent businessman and a baseball fan. "Abe Attell did the fixing," he read from a prepared statement. "The whole thing started when Attell and some other cheap gamblers decided to frame the Series and make a killing. The world knows I was asked in on the deal and my friends know how I turned it down flat. I don't doubt that Attell used my name to put it over. That's been done by smarter men than Abe. But I was not in on it, would not have gone into it under any circumstances and *didn't bet a cent on the Series* after I found out what was underway." As Michael Corleone was forced to ask his brother Fredo, "You believed that story?" The grand jury apparently did. The truth was that so many gangsters had been trying to fix the series, Rothstein found it easy to cover his tracks. As he told one of his protégés, "If nine guys go to bed with a girl, she'll have a tough time proving the tenth is the father!"

Born in Manhattan in 1882, Rothstein was a math whiz and junior conniver who learned to love the rackets before he turned nine, even while his older brother, Harry, was studying to become a rabbi. "Who cares about that stuff?" Arnold spitefully asked his disappointed father. "This is America, not Jerusalem. I'm an American. Let Harry be a Jew." By 1910 Arnold owned several brothels and a prosperous casino in Manhattan, for which he hired the most talented mechanics as dealers, and part of the Havre de Grace track in Maryland, where he and his jockeys fixed a goodly percentage of the races. In 1919, he rigged the biggest sporting event in America. The luck factor in square baseball, as in poker and racing, he knew, was simply too great to risk betting large sums on them. Scott Fitzgerald based his character Meyer Wolfsheim, Jay Gatsby's crooked associate, on Rothstein. Gatsby proudly identifies Wolfsheim as "the man who fixed the World's Series back in 1919."

During the twenties, Rothstein branched out into bootlegging and narcotics, working with Meyer Lansky, Legs Diamond, Lucky Luciano, and Dutch Schultz. Rothstein's nicknames included Mr. Big, the Fixer, the Man Uptown, the Big Bankroll, and the Brain. Whatever they called him, he served effectively as the go-between among the various Jewish, Irish, and Italian outfits and levied handsome fees for the service. This also made him one of the inspirations for Hyman Roth, played by Lee Strasberg in *The Godfather, Part II*. Rothstein's office was Lindy's restaurant, at Broadway and Forty-ninth Street. To foil eavesdroppers, he conducted business standing on the corner surrounded by bodyguards, taking bets and collecting from those who had lost the previous day. At night, to relax, he played in the biggest poker games in the city.

On Saturday, September 8, 1928, he sat down in a stud game hosted by the big, squared-jawed bookie George "Hump" McManus. The other players were California stud artist Nate Raymond, who was in New York on his honeymoon; golf and poker hustler "Titanic" Thompson, up from Arkansas; and New Yorkers Joe Bernstein, Meyer Boston, and Martin Bowe. Though much less an underworld force than Rothstein, McManus was well connected in the city, with one brother serving as an NYPD lieutenant and another as a Catholic priest. The Hump's floating stud action in and around Times Square was a prototype of the Executive Game run by Junior and Johnny Boy Soprano and later by Tony. As host, the Hump was responsible for security, meals and drinks, and making sure the game was on the level and all debts were settled up afterward.

One version of events is that the New Yorkers, the road gamblers, or some combination of the two colluded against Rothstein, perhaps to avenge losses they'd suffered in rigged games on Rothstein's home turf. Whether it was due to collusion, mechanical manipulation by a dealer, or plain old bad luck, Rothstein began to lose early and kept getting second-best hands as the stakes, at his insistence, were steadily raised. As the weekend wore on, he chased his losses by playing more and more recklessly. Long after the others wanted to quit, Rothstein demanded the action continue, which made his opponents nervous for a number of reasons. One was that, instead of cash or chips, Rothstein made his larger bets using chits, small pieces of paper with dollar amounts scribbled above his "A.R." By dawn on Monday, A. R. owed Thompson $30,000, Bernstein $73,000, and Raymond $219,000 in chits.

"I think, my friends, that some of you play cards with more skill than honesty," he said, getting up. "I think I've been playing with a pack of crooks." The clear implication, that cheaters didn't have to be paid, seemed confirmed when he left the room without signing any IOUs. Some say he even had $19,000 in cash in his pockets.

"Is this the way he always does business?" Thompson demanded to know. "Not even a scratch," Raymond said angrily, meaning no scratch of his pen on an IOU. McManus did his best to reassure them. "That's A.R.," he said. "Hell, he's good for it. He'll be calling you in a couple of days."

Yet a couple of *weeks* passed without Rothstein calling. As McManus dunned him more and more aggressively, Rothstein spread the word that the game had been fixed, while the Hump remained adamant it had all been legit. So had the Brain been outplayed or bamboozled? We can never know for sure, but several sharping experts and gambling historians, John Scarne and David Pietrusza among them, have reckoned that Rothstein was cheated. Thompson never made any bones about being a hustler, and all three New Yorkers were known as skillful professionals, which in those days nearly always meant sharps. This also seemed confirmed when Rothstein equated *skillful* with *crooked*. Decades later we even have Bernstein's Hall of Fame bio describing him as "a sharp road gambler."

On the other hand, there has never been a high-stakes marathon, crooked or straight, in which someone didn't lose a lot of money, and the tough competition combined with fairly dealt second-best hands could have been the reasons Rothstein got busted. But like so many players, especially professional cheats, he refused to believe that he'd lost fair and square—that the risk-averse genius who'd paid off the Black Sox had been bitten by a random black swan. (A black swan is a statistically improbable run of good or bad luck, to be discussed in Chapter 43.)

Seeking an expert opinion, Rothstein called on his friend Nicky Arnstein. An aristocratic con man, bond thief, and cardsharp who had done time in Sing Sing and Leavenworth, Arnstein had polished his sleight-of-hand skills in stud games across the country as well as on transatlantic luxury liners. And while he sympathized about Rothstein's losses, he reminded his *chaver* that sharping was part of their business. Hadn't both of them made millions this way? Rothstein supposed that they had. "Arnold, rigged or not, you have to pay it off. Even if it was crooked, no point to your advertising you were a sucker."

If Rothstein could not disagree, nor could he entirely swallow his old friend's advice. And so, without firmly deciding how to proceed, he continued to stiff McManus, hoping to make him sweat and maybe take a smaller amount. "I'm not going to give them a cent," he made a point of saying in public, "and that goes for the gamblers and gorillas. I can be found any night at Lindy's, if they're looking for me. And if I get killed, no one is going to get any money." But money wasn't really the point. Rothstein was worth several million dollars, so it was mainly the principle that stuck in his craw.

Muscling him was thought to be out of the question, so McManus went to Jimmy Hines, his connection in the Tammany political machine and a man who also did business with Rothstein. "They'll get their money," Rothstein told Hines, "but when I want to give it to them and not a minute before." Four more weeks passed. With all the pressure he was under from both Rothstein and his creditors, McManus, a heavy drinker, began to drink even more. One evening, while drunk, he told a gorilla named Willie McCabe he would personally kill Rothstein if he didn't pay up right away.

At 10:15 p.m. on Sunday, November 4, McManus called Rothstein from Room 349 of the Park Central Hotel, where he was registered as George Richards. He requested that Rothstein come over to negotiate a settlement, guaranteeing his safety in what would be a two-person sit-down. Rothstein hung up and handed his gun to a protégé, saying, "Keep this for me, I'll be right back," then made the short walk to the Park Central.

Shortly after Rothstein entered the hotel, a single gunshot clapped through the brisk midtown evening. Moments later, a Colt .38 Detective Special flew from the window of 349. It bounced off the hood of a taxi and clattered across the sidewalk. Inside, hotel employees found Rothstein limping down the service stairs. Clutching his lower abdomen, he asked for a cab to take him home. Instead, a police officer summoned an ambulance, and Rothstein was taken to Polyclinic Hospital, where a .38 slug was removed from his belly. It had entered just above his groin, severing an artery and causing massive internal bleeding. He left the OR in a coma.

After being given a transfusion and morphine, he regained consciousness long enough to tell his wife, Carolyn, he wanted to go home. When the Irish detective Patrick Flood asked who had shot him, he said, "I'll take care of it myself." Pressed further, Rothstein summoned the strength to answer mockingly, "Me mudder did it."

Before anyone could take care of anything, Rothstein died at 10:20 in the morning, November 6, 1928—Election Day. Back in September, he had bet heavily on Herbert Hoover to beat Alfred E. Smith, and in the New York governor's race on Franklin Roosevelt to outpoll Albert Ottinger. He would have collected $570,000, almost twice what he owed McManus, but according to common bookmaking practice, a bettor's death canceled his wagers.

McManus hid out from Rothstein's henchmen for another three weeks before arranging to be safely arrested in a Broadway barbershop. Other players in the stud game were arrested as well, but they all had unimpeachable alibis for the night of November 4 and were quickly released.

When the case came to trial a year later, the state's attorney contended that McManus had murdered Rothstein for welching. McManus's story was that he didn't have the slightest reason to shoot someone who owed him that much money. Although a Chesterfield topcoat with his name sewn into the lining had been found in Room 349, no hotel employee could—or would—place him there at the time of the shooting. Nor were the prosecution's forensic witnesses able to tie him to the .38. Their overall case was so weak, the defense felt no need to call even a single witness. After Judge Charles C. Nott Jr. directed the jury to acquit the accused, McManus walked out of the courtroom wearing the Chesterfield that only moments before had been tagged as a prosecution exhibit.

Whether it was baseball's World Series or the biggest poker game around being fixed, or the sucker was gutshot for welching, the gangster code of silence had prevailed once again with a vengeance. And despite all the progress players like Monty and Herb Yardley had made in reclaiming their game from the outlaws, it was clear that the job wasn't finished.

THE EDUCATION OF A
POKER PLAYER, PART 2

SNSZK KXCHR ZAKDC KNMFH STCDE NQS XK

—WORLD WAR I GERMAN MILITARY CODE

REPRODUCED IN *YARDLEYGRAMS*

I n early 1930, with his esoteric skills no longer in demand and the un-employment rate spiraling toward 35 percent, Herb Yardley couldn't find a job. "I felt very small in my rags and could scarcely open my mouth," he said later. "Poverty had done strange things to me, though only a few months before I had stood at the top of my profession. Now I suddenly found myself with no voice, no matter, no confidence." He probably didn't even consider trying to support his wife and son at the poker table. The games were either too big for his bankroll or too small to matter, and in the bigger ones he could hardly count on a fair shuf-fle. On top of that, gambling was illegal in nearly all jurisdictions. Play-ing square poker as a regular job would have been almost unthinkable.

He finally hit on the idea of a publishing a memoir about his years as a code-breaking spy. After failing to find a ghostwriter, he took a cheap room in Manhattan, rented a typewriter, bought five hundred sheets of paper, and—nothing. "I could do no more than stare into space. For days I pecked out a few lines and threw them into the fire," he admitted to his agent, George Bye. "I utterly detested the job of writing what seemed to me to be one of America's greatest episodes. All that I had done in life had been done well. I had in my possession hundreds of letters testifying to my ability as decoder of cryptograms. But I knew nothing about writing. . . . You cannot know what it means to sit before a typewriter with a tremendous story with no training, no craftsmanship to tell it." Yet his growing desperation spurred him to write by the seat of his pants. He screwed his rear end to the sticking place and knocked out the book in five months.

The American Black Chamber was published in 1931. At forty-two, Yardley had lost most of his hair, and his author photo has him resembling Dwight Eisenhower, one year his junior. Recounting his adventures as head of MI-8, the book dished up juicy details of code breaking, spy catching, wireless and cable interception, secret inks, midnight liaisons. An American bestseller, it was quickly translated into French, Swedish, and Japanese. In Washington, however, the book was considered such a betrayal of intelligence methods that many accused Yardley of treason. While no formal charges were brought, he became persona non grata in military and diplomatic circles. Some officers loathed him so intensely that despite his potential value during a war with Germany or Japan, he was blacklisted from all intelligence jobs. Yardley did his best to defend himself, insisting his motives were patriotic and that he was responsible for turning "intelligence into a significant instrument of war, no longer mistrusted by but accepted and even welcomed by admirals, generals, and statesmen," if not by Henry Stimson.

Even Kahn extends him little sympathy on this issue. He does point out that Yardley "never sold information to Japan or to anybody else, and he never worked against the United States," but adds that he "cheated by working for himself while being paid by the government. Later, he was indeed a hired gun, an opportunist, and he breached the trust his country had placed in him when he published his book. The action was despicable. It was rightly castigated by many people. But it cannot be characterized as treason. Yardley was a rotter, not a traitor." Kahn's more subtly damning conclusion is that Yardley "sold his soul for his book." Being ostracized by former colleagues bruised him to his core, and he never fully recovered his confidence and equilibrium. And the worst was yet to come.

Not surprisingly, the Japanese edition sold like Sapporo in hell. The downside was that it shamed the Imperial military into upgrading its codes and cipher systems. It soon developed an Enigma-type machine code-named "Red," then an even more sophisticated device, called "Purple" by American spies, to encrypt its most sensitive messages.

To escape some of the withering scrutiny he was under in Washington and New York, Yardley moved back to Worthington, where he tried to capitalize on his notoriety by founding Major Yardley's Secret Ink, Inc. While mixing an experimental batch of the stuff he cut his right hand on a shard of glass, and the ensuing infection resulted in his middle finger being amputated. Had the patron saint of intelligence agents mailed him a coded fuck-you? Whether or not it was karmic comeuppance, Yardley remained fairly cheerful about it, signing his letters "Three-Fingered HOY." Ever adaptive, he began smoking with his left hand and learning to type and to peel up hole cards with what was left of the other.

Infected by the writing bug, too, Yardley churned out—with help from two ghostwriters—three pulpy spy novels, *The Blonde Countess*, *Red Sun of Nippon*, and *Crows Are Black Everywhere*, along with radio plays and books of puzzles. *Yardleygrams* collected five stories designed to teach the reader how to decipher cryptographic messages. But none of these sold very well, and the profits from his invisible-ink business remained themselves undetectable. He needed another way to cash in.

As war between the United States and Japan loomed larger during the thirties, Yardley put together a 970-page manuscript titled "Japanese Diplomatic Secrets," hoping to fashion it into a second bestseller. Though his publisher turned down the project, the State Department got wind of it and procured a carbon copy of the manuscript. Upon reading it, the senior Far East adviser warned, "In view of the state of excitement which apparently prevails in Japanese public opinion now, characterized by fear or enmity toward the United States, every possible effort should be made to prevent the appearance of this book." The army dispatched two captains to Worthington to demand that Yardley turn over all government documents in his possession. Thomas E. Dewey, the chief assistant U.S. attorney, acting in concert with the army chief of staff, Douglas MacArthur, informed Yardley's old nemesis Henry Stimson, who was now secretary of war, that the manuscript was "as bad as it could be, just the kind of thing which might be more than the Japanese could stand." It was seized under the Espionage Act of 1917, and Senate and House members met to orchestrate a bill to suppress it. After several revisions, HR 4220, "For the Protection of Government Records," was given to the Judiciary Committee. In part it said, "Whoever shall willfully, without authorization or competent au-

thority, publish or furnish to another any matter prepared in any official code . . . shall be fined not more than $10,000 or imprisoned not
more than ten years, or both."

Among the hundreds of new bills designed to raise America from the
depths of the Depression, few were given higher priority than quashing
Yardley's project. The Judiciary Committee requested its enactment "at
the earliest possible date." After a series of back-and-forth amendments
making sure freedom of the press would not be compromised, the bill
passed both chambers and was enthusiastically signed by President
Roosevelt on June 10, 1933, as Public Law 37. Yardley called it the "gag
bill" and wrote a magazine article about it, but his agent wisely advised
against publishing even that. "I think everybody is pretty well convinced you are a devil-may-care human being. To that impression I
should not like to have added that you are thumbing your nose at con-
stituted authority." There it was. Yardley was finished not only as a
cryptanalyst but also as a writer about those experiences.

It was at this rock-bottom point that Louis B. Mayer suddenly decided he needed the author of *The American Black Chamber* to help develop a Myrna Loy espionage comedy for Metro-Goldwyn-Mayer, one
that would build on the successes of Greta Garbo in *Mata Hari* and
Marlene Dietrich in *Dishonored*. Yardley's agent wired the details in the
telegraphese with which his client had long been familiar: "MGM offered me ten thousand dollars American Black Chamber and Blonde
Countess This is absolutely best I can do STOP Guarantee of ten
weeks at two fifty a week Transportation both ways Please confirm acceptance."

He did. Moving with Hazel into an MGM bungalow, he began work
on an in-progress script involving—what else?—the solution of a cryptogram concerning the whereabouts of German U-boats attacking
American troopships in 1918. His job was to evaluate the plausibility of
certain scenes and sketch a few new ones explaining the technicalities of
wavelength, transposition, and direction finders. Warming to the Hollywood ethos, he drafted a scene in which the hero visits "one of the numerous intimate expensive dancing joints that sprang up in all the
capitals," where he dances with a "cutie." It was also his idea to call the
film *Rendezvous*. Mayer had planned to pair Loy with William Powell,
but when Loy held out for more money, the female lead went to Ros-
alind Russell, whose spy lingo Yardley got to coach—a rather delicious
assignment. Newspaper ads featured the tagline, "He could solve the

most intricate puzzle—unless it was dressed in skirts." The reviewer for *The New York Times* was impressed: "With sleek banter and that blend of bored nonchalance and razored shrewdness that make him one of our most attractive performers, [William Powell] introduces us to the counter-espionage manoeuvres described by Major Herbert O. Yardley in 'The American Black Chamber.'" Though a dozen other writers were involved, screenplay credit went to Sam and Bella Spewack. The publicity kit mentioned *The Blonde Countess* but not the more controversial *Black Chamber*, though the credits say the film was based on Yardley's nonfiction bestseller.

No writer understood the studios' collaborative and crediting practices better than the legendary Chicago journalist and Hollywood script doctor Ben Hecht, who won an Oscar in 1929 for *Underworld* and another in '37 for *The Scoundrel*. "Movies were seldom written," Hecht said. "They were yelled into existence in conferences that kept going in saloons, brothels and all-night poker games." Such locations suited writers like Yardley and Hecht to a T—or a P. Another way Yardley's experience was typical was that after returning from Hollywood in 1937, he and Hazel separated. Within weeks he was living with his longtime lover, Edna Ramsaier. He had hired Ramsaier as a sixteen-year-old typist on his MI-8 staff back in 1920, but she'd since developed into an effective cryptologist in her own right. They were married in Reno on August 29, 1944.

Paying alimony to Hazel and having saved almost no movie loot, Yardley wrote an unproducible play and a novel his publisher flatly rejected. So when an offer came from Generalissimo Chiang Kai-shek to decipher Japanese messages during the second Sino-Japanese War, Yardley leaped at the chance to get back to code breaking. For this ultrasecret mission of espionage, he'd be paid $10,000 per year. Besides the handsome salary, he was motivated by his desire to help avenge the Rape of Nanking, in which as many as three hundred thousand Chinese noncombatants were slaughtered, by his rage over the Japanese sinking of the USS *Panay*, and, worse, the strafing of its lifeboats in December 1937. Like many Americans, he was amazed that President Roosevelt had responded with no more than a letter of protest.

Yardley sailed to Hong Kong by way of Gibraltar, Suez, Bombay, and Singapore, then up the Yangtze fourteen hundred miles to Chungking, the headquarters of the Nationalist government. His cover in China was as "Herbert Osborn," a merchant of skins and hides. While his real job was to teach the Nationalists how to break the Imperial codes, he first had to break one himself. Here Kahn provides a brilliantly incisive account of the sorts of things Yardley picked up on:

> While studying a series of kana [syllabic script] messages transmitted every day at 6 a.m., noon, and 6 p.m., he noticed that of the forty-eight kana only ten were used, perhaps representing numerals, and that the messages were extremely repetitious in format, perhaps therefore meteorological. He arbitrarily converted the kana into figures and studied them. His team's rough direction-finding indicated that the messages were being sent from near Chungking and Yardley concluded that the first group of all the messages, 027, stood for *Chungking*. He further observed that all the messages sent at 6 a.m. had, as their second group, 231, those sent at noon, 248, and those at 6 p.m. 627. The third group in nearly all the messages was 459—except for a message of noon that day, where it was 401. Yardley noted that the light rain of several days had cleared at noon and he concluded that 459 meant *rain* and 401 *fair weather*. It was 1 p.m. He called in his Chinese liaison officer and told him that he believed Chungking would be bombed that afternoon. While he was explaining his analysis, the sirens wailed. Yardley's reputation was made.

The passage allows us to watch Yardley think like a poker maestro as he studied both the cards and the player across from him. Exercising his keen deductive facility, he made strong leaps of insight between numbers and kana, weather and bombers. Like the English major he almost became, he translated script into numbers, numbers into words, and words into meteorological patterns and military game plans, much as he (or we) might interpret a raise in light of a physical tic combined with a glitch in a betting pattern. His work in China was a mature blend of the reads he'd been making since he learned five-card draw from his grandfather, Morse code from his father, and serious poker from Monty, together with what he had taught himself while managing MI-8.

"Osborn" meanwhile was pursuing dangerous liaisons with Chinese and German women and cleaning up in seven-card stud games with expats, double agents, and journalists, including Emily Hahn of *The New Yorker* and Theodore White of *Time*. White called Yardley "an extremely witty man" whose stories of "his bearded grandfather who was a Union veteran" made it seem "wonderfully adventurous to all of us that he should now be here in the mysterious Orient cracking Japanese radio codes for Chiang Kai-shek." Hahn wrote that "everyone knew his real name" and wondered "if he tells his friends the things he used to tell us while playing poker."

When "Osborn" called the bluff of a Brit in a massive pot, the man resentfully exposed his identity. "I'll play with you no more!" the bluffer said, before pausing ominously; then he curled his lips and sneered, "Major Herbert Osborn *Yardley*?" Once word of this got around, Axis counterespionage agents were able to use Yardley's bald head and missing finger to confirm the ID. "I became a marked man in the Orient," he wrote. Anthony Holden has called the Yardley of this period "a proto–James Bond," though at eighty pounds over his high school playing weight, he was more likely to be played by Alfred Hitchcock than by Daniel Craig.

In jeopardy now from Japanese and German assassins, he needed to get back to the States. The Chinese were naturally eager to retain his services, so they stalled with the necessary paperwork while leaning on him to stay the course. When they told him he couldn't board a flight out of the country without approval from on high, Yardley bluffed. If they didn't give him clearance, he said, he would arrive at the airport with a newspaperman and the attaché—in other words, he'd reveal to the world what his job was and what he had learned. And it worked.

Either that or he hadn't been bluffing.

26

THE SECRETARY, THE PRESIDENT, HIS WIFE, AND HER LOVER

> Expert diplomatic poker player that he was, Molotov gave [Ribbentrop] no sign of being in a hurry.
>
> —WILLIAM L. SHIRER,
> *THE RISE AND FALL OF THE THIRD REICH*

To unwind after his grueling days managing a depression and then a world war, Franklin Roosevelt hosted a nightly cocktail hour in his second-floor study. "How about another sippy?" he would ask from his wheelchair before splashing together martinis and old-fashioneds amid the clutter of his desk. Though he seldom had more than one drink, he relished this downtime for the chance it gave him and his staff to recharge their batteries, the better to face the mind-bending decisions the next day would certainly bring. A simple dinner would often be served, followed a few times a week by a game of low-stakes poker.

Eleanor Roosevelt adamantly refused to participate in any gambling game, let alone one whose object was to mislead opponents in order to take their money; nor had she shared Franklin's bed since discovering his love affair with Lucy Mercer back in 1918. The cocktails and poker were organized by presidential secretary Marguerite "Missy" LeHand, whose third-floor bedroom was directly above FDR's. In *No Ordinary*

Time, her superb account of the home front during World War II, Doris Kearns Goodwin reports that "Missy was in love with her boss and regarded herself as his other wife. Nor was she alone in her imaginings." According to senior adviser Eliot Janeway, "In terms of companionship, Missy was the real wife." As to Roosevelt's paralysis, biographer Joseph Persico has discovered that three eminent physicians "found 'no symptoms of impotentia coeundi.' In plain English, he could sustain an erection." Even the Roosevelts' son Elliott seemed to accept that Missy and his father were lovers. "Everyone in the closely knit inner circle of father's friends accepted it as a matter of course."

Regulars in the poker games included Missy and her boss, advisers Harry Hopkins and General Edwin "Pa" Watson, Interior Secretary Harold Ickes, Treasury Secretary Henry Morgenthau, Admiral Ross McIntire (the president's physician), press secretary Stephen Early, Supreme Court Justice William O. Douglas, Attorney General Robert Jackson, and Eleanor's intimate friend Lorena Hickok, a cigar-smoking AP reporter whose bedroom adjoined the first lady's. "I wish I could lie down beside you tonight & take you in my arms," Eleanor wrote in one of the thousands of letters the women exchanged. Their most explicit letters were burned, though not the one in which Hickok wrote, "I remember your eyes, with a kind of teasing smile in them, and the feeling of that soft spot just northeast of the corner of your mouth against my lips." Whatever Kenneth Starr might think of these domestic arrangements, it's clear that neither Hickok nor LeHand required a poker nom de guerre.

Admiral McIntire always insisted that the game end by eleven o'clock so his patient could get enough sleep, though the commander in chief was sometimes able to cajole the admiral into letting him play an extra forty-five minutes or so. When the deal rotated to him, the president usually chose either seven-card stud with the one-eyed jacks wild or Woolworth's, in which fives and tens were wild. The limits were so low that Jackson lost only $2.30 during a weeklong fishing trip in Florida, even though he, the president, and four others played every night. Roosevelt was that week's biggest winner, netting a grand total of $18. On weekends back in Washington, the action often moved to Ickes's Maryland estate, where privacy was easier to come by and the food was much better. (Hemingway called White House cuisine during Roosevelt's tenure "the worst I've ever eaten. We had rainwater soup followed by rubber squab, a nice wilted salad and a cake some admirer had sent in. An enthusiastic but unskilled admirer.") The most expensive poker session at Ickes's home was a $1-limit affair in which Ickes won $53.50 and the president lost $35.

Which was just fine with the millionaire president, who overruled requests to raise the stakes. He wanted to relax, not lose or win anything but trivial sums. Jackson observed that for Roosevelt poker "was a pastime, not a passion," for whom the games were "an exchange of much conversation but little money." General Watson accepted this policy but insisted they abide by "the Powder River rules," which called for him to shoot any player who announced his hand incorrectly. Amid such jocularity, Roosevelt "studied the players as much as he did the cards," though Jackson believed Admiral McIntire was the most skilled of the bunch.

That opinion was colored by the fact that one of the toughest players in Washington at the time, Vice President John Nance "Cactus Jack" Garner, was seldom if ever invited to Roosevelt's games. The son of a Confederate cavalry trooper, Garner (1868–1967) had grown up playing high-stakes draw amply lubricated by bourbon and branch water. He represented his Texas congressional district in the House of Representatives for thirty years, rising to Speaker in 1931. During most of those years, his poker winnings exceeded his congressional salary. As vice president, he dismissed his boss's games as "just for conversation," failing to grasp how necessary they were for exactly that reason.

The fact was, the two men got along poorly on a number of fronts. FDR had invited Garner onto the ticket in 1932 only to reward him for delivering his delegates from Texas and California on the fourth ballot of the Democratic convention in Chicago. Though Garner later called running for vice president "the worst damn fool mistake I ever made" and the job itself "not worth a bucket of warm piss," his legislative experience and personal friendship with scores of congressmen were crucial in getting key New Deal initiatives passed during the administration's first hundred days. But his enthusiasm for the "second New Deal" cooled considerably when, during their second term, FDR pushed for programs that Garner thought smacked of class warfare, and he made sure they didn't get passed. He liked it even less when the president tried to pack the Supreme Court by increasing the number of justices. Roosevelt dumped Garner from the 1940 ticket and, with Henry Wallace as his running mate, went on to win his third term. Having challenged FDR in the Democratic primaries, Garner retired to his ranch in Uvalde. He later became a friend and adviser to both Truman and Kennedy. On November 22, 1963, just before his motorcade left the Dallas airport, JFK called Garner to wish him a happy ninety-fifth birthday. Upon his death at the age of ninety-eight, Garner was described as the last public man linking "America of the Civil War and America of the Nuclear Age."

New Deal, of course, was the poker term FDR had attached to his wide-ranging series of federal programs designed to help the "forgotten man at the bottom of the economic pyramid" make it through the Depression. *How to Win at Stud Poker*, that 1938 primer by James Wickstead, had a similar sense of morality. Wickstead was writing for players looking for convivial entertainment, not stacks of loot. The goal was playing well, not cleaning out your tablemates, most of whom were your friends. Cheating them would be unimaginable—certainly not in the spirit of the popular president.

"Establish a strict limit," Wickstead advised, "either for bet sizes or the total amount a player can lose for the evening." Either type of restriction would act "as a 'governor' and is more consonant with equity and fairness." Lower limits, he said, besides being more fair, made it easier to play good poker. "Oftentimes a player's game is ruined due to the fact that . . . the limit is too steep to permit a free and easy style of play." Worse, the player "loses his ability to diagnose the simplest hands and, as a consequence, becomes prey to fear," when the only thing he should have to fear, of course, is fear itself.

Not that the players in the low-limit White House games didn't want to win. Goodwin provides an example of how competitive FDR and his pals were:

> It was the president's custom each year on the night that Congress was due to adjourn to host a poker game in his study. . . . Whoever was ahead at the moment the Speaker called to say that Congress had officially adjourned would be declared the winner. On this night Morgenthau was far ahead when the Speaker phoned, but Roosevelt pretended that the call was from someone else and the game continued until midnight, when Roosevelt finally pulled ahead. At this point, Roosevelt whispered to an aide to go into another office and call the study. When the phone rang, he pretended it was the Speaker and declared himself the winner. Every-

one was in high spirits until the next morning, when Morgenthau read in the paper that Congress had officially adjourned at 9 p.m. He was so angry that he handed in his resignation. Only when the president called and convinced him it was all in good fun did Morgenthau agree to stay.

Yet anyone who thinks the nickel-ante poker and related shenanigans were merely good fun should consider their underlying purpose—to help the crippled president decompress with friends every night after dealing with the Depression and, in his third and fourth terms, the most devastating war the world has ever known. Even as "matters in Europe became constantly blacker" in August 1939, Jackson observed that Roosevelt "seemed to relax under the stimulus of the game and for the moment we forgot the war."

His teetotaling counterpart in Berlin, on the other hand, had few if any friends and refused to take a break from his responsibilities. As Goodwin put it, "While Roosevelt continually renewed his energies through relaxation, Adolf Hitler diminished his strength through overwork." Joseph Goebbels, the minister for propaganda, wrote in his diary: "The Fuhrer seems to have aged 15 years during three and a half years of war. He does not relax. He sits in his bunker, fusses and broods." Minister for Armaments Albert Speer believed Hitler's failure to relax left him "permanently caustic and irritable," much less effective in managing the Wehrmacht. The Hitler biographer John Toland tells us that even before he started the war, the fuhrer had developed "severe stomach cramps, insomnia and eczema" to go with his "meteorism, uncontrollable farting, a condition aggravated by his vegetarianism." Such conditions only got worse as the Allies advanced into Europe. "I have to relax before [bed] and talk about other things," Hitler told Erwin Giesing, his latest doctor. "If not, I see before me in the dark the General Staff maps and my brain keeps working. It takes hours before I can get rid of such visions. . . . I know where every single division stands—and so it goes on and on for hours until I fall asleep around five or six. I know this is not good for my health but I can't change my habits." When Giesing insisted that he rest in bed for at least a week, the patient flatly refused, shrieking, "You have all conspired among you to make a sick man out of me!"

While the American commander in chief relaxed playing Woolworth's for a couple of dollars a pot, GIs were carrying poker to Europe, North

Africa, China, the Pacific, and finally Japan. The American blender that the British captain Geoffrey "Pirate" Prentiss uses to make his famous banana pancake batter in the opening scene of *Gravity's Rainbow* was won from a Yank in a poker game. The United States Playing Card Company secretly worked with the Defense Department to make special decks to be sent as gifts for POWs. When the cards were moistened, they peeled apart to reveal sections of a map indicating escape routes out of Germany. Other cards, called "spotters," showed the silhouettes of enemy tanks, ships, and aircraft. On many of the thirty million regular decks issued by Allied pursers and quartermasters, FDR was depicted as the king of diamonds, Churchill the king of spades, Stalin the king of hearts, de Gaulle the king of clubs; Hitler, as the joker, had a bomb dropping onto his head.

The general in charge of most of those troops, Dwight D. Eisenhower, had learned to play poker as an eight-year-old back in Abilene. His main teacher was a frontiersman and hunting guide named Bob Davis, who also showed him how to hunt, fish, trap, and cook what he killed. Once the meal was finished and the utensils were clean, Davis made young "Ike" memorize poker odds. "He dinned percentages into my head night after night around a campfire," Ike wrote decades later, "using for the lessons a greasy pack of nicked cards that must have been a dozen years old. We played for matches and whenever my box of matches was exhausted, I'd have to roll in my blankets and go to sleep." As a West Point upperclassman in 1915, he attended "cadet dances only now and then, preferring to devote my time to poker." During World War I, he paid for his dress uniform and courted the hard-to-get Mamie Doud with his winnings. Sitting down in one game with only two silver dollars, he stood up a few hours later with more than a hundred of them, allowing the impoverished second lieutenant from the wilds of Abilene to compete for a wealthy debutante out of the Denver society pages. Among the fancy meals and gifts he lavished on Mamie was her engagement ring. A replica of his West Point class ring, it was an amethyst set in gold that she accepted from him on Valentine's Day, 1916.

Eisenhower was not only skillful at poker, he was also dedicated to keeping the game honest. While stationed at Camp Colt in Pennsylvania in 1917, he learned that a well-connected junior officer had used a marked deck in a stud game. Captain Eisenhower told him to either resign or face a court-martial. The officer chose the former option but reneged even on that. He returned to the base with his father and congressman, who requested that the cheater be transferred to a new post instead. Eisenhower firmly explained that no officer could be effective in the field without personal integrity, and that transferring the culprit would merely be passing the problem along to other soldiers. That was something he wasn't going to do. A more senior officer eventually greased the way for the transfer, but Eisenhower had stood his ground on this principle.

While stationed at Ford Meade under Colonel George Patton, Captain Eisenhower continued to dominate the action among his fellow officers. Their highest-stakes game was reserved for bachelors and married men who could comfortably afford to lose. One player who flouted this rule wound up losing so much to Ike that he was forced to cash in his wife's war bonds to make good on his IOU. Eisenhower reluctantly accepted payment but felt so guilty afterward that he conspired with others in the game to lose the money back to the man. "This was not achieved easily," Eisenhower recalled decades later. "One of the hardest things known to man is to make a fellow win in poker who plays as if bent on losing every nickel." He then persuaded his friend Colonel Patton to immediately ban poker at the fort, if only to keep the same fellow from squandering any more money. The sour experience was enough to persuade Eisenhower that, as an officer, "I had to quit playing. It was not because I didn't enjoy the excitement of the game—I really love to play. But it had become clear that it was no game to play in the Army."

As the supreme Allied commander in 1944, Eisenhower outfoxed the Nazis on D-day with a variety of bluffing maneuvers before taking Normandy Beach. Stephen Ambrose writes in *D-Day* that before the assault "dummy paratroopers dropped by the SAS convinced some German commanders that the whole operation was a bluff." He also reports that as Allied soldiers and sailors prepared for the invasion, gambling "was the favorite boredom killer. There were virtually non-stop poker and crap games." Hemingway, Irwin Shaw, the photographer Robert Capa, Don Whitehead of the Associated Press, and many other correspondents played poker along with the troops. Shaw wrote that while the Luftwaffe was bombing London, "It was considered very bad form indeed to hesitate before placing a bet or to move away from the table, no matter how close the hits or how loud the anti-aircraft fire."

Some of the eleventh-hour action became rather frenzied, "like nothing I'd ever seen before," one Canadian sapper recalled. "There was no use in holding back, nothing made any difference, bet the lot. When officers came around they would sort of cover the money with the blankets they were playing on." *Nothing made any difference, bet the lot*—probably what William Gill had been thinking when he lost his gold watch before the mustard gas wafted over his trench in 1918, and what many blue- and gray-coated infantrymen had felt before each blood-soaked melee.

On June 5, 1944, the night before D-day, Pfc. Felix Branham of the 116th Infantry tried to get everyone on his ship to sign a five-hundred-franc note he'd won in a poker game. Asked why, he said, "Fellas, some of us are never getting out of this alive. We may never see each other again. We may be crippled, or whatever. So sign this." Fifty years later, Branham still had the framed note hanging on his wall, and insisted, "I wouldn't take *anything* for it."

Struggling to describe the brotherhood that developed among the crew of his B-17, the *Memphis Belle*, pilot Robert Morgan said, "I don't know that anybody has ever invented a word that fits what I'm trying to say. Our crew sure as hell never tried to describe it. It was too sacred to have a name, so we played poker and drank whiskey instead." Whatever combination of skill and emotion they shared, nothing conveyed or complemented it better than a few well-timed bluffs and some booze. Morgan added that "it was a way of setting fear aside, and it was inter-dependence—a way of knowing at every instant under extreme duress what the other fellow's function was, and how he was handling it." When Hemingway spoke of a bullfighter's "grace under pressure," and Shaw of the refusal to flinch in the face of a bomb *or* a raise, they were talking about something similar. Part of the secret, as FDR knew, in-volved getting out from under the pressure on a regular basis, prefer-ably in the company of those you were sharing it with.

THE EDUCATION OF A
POKER PLAYER, PART 3

I never limp on the button, 1 off the button, in super high
ante structures, with high cards, when it is my birthday,
when I'm drunk and I could go on. Bottom line: I'm not a
big fan of limping.

— GUS HANSEN, *EVERY HAND REVEALED*

In early 1941, General Joseph Mauborgne, chief signal officer of the
U.S. Army, recommended that his counterparts in Canada, which had
declared war on Germany in 1939, hire Yardley to run their code-
breaking unit. Mauborgne described him as an expert cryptographer
and fine organizer who had "perhaps suffered unduly" for past mistakes. The Canadians took this advice. Relieved to be working for the
Allies again, Yardley and Edna moved to Ottawa. Between June and
December, Yardley built Canada's cryptographic bureau pretty much
from scratch, training its fledgling staff to decode messages intercepted
on their way to and from Germany and Japan. But a few days before the
December 7 attack on Pearl Harbor, the Canadians submitted to pressure to fire him from British and American surveillance officers who
were still angry about what he'd revealed in *The American Black Chamber*. A few newspaper columnists wrote in response that if Yardley
was still working for the United States, "the attack might never have
occurred."

George Bye interceded on Yardley's behalf with Eleanor Roosevelt, who was also Bye's client, but nothing came of it. Yardley was out once again, this time for good. Edna compared their retreat from Ottawa to Napoleon's from Moscow, "with both parties leaving in snow and defeat." Herb later found work building houses and hawking real estate in New York and Florida, but his heart wasn't in it. Kahn's opinion is, "Canada recovered. Yardley did not."

Not right away, at least. It wasn't until his retirement in the mid-1950s, when he and Edna were living in Silver Spring, Maryland, that he decided to write—by himself this time—what would be his final and most famous book. On November 9, 1957, when an excerpt called "Winning at Poker" was featured on the cover of *The Saturday Evening Post*, the issue broke its newsstand record by selling 5.6 million copies. Fed up with cardsharps, the *Post*'s vast middle-class readership was apparently hungry for lessons in tough, honest poker.

A week later the complete book, *The Education of a Poker Player*, was published. Yardley's editor told him that sales immediately took off "like one big-assed bird." A writer for *The New York Times Book Review* declared, "What Goren and Vanderbilt have done for the bridge player, Herbert O. Yardley has now done for the poker player. He has given us dignity, wisdom and philosophy." Three-fingered HOY had come a long way since being gagged by Public Law 37.

That the critical and commercial success of *The Education* occurred during the administration of another bald Midwestern draw player and a Quaker vice president who'd built his political bankroll in navy stud games could not have been entirely a coincidence. Millions of other vets had played the game in Europe, the Pacific, and later in Korea, and they brought it home with them to the affluent new suburbs springing up across the country. By 1957, the public was primed for a serious book about poker.

Most books before Yardley's were either tales of high-stakes action, usually ending with a sucker holding four kings losing everything, or straightforward primers about how to play squarely dealt hands. Part of what makes *The Education* so original is the way it braids racy memoir with rock-solid poker advice. The first half takes place in Worthington around 1906, the second half in China in the late thirties. Each chapter focuses on a particular variant: five-card draw, stud, deuces-wild, lowball, and both straight and high-low seven-card stud, with an afterword explaining less popular variants. Most of the dialogue involves the teenage Yardley receiving sage advice from Monty or, in the later chapters, the worldly spymaster giving similar advice to Ling Fan, his Chinese translator. Ling wants to improve his game without getting fired or executed by his dim-witted boss, who is known as "the Donkey." A big pot always develops in which the psychology of the players is thrown into high relief as the hand tensely plays out. Each chapter concludes with odds tables, a dozen or so sample hands, and a summary of tactical pointers.

Yardley reports that the only "clean" game in Worthington was run by his old mentor, James Montgomery. In 1905, Monty and sixteen-year-old Herb watch a hand of deuces-wild in which an elderly Swedish corn farmer, Bones Alverson, bets the last quarter of his farm against an itinerant theater producer, who wagers a tent show. Bones wins the hand but dies of a heart attack from the excitement while clutching his cards Hickok-style. Unlike the farmer Meredith's chest pains, Bones's were only too real. He bet the farm and won a traveling road show, just before *buying* the farm. Monty delivers the proceeds to Bones's widow. "She'll probably grieve for a couple of days," he says, "then be relieved that he's dead. At least he can't gamble the farm away now." Perhaps A-A-A-2-J, or any quad aces, for that matter, should henceforth be called Bones's Hand.

Yardley also writes of Jake Moses, a traveling salesman who lost ten trunks of shoes, and of players who lost and won horses, cattle, wagons, grain, sawmills, and farming implements. A banker is caught buying in with marked money he had stolen from the bank. The new owners of sawmills and grocery stores show up the next morning and explain to employees what happened. Poker and its open-stakes risks are sufficiently ingrained in the national mind-set by 1907 that such explanations make sense.

In one of the more intriguing asides, Monty claims that one of his favorite writers, Edgar Allan Poe, "was disinherited because of his poker debts." The fact is that Poe did lose $2,500 playing ecarte—a thirty-two-card French game for two players who bid and take tricks—as a freshman at the University of Virginia in 1826. The incident was the catalyst for one of his creepiest tales of Gothic horror, "William Wilson," which concerns cheating at ecarte. Yet none of Poe's numerous biographers mentions him playing poker, and his poems and tales contain not a shred of evidence that he was familiar with the newer American pastime. Monty's cautionary point about poker debt is well taken, but a Poe tale young Herb might have found even more instructive is "The Gold-Bug," which depends on the solution of a cryptogram.

Late in the China section, Yardley provides a suspenseful account of his time under threat of assassination. Moving around incognito, he tracks down a Nazi spy while coaching Ling on seven-card-stud tactics. In a big pot in Hong Kong, he confidently outplays a snobby British "plunger" by counting how many diamonds are out. "Most persons successful in cryptology have what is known as a photographic mind; otherwise they could not retain . . . the long sequences of code words and letters which must be remembered if the cipher is to be unraveled. This is not memory," he adds, "it is mental photography. Without effort I could name every diamond that had been dealt."

Showing a board of four diamonds, the plunger raises Yardley "five thousand Chinese," obviously representing a flush. "Too much?" he sneers.

"Not too much if you didn't make the fifth diamond," Yardley tells him coolly. "And I don't think you did. There's only one diamond left, and unless you have a horseshoe concealed somewhere, you didn't catch it." Holding a straight, Yardley calls. "Because of his insolence I dragged the money in even before he turned his hole cards." The plunger is so enraged that he spitefully blows Yardley's cover. The scene is also instructive to hold'em players who may have forgotten, if they ever knew to begin with, how important memory is while playing seven-stud. If they hope to succeed at H.O.R.S.E., the latest gold standard of poker excellence, Part Two of *The Education* can provide some valuable pointers.

Yardley's general strategy is to minimize risk at all costs. "I do not believe in luck," he writes, "only in the immutable law of averages." As for tactics: "Assume the worst, believe no one, and make your move only when you are certain that you are unbeatable or have, at worst, exceptionally good odds in your favor." He also declines to sit in any game "unless there are at least three suckers" playing.

Not surprisingly, he came to be known as Old Adhesive, presumably because he was too "sticky" to give action without a huge starting hand. As David Sklansky would describe a similar approach in *The Theory of Poker*, "A good player develops the patience to wait for the right situations to play a pot and the discipline to release a hand he judges to be second-best." Yardley, if anything, had even less gamble in him than Sklansky recommends. Yardley's squeaky-tight approach would often be outplayed by today's top-notch pros. They'd steal his antes, fold when he bet, attack whenever low cards appeared on his board. And if

Yardley had learned to play hold'em, he probably wouldn't take enough risks to be a consistent winner in no-limit tournaments. But in pot-limit ring games against undisciplined amateurs in the first half of the previous century, his rocky approach seems to have served him quite well. Millions of his readers have felt well served by it, too.

The Education broke ground for the anecdotal advice of Doyle Brunson and other *Super System* contributors, Barry Greenstein's *Ace on the River*, several books coauthored by Tom McEvoy and T. J. Cloutier (especially the latter's often violent "Tales"), Dan Harrington's wittily quantitative breakdowns of no-limit hold'em strategy, Phil Gordon's debonair primers, Gus Hansen's funny and informative *Every Hand Revealed*, and Daniel Negreanu's *Power Hold'em Strategy*, the Bible of the small-ball approach.

Yardley's book can also be enjoyed for its do-or-die showdowns and worldly philosophy. One British edition included a foreword by Ian Fleming, who wrote of its "smoke-filled pages" containing "a hatful of some of the finest gambling stories I had ever read." He accurately predicted it "would certainly become a classic." An introduction by Al Alvarez emphasized its personal or existential qualities. Alvarez said it helped him grow up, and not just as a poker player.

> I had a marriage I could not handle, a childish desire to be loved by the whole world, and an equally childish conviction that everything would turn out all right in the end. When it didn't I was—simply and profoundly—outraged. I had lived my life as I had played poker, recklessly and optimistically, all my cards open on the table and nothing in reserve. I had also assumed that everybody else was doing the same. I was wrong, of course, and it was about the time I began to realize this that I first read Yardley. . . . What applied so cogently to money in a poker pot applied equally to the feelings I had invested in my disastrous personal affairs: "Do the odds favor my playing regardless of what I have already contributed?" I knew the answer. The only puzzle was why I should have discovered it not in Shakespeare or Donne or Eliot or Lawrence or any of my other literary heroes, but in a funny, vivid, utterly unliterary book by an American cryptographer and intelligence agent. It was the beginning of my real education and I sometimes wonder if that was what Yardley, too, was implying with his title. In the end, what he is describing is not so much a game of cards as a style of life.

Given his parochial beginnings, Yardley turned into a fairly representative man of the first half of the twentieth century. He drank, smoked, played poker, chased skirts, failed and succeeded in a variety of careers, and was honored and shunned while serving in three major wars. He may have sold invisible ink, but he chose to play poker on the level and encouraged his readers to do the same. Like John von Neumann's game theory during the cold war (the subject of Chapter 29), Yardley's pokeraticious logic informed what he did for the military. In his code-breaking work and his books, he unpacked the subtly expedient ways both poker players and intelligence operatives think. As Western democracies struggle to decode Al Qaeda videotapes, jihadi websites, and billions of Internet messages, we could clearly use several thousand more "cipher brains" to translate Arabic word patterns and separate orders from bluffs.

Unlike *The American Black Chamber*, Yardley's poker bestseller cost him no job opportunities; it brought him nothing but royalty checks and prestige. The trouble was that he had only a year to enjoy them. He died on August 7, 1958, a few days after suffering a stroke. Buried with honors at Arlington National Cemetery, he was later inducted into the Military Intelligence Hall of Fame. Though his reputation and influence far surpass those of several members of the Poker Hall of Fame, he has yet to be enshrined there, in spite of the fact that, more than anyone else, Herb Yardley helped usher in the age of square poker.

THE BUCK STOPS WITH VINSON—
OR WINSTON

> Of course no childhood is without its terrors, yet I wonder if
> I would have been a less frightened boy if Lindbergh hadn't
> been president or if I hadn't been the offspring of Jews.
> —PHILIP ROTH, *THE PLOT AGAINST AMERICA*

As the 1944 election approached, the cardiologist treating Franklin Roosevelt for congestive heart failure believed that the president had less than a year to live. While the prognosis remained a closely guarded secret, ordinary citizens could see the darkness beneath Roosevelt's eyes and how badly his hands shook. With both fronts of the war still very much undecided, however, a majority of Americans hoped to retain their commander in chief. Yet if FDR was the favorite as he sought an unprecedented fourth term, the progressive politics of Vice President Henry Wallace had alienated too many Southern Democrats for him to be invited back on the ticket for this crucial election.

At the Democratic Convention in Chicago, most of the delegates and backroom pols correctly assumed they were choosing two presidents—the incumbent and the man who would succeed him before the war ended. But who would it be? Comparing his first choice, Justice William O. Douglas, to the longshot Harry S. Truman, FDR grumbled, "I hardly know Truman. Douglas is a poker partner. He is good in a poker game and tells good stories." Roosevelt was evidently unaware that the jovial Missouri senator loved spinning yarns and playing low-stakes poker with wild cards at least as much as Douglas did—or as FDR himself, for that matter. Even so, in the interests of compromise and party unity, the president allowed a few big-city bosses to maneuver delegates into nominating Truman for the vice presidential slot. In November they handily outpolled the Republican ticket of Thomas Dewey and John Bricker.

FDR was sworn in for his fourth term on January 20, 1945, the first wartime inauguration since Lincoln's in 1865. Eighty-two days later, Eleanor Roosevelt summoned Truman to the White House to tell him the president had died of a cerebral hemorrhage at the "Little White House" in Warm Springs, Georgia, where he'd been receiving polio treatments—and seeing both Missy LeHand and Lucy Mercer Rutherford—for years. At 7:09 p.m. on Thursday, April 12, 1945, Truman became the thirty-third president. When word reached Berlin, Joseph Goebbels cried ecstatically, "Bring out our best champagne!" before phoning Hitler to crow that the demise of the Churchill-Roosevelt juggernaut was a turning point "written in the stars."

Meanwhile, as the Allies pushed deeper into Germany and savage fighting continued across the Pacific, Secretary of War Henry Stimson informed the fledgling commander in chief about a radically new type of weapon at his disposal. The nuclear bomb was the product of the highly classified Manhattan Project, which Albert Einstein and others had urged FDR to create three years earlier. Its primary purpose was to counter Germany's nuclear program, which had discovered fission in 1938 and was working to produce its own bomb when Hitler committed suicide on April 30, 1945, causing every Nazi commander to surrender within a week. So much for Herr Goebbels's astrological forecast.

The Manhattan Project had relied heavily on the expertise of German and other European Jewish physicists—including Einstein, John von Neumann, Otto Frisch, Niels Bohr, Leo Szilard, and Edward Teller—who had fled to the United States and Britain as the Third Reich's anti-Semitism became overtly genocidal. (The first anti-Semitic law Hitler put in place had stripped all non-Aryan professors of their posts back in 1933. Extermination camps for the "Final Solution of the Jewish Question" began operating in 1942.) J. Robert Oppenheimer, the scientific director of the project who is often called the "Father of the Atomic Bomb," was born in New York City, but both of his parents were of German-Jewish extraction. It can certainly be argued that if the Fuhrer hadn't so loathed the Jews, and if he'd managed to relax and recuperate from time to time, as Roosevelt and Truman did, the Axis powers might have won World War II.

When Truman was sworn in, his poker buddies from the previous war were afraid he might stop playing now that he had been "promoted." They need not have worried. The new chief executive even requisitioned a set of chips embossed with the presidential seal for use in the White House, though he tried to avoid being photographed gambling on its premises, however tiny the stakes. The prudes of America would put up with only so much.

Truman had learned to play cards from his aunt Ida and uncle Harry on their Missouri farm back in the 1890s. In a letter to Bess Wallace, the woman he was courting, in February 1911, the sincere twenty-six-year-old suitor painted an accurate picture of himself. Even though he was religious, he wrote, "I like to play cards and dance . . . and go to shows and do all the things [religious people] say I shouldn't, but I don't feel badly about it."

In France seven years later, Lieutenant Truman played about as much poker as Carl Grothaus, Bill Gill, Herb Yardley, Ike Eisenhower, and a million other doughboys did while in Europe. Truman received further artillery training in Montigny-sur-Aube, mastering the specs and capabilities of a new French seventy-five-millimeter cannon called the "Devil Gun" by the Germans, though he also had time to play stud and tour the Burgundian countryside. Promoted to captain, he saw action with Battery D of the 129th Field Artillery in the Vosges Mountains. His horse was hit by an exploding German shell and rolled on top of its rider, who had toppled into the shell's crater. After being rescued by a burly lieutenant named Vic Householder, Captain Truman shocked Householder and the rest of his battery by unleashing a cascade of creatively violent profanity at the Germans. His men, and probably Truman himself, hadn't known he had words like that in him. But they all served effectively in the Meuse-Argonne offensive, which culminated in the biggest battle in history to that point, a gory Allied victory during which more firepower was expended in three hours than during the entire Civil War.

Waiting to sail home after the Armistice was signed in November, Truman and his comrades passed that autumn in the mud near Verdun, much of the time in poker games that went on for decades after they were demobilized. The collection of army gear preserved at the Truman Library includes three dog-eared poker decks. According to Harry Vaughan, a fellow officer in France who later served as the president's chief military aide, it delighted Truman to chase Vaughan "out of a hand and then show me that I had him beat; that was worth a month's pay. And he did it all too frequently."

As a judge back home in Independence, Truman kept up with his army buddies mainly around the poker table. Many sessions took place across the street from his courthouse in a third-floor room at 101 North Main Street. The eighteen regulars dubbed themselves the Harpie Club, after the harmonicas they played at memorial ceremonies, with Truman serving as their unofficial president. Played in the same convivial spirit as games in FDR's White House, Harpie Club action had a ten-cent limit with a three-raise cap, so very few pots amounted to more than a couple of dollars. Until Truman moved to Washington as a senator in 1935, he seldom missed a session, though he never took the results very seriously. Fellow Harpie Bruce Lambert called him a "chump" who called too many bets with weak hands. "He wanted to see what your hole card was, and knew anyone got a kick out of winning from him and he accommodated . . . but if he could whip you he got a big kick out of it."

Truman's preference for poker over fussier country-club pastimes helps explain the temperament of "Give 'Em Hell Harry" during American labor disputes, hot wars with Japan and North Korea, and the cold war with Russia and China. Even so, the game's long, often unfair association with other vices did not apply to Truman. In August 1945, he went to Potsdam to divide up control of Germany with Churchill and Stalin. The ravaged culture in and around that city made prostitutes easy to come by, and a brazen young army public relations officer, noticing that the president was on his way to dinner by himself one evening, told him that if there was anything he needed, the officer would be happy to procure it. "Anything, you know, like women."

"Listen, son," Truman told him. "I married my sweetheart. She doesn't run around on me, and I don't run around on her. I want that understood. Don't ever mention that kind of stuff to me again." Truman got out of the car they were in without saying goodbye to the officer.

Returning from Potsdam by sea, the commander in chief tried to relax in a weeklong stud game with journalists aboard the battleship *Augusta* while awaiting news of the device he had ordered to be detonated above Hiroshima, hoping to spare American troops from having to invade the Japanese mainland. Because Secretary of State James Byrnes bitterly differed with his boss about what to do next—and was not in the game—Merriman Smith, a UPI reporter who was, wrote that Truman "was running a straight stud filibuster against his own Secretary of State." Truman may also have used his tabletop rapport with "Smitty" and other journalists to court their approval after describing "in great detail the development of the atomic bomb and the forthcoming first drop on Hiroshima," wrote one of them. "Once this graphic secret was told to us for later publication, out came the cards and the chips."

After Japan surrendered, Truman and his poker cabinet often cruised the Potomac on weekends aboard the presidential yacht *Williamsburg*. "You know I'm almost like a kid," he told Bess before one such outing. "I can hardly wait to start." Regulars included General Harry Vaughan, Chief Justice Fred Vinson, Admiral William Leahy, Air Force Secretary Stuart Symington, and special counsel Clark Clifford. (Clifford was charged with organizing the games, replacing a naval aide who had told the president he didn't drink or play cards. Truman quickly found the man an excellent job somewhere else.) Shipboard meals were leisurely, with plenty of time for discussions of history and politics. But once the poker began, the stakes were dramatically higher than what Roosevelt's cabinet had played for. Truman's crew started with five hundred dollars in chips, with a one-time option to rebuy. Ten percent of each pot went into a "poverty bowl," a carryover from the Depression, to be distributed a hundred dollars at a time to players who'd lost their initial thousand.

By every account, Truman "loved wild games." According to Robert G. Nixon, an International News Service war correspondent, the president "knew some of the wildest games that I have ever heard of. I don't think you could find them any wilder. Some I even forgot because they were too complicated. There was one that I'll never forget. It was a seven-card game called 'seven card, low hole card wild, high low.'" Apparently, if you hold "a pair of deuces as low hole cards, nothing can undercut you. You are a very lucky man on that hand. If you have a pair of treys or a pair of anything else, and you have matching cards up, you may think that you have three or four wild cards, but the last card that's dealt down can turn out to be a deuce, undercutting the treys, and you're dead. Your hand is worthless." The reporter claimed to have lost large pots "with five kings and a seven, six low. That shows you how *hazardous* this game is and what you must know about it." But Nixon emphasized that such games were all in good fun, that losers were encouraged to replenish their stacks from large pots, and that poker was the president's "only means of relaxation—that and walking. Never did anything else. He never wanted anybody to get hurt in a poker game."

After Truman retired to Kansas City in 1953, he joined a game hosted on a rotating basis by Eddie Jacobson, his old haberdashery partner, and several of his other Jewish friends. One, the prudish A. J. Granoff, recalled that the ex-president would "lean over and look at my cards and say, 'I got you beat already.'" Truman, he said, also tried "to embarrass me by telling some off-color story, then claimed that I blushed. Maybe I did." When Jacobson joined in the teasing, Granoff would blush again, and Truman and Jacobson would both roar with laughter.

Another group of his Jewish friends played at the Oakwood Club. Randall Jessee, a television journalist, claimed the former president was playing as loosely as ever. "Truman just couldn't bear to fold; he wanted to be in to the end. He had a special weapon, though," Jessee said, "which he used to improve the odds. It was called 'Vinson' after his favorite poker companion from presidential days. It's low ball, high ball, I never did understand. He was pretty good at [it], because nobody else understood what we were doing." It was probably the same wild-card game that Nixon described. Each time the deal rotated to Truman, he'd say, "Well, we're going to play Vinson now."

Throughout his eighty-eight years, Truman used poker as both a personal and political means of expression. His motto, "The buck stops here," refers to the dealer's button or placeholder, because during the nineteenth century hunting knives with buckhorn handles often served that function. It was the president's folksy way of letting Americans know he was responsible for what happened on his watch—that he wouldn't "pass the buck" in tough situations. According to the Truman Library archivist Raymond Geselbracht, the president also loved the "vitality in the game that let him share in the lives of people he liked and see them as they really were, underneath whatever formalities they usually had to adopt when they dealt with a judge, senator, President, or former President. Poker also gave him a chance to make his friends happy in some small ways, which was very important to him."

That the game keeps friendly competitors elbow to elbow all evening is one of the reasons it has endured for so long. For Truman and his predecessor, it was a chance to drop the formality of office and kibitz with friends old and new. One of the most famous examples occurred on March 4, 1946, when Churchill joined Truman's game aboard FDR's old armored railroad car, the *Ferdinand Magellan*, for a trip to

Fulton, Missouri, where Churchill was to deliver his era-defining "Iron Curtain" speech.

"Mr. President," said the prime minister, sitting down, "I think that when we are playing poker I will call you Harry."

"All right, Winston," said Truman.

Churchill had downed five scotches before the action began, and now he pretended that he hadn't the foggiest idea how to play. "Harry," he said at one point, "I think I'll risk a couple of shillings on a pair of knaves."

Charlie Ross of the *St. Louis Post-Dispatch* wrote, "We played straight poker. The President and the rest of us would have liked to introduce some wild games, but the Prime Minister thought this would be too confusing." Worried about the reputation of American players, Truman had encouraged them to bring their A game. As the *Magellan* blasted through the heartland, Churchill lost steadily—so much, in fact, that when the great Brit left the table for a moment, Truman told his companions to let up a bit. "But, Boss, this guy's a pigeon," said General Vaughan. "If you want us to play our best poker for the nation's honor, we'll have this guy's pants before the evening is over." Whether or not they let up, Churchill was down $250 when he quit at 2:30 a.m. He needed to get some sleep before giving his speech.

"The United States stands at this time at the pinnacle of world power," he declared the next day. "It is a solemn moment for the American democracy. For with this primacy in power is also joined an awe-inspiring accountability to the future." Three paragraphs later he came to the crux: "From Stettin in the Baltic to Trieste in the Adriatic, an iron curtain has descended across the continent." The West, he continued, must never show weakness or fear in the face of the "Soviet sphere." Afterward, Truman told him the speech would "do nothing but good," though many Americans felt the old bulldog had poisoned the already difficult relationship we had with our other main ally. Eight days later Stalin branded the speech "a call to war," and the cold war was officially under way.

COLD WAR POKER

There's no sense in being precise when you don't even know
what you're talking about.

—JOHN VON NEUMANN

George Orwell first used the term "cold war" in his essay "You and
the Atomic Bomb" in October 1945, ten weeks after Nagasaki and a
year before publishing *Animal Farm*. The essay described a totalitarian
state much like the USSR "in a permanent state of 'cold war' with its
neighbours." As usual, Orwell foresaw what was coming before nearly
everyone else did. The Soviets wouldn't test an atomic device until
August 1949, but when their hydrogen bombs, designed by Andrei
Sakharov, were deployed in the early fifties, the nuclear arms race
heated up quickly. The cold war got colder and radically more perilous.

Two brilliant Jewish professors, John von Neumann and Oskar Morgenstern, helped the United States to eventually win both the race and
the war without a single nuclear shot being fired. Von Neumann was a
Budapest-born physicist and mathematician who had fled Nazi persecution in Germany in 1933. The newly founded Institute for Advanced
Study in Princeton, New Jersey, offered him an appointment alongside Kurt Gödel, Albert Einstein, George Kennan, and Robert Oppen-

heimer. It is difficult to imagine an academic program yielding more momentous yet practical benefits.

The seeds of one of its most fertile collaborations had been sown back in 1928, when von Neumann published "On the Theory of Parlor Games," an elegant, pathfinding paper inspired in large part by poker. The roots of game theory went back to the nineteenth-century economists Augustin Cournot and Francis Edgeworth. It was formally introduced in 1921 by Émile Borel, a French mathematician, who wrote about "*la théorie du jeu*" in a note about bluffing in poker. Seven years later, von Neumann independently arrived at game theory via much the same route. Zero-sum games of complete information, such as checkers and chess, failed to interest him. Why not? Because the correct move is always discernible by both players, leaving no room for deceit. Von Neumann was intrigued by the fact that poker strategy involves guile, probability, psychology, luck, and budgetary acumen but is never transparent; it always depends on the counterstrategies deployed by opponents. Experts misrepresent the strength of their hands, simulate irrational behavior, and deploy other mind games to confuse their opponents. In a nutshell, they bluff. The "Parlor Games" paper was, among other things, von Neumann's first serious attempt to express the tactic of bluffing in mathematical terms. But before he could follow through on its implications, he and his family had to escape the expanding reign of terror in Europe.

By the late thirties, however, this volcanically creative polymath was able to team up in Princeton with the economist Oskar Morgenstern to develop the "Parlor Games" theory. Morgenstern had found safe harbor at Princeton University after being purged by the Nazis from the University of Vienna. The two men first discussed games and economics with Einstein and Niels Bohr on February 1, 1939, at the Nassau Club. After becoming close friends and having lengthier conversations, Morgenstern and von Neumann decided to cowrite a fifty-page manuscript for the *Journal of Political Economy*. But as they bounced more ideas back and forth—with Morgenstern, as midwife, asking provocative questions, von Neumann doing the heavy mathematical lifting—the project mushroomed into *Theory of Games and Economic Behavior*, a seven-hundred-page magnum opus. Though publication was delayed by the wartime paper shortage, when the book appeared in 1946 it not only revolutionized economics and defense strategy but gave rise to a new field of scientific inquiry.

In spite of its fun-sounding moniker, game theory is an unplayful branch of economics in which ruthless self-interest governs every decision. Each kind of contest is expressed mathematically; its rules are defined and a game tree is drawn, from which solutions to winning logically proceed. In practical terms, game theory provides tools for analyzing situations in which players or countries try to make interdependent decisions with maximal utility. It was eventually used to analyze business models, poker hands, presidential candidates, evolutionary biology, and thermonuclear confrontations.

Meanwhile, and with terrible irony, von Neumann in 1943 had become an indispensable member of the ultrasecret Manhattan Project in Los Alamos, New Mexico, serving as a group leader in charge of designing the bomb. Among his most crucial inventions were a potent uranium isotope, the implosion method for causing nuclear fuel to explode, and a binary data-processing program called the "von Neumann machine." Today it is called the computer.

At the end of their eighty-hour workweeks, many of the scientists relaxed the same way Roosevelt and Truman did. The Ukrainian chemist George Kistiakowsky won money in these poker games not only from the inventor of game theory, but also from Stanislaw Ulam, Isidor Rabi, and other world-class mathematicians. Kistiakowsky said their play was so weak at first that he offered them lessons, pointing out that "if they had tried to learn violin playing, it would cost them even more per hour. Unfortunately, before the end of the war, these great theoretical minds caught on to poker and the evenings' accounts became less attractive from my point of view."

Unlike many of his fellow scientists, von Neumann got along famously with military men, especially the poker players among them. (He once told a Senate committee that his political ideology was "much more militaristic than the norm.") One fellow player was Leslie Groves, the no-nonsense general in charge of the entire Manhattan Project. Groves appointed von Neumann to the Target Committee advising the president on sites "the bombing of which would most adversely affect the will of the Japanese people to continue the war." The committee's first choice, Kyoto, was overruled by Secretary of War Henry Stimson, who had spent his honeymoon there. Herb Yardley's old nemesis convinced Truman that Kyoto's religious and cultural significance would be crucial to rebuilding that nation. We needed to make Japan our trading partner, Stimson argued, as well as a buffer against the Soviet Union. In his diary he called the bomb the "master card" in the great game of postwar diplomacy with China and Russia, as well as "a royal straight flush, and we mustn't be a fool about the way we play it."

Von Neumann had always found poker more lifelike than other games, its tactics gratifyingly similar to those deployed by generals, diplomats, and presidents. Indeed, this was probably what gave the fifty-two flimsy pasteboards their uncanny weight in the first place— not unlike plutonium 239, the "royal straight flush" of cold-warfare elements and the one we may still have to answer for.

Von Neumann certainly did. After V-J day he served as a military adviser to both Truman and Eisenhower, and as a member of the Atomic Energy Commission. He was credited with closing our "missile gap" with the Soviets by designing intercontinental ballistic missiles with multiple warheads, and with deterring attack with the game-theory-based strategy of mutual assured destruction. Known as MAD, it assumes neither side will launch a first strike because the other side would retaliate so comprehensively that the populations of both countries would be annihilated. Critics branded his counterintuitive doctrine "inhuman," and it apparently made von Neumann a model for Stanley Kubrick's mad Dr. Strangelove, portrayed with dark hilarity by Peter Sellers. Yet the fact is that MAD kept a single warhead from ever being launched, though a device from that era still might be detonated one day by a terrorist group.

Von Neumann was awarded the Medal of Freedom in 1956, a few months before dying of brain cancer. The harrowing malignancy was probably caused by inhaling plutonium at Los Alamos and/or being irradiated while observing his brainchild, the first man-made nuclear explosion, at Alamogordo Test Range on the Jornada del Muerto Desert on July 16, 1945.

Oskar Morgenstern also advised Eisenhower as the nuclear arms race threatened to spiral out of control. The poker tactics at the cold heart of game theory helped the war-weary president see his way through a variety of crises with the Soviets, when a single miscalculation by either side could have led to hundreds of millions of deaths. General Andrew J. Goodpaster had observed Eisenhower up close both in NATO and White House strategy sessions, and he noted the president's natural affinity for von Neumann's and Morgenstern's thinking. "Anything that's based on the theory of games," said Goodpaster, "fits well into . . . the way General Eisenhower's mind works. He's a great poker player . . . and he's a tremendous man for analyzing the other fellow's mind, what options are open to the other fellow, and what line he can best take to capitalize or exploit the possibilities."

As Morgenstern put it in 1961, "The Cold War is sometimes compared to a giant chess game. The analogy, however, is quite false, for while chess is a formidable game of almost unbelievable complexity, it lacks salient features of the political and military struggles with which it is compared." Because chess is a game of complete information, it provides no opportunities to bluff, leaving it "far removed from political reality . . . where the threatening nation has to weigh the cost not only to its enemies, but to itself, where deceit is certainly not unheard of, and where chance intervenes." Luck, deceit, and cost-effectiveness are basic to poker, a game in which "the best hand need not win." It is the bluff that makes poker the most useful model for "countries with opposing aims and ideals [who] watch each other's every move with unveiled suspicion."

"If chess is the Russian national pastime and poker is ours," Morgenstern continues, "we ought to be more skillful than they in applying its precepts to the cold-war struggle." We need to be strategically astute because "nuclear weapons are spreading ominously while the ability to deliver them anywhere, from any point on earth, is already in the hands of the two super-powers. With bluffs so much easier to make and threats so much more portentous than any previous time in history, it is essential not only for our own State Department but for the entire world to understand what bluffs and threats mean; when they are appropriate; whether they should be avoided at all cost; in short, what is the sanest way to play this deadly, real-life version of poker."

Parallels between poker and nuclear showdowns aren't neat or one-to-one, yet no game more closely resembles military and diplomatic maneuvers. Morgenstern says they are "similar enough so that something substantial can be learned from good poker principles. Corresponding to each player's cards and chips, you have the quantity and quality of a country's weapons, the disturbance which one country can cause another, and the changes in national plans that can be imposed. Bluffs correspond to the numerous threats being made with increasing frequency on the contemporary international scene."

It is worth noting here that the old Germanic word *bluffen* means "to bluster or frighten." The English version, combining both meanings, first appeared around 1665, as bluff-based vying games like *pochen* and brag became popular. No other kind of game so perfectly captured the essence of this deceitful yet potentially lifesaving tactic—of making someone believe you will fight to the death if necessary, without having to actually shed any blood, let alone evaporate cities.

While Stalin seldom bluffed, his successors regrettably picked up the knack. "Unquestionably the most successful bluff, by either side," writes Morgenstern, "was the Soviet Union's threat in 1956 to rain missiles on England unless she stopped her actions in Egypt" during the Suez crisis. He also believed the West was bluffed by the simple roadblocks the Red Army put up around West Berlin. Instead of a massively expensive airlift, all we needed were a few tanks to break through the roadblocks. "We held strong cards but we didn't know how to use them. We fell for a bluff that was easy to recognize as a bluff, even . . . when our total nuclear power was so much greater than that of the Soviets.

"If the Communists," he continues, "seem to be superior players to date, it is perhaps not so much because of their tactics in playing any particular hand, as because of their firmer adherence to sound optimal strategy." Then he presciently adds, "the United States has, with some justice, been criticized for being alternately too uncertain of its line . . . and too rigid, as in our refusal to recognize Red China—the most populous country in the world and, in a few decades, sure to be one of the most powerful."

In March 1955, Eisenhower had pulled off a nuclear bluff against Mao Zedong over the islands of Quemoy and Matsu during a war between China and Taiwan. Secretary of State John Foster Dulles declared that the United States was considering a nuclear strike on the mainland, with Admiral Robert B. Carney adding that Eisenhower was planning "to destroy Red China's military potential." When the Soviets signaled an unwillingness to threaten nuclear retaliation for a U.S. attack, Mao backed down. But in 1960, Eisenhower got called, as it were, by Khrushchev when a U-2 spy plane was forced down in the heart of Russia—on May Day, no less. After initially denying it was a spy plane, Eisenhower was forced to admit that it was when Khrushchev produced the pilot and plane. Morgenstern describes Khrushchev as "alternately acting the clown, the bon vivant, and the ogre, yet never stepping completely out of character and managing to keep his non-Communist audience in a state of chronic uncertainty."

In *Big Deal*, Anthony Holden illuminates the pokerlike nature of the Cuban missile crisis of October 1962. Holden shows how it "can be analysed in almost uncanny detail as a slowly developing hand, involving bluff and counter-bluff, with stakes as high as they go." Khrushchev, like "all the best poker players, was playing the man rather than his hand. He and Kennedy had played an earlier game at their Vienna summit, where the Russian leader had 'read' the new American president as young, inexperienced and easy to push around."

The cold war historian John Lewis Gaddis seconds this view: "In no sense did Khrushchev want, or think the Soviet Union could survive, a nuclear war. He was, however, more prepared than Truman or Eisenhower—or Stalin—had ever been to risk war: to threaten nuclear escalation in the belief that the West would prefer altering over maintaining the status quo. With all the flamboyance of a high-stakes poker player, Khrushchev raised the ante, confident that he could bluff his opponents into backing down." Despite America's superior arsenal—an eight-to-one advantage in rockets, made even more potent by von Neumann's ICBM system—Khrushchev believed Kennedy would prove too weak to keep the Soviets from basing nuclear missiles on Cuba and that his humiliating failure at the Bay of Pigs and in other covert operations had sapped his overall confidence on the subject of Castro's domain. But when the forty-five-year-old president boldly "quarantined" the island and sent uncoded orders putting American bombers on highest alert, Khrushchev, in Holden's phrase, "folded his hand and conceded the pot." During two weeks of military and diplomatic posturing, both sides had engaged in dangerous—some would say reckless—brinksmanship. Even though Khrushchev had "blinked," he still had long-range bombers and submarine-based missiles capable of hitting our cities, so Kennedy needed to let him save face. He authorized a public pledge that the United States was "unlikely to invade" Cuba again if the Russians dismantled the bases. And to seal the deal, he privately promised to remove our fifteen medium-range Jupiter missiles—which were obsolete anyway and scheduled to be removed before the Cuban crisis began—from Turkey within a few months. The lag time was designed to keep the public from understanding that such a deal had been made, at least until after the midterm elections a few days later.

"As in poker," writes Morgenstern, "both we and the Russians must realize the importance of making threats commensurate with the value of the position to be defended, and not bluff so grossly that the raise is sure to be called." He concludes by underscoring the key difference between the two kinds of showdown. "In poker there are always some winners and some losers; in power politics, both sides may lose. Everything."

In the end, of course, mankind was fortunate that neither the West nor the Soviets overplayed their hand militarily. The cold war ended peacefully in 1989, after Mikhail Gorbachev's glasnost and perestroika (openness and reform), aggressively encouraged by Ronald Reagan's political and economic pressure, led to the dismantling of the Berlin Wall, the Iron Curtain, and the Soviet Union itself. We should also be relieved that Orwell's 1945 prediction of "how likely we all are to be blown to pieces by it [the bomb] within the next five years" is one of the few he made that didn't come true. That it hasn't so far has as much to do with von Neumann's ICBMs as it does with his poker-based game theory.

DOWLING AND KRIEGEL, BLOTZSKY AND WITHERSPOON

Soul to soul, our shadows roll
And I'll be with you when the deal goes down.

— BOB DYLAN,
"WHEN THE DEAL GOES DOWN"

In the middle decades of the twentieth century, while presidents, generals, and scientific geniuses were playing poker to unwind after earthshaking workdays, the reporter Allen Dowling and his newspaper cronies were doing much the same thing. The stakes of their jobs may not have involved the survival of civilization, but the dollars and bragging rights they competed for were just as important to them as they were to the millions of other folks playing in kitchens and basements, fire stations and VFW card rooms, not to mention all the games being played in Canada and throughout Northern Europe.

In the press room of Baton Rouge City Hall, the action among Dowling's colleagues usually got under way around noon, though on slow news days the cards could be in the air as early as 9:00 a.m. During their frequent all-night sessions, the players ordered in food and drink, caught catnaps on the wicker couch, and called home only occasionally. When covering an out-of-town story, they'd put up at a hotel or hunting lodge and bring out the cards as soon as they'd called in their copy.

As Dowling writes in *The Great American Pastime*, the spirit of these games was "ask no quarter and give none." No one was interested in what he calls "brother-in-law poker," which would have meant occasionally checking a cinch hand to a crony who was losing, showing him a strong hand after he folded, or not turning over a bluff. "Poker's too deadly an exercise to permit of Pollyannaism," he says, while making the case that poker's manly camaraderie gives players a chance to get a few repressed gripes off their chests with aggressive raising, and to sling witty insults that might amount to fighting words away from the table. Nor should we overlook the game's ancillary benefits, such as poker buddies helping each other away from the table. While Dowling was covering a case of unrequited love that led to a murder-suicide, it turned out that one of his tablemates was friendly with both bereaved families. He not only supplied Dowling with background information on the one-way romance but helped him secure family pictures to illustrate his article.

Perhaps the grimmest game took place at a boardinghouse in the prison town where a sextuple execution by hanging was about to occur. Because rumors of a jailbreak had been circulating, the prison was under guard by the military. Attorneys for the condemned kept access to their clients tightly controlled while exhausting every appeal to get the sentences commuted. Meanwhile, only those with a special pass were allowed into the prison courtyard. Having no pass, Dowling proposed that a poker game would not only relieve the reporters' collective boredom while they waited for the appeals to be heard, it would also let each of them keep a close eye on his scoop-hungry competition. While everyone agreed to this plan, one reporter, pretending to be too drunk to either play cards or conduct an interview, somehow made his way onto death row and "beat the whole crew with one hell of a story." Dowling's luck held, though, because the sneakily intrepid reporter happened to work for the same paper as he did, and Dowling, no less intrepid or sneaky, led their boss to believe that "my efforts to assist in organizing the poker game were part of a subtle plot to keep the others occupied while my confrere scored his coup." He had proved, if nothing else, that there was more than one way to run a bluff or get credit for a scoop.

After landing a seat in a three-handed game in a barbershop, Dowling began to suspect that the barber and the hulking attendant from the gas station next door were colluding against him. Observing the pair more closely, he sensed they were engaged in "knee action," bumping each other to indicate the strength of their hands, then raising and reraising in tandem to build or force Dowling out of big pots. But instead of confronting them or quitting the game, he came up with a better idea: he told each player in private that the other was "setting him up for a trimming." This got them to "quit worrying about my hole card and begin a feud of their own," and to play their own hands incorrectly. When Dowling "had recovered what I'd lost previously, due to their collusion, I shook loose from them."

His experience with lobbyists taught him that, although honest, they were seldom the loose free-spenders one might expect. He found most of them "reluctant to put greenbacks into circulation unless they have what they consider to be an irrevocable understanding for requital in a form that is entirely satisfactory. I've made a mental note of their niggardliness," a trait that extended to the poker table, where they were "tough and unyielding," willing to put money in the pot only when they had a cinch or close to it. He adjusted his tactics against them accordingly.

As for his fellow ink-stained wretches, Dowling was forced to conclude they were "not the world's best players," mainly because of their "very *indifference*," even when nearly every pot in the pressroom was subject to a flurry of raises. Somehow their professional skepticism had caused them to pay "little or no attention to strong representations or to pairs in sight." Dowling therefore played much more conservatively against them, reraising with strong hands and folding close calls. "Thus, while the pots I won averaged as big as the pots won by any other player, I was saving three or four times more money."

After a run of losing sessions, however, Dowling was determined to improve his results—not with marked cards or knee action, but by mending his tactics and strategy. He essentially grabbed himself by the collar, shoved himself against the wall, and wagged a finger in his very own face. Stop drawing to long shots, he told himself sternly. Give more weight to position, because the later you act, the more hands you can profitably play because of the diminished possibility of being raised. Shun straight and flush draws in favor of pairs above nines. Don't guess or hope; rely instead on the immutable law of averages. He "resolved that when my judgment told me I was defeated to throw my hand away. It's really surprising the amount of money that may be saved in that fashion." He also stopped sandbagging in draw by passing with strong hands, hoping to reraise the opening bet—stopped pretending to be, as he called it, an alligator basking on a log, to avoid being stranded with a powerful hand. "I resolved never to pass if my hand warranted opening; but I never opened unless I could stand a raise."

Bankroll management was just as important. Playing with short money made him too likely to fold the winning hand to a bluff, and too scared of being called to run bluffs himself. He also woke up to the fact that each opponent must be played as a distinct personality, with his own set of tendencies, and to how crucial it was to read how each opponent had appraised his own tendencies. "Witherspoon may have you classed as a tough hombre while you're just a soft touch to Blotzsky," he wrote.

On a practical note, he offers advice on starting a home game. The key is to simply start playing, even two- or three-handed, because once a game gets under way, other players will eventually arrive. When the table fills up and a waiting list forms, the host can begin to shape the ideal roster, balancing such factors as friendliness, financial stability, and a willingness to gamble with speculative hands—what we would call giving action. Inviting a garrulous bore, of course, threatens the game's long-term viability. Less obvious but no less important is a strategy for dealing with the legions of men who are reliable at home and in the office but who "fail to keep a poker appointment with calm indifference and never even think of sending notification." Almost as vexing are those with a "pretty definite idea" they won't be able to play yet ask to be counted in on the off chance their conflicting engagements will miraculously disappear by that evening.

The game he holds up as a model has been running twice a week in the home of a retired merchant for twenty-five years, even though several charter members, as well as some of their replacements, have either died or drifted away. The action takes place on a circular table in the corner of a basement kept cool by a ceiling fan in summer and warmed by the furnace during the winter. Each session begins around 7:00 p.m. and concludes when an alarm clock rings five hours later. For the first four hours, the ante is ten cents, bets twenty-five. Although the stakes jump to twenty-five and fifty cents at the end of the evening, everyone at the table can comfortably afford them. Five-card draw jacks-or-better remains the merchant's game of choice. Tigers and skipping straights are part of the hand hierarchy, not surprising in a Louisiana home game. The host doesn't rake any pots but charges a small fee for a cold supper and soft drinks, cigarettes and cigars. Since the players pay for these things whether or not they consume them, "they figured it was their duty to get their money's worth," Dowling reports. "It al-

ways tickled me to watch them stuff themselves then bellow for bicar-
bonate of soda."

As a typical male of this era, Dowling isn't fond of playing with
women. Though not as misogynistic as his fellow Louisianan Stanley
Kowalski, he still looks askance on "boys and girls who combine penny
ante poker and social entertainment under the dubious heading of a
'poker party.' Such functions generally resemble each other, but there
are varying degrees of punishment." Downsides include "silly" games
in which one-eyed jacks are wild, or "if you draw a nine, the hand is
nullified, but if you draw a four, your hole cards become wild, and so
on, ad infinitum," all this on top of the fancy highballs, greasy food, and
"endless chatter, feminine squeals of delight or dismay, and the general
disorderliness of the procedure, such as players paying no attention to
sequence of action, to complete your mental pandemonium."

Dowling feels much the same way about low-stakes men-only games
that exist mainly as "an excuse to exchange gossip or the latest porno-
graphic stories." Such mindless frivolity is not to be confused, however,
with "poverty" or "Depression" poker, egalitarian variants created in
the spirit of Roosevelt's New Deal. Still played in basement corners and
presidential studies, poverty poker gave players who'd lost all their
chips a chance to compete for credit points and eventually, via complex
formulas that varied from house to house, earn back some chips from a
pool fed by regular pots. It wasn't uncommon for a player to be busted
in the first forty minutes, go "on relief," and wind up as the night's
biggest money winner. For this reason and others, Dowling believed
even microstakes games could be compelling so long as everyone—
women included—took the game seriously, and the dealer's choices
were limited to straight stud or draw, with no wild cards. The best
poker action, he said, was "disciplined sternly and woe to the player
who passed or even put up his ante out of turn."

Another crucial thing to decide was how long the game should last.
Five hours must have struck many of his readers as too brief a session,
especially given that the fewer hands played, the less likely it was that
skill would prevail. Yet how much poker was too much? Despite the
addictive appeal of marathon games, Dowling understood how easily
they could spiral down into Dostoyevskian misery. "I don't believe there
is anything equal to the rattle and clatter of early morning garbage
cans," he writes, "especially in bleak or cold weather, when you're leaving an all-night poker game after taking a sound drubbing." Empty
pockets, the afterburn of whiskey and cigarettes, a boss impolitely de-

manding your clear-eyed attention—and these might be the least of your problems. Because even when your poker wad is thick, if "there are any domestic responsibilities whatsoever, your failure to come home is a problem that demands consideration and possibly some nimble thinking."

Dowling tells of a Louisiana state senator, standing in tears before a window as dawn rises over yet another all-night session, eloquently challenging himself and his tablemates to contemplate the folly of playing too much poker. Spurring himself to impressive rhetorical heights, he bemoans missing the finer things in life, the effects of sleep deprivation on soul and body, the moral decrepitude of giving in to what he calls a gambling "infatuation." (In those days it wasn't understood as addiction.) The only hitch to the senator's hand-wringing sermon was that he and his listeners all returned to the felt that same evening.

Meanwhile, thirteen hundred miles north and east, in New York City, Leonard Kriegel's obsession was more—to use a favorite term from those years—existential. His memoir "Poker's Promise" describes the rites of passage of traumatized Jewish immigrants after the Second World War, when the game "eased us into American aspirations, suggesting how each of us might bankroll his sense of belonging."

"Like me," he writes, "the friends who introduced me to poker in the early 1950s were the children of immigrants. And that, I suspect, explains our infatuation with a game that seemed quintessentially American. No game commanded greater loyalty and no game promised more. Along with the intricacies of baseball, poker was a cultural bridge that helped you cross over into a wider world." Kriegel recalls listening as a boy to middle-aged furriers, garment workers, and taxi drivers "vehemently discussing in Yiddish the trials and tribulations of their weekly poker game. I can still hear the echo of those voices dripping with derision as a player's efforts were dismissed with the contemptuous, *'Er spelt vee ah greener.'* ('He plays like an immigrant.') No condemnation could have been more formidable, no dismissal more damning. For to play like an immigrant was to deny the very entitlements America offered. . . . Even in the golden land, one listened carefully to opportunity's knock." Because as David Mamet would later observe about poker, "opportunity may knock, but it seldom nags."

Young Leonard gradually realizes that "no game better embodied the enormous sense of possibility we felt was ours by right of having been born in this America. A man could shed the past in poker. What could possibly be more American than that?"

His most dramatic case in point is a Holocaust survivor. "Defined by the horror of his past and limited by the paucity of his English, he searched our fears as closely as we searched his." One night a mutual friend (not Larry David) brings the survivor to their poker game. "Almost immediately, he established a reputation as a daring, skillful player," writes Kriegel. "It was as if the nightmare of Europe could be expunged by the mundane triumph of drawing an inside straight. I can still see him as he dealt, slamming the cards down, blue numbers tattooed on his arm seeming to quiver beneath the living flesh. I remember him holding his own cards like a sweeping fan of affirmation as he said in his thickly accented yet suddenly triumphant English, '*I* open!'"

THE LEGEND OF JOHNNY
AND THE GREEK

Between legend-making, exaggeration, and fabrication, there
is reason to believe we don't know the accurate story.
— MICHAEL CRAIG

Once we enter poker's modern era, the way individual hands or entire games played out becomes more verifiable. Film, videotape, living
memory, stricter editorial standards, and digital records online all bring
us closer to yesterday's action—who said what to whom, how much was
at stake, who held what hand on the river. Even so, what Michael Craig,
author of *The Professor, the Banker, and the Suicide King*, said about the
celebrated showdown between Johnny Moss and Nick "the Greek"
Dandalos can serve as a caveat to nearly any account of a poker session,
whether it took place in 1827, 1951, or last weekend. We don't know
the accurate story, in part because most players' "need to mislead"—
whether their opponents, their spouses, the IRS, or the fellows to
whom they are bragging—colors nearly every report of how the long
money changed hands.

Unless he was an eyewitness, and sometimes not even then, all a historian can do is sift through what's been written and said about a game,
trying to get a feel for which version of a poker session sounds the least

out of tune or, if he's lucky, has the actual ring of truth. (Online and televised games, of course, leave much clearer evidence trails.) That said, sometime between January 1949 and the spring of 1951 a casino boss named Lester Ben Binion hosted a heads-up, winner-take-all marathon between Moss and Dandalos in downtown Las Vegas. Many of the details, including the year, remain subjects of debate, with one Moss biographer saying it was 1949 and another saying 1951.

What isn't in doubt is that Binion was born in Pilot Grove, Texas, sixty miles northeast of Dallas, in 1904. His grandparents had migrated there from Chicago, and both his parents grew up Catholic and poor. Benny spent his youth punching cattle, trading horses, running numbers, and sitting on the fringes of card games, finally making his bones in the twenties and thirties. Starting with $56, he and his younger brother launched their own numbers policy, a kind of neighborhood lottery, netting $800 their first week in business. His brother died in a plane crash a few years later, but Benny branched out from numbers to dice, running no-limit craps games in the shadow of the Dallas courthouse. Regulars at his casino included H. L. Hunt, Clint Murchison, and Howard Hughes, all of whom rolled the bones for six-figure stakes. They were attracted by Benny's reputation as a "square craps fader," a host who relied on the normal house edge to guarantee profitability, instead of daubing and loading—making his dice slightly tacky or heavy on one side—in ways that disadvantaged the shooter.

Cards were another story. "I was never a real good poker player," he told an interviewer, contrasting himself with friends who made a living at the game. "They know the cards, and know the percentages . . . and how many chances he's got to make it, and this, that, and the other. I can't do that. I don't know that end of it." What he did know was how to create a secure environment for games of skill and chance, and to take a handsome cut for his trouble.

Since the games were illegal, Binion and his fellow racketeers had to police both their clients and competitors. Their weapons of choice included baseball bats, shotguns, and homemade bombs. By nearly every report, Benny was a warmhearted, generous family man who savored his reputation as a cold-blooded killer. "There's no way in the world I'd harm anybody for any amount of money," he declared near the end of his life, this after certain statutes of limitations, and not a few of his enemies, had expired. "But if anybody goes to talkin' about doin' me bodily harm, or my family bodily harm, I'm very capable, thank God, of really takin' care of 'em in a *most* artistic way. And I'm still very capable.

I don't have to hire nobody to do none of my dirty work. That sounds a little bit like braggin', but if they don't think that I can do it, well, just let 'em come on."

Come on they did. As the boss gambler in Dallas during the Second World War, Benny was targeted for hits by his competition and prosecuted by the government on a regular basis. The cumulative heat became so intense he decided to get out of town. "My sheriff got beat in the election," was how he explained it. In 1946 he piled his wife, their five young children, and $2 million in cash into his maroon Cadillac and drove to Las Vegas, where most of his games were now legal.

He first became a partner in the Las Vegas Club with J. Kell Houssels, but Benny's decision to reduce the house edge and remove betting limits led to a split in the merger. And Benny had other big problems. Back in Dallas, the numbers boss Herbert "the Cat" Noble's wife was incinerated by a car bomb meant for the Cat. So certain was Noble that Benny had authorized the hit that he fitted an airplane with bomb racks, got hold of two incendiary devices, and circled Binion's Bonanza Road address on a map of Las Vegas. The sortie was thwarted by Texas police, but word of the bomb racks and map made its way out to Benny. In 1951, the year he took over the El Dorado on Fremont Street and renamed it Binion's Horseshoe Club, Noble—whose nickname referred to the eleven times he'd survived attempts on his life by Mr. Binion—was decapitated by a pipe bomb planted next to his mailbox.

Born on Crete in 1893, Nick "the Greek" Dandalos was a much more refined sort of gambler. He moved to America with a lavish allowance from his godfather, a shipping magnate, and arrived in Vegas in 1949 claiming to have broken every high roller back east, Arnold Rothstein included, winning in the neighborhood of $60 million, though he admitted losing most of it back on the thoroughbreds at Joe Kennedy's Hialeah racetrack. His new game was poker, which he called "the art of civilized bushwhacking," and he said he was looking to play "the biggest game this world has to offer." His problem was that poker in Vegas took place in ring games with limited bet sizes. Asking around, he was told Benny Binion was the man to see about no-limit action. He proposed that Benny match him against "any man around" in a heads-up, no-limit, winner-take-all poker marathon.

The house tends to make relatively little by spreading poker, but Benny sensed there might be other ways to skin this particular cat. He conferred with his friend Jimmy Snyder, who also used "the Greek" as his moniker. Snyder had been saying for years that poker was America's most popular game. Still played mostly in back rooms and kitchens, however, it remained an underground national pastime. All it needed to become more visible, Snyder imagined, was the institutional organization of baseball, and to get that, it needed a forum and some nuanced PR. Snyder also believed the strongest poker players were Texans, in part because of the vastness of their landscape and the scarcity of other amusements. He told Benny that the best man to stand up to Dandalos would hail from that ornery state.

Snyder had also succumbed to his fellow Greek's charm. "He recited poetry," he said. "He was beautiful with women. He made Omar Sharif look like a truck driver." Benny called him "the strangest character I ever seen," and said he would host the game only if it was played at a table near the front of his casino, in full public view. When Dandalos agreed, Benny phoned his friend Johnny Moss, the best poker player he knew.

While the Greek had a degree in philosophy, Moss's formal education had ended, like Binion's, in second grade. After working with Binion as a Dallas paperboy, Moss followed his friend into the gambling rackets, learning to cheat at poker long before he learned to play square. "Dealin' from the bottom of the pack, dealin' seconds, usin' mirrors, markin' cards," he recalled in 1981, at age seventy-four. "We thought we were smart. Everybody we looked at was a sucker. The suckers had money an' we didn't. I could make a livin', but it warn't a good livin'. I could never get hold of a lot of money, like a sucker could, so in time I come to see it was better to be a sucker. For sixty years now, I've been a sucker. But I'm hard to beat." He may never have become a completely square player, but by 1949 he was certainly tired of evading the police while trying to beat other cheats, legitimate players, and runs of cold cards, and of needing to pack a revolver at the table and carry a .410 double-barreled shotgun from town to town because road gamblers were such enticing targets for highwaymen. He was ready to move to Las Vegas.

Legend has it that Moss was already in a pretty good game in Odessa when Benny finally reached him. He'd been playing for three days without sleep, but he still got on the first plane to Vegas, took a taxi to Benny's joint on a crisp Sunday evening in January, and sat down to play. Dandalos was fifty-six, Moss forty-two, so stamina was going to be an issue. So was the ability to concentrate, since their table was soon hemmed in by chattering flocks of railbirds two or three hundred strong. From time to time well-heeled tourists were permitted to "change-in to" the game for a minimum of $10,000, but none lasted more than a day or two.

Early on, the Greek pulled dramatically ahead, threatening to wipe out Moss's more limited bankroll. Apparently the Greek seldom slept, because he spent nearly all of their break time at the craps table. Once, when Moss came back downstairs from a nap, Dandalos joshed him, "What are you going to do, Johnny, sleep your life away?" They are supposed to have played for five months, breaking for sleep only once "every four or five days," as fresh dealers rotated in every twenty minutes to keep the action brisk and precise. (We should bear in mind that playing poker well for days without sleep was a badge of honor back then, so the number of consecutive hours at the table may well have been exaggerated.) Meanwhile, the size of their audience continued to grow. Noting how much the railbirds were wagering elsewhere in his casino, Binion called his new main attraction "the biggest game in town." During one break, while the railbirds headed off to the craps and blackjack tables, Dandalos allegedly chaperoned Albert Einstein along Fremont Street, introducing him to local gamblers as "Little Al from Princeton—controls lotta the action 'round Jersey." It is also said that Einstein, though much amused, managed to keep a straight face. (The factual status of this on Snopes.com remains "Undetermined.")

In one famous hand of five-stud, the up cards were 8-6-4-J for the Greek and 6-9-2-3 for Moss. With more than $100,000 already in the pot, the Greek bet $50,000. Moss, who had a nine in the hole, raised by moving all his available chips in. The Greek had only $140,000 left of what had recently been a seven-figure bankroll. "I guess I have to call you," he said, pushing the last of his chips toward the pot, "because I think I've got a jack in the hole." Moss told him, "Greek, if you've got a jack down there, you're liable to win a helluva pot." Dandalos indeed had the jack, and the pot came to $520,000. The Greek had recklessly chased Moss's pair of nines during the final two betting rounds—hoping for, even counting on, then hitting the miracle jack. "But that's all right," Moss said years later, observing that the Greek's weakness for long shots didn't bode well for him. "I broke him in the end."

It wasn't until the middle of May that Dandalos finally succumbed with a handshake and the famous line, "Mr. Moss, I have to let you go." Legend has it that the Texan took between $2 million and $3 million from the game. Adjusted for inflation, this would be like winning $20 million or $25 million today.

Did it happen that way? If it did, why did Moss then begin taking jobs managing Las Vegas card rooms? To use their "eyes in the sky" to cheat more effectively? "Back then there was lots of cheating, and Moss would cheat," Doyle Brunson told a reporter. Another motivation for taking those jobs—that he needed the salary—was confirmed in 2004, when Brunson told Michael Craig that Moss had promptly lost the entire Dandalos bundle at the craps table. Most people might find this hard to believe, but it is in fact rather common in Las Vegas for a man to win a few million dollars playing brilliant poker for several days, weeks, or months, only to lose it all in as many hours or minutes throwing dice. At some point in their careers, Dandalos, Moss, Stuey Ungar, T. J. Cloutier, Phil Ivey, John Hennigan, Ted Forrest, and dozens of other poker maestros are alleged to have sprung similar dice leaks.

Since that interview, Craig has also offered a variety of reasons to believe that any Moss-Dandalos poker game was probably shorter, with much less at stake. He points out several discrepancies in accounts published decades later (in Jon Bradshaw's *Fast Company* and Don Jenkins's *Champion of Champions*), and notes that articles about Moss or Dandalos from the '50s and '60s fail to mention any showdown between them. Then there is Binion's 1973 oral history interview with Mary Ellen Glass, in which, Craig reminds us, Binion "talks about Nick the Greek in connection with the Horseshoe back then and in later days. . . . But he never mentions (a) Johnny Moss; (b) a poker game between Moss and Dandalos; (c) any big poker game that drew spectators to the Horseshoe; or (d) any poker game from that era having anything to do with the start of the World Series of Poker in 1970." Craig also notes that when Dandalos was buried in Las Vegas in 1966, "the *Sun* and the *Review-Journal* both reported it on the front page. . . . The *Review-Journal* story says, 'The Greek was an attraction here for many years. Local gamblers enjoyed pointing out the legendary "Aristotle of the pass line" to gaping tourists.' There is no mention of poker, Moss, the Horseshoe, Benny Binion, or the legendary game" in either story. Craig now believes "the whole thing wasn't made up, but like many great poker stories, it grew over the years. And as Johnny Moss evolved from a tough old cheater who was banned from Vegas for a couple of decades—banned or in fear for his life—to the 'Grand Old Man of Poker,' what was a big score against Dandalos grew into a battle of the titans."

From Henry Clay and Wild Bill Hickok to Johnny Moss and Annette_15 Obrestad, accounts of the hand-to-hand combat of historical figures have always been embellished somewhat. But it's safe to say that Dandalos and Moss were exceptional high-stakes players who engaged in a midcentury showdown that Dandalos lost. It was apparently something of a spectacle. And the spectacle was hosted by the impresario who would launch the World Series of Poker two decades later. In doing so, Benny Binion and the three dozen original contestants—including Moss, who took home three of the first five championship trophies—introduced to the general public a variant called Texas hold'em.

HOLD ME, DARLIN'

I don't want to push my chips forward and go out and meet
something I don't understand.

— SHERIFF BELL IN *NO COUNTRY FOR OLD MEN*

Given the global popularity of Texas hold'em today, a description
of its rules might not be necessary. But the uninitiated should know that
each player is dealt two cards facedown, to be combined with five community cards dealt faceup in the middle of the table—first three simultaneously (called the *flop*), then a fourth (the *turn*), then a fifth (the
river)—with a round of betting after each of the stages.

Hold'em is often called a variant of seven-card stud. This is mainly
because no draw takes place in either game and players in both games
have a board of exposed cards—four individual cards in stud, five community cards in hold'em—for a total of seven cards from which to
make a five-card poker hand. The key differences are stud's antes versus rotating hold'em blinds; stud's 3-1-1-1-1 pattern versus hold'em's
2-3-1-1; the fact that stud is played with fixed bet sizes, whereas
hold'em, with four betting rounds instead of five, lends itself more
readily to a no-limit format; and the superiority of hold'em as a televised spectacle. Because a hold'em player shares five-sevenths of his

cards with opponents, the difference between the best and second-best hand—all the difference in the world, you might say—is nearly always more subtle than in stud. Hold'em also requires no memory of board cards that were folded, which Yardley and others have shown to be crucial in stud. No-limit hold'em is much more about sizing bets correctly and reading patterns and body language.

Five-card stud was played as early as 1860, with the seven-card version developing toward the end of the nineteenth century. Hold'em wasn't played until early in the twentieth and didn't overtake draw and seven-stud as the most popular game until the late 1980s. By then its original name, Hold Me Darling, had long since been abbreviated to Hold Me, and then, via the twanging vicissitudes of cowboy enunciation, to hold'em.

No one knows for sure where and when the first hand of hold'em was dealt. One plausible guess is that a dozen or so Texas ranch hands wanted to play a little stud but found they had only one deck. The most creative cowboy must've got to thinking: if five cards were shared by all players, as many as twenty-three of them could be dealt two-card hands. While the time and place of this eureka moment are impossible to pinpoint, in May 2007 the Texas state legislature formally recognized Robstown, twenty miles west of Corpus Christi, as the birthplace of hold'em.

> WHEREAS, The popularity of the poker game Texas Hold'em has increased dramatically over the past several years, and each day untold numbers of people throughout the world play this exciting game of skill, intuition, and good old-fashioned luck; and
>
> WHEREAS, A true phenomenon of our time, Texas Hold'em has taken the world by storm, captivating countless card enthusiasts with its deceptive simple format; whether betting and bluffing across casino tables and kitchen tables, raising and folding in the virtual world of online card rooms, or moving "all-in" at charity poker tournaments, poker players everywhere have embraced this fascinating and challenging game; and
>
> WHEREAS, The game's invention dates back to the early 1900s when it is traditionally held that the first hand of the popular card game was dealt in the city of Robstown, and from there it traveled northward in the hands of "rounders" and up the sleeves of cardsharps who quickly recognized the game's potential for mass appeal; and

BARACK OBAMA

UNION SOLDIERS PLAYING POKER

A *MISDEAL* BY FREDERIC REMINGTON

A BOLD BLUFF AND *WATERLOO* BY C. M. COOLIDGE

HERBERT O. YARDLEY

STU UNGAR

PRESIDENT TRUMAN PLAYING ABOARD THE *WILLIAMSBURG*

DOYLE BRUNSON, STU UNGAR, AND JACK BINION AT THE 1981 WSOP

ERIC DRACHE

DAVID SKLANSKY

JOHNNY MOSS

CRANDELL ADDINGTON

TOM McEVOY DEFEATS ROD PEATE AT THE 1983 WSOP.

ANTHONY HOLDEN

HOWARD LEDERER

WORLD SERIES OF POKER COMMISSIONER
JEFFREY POLLACK

DANIEL NEGREANU

JOHN JUANDA

TOM "DURRR" DWAN

WHEREAS, Poker legends such as Crandell Addington and Doyle "Texas Dolly" Brunson helped further popularize the game in and around Texas in the 1950s, and they and others eventually brought Texas Hold'em to Las Vegas, where it was first played at the Golden Nugget Casino in 1967; three years later, the inaugural World Series of Poker was played at the Horseshoe Casino, featuring no-limit Texas Hold'em to determine the world champion, and that annual tournament has continued to grow in both size and stature with each passing year; and

WHEREAS, The popularity of hold'em has no doubt been spurred by the advent of online gaming and by the broadcast of televised poker tournaments, most notably the World Series of Poker's "Main Event," a $10,000 no-limit Texas Hold'em tournament that attracts top poker professionals, talented amateurs, celebrities, and poker wannabes from around the globe to become the next world champion of poker; and

WHEREAS, It is said that Texas Hold'em takes a minute to learn and a lifetime to master, and this telling statement underscores the high level of skill necessary to win consistently; a successful player relies on reason, intuition, and bravado, and these same qualities have served many notable Texans well throughout the proud history of the Lone Star State; now, therefore, be it

RESOLVED, That the 80th Legislature of the State of Texas hereby formally recognize Robstown, Texas, as the birthplace of the poker game Texas Hold'em.

The resolution's post hoc chest thumping may distract us from the fact that the same legislative body has made this "game of skill" illegal in public, including most charity tournaments, and makes those hosting the action subject to civil penalties of up to $50,000. If the Lone Star State wants credit for this "true phenomenon of our time," and especially for no-limit hold'em tournaments, is it too much to ask that her citizens may play them in public?

By dating the birth of hold'em to the early 1900s, the legislators underscored the difficulty of being more precise in fixing the origins of any poker variant. Hold'em seems to have arrived in Dallas, the state's unofficial gambling capital, around 1930. Johnny Moss claimed to have played limit hold'em at the Elks Club and the no-limit version at the Otters Club in the '30s, though there's no record of hold'em being part of the showdown with Dandalos in 1949 or '51.

When *Oswald Jacoby on Poker* appeared in 1940, it mentioned no game called or resembling hold'em. Jacoby's book had a foreword by Grantland Rice, whose 1924 account of a game at the Polo Grounds between Army and Notre Dame and its famous backfield began: "Outlined against a blue-gray October sky the Four Horsemen rode again. In dramatic lore they are known as famine, pestilence, destruction and death. These are only aliases. Their real names are Stuhldreyer, Miller, Crowley and Leyden." Rice had made his own name by mythologizing other athletes, including Babe Ruth, Jack Dempsey, Bobby Jones, and Bill Tilden, so his introduction to a poker compendium was one of the first times the public was encouraged to think of the game as a sport. Jacoby, for his part, was an international backgammon and bridge master, making his verdict all the more credible when he declared poker to be a game of skill. *Jacoby on Poker* focused on draw and stud but did mention two games related to hold'em. Spit in the Ocean was a form of draw in which one faceup "spit" card became part of every player's hand. And in a game called Cincinnati, which presumably arose in that city, each player was dealt five cards facedown, to be combined with five community cards dealt one at a time. It obviously took a very strong hand to win a pot. The biggest full house would often have to be folded to an opponent representing a straight flush or quads.

Foster's Complete Hoyle from 1963 mentions neither Cincinnati nor hold'em but does describe an old variation on draw called Wild Widow. In that game, each player receives five cards facedown, and a "wild widow" card is placed faceup in the center of the table. If the widow is a 5, for example, 5s are wild for that hand. Widow and spit cards almost certainly triggered the idea of community cards in Cincinnati and Texas hold'em, though which game developed first isn't clear.

In *Super System 2*, Crandell Addington recalls that hold'em was played throughout Texas in the early '60s. He lists "Pinky" Rhoden of Lubbock, "Duck" Mallard of Lockhart, Jesse Alto of Corpus Christi, Jack "Treetop" Straus of Houston, and Tom Moore of San Antonio as leading road gamblers and proselytizers for hold'em. What expert, after all, wouldn't want to compete for high stakes against players just learning a game?

Addington says Felton "Corky" McCorkindale (elsewhere spelled McCorquodale) is the man who in 1963—not '67, as the Texas legislature has it—introduced hold'em to Las Vegas, specifically to the California Club downtown at the corner of Ogden and Main Street. Other Texans attracted to Vegas by poker's legal status there included Addington, Straus, Moss, Brunson, "Sailor" Roberts, and "Amarillo Slim" Preston. But since their game at the Golden Nugget downtown tempted few tourists from the Strip to "drop in," hold'em remained an unintentionally well-kept secret for the rest of the decade. Their game was so insular, in fact, that at the height of the war in Southeast Asia McCorquodale reportedly asked Brunson, "Where in the heck is this place Vietnam?"

In 1969, however, these colorfully monikered Texans were invited by Sid Wyman to play hold'em near the entrance of his Dunes Casino, on the site where the Bellagio now stands on the Strip. And in 1970, of course, Benny Binion and his Texas cronies chose hold'em as one of five games in the inaugural World Series of Poker. The following year they picked it to decide the championship event, which made its current status inevitable.

The first nationally published description of "Texas Hold Me" was by A. D. Livingston in the August 16, 1968, issue of *Life*. Livingston called it the culmination of wild-widow poker and characterized its tactics as "poker upside down. The really big action, unlike normal poker, can often come at the beginning of a hand, as players try to bully one another out." He said the game allowed for "great precision in analyzing hands, especially dear to brainy poker experts." Searching through his extensive collection of poker books, Livingston couldn't find a single reference to Hold Me, though he said it had "quickly" become popular in Texas, Alabama, and Colorado, and may have "covered the country" under such names as Tennessee Hold Me, Hold Me Darling, and hold'em.

High-stakes players preferred Hold Me, he said, because while in draw only a royal flush is a lock and in seven-stud it is also quite difficult to have one, "in Hold Me, you can tell if you have a lock after the cards are dealt up." If the community cards have no pair or three of one suit, the highest possible straight is a lock. Even so, Livingston said, "The main reason for Hold Me's popularity is the huge play it gets at the table. The historical trend in poker has always been toward more and more action," and Hold Me continued that pattern. Novelty also counted in its favor: "People have learned to play [stud], and if properly played it can get pretty drab. But Hold Me—with its increased play of straights and flushes—is more lively than stud ever was. Any respectable stud man would quickly fold a diamond 5-6, but such pip cards are often worth a call in Hold Me. So much depends on [the flop] that it is not uncommon for every player at the table to call the first bet." Two years before the World Series was launched, Livingston boldly declared, "I believe the game is a major event in the history of poker and I predict it will replace stud for the rest of the century."

In the meantime, hold'em continued spreading west to California, Alaska, and even Australia. Its popularity accelerated as the WSOP became better known, and especially when the California legislature declared it legal in 1988. From California it bounced back east across the United States and over to Ireland and Britain. Anthony Holden reports that it was introduced to Europe in the 1980s by the Irish bookmaker and poker enthusiast Terry Rogers. "Nicknamed the 'Red Menace' because of his ginger hair and bursts of belligerence," Rogers was one of the first to cross the Atlantic each May for the World Series. At the 1980 main event, he was the only bookmaker not to write off Stu 'the Kid' Ungar, pricing him at 20:1 while most oddsmakers had him at 100:1. Back in Dublin, Rogers founded the Eccentrics Club, where, as Holden reports, "The inaugural Irish Open tournament saw Collette ('Collect') Doherty sent to Vegas as the first European, man or woman, to play in the World Series' main event." Another Eccentrics Club member, the carpet manufacturer J. J. "Noel" Furlong, went on to win the WSOP main event in 1999, with two other Dubliners joining him at the final table. Before Rogers's death that year, he'd handed control of the Irish Open to his friend Liam Flood, who Holden says "really deserves to share the credit for introducing Hold'em to Europe," mainly by televising it on *Late Night Poker* on Britain's Channel 4.

Back in the States, ABC's *Wide World of Sports* had aired a ten-minute segment on the WSOP in 1979. The following year, CBS Sports did fifteen minutes of highlights. Throughout the '80s and early '90s, ESPN broadcast half-hour specials on the tournament, though never in prime time. Well-respected World Series narratives by Al Alvarez (*The Biggest Game in Town*, 1983) and Holden (*Big Deal*, 1990) introduced no-limit hold'em to a different sort of audience while giving its players their first taste of literary cachet.

But hold'em didn't become a mainstream phenomenon until the Holocaust survivor Henry Orenstein invented a poker table with glass panels through which cameras could reveal each player's hole cards. Orenstein had been motivated by the "incredibly boring" coverage on ESPN. "You couldn't see the hole cards!" he complained, echoing bored poker viewers the world over. In 1998, his table was used for *Late Night Poker*, and two years later for the first Poker Mi££ion on the Isle

of Man, broadcast live on Sky Sports 1. In March 2003, the Travel
Channel's broadcasts of the World Poker Tour began using "lipstick"
cameras recessed into the side rail for its own monthly no-limit
hold'em events, and ESPN used almost identical technology for several
events in that summer's WSOP.

Before Orenstein's brainstorm, watching poker on television had been
akin to watching bears hibernate and smoke. Stony professionals mask-
ing their thoughts as the flop hit the table made for excellent poker but
ponderous TV, since the audience had no idea who was bluffing and
who held the nuts, even after most hands were over. The new hole-card
cams gave viewers more information than the players contesting the
pots had. Sidebars displayed relative chip counts, the size of the pot,
and the odds of each hand winning at the showdown. Suddenly, watching million-dollar pots being wrangled over by seasoned road gamblers, talented amateurs, and telegenic young stars proved to be both
dramatic and educational. As Holden points out, "The resulting explosion of poker on cable television turned the leading players into
celebrities—even, in some cases, brands—whom the average Joe could
find himself sitting down next to at a tournament. Joe's liability, what's
more, was limited to the buy-in, which he could win in a satellite, usually online. The new economics of poker were born."

The game played in virtually every televised event continues to be
no-limit hold'em, the form that most consistently rewards an aggressive approach. The leverage it provides to win pots without the best
hand gives forceful risk takers a significant edge. Dan Harrington, the
1995 world champion and author of the definitive series of primers on
no-limit tournaments, helps to explain its appeal: "The best poker variations strike the right balance between hidden and exposed cards. Texas
hold'em lies right in the center of that sweet spot. Two hidden cards allow plenty of room for maneuvering, while five exposed cards allow a
good player to make plenty of deductions about opposing hands."

Tournament hold'em is also a ratings favorite because five of the
seven cards in each hand are faceup in a neat row at the center of the
table (right alongside the sponsors' logos), so it's much easier for a mass
audience to follow than stud action, in which as many as seven four-
card boards compete for attention on an overcrowded screen. But the
most telegenic aspect of no-limit hold'em is that it allows both skilled
and unskilled players to *go all-in*—one of our century's favorite verbs—
at any point in the hand. Time-constrained editors cut past most of
the sophisticated sparring of "small ball" artists to linger on crowd-

pleasing, make-or-break hands, especially those involving poor sports or loudmouths. The judicious use of the all-in "shove" is an important weapon in any skillful no-limit player's arsenal, of course. But far too many of these all-in hands, especially in tournaments, come down to a race between a pocket pair and overcards, which is similar in skill to a coin flip.

The popularity of shoving has accelerated with the publication of *Kill Phil* and similar books, which recommend going all-in as the best way to neutralize the more nuanced skills of Phil Ivey, Phil Hellmuth, and other intimidating professionals. The profligate use of all-in bets before the flop is the reason Furlong and others have called no-limit hold'em "two-card chicken." Their criticism gains force as more and more players, drawn to the game by TV, try to compensate for their lack of postflop talent and courage by pushing their entire stack forward whenever they're dealt a pair or an ace. As Addington scoffs, "This style of play, sometimes referred to as 'catch an ace and take a race,' re-introduces a substantial amount of luck into a game that had always favored the best player over the best card catcher."

However much "killing Phil" has neutralized the skill factor, Texas hold'em remains the clear game of choice in casinos, on television, in home games, as well as at the vast majority of virtual tables, where most pots are contested by folks who are oceans away from each other. All-in online, no one can read your face or body language to get a bead on whether you've flopped a made hand or you're drawing. And in the chat box, of course, no one can tell if you're drawlin'.

THE OPPOSITE OF A PEACE SIGN

Charlie don't surf!

—COLONEL WILLIAM KILGORE

American soldiers certainly played poker in Vietnam—in jungle hooches, Hanoi prison cells, air-conditioned offices in Long Binh and Saigon. The helicopter pilot Jeffrey Tillman described playing conditions at the notorious Dak To airstrip. "Serving the 'Tri-State Area' of South Vietnam, Cambodia, and Laos, Dak To International offers the weary aviator blinding dust in the dry season and bottomless mud during the monsoon," he wrote. "For the sports-minded, there are numerous NVA and Main Force Viet Cong units conveniently located throughout the surrounding countryside for your shooting pleasure. During the peak tourist season accommodations are very limited, so bring your own tent or poncho. Dining is also somewhat limited, with C-rations being the cuisine of choice, though a tasty monkey or dog stew can be had at the Montagnard village next to the river. Warm beer and a friendly game of poker are always available in the Falcons tent, so plan on adding Dak To to your 'must visit' list."

Yet an even more interesting story, perhaps, is how one of the cards in GI poker decks wound up being used as a weapon throughout Vietnam. The U.S. military was constrained from deploying its most lethal weaponry against North Vietnamese insurgents because the commanders in chief—Presidents Kennedy, Johnson, and Nixon—feared China or the Soviets might retaliate with nuclear missiles. So in addition to such devastating conventional weapons as napalm, helicopter gunships, mine-laying destroyers, and supersonic fighter-bombers, Johnson ordered that subtler forms of warfare be ratcheted up. On April 9, 1965, in a classified White House memo from the national security adviser, McGeorge Bundy, to the secretaries of state and defense and the directors of the CIA and USIA, Bundy spoke for the president when he called for "intensified and expanded psychological activities in the Vietnamese conflict."

When the First Air Cavalry Division arrived in-country on September 11 of that year, the Pentagon attached to it the first new psyops unit as a "force multiplier." Trained at the John F. Kennedy Special Warfare Center at Fort Bragg, North Carolina, the twenty-two-man unit under Captain Blaine Revis began its operations by dropping primitive leaflets into the jungle. *What is your girlfriend doing at home while you are here? You will die in the mud a horrible death . . . give up and we will pay you and give you soap.* Eventually they were dropping three and a half million such leaflets per week.

At some point in 1965 or '66, an American soldier came up with the idea of placing a card from a poker deck on a Viet Cong casualty in an effort to taunt or intimidate his comrades. The gesture caught on and was memorably depicted in Francis Ford Coppola's *Apocalypse Now*. When a green GI, the celebrated surfer Lance Johnson, sees his fellow soldiers tossing cards onto dead VC fighters, he asks Captain Willard about them. "Death cards," Willard tells him. "Lets Charlie know who did this."

The psyops of these ground troops apparently led the air force to adapt its own version. According to one report, American planes "sprinkled enemy territory with playing cards, but prior to carpet bombing, they dropped only the ace of spades. Before long, the Pavlovian technique took hold, and just the dropping of aces was sufficient to clear an entire area."

The spade ace had badass cachet five hundred years before Charlie failed to surf Vietnam. French spades from as early as 1460 were stenciled black pikes or spearheads, by far the most deadly image among the four suits. *L'as de pique* was said to represent death in French-Indochinese fortune-telling. As a cooler, more pointed expression than the skull and crossbones, the American military began to deploy it on special-ops patches, on aircraft and trucks, and as "calling cards." But as more troops began displaying the actual card on their helmets, at least one marine warned that they "couldn't afford to part with that ace from every deck we owned. We had to have some complete decks for poker."

Americans came to favor the Bicycle ace of spades because they had somehow gathered that superstitious VC soldiers associated "Lady Liberty" on the back with the goddess of death. Captain Charles W. Brown claimed that his platoon had originated the use of the death card. In 1966 he wrote that while sitting around a poker table, "one of the platoon leaders called our attention to an article in the *Stars and Stripes* [that] pertained to the superstitions of the Viet Cong. The article stated that two of their bad luck symbols were pictures of women and the ace of spades. Later that evening, someone in the group noticed that the ace of spades from a deck of Bicycle playing cards contained a picture of a woman that just happened to be a representation of the Goddess of Freedom or Liberty on the dome of our nation's capitol building."

As soon as the United States Playing Card Company heard about the military's interest in their Bicycle spade ace, the company shipped off cases of decks consisting of nothing but that particular card. In 1966 the company hired the J. Walter Thompson agency to feed what it saw as a feel-good story about its Bicycle brand to UPI and Bob Considine's widely syndicated newspaper column, among other media outlets. USPC soon received thousands of requests for Bicycle decks containing fifty-two aces of spades, especially from mothers of GIs who wanted to send them to their sons. Follow-up stories were soon published in *Life*, *Look*, and *Newsweek*, and broadcast on NBC's *Huntley-Brinkley Report*.

As the PR and psyops campaigns continued, one critical question remained: Were Viet Cong and North Vietnamese troops actually intimidated by the ace of spades—*ach bich*, as they called it—or, for that matter, by any playing card? According to one GI, "The story we heard was that the Vietnamese were inveterate card players—and that was true; I saw mamasans playing cards many, many times in any shade that was available—and that some of the common superstitions about certain cards had penetrated Vietnamese culture, by way of the French.

For instance, the Ace of Spades was a death card. The Queen of Hearts was a love card," and so on. Sergeant Rick Hofmann of the Sixth Psyops Battalion naturally spoke up for the card's ability to intimidate: "We understood the card to be a double whammy. The Ace of Spaces itself was bad luck, reinforced by the standing goddess in the center of it." Another soldier said the card meant "I understand that my job means killing the enemy. I am ready to do so. Think of it as the opposite of the peace sign." The card was often stuck into the mouth of a dead insurgent, and one GI recalled seeing it nailed to the forehead of a Viet Cong tax collector. "The whole idea was to scare the crap out of Charlie," he said.

Yet other reports cast serious doubt on the card's effectiveness. Captain Revis himself called it "a bad idea and a case [of] transposed symbolism. We Americans look at the ace of spades as the death card, but to the Vietnamese it is more like a phallic symbol and if anything might suggest we were involved in necrophilia." Another soldier called it "just another example of cultural ignorance on the part of brass that hardly ever got out of their air-conditioned headquarters and the Circle Sportif."

Yet even if the *ach bich* failed to scare Charlie, many U.S. troops loved the idea of marking their territory with calling cards. As one young grunt put it, "Did it work? I'm not sure. Did it help our morale? I definitely think so! In our company and others throughout Vietnam, I think the cards did something to encourage the men that were just trying to survive during a difficult time." The death-card historian Herbert Friedman wrote that the aces proclaimed the GIs to be "the biggest and 'baddest' varmints in the valley of death. The cards motivated and encouraged American troops far more than they terrified the enemy." He also pointed out that attempting to manipulate another group's superstitions is always a dicey affair. "Tampering with deeply-held beliefs, seeking to turn them to your advantage means in effect playing God. . . . Failure can lead to ridicule, charges of clumsiness and callousness that can blacken the reputation of psychological operations in general. It is a weapon to be employed selectively and with utmost skill and deftness."

Otherwise, it would not only fail to intimidate but could get your own soldiers killed. As one GI complained, "I don't think it scared them at all. In fact, I believe their buddies thought we did it and for about two weeks we had a running gun battle with the sons of bitches! I didn't mind fighting them, but I just couldn't see any sense in stirring them up!"

A postwar evaluation by the USIA noted that the ace of spades was not included in regular Vietnamese decks. "Thus," writes the military historian Robert Chandler, "except for a few Montagnard hill tribesmen, [Vietnamese soldiers] were unfamiliar with its meaning as a death omen." (He is referring to tribespeople similar to those seen worshiping Colonel Kurtz in *Apocalypse Now.*) Friedman emphasizes that more than one U.S. military survey concluded that "the ace of spades does not trigger substantial fear reactions among most Vietnamese because the various local playing cards have their own set of symbols, generally of Chinese derivation." The bottom line on the *ach bich*? "It did not work."

Films such as Michael Cimino's *The Deer Hunter* and the real-life POW experiences of men like John McCain contribute to our sense of what captured Americans must have endured in Vietnam. Fighter-bomber pilots like McCain, whose mission was to deliver destruction and death from on high, often causing hundreds of collateral civilian deaths, were treated more harshly than most. McCain fractured both arms and a leg after being hit and ejecting from his plane on October 26, 1967. He nearly drowned after parachuting into Truc Bac Lake in Hanoi. When he regained consciousness, soldiers vengefully spat on, kicked, and stripped him of his uniform. Others crushed his shoulder with a rifle butt and drove a bayonet into his abdomen and foot. He was taken to Hanoi's main prison, where his captors refused to put him in the hospital; instead, they continued to beat and interrogate him. His dark hair turned white. He was later offered an early release because of his father's high rank in the navy, but the junior McCain gallantly refused to break the code of "first in, first out." He wasn't released until March 1973.

During the '60s, most POWs were confined alone or in two-man cells scattered throughout the North. After a few were freed by American raids in 1970, nearly all were removed to communal prisons in Hanoi, where security was tighter. With two or three dozen of them now confined in each room, the POWs were grateful for each other's company but soon became desperate for ways to relieve their homesickness, claustrophobia, and boredom.

The air force lieutenant John "Spike" Nasmyth had been an F-4 pilot in the 555th Tactical Fighter Squadron, the famous Triple Nickle. Shot down and captured more than a year before McCain, Nasmyth spent 2,355 days as "Uncle Ho's guest," as he put it. "The Vietnamese gave us playing cards," he recalled of his time in Room 6. Made of stiff cardboard, they couldn't be shuffled without cracking them, so the men swished them around for a while before cutting and dealing again. The chips in Room 6 were hand-baked by the air force captain Dick Bolstad, a pilot Nasmyth aptly calls "a very inventive guy." Bolstad mixed bread and water with ground-up roofing tiles to make orange chips, with leftover medicine for purple ones, and coal dust for blacks. And just as they were in Las Vegas, purple chips were harder to come by. It was only when "Dick could convince Zorba the Gook that he was suffering from a foot fungus and score a little foot medicine" that he was able to cook up the purples. All of his chips, though, were "perfectly round, perfectly decorated, perfectly colored, and hard as a rock." The only problem was that when "the semi-finished chips were laid on the window sill to dry, there was a fairly good chance that the rats would carry them off or just take a bite or two." The resourceful Bolstad came up with a "secret ingredient" to add to his chip recipe that even rats found distasteful (it was probably urine or feces). "This discovery," writes Nasmyth, "kept his chips in top quality."

With poker sessions lasting for days, senior officers mandated a maximum loss of $1,000, though Nasmyth reports that "some guys hit their max in several rooms over the years." Nasmyth was one of the "poker czars" in charge of keeping tabs of who owed whom what. He meticulously kept the tally on a crumpled piece of cigarette paper, which he hid in his ear and managed to smuggle out upon their collective release in 1973. "When we got home, I mailed IOU letters to the losers. Everyone paid up, and every winner got paid." We suspect that his follow-through would have been equally diligent even if his own winnings hadn't come to $3,740.25.

Creative poker thinking in prison was hardly limited to Bolstad and Nasmyth, especially during the holidays. In *Faith of My Fathers*, McCain recalls that he and some fellow POWs gave one consistent loser "an IOU for another $250 in imaginary chips" as a Christmas gift. On Christmas Day 1971, Dwight Sullivan presented his friend Ted Ballard with a tiny poker table he had fashioned from bread and sticks. "It even had ash trays," said Ballard. "I kept the table for almost a year until the guards finally found it and took it away." Despite years in captivity, during which he was forced to play with breakable cards for money he and his buddies figured they might not live to spend, Ballard never lost his barbed sense of humor. He proved it by giving his fellow prisoner Leroy Stutz "an imaginary book" as a Christmas gift, to go with Stutz's mounting IOUs. The title? *How to Play Winning Poker.*

TWO BURN HOLES IN A BLANKET

And it's one, two, three,
What are we fighting for?
Don't ask me, I don't give a damn,
Next stop is Vietnam.
— COUNTRY JOE AND THE FISH

Massachusetts congressman Thomas "Tip" O'Neill was no peacenik or Viet Cong sympathizer. Although his congressional district included twenty-two colleges, with more students and professors than any other district in America, the majority of this burly Irish Democrat's votes came from the working-class precincts of Boston and Cambridge, where in the mid-1960s support for the war was close to unanimous. The result was that very few members of Congress spoke up more strongly for President Johnson's troop escalation.

O'Neill recalled being briefed on the latest numbers and tactics by Secretary of State Dean Rusk at the White House in 1966. When Rusk was finished, O'Neill "moved that all of us at the briefing should stand and give him a rousing vote of confidence for the way he was handling things. A few hours later, the president called me to express his appreciation." After that, O'Neill was regularly briefed by Rusk and General William Westmoreland, especially before he was to speak on college campuses, where the questions were increasingly hostile. That way,

O'Neill's replies to the antiwar students could be backed up by valid claims of having new information from the most highly placed sources.

When he got home at night, O'Neill's college-age children continued to pepper him with questions. A few of his son Tommy's friends had recently fled to Canada to avoid being drafted, and O'Neill told Tommy he thought such decisions were shameful. "You'd be breaking my heart if you did that."

"I wouldn't be breaking your heart," Tommy shot back. "I'd be hurting you politically."

When challenged by his son and other young constituents, O'Neill would say, "I think I know more about this situation than you do. I've been briefed forty-three times. I've been briefed by Robert McNamara. I've been briefed by General Westmoreland. I've been briefed by the CIA. I've been briefed by Dean Rusk. And I've been briefed by the president of the United States."

"That's a lot of briefings," one student, Pat McCarthy, sardonically remarked. "But how many times have you been briefed by the other side?"

McCarthy's question kept O'Neill awake that night. He couldn't fall asleep until he'd promised himself to take "a good look at the other side of the issue." And the other side happened to make itself heard during a poker game that week at the Army and Navy Club. One player, General David Shoup, had recently retired as commander of the Marine Corps because he disagreed with Johnson's approach to the war. O'Neill felt he could rely on Shoup's opinions because the general obviously had high-level inside information untainted by pacifist ethics.

Born in Battle Ground, Indiana, of all places, Shoup had led the attack on Betio Island, the first amphibious assault of World War II. For this and other heroics, he'd received the Medal of Honor and two Purple Hearts. *Time* correspondent Robert Sherrod called him a "squat, red-faced man with a bull neck, a hard-boiled, profane shouter of orders [who] would carry the biggest burden on Tarawa." Another writer described Shoup as "a Marine's Marine," a leader the troops "could go to the well with." Sergeant Edward Doughman called him "the brainiest, nerviest, best soldiering Marine I ever met." Shoup wrote poetry to relax between battles and was also considered "the most formidable poker player in his division," a man who stared down opponents with eyes "like two burn holes in a blanket."

He also had earned the respect of three presidents. Appointed commandant of the Marine Corps by Eisenhower in 1959, he was later known as the "favorite general" of O'Neill's friend Jack Kennedy. As a trusted military adviser, Shoup told the young president, "The commonest mistake in history is underestimating your opponent—happens at the poker table all the time." When LBJ pinned the Distinguished Service Medal on Shoup in '64, he described him as "strong enough to prevent a war and wise enough to avoid one."

Retiring two years later in protest over LBJ's measured approach, Shoup said, "Every senior officer that I knew said we should never send ground forces into Southeast Asia." He went on, "I believe if we had, and would, keep our dirty, bloody, dollar-crooked fingers out of the business of these nations so full of depressed, exploited people, they will arrive at a solution of their own. That they design and want. That they fight and work for. . . . Not one crammed down their throats by the Americans." This is pretty much what he told Tip O'Neill during that poker game and afterward. "It curdles my blood to think we're sending our boys on a mission we're not out to win," he also confided. "But that's what's going on. The will to win just isn't there. The president is afraid that if he pushes too hard, he'll start the next world war."

Nor was Shoup the only military leader who felt this way. O'Neill was soon meeting with Pentagon and CIA experts who supported their commander in chief in public but over beers or across the poker table said the war was unwinnable. Several complained that their memos to Johnson were screened by Bundy and other top advisers. They wanted O'Neill to relay their memos to Speaker John McCormack, one of the most avid hawks in Washington.

Then there was the South Vietnamese prime minister, Nguyen Cao Ky, who played poker with reporters during the thirteen-hour flight from Saigon to Honolulu, where he conferred with Johnson and his admirals in 1966. Nguyen later said, "The U.S. was and is the world's leading naval power, but, fearing to offend the Soviets, failed to blockade Haiphong. A river of munitions flowed through that port to be used against South Vietnam and its allies."

By September 1967, O'Neill had made up his mind that "the Vietnam conflict was a civil war, and that our involvement there was wrong." In a letter to his constituents, 85 percent of whom still supported the war, he wrote, "We were paying too high a price in both human lives and money." We should instead "promote an Asian solution to what was essentially an Asian problem."

On the evening of September 14, as headlines such as O'NEILL SPLITS WITH LBJ OVER VIETNAM began rolling off the presses,

O'Neill's poker game at the University Club was moved at the last minute to the Metropolitan Club. But it wasn't because O'Neill wanted to avoid reporters; Iowa congressman Ben Jensen "had been losing more than he could afford . . . so for a few weeks we played hide-and-seek with him." The new location was so secret that even the president couldn't reach the players that night. An angry LBJ tried to put through four calls to O'Neill, who, as it happened, was just across the street from the White House at the corner of 17th and H. When O'Neill finally got home from the game around 2:00 a.m., Secret Service agents were waiting in his driveway with orders for him to be in the Oval Office at nine o'clock sharp. He had some explaining to do.

The man who had summoned him was very much a poker player himself. According to *The Best and the Brightest*, David Halberstam's definitive account of how America became involved in Vietnam, Johnson "always liked to talk in poker terms and analogies." Robert Caro's multivolume biography *The Years of Lyndon Johnson* makes clear the extent to which the game influenced LBJ and his forebears and colleagues. On an 1867 cattle drive, writes Caro, "the Johnson boys loved poker." As both card players and ranchers, "the poker-playing Johnsons shoved into the pot their whole pile." Lyndon's father, Sam, taught him to play when he was five, and he soon "more than held his own" against much older boys. But it was as a networking tool that Lyndon found poker most useful. In 1946, the up-and-coming Texas congressman tried to get himself invited into President Truman's game on the *Williamsburg*. When those efforts failed, he started his own game, though he did play with Truman "two or three times" at the home of Treasury Secretary Fred Vinson. Since access to your party's president was politically crucial, Johnson understood that a seat in his regular poker game would have been an indispensible asset.

Sworn in as president after Kennedy was assassinated on November 22, 1963, Johnson was elected on his own in a landslide over Barry Goldwater the following year. After decades as a power broker in the House and Senate, Johnson was able—as Kennedy had not been—to maneuver their civil rights and Great Society initiatives through both branches of Congress and sign them into law. By 1966, the voting rights of black citizens in the South had expanded dramatically, U.S. wages were the highest in history, unemployment at a twelve-year low. Johnson's only major political error was his belief—shared by both Kennedy and Nixon—in the domino theory. "If we allow Vietnam to fall," he would say, "tomorrow we'll be fighting in Hawaii, and next week in San Francisco." Diplomat George F. Kennan's more seasoned opinion was that "we would do better if we would show ourselves a little more relaxed and less terrified of what happens in the smaller countries of Asia and Africa, and not jump around like an elephant frightened by a mouse every time these things occur." And as Oskar Morgenstern had made clear back in 1961, the game the superpowers were engaged in was poker, not chess or knock-over-the-dominoes.

"Tip, what kind of a son of a bitch *are* you?" Johnson demanded to know when O'Neill appeared in the Oval Office the morning after his poker game. "You, of all people! You and I have been friendly since the day you came to Washington. I expect something like this from those assholes like Bill Ryan [a New York congressman who had long opposed the war], but *you*? You're one of my own." He brought O'Neill over to a high-tech map of Vietnam with American positions indicated by colored lights. Pulling rank in much the same way O'Neill had with antiwar students, Johnson said, "Tell me, do you think you know more about this war than I do?"

O'Neill's response echoed what General Shoup had told him. "You can't win this war if you're not mining the harbors and knocking out the bridges and the power plants."

"I *can't* do those things," Johnson protested. "They're just too dangerous. I can't risk involving the Soviets or the Chinese." He was admitting that the larger, more strategic poker game—the one dominated by game theory and John von Neumann's MIRVed warheads—took precedence over tactics for defeating the North Vietnamese insurgents.

"Then let's get out of there," O'Neill responded. "If we really can't win, we shouldn't be there in the first place."

While insisting the war was still winnable, Johnson told O'Neill they would always be friends and thanked him for explaining his new position. If either man suspected it would help turn the public against Johnson's war, both were also aware that several congressmen had already been voted out of office because their opposition to the war was branded "anti-American." While O'Neill's change of heart—originally prompted by Tommy O'Neill's and Pat McCarthy's questions—cost him plenty of support, he picked up at least as much on campuses within his district. In the highest political circles, Shoup's conversion of O'Neill and other congressmen snowballed into an avalanche of skepticism about LBJ's war policy.

Aaron Brown has suggested that a better student of history than Johnson would have realized "China was more likely to enter the war against the North Vietnamese than resent aggressive U.S. action, and bad relations between Moscow and Hanoi offered diplomatic options far superior to war." In any case, Johnson's read of the other superpowers' tendencies and objectives may have been off, but his sense of domestic opinion was—to use a phrase of the campus protestors—right on. After narrowly defeating one antiwar Senate Democrat, Eugene McCarthy, in the New Hampshire primary and watching another, Robert Kennedy, launch an immensely popular candidacy four days later, Johnson stunned the country on March 31, 1968, by going on television to announce, "I shall not seek and I will not accept the nomination of my party for another term as your President."

Sometimes it's poker strategy, such as the nuclear bluffing deployed by Western and Communist leaders throughout the cold war, that alters the course of events. Other times it's poker-table camaraderie, as it was between Shoup and O'Neill. And while the game's tactics *and* camaraderie informed the masterful parliamentary horse trading that enabled passage of Johnson's most enlightened social legislation, he probably would have been even more effective if he wasn't bogged down by the war. O'Neill's opinion—"If it hadn't been for Vietnam, Lyndon Johnson could have gone down in history as another Roosevelt"—is still widely held. David Halberstam also made clear that Johnson got plenty of good advice about withdrawing from Vietnam, but that by 1968 he was "too deep into the war and he was not anxious to admit that this ally [the government of South Vietnam], for whom he and his country had sacrificed so much (an ally which had in effect cost him his Presidency), was not a worthy ally." Halberstam concluded: "With so many more chips already in the poker game . . . it was too painful for Johnson to accept the argument of cutting his losses."

35

THE WORLD SERIES OF POKER, PART I

In poker the thickness of a card, the luck of the draw, can make you rich and famous or send you to the rail whimpering and broke. If a diamond had come, you'd be the world champion—but it didn't and so you aren't.

—BYRON "COWBOY" WOLFORD

Twenty-three hundred miles west of the White House, Corky McCorquodale was sitting in the Golden Nugget with his fellow hold'em players, wondering where in the heck this Vietnam place was. Directly across Fremont Street, Benny Binion's Horseshoe Casino continued to dominate Glitter Gulch, as the gambling section of downtown Las Vegas was known. Yet Binion still had to compete with the Rat Pack, Folies Bergère, Elvis Presley, and all the Jetsonsesque architecture going up a few miles south on the Strip. True to his Texas roots, Benny had carpenters fashion a nine-foot-tall golden horseshoe to display behind Plexiglas his collection of one hundred $10,000 bills, which remained legal tender until 1969. Tourists flocked to see it, drawn by the opportunity to be photographed in the presence of a million bucks. So near, yet so far! The Horseshoe vault soon housed thousands of Kodak negatives, including one of the Manson family posing in front of the money, psychotic little Charles front and center.

Yet Benny understood that joints like his could always use another spectacle, something not only to get working-class tourists talking and posing, but to draw in high rollers as well. The idea of a poker World Series may have been percolating in the back of his mind since the Moss-Dandalos showdown—a no-limit match attracting hundreds of spectators, many of whom would also play the pit games and slot machines. If it had been, however, he let a couple of decades go by before finally acting on it.

The catalyst arrived early in 1969, when Benny and his sons were invited by Tom Moore to attend the Second Annual Texas Gamblers Reunion at the Holiday Hotel up in Reno. Moore's goal was to attract as many high-rolling craps and blackjack players as possible into his new casino. The first reunion had been the idea of his adviser Vic Vickrey, who imagined it would help drum up business during the slowest time of the year. After the event met with limited success, Moore's wife, LaFayne, had the idea of changing the focus the following year to a series of high-stakes poker games. Vickrey recalls that the Holiday "had a couple of old poker tables over there in the corner, and I tossed in $3,000 of the hotel's money just so's these fellas would have a little somethin' extra to try shootin' at."

Dandalos had been dead for three years, but among the Texas road gamblers who showed up were Moss, Brunson, "Amarillo Slim" Preston, Jack "Treetop" Straus, Felton McCorquodale, Brian "Sailor" Roberts, the spiffily dressed oilman Crandell Addington, and Charles Harrelson, who would later be convicted of the contract killing of U.S. District Judge John H. Wood. The non-Texans included Walter "Puggy" Pearson out of Tennessee, the talkative Ohioan Jimmy "the Greek" Snyder, the New Yorker Jimmy Casella, and a pool hustler by the name of Rudolph Wanderone Jr., also known as "Minnesota Fats."

To avoid giving an advantage to single-game specialists, the players decided to alternate among five-card draw and stud, seven-card stud high and high-low, and the new favorite game of most of them, no-limit Texas hold'em. After playing for six or seven days, Moss was either voted or named "King of Cards" and presented with an engraved silver platter. Addington was honored as "Mr. Outside," which designated him as the best road gambler. ("Inside" gamblers tended to host their own games.) Moss's platter has apparently been lost, but the engraving on Addington's reads

19 ~ THE HOLIDAY HOTEL ~ 69

2ND ANNUAL

GAMING FRATERNITY CONVENTION

MR. OUTSIDE

CRANDELL ADDINGTON

By Addington's account, it was he who won the most money that week, which is why he received the platter. Vickrey's $3,000 sweetener, he said, "didn't happen. Vic is a friend, but he is a bit off here." As far as a trophy for the King of Cards, he said, "I don't know if Moss got any such trophy, but it certainly was not by vote of the players." Suggesting that it might have been an honorary title bestowed on Moss by his friend Moore, he asked, "Can you imagine poker players with their egos 'electing' another player their 'King'?"

In any case, Moore and Vickrey were disappointed with how seldom the high-stakes gamblers strayed from the poker tables into the casino pits, even though all their suites and meals had been comped. Benny Binion, however, was plenty impressed with the gathering. "That was a good thing up there in Reno," he said. "It sure brought in a lot of people, and I'm certain there will be even more next year. The more I think about it, that might be a good thing to have here at the Horseshoe."

After Benny and Jack confirmed that Moore had no plans for another reunion, they decided to host one themselves. Their enthusiasm for a poker convention on Fremont Street was shared by Jimmy Snyder, who had just opened a public relations office in Las Vegas, with Howard Hughes as one of his clients. After Snyder volunteered to promote the event gratis, he and the Binions invited most of the men on Moore's list to the Horseshoe in May 1970 to compete in what they grandly decided to call the World Series of Poker, in spite of the fact that there were fewer than fifty poker tables in all of Las Vegas then. Among the three dozen or so men who showed up were Moss, Brunson, Casella, Preston, Straus, J. R. Green, Don Howard, Joe Floyd, Bob Hooks, George Barnes, Curtis "Iron Man" Skinner, and the singer and actor Chill Wills. Also on hand were Titanic Thompson and Joe Bernstein, two of the men who had taken Arnold Rothstein to the cleaners back in 1928, though they never collected their money.

Because the Horseshoe had no poker room—floor space for pit games and slot machines was simply too lucrative—the baccarat alcove was temporarily fitted out with three tables. For ten or eleven days the invitees played five forms of poker: five-card draw high, deuce-to-seven draw, seven-card stud, razz, and no-limit hold'em. The stakes amazed the railbirds, including a group of potential muggers pressing up close to the tables. Seeing that some of his contestants were getting nervous, Benny asked the outlaw types to step back from the rail. When they refused, he sidled up to their leader. "I know you're a young man who thinks he's tough," the sixty-six-year-old Binion told him. "I'm an old man and I know I'm tough. If you want to see who's tougher, let's go to the garage and figure it out."

"Right about then," Brunson recalls, "those guys left."

And it was another tough old Texan, sixty-three-year-old Johnny Moss, who dominated his mostly younger foes at the tables. At the dinner afterward in the Horseshoe's Sombrero Room, they voted him the champion. Jack Straus was voted Most Congenial, while Slim Preston seemed to be campaigning for Least—or Most Honest. "I couldn't understand why the fuck anybody would vote," he presciently complained. "We played for a lot of money, and that was the vote." Moss, in any case, received another silver trophy and kept what he'd won at the tables. "In those days it warn't no one game and it warn't no freezeout," he told Al Alvarez in 1981. "You had to win all the games, win all the money. Then you're the best player, an' they vote on you. A lot of gamblers hate me, but they still vote on me being the best player in the world."

For the Binions and Snyder, the goal had been to garner publicity. The problem was that, three decades before hole-card cameras, watching high-stakes pros play mostly expressionless poker just wasn't all that exciting. Among the bored observers was Ted Thackrey Jr., who'd been assigned by the *Los Angeles Times* to cover the event. Afterward, he advised the Binions to "make it a contest" somehow. "If you want to get the press involved and turn the World Series into a real sporting event, you need to give it some structure, create some drama, and make it a real tournament."

Seconding Thackrey's opinion, Preston and Pearson persuaded Benny that, instead of voting for the winner, the players should compete in a no-limit hold'em "freeze-out"—that is, with no chance to rebuy and the blinds rising every two hours, the action would proceed until one player had all the chips. In 1971, six starters put up $5,000 apiece and played for two days. Once again, Johnny Moss won, pocketing the entire thirty grand.

The next year a pair of winner-take-all events were scheduled, and both attracted eight players. The five-card-stud tournament with a $5,000 buy-in was won by Bill Boyd. And this time the buy-in for the no-limit hold'em event was doubled, with Benny putting up the extra

$5,000 for each of the entrants because he and Snyder figured the rounder number would snag more publicity. The $80,000 prize was won by Preston, whose idea it had been to double the entry fee.

A more seductive raconteur than the taciturn Moss, the tall, rail-thin Preston wrote a quickie bestseller, *Play Poker to Win*, and went on the talk-show circuit. His first appearance on Johnny Carson's *Tonight Show* was such a hit that he was invited back eleven more times. He also appeared three times on *60 Minutes*, made speeches to the National Press Club in Washington and one from the floor of the Senate. Far and away the world's most famous player now, he was able to boost exponentially the public's interest in, or at least its awareness of, tournament poker.

Preston became such a sought-after guest that Tom Snyder gave him, Binion, and Bernstein an entire *Tomorrow Show*, during which they put on what Slim called "an hour's commercial for the Horseshoe."

"Benny," asked Snyder at one point, "why is it that those places out there on the Strip in Vegas have a $500 limit and you've got no limit?"

"Well, they got great big hotels and little biddy bankrolls," drawled Benny. "I got a little biddy hotel and a great big bankroll."

"But aren't you afraid someone will break the bank?"

"Well, not really. I got a darned good head start on 'em."

Both the Horseshoe and its World Series were now on the map.

Puggy Pearson took nineteen hours to win the championship in '73, when thirteen entrants (none subsidized by Benny this time) contributed to a purse of $130,000. The relentless Mr. Moss finished second. Pearson also won two of the other five events, which this year included razz, five-card draw high, deuce-to-seven draw, seven-card stud, and a smaller no-limit hold'em event.

With the World Series doubling in size, Jack Binion hired Eric Drache, a young stud player from New Jersey who had learned to play seriously as an MP in Vietnam, to organize the various tournaments. Snyder meanwhile had persuaded CBS to film a documentary of the main event, to be narrated by Snyder himself. Watching the action in person, Al Reinert of *Texas Monthly* described Pearson as looking "like he's between acts as a circus clown" and Moss's face as "transparently blank, the practiced result of 50 years of self-induced rigor mortis." After Straus's flush on the river sent Preston to the rail, the loquacious Texan began hawking autographed copies of *Play Poker to Win* for $50 apiece.

"This poker game here gets us a lot of advertisement, this World Series of Poker," Benny told the oral historian Mary Ellen Glass in May

1973. He wasn't exaggerating. Thanks to Preston and Snyder, seven thousand stories about the World Series had already appeared in newspapers and magazines, not to mention the TV coverage. Yet Benny was just getting started. "We had seven players last year," he said, "and this year we had thirteen. I look to have better than twenty next year. It's even liable to get up to be fifty, might get up to be more than that . . ." He paused, gazing beyond Glass for a moment. "It will eventually."

Moss outlasted fifteen other players in the '74 main event, finally defeating Addington heads-up for the $160,000 prize. He received yet another silver trophy to go—with a manly gold bracelet commissioned from Neiman Marcus. It was the first time these bracelets were awarded, and they've since become the symbol of excellence in tournament poker. Boyd had won his own bracelet in the five-stud event, Preston in the smaller no-limit hold'em, Roberts in deuce-to-seven draw, and Casella a pair of them in razz and seven-stud. As usual, though, there was more money at stake in the side games, where some individual pots dwarfed what tournament winners took home.

The tournaments were still winner-take-all when Roberts earned $210,000 in the 1975 main event and Brunson $220,000 the following year. When Brunson became the second repeat champion, in '77, thirty-four players had entered, so his prize money mushroomed to $340,000, a considerable sum when the median family income was $14,000. Both years his hole cards on the final hand were 10-2, and both times he came from way behind on the flop to river a full house. Jesse Alto, a Houston car dealer and regular final-tablist, was his unlucky victim in '76; the next time it was Gary "Bones" Berland, a Los Angeles pro who eventually won five bracelets, though never in the main event. At crunch time in the Big One, Brunson's miracle river cards came sliding off the deck two years running. Alto's and Berland's stayed buried, the main reason far fewer people have heard of them.

By this point Benny Binion, at seventy-three, had come to prefer the kitchens as his bailiwick. His motto was "Good food cheap, good whiskey cheap, and a good gamble." He also insisted on cleanliness. "My kitchens get dirty," he threatened with weirdly draconian logic, "I'll call the health department. They'll straighten 'em up pretty quick." All beef served at Horseshoe restaurants, from the ground chuck in burgers and chili to the prime rib in the steak house, was raised on his four-hundred-thousand-acre ranch in Montana. Quality nonbeef selections also appeared on the menu. T. J. Cloutier, a younger Texas pro, noted that Benny "always had some oddball item in the players' buffet line—buffalo steak, rattlesnake, bear meat, this and that—and the main courses were never repeated during the series." The players loved him for inventing their annual championship and get-together, and they loved the down-home hospitality with which he continued to host it.

When Benny died on Christmas Day 1989, Preston proposed an epitaph for his friend: "He was either the gentlest bad guy or the baddest good guy you'd ever seen." He was certainly the impresario who nurtured Vic Vickrey's and LaFayne Moore's brainchild of a few Texans gambling "over there in the corner" in Reno into a million-dollar poker tournament covered on network TV. Even so, it's doubtful he ever imagined the nine-figure international spectacle his World Series would become.

36

GARDENA, THAT SEVENTIES POKER CAPITAL

[My brother] liked the notion of the outlaw—not the mean outlaw who is rude to the saloon lady, but the Robin Hood kind: the outsider, the existential hero. . . . Poker fulfilled that role for him, I think.

—AUGUST KLEINZAHLER, *CUTTY, ONE ROCK*

By the mid-1970s, poker had two distinct capitals. The Texas road gamblers' no-limit hold'em sanctuary in downtown Las Vegas was active most weeks of the year but focused on the World Series in May, while the licensed card rooms of Gardena, a working-class suburb of Los Angeles, hosted hundreds of five-card-draw players every day except Christmas. Poker was still for the most part an underground national pastime, but its lawful status in these far Western towns was a double blast of oxygen for high-stakes professionals and recreational players alike.

In *Poker Faces: The Life and Work of Professional Card Players* (1982), David Hayano painted a vivid group portrait of men struggling to make a name for themselves, or at least a decent living, in Gardena. Hayano had a Ph.D. in anthropology from UCLA. His dissertation on the Awa and Gimi people of Papua New Guinea had landed him a teaching job at California State University, Northridge. For his next project, he immersed himself in the indigenous tribe of Gardena draw players, becoming what he called an "autoethnographer." It was the first time a significant corner of the poker world had been systematically analyzed.

Some background: In 1872, California's poker-playing legislators passed a statute outlawing "stud horse poker," a casino game with a built-in house edge that was stud poker in name only, while intentionally omitting five-card draw from the list of prohibited games. In 1891, however, a new legislature banned all gambling, poker included, anywhere in the state. But in 1911, Attorney General Ulysses S. Webb (born in 1864 and named for Ulysses S. Grant) exempted draw poker from the ban, arguing that it was a "game of science rather than chance." Plenty of poker was played in California, but it wasn't until the Depression that commercial card parlors began to spring up around the state, usually as efforts to expand the meager tax base. No fewer than six—the Rainbow, Monterey, Gardena, Horseshoe, Normandie, and El Dorado—would open in cash-poor Gardena, whose city council explicitly made poker welcome there in 1938. (The game had been legal in Las Vegas since 1931. It would not become legal in Atlantic City until 1977; in Tunica, Mississippi, until 1990; or at Foxwoods in Ledyard, Connecticut, until 1996.)

The Gardena clubs prospered by featuring posh restaurants with crystal chandeliers, while the draw games down the hall proceeded in briskly unglamorous fashion. The clubs' gaming licenses were usually held in the name of the local VFW or American Legion posts. To further insulate them from charges of fostering vices like prostitution and loan-sharking, their owners promoted them as friendly places to have an inexpensive meal and as tax-paying businesses that employed hundreds of citizens and kept property taxes low. The clubs made money not by raking a percentage of each pot but by renting seats for between $1 and $10 per half hour, depending on the stakes.

Without professional dealers, the deal rotated among the eight players. Even so, Hayano describes the action as "a no-nonsense, speedy affair," with as many as sixty hands per hour being dealt, though the average at full tables was closer to forty. "In contrast with the staged scenes of poker games in popular novels and films, commercial cardroom players never make long-winded speeches about calling, raising, or folding because other players would not allow them," he writes. "Nor can players run to the bank or sell their houses for more money while involved in a hand, for the law prohibits playing with any money that is not on the table."

Security personnel banished troublemakers—drunks, cheats, thieves, anyone who started a fight or otherwise disturbed the peace of regular rent-paying customers. Floor people made sure open seats were filled efficiently on a first-come-first-served basis. "Chipgirls" in large, bulging aprons exchanged cash for "checks," getting players into action more quickly. The clubs also hired proposition players to help games get started and fill seats at short tables to keep those games from breaking up. Then as now, a "prop" received a salary (up to $150 per day) but had to risk his own money in whatever game the floorman directed him to play. The main games were five-card draw jacks-or-better, high-low, and lowball.

The clubs were limited by law to thirty-five tables apiece, for a total of 1,680 players—a critical mass whose gravity attracted the toughest poker pros in the country. There were reputations to be made in Gardena, plus all those extra hands dealt per hour multiplied the expected value their edge in skill already gave them. The amateurs they feasted on included businessmen, housewives, retirees, and students.

Hayano reports that 90 percent of the players are men. Forty-six percent of the men and 74 percent of the women are over sixty. Older players patronize clubs offering the best low-stakes action. Younger men like to play higher, often through the next morning, or longer. The high-stakes tables are in corners less accessible to railbirds and other distractions. They receive better service and "their players are generally accorded some degree of curiosity and respect by small-stakes players." A player's preferred game and stakes tend to be so consistent that "two men may play in the same club for ten years, only twenty feet apart, one in a high-stakes draw game, the other in a small-stakes lowball game, yet they may never recognize or interact with each other."

The smaller games are beatable, says Hayano, by passively waiting for strong hands and betting them aggressively—that is, by playing ABC poker. Bigger games tend to have wilier players, many of whom are professionals. The toughest pros are inclined to raise and reraise before the draw, sometimes without even looking at their cards, and to stand pat "with absolutely nothing at all." Instead of waiting for strong hands, pros "manufacture" or represent them with a variety of betting and acting maneuvers, which of course make them harder to play against.

Hayano reports that before the emergence of draw in Gardena, the typical pro had been born in the rural South, most often in Texas.

Shotgun-packing road gamblers like Moss, Titanic Thompson, and Bet-a-Million Gates, or *The Sting*'s Doyle Lonnegan and Henry Gondorff, all had a strong outlaw stigma that transferred even to married men playing for pocket change in wood-paneled rec rooms. But as licensed card rooms began deploying security systems and PR departments, playing poker began to seem a little less socially deviant. A related result was Gardena's "more heterogeneous modern class of professional poker players. Members are drawn from almost every segment of the socioeconomic, ethnic, religious, educational, and occupational ranks of American society."

The downside of making poker your job includes the distinct possibility of working longer hours and winding up deep in the red. "I thought it would be fun doing this for a while. You know, come and go any time you want. But it's really a nightmare now," one pro admits to Hayano. "When you get stuck you stay all day and night and don't make a damn buck. I'm still here from two days ago. Maybe I'll get back into business and not fuck around coming down here all the time."

The group Hayano classifies as "subsistence pros" must win week after week just to cover their living expenses. They tend to avoid other pros and seek out the weakest opposition, nearly always found in lower-stakes games. Those he calls "career professionals" choose the highest-stakes action, hoping to sharpen their skills against the stiffest competition available. Besides money, they're intensely interested in peer recognition. In ethnographic terms, they engage in a considerable amount of *face work*, efforts to build or maintain their status. They like to emphasize how difficult yet rewarding their chosen career is. "You can't just sit down and play," says a pro named Rick H. "I go and think about the players and the game for a while and draw up a game plan. I don't like to play long hours because I'm concentrating and figuring the odds all the time. Hell, I work less hours a month than a doctor, and I can take vacations any time I want to."

During the years Hayano reports on, few pros in Gardena have more than two years of college. Most are white. The next-largest ethnic group is the Asians, followed by blacks and Latinos. Despite the fact that many pros often play for days at a time, not one sees himself as a compulsive gambler. Largely because of the hours they keep, almost two-thirds are either unmarried or divorced. "I see these guys down here more than my wife and kids," one admits. "I've sure been screwed a lot, but never been kissed."

In the end, Hayano calls poker "the existential game" and defends it on the grounds that in the small world of "the green-felt tables . . . with all their arcane symbols and skills," a professional player "tests his inventive adaptiveness at every moment." To critics who complain that the pros are doing nothing worthwhile, Hayano says "it is unfair to question the ultimate meaning of any individual's way of life." He suggests that, "like formal religion," a full-time commitment to poker can "provide solace from the ultimate certainty of death." Neither of these "neuroses," as he calls them, whether a devotion to God or to cards, is necessarily more soothing than the other. And while Hayano doesn't mention it, there seems to be a fair number of those who choose both.

We are lucky to have a draw-playing anthropologist's account of Gardena in the '70s, but to see that lost world even more in the round we also need to read the Gardena chapter of Aaron Brown's *The Poker Face of Wall Street*. In 1976, as a nineteen-year-old Harvard undergraduate, Brown was able to pass as twenty-one in a few of the clubs. He describes them as having "the ambiance of airport gate waiting areas," his competition as looking "like midlevel office workers after a two-day bus ride." The management seemed "anxious to preserve a friendly image, advertising good meals and companionship rather than excitement and sex, like Las Vegas did at the time." Gardena, Brown recalls, was "not a place to play poker for fun."

At the top of its pyramid were the winning career professionals, to whom the floormen kowtowed, he says, "as if they were star athletes." The winners' main function was "to protect the community from tourists. Most tourists can be handled by the hobbyists. If they start to win, subsistence pros take over. But if that doesn't work, each card room needs to have some of the top players in the world to bring in." Brown explains that if "a tourist keeps winning, he will come up against his match. If that weren't true, top players from all over the world would keep showing up in Gardena until the game had such negative expectation to the community that it would fall apart. The winners are the hired guns elected sheriff to keep other gunmen away." Winners were nearly always younger men and usually "the best educated group within the community. Unlike most of the other regulars, who have arrived at their destinations in life and will likely go down rather than up in the future, winners are usually on their way to something."

Among the players Brown met were David "the Arm" Hayano himself, so-called because of the way he slammed chips into the pot. Also lurking at the tables were David "Einstein" Sklansky, hard-drinking

Steve Margulies, and "Crazy Mike" Caro. If Caro's nickname "makes you think of a cheerful eccentric, always joking around, you're mistaken. His manner suggested serious clinical issues, and his play was wildly erratic." Brown adds that Caro "was among the best players I've ever seen, but I honestly don't think it was an act."

Brown had been warned to look out for mechanics and colluders, but the first thing he noticed was that some of the floormen allowed their friends among the regulars to swipe chips from tourists away from the table on bathroom breaks, and to pass cards or signal the contents of their hands to each other. Brown also caught some regulars raising and reraising in tandem when strangers like him were in a pot against them. The amount of the raises is limited, but not their number, so that "two players against me can play effective table stakes poker whenever they choose, while I can only play limit." Although he observed more of this behavior than would be tolerated in card rooms today, he says he found most Gardena players to be friendly and honorable.

Intriguing as his reports of gunmen, cheats, and thieves are, it's at the macroeconomic level that Brown make his most telling points. By the time he published *The Poker Face of Wall Street* in 2006, he was a senior executive at Morgan Stanley and a widely respected quantitative analyst, so he looked back on Gardena through the eyes of an investment banker. Crunching data from Hayano and other academics, he concludes that the winners comprised barely 2 percent of the players but reaped the (male) lions' share of the profits. Break-even players filled about 10 percent of the seats. At the bottom were the action players, the 2 percent who played wildly and were "by far the biggest losers in the card room." He says a typical high-stakes table had one winner, one action player, and five break-even players.

At the lower-stakes tables, subsistence pros (10 percent of all players) were the most consistent winners. Hobbyists (40 percent) usually broke even or lost small amounts. Tourists (30 percent) were at the table to have a good time, but they lost even more consistently than the action players, while competing for smaller amounts. The action players' loud, flashy play made them the easiest group to identify. The other groups blended into each other as skill and luck built and shrank bankrolls.

Brown reckons that during the '70s a typical club had annual revenues of $5 million. It was home to about ten winners and fifty subsistence players, with a thousand break-even hobbyists dropping in for shorter sessions, along with three thousand tourists playing even more sporadically. Winners made about $50,000 a year, with subsistence players averaging $10,000. He acknowledges that the "actual amounts varied widely. Some tourists showed up once and won, and some break-even players had a substantial profit for the year. Other players dropped $10,000 or more." (For context, in 1975 a family of four needed $5,050 to stay out of poverty, a single male even less. The median family income was $13,719.)

Small money generally flowed from tourists through break-even hobbyists to subsistence grinders, big money from action players to winners like Sklansky and Caro. Measured pot by pot over the course of a year, Brown says about $2 billion was won and $2.006 billion was lost per card club. Each club took $5 million of that for taxes, expenses, and profit, leaving $1 million to be divided up by the winners. Multiply these numbers by six to get a sense of the entire Gardena "pokonomy."

The bottom line was that half a dozen poker parlors financed 25 percent of Gardena's city budget during those years. Joints like the Normandie, Rainbow, and Monterey also provided employment for hundreds of chip runners, brushes, props, cashiers, floor managers, security guards, bean counters, restaurant and maintenance workers. They provided pricey entertainment for thousands of recreational draw players, a living wage for three hundred grinders, and a handsome income for maybe sixty winners.

Mason Malmuth didn't arrive in Gardena until 1981, by which point he says that women made up at least 20 percent of the players. He adds that "almost all" the pros worked as props then, some for as much as $300 a day. They could also get a letter from the club declaring the half-hourly collections to be a necessary expense of their job. "Thus they became tax deductible," says Malmuth. "Since collections were roughly equal to the prop's salary, if he didn't report his winnings (or claimed he lost) the prop could pay almost no taxes." He claims that more than a few props would collude against tourists, soft-playing each other and splitting the profits of tag-team reraises when only one of them had a strong hand—although offering the tourist two-to-one odds on each bet, he adds, was often an expensive mistake.

Malmuth also takes issue with Brown's small percentage of winners, or at least with the way he defines what a winner is. "If I play one thousand hours a year and win, and you play ten hours a year and lose, if you count as one loser, I should count as one hundred winners. My guess, and this still applies today," he adds, is that in card rooms "approximately seventy percent of the people playing are winners (to at least some small degree)."

Caro, who played as "Crazy Mike" in Gardena for fourteen years and now prefers to be called "the Mad Genius of Poker," saw many more cheaters than Brown did. "At the old Rainbow Club," he insists, "there were always colluders—people working in teams, with signals and codes. The club generally ignored it, but there got to be so many of them that the management finally felt they had to do something." The club issued an edict with a printed list of names, declaring that "only three of the people on this list could be in one game at any one time. Well, of course, we were outraged! They were giving us a list of the guys they knew to be cheaters, and saying they could only work in teams of three. So to calm us down, they modified their decision: only *two* of those guys could be in a game at a time."

After Caro became director of poker operations at the Huntington Park Casino in 1986, several Gardena players came in and confessed they had cheated him, adding, "but I swear I'm straight now." He says the cheaters "wanted to make sure I'd let them play. But I had no idea how severely I'd been cheated until they confessed to me! In the bigger games, a poker professional is supposed to average $450 an hour, but I usually wasn't at that level. I probably lost $100,000 a year to cheaters."

As to the styles and skills of the square players, no less an expert than Sklansky writes, "I intuitively suspected I was better off playing in games with the typically tight Gardena players than in the looser games with players who played too many hands. I now realize what the difference was. The tight players never bluffed, which was profitable for me, whereas in the looser games players were bluffing more or less correctly—and that hurt me."

Gardena is no longer a poker capital, though L.A.'s landmark rooms haven't moved very far—to Bell Gardens and Commerce, specifically. In 2000, *Hustler* publisher Larry Flynt opened a new $40 million poker room in Gardena on the site of the old El Dorado, naming it after his magazine.

Draw poker, too, has given way to flop games and stud. Even so, it was during his years playing limit five-card draw in Gardena that Sklansky began to develop the ideas in *The Theory of Poker* and a dozen other bestselling primers. These books continue to educate millions of players, particularly those specializing in the five limit games comprising H.O.R.S.E.

Cameras and professional dealers have also reduced the collusion and chip swiping. Los Angeles card rooms may no longer have crystal stemware, but the food they wheel up next to the tables is tasty, nutritious, and free. There's plenty of face work still going on, too. Television exposure and online sponsorship deals provide hundreds of players with lucrative incomes over and above what they win or lose at the tables. Many of the younger ones know all about the Texans in Las Vegas but remain unaware of the trails blazed for them by the early poker pros in Gardena.

THE WORLD SERIES OF POKER, PART 2

Good high-stakes poker players are neither noble nor greedy. They've sized up their fellow players, know a good deal about probabilities and tendencies, and wish like poets that their most audacious moves be perceived as part of a series of credible gestures.

—STEPHEN DUNN, *WALKING LIGHT*

By the late 1970s, Benny Binion's two sons were running the tournament, with Eric Drache as their principal lieutenant. The older son, Jack, who resembled Ron Howard in both looks and easygoing respectability, was in charge of general casino operations, with Ted, a bushy-haired, hard-living rocker whose hero was Jim Morrison, serving as host on the gaming floor. Ted was more rakishly handsome than his brother—toothier, with longer, thicker hair. Inclined to dark business suits, Jack was a brilliant executive—World Series revenue multiplied a hundredfold during his tenure—while Ted preferred dressing down while mixing it up with high rollers.

"Jack is the boss," said their father. "Ted's next boss." The basic division of labor had Jack around during regular business hours and Ted running things after dark. Jack was a natural CEO who eventually grew the Horseshoe brand into a $1.45 billion string of casinos. The "next boss" was called Ted after his mother, Teddy Jane. (Ted may have grown into his father's hat and shoe size and big, moon-faced features, but not into his commanding personality. He was also too fond of narcotics and dangerous women.) Following the same reverse-gender system, daughters Barbara, Brenda, and Becky got soundalike versions of their father's name but were apparently never considered boss material by their old-school Texas Daddy.

In 1979, the Binion men instituted the Poker Hall of Fame, essentially a row of plaques hung along a wall of the Horseshoe—a Wall of Fame, then, in the cathedral of tournament poker. They put their heads together with Drache and inducted four fairly obvious charter members: Moss, Dandalos, Felton McCorquodale, and Wild Bill Hickok. Somewhat more eccentrically, they added "all-around player" Red Winn, about whom little else is known; casino owner and high-stakes player Sid Wyman; and Sir Edmond Hoyle, the white-wigged London authority on whist and other card games who died in 1769, decades before the first hand of poker was dealt.

The Binions also realized that a legitimate world championship needed to involve more than two or three dozen contestants. Because only a few leading pros and wealthy amateurs could afford to risk $10,000 in a winner-take-all freeze-out, what was to be done? They turned to Eric Drache for the answer.

Drache claims he came up with the idea of one-table, thousand-dollar winner-take-all feeder tournaments by accident in either 1978 or '79. One day he noticed that about $10,000 in chips was at stake on one of the Horseshoe's no-limit tables, and the lightbulb switched on. He simply suggested that the players put up $1,000 apiece and play winner take all for a seat in the main event, which they did as soon as ten had agreed. And it was definitely '78 when Drache began paying the top five places, instead of just a single survivor. He figured a more gradual payout structure would tempt a few extra players to try their luck against the veteran road gamblers. It worked. Fifty-four hopefuls entered the main event in '79, when 9 percent of the field was paid, ranging from $27,000 for fifth (Johnny Moss) to $270,000 for the winner.

The kicker was that first-place money and the bracelet went to Hal Fowler, a public relations executive in his late fifties from Ventura, California. In a bona fide secular miracle, the PR man had arrived at the final table with only $2,000 of the $540,000 in play. Making the odds against him even more prohibitive, he was up against the likes of Moss, Addington, Bobby Baldwin, and a young, cocaine-addicted poker genius out of Houston by the name of Bobby Hoff. Yet Fowler somehow managed to surf a tsunami of luck—hitting inside straight draws, backdooring flushes, sucking out in huge hands, all this while popping as many as twenty Valiums for his nerves—to a showdown with Hoff. Handicappers rated Hoff, called "the Wizard," among the strongest no-limit hold'em players alive at the time. It was laughable to believe he would have any trouble with Fowler.

Three decades later, long after he had kicked his drug habit, Hoff still gets emotional about the result. Heads-up, he had used his talent and experience to chop away at the overmatched amateur's chip stack. "I won all of the little pots, but every time we had a big confrontation and a big pot, Hal won every single one."

We can hear the pain in Hoff's voice as he recalled for the journalist Dana Smith the nastiest series of beats ever suffered at the main event's final table. To take but one example, Fowler called all-in with second pair against Hoff's top pair. "With one card to come, I had two queens and a six kicker," said Hoff. "Hal had two jacks and a king kicker. He had all of his money in the pot, and I still had $150,000 in chips." Fowler, of course, caught a king on the river. In the next big hand, both players pushed all-in on the turn with the same straight, but Hoff had a diamond flush redraw—and no diamond came. As the rodeo rider and bracelet winner Byron "Cowboy" Wolford observed fatalistically, "In poker the thickness of a card, the luck of the draw, can make you rich and famous or send you to the rail whimpering and broke. If a diamond had come, you'd be the world champion—but it didn't and so you aren't."

Yet the final hand really took the cake. Hoff squinted down between his knuckles at the ace of hearts and the . . . ace of clubs. He made a substantial preflop raise, which Fowler impetuously called with 7-6 off-suit, a reasonably good hand with several players in the pot, but a terrible hand to call a raise with heads-up. On a flop of J-3-5, Hoff bet half his remaining chips. Fowler thought for a moment, dragging deeply on a cigarette, then made the call with nothing but an inside straight draw: four outs. When the inevitable 4 of spades appeared on the turn, the rest of the money went in. As Slim Preston put it, the lamb had just slaughtered the butcher. T. J. Cloutier called it the biggest upset in the history of poker. "You could've played as good as God can play and still not have beaten Hal on that day." The men and women who actually turned the tide in most of the big pots that day were the human randomizers in the white shirts and black BINION'S HORSESHOE bow ties. There's also no doubt that thousands of ordinary players found it cause for a compensatory toast.

Fowler defended his clearly incorrect calls with the classic novice's rationale: "I had a feeling [a 4] was going to fall on fourth or fifth street. I play my hunches. Sometimes when you have a hunch, it means something." Not surprisingly, the '79 main event would prove to be the only WSOP tournament in which he ever cashed. It would be another twenty-three years before so rank an amateur would win it again.

In part because of "the Fowler Effect," seventy-three players proved willing to risk $10,000 to challenge the bracelet-laden Texans amid the stagflation of 1980. "Ten dimes" wasn't what it used to be, and besides—if a short-stacked novice like Fowler had beaten the likes of Hoff, Moss, and Brunson by catching some cards, a lot of serious amateurs thought, Hell, I can too! They included a pair of Nebraska ranch hands calling themselves "Maverick Mike" and "Buffalo Butch," San Diego's Barbara Freer, Ireland's Colette Doherty, the fierce and beautiful Betty Carey, and the thirty-five-year-old star of *Welcome Back, Kotter*, Gabe Kaplan. Meanwhile, the Binions had struck a deal with a start-up cable outfit unpromisingly called the Entertainment and Sports Programming Network to broadcast the poker World Series.

This was also the year in which Stuey "the Kid" Ungar arrived at the Horseshoe. He also quite simply *arrived*. An out-of-control sports bettor and nearly unbeatable gin artist from the Lower East Side of New York—"hands down the greatest player that's ever lived or maybe that will ever live," said an expert who saw him play many times—Ungar had recently taken up poker because he'd run out of gin victims, even when he spotted them a peek at the bottom card of the deck. Gin tournament officials banned him because people avoided any events that he played. He was also an obnoxious winner and a terrible sport when he did lose the occasional match.

But gin was one thing; no-limit hold'em was dominated by Texans who had more or less invented it. These were tough, savvy veterans who tended toward physical amplitude. Brunson was six three and three hundred pounds, Hoff and Baldwin about the same height. Preston was a lanky six five in his custom cowboy boots with SLIM stitched in contrasting leather up their sides. In stocking feet, Treetop Straus was six six. Ungar was barely five four and weighed 110 pounds. At twenty-five, he was the youngest player in a field that believed hard-bitten experience was the only way to learn what they called "the Cadillac of Poker Games." In his Rolling Stones haircut and skinny black pants, the Kid could have passed for eighteen, and he'd been playing hold'em for only a few months. The photographic memory he deployed to annihilate gin opponents would have been invaluable if the WSOP championship were decided by stud, but in hold'em it was relatively useless.

Yet Ungar's phenomenal card sense and IQ of 185 helped him in all games, of course. And even though a freeze-out didn't allow him to buy more chips if he lost his initial $10,000, he began the main event with his usual hell-bent aggression. "I just have to make myself hate my opponents," he said. "I just want to rip their throats out." Once he had doubled through to $21,000, the freeze-out aspect worked even more heavily in his favor. Nolan Dalla and Peter Alson's biography perfectly captures his tablemates' predicament: "Many players who bought in for $10,000 and a chance to play in the world's most prestigious poker event wanted to savor the experience for as long as possible. Their fear of elimination played right into the hands of Stuey, whose cutthroat style definitely served him well. He immediately sized up those players who were content to wait patiently for a good hand—and even then were loathe to lose too many chips to it—and when he sensed any weakness in them, he put them to the test."

By the end of day two, Ungar was in second place among sixteen survivors, with $93,500. Holding better than a two-to-one chip lead, however, was the crowd favorite, Kaplan, a talented mimic of Texans and Irishmen who also did a mean Groucho Marx. His biggest hand so far had come against Robert "Red" Bone, an Arkansas commodities trader and friend of Governor Bill Clinton who was advising Hillary Clinton as she traded cattle futures, occasionally executing orders when her account had insufficient funds to cover them. Bone, in any case, flopped a set of tens against Kaplan and bet out on every street, pushing all-in on the river when he made a full house. Kaplan, who had slow-played aces full, was only too happy to call, knocking out Bone and taking the lead in the tournament.

On the young side but no beginner, Kaplan had recently beaten the stud artists Baldwin and Bill Boyd in $100,000 heads-up matches and won the Super Bowl of Poker in Reno, outlasting a no-limit hold'em field even tougher than the one here at Binion's, which now included a sizable fraction of tourists. If Kaplan could hold on and win the main event, as bookies had made him a five-to-two favorite to do, it would be a major PR coup for the series.

On day three, however, the bearded comedian suffered a string of bad beats that not only kept him from winning but made him the Bubble Boy—eliminated in sixth place, that is, when only five would be paid. What Kaplan called "the last straw" was a hand against Moss, who had raised on the button with the A-8 of diamonds. Kaplan, in the big blind, just called with 4-4. When the flop came with the 4 of hearts and 6 and jack of diamonds, Kaplan led out with a sizable bet. "Moss thought for a few seconds," says Kaplan, "and then in his Texas drawl said, 'All raht, Ah'm all in.' He even removed his Rolex and put it on top of his chips." Kaplan called with the rest of his chips, adding his own watch and ring for good measure. "John, if you have three jacks you might as well take my ring also." (Jewelry, of course, doesn't actually play in a tournament.) After the hole cards were exposed, Kaplan, a three-to-one favorite, watched the dealer turn a fatal diamond then fail to pair the board on the river. Moss chuckled as he raked in the chips. "If you'd had a Rolex, Ah'd have to let that bet stand too."

The other finalists were Ungar, Brunson, the New York beer distributor Jay Heimowitz (who'd already won a bracelet in a $5,000 no-limit hold'em event), and another talented semipro, Charles Dunwoody. Brunson trailed the field with $44,000 at a point when Ungar led with more than $300,000, but he managed to outplay and outdraw the other veterans to finish heads-up with the Kid.

With $310,000 to Ungar's $420,000, Texas Dolly was still made a six-to-five favorite by bookie Jackie Gaughan to win his third championship. Dolly took $50,000 of that action, though he had plenty of respect for his diminutive opponent. "In all the years I've played poker," he said, "I don't think I've ever seen another player that actually improved as the tournament went along. He used the World Series and all of us as a training ground."

Ungar also got lucky, as anyone who wins any tournament must. On the final hand, with the chips fairly even, Brunson was dealt the A-7 of hearts, Ungar the 5-4 of spades. As Brunson recalled with impressive humility, "I made two mistakes in the same hand, one of the worst plays I've ever made. Before the flop I brought it in for a raise and Stu called, making about $17,000 in the pot." The flop came off A-7-2, giving Brunson the top two pair, Ungar an inside straight draw—the same four outs Fowler had against Hoff. "A lot of time in this situation," Brunson said, "I would bet big (overbet the pot) to throw off my opponent, but this time I decided to trap Stu and so I only bet the size of the pot, $17,000. Stu called. That was my first mistake." He went on: "When a three came on the turn, Stu led at the pot for around $30,000, and I moved all-in. Stu called. That was my second mistake. I should've just flat called because at the river, when a deuce fell that paired the board and also made a flush possible, Stu would've shut down—and I wouldn't have got broke to the hand."

Having played no-limit hold'em for just a few months, Ungar had beaten a field that had been playing, on average, for at least a dozen years to become poker's youngest, and still most notorious, champion. The next afternoon he lost the entire $385,000 prize gambling with Brunson and others at golf, a game he had never played before in his life.

The 1981 series was covered by hundreds of journalists, including Curt Gowdy for NBC Sports and for *The New Yorker* by, of all people, a London poet and critic by the name of Al Alvarez. The book he produced, *The Biggest Game in Town*, is a comprehensive account of the championship as it began to mature into its second decade. Few books on any game have been received with as much enthusiasm over so long a period. Casual poker players and world-class professionals continue to revel in its lapidary prose, sage hold'em insight, and droll use of cowboy patois.

The Biggest Game naturally concludes with the main event, in which seventy-five players competed for shares of a record $750,000 purse, half of it reserved for first place. Infusing the hand-to-hand combat with as much drama as any sporting event, Alvarez demonstrates once and for all that an understated prose account of poker action is quite a bit more exciting than watching the game in person, or even on television with hole cards revealed. His book has no weaknesses, really, though it does involve a missed opportunity. Ungar could not have been easy for a reporter to get next to—few self-destructive, semiliterate, monomaniacal gamblers and cocaine addicts are. Compared to the soul baring Alvarez coaxed from subjects like Moss, Brunson, Jack Straus, Eric Drache, Jack Binion, and the young New Yorker Mickey Appleman, Ungar's crude, inarticulate psyche amounts to fingernails down a blackboard. The result was that the Kid got much shorter shrift from Alvarez than he otherwise might have received.

Perry Green, a big-hearted Orthodox Jewish furrier from Anchorage, outlasted every pro to finish heads-up with Ungar—who was Jewish himself, though extravagantly not Orthodox. Green even managed to build a sizable chip lead, but one huge late hand put Ungar in the driver's seat. "Perry had more chips than Stuey when they got it all in," the ever-present Brunson recalled. "The flop came J-9-8 with two clubs. Perry had the 10-2 of clubs, but Stuey had the A-J of clubs. The fourth card was a 6 and the last one was a blank—but if that 6 had been a 7, Perry could have won the tournament with a straight and it would have been the third time that a 10-2 had won it. As it turned out, Stuey won a $560,000 pot that turned the tide."

On the final hand, Ungar was dealt the A-Q of hearts, Green the 10 of clubs and 9 of diamonds. When Green raised to $16,000, the Kid reraised him to $41,000. Looking unhappy, Green called. On a flop of 8 and 4 of hearts and 7 of diamonds, Ungar, with the nut flush draw and two overcards, bet the last $78,000 his opponent had left. Green, with an open-end straight draw, reluctantly said, "I call." When the straight failed to materialize and another queen needlessly spiked on the river, Ungar leaped from his seat and said, "Hey!" He'd been playing hold'em for only about a year and a half, but he'd just notched his second world title.

THE WORLD SERIES OF POKER, PART 3

They all know me as a small-timer, but that's about to change.

—MIKE MCDERMOTT

Eric Drache's one-table satellites to the main event steadily increased the number of entries—to fifty-four in 1979, seventy-three in 1980, seventy-five in 1981, one hundred and four in 1982. Nineteen eighty-two was also the year Treetop Straus won the Big One after being down early on to a single $500 chip, giving rise to the expression "all you need is a chip and a chair," the mantra of every contender sitting behind a short stack. Meanwhile, next door to the Horseshoe, the Mint's poker manager, Jim Albrecht, followed suit by spreading WSOP satellites of his own. At the old Bingo Palace out on Sahara (today's Palace Station), Tom Bowling spread hundred-player "supersatellites" with $110 buy-ins and one very fortunate winner. Albrecht and Bowling encouraged other card-room managers to follow their lead, and the snowball began to get bigger.

While the prize pool increased by $10,000 with every satellite winner, the downside, at least for the original coterie of Texans, was that it was increasingly difficult for any of them to win what they considered to be *their* event. Whatever their advantage in skill, it was now taking more and more luck to survive the long gauntlet of bad beats and coin flips the larger fields forced them to run.

A more practical problem was that by 1983 the Horseshoe didn't have enough space for all the players lining up to register—234 in the limit hold'em event, 108 in the no-limit championship. The Binions not only had to borrow poker tables from neighboring casinos, but in the opening rounds they had to seat much of the field across the street at the Golden Nugget, the Fremont, and the Four Queens. Only after a sufficient number of starters had been eliminated was everyone finally moved, under the supervision of officials with walkie-talkies, over to the Horseshoe. Every player's dream had been to make the final table of a World Series event, and the joke among the survivors was that at least they had "made the final casino." Amid all these growing pains, it was only fitting that the winner, the Grand Rapids accountant Tom McEvoy, had earned his seat in a Horseshoe satellite, with the runner-up, Rod Peate, a medium-stakes player from Los Angeles, gaining entry to a Bingo Palace super.

After Brunson, the Irish pro Donnacha O'Dea, and five other final-tablists had been eliminated, the heads-up struggle between McEvoy and Peate lasted more than seven hours. Many of their hands have been recorded and analyzed, but it's a photograph by the Binions' young dealer Pamela Shandel that most vividly captures in classic black-and-white the moment Drache's project of democratizing the World Series finally achieved liftoff (see insert).

It's Friday, May 20, 1:45 a.m. Shandel had dealt earlier rounds of the tournament, but now she was off the clock, wielding her Nikon. After clawing his way back from a four-to-one chip deficit, McEvoy had just taken a $630,000-to-$450,000 chip advantage. And now he had found pocket queens, his opponent the K-J of diamonds—two very strong hands when heads-up, though McEvoy's was a two-to-one favorite. With the blinds at $8,000 and $16,000, Peate, on the button, raised to $40,000, and McEvoy reraised all-in. Peate quickly called—too quickly, he later admitted—and discovered he needed a king or a flurry of diamonds. The fatal race was on as Shandel composed her shot and refocused. After a flop of 6-6-3, a jack on the turn gave Peate two more outs, but when the trey of spades failed to save him on the river—*click*—McEvoy's life changed forever.

Shandel's photograph illuminates both sides of the heart-pounding dynamic that ABC in those years used to trumpet in its coverage of

Olympic events: *the thrill of victory and the agony of defeat*. But while sports broadcasts often require an evening of action, color commentary, and interviews, Shandel's single image delivers the ecstasy and pain simultaneously. The moment that final trey hits the felt, McEvoy springs from his chair, grabbing his cowboy hat in one hand and punching the air with the other, while Bobbi, his wife, clutches his pants pocket and the small of his back. "I did it! I did it!" he gasps. Peate, stunned and sickened, can't bear to look anymore as his last chance to be the world champion—*a king, please, a king!*—gets snatched out from under his mustache. He probably wasn't even thinking about the $216,000 he'd receive, compared to McEvoy's $540,000, a much steeper plunge between first place and second than in payout structures today. But at least, for Peate's sake, they weren't playing winner-take-all anymore.

(A note about deals: to insure themselves against getting unlucky at the final table, or to flatten out the sharp income spikes of tournament poker in general, many players legitimately trade or sell percentages of their action either before the tournament begins or upon making the final table. In 1983, for example, Johnny Chan had 20 percent of both Peate's and McEvoy's action. Because each finalist had sold other pieces of himself before the tournament, the still unknown Chan netted more than either of them.)

Standing on a chair above Peate's left shoulder, Shandel had composed her shot wide enough, and with enough depth of field, to manage candid portraits of both finalists while conveying the stature of the event in the rapt attention of the other photographers. A score of telling details put us squarely back in the poker world of 1983: the haircuts, the modest number of chips in play, the cigarette in the comforting hand on Peate's shoulder, Bobbi McEvoy sitting right at the table while "sweating" her husband. (Other Shandel photos capture Bobbi stacking Tom's chips and rubbing his back, and Peate's girlfriend, Janice, doing similar things.) This was the last year in which at-the-table sweating was permitted.

Above all, the photograph shows us two guys who didn't have ten thousand bucks to casually peel off beforehand, one of them crossing poker's ultimate finishing line slightly ahead of the other. Without the satellites that put them both in contention, high-stakes tournament poker might have devolved into a faux cowboy parlor game for a few dozen affluent rounders. Without Shandel's picture, it would be harder to appreciate the look and feel of the instant Eric Drache's brainchild first realized its egalitarian potential.

· · ·

As the main event garnered more print and television coverage, the number of entries rose to 132 in 1984, 141 in '86, and 167 in '88. The other big growth factor besides media attention and satellites was the availability of Brunson's *Super System*, Sklansky's *Hold'em Poker*, and other quality advice books. First published in 1978 with a $100 price tag, *Super System* sold out almost immediately and changed the face of poker forever. With experts such as Caro, Sklansky, Chip Reese, and Bobby Baldwin writing about the other variants, Brunson himself covered no-limit hold'em. In his ninety-seven-page chapter, the longest in the book, he recommended constant aggression, though his advice was also highly specific. Almost by himself, he taught a generation of players how to play suited connectors, and to bust the conservative players who waited for big pocket pairs before entering a pot. His advice, of course, had maximal authority because he had just won the WSOP no-limit hold'em championship in '76 and '77 and narrowly missed a three-peat in '78 a few weeks after the book was published. He finished second that year to Baldwin and then second to Ungar in '80.

McEvoy went on to cowrite more than a dozen primers after his win, which he said "changed my life overnight. It gave me instant recognition and opened other doors for me, including some tournament buy-in sponsorship deals. When I decided to write books, I had instant credibility, and many students came to me for private lessons." Who can doubt him when he says his career would have been dramatically different if he'd finished "only" second? The fates of Rod Peate, Perry Green, Bones Berland, Jesse Alto, and other runners-up may remind us of the Jerry Seinfeld routine in which he calls the winning Olympic sprinter "Greatest Guy in the World," while the guy who finished a nose behind becomes "Never Heard of Him."

The availability of so many state-of-the-art advice books probably changed the landscape of tournament poker as much as the satellites did. "The astounding volume of how-to literature that is a by-product of the boom in poker's popularity has helped narrow the gap between so-called professionals and amateurs," Drache observed in 1984. "A decade ago probably 75 percent of the people at the World Series were professionals. It's a lot less than that now." The ratio of pros to amateurs has dwindled ever since, to the point where few pros even make the final table anymore. Viewed individually, any book-learned or seat-of-the-pants amateur who wins a satellite or has ten thousand bucks burning a hole in his pocket might be considered dead money in the tournament—that is, a person with almost no chance of finishing in the top 10 percent—but taken collectively as an ever larger fraction of the field, the odds are increasingly good that one of them will win the whole thing. (The shifting combinations of book learning, practical experience, timing, and other factors required to succeed in these tournaments is the focus of Chapters 42–44.)

By purchasing the Mint in 1988, the Binions nearly quadrupled their number of hotel rooms, from 81 to 296, to go with a sundeck and swimming pool on their new tower's roof. Rooms in the twenty-five-story tower were also quite a bit spiffier than those in the old wing. Even better, in May the entire field of every event could now be seated in a single high-ceilinged room in the second-floor annex, with thirty-eight tables and three times more floor space than the cramped alcove used for previous World Series. The size of a grammar school gym, the room had a ceiling fitted with cameras and monitors but not nearly enough ventilation for the number of players who smoked.

First prize in the main event rose to $700,000 that year, when Johnny Chan, a Chinese-born former cook, outlasted a record field to become the third—and almost certainly the last—back-to-back winner of the main event. This time "the Orient Express" narrowly defeated Erik Seidel, a tall, pensive backgammon pro who had traded for Paine-Webber on the American Stock Exchange before most of those jobs expired in the market crash of 1987. In the first poker tournament of his life, Seidel outplayed everyone when the tables were full but admitted he had little idea how to compete heads-up, especially against the reigning title holder. "I didn't have any feel as to how I should be playing the structure or the relative hand values," Seidel admitted in a rare display of modesty by a successful poker player. On the final hand, already down $300,000 to $1.4 million in chips, he flopped the top pair; his problem was that Chan had flopped the nut straight. The short, crafty champion was able to trap the six-foot-six New Yorker into going all-in on the turn with his pair of queens. Even more unfortunately for Seidel, this was their only hand to be featured in *Rounders*, which ends with Mike McDermott (the clean-cut, all-American Matt Damon character) heading to Binion's from New York City with ten grand in his pocket, bringing the lure of the World Series full circle.

Seidel was only one of several remarkable tournament players to emerge from the Mayfair Club, a small, private card room beside

Gramercy Park in Manhattan. The alumni of its big hold'em game include Dan Harrington, Jay Heimowitz, Howard Lederer, Mickey Appleman, Jason Lester, Paul Magriel, and Steve Zolotow. It was Seidel who had discovered hold'em on a trip to Las Vegas in the early 1980s and introduced it to a few of the high-stakes players at the Mayfair, where it was originally played with backgammon checkers and analyzed in exhaustive detail once the club closed at 4:00 a.m. By the late '80s there was probably as much hold'em prowess concentrated in that club as in any game spread in Las Vegas.

In 1989, the WSOP comprised fourteen events running May 1–19. Limit and no-limit hold'em attracted by far the most entries, though bracelets and serious money could also be won in seven-card stud high and high-low, razz, ace-to-five draw, deuce-to-seven triple draw, and both limit and pot-limit Omaha. Altogether the series offered more than $6.2 million in prize money, with probably three times that much at stake in the side games.

Now that Eric Drache had left to run poker operations at the Mirage, Steve Wynn's new property on the Strip, the Binions hired the Mint's Jim Albrecht to help run the show with their own Jack McClelland. Together they fine-tuned the blind structures and introduced $220 supersatellites with unlimited optional rebuys during the first two levels and double add-ons after that. They also paid the winners in tournament chips that could either be sold or used to enter any WSOP event, not just the Big One. These new wrinkles doubled satellite participation, which in turn swelled the entries and purses of bracelet events.

The Albrecht-McClelland team also worked hard to preserve a welcoming atmosphere for all the new female and international players who were now showing up. Having been a Horseshoe dealer and shift manager since '84, McClelland used his supervisory talent and dry sense of humor to help maintain order and calm amid the sometimes belligerent World Series tension. "If you don't know the rules as well as you should, they'll use a technicality to try to win a pot. And we had a lot of characters back then, like Johnny Moss, Stu Ungar, who were sort of bigger than life. You had to use a firm hand. You had to spank them then give 'em a little sugar. You're part psychologist, part kindergarten teacher, part priest." In fourteen years running the series, during which he kicked off every tournament with his signature "Shuffle up and deal," McClelland watched several players go from nowhere to millionaire poker star and (often) back again. "There was more of a family atmosphere," he recalled of the late '80s and early '90s, "but it was really hard to make a living as a player because there weren't many [novices] in most of the tournaments."

Chan's poker star hadn't faded, of course. His remarkable run at the end of the Reagan years continued through the '89 main event, when he buzz-sawed his way through a field of 178 to get heads-up with Phil Hellmuth, a brazen twenty-four-year-old from Madison. The six-foot-five college dropout—from the University of Wisconsin, where his father was a dean—had late-blooming acne and a habit of loudly informing everyone within earshot how great a player he was. That is, how great he, Phil Hellmuth, was—not Johnny Chan, for example, the player on the verge of an unprecedented threepeat, or any of the other former champions who might have been listening. And much to many people's chagrin, Hellmuth took a pair of pocket nines all-in against Chan's A-7 of spades to become the youngest WSOP champion to date. "The Poker Brat" had come, seen, and conquered, and the whole world would now have to hear about it.

Though Hellmuth continues to be among the poorest sports in poker, marriage and fatherhood seem to have matured him somewhat. "Having such big success so early, I thought I was some sort of poker god," he admits. "I guess my ego got out of line." He attributes this to his efforts to compensate for low self-esteem as a kid, as well as to a mild form of attention deficit disorder, though it also involves what can only be called phosphorescent hubris. "In ten years," he would gloat not long before breaking Chan's and Brunson's shared record of ten WSOP bracelets in 2007, "I want people to say Phil Hellmuth broke every record in poker, and no one even comes close." And if people don't say that, it seems a safe bet that wild horses couldn't keep Hellmuth from saying it for them.

When evaluating the significance of overall bracelet counts, we should note that Doyle Brunson, Chip Reese, and other friends of Jack Binion would boycott the series for several years beginning in 1998, when Jack lost control of the Fremont Street flagship amid bitter legal wrangling among Benny's heirs and in-laws. Many pros have also neglected to play some or all WSOP events because the stakes were lower and the luck factor higher than in the cash games they feasted on. Only in the current age of endorsement deals, as one's bracelet count emerged as a prime if imperfect measure of poker greatness, have many brilliant live players begun to focus (or refocus) on winning them. We should also bear in mind how much tougher it is to win bracelets in the twenty-first century, when more than twenty-five hundred players routinely enter the no-limit hold'em events, compared with outlasting the tiny fields of the '70s and '80s. This is offset, however, by the sixty or so events that can be entered these days at the Rio and in London, compared with the five or six in the earliest years at the Horseshoe.

Another development from the last two years of the '80s was that Anthony Holden took a thirteen-month sabbatical from literary London to play the pro tournament circuit, bookended by a pair of World Series championships. *Big Deal*, his account of his frenetic high-stakes odyssey through Britain, Malta, Morocco, and the United States, makes for spirited, often hilarious reading. On the very first hand of the '88 championship, Holden found himself in a showdown with Ungar, whom he described as "a diminutive stick-insect of thirty-four-going-on-twelve . . . his wrists so emaciated that his championship bracelets all but pinned them to the table." Holden acquits himself impressively in the hand, relieving the emaciated insect of $1,850. The author even survives the first day of the tournament (as Ungar does not), going to bed with $8,000 in chips. Yet his luck doesn't hold and the best he can manage in two tries in the main event is ninetieth out of 167. Chastened, he goes back to writing full-time, restricting his poker to the regular Tuesday night game with, among others, his mentor Al Alvarez.

While Alvarez had played low-stakes side games while covering the WSOP in '81, he entered no bracelet events. Continuing his protégé's insect motif, he admitted he was simply too "bug-eyed with wonder" during his first assignment to function effectively with both notepad and chips. But thirteen years later he ventured into the Big One as both reporter and player. Before putting up the $10,000, he had practiced on a computer program and played in small British tournaments, steeling his no-limit game while trying to stay realistic. "Although I often reached the final table and occasionally won an event, I knew that in Vegas they marched to a different tune. I would be like a good club tennis player with a wild-card entry to Wimbledon: the game played by the top players has no relation to the game played by the likes of me; it just looks the same." Unfortunately, he lasted less than four hours, losing a third of his chips when he slow-played a straight, greedily checking in hopes of building an even larger pot, only to be counterbushwhacked on the river by Barbara Samuelson's higher straight. (Samuelson used his chips to help her place tenth, at that time the highest finish ever by a woman.) Alvarez surrendered his final $6,000 when his pocket queens got ironed out by the ace-king he "knew" his opponent was holding, especially after a king hit the board. "I had been preparing for this day for fifteen months," he sheepishly confessed, "and when it came I blew it. I had made the classic mistake of a newcomer to the big league: I played what the pros call 'tight-weak'—afraid to bet without the stone cold nuts and easily scared out. But at this level players can smell your fear, and they run all over you."

Other British and Irish players, however, along with some talented Vietnamese and Iranians, were catching up fast to the Texans and the guys from the Mayfair. But nobody ever caught up to the Kid from the Lower East Side.

39 ♣

THE WORLD SERIES OF POKER,
PART 4

The last thing I took away from the yeshiva is this: we can't
run from who we are.

—JUDGE ABE PETROVSKY IN *ROUNDERS*

In 1990, the first non-American player, an Iranian-born resident of
Wales named Mansour Matloubi, won poker's world championship.
Chan had been born in Guangzhou, a Chinese city not far from Hong
Kong, but was raised for the most part in Phoenix and Houston, where
his family owned restaurants. He was an American citizen living in Las
Vegas and had been playing professionally there for nine years when he
first won in 1987.

On the key heads-up hand of the 1990 main event, with the blinds at
$15,000 and $30,000, Matloubi raised to $90,000 from the button with
pocket tens. Holding a $1.1 million–to–$840,000 chip advantage, Hans
"Tuna" Lund called with A-9. Playing out of Sparks, Nevada, Lund was
six seven in his two-tone trucker's cap and well over three hundred
pounds. Matloubi was a chain-smoking, hatlessly dapper five nine. The
flop of 9-4-2 gave Lund what he thought was the best pair and best
kicker. Hoping to check-raise, he knocked the felt twice with his fist.
When Matloubi obliged him by betting $100,000 on his overpair, Lund

raised him to $350,000. The move sent the olive-skinned Brit into the tank—the think tank, that is—for almost five minutes. Dragging contemplatively on a thin Capri cigarette, he finally concluded that Lund would have reraised before the flop if he had a pocket pair above tens; if he'd flopped a set of nines, fours, or deuces, so be it. Stubbing out his Capri, Matloubi pushed forward the rest of his chips, which constituted a raise of $378,000.

Lund now understood that he probably had the second-best hand, but the pot seemed too big to fold the top pair and top kicker. He shrugged his big shoulders and called. When the hands were turned over, Lund slapped the side of his head. Matloubi stood up and began pacing behind his chair—until an ace spiked on the turn and he angrily kicked it over. Tuna's pot-committed crying call had paid off, leaving Mansour with only two outs among the forty-four unseen cards. The crowd, mostly fellow Nevadans pulling raucously for Lund, was still cheering the turn card when the ten of spades peeled off the deck. Lund slumped back into his chair as Matloubi yelled, "Oh my *God!*"

Describing the swings of fortune after each of the four rounds of betting, ESPN color commentator Chip Reese told the audience, "This is without question the most incredible hand in the World Series of Poker." With a six-to-one chip lead, Matloubi needed only a few more hands to bring the championship of America's national pastime home to Great Britain, along with the gold bracelet and $895,000. "When I got to the final table, I thought I had made it as far as I could go," he said of being up against the likes of Lund, Peate, the aggressive and cantankerous John Bonetti, and the '86 champion, Berry Johnston. "I entered hoping to get a piece of the pie, and I got it all."

It had certainly helped Matloubi's cause that Stuey Ungar was busy cementing his reputation that week as the Keith Richards of poker. Ambushing pots with his usual pirate's abandon, he had intimidated and outmaneuvered opponents on his way to an early chip lead. Halfway through the second day, he and many others believed that he had his third championship all but sewn up. Calling a raise with pocket tens against another good-sized stack, he watched the flop come with an ace, a ten, and a small card. He was even more pleasantly shocked when his nervous opponent pushed all-in. "I called him in a heartbeat," said Stuey. "He had a king and a jack. On the river a queen came. He hit the gutter ball. If I had won that pot, I would have had five hundred thousand in chips early in the tournament! It would have been all over. I mean, over. Done! . . . There was no way I'd lose if I won that pot. But those are the bad beats you have to take."

Yet it seems that the Kid didn't take this one especially well. Still among the leaders after two days of play, he failed to appear at high noon on day three. A few minutes into the action, Jack McClelland phoned Billy Baxter, who had put up Stuey's buy-in (in exchange for half of whatever he might win) and was paying for him to sleep across the street at the Golden Nugget, to say that his horse hadn't shown.

"How could he not be there?" asked Baxter. "He's one of the chip leaders in the goddamn World Series of Poker!"

It turned out that Stuey was lying close to death in Room 341 of the Nugget. His cocaine habit had been costing a steady $1,200 per week, but perhaps he had overindulged the night before to ease the pain of losing that pot to the gutter ball. Or maybe his Tuesday night dose had been cut less than what he was used to. Whatever the reason, after Baxter got Nugget security to unlock the door, the unconscious thirty-six-year-old addict was taken by ambulance to University Medical Center. While his seat remained empty for the final two days, his stack was blinded and anted off round by round, though enough chips remained for him to finish ninth and win $20,050. To his other World Series accomplishments was now added the dubious distinction of making the final table from the intensive care unit—a record unbroken even when Paul "Eskimo" Clark suffered a pair of small strokes during the 2007 razz event in which he finished fourth; only after he'd been eliminated would Clark accept medical attention. While Baxter had managed to recover his investment, he undoubtedly swore never to back Stuey again.

Much farther out of the spotlight that May was a poker variant Ungar never took to—Omaha eight-or-better, a high-low split game requiring the winner of the low half of the pot to show down five different cards below nine. Because of the patience and technical skill it required, its popularity had expanded throughout the 1980s as a less rowdy alternative to the Texas bluffers' darling. The $1,500 event at the '90 World Series was the first time it was played for a bracelet, which was won by the Vegas pro Monte Kouz. Other bracelets were awarded that year to Shawqi Shunnarah, an American of Persian descent, for pot-limit Omaha, the most popular form in London and other European cities; Slim Preston in the larger pot-limit Omaha event; Houston's John

Bonetti for deuce-to-seven draw, also called Kansas City lowball; another Houstonian, Allen Baker, in the smaller no-limit hold'em event; and Berry Johnston for limit hold'em, a more technical variant increasingly prevalent in California.

On May 14, Benny Binion was posthumously inducted into the Hall of Fame. Though he had played fairly seldom and by his own admission not very well, the citation called him a "tempered player who was skilled at all forms of poker." The real and legitimate reason was that he had ushered a game played by a few of his Dallas cronies into the modern age of televised tournaments, making no-limit Texas hold'em by far the most popular variant of the national card game.

In promoting his World Series, round numbers had always been crucial. Since 1972, when Benny subsidized 50 percent of each buy-in to attract more publicity, the price of admission to the main event had been (and continues to be) the iconic $10,000—ten large, big heap wampum, long money. Ten dimes, others call it, using deflationary gamblers' lingo to show off how little they value it, or to reduce the emotional impact of losing it. For perspective, it's what Robert Ford was paid to kill Jesse James in 1882, and what John Backus cheats the cheaters out of with a double cold deck during the voyage to San Francisco in Twain's "The Professor's Yarn." It's what MGM paid Herbert Yardley to help write a spy movie in 1934, what Chiang Kai-shek paid him four years later to break the Japanese code, and what Richard Nixon needed to bankroll his 1946 congressional campaign. It was the bounty Quint demanded of Chief Brody and Amity's business owners to kill the marauding white shark in 1975. "I value my neck a lot more than three thousand bucks, Chief," growls Quint after scraping his fingernails down a chalkboard to get their attention. "I'll find him for three, but I'll catch him, and kill him, for ten. But you've gotta make up your minds. If you wanna stay alive, then ante up."

In the 1990s, that same three-eighths-inch stack of C-notes was called "high society" by Mike McDermott, who is packing a wad just that thick as he heads for the Horseshoe. Anteing up against Chan and the other great whites is what separates Mike from the unheroic "grinders" who eke out a living at poker. Ten thousand dollars had been roughly the median family income when the World Series began in 1970, and despite inflation the sum will still buy a year's tuition at an excellent state university, a used VW Beetle in pretty good shape, or a family vacation to Hawaii. It's also the amount won by the high-stakes pro Howard Lederer, a vegetarian, from his fellow pro David Grey, who had bet him that he wouldn't eat a cheeseburger.

In 1991, the WSOP introduced a longer round number when first prize in the main event rose to $1 million. The cash and bracelet went to Brad Daugherty, a former construction worker living in Reno, who had outlasted the likes of Perry Green, Donnacha O'Dea, and Ali Farsai of Beverly Hills. Second-place money of $402,000 went to the Vegas professional Don Holt, who had won a bracelet in stud two years earlier.

First prize remained at a million for the rest of the decade, as prize money for the other finalists continued to rise. (The junk bond analyst Alan Goehring won $768,625 for finishing second in '99.) The sums awarded in the championship and even in some of the preliminary events were now dwarfing the purses of Wimbledon, the Masters, and the Kentucky Derby, not to mention baseball's World Series. The dream of Mike McDermott was increasingly shared by the average American guy. More and more women were also being inspired, especially after Barbara Enright outlasted 269 players to finish fifth in '95. (She would have finished higher if the Illinois pro Brent Carter hadn't bizarrely called her all-in preflop raise with a 6-3 and outdrawn her pocket 8s.) The winner that year, Dan Harrington, a chess and backgammon master, went on to establish a record in large-buy-in no-limit hold'em tournaments bested only by Ungar and a couple of others. In 2004, he began writing the definitive series of primers on how to play them.

Two years after Matloubi won the main event in 1990, a second Iranian player, the real estate investor Hamid Dastmalchi, took home the bracelet. He had learned to play at age twelve in his native country before moving to San Diego. Having won a bracelet in a smaller no-limit event in '85 and a pot-limit hold'em bracelet in '93, Dastmalchi went on to take fourth in the '95 main event.

Since then, pros such as Farzad Bonyadi, Korosh Nejad, Ben Roberts (born Mehdi Javdani), Antonio Esfandiari, and Amir Vahedi have impressively extended the Iranian poker tradition. Born in Tehran in 1961, Vahedi enlisted in the army during the war with Iraq. After he'd served for two years in that hideous bloodbath—poison gas was deployed, martyrs' brigades of children marched across mine fields— Vahedi's mother begged him to desert his unit and leave the country. Despite his determination to serve with honor, he decided to obey his mother's desperate plea. He was imprisoned in Afghanistan but upon his release managed to obtain a forged passport, make his way to East Berlin, slip into West Berlin, and eventually arrive in Los Angeles. There he drove limos and learned to play tournament poker, achieving enough success in the latter—his lifetime earnings exceed $2.5 million—to be immortalized with a cigar-chomping bobblehead. He also coached Ben Affleck before the actor-director won the 2004 California State Championship. Affable and gregarious away from the tables, Vahedi can be almost recklessly aggressive while playing hold'em. "To live in a no-limit tournament," he has famously observed, "you have to be willing to die."

Meanwhile, after his victory in 1990 and a dominant run in the cash games, Matloubi began to be spoken of as "the new Stuey Ungar." Ears burning, pride singed, Stuey challenged Mansour to a series of heads-up, winner-take-all matches for $100,000 each during the Four Queens Poker Classic in February of '91. Brimming with confidence, Mansour happily put up $50,000 and sat down to play. After a seesaw sparring match between two aggressive champions, Stuey had built up his stack to $60,000 when he opened a pot for $1,600. (The blinds were $200–$400.) Mansour called with 4-5 offsuit. On a rainbow flop of 3-3-7, Mansour checked to Stuey, who bet $6,000. Mansour, sensing that Stuey had neither a 3 nor a 7, and hoping to hit a 5 for a straight, called again. Both players checked the king on the turn. When a queen appeared on the river, Mansour had missed his draw. Even so, he continued to smell weakness in Stuey and moved all-in for more than twice the size of the pot. Stuey stared him down for ten or twelve seconds. "You have 4-5 or 5-6," he coolly announced. "I'm gonna call you with this," though all he could show Mansour was 10-high.

When the railbirds saw the two hands, even Phil Hellmuth was startled. "Wow, what an unbelievable call! Stuey can't even beat a jack-high bluff." Mansour later said he felt "like a bulldozer just ran over me. I still love Stuey, but what the heck is going on!" As Barry Greenstein and others have noted, Stuey "was a hard player to bluff, since he was an expert at figuring out when his opponent was on a draw that didn't get there." The extremely narrow range of hands Stuey had put Mansour on, 4-5 or 5-6, were just about the only two he could beat in a showdown, so it took complete confidence in his read to call a bet of that size. "When a guy makes a call like that against you," Matloubi admitted to Hellmuth, "you just give up. It's like he's taken all of the wind out of your sails. I decided that I couldn't play any more heads-up no-limit hold'em, at least not that day, if not forever." Stuey's defeat of Mansour and the way he'd accomplished it cemented his reputation as the game's reigning genius.

By 1997, however, the former back-to-back champion hadn't won a tournament in over six years. He couldn't even scrape together the bankroll to play in the black-chip game at the Bellagio, which had replaced the Mirage as home of the highest-limit action. Decades of snorting cocaine had caused his nostrils to partially collapse, which he tried to conceal behind oversized round blue sunglasses. On May 15, he was so obviously strung out that twenty minutes before the main event he hadn't found a backer to put up his $10,000 entry fee. Desperate, he called Billy Baxter and pleaded with him to forget the ICU final table experience seven years earlier. "I knew Stuey was having problems and wasn't in great shape," Baxter said later. "But he was always hard to say no to. It just seemed from his tone that he wanted to play in that tournament more than anything, and in the end I didn't have the heart to tell him he couldn't. What the hell—I done worse things with my money."

Though it was a struggle for Stuey to focus or even stay awake for most hands—many recall that he looked like a corpse—his aggression and talent against a field consisting mainly of players trying to survive were enough for him to finish day one in seventh place with $41,175 and day two in second with $232,000. The luck of the draw on day three put him at a table with Brunson, Hellmuth, and Chris "Jesus" Ferguson. Hellmuth took the opportunity to try to dominate these former and future champions, but it was Ungar who responded most effectively by playing back—that is, reraising—almost every time Hellmuth came in for a raise. "Stu's very good at looking at a player and knowing what he has," Hellmuth admitted. "I know because I personally bluffed off two hundred thousand to the guy during the tournament. In fact, my bluffing him so many times kept him going strong and knocked me out."

When the final table was set late Wednesday night, Stuey had a sizable chip lead. Not surprisingly, Baxter and Mike Sexton made a bed check of his room at the Horseshoe. Baxter was only half joking when he told Stuey that if he didn't show up on Thursday, "I'm going to kill your ass." But he was serious when he added, "It's all over. The rest of them—they're playing for second place."

"You have to appreciate the beauty of what Billy did for Stuey that night," Sexton said. "I mean, Stuey was so fragile at the time; that comment was just the perfect boost to get him ready and keep him straight." And his friends' little pep talk did keep him straight, at least for the next eighteen hours or so, long enough for Stuey to blitz through the other finalists and become the only player ever to win three WSOP main event championships. (Moss was elected to his first; in the next two, he vanquished fields of eight and sixteen.)

In keeping with a no-frills Horseshoe tradition, the million dollars in cash arrived at the table in a cardboard Chiffon toilet paper box. Baxter's faith in Stuey had finally paid off in spades, but Stuey's half share would be gone within a couple of months, most of it spent on long-shot sports bets and baggies of cocaine. Because his ruined nostrils kept him from snorting the powdered form, he was now smoking crack and swallowing Percodan tablets. When it came time the following May to defend his title, he was too strung out to walk upright into the tournament room, let alone play, even though Baxter was more than willing to front his buy-in again.

Six months later, on November 22, 1998, Stuart Errol Ungar, forty-five, who had won in the neighborhood of $25 million playing poker and gin, was found dead in Room 16 of the Oasis Motel, a $58-per-night dive in the no-man's-land between downtown Las Vegas and the iridescent gleam of the Strip.

Of the thirty major no-limit hold'em events he entered in his life, Stuey won an astonishing ten of them, a percentage that will never even be approached. "At least three of those tournaments," adds Brunson, "he was stoned out of his mind and went out immediately. So that makes ten out of twenty-seven." Players in the next highest echelon, Brunson included, win roughly one start in forty.

The Kid's near-suicidal approach to playing hold'em, betting sports, and getting high had positive results only in the card game. His weaknesses and strengths, though, were often two sides of the same purple chip. Addiction and mental illness remain disgracefully misunderstood in our culture, but it seems increasingly clear that the headlong talent of people like Ungar has to do with unusual—some would call it freakish—neural chemistry. Behind the forehead, more specifically in the anterior cingulate of the frontal cortex, they have more vulnerable dopamine systems, "psyches" (as we used to call them) more easily hijacked by rewards like sex, dope, money, or laurels. In poker, successful bets and raises can trigger overpowering pleasure, and this dopamine rush gets deeply embedded in the memory of the most talented players.

Normal brains work this way, too, but they tend to operate within milder and narrower "mood swings," with lower-intensity jolts of pleasure and insight. "The same neural circuitry involved in the highs and lows of abusing drugs," says the Harvard neuroscientist Hans Breiter, "is activated by winning or losing money." The difference is that while geniuses work hard at their art form or game, the neurobiologist Steven Pinker reminds us they "may also have been dealt a genetic hand with four aces." It may be in chess, painting, business, or poker, but impossible, even deranged leaps of insight—calling Matloubi's all-in bet with 10-high, for example—are what separate ordinary artists from great ones. Then there's the fact that, more than any other poker variant, no-limit hold'em rewards fearless, even "crazy" aggression. When played in single-elimination tournaments, with many players just trying to survive but most of the prize money at the top of a steeply ascending pyramid, there is even more of a premium on putting opponents to the test. The bottom line is that Stuey's natural recklessness and freakish neural circuitry not only broke him and killed him, they were also what made him unbeatable.

THE WORLD SERIES OF POKER, PART 5

The best way to play poker is to act like Jesus but play like the Devil.

—TOMMY ANGELO

In 1997, at least twelve of the twenty-one bracelets were captured by foreign-born players, confirming that the Texas gamblers' reunions in Reno and Las Vegas had evolved into an authentic World Series. (We must say "at least" because a birth certificate has never been required for entry.) The next year produced at least ten non-American winners, with the championship bracelet going to Thuan "Scotty" Nguyen, a thirty-five-year-old pro sporting gold chains and Buddhist medallions to go with his curly gelled mullet and often churlish behavior. Two decades earlier, he had escaped in a small boat from Communist Vietnam. He, his younger brother, and a dozen other refugees were chased by a police cruiser and spent twenty-three days lost at sea, almost starving to death before a passing Taiwanese ship finally picked them up. Six months later he finally arrived in California. In Nguyen and other Vietnamese refugees, we may never find a better example of the immigrant's dominant poker gene expressing itself in America.

1.	Scotty Nguyen	$1,000,000
2.	Kevin McBride	687,500
3.	T. J. Cloutier	437,500
4.	Dewey Weum	250,000
5.	Lee Salem	190,000
6.	Ben Roberts	150,000
7.	Jan Lundberg	112,500
8.	Marc Brochard	75,000
9.	Paul McKinney	57,500

The following day, however, another of Nguyen's brothers still in Vietnam was killed in an automobile accident. Since receiving that horrible news, Nguyen has refused to wear his championship bracelet, though he now has four others to choose from. He remains one of poker's most talented players, as well as one of the most obnoxious when drinking.

In 1999, three of the final seven finishers in the main event hailed from Dublin, including the winner, carpet manufacturer J. J. "Noel" Furlong. The champion's nickname referred to his birth on December 25, 1937, though it was the horse trainer and racing fan's last name that secured his place on the unofficial WSOP all-name team. The debonair sixty-five-year-old George McKeever took seventh, and Padraig Parkinson, a cunning but good-humored Irish pro, finished, as he put it, "t'ird."

1.	J. J. Furlong	$1,000,000
2.	Alan Goehring	768,625
3.	Padraig Parkinson	489,125
4.	Erik Seidel	279,500
5.	Chris Bigler	212,420
6.	Huck Seed	167,700
7.	George McKeever	125,775
8.	Paul Rowe	83,850
9.	Stanley Bayne	64,285

Parkinson used his prize money to finance a move to Paris, but he arrived back at Binion's the following year determined "to win the damn t'ing." At forty-two he had committed himself to a regimen he admitted would never have occurred to him in his younger days. Eating less meat and getting more regular exercise were the easy parts, he said. A devoted imbiber of spirits, he woke up on January 1 with a hangover but resolved to not touch a drop until the main event ended on May 18. "If you want to be a champion, I t'ink you have to behave like one," he said, with no small regret in his voice.

After being dominated by sons of the American South in its formative years, by 1999 the World Series had crowned champions from the Bronx, Brooklyn, Boston, Grand Rapids, China, Iran, Vietnam, and Ireland. And in the first event of 2000, limit hold'em with a $2,000 buyin, the soft-spoken gentleman Hieu "Tony" Ma, another Vietnam-born maestro, defeated a record field of 496. The other names at this final table proved yet again what a melting pot the poker community had become.

1. Hieu "Tony" Ma	$367,040
2. Roman Abinsay	188,480
3. Hung "Peter" Tran	92,240
4. Ray Dehkharghani	59,520
5. David Stearns	44,640
6. Jimmy Athanas	34,720
7. Kevin Lewis	24,800
8. Reinhold Schmitt	19,840
9. Scott Brayer	15,875

A few days later, Jerri Thomas, a commodities trader from Hamilton, Ohio, won the $1,500 stud bracelet. Her victory was all the more impressive because she had given birth to her second child only three months earlier. Clearly back in shape both mentally and physically, she wore a close-fitting hooded red sweatshirt, a diamond necklace, and her big diamond engagement ring to the final table, where she began play far behind the chip leader. As her husband, Harry Thomas Jr., and young Harry III looked on from the stands, she coolly dispatched her seven male opponents. Her sister Mel and twelve-year-old son, Mark, helped Harry with the babysitting, but during the fifteen-minute breaks granted every two hours, Jerri took "Trey" to the women's room herself for a diaper change. The Thomases' teamwork paid off in other ways, too. Harry had taught Jerri to play stud seven years earlier, and now they were only the second married couple with a WSOP bracelet apiece. (Max and Maria Stern were the first.) Harry, a Cincinnati developer who won the $5,000 stud event in '85, had undergone a quintuple bypass the previous September, when Jerri was five months' pregnant, but he was fully recovered. Devout Christians, the Thomases credited Danny Robison, their Bible course instructor, for fundamental guidance with their poker games as well. Harry emphasized that he and Jerri try to compete only against people who play for sport or entertainment, not from financial necessity, though of course they have no control over who else enters these tournaments.

"This has been a dream for a long time," Jerri told reporters while being photographed with the bracelet. "I don't think the layoff really hurt me. Harry getting well was such a blessing, and the baby has brought so much joy into our lives, that maybe it helped. It has really been a wonderful year."

And then, on May 5, Jennifer Harman took home the no-limit deuce-to-seven bracelet. Because of this variant's degree of difficulty and the fact that few people play it, the event drew only thirty entrants and paid just five places. Yet the Deuce (in which the lowest hand wins, and aces and straights both count as high) is a title that poker pros covet almost as much as the Big One. No satellites are spread for it, which serves to exclude nonprofessionals. Only the fourth woman to win a World Series bracelet (not counting women-only events), Harman became the first to take a no-limit contest. The lean, blond thirty-six-year-old exudes the aura of a cute but naïve li'l sis, often sighing like a frustrated schoolgirl, though opponents who read her as such are in for some expensive lessons. Her short-sleeved Lycra tops reveal a Y-shaped scar on her left triceps, earned while protecting a friend's child from one of her ornery Australian blue cattle dogs. Even when Harman isn't in a hand, the fine blond hairs along her forearms bristle with static. Her nerves had been steeled in nightly high-stakes games with the likes of Brunson, Lederer, Reese, Chau Giang, and Annie Duke, but until that week Harman had never played no-limit deuce. Neither had Duke, for that matter, but that didn't faze either one of them. They took a ten-minute lesson from Lederer, Duke's older brother, and put up their five grand apiece.

1. Jennifer Harman	$146,250	
2. Lyle Berman	81,250	
3. Steve Zolotow	48,750	
4. Bruce Corman	33,500	
5. Lamar Wilkinson	16,250	

In his wrap-up report on the Deuce, Andy Glazer, the dean of tournament reporters, risked PC citations by referring to Harman as "a stunningly beautiful woman," then hastened to remind his readers that he'd called a male player "ruggedly handsome" three reports earlier. Glazer was somehow able to post his insightful and punny four-thousand-word accounts within a couple of hours of each event's final hand. Before he sat down at the keyboard, the former Atlanta defense attorney hovered above the final table with a gray legal pad for as long as ten hours, furiously jotting down chip counts and bets while also devising his narrative and headline—MOM DEFEATS THE SEVEN STUDS, for example, for the story of Thomas's victory. As far as the runners-up were concerned, the headline of another witty reporter, Mike Paulle, was a pip more emasculating: SNOW WHITE FENDS OFF SEVEN DWARVES.

1. Jerri Thomas	$135,975
2. Bill Gibes	69,825
3. Phongthep Thiptinnakon	34,910
4. Stan Goldstein	22,050
5. Richard Tatalovich	18,375
6. David Chiu	14,700
7. Dale Phillips	11,025
8. Rafael Perry	7,720

Fending off dwarves or studs, it had taken Thomas and Harman only nine days to double the women's bracelet count of the previous three decades. And then, in the $5,000-limit hold'em event, Melissa Hayden came within a couple of hands of making it five. The red-maned Manhattan photographer ultimately lost to Jay Heimowitz, who captured his personal fifth. Heimowitz had also finished third behind Brunson and Ungar in the main event of 1980, when he took pocket aces all-in against Brunson's pocket jacks but got beat.

1. Jay Heimowitz	$284,000
2. Melissa Hayden	142,000
3. Men Nguyen	71,000
4. Steve Zolotow	42,600
5. Gus Echeverri	31,950
6. Frederick Brown	24,850
7. Michael Danino	17,750

8. Hung La	14,200
9. Harry Thomas	11,360

Aside from the former champions, the male player generating the most buzz was Chris "Jesus" Ferguson. Long and exceptionally lean, with three-foot chestnut locks, a full beard, and Jesus-like features, Ferguson was even more striking in his poker regalia: a Black Stallion cowboy hat adorned with silver medallions and wraparound mirrored shades in whose reflection the action on the table was regularly captured by photographers. Though he could have passed for Richard Petty's hippie nephew or the rhythm guitarist of the Youngbloods, the thirty-seven-year-old stock trader and swing dancer from Pacific Palisades had in fact been toiling studiously that spring at UCLA, completing work on his Ph.D. in computer science and game theory. In the meantime he'd managed to crossbreed poker's traditional Marlboro Man persona with its nonsmoking, more halcyon L.A. component. Modest and soft-spoken, he listed his occupation as "student" on questionnaires, despite having just been named Best All-Around Player at the California State Poker Championship back in February. Here at Binion's in May, he had already reached three final tables and won the $2,500 stud event.

1. Chris Ferguson	$151,000
2. Al DeCarlo	75,500
3. Perry Friedman	37,750
4. Kevin Song	22,650
5. Kim Nguyen	18,875
6. Frederick Brown	15,100
7. Pierre Peretti	11,330
8. Laurence Kantor	7,555

Continuing the brainy-guy trend, the bracelet for $1,500 Omaha was captured by Ivo Donev, a forty-year-old chess player from Rousse, Bulgaria. His father, I. M. Donev, had been the national champion of Austria and later trained the East German chess team in the early 1980s. Ivo won the Moscow International Youth Tournament in '89 and quickly rose to the rank of International Master. His final step up to Grand Master was impeded by the collapse of the Soviet Union, during which chaos and inertia ruled for three years in the chess world. In

'92, Donev and other young players tried to revive the game in Bulgaria, but, as he said, "somehow the magic was gone." Two years later he immigrated to Virginia with his wife and daughter. To support them while studying electronics, he taught at an online chess school, offering students close tactical analyses of the Fianchettoed King's Bishop, the Maroczy Bind Formation, and the Hanging Center, all for $30 an hour. Unchallenged by the level of chess competition he found in his adopted country, he decided to take up an American game. Already steeped in a training discipline that used books and computers, Donev learned poker by studying Sklansky and Malmuth, Cloutier and McEvoy, and *Super System*, and by practicing on Wilson Turbo software. Playing at Binion's in crisp white button-down shirts, Donev was the picture of masterful concentration, in contrast to some of his opponents, with their loud shirts and motormouth prattle, chest hair atwinkle with jewelry. Salt-and-pepper hair neatly groomed, Donev kept his lucky blue-and-gold tie in a neat Windsor knot at all times.

1.	Ivo Donev	$85,800
2.	Thor Hansen	42,900
3.	Martin Oliveras	21,450
4.	Hassan Igram	12,870
5.	Ben Tang	9,652
6.	Charli Brahmi	7,510
7.	Mark Scott	7,510
8.	Barry Shulman	7,510
9.	Dan Heimiller	3,430

Poker's evolution made even more headway when twenty-three-year-old Phil Ivey took home the $2,500 Pot-Limit Omaha title, becoming the second African American with a World Series bracelet. (The first was Walter Smiley, a Gardena pro who took the $5,000 stud title in 1976.) Playing out of Atlantic City, Ivey had been on the tournament circuit for less than a year, but his triumph was hardly a fluke. Four weeks earlier he had become the youngest titleholder at the World Poker Open in Tunica, winning a hold'em event and cashing in three others. In the PLO event at the Horseshoe, he had to come back from an $85,000-to-$400,000 chip deficit to defeat Amarillo Slim Preston, all the while pointedly ignoring Preston's "friendly" verbal jousting designed to distract his opponent and pick up a read based on how he responded. In thirty years of World Series play, during which he had won four bracelets, Preston had always finished first after making a final table.

1.	Phil Ivey	$195,000
2.	"Amarillo Slim" Preston	97,500
3.	Markus Golser	48,750
4.	Phil "the Brat" Hellmuth Jr.	29,250
5.	Dave "Devilfish" Ulliott	21,940
6.	Dave Colclough	17,065
7.	Hassan Kamoei	12,190
8.	Ali "Baba" Sarkeshik	9,750
9.	Chris Bjorin	7,800

The straightshooting Glazer toasted Ivey's achievement. "Poker doesn't belong to white American males anymore," he wrote. "Poker books, computer programs, and worldwide legal cardrooms with codes of conduct have cut the head off the 'good old boy' network, even if the body does keep flopping around for a while. Poker now belongs to anyone with the brains, guts, and nerves to play it, and there's something about that level playing field that feels great, even to a white American male writer."

Altogether in 2000, there were twenty-three bracelet events, the smallest of which yielded more prize money than the main event of most competing tournaments. Copying the WSOP's freeze-out format, with a $10,000 no-limit hold'em event as the finale, they included Jack Binion's World Poker Open in Tunica; Amarillo Slim's Super Bowl of Poker, hosted by various casinos in February; the Diamond Jim Brady in August at the Bicycle Club in Los Angeles; and the United States Poker Championships, mid-September to mid-October at the Taj in Atlantic City. National championships were also being held in a dozen European cities, including the Helsinki Freezeout, the Irish Open at the Merrion Club in Dublin, and the Euro Finals of Poker at the Aviation Club on the Champs-Élysées. The Australasian Championship took place in Melbourne, along with smaller events in New Zealand, South Africa, and Costa Rica.

But as far as prestige was concerned, when fifteen top touring pros were asked to rank the fifty most important tournaments worldwide, the WSOP main event received every first-place vote, giving it a perfect aggregate score of fifteen. Twenty of the next thirty best scores went to preliminary WSOP events. At the turn of the millennium, then, golf and tennis had four majors apiece, horse racing three, boxing a shifting variety of sanctioning bodies and belts. But like America's major team sports and the world's most popular form of football, poker still had only one.

Yet there was also much less of a family atmosphere at the Horseshoe these days, and it wasn't solely due to the size of the fields and the crowds. Benny had passed away, and Jack was forced out by his sister and brother-in-law. In the same year, 1998, Ted died a horrible death— either the victim of an Ungaresque overdose or murdered by his live-in girlfriend and a male friend who was later caught digging up forty-eight thousand pounds of silver Ted had buried on his ranch in Pahrump. Becky Binion Behnen was accused of cutting too many corners, from serving mediocre food in the buffet to reducing the gold in the bracelets from eighteen to fourteen karats. They were no longer fashioned by Neiman Marcus, either; their new design was flimsier and less elegant. On her husband Nick's advice, she had sold the bills in her father's million-dollar horseshoe display. Before the '99 series, she and Nick replaced nearly every employee associated with her brothers, including poker room managers Jim and Susan Albrecht and tournament director Jack McClelland, who now ran the World Poker Open. It was out of loyalty to Jack and his team that Brunson, Reese, and other top pros were boycotting the series. In May 2000, there was also a jury deliberating charges of first-degree murder against Ted's friend and consort two blocks away from the Horseshoe.

Even so, most former champions, and plenty of others, had put up their $10,000. Johnny Chan's red Mercedes SL was back in valet parking, with its California plates reading 333JJ—treys full of jacks. Also on hand was *Card Player* editor Linda Johnson, resplendent in silver-and-black geisha garb to set off her bracelet in razz. Beside her stood Puggy Pearson, decked out in a lemon silk Genghis Khan outfit, including a crown with tasseled earflaps, to go with his pug nose and Abe Lincoln whiskers. "Some crowd here this mornin'," he observed with a twang. "Lotta pretty ladies, all raht." A few of the female players had on what could only be called boudoirwear: lacy nothings hung with spaghetti straps over flamboyant tattoos and plush torsos. But despite the tradition of look-at-me threads on day one, the leading sartorial choice for the men remained poker practical: baseball cap, sunglasses, sateen casino jacket, sweatpants or khakis or denim.

The field was an ecumenical crazy quilt of players from two dozen countries, among them Hasan Habib from Karachi and Jason Viriya-yuthakorn from Bangkok. Any all-name team would also have to include Chip Jett, Exxon Feyznia, Sirous Baghchehsaraie, Toto Leonidas, Somporn Li, David Plastik, Lin Poon Wang, and Spring Cheong, while certainly not forgetting the 1996 champion, Huckleberry Seed. Evangelical Christians would be competing this year with Larry Flynt and Devilfish Ulliott, CEOs and dot-com zillionaires with blackjack and poker dealers, gay men and lesbians, cowgirls and golfers and artists, black poker professionals and Jewish physicians, Jewish pros and black docs, at least one Aramaic scholar and rabbi, and several Vietnamese boat people. Altogether they numbered 512, breaking the previous record by 119 and bringing the purse to $5.12 million. Five tables would be paid instead of four—nine players more than the usual thirty-six. First place would bring $1.5 million, second almost $900,000, and all other payouts would escalate. Places 45–37 would be paid $15,000 apiece.

Phil Hellmuth was on hand, of course, hoping to increase his bracelet count to seven. The previous year he had boorishly challenged the guy who knocked him out of the main event to play heads-up for a million dollars. Once he calmed down, though, he checked himself into Esalen to work on his temper, having promised Linda Johnson to control it as a condition of writing for *Card Player*. But he still made no small plans for himself. "If I could stay healthy and get lucky and win twenty-five WSOP bracelets over my lifetime," he posted modestly on philhellmuth.com, "then I may well be considered the best poker player of all time." This year he had pulled out every stop, budgeting almost $200,000 for the World Series month. He was spending $1,000 a week to have access to the Bellagio's health club and swimming pools, not counting what he called "the world's most expensive room service," plus $1,800 a week to rent a Lincoln for the seven-mile commute to the Horseshoe and $90,000 for tournament buy-ins and rebuys. He even decided to skip the $5,000-limit hold'em event because its final table was scheduled for the night before the Big One. Instead he flew home to Palo Alto to relax with his wife and young sons, then flew back to Vegas on Monday morning. But at least he had managed to show up on time for the tournament. He often sleeps through the first hour or two, letting 5 percent or more of his chips be blinded off, a display of hubris his opponents both savor and resent.

Many reporters considered 512 entries more than a little flabber-gasting, not only because of the five-figure buy-in but also because the World Poker Open had ended only a week before the World Series began. "All that money hasn't had time yet to filter back down into the poker community," one of them observed. "Most of it's still deep in the pockets of the winners." Others noted that hundreds of other tournaments now competed with the WSOP. There was also the relative decrepitude of the Horseshoe facilities and the fact that most affluent players would rather stay—and play poker—at the Mirage or Bellagio, out in Los Angeles, back east in Atlantic City, or in Europe. But Glazer cited the NASDAQ being "north of four thousand," the prestige of being the oldest and largest tournament, and the extra week of satellites Becky had scheduled. And as Preston pointed out, "The Series is so big and successful you could hold it in Pahrump, out there where Teddy had his silver buried, and people would show up."

The $1.5 million first prize would be one and a half times the previous record, and the most money ever awarded to a single winner of a sporting event. (Boxing purses have to be split with small armies of trainers and managers.) The player who lost the last hand would still receive $896,500 to salve the pain. The winner of that year's Masters, Vijay Singh, had earned $828,000, and the owner of Fusaichi Pegasus got $888,400 for winning the Kentucky Derby.

Appleman, Duke, Kathy Liebert, Mike Sexton, and *Card Player*'s Jeff Shulman all made strong runs, but by the end of day four only Cloutier and Ferguson were left. Ferguson had once held a fourteen-to-one chip lead over Cloutier, but the former tight end gradually built up his stack while waiting for the other finalists to be eliminated. After a two-hour heads-up match, Cloutier was only slightly behind, $2.5 million to $2.6 million, when he raised to $175,000. Ferguson thought for a moment, took another peek at his cards, and reraised to $600,000. Cloutier moved all-in like a shot.

Chris now went into the tank for a couple of minutes. He scratched his cheek through his beard, shook his head, exhaled. Then he agonized for another five minutes. He took off his mirrored shades and rubbed his bloodshot eyes before finally calling the raise. As the buzz of the crowd rose to a crescendo, he turned over the ace of spades and the nine of clubs. When T.J. showed him the ace of diamonds and the queen of clubs, the spectators whistled and gasped.

The flop—four of hearts, deuce of hearts, king of clubs—kept T.J. in the lead, amid much delirium. Neither T.J. nor Chris held a heart.

The king of hearts fell on the turn. So now any deuce or four would produce a chopped pot. Exuberant Ferguson fans yelled for a nine, though surely Chris himself would have felt lucky to gain a split pot. But he suddenly leaped from his seat with his fists in the air, this as T.J. thrust a huge paw across the table, as the nine of hearts spiked on the river. Chris reached back across the fatal card to clasp T.J.'s hand. "You outplayed me," he said in the din. T.J. shook his head, disagreeing, although Chris was correct. That T.J. had just been harpooned through the ventricles didn't register on his craggy features. He smiled!

Chris made his way around the table to where T.J. was standing with his pretty wife, Joy, inside a crush of reporters. Although Chris was almost as tall, when the two men embraced, their difference in mass was straight out of vaudeville: mesomorph-endomorph, steel-wool ringlets meshing with yard-long chestnut locks, the burly tight end held by the sinewy swing dancer.

"Are we still friends?" Chris asked.

"Of course! Don't feel bad. You played great." But once they let go of each other, T.J. asked, "You didn't think it would be that tough to beat me, did you?"

"Yes, I did. *Believe* me, I did."

By now Glazer and Hellmuth, each brandishing a microphone, had latched onto T.J. "Chris is the one who should be getting the attention," he told them. "There's a lotta luck in poker, and if you're gonna play this game you better get used to it." When asked about the river card, he said, "I felt the nine coming off at the end. When I get in that zone, I can feel the cards coming. But you should be talking to Chris. He's the champion."

Directly behind him, Sexton was explaining to the French TV audience that not only was Cloutier the all-time World Series money leader, he was also the leader in overall tournament winnings. "Nobody's even close." Glazer was nodding, but added, "All true, but Chris earned this title. He walloped the little stacks when he was supposed to, he played cautious when he was supposed to, when he didn't want to give T.J. easy double-throughs. He was also more aggressive when the two stacks got closer, and when it was finally time to gamble, he picked the right moment."

Others, close by, expressed the opinion that Chris had made "a terrible call."

That Ferguson made clear he realized how lucky he was on that hand made it easier to appreciate how brilliantly he'd played throughout the 2000 World Series: four final tables, two first-place finishes, $1,672,260. "I really feel terrible for T.J.," he said. "I can imagine how brutal losing like that can be. He was definitely the best player today." It was the sort of modesty and acknowledgment of the luck factor too seldom heard at these events, then or now.

That final table had been filmed in the traditional way, with the audience never finding out what the hole cards were unless there was a showdown. But six months later a milestone occurred when hole-card cameras were used to broadcast the inaugural Poker Mi££ion live from the Isle of Man—though of course there was much else at stake in November 2000. Supreme courts in Tallahassee and Washington were about to decide whether chads had been dimpled, pregnant, or hung. The lead in New Mexico had already changed hands three times, with one recount putting George W. Bush ahead of Al Gore by four votes among the nearly six hundred thousand cast. This photon-thin margin was made all the more interesting by a statute decreeing that, should the final tally end in a tie, all five of the state's electoral votes would go to the winner of a mutually agreed-upon game of chance.

The organizers of the Mi££ion had crossbred the WSOP format with a version of Henry Orenstein's under-the-table cameras, which had already proved successful on Britain's *Late Night Poker* broadcasts. Determined to call their event the Poker Mi££ion, Ladbrokes Casino and Sky Sports guaranteed the winner £1 million. The pound was then worth about $1.50, and they wanted to keep pace with the $1.5 million prize Ferguson had won back in May. The problem was that even after the sponsors added £250,000 to the purse, everyone but the winner would be competing for the relatively paltry sums left over for places two through nine. The world watched London television director John Duthie put on a spectacular display of bluffing to win the event going away. Second prize, a mere 10 percent of what Duthie took home, went to Israeli pro Teddy Tuil. For finishing ninth, British pro Simon "Aces" Trumper actually lost money.

1.	John Duthie	£1,000,000
2.	Teddy Tuil	100,000
3.	Ian Dobson	50,000
4.	Tony Bloom	25,000
5.	Gary Lent	15,000
6.	Barney Boatman	14,000

7. Mohammed Barkatul   10,000
8. Ali "Baba" Sarkeshik   8,000
9. Simon Trumper   6,000

Unfairly top-heavy as the payout structure was for the 156 players putting up £6,670 apiece, the promoters' magic round number for first place had been realized. Final-table action was broadcast live to three hundred million households in 140 countries, then rebroadcast in the United States in prime time on Thanksgiving evening. One of the upshots was that by 2002, the World Poker Tour, a rival series of tournaments that also cloned the WSOP format, was deploying hole-card cameras for its highly rated shows on the Travel Channel, and ESPN followed suit in '03 for its popular coverage of World Series events. The age of respectable Nielsen ratings and new poker millionaires being minted at monthly or even weekly events was now under way.

SMALL BALL, THE BLUFF, AND THE BOOM

How great would it be, like in the World Series of Poker, that at the first tee of the Tour Championship, that's all you see is the ten million dollars stacked up there and that's what you're playing for.

—TIGER WOODS

The poker boom unofficially detonated on the evening of March 30, 2003, with the Travel Channel's first broadcast of the Five Diamond World Poker Classic at the Bellagio in Las Vegas. Produced by Steve Lipscomb, the show's lavish production values blended tabletop hole-card cameras, informative sidebars (amount in the pot and in each player's stack, odds of each hand winning at a showdown), and beginner-level explanations from Mike Sexton and Vince Van Patten, all of it hosted by *Playboy* cover girl Shana Hiatt, who sometimes wore just a bikini. The commentary by Sexton and Van Patten would become more sophisticated as casual viewers began to pick up on the tactics and lingo of tournament hold'em.

The World Poker Tour also hosted events in Paris, Los Angeles, Reno, Mississippi, Connecticut, Costa Rica, the Bahamas, and on a cruise ship off the west coast of Mexico. The broadcasts of those tournaments averaged 1.1 million viewers during its first season, with reruns often attracting three times that number. Forced to play catch-up,

ESPN combined similar hole-card technology with a Wild West ambience for its nearly round-the-clock broadcasts that fall of the World Series (taped at Binion's back in May), drawing even larger audiences. Capping that milestone year, NBC aired the WPT Battle of Champions on Super Bowl Sunday 2004. Twenty-five years earlier there had been a single event with a $10,000 entry fee; now there was one every couple of weeks, and pros wanting to compete in them all had to budget close to a million dollars a year for travel and buy-ins.

By bluffing his way to that first WPT title, a handsome young Danish tennis and backgammon champ named Gus Hansen became an overnight heartthrob, as well as the poster boy for a relentless approach to no-limit hold'em called "small ball." Variations on the style had actually been played for years—though seldom on television—by Brunson, Ungar, Chan, Hellmuth, Negreanu, Ivey, David Pham, John Juanda, Alan Goehring, and others. Now, with the poker world seeing the hole cards, Hansen and his fellow small-ball artists would make or call a modest preflop raise (usually two and a half times the big blind) with just about any two hole cards, aiming to bust the rocks who patiently waited for big pocket pairs. Even when the flop missed his hand, the small-ball artist proceeded on the assumption that it probably missed the rock's, too, and attacked with a bet, though he usually tried to keep the pot small in case his opponent had flopped a big hand. Brunson had described an earlier version of the strategy in the original *Super System*, but the new hole-card cams visually introduced it to millions of players who never had opened that bible.

The boom began to mushroom in May 2003, when Tennessee accountant Chris Moneymaker entered a $39 satellite on PokerStars.com and won a $10,000 seat in the WSOP main event, his first live tournament ever. More startling still, the well-named amateur outlasted 839 players and found himself heads-up against Sammy Farha, a charismatic and intimidating Lebanese pro, for the $2.5 million first prize. Even though he had the chip lead, Moneymaker offered to split the $1.2 million difference between first and second prize and play for the bracelet only. As by far the more experienced of the two, Farha said thanks but no thanks.

As the definitive hand of their heads-up endgame was dealt, Moneymaker had $4.62 million in chips, Farha $3.7 million, though most observers made Farha the favorite. The blinds were $20,000 and $40,000 with $5,000 antes. With the king of spades and 7 of hearts, Moneymaker gathered enough chips in his right hand to make a small raise to

$100,000. "Don't do it!" joked Farha, like a tomcat poised above a mouse hole with an unlit cigarette dangling from his lips. (Farha didn't smoke but seemed to feel his ever-present cigarette enhanced his Bogart-like table image.) Moneymaker did it anyway, and Farha called with the queen of spades and 9 of hearts. The flop came 9 of spades, 2 of diamonds, 6 of spades. With the top pair, Farha checked—hoping, he said later, to check-raise—but that plan was thwarted when Money-maker checked behind him.

The turn was the 8 of spades. Farha still had the top pair, but now he was looking at some scary straight and flush possibilities. Since he couldn't afford to let Moneymaker see another card, he made an over-bet of $300,000 into the $210,000 pot. But instead of folding, the ac-countant surprised him by raising to $800,000. "We said it was going to be over soon," said Farha, calling the extra half million. He was right. Whoever won this pot would have a lock on the money and bracelet.

When the 3 of hearts appeared on the river, Moneymaker had missed all his draws. With a paltry king-high, the only way he could win this pot was with a bluff. Once again, Farha checked, planning to call when Moneymaker bluffed all-in—which is exactly what the goateed Kentuckian did. Even so, Farha hesitated. "Must've missed your flush, eh?" he said. Another good guess. His brain and mouth were playing perfect poker, but his heart and right hand were having trouble follow-ing through. Afraid of a straight or a flush and faced with losing his chance at the title if he made the wrong decision, he tried again to get a read. "I could make a crazy call on you," he said, watching for a reac-tion. "It could be the best hand . . ." But Moneymaker gave him not a word or a twitch to interpret. (He later said he was concentrating on his trip home and how dramatically his life would be improved by second-place money.) Farha finally picked up his cards—the winning hand by a mile, his ticket to poker immortality—and winged them into the muck.

Moneymaker exhaled but said nothing while pulling the pot in and stacking the chips. ESPN commentator Norman Chad called it "the bluff of the century." And even with ninety-seven years to go, the claim didn't seem that preposterous.

Flush with new confidence and a two-to-one chip advantage, the mouse made short work of the cat, and the poker world would never be the same. Millions of online amateurs around the globe got to watch one of their own parlay $39 into $2.5 million by getting lucky—though no more so than anyone who wins this event—as well as by outplaying Farha and other veterans, including Harrington (who finished third),

Ivey, Hellmuth, and Vahedi. Internet poker sites boomed, in part by offering inexpensive (occasionally free) satellites into the 2004 main event, for which entries tripled to 2,577. And presto: Another Poker-Stars qualifier, the patent attorney Greg Raymer, won the $5 million first prize. The depth of the prize pool and the number of online opportunities to win a cheap seat expanded the field to 5,619 in '05 and 8,774 in '06. But it was primarily the bluff against Farha that had launched what the poker industry calls the Moneymaker Effect.

How did he do it? Like any successful bluff, it was an artful blend of nerve, timing, math, scare cards, pattern recognition, and what might be called recumbent method acting. Because at the most basic Stanislavskian level, a tournament-deciding bluff works like this: if losing the pot and taking second-place money will make a bluffer happy, he will also look happy to be called.

A brilliant bluff also requires a coherent story line. It may mislead the opponent but shouldn't confuse him; otherwise he might call just to satisfy his puzzled curiosity. The most artful bluffs also require a smart, even ingenious bluffee, such as Farha. Facing a reckless donkey with no imagination, it's better to wait until you have a real hand. Your opponent must fear losing his chips (and, ideally, his shot at a bracelet) and be able to imagine you having the hand your body language and bets represent. So the story you tell him must be not only coherent but also credible. As you lie to his face, after all, you're counting on him to believe you. Moneymaker's bets and calm demeanor combined with the cards on the board to say, "I have a straight or a flush." Farha's fold said, "If you say so . . ."

In late 2004, Becky Behnen, under a mountain of debt, sold the rights to the World Series to Harrah's Entertainment. Harrah's was the world's largest gaming company and, as many poker players were quick to complain, the one most obsessed with the bottom line. It had a corporate ethos much more interested in mindless pit and slot players than in hosting the championship of a game based on skill.

The first change Harrah's made was moving the event to the Amazon Room of the Rio, its midmarket property on Flamingo Road about a mile west of the Strip. Anthony Holden and others compared it to moving the British Open Tennis Championship from Wimbledon or the Masters from Augusta National. Yet it was also true that the Horseshoe facility was simply too small and decrepit to accommodate the enormous WSOP fields of the boom years. Benny, Jack, and Ted were out of the picture, the Horseshoe was falling apart, and the Binions' chapter in the history of poker was written.

The Amazon Room, the Rio's hangar of a convention hall, seated up to 2,430 players and dealers at 213 oval tables, each one lit by a white Noguchi-esque lantern and far above that by scores of spotlights hung from black scaffolding along with surveillance cameras, ad banners, air ducts. As chips clacked and clattered, many thousands of cards were shuffled and pitched, peeked under, fingered, and mucked, always clockwise. A tented annex outside seated another three hundred or so. Instead of April and May, the 2005 World Series was scheduled for July and August, when Harrah's had more rooms to rent and more players were able to spend some vacation time taking a shot in the Big One. Unfortunately, this was also the height of the Mojave Desert summer, when the breeze above the asphalt is like a hair dryer held an inch and a half from your nostrils. Inside, the Amazon Room was kept brisk enough to make many players shiver in their heavyweight fleece. The forty-four other bracelet events included a glut of interchangeable no-limit hold'em tournaments with affordable buy-ins. And for that year only, the final two days of the main event would be played back downtown at Binion's—a nod to World Series tradition as well as a way to mark the centennial of the founding of Las Vegas.

Harrah's also hired Jeffrey Pollack as the first WSOP commissioner. At forty, Pollack had established himself as an innovator in a range of industries: politics, publishing, sports, and new media. After his brother, Gary Bettmann (same mother, different father), was appointed commissioner of the NHL in 1993, he began to see sports as an integral part of the entertainment industry. He soon went to work for David Stern, who needed someone to help him manage communications during collective bargaining with NBA players in 1998. By 2001, Pollack was working at NASCAR, trying to usher a tobacco-stained, good-ol'-boy pastime into the digital age. Having never seen an entire race in person or on TV, Pollack helped transform stock-car racing into a major general-interest sport. His technical innovations included an interactive television show featuring in-car cameras, which boosted ratings and earned him a Primetime Emmy for Interactive Television Programming and a Sports Emmy for Outstanding Innovative Technical Achievement.

So no one should have been very surprised when, soon after purchasing the rights to the World Series of Poker, Harrah's asked Pollack to do for poker what he'd done for the racing set. Although critically and financially successful at NASCAR, he took the job in part because he saw the World Series of Poker as being, at least potentially, "more about sports than about gaming." The annual championship of America's national pastime, successful as it had been, still seemed to him like "a thirty-five-year-old start-up."

The new commissioner's natty grooming and Ralph Lauren Purple Label suits made him stand out amid all the sunglasses, hoodies, and logo'd baseball caps at the Rio. The first thing he wanted to change was the atmosphere. Not that everyone had to wear pinstripe, but as Pollack walked among the hallways of the Rio and the tables of the Amazon Room in June 2005, he brushed past groups of nearly naked women handing out vouchers for either light beer or free limo rides to a strip club—maybe not the least attractive sights to the average poker player but still something that struck Pollack as "not quite the right vibe" for what was supposed to be a world-class sporting event that welcomed both women and men.

He also made it his business to listen to the players. They were funding the prize pools for Harrah's, and he wanted them treated as customers. Better food, more skill-friendly tournament structures, longer training for dealers, and more space between tables all followed. Pollack was quick to credit the best players' very high poker IQ. He called Negreanu and Lederer "wicked smart" and invited them and a dozen other pros and amateurs onto his Players Advisory Committee. In the face of increasingly stiff competition from the WPT and other televised franchises filmed in exotic locales, Pollack emphasized the WSOP's lore and history. "It's all about the gold bracelet," he said. "Players measure themselves against each other by how many bracelets they have, not by how much money they've won. And we're the only place where you can win one."

Within two years the WSOP had a new five-year deal with ESPN, a presenting sponsorship with Miller Brewing, and marketing sponsorships with Hershey's, Planter's, Hertz, and Corum Watches. Pollack had also arranged new media alliances that put the WSOP on the Internet, Xbox, iTunes, and mobile phones around the globe. By 2008, the franchise was ranked as one of the most admired sports brands, and the ratings for the final table of the main event on ESPN had risen by 46 percent.

While competing in the early rounds of the 2005 main event, Jack McClelland had observed that there were "fifty-six hundred players—

probably three hundred professionals and maybe another three hundred serious amateurs and five thousand guys named Joe. I put myself in the experienced amateur group, and if you're in that group, you feel like, 'Wow, I've really got a chance this year.' And that's what's really made poker boom. It's not watching the same ten pros play every week; it's watching the unknown guy come out and win." Having awarded hundreds of bracelets and close to a billion dollars in prize money, first at the Horseshoe and since 1998 at the upscale Bellagio, McClelland had invaluable perspective on defeating a field of that size. "The number one thing in winning tournaments is being aggressive. If you're aggressive, you're going to win a tournament once in a while because gathering chips is the most important thing. Surviving is good, and getting into the money is fine, but it's better to win once and get seven-point-five million than to be in the money for five thousand a hundred times and end up with half a million."

As it turned out, the $7.5 million first prize in that year's main event was won by a professional who was also a Joe—Joe Hachem, a Lebanese-born Australian living in a suburb of Melbourne. The genial thirty-eight-year-old chiropractor had been forced to stop practicing in 2002 because of a rare blood disorder affecting his fingers. The decision to turn his poker hobby into a full-time job, especially risky because he had a wife and four children to support, led to him winning almost $11 million in less than three years, on top of a lucrative sponsorship deal with PokerStars. "Pass the sugar," his signature expression when raking in a pot, seemed also to describe his new career path fairly well.

At the 2006 World Series, Jon Friedberg, an MBA from Pepperdine who cofounded the interactive media company Reactrix, won his first gold bracelet and $526,185. He outlasted 2,890 opponents in Event 17 playing small ball—measured bets, dead-on reads, and perfectly executed bluffs.

With four players left, he pulled off a classic semibluff reraise with the 6 and 7 of hearts. Two opponents had folded to him in the small blind, and he decided just to complete the half bet to $30,000. The guy in the big blind was the hyperaggressive John Phan, runner-up for 2005 Player of the Year, who raised to $90,000. (Phan had $1 million in chips, Freidberg $1.8 million.) Friedberg called the raise and watched the flop come 4-8-9 with two hearts. With both a flush draw and an open-ended straight draw, he bet $120,000. Phan raised to

$300,000. After noting that Phan would have $600,000 left—enough to regroup and play on—if he folded, Friedberg reraised all-in. And Phan mucked.

"I rarely bluff without some kind of draw to the best hand in case I get called," Friedberg said afterward, "except when I'm ninety percent certain my opponent has absolutely nothing." Such was the case when, with three players left, Friedberg had $1.7 million, Phan $700,000. With an unsuited 2-3, the worst possible hole cards three-handed, Friedberg raised to $60,000. Phan called. On a flop of A-A-5, Friedberg bet $80,000. Phan called. The turn was a 6, and Friedberg decided to go for a check-raise. When Phan obliged by betting $80,000, he raised $220,000, about half the size of the pot—"an amount that appears as if I want John to call." Buying this story, Phan folded. "I was confident John didn't have an ace, based on his betting patterns and body language," said Friedberg. "After I had raised preflop, made a standard continuation bet on the flop, then check-raised the turn for a nominal amount, I was certain he would surrender, thinking I had an ace."

Like many young women in poker, the Amarillo-born artist Shawnee Barton favors short tops that either go or clash with her pink-tinted ponytail. With ten players left in the '06 women's championship, Barton's lime green tank top helped determine where she would finish. The action had folded to her on the button. Even though she had nothing but an unsuited 10-7, she tried to steal the antes and blinds by raising three times the big blind. Sitting in the big blind, Laurie Scott had the largest stack of chips at the table. As Scott called the raise, she asked, "You're not trying to steal the blinds, are you?"

"She had called me out and both of us knew it," Barton said later. "My move was just too obvious. But when the flop came down K-5-2, I still bet about 60 percent of the pot because I wanted to stay in control of the hand and because I knew she'd either fold or go over the top of me. She was a really aggressive player who rarely just called. If she raised, I would fold. She stared me down for what felt like a couple of hours, but she finally mucked. I took a deep breath. 'You could probably beat my jack, couldn't you?' she asked me. I told her I probably could."

During the next break, the male dealer, breaking protocol, came up to Barton and said, "I like your game, girl. I saw you bluffin' and I thought, 'That girl's got balls,' but I was hoping the other woman didn't call 'cause I knew you were beat. Your heart was pumpin' and your stomach was goin' up and down. I *knew* you were bluffin'. You gotta put on a big sweatshirt, girl." Barton dug through her backpack, draping herself with what she called the "frumptastic outfit" she wore for the rest of the tournament. Flesh duly covered, she bluffed her way to a substantial chip lead when only two players were left. She got mind-bendingly unlucky on the final three hands when her heads-up opponent, Mary Jones, called three huge bets from way behind before hitting miracle rivers, but "Amarillo Shawnee" still finished second and took home $123,178.

In the main event, with six players left of the 8,773 starters, the Malibu agent-turned-producer Jamie Gold raised to $750,000. San Antonio's Richard Lee, who was playing his first poker tournament, called from the small blind. Paul Wasicka, a young pro from Dallas, called from the big blind. The flop came queen of diamonds, queen of spades, jack of clubs. Check, check, check. The turn was the jack of spades, putting a second pair on the board. Lee checked. So did Wasicka. Gold bet $800,000 into the $2.3 million pot, representing a queen or a jack. As an agent, Gold had represented James Gandolfini, Lucy Liu, Jimmy Fallon, and Felicity Huffman. With his dark hair and brash irreverence—some called him an obnoxious motormouth—he reminded many folks of Ari Gold, the agent played by Jeremy Piven on *Entourage*. But earlier that year the real agent had switched careers and begun to make his way as a producer.

The question for Lee and Wasicka was, Did Gold have a queen or jack in his hand, or at the very least an ace? Both scanned Gold's face long and hard for a tell, and both folded. Before hauling in the mountain of chips, Gold showed them the 3 of spades and 2 of hearts: a stark naked bluff. With more than his share of good cards and a number of similar bluffs, Gold went on to win the $12 million first prize. But it soon turned out that before the tournament, when Gold had allegedly promised Bruce Crispin Leyser, a business partner, that they would evenly split whatever money he won, Gold may have been bluffing then, too. Leyser filed suit in Las Vegas District Court asking for $6 million, and the case was settled out of court the following February.

The final distribution of the $12 million remains undisclosed, but the financial upshot of pocket cams, cheap online satellites, and Moneymaker's parlay secured by his bluff against Farha could not be more clear. A decade-by-decade table shows not only the steep upward curve of WSOP prize money, even as the buy-in remains $10,000, but the increasingly flat payout structure of almost every big tournament, which in turn allows hundreds more players to enter future events on the never-ending world poker tour.

1976	1986	1996	2006
1. $220,000	1. $570,000	1. $1,000,000	1. $12,000,000
	2. 228,000	2. 585,000	2. 6,102,499
	3. 114,000	3. 341,250	3. 4,123,310
	4. 62,700	4. 195,000	4. 3,628,513
	5. 51,300	5. 128,700	5. 3,216,182
	6. 39,900	6. 97,500	6. 2,803,851
	7. 34,200	7. 78,000	7. 2,391,520
	8. 22,800	8. 58,500	8. 1,979,189
	9. 17,100	9. 44,850	9. 1,566,858
			10. 1,154,527
			11. 1,154,527
			12. 1,154,527
			13. 907,128
			14. 907,128
			15. 907,128
			. . .
			200. 42,882
			. . .
			600. 20,617
			. . .
			876. 10,616

DRAWING RED LINES IN THE DESERT, OR HOW (NOT) TO BLUFF A MARTYR

> The great gamblers, and there are not many, don't need anything. They simply wish to prevail. And we know how dangerous people are who don't need anything.
>
> — STEPHEN DUNN

The 2006 World Series had taken place during the summer of Hezbollah *v.* Israel, the foiled Al Qaeda plot to blow up jetliners with liquid explosives, and the UN Security Council's ultimatum to Iran to stop enriching uranium. A few weeks earlier, on April 11, the Iranian president, Mahmoud Ahmadinejad, had staged a pep rally in his country's holiest city, Mashhad, which means "Place of Martyrdom." Wearing traditional Persian garb, bearded young men whirled about among fluttering doves, chanting "God is great!" and brandishing silvery tubes of uranium hexafluoride. Their joyous danse macabre served as the overture to Ahmadinejad's triumphant claim: "Iran has joined the club of nuclear nations."

President Bush implied that this claim was premature. "We want to solve this issue diplomatically," he said, but he refused to rule out the use of force "to prevent Iran from developing" weapons-grade fuel. "All options are on the table," he warned, presumably including a nuclear strike. In response, Ahmadinejad rattled his scimitar, vowing to "cut off the hands of any aggressor." It also seemed relevant that his boss, Ayatollah Ali Khamenei, had called those who sought reconciliation with America "simpletons and traitors." The two countries hadn't officially spoken since 1979, when Islamist radicals—the twenty-three-year-old Ahmadinejad among them—seized the American embassy, took fifty-two hostages, and clinched the revolution that put the mullahs in power. Now, as president, Ahmadinejad had taken the position that shutting down the uranium-enrichment program "is our red line, and we will never cross it." To those who might be angry about the program, "We say, be angry at us and die of this anger."

"Ahmadinejad and the Iranian regime are bluffing," at least according to Gerald Steinberg in Toronto's *Globe and Mail*. "Rather than a sign of strength, the premature and exaggerated boasts appear to reflect weakness." Whereas the headline above an op-ed piece by Martin Indyk in the *Los Angeles Times* declared, IRAN'S BLUSTER ISN'T A BLUFF. Despite these diametrically opposed views, each writer, like thousands of fellow journalists on either side of the question, correctly assumed his readers understood what a bluff is.

Such statements should also remind us that at least two hundred years before America was founded, Persian courtiers were playing bluff-based card games, and that during the 1990s two ethnic Persians had won the World Series of Poker. In 2006, Ahmadinejad seemed to have adapted his countryman Amir Vahedi's motto: "To live in a no-limit tournament, you have to be willing to die." The Iranian president, after all, had been a Basij recruiter during the war with Iraq and was extravagant in his praise for human mine detectors and, later, suicide bombers. In his inauguration speech, he asked, "Is there any art more beautiful, more divine and more eternal than the art of the martyr's death? A nation with martyrdom knows no captivity." And if, as he believed, the Twelfth Imam was about to return to destroy the world's infidels, why should Iran's president compromise with the West, especially when a reported nine million Basiji had formed a human chain fifty-four hundred miles long to support his nuclear program?

But was Ahmadinejad really a martyr himself, or did he just play one on TV? More crucially, could the West accept nuclear weapons in the hands of a demagogue obsessed with self-slaughter? Even though his regime probably had no warheads yet, it was counting on belligerent pronouncements toward Israel—which "must be wiped off the map"— and America to rattle world energy markets, raising fuel prices while enriching Iranian coffers at the rate of billions of dollars per week. This in turn enabled it to fund Hezbollah and Hamas, and pay hefty sums to import nuclear expertise, and made it less vulnerable to the UN's economic sanctions. In this sense, Ahmadinejad's posturing put us almost literally over a barrel. Even worse, Iran's nuclear program kept edging closer to yielding the fifteen or twenty kilograms of U-235 necessary for a warhead or suitcase bomb. Ahmadinejad and the atomic ayatollahs who controlled him may have banned gambling card games, but they had signaled a willingness to risk many millions of lives—Muslim, Christian, Jewish, and otherwise—in the ultimate no-limit staredown. On top of which, other nuclear powers needed their oil just as much as we did, and one or two of them might be willing to barter oil for warheads. Suddenly the cold, ashen postapocalyptic world Cormac McCarthy had so meticulously imagined that year in *The Road* didn't seem quite so far-fetched anymore.

Parallels between poker and nuclear showdowns are never neat, but the faceoff between Iran and the West clearly required a keen understanding of the deceitful yet potentially lifesaving tactic of bluffing—of making someone believe you will fight to the death without actually having to shed any blood, let alone evaporate cities. As Oskar Morgenstern reminded us back in 1961, it is the bluff that makes poker the most useful model for "countries with opposing aims and ideals [who] watch each other's moves with unveiled suspicion."

Our country was naturally suspicious when we learned that Iran had sought warhead designs from Pakistan while developing long-range missiles capable of delivering those warheads. According to Raymond Tanter, a former member of the National Security Council, Iran had also used reverse engineering of hardware secretly purchased from Ukraine to move "a screwdriver's turn away from having a nuclear-capable cruise missile system."

Back in March 2003, while attempting to enlist allies for a war with Iraq, President Bush implied he would call France's bluff in a Security Council vote on whether to support an invasion. "It's time," he said, "for people to show their cards." CNN's Bill Schneider called Operation Iraqi Freedom "Texas political poker, the ultimate high-stakes gamble, because President Bush has put everything on the line with this war."

After the situation in Iraq began spiraling out of control, many Americans also wondered whether Mr. Bush had artfully countered the bargaining chips in Iranian and North Korean arsenals while playing

"Plutonium Poker" (the term is Fred Kaplan's, in *Slate*). Pyongyang, Tehran, and Al Qaeda, as well as Afghan and Iraqi insurgents, all may remind us of what Crandell Addington said during the 1981 World Series: "Limit poker is a science, but no-limit is an art. In limit, you are shooting at a target. In no-limit, the target comes alive and shoots back at you." The Bush administration's credibility, and thus its ability to bluff, was also undercut when its claims that Saddam Hussein had weapons of mass destruction, was linked to Al Qaeda, and had sought uranium from Niger all turned out to be false.

Iran's credibility was also in doubt. It had been cited by the International Atomic Energy Agency for hiding enrichment activities since 1985. The question had become, Did the current regime want to join the nuclear club mainly to generate electricity, or to wield a nuclear club of its own? One clue was provided when Ayatollah Hashemi Rafsanjani, a moderate in Iran's political spectrum, observed that "a single atomic bomb has the power to completely destroy Israel." He and other mullahs even issued a fatwa sanctioning the use of nuclear weapons. Iran's vast oil reserves also undercut its claim to need a peaceful source of new energy. Much more revealing, however, was the admission by A. Q. Khan, godfather of Pakistan's bomb, that he had smuggled into Iran both a spherical warhead design and P-2 centrifuge technology capable of quadrupling its nuclear enrichment capacity. Poker players call such things halogen tells. Taken together, they comprise persuasive—some would say foolproof—evidence that Iran's goals were measured in megatons rather than kilowatts.

Yet how far could we push the Islamist regime? "Do not press a desperate foe too hard," Sun Tzu counseled around 300 BCE. Why not? Because a wounded animal is often more dangerous than a healthy one, which can run for its life. Likewise, a desperate human may act spitefully rather than pragmatically, choosing a martyr's death (and taking others down with him) over a lifesaving retreat. If your opponent has been bullied of late, it's probably best not to bluff him.

Iran seemed to feel that the West had been pushing it around since the Mossadegh government was overthrown in 1953 and the shah was installed. More recently, Javad Vaeidi, deputy head of the Supreme Security Council, admitted that giving up the enrichment program would be a national humiliation. To keep from losing face, the regime might be willing to go down in flames, taking with it as many infidels as inhumanly possible. Or it might only *pretend* to be willing to do that. How could one tell the difference? In the nuclear age, the ability to distinguish a genuine threat from a bluff may be the most important skill a president or secretary of state can possess.

With an opponent who is truly committed to martyrdom, we have all the more reason not to humiliate him. We need to understand his psychology in order to know which of his buttons we can and can't push. How did the atomic ayatollahs feel, for example, about being publicly dressed down by females? In 2006, the Security Council's position was represented by Secretary of State Condoleezza Rice and British Foreign Secretary Margaret Beckett. After saying they would negotiate face-to-face only if Iran suspended enrichment, both women warned that "further steps" would be taken should the offer be refused. Might not the sex (or race) of our leading diplomats have made our demands even harder to swallow? What self-respecting white-bearded mullah backs down, after all, from a petite Mozart-playing black woman? The role of women in society wasn't officially on the table, of course, but no issue more succinctly epitomizes the chasm between radical Islamism and the liberal West. If Iran's leaders shared more of our values—as Israel's, India's, Brazil's, and now South Africa's do—we would probably be much less adamant about keeping their hands off the bomb.

Ahmadinejad and like-minded heads of state have made it illegal under shariah even to own a deck of playing cards, let alone gamble with them. In August 2005, an Islamist judge in the Indonesian province of Aceh sentenced four women to be publicly beaten for participating in a card game involving 65,000 rupiah, about $6. More than a thousand people gathered after Friday prayer sessions to watch the women receive seven vicious blows apiece across their backs with a long rattan cane. Another judge blamed the tsunami, which took twenty-five thousand lives and destroyed much of the Acehnese economy, on women who didn't wear the chador.

More general bluffing guidelines our leaders would do well to recall include **bluster = weakness**. If Ahmadinejad claims to already have "the full gamut of nuclear technology," a pokerticious diplomat will infer that he doesn't. She'll put him on a much weaker hand and reraise. If a leader in Pyongyang or Tehran tries to stare her down, she'll remain serenely confident that people holding powerful cards tend to downplay or even—the Israelis again come to mind—deny the existence of a nuclear arsenal.

Isolate your opponent. One player is a lot easier to bluff than two or three. This is why Condoleezza Rice tried to isolate Iran by accepting Chinese and Russian demands to limit sanctions against their affluent client.

Project strength. After defeating Saddam's army, our failure to create a stable peace in which democracy could thrive made us look weak. So did Israel's failure to defeat Hezbollah. So did our failure to capture Osama bin Laden.

Seem to mean it. As the physicist and historian Jeremy Bernstein observed, "The Israelis seem to mean it when they say they would not allow the Iranians to have nuclear weapons." Harry Truman clearly meant it in August 1945, as John Kennedy also appeared to in October 1962. Indeed, the entire First and Second World Wars and the cold war, as well as Operations Desert Storm and Joint Endeavor, made U.S. leaders appear to very much mean it, although Vietnam, Lebanon, Somalia, the fiasco in Tora Bora, and the occupation of Iraq all cut in the other direction. For his part, Ahmadinejad seemed to mean it when he took over our embassy, recruited children to march across minefields, stonewalled IAEA inspectors and, more recently, when he arms and funds Hezbollah, Hamas, and countless Shia suicide bombers.

Expect duplicity. Former secretary of state Warren Christopher, who negotiated for the release of American hostages in 1979, warned that Iranian negotiators would deploy "bazaar behavior" resembling that of "a Middle Eastern marketplace, with outlandish demands, feints at abandoning the process and haggling over minor details up to the very last minute." He counseled our negotiators to remain steadfast but realistic. Or as Doyle Brunson once put it, "Luck favors the backbone, not the wishbone."

Keep all options on the table, even the most baldly Strangelovian.

The most spectacular upside of a nuclear bluff is avoiding war altogether, not to mention preserving the planet's economy and ecology. If the United States or Israel convinced Iran's leaders that Natanz and even a city or two might be bombed if they don't halt enrichment, it could short-circuit Iran's quest for weapons-grade material *and avoid having to harm a single Iranian*. The downside, of course, is increasing the risk that we'll overplay our hand and push a desperate opponent too hard, unleashing a whirlwind of suicide bombers, disrupting the flow of oil, or worse.

In August 2006, two weeks after the World Series ended, Iran re-raised the Security Council by announcing that it would ramp up enrichment activities, not cancel them. Ahmadinejad italicized the point by inaugurating a new heavy-water reactor, the kind that specializes in weapons-grade plutonium rather than electricity. This belligerent gesture came during large-scale war games named after Zolfaghar, "the Sword of Ali." (Ali is revered by Shiites as the successor of Muhammad.) Ali Akbar Hashemi Rafsanjani, a senior cleric who heads the powerful Expediency Council, declared, "We hope America has learned a lesson from the war in Lebanon and refrains from getting involved in another conflict." Underscoring this veiled threat with violence, Iranian state television showed troops firing live ammunition from helicopters, dropping large bombs in the desert, and launching medium-range radar-evading missiles, called Saegheh, which means "thunder" in Farsi. Brigadier General Muhammad Hassan Dadrass took pains to emphasize that Iran was not revealing "the major part of its military capability." By alluding to vastly more serious thunder, was the general saying that Iran already had a nuclear ace, maybe two, up her sleeve—or, à la Jamie Gold and Jon Friedberg, just a trey and a deuce?

FOOLED BY RANDOMNESS

There's a lotta luck in poker, and if you're gonna play this game you better get used to it.

—T. J. CLOUTIER

Like many tacticians before him and since, James Wickstead naïvely downplays the luck factor. "In philosophy there is no such thing as 'luck,'" he confidently states in his 1938 primer on stud. "'Luck' is purely subjective, in the eye of the beholder. The amount of 'bad luck' that a player has over a period of time is practically negligible. He holds average cards and his winning or losing is contingent on how he plays them." What Wickstead seems not to understand is that while playing well is essential, for a player to hold average cards—that is, for the variance to become perfectly flat, canceling every last outlier—the universe of hands must be vast, well into the millions by most estimates and more than most players will see in their lifetime, let alone in one weekend or tournament. When you consider the random fluctuations of several opponents' cards, the luck factor spikes through the ceiling. So that when Wickstead tut-tuts, "Viewed through the lorgnette of careful reasoning, we must reach the conclusion, namely, that 'luck' or any other exterior factor counts for very little," experienced players might quote

Joseph Conrad: "It is the mark of an inexperienced man not to believe in luck." Or at least they might ask, "What the hell's a lorgnette?"

Or as the narrator of Rick Bennet's novel *King of a Small World* astutely observes, "In the long run there's no luck in poker, but the short run is longer than most people know." The narrator of Jesse May's *Shut Up and Deal* seems to respond directly to Wickstead: "People think mastering the skill is the hard part, but they're wrong. The trick to poker is mastering the luck. That's philosophy. Understanding luck is philosophy, and there are some people who aren't ever gonna fade it. That's what sets poker apart. And that's what keeps everyone coming back for more." If it were purely a skill game, like chess, it would be quite a bit less lucrative and popular. When the nature of a game allows its best players to win every time, the line to bet against or challenge them becomes very short.

While it's difficult to put a finger on exactly where luck, good or bad, works its magic in poker, let's look at the stages of fortune in a fairly typical tournament hand. Lucky to be dealt pocket jacks near the bubble of a no-limit hold'em event, Jackson is unlucky to have an opponent named Quinn peer between his knuckles and find pocket queens, especially because Quinn's stack is bigger than Jackson's. When Jackson raises to three times the big blind, Quinn considers reraising with queens, but respects the early-position raise and just calls. On a rainbow flop of 4-7-9, Jackson thinks he's lucky that not a single overcard to his jacks has appeared, but in fact he is unlucky that the texture of the flop encourages him to bet into queens. Depending on his chip count, Jackson may very well go all-in at this stage, even if he checks first and Quinn makes a sizable bet. Granted, the play of such hands can be complex. A supremely observant and disciplined player may somehow put Quinn on a bigger overpair, check, and fold when Quinn bets. Or Quinn's acting skill might convince Jackson that Quinn had called before the flop with a much weaker hand than Q-Q. But what nullifies almost every complexity is that a short-stacked Jackson will correctly feel the need to go all-in before or after this flop. He will then be called by Quinn, and 90 percent of the time he will lose all his chips. Note as well that Jackson wasn't unlucky that a jack didn't flop; he just wasn't lucky *enough*. But if a third queen also appeared on the board, flopping a set of jacks would be very *un*lucky. Either way, getting busted near the bubble will be sickeningly unfortunate for Jackson. For Quinn, Jackson's bad luck will probably be worth at least several thousand dollars in prize money, though Quinn will probably think his windfall of chips was due mainly to skill.

When getting dealt a worse hand (an unsuited 4-7, for example) would have led to a better result (folding before the flop), we say that Jackson's timing was off. Quinn's timing was perfect. But instead of Quinn's poker skill, it was the dealer—the human randomizer in a clip-on bow tie—who literally and figuratively pushed all those chips to him. Seven or eight times out of ten, this is who determines who wins the make-or-break tournament hands, especially when we count all the races decided by that same human shuffle machine.

Now let's compare some inflection points in baseball, since the valences of our national pastimes are surprisingly similar. Both are played nine- or ten-handed but place a huge premium on individual success: it's the whole ball game at the poker table, of course, and while a baseball team competes for a pennant, it's the veteran sluggers and strikeout artists who make the long money. Sample size is crucial in gauging the luck factor in either game. The best football teams and tennis players and boxers win 90 percent of their matches, while the best baseball team wins only about 60 percent of its games. During the playoffs, against other strong teams, this percentage should drop even lower, and the difference in overall team skill often is not enough to overcome the luck factor.

It shouldn't be surprising, then, that the tactics of both baseball and poker are dominated by probability. Managers maneuver to achieve or avoid lefty-righty matchups, and they count on statistics to establish rotations and batting orders. Poker players gauge pot odds, randomize bluffs, fold when their hand is a statistical underdog, raise when it's the favorite. In both contests, decoys and stealing are crucial, but patience is just as important. Baseball and poker players spend most of their time picking up signs, moving into position, and working the count, but once every nine plays or so, on both offense and defense, their skills really have to pay off. Yet more than in most competitions, luck becomes pivotal.

Imagine there are two out, bases loaded, late in a close playoff game, as Arnold Rothstein certainly did before the 1919 World Series. With a full count, the pitcher unleashes a nasty two-seamer tailing in on the hands of the opposing cleanup man. The dozens of possible outcomes include the batter taking a close pitch for ball four—or strike three. On a perfect pitch, luck—or the ump's fallibility—is involved in getting, or not getting, the call. (An obvious parallel is a race between pocket queens and A-K.) Or the batter might swing—pull in his hands and skillfully make hard contact, driving the ball just over the left field wall; or to nearly the same spot, where the left fielder is able to make a snow-cone catch; or an inch to the left, where the fielder gets his glove on it before it caroms away for a bases-clearing double. The wind, at least as much as the fielder's glove skill, will determine the outcome. Or the batter might swing and make feeble contact, resulting in a foul tip caught or dropped, a swinging bunt, an easy three-hopper to short, a seeing-eye single, a pop-out, a duck snort just out of reach of the second baseman, and so on.

Poker luck is even more egalitarian. The genes of very few of us produce Randy Johnson's seven-foot left-handed wingspan or the eyesight and coordination of Henry Aaron, but we all have the same chance of being dealt a timely hand when the money is on the line. And of not being dealt one.

In no-limit hold'em tournaments, novices with excellent timing routinely destroy famous pros. They also lose to two-outers and finish 100th out of 1,007—when 99 places are paid. For the pros it's no different. Among the top three hundred tournament specialists, the differences in skill are quite small. Whoever "runs good" for a few months will make televised final tables, win major titles and millions of dollars, and be hired, as Martin de Knijff was in 2004 and Michael Mizrachi was in '06, as pretty much the sole face of a big online site. A lot of folks must have been sold on the idea that de Knijff or Mizrachi was notably more skillful than the pros who, by winning a few extra coin flips, would have earned those same titles.

Netting a profit in poker tournaments year after year definitely requires plenty of skill, but by far the most important factor determining who wins one is luck. Too few winners acknowledge this, though, and the winners are who most people want to hear from. TV producers and magazine editors operate on the assumption that poker fans don't want to hear that a black swan took down those photogenic bundles of Benjamins. No, it was their hero's laser focus on an opponent's pulsing vein late on day six that earned him the cash and the bracelet.

What the hell's a black swan, you ask? Astonishing luck, good or bad. According to Nassim Taleb, the trader who made them notorious in his books *The Black Swan* and *Fooled by Randomness*, "A black swan is an outlier, an event that lies beyond the realm of normal expectations." He was writing in response to the 9/11 Commission, criticizing its failure to understand risk. "Most people expect all swans to be white," he continued, "because that's what their experience tells them; a black swan is by definition a surprise. Nevertheless, people tend to concoct explanations for them after the fact, which makes them appear more predictable, and less random, than they are. Our minds are designed to retain, for efficient storage, past information that fits into a compressed narrative. This distortion, called the hindsight bias, prevents us from adequately learning from the past."

Hindsight bias also happens to be a polite term for calling an all-in preflop raise with A-7 suited, rivering a straight, and yelling, "*Yeah, baby! Ship it!*" Of adolescents such as these, Taleb writes: "Lucky fools do not bear the slightest suspicion that they may be lucky fools." And why not? Because their "strings of successes will inject them with so much serotonin [the hormone of pleasure] they will fool themselves about their ability." And also because "our hormonal system does not know whether our successes depend on randomness." In other words, it feels so darn good to win a big pot that we prefer to give our favorite player the credit, even when all he's done is hit the bull's-eye of the target next to the one he was aiming at.

Another reason we're so easily fooled by random success is that poker movies and television broadcasts tend to equate getting lucky with tactical prowess. As Mike D'Angelo pointed out in *Esquire*, directors "try to create excitement by emphasizing luck rather than skill—or, more accurately, by treating luck as if it were skill." It's a crucial distinction, of course, but one that a sizable fraction of the audience is unable to make. D'Angelo points to the climactic hand of the $150 million tournament in *Casino Royale*: "While the icy arch-villain's full house bests a flush and a smaller full house, it's no match for 007's improbable straight flush, which he smugly unveils as if he'd somehow willed this result rather than just winning the poker equivalent of the state lottery."

D'Angelo adds that the phoniest hand ever filmed is the last one in *The Cincinnati Kid*, in which the Kid's full house loses to the Man's straight flush—in short stud, no less, when the chance of making such powerful hands is exponentially smaller. D'Angelo puts the odds against aces full losing to a straight flush at "roughly 45 million to 1." *Card Player* columnists Roy Cooke and Michael Wiesenberg, however, have explained in great detail how the play of this hand makes more sense than some of the movie's critics have claimed. They agree, though, that the only way the Man busts the Kid on that hand is by getting, in Wiesenberg's word, "superlucky."

While the Man's and 007's exceedingly well-timed straight flushes are perfect examples of a black swan, it's important to realize that every winner of an actual grudge match or tournament has also been blessed by at least one or two of these life-changing fowl. Phil Gordon is among the more thoughtful pros who believe that randomness is a much bigger factor than most players realize or are willing to admit. "Change ten river cards in any poker player's tournament career," he says, "and I would bet that they would be a losing tournament player for their career."

Again, this is not to suggest that skill isn't crucial in tournaments. But when 75 or 80 percent of the entrants are skillful *enough* to win if their timing is exquisite, it may be foolish to give so much credit—and such a large percentage of the prize money—to the player who wins the last hand. This is perhaps the main reason that the winner's share of most prize pools keeps dropping year after year, from 100 percent in the early 1970s to around 20 percent in the boom years. The incentive to enter will be reduced if it goes much lower than that, but most players agree that the trend has been a healthy development.

We can also get a sense of the luck factor from poker's elite. Daniel Negreanu was the highest-ranked tournament player in 2004, but the charismatic and talented Canadian didn't win a single event in 2005. Did his acumen suddenly wither? Of course not. His luck just regressed a bit closer to the mean. In his always frank blog, Negreanu walked his fans through two key hands against Erik Seidel during the '05 World Series. Both times Negreanu was a slight favorite when the big money went in the pot, and both times he lost. "Those hands in particular have been the difference in my year this year vs. last. Playing the hands is unavoidable, but if you never hit one it's impossible to win. Plain and simple."

Seidel, who used to work in Taleb's business and now has eight WSOP bracelets, is ironically more famous for losing the '88 championship to Johnny Chan when Chan was fortunate enough to flop a straight on the final hand. Film of the hand was used in *Rounders* to show how skillful Chan was. Not that Chan *wasn't* skillful, but slow-playing the flopped nuts hardly proved it.

Jesse Alto is one of thousands of highly skilled WSOP regulars who never won a bracelet. Alto cashed in ten of the early tournaments, most notably in the main event of 1976, when he finished ahead of every

FOOLED BY RANDOMNESS ♣ 343

player but one, yet he lost the bracelet and the entire $220,000 purse to Doyle Brunson. In the final hand, Alto was dealt the ace of clubs and jack of hearts, Brunson the ten and deuce of spades. The flop came ace of hearts, jack of spades, ten of hearts, giving Alto the top two pairs and a backdoor heart draw, Brunson a third pair with no kicker, no heart. The reigning champion had less than a 12 percent chance of winning this pot at a showdown. He had plenty of poker heart, though. When Alto led out with a pot-sized bet, Brunson responded by moving all-in. Even though Alto was covered, he was only too happy to call and over-joyed when he saw Brunson's hand. What Brunson now needed was neither courage nor skill but simple dumb luck. The turn was the 2 of clubs, giving him two pairs but leaving him an even bigger underdog than he was after the flop—until the 10 of spades on the river, a black swan if ever there was one, gave him a full house and, with it, the bracelet and prize money. Alto's share was zero. The lives of these play-ers significantly diverged at this point.

T. J. Cloutier has won more tournaments than anyone and would have won the 2000 world championship if Chris Ferguson hadn't spiked his three-outer on the river. The following summer virtually the same thing happened to Cloutier when he got heads-up with Brian Saltus in the Tournament of Champions. In both cases, Cloutier smiled as he shook the lucky winner's hand and told him how well he had played. "That's poker," he added. His thoughts about vicious black swans might be called Texas fatalism: "You can set up all the plays in the world, you can play perfectly on a hand, and you can still lose. And there's nothing that you can do about it."

Then there's Dan Harrington, who has had as much success in, and with as deep a mathematical understanding of, no-limit hold'em tour-naments as anyone alive. "The volatility in tournaments is out of sight," he says bluntly. "I don't think you can consider playing tournaments for a living. I think that is impossible. Even if you are a world-class player, the expenses are just too high. . . . If you're going to play poker and fo-cus on tournaments, you better be wealthy, and if you're wealthy, why are you playing poker tournaments? Sure, you see some names repeat-ing as winners. They are truly great players. But the problem is, there are lots of other truly great players you haven't seen at all. And it's not because they are playing badly. It's the variance. You need to be extremely lucky."

What Harrington fails to mention, of course, is the damn-the-expenses appeal of winning millions of dollars at a televised final table, the sponsorship deal that often goes with it, and the sweet rush of finishing first. But the bottom-line fact is that not even the very best players can count on turning a profit in tournaments unless they get freakishly lucky—or until they are sponsored into the televised events. Once a player is talented, lucky, and/or charismatic enough to have his buy-ins and travel expenses covered in exchange for wearing a logo or two, it becomes almost impossible for him to lose on the circuit. For everyone else, though, Harrington's points remain valid. Yet there are plenty of other ways to think about variance, as we'll see in the following chapter.

BUNCHES OF LUCK

Mr. Jinx and Miss Lucy, they jumped in the lake.
—BOB DYLAN, "THINGS HAVE CHANGED"

A deck of fifty-two cards can be shuffled into 52! sequences: 52 × 51 × 50 × 49, and so on down to 1, which comes to 80,658, 175,170,943,878,571,660,636,856,403,766,975,289,505,440, 883,277,824,000,000,000,000. (The final 12 zeros are *not* due to rounding, by the way.) Among this dizzying number, poker players, if they live long enough, will find every last combination of hole cards, burn cards, flops, turns, and rivers. With our short-term perspective, however, we tend to be furious when, with all of these possible variations, we're dealt a dozen hands in a row that are more or less the same, without a single card higher than 7—unless we're playing lowball, of course, in which case we're thrilled. The length of this number has a lot to do with why the winner of the World Series main event is no longer thought of as poker's best player. When decks are well shuffled, the laws of randomness produce wildly unpredictable results on a regular basis. And the larger the field, the less likely it becomes that the best player in any tournament will win it.

Serious players are at war with the shuffle. Many of them prefer no-limit or pot-limit games because big-bet poker gives them more leverage to win pots without the best hand. Other strong players prefer a mixed limit game such as H.O.R.S.E., in which the money usually goes to those who make a series of small, correct decisions over a number of hours or days. Among high-stakes professionals, the $50,000 H.O.R.S.E. event at the WSOP has become the gold standard of tournaments. But the very best players, of course, do well in both kinds of games.

In the previous chapter, we saw how much luck is necessary to win a no-limit tournament, especially now that the fields routinely exceed two thousand players. A high degree of skill is required to play these events for a profit, but it's also true that a growing percentage of players are capable of winning if their timing is exquisite. Skill remains paramount, but the luck factor—usually in the form of bad timing in a single key hand late in the tournament—prevents the most talented players from finishing first as often as they do in golf, chess, tennis, boxing, or Scrabble.

Even so, David Sklansky, Howard Lederer, and Annie Duke have made a convincing argument that in both cash games and tournament poker, a preponderance of skill wins the money. Their point is fairly simple: you cannot intentionally lose at games of chance such as bingo, lotteries, craps, or roulette, but a poker player can easily lose on purpose if he wants to. Lederer adds that most no-limit pots are won without a showdown, and it is clearly the bettor's skill in deciding when and how much to raise that determines the outcome of those hands.

For historical perspective, we also have Mark Twain's famous report in *The Galaxy* of October 1870. "Science vs. Luck" describes a legal dispute in Kentucky, where the law against games of chance was quite strict. About a dozen young men had been indicted for playing a variant of seven-card stud called seven-up or, sometimes, old sledge. Twain says it was so clear the players would be convicted that their attorney, Jim Sturgis, was the object of great public sympathy. "People said it was a pity to see him mar his successful career with a big prominent case like this, which must go against him," he writes. "But after several restless nights an inspired idea flashed upon Sturgis, and he sprang out of bed delighted."

When the trial began, Sturgis acknowledged that his clients had played poker for money. His entire defense consisted of the argument that seven-up was not a game of chance. The jury and judge all smiled at his effrontery. The prosecuting attorney ridiculed him. Finally, the judge "lost a little of his patience, and said the joke had gone far enough. Jim Sturgis said he knew of no joke in the matter—his clients could not be punished for indulging in what some people chose to consider a game of chance, until it was proven that it was a game of chance." The town's deacons were all happy to testify, "unanimously and with strong feeling," that it was a game of chance.

Undeterred, Sturgis brought in "a cloud of witnesses, and produced an overwhelming mass of testimony" that it was, in fact, "a game of science." He then asked the judge to "impanel a jury of six of each, Luck versus Science—give them candles and a couple of decks of cards, send them into the jury room, and just abide by the result!" The judge agreed. After swearing in the deacons as "chance" jurymen and six "inveterate old seven-up professors" as the "science" jurors, he instructed them to play seven-up throughout the night.

In the morning Deacon Job, the foreman, read the verdict: "We, the jury in the case of the Commonwealth of Kentucky vs. John Wheeler et al., have carefully considered the points of the case, and tested the merits of the several theories advanced, and do hereby unanimously decide that the game commonly known as old sledge or seven-up is eminently a game of science and not of chance." During the entire night, said the deacon, "the 'chance' men never won a game or turned a jack, although both feats were common and frequent to the opposition; and further more, in support of this our verdict, we call attention to the significant fact that the 'chance' men are all busted, and the 'science' men have got the money. It is the deliberate opinion of this jury that the 'chance' theory concerning seven-up is a pernicious doctrine, and calculated to inflict untold suffering and pecuniary loss upon any community that takes stock in it."

After a lifetime of poker on three continents, Herb Yardley reached this conclusion: "I do not believe in luck—only in the immutable law of averages." The high-stakes cash player Brian Townsend is one of dozens of twenty-first-century pros who echo Yardley. "I don't believe in luck. It's all mathematics," says Townsend. "Everybody runs the same. I believe in taking personal responsibility for my play. I see too many posts in which people say they run bad or are unlucky. I believe that you make your own results, and that everything comes down to your decisions. No one else is in control but yourself. People think that the cards have a role in the results, and they do in the short run, but in the long run, it'll all even out. If your results aren't good, it's most likely because you're not playing well."

Crandell Addington insists that luck is not a major factor in no-limit hold'em "if you include cash games in the generalizations about luck and randomness. Yes, randomness has become a major factor in the NLH tournaments televised today, which is an aberration of the pure form of the game. But that is not true, nor has it ever been, in the pure form of the game, i.e., the cash game." Addington adds that he and several of his old road-gambling cohorts "never had a losing year as we played throughout the country. Those were cash games in which Lady Luck occasionally found a seat at the table, but for the most part she was barred from the games. Although I cannot express an opinion about the skills of some of today's younger professionals in cash games, since I have not played with them, I notice that some of them struggle in the $100,000 change-in cash NLH that is currently televised. Quite a different game from tournament poker."

Says the writer and inspired amateur Peter Alson: "Tournaments are more luck-dependent than cash games for the simple reason that the blinds keep increasing, which forces one to commit chips with perhaps only a very small edge or no edge at all. If the blinds did not increase, tournament poker would be very similar to live play in terms of luck." He goes on: "People talk about the long run. I think most of the mathematicians out there will agree that the long run can be a very long time, and that while things will usually even out, this is not always the case. Although luck will average out as a whole among the poker-playing population, there are individuals who will be unlucky for life and others who will be lucky for life. If you are very skilled but luck goes against you over the course of a lifetime, you might still be a winning player, just not as much of one as you might have been if luck had broken even or slightly favored you. In every bell curve there will be losers and winners in the distribution of luck."

English pro Barney Boatman: "I think you'll find that there is an inversely proportional relationship between the amount of success a player has had and the importance he attaches to luck. You will not be surprised therefore to know that I think luck is a big factor in NLH tournament play. Even though luck evens out in the sense that you win roughly half your coin flips, etc., there is no guarantee that you win your share of the few key hands that come late in big events. This is my view because the alternative, that I am not quite good enough, is too horrible for me to contemplate!"

Mason Malmuth: "The right way to answer this question is to compute the coefficient of variation (CV) based on a good player's results.

And the CV is just the win rate divided by the standard deviation. All of this and how to compute it is in my book *Gambling Theory and Other Topics*. . . . As a rough guide, if the CV is over 10 percent, the luck factor is low, and under 10 percent the luck factor is high. I would expect the CV for a good no-limit hold'em player who plays in reasonable games to be at least 20 percent, meaning a very low luck factor, especially in comparison to limit games."

Writing with the high-stakes pro Brandon Adams, Aaron Brown broke down the odds of great players making a major final table, where the big money is, with a phenomenal degree of precision. "Before the 2006 WSOP main event, I went to Betfair.com to get pretournament betting odds of various players making the final table. Phil Ivey was the favorite at 22 to 1; it should have been 877 to 1 if poker is a game of pure luck. Of course, the Betfair bettors might be mistaken but they have proven remarkably accurate in general. Also the player with the 8th best odds, Allen Cunningham, paid off. If things were random, there would only be 1 chance in 88 that anyone from Betfair's top 10 would make the final table. Betfair quoted odds on only 114 of the 8,773 entrants, I assume the ones their customers thought were the best. The implied probabilities of making it to the final table followed a power curve closely: Probability = $0.02334 * R^{-0.3860}$, where R is rank (so R = 1 for Phil Ivey, R = 2 for Daniel Negreanu, . . . R = 8 for Allen Cunningham). This implies a Gini coefficient of 24%. Making the series of bets described above, $8,773 to $1 with the worst player, $8,772 to $2 with the second worst, and so on, produces an expected profit of $9.13 million. That leads me to say success in the WSOP main event is 24% skill and 76% luck."

Chris Ferguson, with a Ph.D. in computer science and game theory to go with his five bracelets, puts the ratio of luck to skill in poker at "pretty close to fifty–fifty." Chau Giang, on the other hand, told Dana Smith of *Card Player*, "At the table I hear people say, 'Poker is luck.' That is 100 percent wrong. If they are losing, it is because they're doing something wrong. Poker is skill, it isn't luck. In the long run, day after day, you cannot get lucky all the time." If you're not exactly sure what ratio Giang is proposing, even though you think you agree with him, perhaps you'll agree with Tom McEvoy: "Poker is a hundred percent skill and a hundred percent luck."

Andy Beal is the Dallas banker famous for not only taking on the high-stakes Bellagio pros in a series of heads-up limit hold'em showdowns for as much as $40 million per match, but also for his tough negotiations to have the matches played on his terms (the subject of Chapters 46 and 47). Discussing the luck/skill ratio in those games, Beal says, "The luck factor influences more than the distribution of the cards falling. The biggest impact of luck for skilled long-term players will reside in environmental stuff: I was lucky I got an extra-good night's sleep last night; I was lucky I was 'in the zone' and playing optimally; I was lucky I didn't get mad and let it influence my play; I was unlucky that my girlfriend called in the middle of the game and told me she was leaving with my best friend, etc. I think these are more material to long-time players. Yes, the pro doesn't let emotion into the game, but we're all human—we're lucky when the human factor doesn't become involved in our game."

Beal's opponent and friend Doyle Brunson admits he's "got no idea" to what extent luck is a factor. "I play and do what I feel is right at that particular moment. I do know there is a lot of luck in the short term, hardly any luck in the long run."

When played well enough to consistently overcome the luck factor, poker becomes an art form. Although he's had plenty of luck in his poker life, Brunson certainly qualifies as an artist; so do Chip Reese, Stu Ungar, and a number of people still playing. By the time they turn twenty-five, Annette Obrestad and Tom Dwan may be in this fast company, too. Fearlessless, brains, and panache are crucial in sizing up players as artists. Another way to say this is that poker artists have fine-tuned their knack for leveraging the uncertainty inherent in the face-down and still unseen cards into subtle but decisive advantages.

In *Bigger Deal*, Anthony Holden writes: "The mystery of poker, and so its infinite fascination, lies in the element of chance, otherwise known as luck. The art of the game lies in minimizing it." Putting technical skill in perspective, Howard Lederer quotes D. T. Suzuki: "If one really wishes to be master of an art, technical knowledge of it is not enough. One has to transcend technique so that the art becomes an 'artless art' growing out of the Unconscious." Adds Lederer, "Staying in the moment is the path to poker success," though we need to remain realistic. "Have I succeeded in staying in the moment at the poker table? Almost never; but I have had some success. In a recent tournament, I was sitting next to a player who, near the end of play that day, told me that he thought I had played well except for a really bad play I had made about 30 minutes earlier. I didn't remember the hand, but after he refreshed my memory, I could only agree with his assessment. I was pleased that only 30 minutes after what might have been my worst play of the day, I had already completely let go of it. I see this as a major stride in my development as a player. Beating myself up over a bad play serves almost no purpose other than distracting me from the task at hand."

In *Zen and the Art of Poker*, Larry W. Phillips writes, "experienced card players believe in the bunching of luck. They have seen it. They have felt it. They know it is not a pipe dream or a mirage. Ignore this phenomenon at your peril. Even the mathematicians admit that it can happen, will happen, does happen." The Chicago attorney Jim Karamanis, who has played recreationally since his college days in Madison, expands on Phillips's idea: "At least on some level, I attempt to gauge who is having a good (or lucky) night and who is not. I factor the luck of a particular player into my calculation of pot odds, etc., in determining whether to make a call or how to play a hand. It is no different than knowing a person who is playing a rush is more likely to call a raise with an inferior hand than one who is not. It is obviously not a scientific calculation, but it is a necessary one." Karamanis adds that he is "more apt to play into a player running badly or draw to unfavorable odds against that player than into a player having a good night. This calculation also changes during the course of an evening, as a player's luck is bound to ebb and flow. Randomness encompasses disproportionate groupings of good or bad hands that manifest themselves at different times and in different sessions of poker. To ignore the disproportionate groupings in your play, to me, is foolish. That's why I am not bothered as much when a poorer player has a run of good cards. My job is not to be affected by it but to observe what is transpiring and position myself accordingly." He concludes: "I may not be able to control luck, but I can certainly maximize my return by observing its effect on the game."

After losing yet another big pot to one of his Thursday-night game's braying donkeys, Karamanis likes to recall a passage from R. L. Wing's commentary on the Tao: "Those who follow the Tao continually look beyond the present reality in an attempt to perceive the seeds of change. They have complete faith in physical laws that demonstrate that all of reality is in a process of change and all processes cycle in the direction of their opposite—from life to death, positive to negative, energy to matter—and back again. Because they learn to recognize and understand the law of polarity, they gain extraordinary insight into worldly affairs," poker included. In other words, maybe, just maybe, the fortunate Thursday-night donkeys will eventually get their comeuppance.

45

THE BIOLOGY AND EROS OF
NO-LIMIT HOLD'EM TOURNAMENTS

The woman with five hearts knew what she had,
knew what we lacked. She bet high and then
higher; it was what any of us would have done.

— STEPHEN DUNN

Women have yet to achieve parity in poker, but they've come a long way since the days when no women played, or even since the era of *Roe v. Wade* and *Riggs v. Court*. In 1977, gaming journalist David Spanier could write in *The Independent*, "No girl I have ever seen at a poker table has ever managed to win consistently. There are plenty who try, in the gorgeous palaces of Las Vegas and in Gardena, and in the workaday casinos of London, too. Women players, typically, are tense, beady-eyed, chain-smoking ladies . . . a far cry from the languorous cuties you see displayed in casino ads." Eyebrow-raising stuff, even coming from a spiny old-school stegosaurus, though for the most part it was an accurate account of the times. But Spanier didn't stop there. "There are often girls around," he continued, "but a girl's fate is to sit on the fringe of the action waiting for her man to finish the game, which inevitably means waiting up half the night. By that time the girl is just about dropping with fatigue and looking like last week's laundry."

Just before he died in February 2000, Spanier surveyed the new landscape: "Women are no longer considered as accessories to be brought to the poker table, but as equals at the game." His opinion was borne out three months later at the World Series, where the women's bracelet count doubled from two to four. The count grew steadily through 2004, with other women consistently making the money. Despite all this progress, however, the winner of every WSOP event in '05 and '06 was a man, as were all eighteen final-tablists in the main event of those years. The '07 razz event was won by Hamburg native Katja Thater and the no-limit hold'em championship event in London by the eighteen-year-old Norwegian phenom "Annette_15" Obrestad. But every other '07 bracelet went to a man, as did the top thirty-six spots in the main event. Not a single woman won a bracelet in 2008.

Linda Johnson, Jennifer Harman, Cyndy Violette, Kathy Liebert, Annie Duke, and Nani Dollison all have won bracelets; they and a few dozen other women, including Liz Liu, Erica Schoenberg, Millie Shiu, and Anna Wroblewski, seem to earn handsome livings at poker. Harman, in fact, more than holds her own every night in Bobby's Room at the Bellagio, home of the toughest ring game on the planet. Even so, a woman has yet to win the WSOP main event; only Barbara Enright, who finished fifth in 1995, has made a final table. Nor has a woman won a single WPT event.

Why the drought? One reason may be that the game played in almost every major tournament is no-limit hold'em, the form that most consistently rewards an aggressive approach. The leverage it provides to win pots without the best hand gives forceful risk takers a significant edge. Yet the biggest obstacle keeping more women from bracelet ceremonies or the top of the POY leaderboard is neither skill nor the need to be aggressive, but the fact that so few of them choose to compete in the major events. Those fields very seldom consist of more than 5 percent women, and often much less. And you've got to be in it to win it.

Tournament-style gambling apparently isn't something the average woman is biologically inclined to sign up for. In a 2005 University of Pittsburgh study, women did just as well as men, both individually and on four-member teams, in a math game that paid $2 for each correct answer. But when offered the chance either to consolidate their profits or risk them in a tournament with much more at stake, most women declined to compete, even the ones who had previously done best in the game. Most men chose to enter the tournament, even those who had fared poorly earlier.

"Even in tasks where they do well, women seem to shy away from competition, whereas men seem to enjoy it too much," the researchers concluded. "The men who weren't good at this task lost a little money by choosing to compete, and the really good women passed up a lot of money by not entering tournaments they would have won." The anthropologist Helen Fisher, author of *The Sex Contract: The Evolution of Human Behavior*, puts these findings in context: "Evolution has selected for men with a taste for risking everything to get to the top of the hierarchy, because those males get more reproductive opportunities. Women don't get as big a reproductive payoff by reaching the top." This anticompetitive bias might be an even bigger impediment to entering poker tournaments, because money not only flows to the top of a pyramid of risk takers but is the game's very language. Aggressively competing for it might simply feel too unladylike for the average woman, even in 2009.

Balancing this bias, perhaps, is the fact that poker also rewards patience and what is often called women's intuition, the empathetic ability to read what others are thinking or feeling. There are plenty of aggressive women, of course, in poker and other arenas, as well as patient, intuitive men. Yet the fact that young men produce about twenty times as much testosterone, a hormone closely linked with both stamina and competitiveness, probably makes it easier for them to stay aggressive for the week or so that it takes to win a major no-limit event.

Age is also a factor. Testy young males not only lust for tournament action, they have or make time for it. As a group they have fewer family responsibilities than women, or than men over, say, thirty-five. Young men are also better able to cope with the physical toll of traveling from event to event.

While Danica Patrick, Kerri Walsh, Candace Parker, and others have proved that women can compete against men in some physical sports, pokeristas are closer to achieving parity and should get even closer as reinforcements arrive. Women already comprise roughly a third of Internet players. Anxiety about competing is presumably less of a factor online, even though intuition is thwarted. But as women learn the game in small-buy-in tournaments online, more might be willing to risk part of their bankroll in lucrative on-land events.

Then there is what might be called the eros of no-limit hold'em, and all of its pluses and drawbacks. Poker players in general often report the game to be more stimulating than amphetamines, alcohol, or even sexual intercourse. When all of our money goes into the pot, electrons and corpuscles rush to the pleasure centers of the cerebral cortex, and others rush lower. To modulate our breathing becomes a pivotal challenge. We blush.

When declaring women equals at the table back in 2000, Spanier slyly added, "This is not to say that sex cannot enter poker. A woman at the table can alter the chemistry of the game," he suggested. "If a woman can exploit her sexuality by a certain smile, a look, a little flirting, to put a male opponent off his game, she is entitled to do so. Any man who responds, in the spirit of the occasion, should be even more on his guard. The object on both sides (one must assume) is to win the pot."

It was in much the same spirit that in 2005 Mayer Labs aired a commercial for Kimono condoms designed to capitalize on the sex appeal of no-limit hold'em. "Poker is fun, tense and exciting," Mayer explains on its website, "just like sexual relationships. Smart, fun people who like sex, like safer sex, and they like it more with Kimono."

Cut to a beautiful woman betting her last chip against a dangerously handsome stud sitting behind a big stack. Making meaningful eye contact, the stud calls her bet and raises one chip. Unpregnant pause, sultry stare, before the woman pushes a Kimono condom—still in its wrapper, of course—into the pot. As three schlubs look on, the stud shoves in the rest of his chips. Packs of Kimono condoms appear on the screen, with the tagline: "When the Stakes are High."

Wink.

No doubt some women will resent, or at least regret, this ad's innuendo. Others will smile, maybe blush. Still others will nod at its accurate reflection of poker's racy ethos and jargon. Extortionate reraises, after all, have long been called "coming over the top" of the initial bettor, often abbreviated to, simply, "coming." To come nearly always requires pushing in all of your chips.

This isn't to deny that all the sparsely clad bimbos posing in ads for online poker sites is an unfortunate, if predictable, trend. At the very least, we should ask ourselves how the Kimono spot would read if the man, with nothing left to bet but a condom, was facing a woman with—wink—an oversize stack. As the old poker Freudian slip goes, "She's got a full blouse—I mean, house."

One response to such innuendos appeared in *Woman Poker Player* in an ad for Interpoker.com. "Weaker sex? I don't think so!" it declares as a blonde in a camisole confidently fingers her hole cards while sitting behind a big stack. "Men," snorts the copy below. "Simple creatures, aren't they? A flutter of your eyes, a flash of leg and they're easily distracted. Well, now it's time to take that female advantage to the poker tables and relieve them of some cash!"

The siren's MO is also endorsed by Toby Leah Bochan in *The Badass Girl's Guide to Poker.* Don't just take men's money, says Bochan. Romance them! In the chapter "Lucky at Cards, Lucky in Love: Meeting Men Through Poker," the newly single author admits that "being hetero, it wasn't like my all-female book club was crowded with possibilities." She recommends that women take advantage of the doubly improved dating odds of late-night action, since more men than women play poker and more single than married men stay out past midnight. Yet whatever the hour, the game provides natural icebreakers. "The mood is energized—there's money at stake," Bochan writes. "And it's easy to tease as you raise and flash a coy smile as you call. Flirting goes with poker like ice cream goes with pie—both are good on their own, but much more delicious together." Old-school feminists and demure pokeristas might try this Bochan line on for size: "I bet you're hiding something big in that pocket." Even less charming are her tactics under the heading, "PMS anyone?" These include: "Revel in being a bitch. Smirk as you pull in pots—gloat. Yell when you suffer a bad beat."

Whatever we think of such advice, we should remember that the cards themselves have long represented gender-based stratagems. Sixteenth-century Swiss decks featured eye-pleasing consorts and bare-breasted dancers, while on Tuscan cards the ladies and dancers were naked. Queens may be clad now and dancing girls chastened to Arabic 10s, but the modern poker deck continues to represent ancient erotic priorities. Kings, queens, jacks, and 10s still combine with themselves and the other cards in untold, and unfair, variations. Why else should a set of queens, for example, beat an equally rare set of jacks? Why should it lose to three kings? Yet poker's long-standing hierarchy of hands, based in part on the sexual politics of European royalty, somehow feels right in our marrow.

In *Sociobiology,* Edward O. Wilson observes that "the more intelligent and social the species, the more elaborate the play." He notes that when playing or pair-bonding, it is "possible for hostile and submissive displays to be combined" to "create a message containing a high level of ambiguity": the fearful but threatening posture of a Halloween cat, for example, or the end of the condom commercial, or Bochan's belligerent flirting. "By combining signals," writes Wilson, "it is possible to give them new meanings."

Nor should we be surprised when some cards pick up bawdy nicknames. A hold'em starting hand of 2-9 is often called Twiggy; 3-8, Raquel Welch; 6-9, big lick; Q-Q, four tits; A-Q, little slick; and much worse. The queen of hearts continues to represent love, while her counterpart in spades remains the predatory, peremptory bitch.

Another of Spanier's eyebrow-raising claims in *Total Poker* is that the game "has an intimate connection with sexual drives." He quotes the psychoanalyst Ralph Greening on its procreative cadence: "There is a rhythm of tension-discharge, which is constantly repeated." Spanier even proposes that poker showdowns are equivalent in the unconscious to comparing penises with other men, although what a showdown might signify to a badass brunette becomes a little harder to say. But the game in Spanier's view certainly involves titillation. "Playing with poker chips, counting them out, stacking them up, the smooth shapes and glistening colors, the sensual pleasure of handling the cards . . . it's all of a piece." With what? Masturbation, he says, most often related to submissive or dominant urges. After making his case in more scholarly terms, he cites an unnamed bisexual friend who confided to him, "I got a huge erection when I was losing one night really heavily. . . . In a dreadful way it was pleasurable. But then when I managed to win some of the money back, the excitement faded."

When the woman in the Kimono spot wagers that condom and the man calls all-in, they are taking Wilson's and Spanier's and Bochan's ideas to their logical if naughty conclusion. Unfortunately, none of these commercials or bimbo-laced ad campaigns—not to mention such flagrantly adolescent sites as NakedPoker.com—are likely to encourage women to play more poker or enter more tournaments.

Harman, for one, is impatient. In 2006, she bemoaned the fact that many women still seem intimidated by men at the table. After granting that women had made progress over the previous decade, she added, "At this rate it'll be a couple hundred years before we're winning half the events."

More than a few people hope that Harman's prediction is off by a century and three-quarters or so. The optimists among them tend to cite the generally upward trend and mention that when "Annette_15" turns twenty-one on September 18, 2009, and becomes eligible to play in American tournaments, progress should greatly accelerate.

46

THE ANDY GAME, PART I

If I can't be a banker, I don't wanna live.

—COSMO KRAMER

Wednesday, May 12, 2004, the Bellagio Resort and Casino. Resting elbows and forearms on the spongy beige cushion, two men face off at a table designed for ten players. The dealer lifts the green deck from the shuffling gadget recessed into the baize on her left, slides in the brown deck she used for the previous hand. She cuts the green deck. The freshly unknowable sequence of the fifty-two cards will determine who wins the next pot.

Or it won't. The man on the right, Todd Brunson, will have something to say about that. He's been doing this for a living since he turned twenty-one thirteen years ago, and he's earned a reputation for playing what is called smash-mouth poker. Riffling together a stack of cranberry-and-white $25,000 chips, he shifts his weight in the chair to get comfortable. At six feet, 260, he calls to mind a retired fullback still issued plenty of meal money. Above his ginger beard and what appear to be baize-colored eyes, he sports a conventional haircut—until you spot the ponytail plunging to the small of his back, which makes it a *mulletus maximus.* Instead of waiting for the shuffle to favor him, Brunson prefers to run over opponents with a ferocious assault of raises, irrespective of the cards he's been dealt.

Andy Beal, the man in the black headphones, is an unlikely candidate for road kill. Eighteen years older than Brunson, he is six two and broad shouldered, in exceptional trim for a middle-aged guy with a desk job. He recently lost thirty pounds on the Atkins diet, and two years earlier he survived a broadside collision in which both vehicles were totaled. He flew in on Tuesday from Dallas, where he normally starts work at Loan Acceptance Corporation by 7:00 a.m. Vegas (Pacific) time. With coffee-brown hair swept back from a ruddy forehead, he could be either a cowboy financier or a family guy on a Vegas vacation. He's both. Poker is something he does for enlightenment and to challenge himself. It's a math- and money-based contest in which he has less of a pedigree than Brunson, whose father happens to be the back-to-back world champion who literally wrote the book on how to run over a game. Yet Beal has at least as much computational firepower as his opponent, and much deeper pockets. Loan Acceptance is a subsidiary of Beal Bank, with assets of $7.2 billion, and Andy isn't the guy who pours quarters and dimes into the coin-counting machine.

The game he is playing with Todd is heads-up limit hold'em, with fixed bets of $100,000 before and after the flop and $200,000 after the turn and the river. No one has ever played poker this high, with $2 million pots being won every ten minutes or so. Right now Todd holds about a two-to-one lead: $15 million to just under $8 million. Andy bought in for $10 million—four racks of cranberries—and has another $5 million on reserve in the cashier's cage. Todd went to the cage with $11.9 million, but the Bellagio had only about $5 million in cranberries left, so he had to settle for $7 million in flags—fourteen hundred-chip racks of the red, white, and blue $5,000 chips. Whenever he runs low on big chips, he slides two racks of flags over to Andy in exchange for two twenty-chip stacks of cranberries.

The match on Table 1 has drawn an audience of a hundred or so, half of them standing on tiptoe along the rail, others craning their necks from seats at adjacent tables. A few of them, including Todd's father, have shares in Todd's action. The stakes are so high that no single player besides Beal can afford them. The Brunsons and several other pros—including Chip Reese, Jennifer Harman, Howard Lederer, Chau Giang, David Grey, and Barry Greenstein—have been forced to pool their resources to be able to compete as a tag team against the lone

Texan. Along with Lederer and Harman, the younger Brunson has been their most successful representative.

Although he is winning and playing well, Todd hasn't been able to concentrate at anything close to 100 percent. He can't get his mind off the death a few days ago of his best friend's Russian-born wife. Todd's wife, Angela, was also born in Russia, and the two couples have been close since they met. Todd still doesn't know whether he should be playing this career-defining match or home with his wife and their friend.

Perhaps in part because of Todd's grief and distraction, Andy roared back over the next ninety minutes, catching hands, keeping the pressure on, and moving ahead—or, as the pros like to say, "getting winner"—by just over $7 million. But then Todd caught some hands, regained his focus, and staged a healthy comeback. By 9:50 p.m. he was $1.1 million ahead—five and a half big bets, about the size of an average pot. Having regained the momentum, Todd preferred to keep going. "Once I get rolling and draw a bead on a guy," he said later, "I wanna play for three days." Andy, on the other hand, felt himself hitting a wall. His body clock, set on Central Time, registered midnight. He was also aware that his opponent's poker day usually began around 5:00 p.m. In terms of their habits and biorhythms, this was bedtime for him and prime time for Todd, so he decided to call it a night. He thanked Todd and his partners for the competition and arranged to resume the match at seven the next morning, when he'd face a new player while enjoying the circadian advantage.

When the series of heads-up showdowns began in December 2001, Andy Beal had been playing blackjack at Strip casinos for twenty-five years and doing pretty well for himself. His numbers-crunching acumen and Xerox recall enabled him to count into a six-deck shoe, giving him about a 3 percent edge against the house. By the late '90s, however, the casinos were starting to flat-bet him—barring him from raising his bet when the count was in his favor. After some testy exchanges with pit bosses, Beal took his chips to the Bellagio's poker room, tucked away next to the sports book of that posh, almost tranquil casino. The games on the main floor ranged from $4/$8 to $30/$60. Two steps up, in the corner, was the high-stakes area, five tables segregated from the sixteen others with a hip-high row of pillars. Flat-screen TVs shared wall space with murals of masked Venetians trysting, playing cards, toting up stacks of gold lucre. The first seat Beal found was in an $80/$160 hold'em game. He exchanged one of the flags he'd been betting on single hands of blackjack for two and a half racks of orange $20 chips. Expertise wouldn't be held against him in this nine-handed game. The only problem was, he didn't have any.

Learning the rules and basic tactics of limit hold'em by the seat of his pants, Beal quickly gathered that solid play at a full table involved folding most of your starting hands. But while conservative play might have saved him a few orange chips, the $5,000-per-hand blackjack player in him was getting impatient. He also observed that at Table 1 over in the corner, two men—Ted Forrest and Chip Reese, as it happened—were waiting for the nightly white-chip game to start. (The Bellagio's $500 chips are white, and this game had betting limits of $2,000 and $4,000.)

Down sat the well-bankrolled novice. Playing Reese and Forrest three-handed is usually quicker than filing a Chapter 11 petition, but since Beal didn't know them from Adam and would be risking but a small fraction of a normal day's income, he was hardly afraid. He just wanted to play for more interesting stakes and not have to fold 80 percent of his hands. He also found the slippery intricacy of three-handed-poker decisions a lot more challenging, in terms of both math and psychology, than those he'd been making in blackjack. With the help of a warm run of cards, he managed to hold his own until the other white-chip maestros began to arrive—the Brunsons, Giang, Harman, and Greenstein. They introduced themselves and invited him to play in their game.

Unfortunately for them, or for him, Beal had a plane to catch. He explained that his family and business responsibilities required him to head for the airport. But he proposed that during his next trip, three months or so hence, one of them play him heads-up with limits of $10,000/$20,000. Todd Brunson assumed Beal was kidding but told him, "I'll be sitting right here at this table."

Back home in Dallas, Beal picked up *Super System* and a few other team-written primers by McEvoy and Cloutier, Sklansky and Malmuth. He was impressed by the rigorous logic but disappointed by how little attention they paid to heads-up strategy. Reading the no-limit section of *Super System*, he recognized a kindred spirit in the senior Brunson's creative attack mode. He was also much taken with Sklansky's definitive wonk treatise, *The Theory of Poker*. The more Beal studied these books, the more poker felt like an extension of his commercial and other endeavors.

Beal had stuck his toe into Texas real estate back in 1976 while still an undergraduate at Baylor, where he majored in business and math. His watershed deal was buying, sight unseen, a 150-unit apartment building in Waco. Barely outbidding his competitors, he effectively went all-in, risking his life savings and then some. Within months he had made his first million and discovered his knack for evaluating the fundamentals of real estate, reading economic terrain, extrapolating a deal's future upside. By 1988, when the savings-and-loan crisis was bankrupting thousands of financial institutions, Beal decided to open one. He launched Beal Bank with a $3 million investment and began buying defaulted loans for forty cents on the dollar. Six years later the bank's capitalization reached $1.5 billion, with assets of more than $7 billion.

There was more to Beal's life than making money, however. A math geek since high school, he continued to brood over Pierre de Fermat's famous Last Theorem, that $A^x + B^x = C^x$ is impossible if x is a prime number. Who cares about such things? Theoretical physicists and mathematicians, the kind of folks who discover gravity, relativity, quantum mechanics, black holes, and nuclear fusion. Beal constructed several algorithms and programmed a dozen of his bank's computers to test a related but brand-new hypothesis, that if $A^x + B^y = C^z$, where A, B, C, x, y, and z are positive integers and x, y, and z are all greater than 2, then A, B, and C must have a common prime factor. When his computers kicked out no exceptions, the discovery was enthusiastically hailed by the math world. In 1993, under the auspices of the American Mathematics Society, Beal endowed a prize (originally $5,000, eventually rising to $100,000) to encourage young mathematicians to prove or disprove what is now called the Beal Conjecture.

Meanwhile, in 1995, he launched Beal Aerospace with the goal of producing expendable rockets. Not only could their payloads be profitable, but he believed they could serve as prototypes for intergalactic escape-and-rescue vehicles. NASA's progress in both of these areas had failed to impress him, but instead of writing his congressman or griping to dinner guests, he invested $200 million in an effort to do a better job. While NASA, Boeing, and Lockheed Martin had put their faith in reusable shuttles, Beal focused on what he called "evolved expendable launch vehicles." The project had sprung from his conviction—a "mathematical certainty," he said—that an asteroid will eventually strike Earth, destroying all but the most primitive forms of life. To avoid extinction, humans will need to colonize other planets.

The aerospace venture failed for a number of reasons. One was a territorial dispute between Guyana and Venezuela about the site of the spaceport. (The site must be near the equator, where much less fuel is required to launch a payload into orbit.) And not only did the federal government subsidize Beal's rivals, but the State Department refused to grant him an export license to launch from outside the United States, citing the Missile Technology Control Regime, an outmoded 1987 treaty which, as Beal pointed out, fails to distinguish between ballistic missiles and peaceful uses and is ignored by rogue states and terrorists, anyway.

As Beal saw his poker experiment, taking on the world's best hold'em players wasn't all that different from buying and selling real estate, starting a bank, building a deep-space rocket, or probing the conundrums of theoretical mathematics. They all required intelligence, curiosity, foresight, and creative risk management, not to mention being "kinda fun."

Yet why aim so high, we might ask, and on so many fronts? Too much money on his hands? Ego tilting out of orbit? One clue may be found on the wall of Beal's office, which features the usual photographs of family, friends, and business associates. Above everything else is a framed sheet of white paper with twelve printed words: *Only those who attempt the absurd will achieve the impossible. —Albert Einstein.*

When Beal returned to the Bellagio in March 2002, he insisted that, in exchange for the opportunity to play a newbie like himself for huge stakes, the pros would have to accept a few ground rules. Instead of their usual nine-handed mixed game, one of them would play heads-up limit hold'em against him, with limits of $25,000 and $50,000. The stakes themselves, in fact, would dictate one-on-one action, since only by pooling their bankrolls could the pros compile one big enough to withstand the variance of playing that high.

The players who accepted Beal's challenge—the Brunsons, Harman, Giang, Reese, Lederer, and Greenstein, as well as David Grey and Lyle Berman—were used to competing most nights in the toughest ring game on the planet. The mix of games they play is designed to keep a specialist in hold'em, say, from sitting down with even the tiniest of edges. To have even the ghost of a chance in their game, you need to master half a dozen variants, readjust every round to radically different hand values and betting strategies, and put a minimum of $100,000 in action. Who had the chutzpah and bankroll to challenge them? According to Reese, it was mainly the young winners of no-limit hold'em events. "You have a million dollars in tournament winnings in your pocket, you're not going to play $100/$200. What'll that do for you?

You've been hit by the deck for five days, you think you're a really good player, and you want to try playing high." Barry Greenstein finished the thought: "As a group, tournament winners are losing players in the Big Game." Why? "We make you think," Greenstein said, "and we make you change the way you think."

Nor was this cunning crew of wizards incapable of colluding against a rich tourist, either by playing softly against one another, signaling hand strength, or ganging up two or three at a time to raise him out of pots. There is no shred of evidence that they even considered doing this, but Beal had to realize they were capable of it, especially if their collective bankroll was in jeopardy. The mere possibility was at least part of the reason he insisted on playing heads-up.

To compensate for their big edge in poker skill, Beal wanted to push the stakes high enough to make them sweat, making it harder for them to play their normal, aggressive A game. In other words, to change the way they thought. Not only did they have centuries of experience and a drawerful of WSOP bracelets among them, but most of the games discussed in the original and second edition of *Super System* had been covered by a member of their team: no-limit hold'em by Doyle, stud high-low by Todd, seven-card stud by Reese, limit hold'em by Harman, pot-limit Omaha by Berman.

Yet neither edition of the venerable classic included a chapter on playing heads-up. Competing against a single opponent, the standard for playable hands is dramatically lower, of course, since you have only one hand to beat. It's less about the strength of your own hand, more about sussing the odds that your opponent will fold to a raise. Maximal strategy in heads-up limit hold'em is something a brilliant amateur like Beal could learn rather quickly, and he wouldn't be sweating the variance while he learned on the job. Yet the Table 1 pros accepted his terms for a chance to leverage their edge in general poker experience. They also bolstered their common bankroll with a few nonplaying investors kicking in a minimum of $100,000 apiece.

Putting egos aside as much as possible, they decided that either Reese or Lederer should have the first crack at the banker. Reese won their coin toss—or lost it, since Beal had stipulated that the match begin at the unheard-of hour of 7:00 a.m. Pacific, when Dallas bankers normally begin their workday. Reese had to set his alarm for an hour not long after he usually climbed into bed.

Beal started fast, catching cards and playing key hands more aggressively—and perhaps with better concentration—than Reese. Three and a half hours later, Beal was ahead by several racks of $5,000 chips. The total bankroll of the Table 1 pros was estimated to be $7 million, and the challenger from Dallas had about six of it. Beal didn't know it at the time, but he was *that* close to busting the most impressive brain trust in poker history.

Enter Ted Forrest, who wasn't even part of the team when the session began. He hit several big hands, extracting the maximum almost every time, while losing the minimum when the cards were unfavorable. Within four hours he had won it all back, plus $1 million. Disaster had been averted, if barely.

Despite Forrest's comeback, Beal was confident that his tactical skill, at least in this version of poker, was equal or superior to his famous opponents'. Over the next three and a half years, he returned to the Bellagio about a dozen more times, always negotiating to set the stakes as high as possible. Even after falling behind several million dollars, he was always threatening to win it all back and then bust them by improving his game while raising them out of their comfort zone.

The first time Barry Greenstein represented the pros, the team had agreed the night before to play no higher than $25,000/$50,000. But when Beal arrived at the table bright and early, he insisted the agreement had been to play $100,000/$200,000. "I didn't fly all the way out here to play twenty-five/fifty," he said, threatening not to play at all. With the rest of his team still asleep, Greenstein settled on $30,000/$60,000, having decided not to call Andy's bluff.

It was around his time that Greenstein was earning his reputation as the Robin Hood of poker by donating his very substantial tournament winnings to charity. Half went to Children Inc., the rest to a rotating group that includes Guyana Watch. In addition to putting up the buy-ins, Greenstein assumed the tax liability for his prize money, so the charities got every penny, which has come to almost $3 million.

To maximize the charitable opportunities, Greenstein plays in about two dozen WSOP events and a dozen more on the WPT circuit. This adds up to hundreds of hours away from the lucrative white-chip game at the Bellagio and Larry Flynt's private stud game in Los Angeles, in either of which he can earn as much as $300,000 per session. "I didn't want to throw my whole life away in the poker room," he told one reporter. "I was making a lot of money, but I wasn't the greatest example

I could set for my kids. I reminded myself sometimes of Nick, the Russian-roulette addict [played by Christopher Walken] in *The Deer Hunter*, sending money back home to his friends."

Greenstein was also inspired by his former girlfriend Mimi Tran, a high-stakes player who provides funds for housing in the Vietnamese village she grew up in. Their first relationship was as mutual exchange students: Barry gave Mimi poker lessons in exchange for her teaching him Vietnamese. Although they have traveled the world together, Barry didn't make the trips to her village. "If she showed up with me, some of them would assume I was her sugar daddy, or that she was a prostitute. I don't want to steal her thunder."

For all his philanthropic largesse, Greenstein was blunt when asked to appraise Beal's poker skill during the earliest matches. "His biggest disadvantage was a tendency to steam off even more chips. When he gets stuck, his game deteriorates." He compared him to "a loose forty-eighty player, with obvious tells. When he had a weak hand, he bet aggressively; he acted scared or uncertain when holding the nuts." Whether or not this was accurate, the tilt-prone, tell-ridden sheriff of Nottingham moved ahead by $2 million the first morning they played. By the time their match was over, Robin Hood could do no better than break even.

At this stage of the series, Beal had taken to wearing sunglasses and a baseball cap with the brim pulled forward. To filter out distractions, and to keep the pros from picking up conversational tells, he also put on big black headphones. What was playing? "Elevator music," he said. "No lyrics, nothing loud or dynamic, just a sound track for counting live outs."

Comparing heads-up hold'em to his day job, Beal said, "Bankers in Texas have a saying. If you're right a hundred percent of the time making loans, you'll make money. Right ninety-nine percent of the time, you'll break even. Right ninety-eight percent of the time, you'll lose money. Right ninety-seven percent of the time, you'll go to jail." So he was quick to recognize that avoiding careless mistakes in a game such as this was "just crucial. When you're in a big pot and you get stubborn, knowing you're beat but still chasing, you can lose a huge amount. You have to play brilliantly for days to win back what you lost in one poorly played hand."

Another challenge for him was that as a blackjack player, he got used to attacking a single, dispassionate opponent across the felt. He never had to scrutinize him or her for facial tics or body language, or avoid betraying information about his own hand. Playing hold'em against some of the most observant pros in the world, he had to work triply hard to eliminate or camouflage tells.

One pattern Beal knew they'd picked up was that he was aggressive and hard to read early on, but once he got tired or fell behind, his game, as Greenstein had noted, often deteriorated. And the longer a match went on, the more sharply focused his tells came into focus, since they were repeated on nearly every hand. He also had a habit of taking a second or two to decide what his play was, slightly longer when he had a close call. But once he gathered that the pros, especially Harman, Lederer, and Todd Brunson, were timing the interval to gauge the strength of his hand, he began wearing a battery-powered device on his calf that vibrated every eight seconds. By always waiting until he felt the next buzz, he effectively randomized his reaction time, making it much harder for them to decipher how much he liked his hand.

Despite the low tech, high stakes, and escalating tension, the match produced moments of humor. During one session, David Grey built a small lead over Beal, but when Grey went to the men's room, Lyle Berman took the opportunity to sit in his chair and play a few hands for the team. Four, to be exact. In which he lost $900,000. Doyle Brunson, watching from one table over, asked, "So, Lyle, did you have fun?" As Michael Craig reports in *The Professor, the Banker, and the Suicide King,* his comprehensive account of the match, "Even Andy Beal, stone-faced behind dark glasses and his ears covered by noise-reducing headphones, started cracking up." Berman, to his credit, also "grinned sheepishly, as players at adjoining tables joined Brunson in a laugh," even if such moments "were becoming few, far between, and (in this case) expensive."

When it was Todd's turn to play his first 7:00 a.m. match, a $10 million freeze-out (with each side putting up half that amount and playing until one had all the chips), he guzzled fifteen Red Bulls to help him wake up. Instead "they almost killed me," he said. He excused himself and hustled to the men's room. The way his stomach was burning and cramping, it felt like he'd given himself a bleeding ulcer. He was still wincing in pain when he finally returned to the table. One of his backers, Johnny "World" Hennigan, chose this fraught moment to sidle up next to him. "I don't wanna put any pressure on you, but if you lose to this guy I'm gonna kill myself. And I'm serious." It was going to be that kind of morning. Even though Johnny World was pulling his leg, the fact was that Todd stood to lose several million of his backers' dollars long before lunchtime, which didn't make his job any easier. And if Beal happened to go on even a three- or four-day hot streak, he could wipe out virtually the entire bankroll of "the Corporation," as the pros and their various backers were called, and drain $30 million from the Las Vegas poker economy.

Even so, both Todd and his father remained unconvinced that any pressure the stakes put on their team was a negative factor. They had, after all, played high all their lives. "Some people play *better* when the pressure is on," Todd insisted. Howard, for his part, said he "felt honored to be trusted by my peers to be one of the main players. But I also felt pressure that I never felt before. It wasn't the stakes. It was playing for everyone else. That's tough."

Yet no matter how well a player handles pressure, he must also avoid getting unlucky. In one crucial hand of another $10 million freeze-out, Todd held the A-3 of clubs, Andy an unsuited K-8. The flop came 8-high and all clubs, giving Andy top pair and Todd the nut flush. "Cap, cap," Todd recalled in his play-by-play voice, meaning that a bet and four raises had been made both before and after the flop. "Turn comes a king, giving Andy top two pairs. We cap it again. River comes a second king. *Pow!*"

Four hands later, Todd was dealt a 6-4 offsuit, Andy a 10-5. The flop came 10-2-3, and the 5 on the turn gave Andy top two pairs again and Todd the nut straight. Bet, raise, raise, raise, which put Todd all-in. "Then here comes a five on the end." Ten-million-dollar game over.

In the key hand of another freeze-out, Todd limped in from the small blind with the 5-7 of hearts. When Andy, holding two black kings, raised, Todd reraised to make Andy put him on a big pair. Andy just called. The flop came 8 and 6 of hearts and 2 of spades, giving Todd an open-ended straight flush draw. Andy bet, Todd raised, Andy reraised, a sequence they repeated until twenty more bets were in the pot. Andy's kings looked especially strong because the board was ace-free, but he needed to make any draw Todd was on as expensive as possible. With seventeen outs on both the turn and the river, Todd figured he was "at worst even money to hit one of the draws." Even if he missed them both, he knew the action he was giving on the hand would "loosen Andy up even more in future hands." The fact that Todd had won a $10 million match the day before and was already ahead in this one also figured into his thinking.

The turn came a black 7, giving Todd what he knew to be a worthless pair. Andy bet and Todd called. When the river missed Todd altogether, Andy raked what was then the biggest pot in poker history.

Despite being Doyle Brunson's son, Todd didn't start playing until he was nineteen or twenty. "Neither of my folks wanted me to play poker," he said. He laughs while adding that his mother, Louise, is notoriously "cheap," which, because his conception was an accident resulting from her thriftiness, was lucky for him. Having already given birth to three daughters and decided that her family was complete, Louise started using a contraceptive foam that, with a coupon, was priced ten cents lower than her regular brand. Seventeen years later, even after she had made millions on her own in Hawaiian real estate, she still bought what her son calls "sandpaper" to save three cents a roll on toilet paper, an especially abrasive bargain while Todd was running cross-country in high school. His father, on the other hand, has always been generous to a fault and doesn't see many propositions on which he doesn't want to make a healthy bet. Splitting the difference between them, Todd has been known to haggle with some belligerence over lawn care fees. "But once we finally agree on sixty-five," he admits, "I hand the landscaper a C-note and wave off the change. And he says, 'What, are you loco, amigo?'"

By contrast, Andy Beal always flew coach, drove a Ford, shopped around for estimates to shore up the retaining wall at his summerhouse in Michigan. In post-Enron Texas, he wanted to be as thrifty a model as possible for his colleagues and employees. If not the anti–Ken Lay, he was certainly known to be frugal.

Compared to most of the Table 1 pros, Todd said, "My nature is closer to Andy's." Both men are extremely aggressive and prefer to play huge pots instead of patiently chiseling away with a narrow edge in skill. And Todd was less than thrilled with his team's policy of rotating new players in. He preferred to develop momentum and feel, then play for sixty hours nonstop. But as the junior member of the team, he respected his elders and abided by their decisions. He was also forced to realize he couldn't simply run over a billionaire. If he wanted to protect his team's bankroll, he needed to mix up his tactics. "But you're always making adjustments in this kind of game. Bottom line, I had to let him run over me a while, knowing I'd get it back eventually." He did. After facing off with Andy eleven times, Todd's records showed he was $20.5 million ahead.

. . .

How had he managed to do this? Along with Jennifer, Ted, and Howard, Todd had slowly drawn a bead on Andy's body language. How did his fingers release the chips when he turned out to be bluffing? Did his nose or mouth crinkle when betting a monster? Picking up usable tells is more doable in a one-on-one match because you're studying the same opponent hand after hand for several hours or days. His tics get repeated and magnified. There is more to learn and there are more opportunities to use what you've learned. By zooming in on how Andy bet out or hesitated, then connecting that to the strength of his hand once they'd seen his hole cards, the best of the Table 1 pros learned to translate his tiniest idiosyncracies into lucrative information about how best to proceed in each pot.

Another edge they enjoyed was their ability either to put in a fresh player or stick with whoever was hot. Running hot or cold, playing well or steaming off tall stacks of cranberries, Andy was always stuck with one choice: himself. Still another big factor was the pros' home-court advantage. Andy had to fly in for the matches. His biorhythms remained in sync with Dallas banking hours, and even on the Bellagio's pillow-top mattresses, he never slept well in Las Vegas. "They all get to sleep in their own beds, eat home cooking," he complained, particularly after they refused to play even a single match in Dallas. And of course he missed his beautiful Estonian wife, Simona, and their four young children.

All these factors began taking their toll in the summer of 2003. Playing $30,000/$60,000 straight up (not as a freeze-out, that is), Jennifer beat Andy for $9.25 million, Todd for about $7 million, netting the Corporation's thirteen shareholders well over a million apiece.

Before his fall trip, however, Andy persuaded them—by proposing to stay home if they didn't agree—to raise the limits to $50,000/$100,000. When he won enough to wipe out most of their previous profits, a few of them complained that the escalating stakes amounted to a slow-motion version of double or nothing. How could they expect to beat a talented, well-funded challenger who kept pressing his bankroll's advantage?

Andy, meanwhile, had beaten Phil Ivey for about $4.5 million. Ivey stuck with his usual hyperaggressive approach, staring blankly ahead in one of his vintage NBA game jerseys, raising and reraising with almost any two hole cards. He had far less leverage in limit hold'em, though, than he does in no-limit, a game in which he preys on his opponents' uncertainty and, in tournaments, their fear of elimination. Andy's bankroll shielded him from the onslaught while he figured out ways (mostly slow-plays and check-raises) to use Phil's auto-raise tactics against him. When the session was over, he said, "Phil played me way, way too loose."

His next opponent was Johnny Chan, who might be even more of an intimidator than Ivey. In the 2002 WSOP heads-up championship, the Orient Express had blasted his way through the elite twenty-eight-player field (open to bracelet winners only) and eviscerated Hellmuth in the final to take the $34,000 first prize. But in a three-day marathon played a year and a half later, he lost between $3.5 and $5 million to Beal. The banker also claimed that Chan shot a few angles against him. With Beal acting first, Chan sometimes bet out of turn—"accidentally on purpose," according to Beal. After Chan pulled this three or four times, Beal found strong hole cards and raised him. When Chan complained that his out-of-turn bet should not have counted, Beal told him sarcastically, "Bet whenever you're ready." The Bellagio floor man ruled that Chan's bet would stand, as would Beal's raise. Chan thought for a moment, then folded. According to Beal, Chan stopped betting out of turn after that.

Before arriving at the Bellagio in May 2004, Beal negotiated the stakes up to $100,000/$200,000. He would play for two days for a total of at least ten hours, and would have to face only one player per day. Perhaps the most important concession he got was that he wouldn't have to play Howard Lederer, who had beaten him handily each time they faced off. Andy had come to believe that, even on his best day, he couldn't beat Howard. Howard's opinion was that he and a couple of his teammates "got in Andy's head. Heads-up is pure mental combat, and once you get inside someone's head, it's tough for them to get you out." He also thought the reason that Doyle, at seventy-three, chose not to face Andy more than once or twice was that "he simply didn't like how much work went into playing heads-up. You are constantly doing something, and I think he found that tiring. In a ring game, you have plenty of downtime." When filling out his lineup cards, though, Doyle called Howard—who was only thirty-seven when he first took on Andy—the best limit hold'em player around. Andy could not disagree.

It was Todd Brunson, though, who moved the Corporation ahead by $1.1 million on May 12, 2004, when the stakes were the highest. The night before the follow-up session, Chip Reese again drew the short straw, forcing him to get out of bed before dawn and begin playing at

7:00 a.m. And once again, Chip started slow, falling behind more than $2.1 million within the first hour. The man generally called the world's best all-around player had on a powder blue track suit, while Andy wore black slacks, a white dress shirt, a black baseball cap, and sunglasses. More significantly, Chip had also donned sunglasses. As Michael Craig reports, "Andy couldn't help but feel a little flattered that Chip thought that highly of his observational abilities."

David Grey sat at an adjoining table, eating breakfast and fielding phone calls from other backers anxious for updates. Doyle, Howard, Gabe Kaplan, and Gus Hansen swung by in person, doing their best to seem confident.

Andy meanwhile had gathered that Chip was folding too often on the turn, which gave him, as the aggressor, four- or five-to-one pot odds, even when betting with nothing. Sweating the match from close by, Howard also thought Chip was "playing way too tight." Whatever the tactical reason, by 11:45 Chip and his backers were stuck $8 million, having lost forty big bets in less than five hours.

Trying not to show how elated he was, Andy headed off to lunch with Steve Wynn, the man who had built the Bellagio and was working on an even more lavish resort that Beal Bank was helping to finance. The Corporation gathered at Table 1 to plan its next move. Was Chip playing too tight, or was it mainly the cards' fault? He later told Craig that three members of the team critiqued his play in a manner that was, to put it mildly, not helpful. "One said he played exactly right," Craig reported. "The second said he played too aggressively. The third said he was not aggressive enough." Chip agreed that someone else should face Andy after lunch, but he also asked, "What's the big deal? Andy's been here all this time and he's never won. Let him take this win and we'll take our loss and go on." He would leave it up to his partners as to who should replace him.

When Andy got back to the Bellagio at two o'clock, Chip had gone home. Sitting behind the Corporation's $3 million stack was a man with dark hair and an olive complexion who introduced himself as Hamid and declared he was ready to resume in Chip's place. Andy had faced at least a dozen members of the team by now, but he'd never laid eyes on this gentleman. As Andy recalls the conversation, he reminded Doyle that he'd promised not to change players during a day's action. Doyle admitted this was true but reminded Andy that they'd also agreed "that either side could quit whenever they wanted to and so the team would simply elect to quit if I didn't want to play anymore." While Andy didn't really buy this interpretation of the rules, he agreed to play on against Hamid.

It turned out his opponent was Hamid Dastmalchi, the 1992 world champion of no-limit hold'em. Born in Iran in 1952, he was now developing real estate in southern California and playing in the biggest heads-up side games and tournaments. Within fifty minutes, while knocking back a series of Courvoisiers chased with Budweiser tall boys, he won back 70 percent of the chips Reese had lost. But then, just as suddenly, Andy began catching cards and won it all back again. The Corporation members watched with redoubling horror as Hamid kept on drinking and losing.

When David Grey called Jennifer at her doctor's office to bring her up to speed, she could barely believe what he was telling her. Even though her renal system was so compromised that she was about to receive her second kidney transplant, she told David, "I'm on my way. I'll play him if I have to."

Andy, for his part, believed all the liquor Hamid was putting away wasn't real, or was at least watered-down—a ruse to get him to lower his guard. Though his read on the booze was dead wrong, his reads of Hamid's poker moves were usually dead on. By 4:30, he was once again ahead $7 million.

Hamid was no match for Andy that day, or was too drunk to play him effectively. With Todd competing in a WSOP bracelet event and Howard ruled out in advance, Doyle had to decide whether to go with the extremely ill Jennifer or Gus, whose specialty was no-limit poker.

"Who the fuck negotiated these circumstances?" fumed Jennifer, though she knew it had been her great friend and poker dad, Doyle. Standing between them, Gus declared himself ready to play but agreed to a stop-loss cutoff. "If I lose two million," he told them, "I'm done."

Since winning the World Poker Tour's first event in '02, the Great Dane had become so notorious for playing "any two" hole cards that when a player turned over, say, an offsuit 9-3 to rake a big pot, he was said to have won with "a Gus." Hansen's wiry torso and model-caliber cheekbones and chin had also won him far more than his fair share of feminine hearts. His problem was that Beal was immune to both his bone structure and single-bet raises. Almost literally licking his chops, the banker needed fewer than ninety minutes to foreclose on $2 million more of the Corporation's dwindling assets.

At six o'clock, Jennifer finally took over. The last time she'd faced

Andy, she had delicately pillaged him for $9.25 million. But now she was sick, weak, and shivering, wrapped in three layers of clothes against the Bellagio's cryogenic AC. She also had a case of the flu, with a temperature of 102. Yet somehow, within thirty minutes, she won twenty-six big bets from Andy, a net gain of $5.2 million.

Although Andy was eager to keep playing, he had an 8:15 plane to catch. "I had a campout with my twin eight-year-old daughters the following morning," he said. The bunkhouse they would sleep in assigned beds on a first-come, first-served basis, and one of his daughters had her heart set on a particular bunk. "I simply wasn't going to miss the last flight out and risk being late with the girls." Since he'd turned fifty, his enthusiasm for campouts had been dwindling, but a date was a date.

With his packed suitcase waiting outside in a limo, he and Jennifer played until 6:45, with Andy steadily reducing her stack and adding to his lead for the trip. "I felt good," he said later. He also understood that Jennifer wasn't feeling well, but at that point he didn't know the details. He proposed that they play another few hands, which turned into five minutes, then ten, then fifteen, during which he kept running hot. Holding A-Q with a flop of Q-2-2, he bet out while tilting his head at a slightly unnatural angle, hoping to convince Jennifer he was bluffing. She raised him, without a queen or a deuce. After one other similar play and more than his share of good luck, he won back the $5 million and then some. When he finally forced himself out of his chair at 7:08, he was $11.7 million ahead. Minus the $1.1 million he'd lost the day before, he was the $10.6 million "winner" for the trip. He thanked Jennifer, Doyle, and their partners for the competition, posed for a photo, and headed back out to McCarran.

Jennifer was actually tickled to see how happy he was. "It's good, you know, that he wins," she said later. "He's a nice guy. He's allowed to win." Under the circumstances, her magnanimity should inspire just about everyone, not just the poker players who might have taken such a loss with less grace. "I knew he'd be back," she added with a Cheshire cat grin. "He was way too excited."

She was certainly right about how excited he was. Discussing the results at his Michigan summer home, Andy's pride in winning the biggest poker match ever played was abundantly clear. "I gotta say," he said, "that was the tits." What wasn't so clear was whether he and the pros could agree on the terms for a rematch.

47

THE ANDY GAME, PART 2

It's a poker game, and I'm kickin' some serious butt!
— COSMO KRAMER

After dozens of sessions over the course of three and a half years, the Table 1 pros were between $20 and $26 million in the black against the Texas billionaire. As far as bragging rights were concerned, did it make more sense to think of these matches as one long game, with the net result the only fair measure of victory, or was it reasonable to call Beal's final session a win when it counted the most?

However we answer this question, everyone agreed that Beal had acquitted himself with honor against the most talented tag team of poker studs ever assembled. Almost to a person, his opponents liked him as a man, respected his heads-up limit hold'em skill, and relished the money he contributed to their bankrolls. Few if any would concede that Beal had an edge over him or her, even those he had consistently beaten for racks full of cranberries.

Beginning in June 2004, the negotiation between Andy and Doyle about the location and stakes of the next match, or even whether there would *be* a next match, became its own kind of poker game. The Corporation's lineup had changed, but its new and old members alike wanted the series to resume ASAP. Andy's position was that it was impossible for him to maintain his poker skills while attending to his other interests and responsibilities, especially while his opponents kept honing their edge by playing for high stakes every day. While refusing to say he got bored, he compared his side of the matches to "playing a new golf course. You're juiced. But by the third or fourth round, the thrill has worn off. Same with chasing around sweet young things you're not married to. There's no future in it." He repeatedly told the pros he had retired from serious poker, though he also invited them to play one final session in Dallas. He had, after all, traveled to their home court more than a dozen times, and he was ready to satisfy whatever concerns they had about decks, dealers, rules, and security. "If not, then God bless 'em," he said. The series, in other words, would be over.

After conferring for a couple of weeks, Doyle's team declined his invitation. They had already added millions to their bankrolls, so they weren't feeling much pressure to travel. And why press their luck, especially with an eight-figure variance and what seemed to be a marginal advantage in skill?

In July, however, Jennifer Harman insisted that she and a few other teammates still had a viable edge. "I'd go down and play Andy myself if my bankroll could handle it," she said. Much more important, Jennifer looked like a new human being. Clear eyed and pink cheeked, her short white blouse revealed the fresh scar where her cousin's kidney had been implanted on May 24. "I feel great," she said, and she looked it. "I'm gonna talk to Doyle again, see if we can get this show on the road."

Todd Brunson felt differently. "Wiring twenty million dollars to Dallas would trigger an IRS audit for sure. It might involve ten or fifteen people putting up a couple million apiece, but you gotta have a name on the transfer, so it looks like one person is moving that amount." Twenty million in cash was far too bulky to carry on a plane. They also might get cheated when playing outside a licensed casino, though no one in the Corporation was suggesting that Andy himself was dishonest. Todd simply noted that "the game could get busted by Dallas police on some technicality," since poker was illegal in Texas. "We don't wanna risk getting robbed by the cops *or* the robbers," he said. He reminded people that Andy had promised to quit the game before, only to change his mind. "The guy obviously loves to play, so what's he gonna do with that urge?" Barry Greenstein agreed. "There are problems playing him in Dallas since it is not convenient for a quorum to travel there and make certain team decisions." He also predicted the banker would come back to Vegas. In other words, Andy was bluffing.

Andy countered by saying they could "just play for chips" and settle up with real money later; Beal Bank would handle the transfer. "If Doyle's team really believed they're still a big favorite against me, they'd figure a way around these obstacles and get one of their butts down to Dallas." When the pros continued to RSVP in the negative, he pointed out that he'd played on their home court for four years, so it was time for them to reciprocate "at least *once*, for Chrissake."

In September he published an open letter in *Card Player* addressed to the Brunsons, Reese, Harman, Lederer, Chau Giang, Ming La, Lee Salem, Greenstein, Forrest, Hansen, Hennigan, Berman, Ivey, Chan, and Dastmalchi. He began by complaining about a story in the New York *Daily News*, calling some of the quotes in it "an unfair mischaracterization" of the matches. "No mention was made that I won more than $10 million in the largest game ever played, $100,000/$200,000 limit hold'em, on May 12 and 13, 2004. No mention was made of the fact that most of the above-mentioned professional players have substantial overall individual net losses after having played many hours against me. I concede that I am a net overall loser in the Bellagio games, although the extent of my losses is often exaggerated and mischaracterized. These stories have become like fishermen's tales, in which the fish is always getting bigger every time the story is told. I spent four years learning the game from the best. Does it surprise anyone that I was an overall net loser during that period?"

Addressing Doyle directly, he wrote, "Now, you want to reduce the stakes and refuse to continue to play at the previous betting limits. Does it surprise anyone that I have little interest in traveling to play in smaller games? My interest has always been the intellectual challenge of competing with the best, in games in which the amount bet is material to the people involved. I have played the best in the largest game ever played, and I won. I had a great time and a wonderful experience, but I have little interest in continuing to play the game, because of the time commitment and travel required to maintain excellence. Call me naïve (I've been called worse), but I believe that I am the favorite in a heads-up limit high-stakes game against most of you. For the record, I challenge you to put up or shut up about your 'professional play.' Come to Dallas and play me for four hours a day and I will play until one of us runs out of money or cries uncle. If your play is so great and your wins have been as large as you claim, you should have plenty of bankroll and be jumping at the chance to come and play another $100,000/$200,000 game and win a lot more money. I should add that you can bring your own independent dealers and your own cards, and can play in a different location of your choice every day if you wish. You should provide a slate of any six or more of the above players and I will pick from your slate who plays. Observers should be free to attend in order to record exactly what happens at this game, so it won't turn into another fisherman's story. My money says you will decline, and that says it all. If you accept, the resulting game will say it all. Either way, I will get to stop reading fishermen's stories." In a P.S., he added, "This challenge is for now (starting September 2004), not weeks, months, or years from now."

Before Doyle had a chance to respond, David Sklansky posted a prediction on the 2+2 Forum, in which he apparently assumed that Andy was proposing a freeze-out. "The problem that the pros have is not bankroll. Rounding up the necessary hundred million or so would be easy. But if they can't quit unless they lose it all, they risk the possibility that they are playing with the worst of it, yet are forced to play on. The chances of that are small but the chances of an almost-as-bad scenario are not. That scenario is that they are favorites by a mere (and unacceptable) eyelash." Sklansky went on to say that "these players are, for the most part, not the absolute cream of the crop limit hold'em players," though he failed to say who those might be. "I think that Andy is slightly ahead of at least half of them. Second, playing heads-up limit hold'em is especially problematical for most of them since they have largely made their way to the top by playing aggressively and fearlessly which is NOT, I hear, the best strategy against Andy." He suggested that "the major threat is that heads-up hold'em is simple enough that a good approximation to the 'solution' to the game, from a game theory perspective, is attainable if you have a few million bucks to spend paying the appropriate experts. Put another way, I believe a computer program, possibly with randomizing features, could be developed that would be favored, or at least about even with any human playing today." Didn't Sklansky himself qualify as such an expert? While his posting wasn't clear about that, his crystal ball told him that because "it is highly possible that Andy has, or will, come up with such a program, these poker players may be facing a $100 million coin flip. Some of them realize that. Thus I predict the match will not happen."

Paul "Dotcom" Phillips was one of most successful young players on the circuit in 2004, though he skipped many tournaments while starting a family and pursuing a range of other interests, including tournament Scrabble. He was also like Beal in that the fortune he made in business (having written the Web server Boa and served as chief technical officer of Go2Net.com) insulated him from poker's inevitable runs of bad luck. Phillips blogged that Beal's challenge was "a poorly disguised attempt to bust the Corporation via variance." Because Beal had much deeper pockets than the Table 1 pros, "the bigger they play, the better the chance that he will break them. It is unlikely anyone has a huge edge in the matchup so the normal swings of 100K/200K could easily hit tens of millions in a short period: $10 million is only 50 big bets. The letter is calculated to get their egos to overrule their other sensibilities." He went on: "As I understand it, he only got them to play 100K/200K last time by refusing to play any smaller, and they got greedy and accepted. He won and wiped out a substantial portion of their overall win at the smaller limits." Phillips closed by admitting that, like most of the poker world, "I will be amused to see where they go from here."

In the next issue of *Card Player*, Doyle spoke up for his teammates in a letter to Andy. "I'm very surprised at the hostile tone in which you wrote this open letter to us. It doesn't reflect the true character of the man all of us have learned to respect and admire. While I haven't talked to everyone concerned in this, I believe I speak for most. First, I would like to apologize for any 'fishermen's tales' that have been told. . . . As far as your challenge goes, we concede that you have more money than all of us put together. So, why would we want to get into a $100,000/ $200,000 game in which we would be underfunded?" Instead, he made a four-point proposal. "1. We will raise a $40 million bankroll and post it along with yours. . . . 2. We will play $30,000/$60,000. If either side loses half of its post-up money, it can raise the stakes to $50,000/$100,000. . . . 3. We will choose who plays and when. 4. We prefer to play in Vegas, the gambling capital of the world. Most of us live here, and what would we do in Dallas when we weren't playing? This is negotiable. The first three points aren't." He concluded with friendly riposte: "Andy, I'm chuckling as I write this closing paragraph. If Bill Gates came to Dallas and wanted to flip coins for $100 million per flip for four hours a day until one of you ran out of money or cried uncle, would you do it? My money says you would decline. Respectfully, Doyle Brunson."

Gabe Kaplan, smiling and shaking his head at the published back-and-forth, quipped that a $100 million showdown involving some of the toughest poker players in history had somehow devolved into "an essay-writing contest."

Doyle's coin-flip reference and counterproposal made clear that the variance in a $100,000/$200,000 game was too high for the modest edge even his best players might enjoy, and that, in any case, they all considered Andy a much more formidable opponent now than he had been in 2001. His third point raised the specter of Howard returning to action, which Andy would almost certainly have opposed. Yet if Andy truly relished "the intellectual challenge of competing with the best," he might have to face Howard again.

Another question: Which side had so far been luckier? "Andy played good enough to win" was Chip Reese's opinion. "The truth of the matter is that he probably played unlucky to get behind as much as he did. He didn't even play that bad in the beginning and he could have easily won." Ted Forrest admitted that "the luck has probably broken in our favor." Andy, to his credit, refused to make excuses for his early losses. "Playing forty or fifty hours, fourteen or fifteen hundred hands in a session," he said, "is enough of a universe that luck isn't much of a factor." But he didn't agree with Doyle that the series of matches amounted to one long poker game. He preferred to think of each match as a separate contest. And he was quick to point out that not only was the trend in his favor, but in the game in which the stakes were the highest, he won.

Meanwhile, Danny Payne, head of the Texas Savings & Loan Department, phoned a Beal Bank official to voice concern about the boss's poker habit. "We normally don't interfere with someone's private life," Payne told *The Wall Street Journal*. "But there is some concern about public perceptions in this case, and we shared that."

A few of Andy's friends also hoped he would stay retired from poker. The *Journal* reported that some of them "see him as banking's eternal teenager: strong-willed, rambunctious and defiant of industry traditions. In a series of interviews, Mr. Beal railed against mainstream banking as stodgy and lethargic. 'If people say I'm doing something crazy,' he said, 'that's usually a good sign.'"

"I'm the fretful uncle about this," said Larry Fowler, a Michigan attorney and longtime friend of the Beals. "I tell him: 'Now, Andrew, don't get carried away too much with this. You get on the radar screen and the bank examiners are going to take a dimmer view of a guy who runs a bank and is gambling for high stakes.'" But Fowler also said, "I think Andy has a capacity to keep things under control. If he loses a few dollars, he's not going to chase it."

Even so, the temptation to keep playing in the world's biggest poker game proved to be overwhelming. "All right, Doyle," Andy wrote in another open letter to *Card Player*, "*I accept your challenge* that we play a $40 million each freeze-out with one modification and several clarifications that follow." Before listing them, he aired a few more complaints about fishermen's stories. "I just read the draft version of a new book [*The Professor, the Banker, and the Suicide King*] that repeats many of these stories, and this book even has Chip Reese claiming poker wins that absolutely never occurred. While my win of our two-day biggest game is reasonably accurately described, the win is materially diminished by ancillary stories that your side was hampered by players being tired or sick or drunk or whatever. Imagine that: little ol' me against all of you in our biggest game ever and you're supposedly unable to find players who are ready to play. So, I guess I can't really beat you guys even when I really beat you guys?" After admitting, "I have an ego, too," he insisted again that he was "an overall net winner against a majority of the [Corporation's] players." He again acknowledged that "my losses to a minority of the above-listed players exceed my wins from the majority," while regretting "that every story has as many different versions as there were people involved, and the most repeated, exciting, and exaggerated version becomes accepted as the truth." He reminded his opponents that "having multiple sources repeat the same story doesn't make the story true," before inviting them to "play a new game that is bigger and better, and we can document exactly what happens. Hopefully, over time this well-documented new game will overshadow the fisherman stories from the old games."

After a few more ground rules and scheduling details were negotiated, Andy arrived at the newly opened Wynn Las Vegas on February 1, 2006. As Barry Shulman put it in *Card Player*: "*Andy is back*, and he has given ground on all fronts, [agreeing] to Doyle's basic requests—those being the sum total ($40 million from each side) and the stakes ($30,000/$60,000, conditionally climbing to $100,000/$200,000). Surprisingly, he even agreed that Doyle could pick his group, but Andy wants any player picked to play until he wins or loses exactly $8 million."

After all the sturm und drang over an $80 million freeze-out, the parties agreed simply to play straight heads-up poker with relatively modest limits (for them) of $50,000 and $100,000. Just across the hall from the in-house Ferrari dealership, in a roped-off section of the Wynn's plush wood-and-leather high-stakes area, Andy proceeded to lose a very modest $3.2 million to Todd, Jennifer, Ted, and David Grey over the course of five days, with Ted's win on February 3 constituting the bulk of their profits. And the next thing anyone knew, Andy was headed back to Dallas. Craig Singer of Beal Bank, speaking on his boss's behalf, issued a statement: "Andy is done with poker for good." That was it?

Todd took this opportunity to remind the 2+2 Forum that Andy had quit poker a few times already. "He is very eccentric and he may be back to Vegas tomorrow, or we may never see him again. Who knows?"

With the over-under on how long Andy would stay away fixed at six months, he startled the pros by returning to the Wynn in less than a week—and immediately went on a heater. On February 12, he won $4.9 million from Jennifer, $1.2 million from Todd on the 13th, and $3.9 million from Ted over the following two days, for a profit of $10 million.

The only nonparticipant at the table during these matches was Michael Craig, who reported not only the board cards and pot sizes but also said that the Corporation's bankroll would need to be replenished. Doyle declared that the match would continue only if the stakes were reduced to $30,000/$60,000 and they could use any player they wanted. When Andy asked for a list of possible names, they gave him four: David Oppenheim, David Benyamine, and Erik Sagstrom—three tough young pros from Los Angeles, Paris, and Gothenburg, Sweden, respectively, all of whom specialized in heads-up cash games—along with Phil Ivey.

Andy agreed to these terms and wasn't particularly worried when, just after 7:00 p.m. on Tuesday, February 21, his opponent turned out to be Ivey. Craig reported that, beginning with limits of $30,000 and $60,000, Ivey "raised 21 of 24 hands on his button." In other words, almost each time he had the advantage of acting last. "Every time he raised, he would lead out on the next bet." Andy's plan was to counter-punch only when he had decent hole cards. On his twenty-fifth button hand, Ivey raised and Beal called. "After a flop of K-K-3, Beal check-raised Ivey's bet but Ivey responded by reraising." When a 4 appeared on the turn, Andy checked, Phil bet, Andy raised, and Phil folded. No one besides Andy knows whether he had a king, a full house, or just chutzpah.

Phil kept it on auto-raise, though, which inflated the pots he won when he actually hit a flop. Raising with K-7, for example, he got Andy to check-raise a flop of 7-7-3, and then to bet the turn. A few hands later, Phil won a $540,000 pot with A-Q after catching a queen on the turn.

Back on his heels only briefly, Andy decided to fight fire with fire. Toward the end of their session, after Phil made his usual button raise, Andy check-raised the flop of J-8-4. Phil reraised, Andy called. After a 10 on the turn, Andy check-raised again and Phil mucked, conceding a $420,000 pot. By the time they stopped for the night, Phil's lead had shrunk to $1.96 million.

As their match resumed on Wednesday morning at 9:45, both men seemed content to spar for a while, with several hands beginning without preflop raises. On one of them, the flop came out J-8-2 with two hearts. Phil bet, Andy called. When another deuce came on the turn, Phil bet again, Andy raised, and Phil reraised. "The river card was the jack of clubs," Craig reports. "Phil bet and Andy, after thinking for a long time, raised. Ivey, too, took a long time to think about it, riffling eight chips—the amount of a reraise—and looking at Beal, hard, before conceding the $600,000 pot." From this and other indications, it was going to be Andy's day—until a few hands later, when Andy called Phil down all the way on a board of 10-10-2-10-7 and Phil showed him quads.

Four hours into the slugfest, the heavyweights were just about even on the only judge's scorecard that mattered. But over the next two hours, Phil kept the heat on and, as Craig comments, "As if he needed it, he also started getting lucky." By 4:20, Phil was up $3.125 million. When Andy said he was ready to stop for the day, Phil (with his teammates' permission) offered to raise the stakes. "I believe in giving a guy a chance to get even," he said.

Resuming the next afternoon at $50,000/$100,000, Andy built a lead of sixteen big bets. Craig provides a telling example of their banter, if that's the right word for it, at this critical stage of the match. "If I lose today," said Phil, "I'll go to school and work for you."

"You can actually make more money on Wall Street than playing poker."

"I know," said Phil. "I just never got into that."

"We could always use smart people on our team. But now I have to stop talking. Otherwise I'll lose millions of dollars." Having said that, Andy put his headphones back on.

Phil smiled, cocked his head, and said, "That was my plan."

It was right around then that Phil won a $1.6 million pot with 5s full of kings. A few hands later, he made quads when Andy filled up, stretching his lead another $1.1 million. The pattern was set. To Craig, "It seemed Phil Ivey caught every possible break in the last two hours." Forced to play catch-up, Andy got more and more reckless. The backbreaker came when he was able to take charge with pocket kings against Phil's measly Q-3 and a board of Q-5-2-6, but a trey on the river gave Phil yet another monster pot.

And then it got worse for the Texan. In a single twenty-seven-minute stretch, Andy lost forty more bets. When it was over just before five o'clock, Phil was up $9.8 million. Refusing to complain about all the miracle cards his rival had hit, Andy shook his hand and said, "Good job, Phil. I'm heading back to Dallas."

Having finished his twelve-day visit stuck $8.1 million, Andy told Michael Craig, "I really feel like I snatched defeat from the jaws of victory. I just feel embarrassed that I stayed too long and got stupid on the last afternoon." But his "biggest mistake," he said, "was coming to Vegas in the first place. When I was ahead, I should have made them come to Dallas." And he wondered aloud whether Phil would ever agree to that.

That match has not happened, in Dallas or anywhere else. Nor does it seem very likely to, given Phil's comfort zone in Las Vegas and Andy's restated commitment to retiring from the big game. What *has* happened, though, is a surge in the popularity of heads-up poker, albeit at much lower stakes. Almost without exception, home games are still played on full tables, mainly because two-person games aren't very sociable, besides being a prescription for carpal tunnel syndrome with the incessant shuffling required. It's just too much work to make decks and deal every other hand while trying to play the present one. Heads-up action in a casino is nearly as slow, even with shuffling machines. Online, however, with a computer to shuffle and deal in a flash, two-player poker is mushrooming. And at the top of the brick-and-mortar world, Jack McClelland added a heads-up tournament to the Bellagio's Five Diamonds event, calling it "our Andy Beal tournament," though Andy himself did not play. Dozens of other casinos naturally followed suit. In 2005, NBC launched its own heads-up championship, which is televised in prime time on consecutive early spring Sundays. The WSOP continues to raise the buy-in for its heads-up bracelet event, which reached $10,000 in 2008. In the same year, online, Full Tilt hosted a heads-up tournament with a $25,000 entry fee.

Meanwhile, the Table 1 pros have moved about forty feet over into the Bellagio's posh new high-stakes area. Called Bobby's Room after the CEO of MGM Mirage, 1978 world champion Bobby Baldwin, it features a Leroy Neiman painting of several of the team's members hanging above the table they play on. Most of the cranberries they won from Andy are either in their lockboxes behind the cashier's cage or invested in real estate. That they have plenty of flags and $1,000 yellow chips left over can be seen through the frosted glass walls as their mixed game continues, often for stakes of $4,000/$8,000. Unless and until Mr. Beal returns to action, this was by far the biggest game in town, though the action on Full Tilt's high-limit tables has lately begun to surpass it.

The fact remains that no combination of friends, family members, journalists, banking regulators, or poker pros has been able to predict what Andy Beal will do next, at least as far as poker is concerned. From year to year and sometimes from week to week, Andy often seems not to know the answer himself.

A closely related question is, Why play these matches at all? For poker pros like Ivey, the answer is clear: to make money. But as Andy asked rhetorically in his letter to *Card Player* before the games at the Wynn, "Isn't there a much better use for the time and money? My first thought is the old quote about why people climb mountains or parachute from airplanes: 'Anyone capable of even asking such a question could never possibly understand the answer.' But my second thought is to attempt to explain. It will be fun and exciting, and it will demonstrate that an amateur can take on the pros over a long-lasting game and either put up a real battle or win the war. It also seems more humane than the dueling pistol matches of the old days, where men defended their honor by taking 20 paces, turning, and shooting: I can defend my version of the fisherman stories without anyone getting shot. And to anyone actually asking the 'better use of time and money' question, the best answer of all is: approximately $15 million of the spoils will go to the largest charity in the world, the U.S. government, in the form of income taxes."

Putting aside the tax implications, Howard Lederer says, "It was a thrill to be a part of those matches. You really felt like each and every session was 'historic' when we played him."

A few of Howard's teammates felt that way, too. So did Andy. But when pressed for the umpteenth time about whether he has really retired from poker for good, he shook his head, nodded, and said, "You just don't keep climbing Mount Everest."

LH AND AI

Anyone who attempts to generate random numbers by de-
terministic means is, of course, living in a state of sin.

—JOHN VON NEUMANN

While Andy Beal and the pros were playing limit hold'em for stag-
gering sums, researchers in artificial intelligence, including Daphne
Koller at Stanford and Darse Billings at the University of Alberta, were
using that variant as a model for computerized systems of incomplete
information. By the age of seventeen, Koller had already taught a data-
base course at Hebrew University before earning her M.A. and enlisting in the Israeli Army. With no personal interest in poker, her goal as
a Ph.D. student at Stanford in the early 1990s was extending the frontiers of game theory and artificial intelligence. Billings was a poker pro
who went back to grad school in '92 to study his vocation more formally. It soon turned out that there was plenty to learn from studying
hold'em besides who held the edge in a freeze-out.

One of the first programs Billings worked on, under the direction of
Professor Jonathan Schaeffer, was called Loki, after the Norse god of
mischief and chaos. Strategically, it followed Sklansky's *Theory of Poker.*
Able to consider billions of possible hands in a flash, the program made

a probabilistic estimate of what hole cards it was up against, then played its own hand correctly according to Sklansky. Loki won money in low-limit Internet games but didn't stand a chance against experts. Its advantages over most other programs at the time included an ability to make tactical adjustments based on an opponent's previous patterns. It bluffed with optimal frequency and learned from its mistakes. It even told pre-scripted jokes, quoted the comedian Steven Wright, and responded to conversation on the Internet server, where it ranked in the top 5 percent of limit hold'em players in ring games.

Poker is relatively meaningless without money, of course, but no person or institution had volunteered to put up Loki's bankroll to compete for high stakes with strong players. And heads-up against a live expert, Loki got handed its lunch. Even though its math skill was flawless, it couldn't make logical leaps or have insights. When an expert reraised preflop with 7–2, it was either a mistake or a move designed to pay off twenty hands later. Loki couldn't tell which it was; nor, without being told to, could it make moves like this. Billings conceded that Loki had to do a better job of accounting for opponents' unpredictability and generate some of its own. It needed to learn to think for itself. It never slow-played a strong hand, for example. Even average human players would be quick to pick up on this pattern and refuse to give Loki much action. "Computers are very dumb," he admitted.

As early as 1979, Doyle Brunson had predicted, "A computer could play fair-to-middling poker. But no computer could ever stand face-to-face with a table full of people it had never met before and make quality, high-profit decisions based on psychology. To do that requires perception and judgment. It requires a human mind." What humans have always had in spades is the capacity to learn strategic flexibility—to "playfully" randomize tactics. Pros call such tricks "changing gears," suddenly playing much more passively or aggressively to keep their opponents off balance. The most talented players do this by feel, making shrewd leaps of faith about what move will work best in a particular situation as it comes up, sometimes flying directly in the face of the odds.

By the late '90s, however, Billings and others had begun to insist that computers were catching up fast. What their machines already had, of course, were vast and perfect memories. IBM's Deep Blue, Loki's famously dominant cousin, could analyze in less than a second two hundred million chess positions, and in 1997 it used this brute computational force to overwhelm world champion Garry Kasparov. That was chess, though, a game of complete, undisguised information. Poker was much less straightforward. Yet if Billings and Schaeffer could somehow blend computational firepower with creative flexibility, they would have an invincible program. "Somehow" and "if" are big caveats, though. "When it comes to imperfect information," Billings wondered plaintively, "how do you get around that? How do you deal with information that is possibly in error, or is deliberately deceptive?" As the Internet poker boom expanded in the wake of Moneymaker's WSOP victory in 2003, the software developed by Billings and Schaeffer was still unable to account for human insight and creative duplicity.

Daphne Koller and her colleagues in Stanford's robotics program deemphasized opponent modeling in favor of classical game theory. Opponent modeling was important in chess, she admitted, but "chess-playing computers don't do that, and they do very well despite that limitation." She called her program Gala, short for game language. Her goal was to solve the general problem of finding optimal strategies in large games of imperfect information. She and her team developed an efficient search algorithm for determining the best possible play in each of the four basic hold'em situations: preflop, flop, turn, and river. Even bluffing, often assumed to be the most innately human and least programmable of tactics, emerges naturally from game theory in her algorithm. The architecture of her system looked like this:

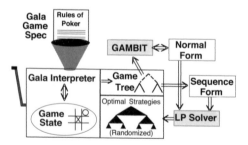

In the July 1997 issue of *Artificial Intelligence*, Koller reported that Gala was exponentially faster than the standard search algorithm, and that its imposing speediness would eventually allow for the solution of games, such as no-limit hold'em, that were orders of magnitude larger than previously possible. (An example of a "smaller" game is limit hold'em, with its preordained bet sizes, the only version of poker that Loki could come close to solving.)

Gala was based on concise declarative language for representing hold'em by its rules. Sevens beat sixes. A flush beats a straight. Players act in a clockwise order. Each path of its game tree was then subdivided into products, each of which could be "re-expressed as the product of the realization weights of all the players' sequences on that path, times the probability of all the chance moves on the path."

Confusing to nonspecialists, maybe, but like every algorithm, Koller's was simply a set of rules for finding an optimal strategy in the smallest number of steps. And it was around this time that the mathematician David Berlinski found a way to humanize algorithmic logic by describing it as "a recipe," as well as "an ambidextrous artifact, residing at the heart of both human and artificial intelligence." Cutting through the intimidating formulas, Berlinski helped laymen understand that algorithms "belong to the world of memory and meaning, desire and design," things that a chef, investor, or hold'em player might employ as naturally as would a Silicon Valley wonk. He also made Koller's working assumption—that a deep mathematical understanding of a game's rules reveals the best tactics for beating it—shine through even more clearly.

Koller's work on Gala assumed that the more we know about one game, the better we understand all of them, including social, financial, and military contests. "For me," she said, "this is more of an exercise in pushing the boundaries of game theory than in specifically solving poker." In Gala's largest possible application, one could extrapolate from poker to what she called "an automated game-theoretic analysis of complex real-world situations."

In practical terms, poker takes nerve, smarts, art, and good luck, yet a grounding in pointy-headed academic theory apparently doesn't hurt, either. Game theory and artificial intelligence were the subjects of Chris Ferguson's dissertation at UCLA. On May 3, 2000, a few days after being awarded his Ph.D., Ferguson won the $2,500 seven-card-stud event at the WSOP. Fifteen days later, he won the no-limit hold'em world championship. Pure serendipity? Probably not.

Ferguson had learned to play no-limit hold'em online long before most people even imagined that was possible. In 1989, during his early days as a grad student, he and a few of his fellow geeks discovered a site called IRCPoker.net. Apparently developed up at Berkeley, the site provided the first computer program capable of dealing, keeping track of bets, and awarding pots to the player with the best hand. In the beginning, betting commands had to be typed in, but the site soon developed point-and-click graphics. Even so, its primitive tournament software was unable to raise the blinds every round, so one player had to use his watch to monitor and announce when the small and big blinds would voluntarily double in size. There was also no bank on the site, so the payouts were in "ether bucks" only.

All this took place in the days when there were very few opportunities to play a no-limit hold'em tournament of any sort. Nearly all games and tournaments in California were limit affairs; the only no-limit hold'em events were the expensive finales of the California State Poker Championship and the World Series over in Vegas. Ferguson was twenty-six at the time, more of a game enthusiast than a dedicated poker player, but he recognized that the ability to learn even rudimentary tactics of NLH while playing online for free was a golden opportunity. The winner of the WSOP, after all, was taking home close to $1 million every spring. The problem was that the caliber of the competition on IRC was so awful. The players had almost no experience with this form of poker, and because the site would replenish their one thousand ether bucks almost as soon as they lost them, they had little incentive to play correctly. The games and tournaments tended to be silly all-in fests, hardly the sort of learning experience necessary to face off with Las Vegas pros.

The designers of the site recognized this, too, and made several savvy rule changes. They raised the buy-in of their no-limit and pot-limit tournaments to two thousand ether bucks and forced players to compete in 10/20 limit games to build up their stacks. Once you'd earned your tournament buy-in, fear of returning to what Ferguson calls "limit hold'em hell" was a powerful incentive to play smart poker in the big-bet events. Granted, there was no real money to be won, but the accumulation of tournament points was a matter of status and pride, especially within the geek community. IRC also maintained lists of who was winning the most bets per hour in the "hold'em hell" action. "It gave the games drama," Ferguson recalls.

It was mainly by this means that the man universally recognized today as a no-limit tournament genius, who has won roughly ten million actual dollars competing in them and probably earned a lot more by hosting them on FullTiltPoker.com, learned to play. The IRC experience also motivated him to start with zero dollars in his personal account on Full Tilt, the site he cofounded in 2004, and to build a stack of $28,000, mainly from tiny cash prizes for finishing high in play-money events, simply to prove it could be done. He donated those profits to charity.

On July 23 and 24, 2007, poker pros Phil Laak and Ali Eslami played four heads-up matches against Polaris, the University of Alberta's latest limit hold'em program. Billings and Schaeffer had once again been the chief architects, but this time, after fifteen years of tweaks and fine-tunings, they were somewhat more confident. And because Polaris had won quite a bit of money online, they were much better funded as well.

The ground rules called for the same cards dealt in one session to the humans to be dealt to the computer in the other, and vice versa. The result would be the sum of the two humans' scores versus the sum of Polaris's. The format, inspired by duplicate bridge, all but guaranteed that skill would be the dominant factor. The contest was held at the American Association for the Advancement of Artificial Intelligence conference in Vancouver. Four 500-hand sessions of $10/$20 limit hold'em would be played. If the humans won a total of twenty-five small bets or more from Polaris in a session, they would split $5,000. If neither the computer nor the humans managed to win that many bets, the session would be considered a draw and the humans would split $2,500. (Smaller wins were considered insignificant because of statistical variation.) If the humans swept all four sessions, they would split $50,000.

Laak, who wore sunglasses indoors against his sightless opponent and often had his trademark "Unibomber" sweatshirt hood pulled up over his dyed-blond hair and black roots, studied every postflop decision for about five minutes in an effort to make the right move. Even so, the first session ended in a tie: Eslami won $465, but Laak lost $395. The second session was won outright by Polaris, which beat the humans for a combined sum of $950 and left them visibly demoralized. "Polaris was beating me like a drum," said Eslami. "They just spent all their freaking time perfecting heads-up limit poker," said Laak, who had crushed a less advanced program, Vexbot, two years earlier, though he admitted he was dealt better cards. Speaking of Polaris, he said, "That thing just beat us."

According to reporters for *Card Player*, Polaris had been successfully designed "to bob and weave like a real player, adjusting to a player's styles and recognizing weakness. Polaris plays such perfect heads-up poker that its main strategy is the same as that of many pros: It tries to play basic solid poker and wait until its opponent makes a mistake."

After recalibrating their tactics, however, the humans mounted a comeback on day two. In the third session, Laak won $1,455 while Eslami lost $635, for a net profit of eighty-two small bets. In the final match, Eslami won $460 and Laak won $110, netting fifty-seven more bets. The final score of the match was humans, two wins and a tie; Polaris, one win. Laak and Eslami split $12,500 for the wins and the draw, but they both admitted Polaris had challenged them far more than typical human opponents. Both play limit and no-limit hold'em professionally, yet even after narrowly defeating Polaris at limit, Laak acknowledged, "The bots are closing in."

Updating what von Neumann and Morgenstern first made clear in the 1940s, Schaeffer, a national master in chess, noted that "poker is harder than chess for computers, and the research results that come out of the work on poker will be much more generally applicable than what came out of the chess research." In other words, scrutinizing the math, logic, and psychology of poker will generate more of what we call killer apps—from nuclear deterrence strategies to computers that think, see, and talk—than studying chess will. A decade after Deep Blue had humbled Kasparov, one of the greatest players in chess history, the most advanced poker program still lost to above-average humans, even at the relatively simple variant of limit hold'em. If nothing else, the results of the Polaris-Eslami-Laak match seemed to confirm that those who see no-limit hold'em as less complex than chess were mistaken.

Then it happened. Over the July Fourth weekend during the 2008 WSOP main event, an updated version of Polaris was brought to the Rio, where it defeated a team of online professionals. The victims were Victor Acosta, Nick Grudzien, Matt Hawrilenko, Kyle Hendon, Mitch McRoberts, IJay Palansky, and Bryce Paradis. All worked as coaches on Grudzien's website, stoxpoker.com, which charges about $30 a month for access to its instructional videos. In six heads-up matches, with limits of $1,000/$2,000 and duplicate hands dealt to each team, Polaris 2.0 chalked up three wins, two losses, and a tie, netting $195,000. Members of Team Polaris were modest in victory, admitting they still had numerous kinks to work out. Critiquing his own play, Hawrilenko quipped, "My navigation system could have played that hand better."

Because Billings had completed his dissertation, Professor Michael Bowling supervised the Alberta grad students who reprogrammed Polaris, though Billings and Schaeffer remained integral parts of the team. "There are two really big changes," said Bowling. "First of all, our poker model is much expanded over last year—it's much harder for humans to exploit weaknesses. And secondly, we have added an element of learning, where Polaris identifies which common poker strategy a human is using and switches its own strategy to counter. This complicated the human players' ability to compare notes, since Polaris chose a different strategy to use against each of the humans it played."

How Polaris might fare against the likes of Todd Brunson, Howard Lederer, Jennifer Harman, Phil Ivey, or Andy Beal has yet to be determined. And despite its impressive accomplishments, it would have almost no chance against elite pros if the format were changed to no-limit.

Ian Ayres, author of *Super Crunchers*, sees a much darker side to all this. A year before Polaris 2.0 beat the humans, he was calling computerized poker "one Darwinian struggle where the unaided human mind is definitely not the fittest." While claiming to be agnostic about whether online poker should be legal, Ayres made a dire prediction in November 2007: "In the very near future, online poker may become a suckers' game that humans won't have a chance to win. Bots are quite scalable and it will be virtually impossible to prohibit computer or computer-assisted online playing." What about the online sites' commitment to identifying and banning the bots? "Unlike the statistical trail left by crude poker cheats at Absolute Poker," says Ayres, "it is possible for bots to randomize their strategies and even hire individual humans to run them," making it harder for sites to detect them.

One reason the best bots are so tough to beat is that, without the possibility of visual tells, they are better at predicting an online rival's hand from his or her previous action. They never get tired or intoxicated, never need a bathroom break, never go on tilt. They are also much better, says Ayres, "at confounding the expectations of their human opponents. Computers can play randomized strategies much better than we can. Our brains are so hardwired to see patterns, it's devilishly hard for most of us to generate random behavior." Our biggest tells, he says, "aren't facial tics but that we just can't stop ourselves from playing non-randomly. With training, we can get better, but we shouldn't fool ourselves. The handwriting is on the wall. High quality bots are an online gambler's worst nightmare."

The good news, according to Ayres, is that bots won't kill poker, they'll just drive it offline; live, "humans-only" action will continue to thrive. Even if he's being unduly pessimistic about Internet poker, it's clear that for the game to keep thriving online, not only must it be exempted from the UIGEA (or the entire act must be repealed), but the sites must figure out better ways to make virtual action more botproof.

A postscript: Much like Crandell Addington, the former road gambler who in 2003 launched a company devoted to medical research, Daphne Koller has shifted her focus from poker to cancer research and computerized vision systems. Addington's Phoenix Biotechnology has developed a drug, PBI-05204, designed to inhibit a molecular pathway necessary for cancer cells to survive; it's already in FDA clinical trials at the M. D. Anderson Cancer Center in Houston. Koller's work with molecular biologists has produced a new type of gene map based on the behavior of genes active in a variety of tumors, which in turn has led to a better understanding of how breast tumors spread into bone.

While many of her best graduate students have been recruited by Google, Koller tries to persuade undergraduates to stay in school and put off, at least for a while, the lucrative salaries and stock options offered to Stanford's most talented software engineers. "My husband still berates me for not having jumped on the Google bandwagon at the beginning," she says, but insists she doesn't regret staying in academia. Her decision must have been easier on her husband after she received a $500,000 "genius" grant from the MacArthur Foundation in 2004 and another substantial award from the Infosys Foundation this year. The total amount, $650,000, on top of her Stanford salary, is still but a fraction of what she might have netted by jumping to Google back in the days she was programming the rules of limit hold'em into her search algorithms. Unlike in poker, however, the bottom line can't always be measured in dollars. "I like the freedom to explore the things I care about," she says.

At least in the cases of Addington and Koller, poker's loss has clearly been humanity's gain. Online hold'em players can also take comfort knowing Koller is no longer upgrading the state of the art of the bots.

THE POKER WORLD IS FLAT
(IN SPITE OF THE UIGEA)

omfg!!!! u call my allin rerais w/ kj soooted u phucken mo-
ron donk!?!?!?!?

—ANONYMOUS

How flat is the poker world these days? It's as flat as the so-called Meadows of the Mojave Desert sprinklered into bloom by Las Vegans, or as the smogbound pavement of Los Angeles and the felt on the thousands of tables in its Costco-sized card rooms. It's even as flat as the alluvial mud of Shreveport and Tunica, as well as more civilized river towns like Dublin and London, Budapest and Paris and Prague, Melbourne and Seoul and Manila—or as the beaches of Punta del Este, the Uruguayan stop on the circuit. It's exactly as flat as those Mercator projections of Earth near the back of airline magazines, the ones with the route lines connecting hub cities that look like they're drawn with a protractor. But of course those are drawn by computers.

And now that most hands are dealt by and played on computers, the poker world is surely as flat as anything in what Thomas L. Friedman calls Globalization 3.0 in his optimistic bestseller *The World Is Flat*. Friedman uses flat as a synonym for connected—digitally, that is, by fiber-optic cables. His exuberant, well-informed book makes a compelling case that a "triple convergence" of Internet technology with economic and political events at the dawn of the twenty-first century generated "more horizontal and collaborative" means of creating value. While warning of several dangers lurking in this global topology, Friedman celebrates the more level playing field and breathtaking variety of opportunities for those with the imagination and training to seize them.

His book rightly emphasizes the role Indians have played in this process. Even so, in 608 pages it never mentions Anurag Dikshit, the software whiz educated at the Indian Institute of Technology who in 2000 created the platform for PartyPoker.com. Party quickly became the world's busiest site by enabling tens of thousands of players to compete in real time at virtual nine-handed tables. The site supercharged a new industry and generated an eleven-figure stock valuation for its shareholders. That industry has been under fire in the United States since the Unlawful Internet Gambling Enforcement Act was signed by George Bush in 2005 (as we'll see further on in this chapter), but whether or not playing our national pastime online turns out to be legal, Internet poker is without question among the killer apps of Globalization 3.0. You'd never guess it, though, from reading Friedman's otherwise reliable book.

An equally glaring oversight occurs when he mentions Bill Gates seventeen times, always in a positive light and often quoting him at length, but poker not once, in spite of the game's famously seminal influence on young "Gator" during his two years at Harvard (1973–1975). Twenty years later, in *The Road Ahead*, Gates recalled the marathon dorm sessions that he believes were at least as productive and intellectually stimulating as his time spent in class. His dorm-mate Steve Ballmer says Gates "played poker until six in the morning, then I'd run into him at breakfast and discuss applied mathematics." Ballmer has called Microsoft's early organization and business plan "basically an extension of the all-night poker games Bill and I used to play back at Harvard." He went on to say, "Sometimes whole divisions would get moved just because someone bet two pairs against an inside straight. People were always wondering why [Microsoft copresident] Jim Allchin ended up with so much power. What can I say? He bet big and won big. It's not always pretty, but it's not a bad way to keep the troops from getting complacent. And I can't say I'm unhappy with how things have worked out for me. I did pretty well one night and ended up becoming President myself." His conclusion? "You gotta know when to hold 'em and when to fold 'em."

Chairman Gates put it this way: "In poker, a player collects different pieces of information—who's betting boldly, what cards are showing, what this guy's pattern of betting and bluffing is—and then crunches all that data together to devise a plan for his own hand. I got pretty good at this kind of information processing." In fact, the planet's reigning e-businessman—and most copious philanthropist—won a significant portion of Microsoft's start-up costs in those dorm games. And it wasn't just dollars reaped to be parlayed a millionfold; it was mainly, says Gates, that "the poker strategizing experience would prove helpful when I got into business."

The business of poker has expanded dramatically since Gates left Harvard, of course, and even since Dikshit wrote the platform for Party. Though estimates vary, there now may be $100 billion—two hundred million players worldwide with an average bankroll of $500—annually in play on live and virtual tables. With the rake in cash games amounting to as much as $3 per pot and up to 10 percent of the buy-in for tournaments, there's a lot of money to be made hosting poker.

Several factors make online action appealing for players: speed, convenience, game selection, weaker competition, dealers who don't need to be tipped. Novices can compete for pennies or play money, or enter the freerolls designed to attract newer, less affluent players. As an experiment to prove he could build a $10,000 bankroll from nothing, the Full Tilt pro Chris Ferguson, already a poker millionaire several times over, took seven months of steady play just to get his balance to $6.50. After another nine months, however, he had reached his goal and donated the entire sum to the Save the Children Foundation. Even more dramatically, Annette Obrestad, who won a WSOP bracelet at the main event in London before turning nineteen, claims never to have deposited money at a site. She did well in freerolls and built her bankroll from there, winning more than $500,000 on PokerStars, $200,000 on UltimateBet, and $136,000 on Full Tilt. In spite of all that, as of 2008 she was only the fifty-first-most successful Internet pro, which means that quite a few people were making excellent livings in virtual cash games and tournaments.

The big sites let their customers choose among thousands of games, from freeroll tournaments with sizable cash prizes up to seven-figure showdowns in the pot-limit Omaha games on Full Tilt. And with action a click or two away around the clock, there's no need to deal with two airports, drive to a casino and sit on a waiting list, or even put on a clean shirt. Most sites provide hand histories to help us track tendencies and plug leaks in our game, and to profit from those of our opponents. Even more crucial is the absence of physical tells, so that reckoning pot odds and betting patterns replaces raw psychological acumen. There's no intimidating eye contact here, either. Comments in the chat box may be withering or sophomoric (and nearly always misspelled), but it's easy to shut them off if we want.

Blogs and chat boxes also teem with allegations of dealing programmed to give multiple players good hands, thereby increasing the bets and the rake, and of sites rigging the deal to prevent new players from losing so quickly that they become discouraged. No hard evidence, however, has ever been produced to back up such claims. The busiest sites rake $1,000 a minute twenty-four hours a day, after all, and nonrandom dealing or other integrity problems would slaughter their platinum goose. (A few cases of in-house cheating will be discussed in Chapter 50.) Those who claim to see far more bad beats online should remember that virtual dealers pitch about four times as many hands per hour. The more hands you play, especially against weak players who "chase" long-shot draws when the pot odds don't justify it, the more bad beats you will suffer. Sophisticated software also lets the sites check hand histories and IP addresses for evidence of player collusion, the other subject of Chapter 50. At the vast majority of tables, Internet players can expect a square deal.

The world can seem tiny, and timeless, while playing online. As we chat and compete, our opponents could be sitting in a Russian dacha, a Midwest college dorm, or three gates down the concourse from us. It isn't unusual at a nine-handed table for a half dozen countries to be represented, which causes a lot of folks besides federal prosecutors to wonder exactly where all this virtual action takes place. In satellites orbiting five hundred miles above Earth? In optical fibers buried beneath the oceans? Wherever a circuit court judge in Kentucky happens to say that it does? In the case of Full Tilt, the corporate office is in Dublin, the players in twenty-four time zones across all six inhabited continents and scores of ships at sea.

As the poker boom continued online and on land, President Bush and his allies tried to criminalize Americans who played their national card game on the Internet. The Unlawful Internet Gambling Enforcement Act of 2006 was one of the more disgraceful statutes passed and signed during his administration, a period already notorious for ill-conceived laws, wars, tax codes, and social policies. The UIGEA ban on some but not all games "subject to chance" primarily targeted online poker sites. When the bill failed to attract enough support on its own merits, Senators Bill Frist (R-TN) and Jon Kyl (R-KY) cynically attached it to a worthier bill designed to improve security at American ports.

Senator Frank Lautenberg (D-NJ) stated that no one on the Senate-House conference committee had even seen the final language of the entire bill, and that many senators were probably unaware of its gaming provisions when they voted to protect major ports from terrorist attack. Even if they were, they may not have known what to make of it. Gambling law expert I. Nelson Rose found parts of the UIGEA "indecipherable" and wondered whether the confusion stemmed from typos or proofreading errors, "since the bill was rushed through without an opportunity to even be read." The attachment maneuver took place in the eleventh hour of debate on the Safe Port Act, which finally passed on a midnight vote by frazzled senators eager both to protect the nation's ports from terrorists and begin their election-year recess. President Bush enthusiastically signed it into law on Friday the 13th of October 2006.

The New York Times pointed out that the law "did not make it impossible or illegal for Americans to bet online, but it did make it trickier for players to get their cash to the offshore casinos that run the Internet sites." More than a few people saw the UIGEA as a convenient distraction from the war in Iraq. It also fit the Bush-Rove pattern of supporting moralistic initiatives designed to gratify the archconservative base of the president and like-minded congressmen, and of parlaying fears about national security into support for other items on their agenda.

"Frist's last-minute addition of this amendment to a completely unrelated bill should be seen by all poker players as an underhanded, purely political move designed solely to shore up Frist's dwindling right-wing, out-of-touch, conservative base," Phil Gordon scoffed. "As a lifelong poker player," said Doyle Brunson, "I can't believe the underhanded way this new bill restricting online poker was passed through Congress. What does Internet poker have to do with the Safe Port Bill? We Texans don't like this kind of trickery. Texas is a state where you can see an enemy coming, a friend is a friend, and you look someone straight in the eyes." Ethan Ruby, unable to play in casinos since being paralyzed in an automobile accident, can play only online. "Internet poker is a great source of enjoyment and allows me to compete on an equal playing field with people from around the world," he said. "I can't understand how President Bush would take this game away from me and millions of other Americans."

"This last-minute deal reeks of political gamesmanship," concluded Michael Bolcerek, president of the Poker Players Alliance. "The American people should be outraged that Congress has hijacked a vital security bill with a poker prohibition that nearly three-fourths of the country opposes." Bolcerek predicted that the UIGEA would "damage an already fractured relationship between government and the electorate."

The act's effect in the online poker community was debilitating, at least temporarily—an expensive hassle to be sure, but hardly the fatal blow its proponents had hoped to deliver. Sites listed on the London Stock Exchange, such as PartyPoker, by far the busiest virtual card room at the time, were forced to stop serving American players in response to the act. The stock of PartyGaming PLC, which runs Party-Poker, lost 60 percent of its value the day after the bill was passed. Other sites, such as DoylesRoom, also stopped serving American customers for a number of months, though players in the United States quickly found other sites, especially Full Tilt and PokerStars, that were more than happy to take their action. Yet because of the net loss of online satellite opportunities, the number of entries to the following World Series main event dipped significantly (from 8,773 to 6,358 in 2007) for the first time. Entries rebounded slightly to 6,844 in '08.

Card Player's legal analyst Allyn Jaffrey Shulman wasn't alone in pointing out that even though annual gambling revenues online had surpassed $12 billion, the UIGEA was futilely attempting to ban rather than regulate and tax it. And while the act prohibited American banks from transferring money in or out of the sites, the sites themselves are located in countries in which gambling is legal, and the United States had no power to make laws affecting companies such as PokerStars or Neteller legally doing business offshore.

The controversy took on a global dimension when the World Trade Organization ruled in favor of Antigua and Barbuda, which had claimed that aggressive efforts by the United States to shut down the sites unfairly discriminated against offshore online gambling companies. When the WTO ruled that the United States must bring its laws into compliance with its decision, *The Wall Street Journal* reported that the decision would have wide-ranging implications in favor of Internet gambling. Mark Mendel, the lead counsel representing Antigua, noted that the UIGEA exclusions highlight the discriminatory trade effect of the U.S. prohibition. "By creating carve-outs for certain domestic re-mote gambling opportunities . . . the legislation flies directly in the face of the WTO ruling. The economic basis of the U.S. restrictions simply cannot be more obvious."

Representative Bob Goodlatte (R-VA), who had led the push for the UIGEA in the House, conceded that "under current federal law, it is unclear whether using the Internet to operate a gambling business is il-legal. The closest useful statute currently is the Wire Act, which pro-hibits gambling over telephone wires. The Wire Act, which was written well before the invention of the World Wide Web, has become out-dated." Goodlatte proposed to amend the Wire Act "to make it clear that the prohibitions include Internet gambling and the use of other new technologies."

"There has never been legislation that would ban online gaming," Shulman said in response. "Bills have been introduced that affect the transfer of moneys from U.S. financial institutions to online gaming sites, but this is quite different than banning online gaming. The proper language always should have been that legislation has been in-troduced in an attempt to curb the rapidly growing online gaming in-dustry. The current bill attempts to ban certain forms of online gaming while sanctioning others. Although Goodlatte claims that the current bill prohibits all gambling on the Internet, it does no such thing. While this bill is admittedly more ambitious than past attempts, it is fraught with built-in, foreseeable problems and contradictions." She noted that the bill prohibits gambling businesses from accepting online bets where a person risks something of value "upon the outcome of a contest of others, a sporting event, or a game predominantly subject to chance." So the issue is not whether the game contains an element of chance or an element of skill, but whether chance or skill is the dominant factor in determining the outcome. Shulman, Howard Lederer, and others have pointed out that when so many pots are won by a bettor who gets no callers, and when the best players consistently win in the long run, it's absurd to deny that skill is the dominant factor in poker. Like chess, bridge, or managing a business or sports franchise, poker is a thinking person's game that relies on logic, intelligence, psychological insight, money management, luck, and the ability to adjust our tactics to what our opponents are doing. To compare it to playing the lottery, bingo, slot machines, blackjack, or craps couldn't be much more ridiculous.

Shulman also reminds us that the Supreme Court has already held playing poker to be a profession, which clearly implies a preponderance of skill. In *Commissioner of IRS v. Groetzinger* (1987), the Court held that since nearly all states permit some form of gambling, if a taxpayer "devotes his full-time activity to gambling, and it is his intended livelihood source, it would seem that basic concepts of fairness (if there be much of that in the income tax law) demand that his activity be regarded as a trade or business just as any other readily accepted activity, such as being a retail store proprietor or, to come closer categorically, as being a casino operator or as being an active trader on the exchanges."

Under most jurisdictions, the term "game of skill" is reserved for those in which skill determines the result more than luck does. Chess, bridge, poker, and most physical games qualify; bingo, blackjack, craps, roulette, and lotteries don't. Even so, there are plenty of U.S. jurisdictions in which betting on lotteries and bingo is legal and betting on skill-based games is not. This has been true since the country was founded—lotteries funded the Continental Army as well as most universities, state governments, and the District of Columbia—and will stay true for some time to come. One reason is that old habits die hard. The chief political criterion has usually been who will benefit from the wagering, not how much skill is involved.

Another question raised by Shulman is why the federal government should expend resources to ban some forms of gambling while permitting and even encouraging others. Frist, Kyl, Goodlatte, et al. argued that gambling destroys the moral fiber of society, only to cynically carve out exceptions for online betting on horse races, the stock market, and lotteries. Lotteries, of course, are nothing but long-shot schemes based entirely on chance, yet they legally siphon billions of dollars—mostly from the pockets of those who can least afford it—into the coffers of thirty-one states and counting.

Among the many members of Congress opposed to the UIGEA, the House Judiciary chairman, John Conyers (D-MI), noted an obvious and ominous parallel. "You might remember a failed experiment the U.S. government tried in the 1920s called Prohibition." He said that supporters of the UIGEA "believe they can stop the millions of Americans who gamble online by prohibiting the use of credit cards to gamble on the Internet. Just as outlawing alcohol did not work in the 1920s, current attempts to prohibit online gaming will not work, either." Instead of a prohibition that drives gambling underground and into the hands of unscrupulous operators, Conyers proposed that "Congress should examine the feasibility of strictly licensing and regulating the online gaming industry. State regulation will ensure that gaming companies play fair and drive out dishonest operators," adding that it could also provide "tax revenue for financially strapped states." Referring to the billion of dollars vacuumed from the U.S. economy into offshore gambling sites, Shulman agreed with Conyers by proposing that the government "regulate and benefit from the taxation instead of generously making offshore governments rich. Why keep trying to legislate morality," she asked, "and, instead, keep all that money in the United States, where it belongs?"

Meanwhile, Wayne Abernathy of the American Bankers Association was warning that the UIGEA was so unclear and sweeping that it threatened to cause "an erosion of the performance of the financial system." Not only were banks not equipped to examine every last financial transaction to make sure they were not for online gambling, he said, but the act failed to clearly define what online gambling was. Instead, it left it up to banks to decide which transactions to allow, which to block, putting them in the business of law enforcement agencies like the FBI. Even if the government were to provide a list of restricted online gambling companies, banks would still find it impossible to ensure that every transaction was legal because there are so many different ways to transfer money online and because of how quickly the Internet changes.

In April 2007, Representative Barney Frank (D-MA) introduced a bill to overturn the UIGEA, calling it "an inappropriate interference on the personal freedom of Americans." In its place, Frank's Internet Gambling Regulation and Enforcement Act (HR 2046) would construct a viable framework for taxing and regulating online gaming. It would establish criteria to distinguish between legitimate sites and those engaged in unscrupulous practices, and would put in place mechanisms to block minors and problem gamblers while allowing responsible adults to play poker online.

The Poker Players Alliance, under the direction of the former senator Alfonse D'Amato, made a commitment to help Frank overturn the UIGEA or at least exempt poker from its provisions. The PPA keeps voters informed on a range of related issues, including the latest age-verification software. It estimates that more than $4 billion in revenue is lost every year because of the attempt to ban online poker instead of regulating and taxing it, in spite of polls showing that 75 percent of Americans oppose such a ban. Most of them believe that because online wagers on lotteries are legal, a skill game like poker certainly should be as well. The PPA also notes that poker tournaments have raised millions of dollars for charity, citing an event featuring fifteen members of Congress that garnered more than $288,000 for cancer research.

As we've seen, the game has been played by presidents, congressmen, justices, generals, captains of industry, and ordinary Americans for almost two centuries now. Virtual poker simply extends that tradition as the game and the country evolve in the twenty-first century— a point apparently lost on President Bush, though not so among the leaders of most other democracies. Since poker's popularity plateaued in the United States in 2006, it has continued to grow in Europe, Asia, Australia, and South America, especially in those countries where playing online remains legal.

As we watch to see what happens next with the UIGEA, we may recall how back in 1840 the Illinois congressman Abraham Lincoln weighed in on a bill proposing to ban the consumption of alcohol. Prohibition, said Lincoln, "goes beyond the bounds of reason in that it attempts to control a man's appetite by legislation and makes crimes out of things that are not crimes. A Prohibition law strikes a blow at the very principles upon which our government was founded."

CHEATING 2.0

What a JERK OFF! ☹ It's hard enough to beat the Odds
once in a while, LET ALONE beat the Odds and a SCUM-
BAG CHEATER on the inside at the same time!

—THE_CPA

Two hundred years after the Cheating Game steamed up the Mississippi from New Orleans, most poker is played on the square. As Anthony Holden wrote in 2007, "Today, in a regulated casino, it is very
unusual to get cheated; online, it's increasingly less likely, with pro-
ceedings strictly monitored by the Web sites." The busiest, most responsible sites have continued to develop their software for identifying
play by bots, all part of their effort to keep virtual poker as much of
a human-to-human experience as possible. *Card Player*'s Justin Marchand adds that the sites "use a certified and independently tested random number generator (RNG) in order to provide players with an
unpredictable game and programs to detect play patterns that suggest
collusion."

Nonrandom dealing, holdouts, card-marking schemes, and cold
decks are all but impossible to pull off anymore in commercial card
rooms, with house dealers changing tables and decks every thirty minutes and everyone surveilled by the eyes in the sky. Cheating still hap-

pens, of course, though probably less than it does in sports, marriage, business, elections, or classrooms, let alone on tax returns, nuclear proliferation treaties, or Wall Street.

The most common form of cheating at poker these days is collusion. At a live table, colluders can signal the contents of their hands to each other, building pots when one of them has a strong hand. During tournaments, teams of cheaters pass around chips, usually from the members who have fallen behind to the one with the largest stack. The chips can be transferred by hand during a break or, at the table, by raising up a pot together before one of them folds, a maneuver called dumping. In either case, the beneficiary is given a big leg up toward reaching the final table, where whatever prize money he wins will be split with his cohorts.

Online, two or more of these cowardly frauds will compete from the same room (or over the phone, or with an instant-messaging system) while playing at the same table. They compare hole cards and whipsaw unwary opponents out of pots with tag-team betting and raising, or simply fold the worst hand and split the profits of always playing the best one. Some players now limit their action to heads-up tables, not only to thwart potential colluders but also because the six- or nine-handed tables are often filled with inconsiderate folks playing half a dozen games simultaneously, slowing the action on all of them to an exasperating crawl.

Veteran journalist Lou Krieger isn't alone in pointing out the enormous incentives the sites have to keep their games legitimate, and that their random-number generators are audited by reputable accounting firms. "Any of them would be crazy to maximize their short-term gain when they are making plenty of money on the up and up," Krieger notes, adding that their "strong vested interest in retaining their customer base" makes them "go to great lengths to ensure that their shuffle is random and impervious to hacking."

While occasionally expressing their doubts—almost always during or after a losing session, when objectivity is never at a premium—the majority of players seem to trust that online poker is dealt fair and square; the $100 million or so they wager every day expresses that confidence.

Collusion, however, is a different sort of problem. Michael Wiesenberg isn't the only industry observer who worries about it. He remains "quite convinced—but can't prove—that undetectable collusion exists at the medium to highest levels of online poker." He claims that it wouldn't be difficult to devise undetectable or difficult-to-detect schemes for cheating online. "If I could do it, then surely others actually have. I'm also convinced that the larceny factor overcomes morality in the biggest private games. I've known many thieves and their mentality, and I don't think that mentality has died out. Now, cheating in well-known tournaments and large public games has probably been significantly lessened, but I doubt it has disappeared." He adds that the technology of cheating "has improved considerably from the sawdust joint and backroom days to where at least some of the highest rollers are getting boosts beyond their capabilities. Again, I have no personal proof of any of this [but] I knew too many thieves in the days I played full time to think they just quietly passed on and no one filled the breach."

In September 2007, something more ominous came to light. An employee of Absolute Poker playing under the account name "Potripper" was apparently able to see the hole cards of his opponents, from whom he had "won" an estimated $700,000. After strenuously denying that foul play had or even *could have* occurred, Absolute apologized and returned all funds, plus interest, to the losing players. The company thereby acknowledged that the integrity of its software had been compromised. Meanwhile, plausible allegations emerged that a player calling himself "NioNio" could see his opponents' hole cards on UltimateBet.com, a sister site to Absolute. Both sites were managed by Tokwiro Enterprises, a Canadian company owned by the former Mohawk chief Joe Norton. Absolute was fined $500,000 by the Kahnawake Gaming Commission (KGC) in February 2008, after an investigation revealed that at least two players had gained access to other players' hole cards. On top of the fine, Absolute had to put up a hefty security deposit and became subject to random audits.

In May 2008, Tokwiro released an even more damning statement. This one admitted that cheating on UltimateBet had been perpetrated by employees who "worked for the previous ownership of UltimateBet prior to the sale of the business to Tokwiro in October 2006." *Card Player's* Bob Pajich reported that the "player or players behind the 18 screen names that were identified as being corrupted have not been named. Tokwiro will refund players their losses once the investigation is complete." The cheater(s) had apparently gained access to what the company called an "unauthorized software code" that allowed them to see all the hole cards. The code had been operative between March 2006 and December 2007, if not longer.

In September 2008, after months of brilliantly creative statistical analysis by David Paredes and a player whose screen name was "trambopoline"—both of whom suspected they had been cheated by "NioNio"—Paredes posted on TwoPlusTwo.com that "NioNio" was winning seventy-five big blinds per hour, this when the most successful pros seldom average more than five or six blinds per hour. His rate of success was nine standard deviations above the mean, which another poster, Michael Josem, said was about as likely as winning a million-to-one lottery three times in a row. Then there was the *way* "NioNio" was winning. Entering pots indiscriminately, he folded every time Paredes or "trambopoline" had a strong hand, raised whenever they were on a draw, and generally played as though he knew exactly what his opponents' hole cards were. Subsequent posts on TwoPlusTwo (many of them contributed by Steven Ware, Cornell Fiji, and Kevin Mathers) provided more detailed evidence in support of Paredes's allegations.

But by far the most dramatic development came after the KGC hired the former New Jersey state gaming regulator Frank Catania to investigate these off-the-charts win rates. Catania alleged that it was Russ Hamilton, the 1994 WSOP main event champion who parlayed that win into a lucrative deal to represent UltimateBet, who'd been cheating the site's players out of millions of dollars. Catania was able to link Hamilton's home in Las Vegas to the "Sleeplesss" account, which was winning huge amounts with suspicious regularity. He also linked the account to an auditing tool, called a super-user account, which had access to an entire table's hole cards in real time. It remains unclear whether such tools were originally designed to cheat or to help repair glitches in the system, but any player wielding this tool could easily "outplay" even the luckiest and toughest opposition in the biggest games UB had to offer. Yet wouldn't it be obvious what was happening if the same player cleaned out his opponents day after day, year after year? It would. Which is why it shouldn't be surprising that Catania discovered that nineteen different player accounts and eighty-eight user names were involved in the scam.

Did this mean that eighty-eight players were in on the rip-off, or even nineteen? Probably not, said Catania. Instead, his report "found clear and convincing evidence to support the conclusion that between the approximate dates of May 2004 and January 2008, Russell Hamilton, an individual associated with UltimateBet's affiliate program, was the main person responsible for and benefiting from the multiple cheating incidents." His report went on to say the KGC "is currently in contact with the appropriate law enforcement agencies and intends to fully cooperate in the prosecution of all individuals involved in the UB cheating incidents." UltimateBet had been slated to merge with Absolute Poker to form the Cereus Network, but the merger was put on hold pending Catania's final report.

After months of denying the very possibility that hole cards could be spied on by hackers or employees, UltimateBet quietly began to refund money—$21.1 million as of November 2008—to players who had lost pots to the suspected cheaters. It also paid a $1.5 million fine and turned over its user records and hand logs to Catania. The investigator's ultimate objective, he said, was to verify that Tokwiro had eradicated the breach in its software's integrity. Meanwhile, Blast-Off Ltd., a Maltese company with an ownership stake in UB, filed a $75 million lawsuit against the site's former owners. (Since the UIGEA was signed by President Bush, more than a hundred online gaming sites had established their headquarters on the tiny island nation of Malta, with its favorable tax codes and gaming laws.)

Other questions focused on the pros representing the pair of tainted sites. While no player besides Hamilton was named in the investigation, a blogger named Marc put it bluntly: "What did Phil Hellmuth and Annie Duke know, and when did they know it? Russ Hamilton is their friend and partner in the UltimateBet business after all. He recruited Phil to UltimateBet in his role as a consultant for the site." Seamarfan269 posted on CardPlayer.com: "WOW!! Thanx for setting poker back 25 years Russ. WTG!!"

As of early 2009, no one seemed to have a clear idea of which jurisdiction Russ Hamilton might be indicted in, despite "clear and convincing evidence" of his guilt. We can only imagine how Lincoln's knife-wielding roughs or any of the frontier vigilantes would have dealt with someone alleged to have cheated on so grand a scale. In our more litigious era, the consensus is that the black eye this WSOP champion had inflicted was the very last thing poker needed as repeal of the UIGEA was being debated in Washington—though many people also believe that Hamilton could serve as Exhibit A in the case for regulating and taxing online poker sites. While Hamilton had not been arrested, he was refusing all interview requests, including one from Steve Kroft of *60 Minutes*, who suggested in a November 30, 2008, report that Hamilton had been able to "get away scot-free." Duke, on the other hand, seemed both upset and surprised by Catania's report. "Huge sums of money were transferred," she said, "and they should have been investigated. But because the person doing the transfers was a friend of the site, they did not get looked at. That should have raised red flags."

High-stakes players avoided Absolute and UltimateBet in droves, most of them deciding that the games on PokerStars and Full Tilt were more trustworthy. Chris Ferguson, who had helped to develop the software and general ethos of Full Tilt, said the site had gone to great lengths to guarantee that no one would ever have access to hole cards in real time. "We do not have super-user accounts, and that was very intentional," he told the reporter Michael Kaplan, adding that there was "a very thick wall between player knowledge and people who play on the site. We use the same encryption codes that banks have." With as much as a million dollars in action most evenings on Full Tilt's six-handed pot-limit Omaha and no-limit hold'em tables, it seems that the players with the most to lose had faith in the software's integrity.

A less monetary drawback to online poker may be the way some of the sites choose to promote themselves. The owners of NakedPoker.com, for example, used the tactics of pimps and pornographers to attract business. They hired Ron Jeremy to appear at promotional events and promised to help arrange dates for its players with famous women, though Jessica Simpson's asking price of $2 million was considered "out of the question." The business plan was representative of what Bob Pajich described as "a small but expanding family of a new type of online poker site, one that mashes sex and poker together into one pulsation package. Instead of brilliant middle-aged men wearing golf shirts, these sites feature topless women in high heels. Instead of tons of pages dedicated to poker strategy articles, these sites feature high-resolution galleries of hot babes in bikinis, hot babes in un-buttoned shirts, hot babes lying on poker tables, and hot babes doing what hot babes do best: look hot." Guys who deposited money at NakedPoker.com could enter weekly freerolls with such prizes as an evening with *Playboy* Playmate Stephanie Larimore, a "34C-24-34 brunette beauty from Fort Wayne." Other prizes included a trip to the Hedonism Resort in Jamaica.

Not many players were buying such come-ons, however, and few in the industry were surprised when the site closed a few months later, failing to refund the money in several accounts. In a similar spirit, PamelaPoker.com featured a gallery of seminude photos of Pamela Anderson and other bimbos, but it was laughed out of cyberspace after four months. TropicalPoker.com didn't last much longer after hiring model Cindy Margolis instead of spending money on customer service and other essentials; even at its high-water mark, it seldom had more than 150 players in action. Likewise, BombshellPoker.com resembled a site to troll for strippers and prostitutes, offering very little in the way of poker action. "Models by day, poker players by night. Besides being extremely easy on the eyes, our Bombshells are professionally trained poker players," claimed the site.

Poker.BodogLife.com appeared to have similar, if marginally more subtle, priorities. Founder Calvin Ayre's advertising featured handsome young studs with long cigars spiriting beautiful women out of town on the backseat of a motorcycle or in the shotgun seat of a convertible. Bodog men are so ruthless at poker, the ads implied, they'll take not only your money but your lady as well. And yet after Jamie Gold, who was sponsored by Bodog in the 2006 main event, said he would use the millions he won to make his father, who has Lou Gehrig's disease, as comfortable as possible, Ayre was unashamed to add, "Jamie truly epitomizes the Bodog spirit." Its actual spirit was epitomized in full-page ads in *Maxim*, *Esquire*, *Blender*, and *Vice* featuring either the woman-stealers or some shady-glamorous Poker Predators facing off against Ayre, with the tagline, "Be the king of your jungle." Effective advertising for womanless, status-hungry adolescents, perhaps, but whatever the opposite of humane generosity and a pure love of poker is, the Bodog spirit is it. Ayre terminated his relationship with Gold a few months later.

Fortunately, several more savory developments were under way while "Potripper," "NioNio," "Sleeplesss," and the cynics at Naked-Poker were doing their thing, as we'll see in the final two chapters.

POKER SCHOOL, POKER LAW, POKER ETHICS

Poker teaches strategy.

—CHARLES NESSON

The Global Poker Strategic Thinking Society was founded by Harvard Law School professors Charles Nesson and Lawrence Lessig, communications maven Jonathan Cohen, and Andrew Woods, a second-year law student. Nesson and Lessig had already launched Harvard's Berkman Center for Internet and Society, and Nesson had famously defended Daniel Ellsberg in the Pentagon Papers case and consulted on the case against W. R. Grace, an early environmental lawsuit that was the subject of Jonathan Harr's *A Civil Action*. Lessig, the author of *The Future of Ideas* and *Code and Other Laws of Cyberspace*, is an expert on Internet law. Cohen helped create United Nations Watch and has built a variety of software and communications companies. Woods graduated magna cum laude from UCLA, where he started the Bruin Casino Gaming Society, the first officially recognized student organization devoted to the study and teaching of poker. Together they launched the GPSTS at the State of Play conference in Singapore in August 2007.

Even a quick browse of the Society's Web page, gpsts.org, makes it clear that poker is more central than ever to the way we educate and entertain ourselves, make laws and contracts, and communicate online or in person. The Wiki-style site features essays, documents, reading lists, and recorded interviews about strategy, game theory, Texas hold'em, presidential poker, and quite a bit more. It encourages us to think of the game as an educational tool, as preparation for careers in business and law, and provides links to various statutes and Supreme Court decisions. And it reminds us that, in spite of the UIGEA, there is no federal law against individuals playing poker online.

The society views poker as "an exceptional game of skill that can be used as a powerful teaching tool at all levels of academia." It uses the game "to teach strategic thinking, geopolitical analysis, risk assessment and money management" and sees it "as a metaphor for skills of life, business, politics and international relations." Its ultimate goal is "to create an open online curriculum centered on poker that will draw the brightest minds together, both from within and outside of the conventional university setting, to promote open education and Internet democracy." The site is already so comprehensive that it includes four different translations of the Koran's opinion of gambling.

Nesson and Woods want to develop chapters at universities around the globe, with seminars, panel discussions, and lectures. Nesson believes that teaching poker as a skill helps students to see the world from others' points of view. In his own classes, he teaches them "to see in the game a language for thinking about and an environment for experiencing the dynamics of strategy in dispute resolution."

The GPSTS holds conferences focusing on the educational value of poker, poker and the law (including Antigua's victory over the UIGEA before the World Trade Organization), and ways of building a business around poker. At the simplest level, it has shown how the game's tactics can help middle-school students better understand fractions, percentages, budget making, and nonviolent problem resolution. But it also promotes lower-stakes competition in higher academia. It has already hosted matches between Harvard and Yale, UCLA and USC, and is in the process of adding chapters at Stanford, Dartmouth, NYU, Carnegie Mellon, Tufts, Cornell, Michigan, Indiana, George Washington, the Wharton School of Business, the National University of Singapore, and at least three Big Ten universities.

The Poker Players' Alliance is a like-minded lobbying group devoted to protecting Americans' right to compete on land and online, and to

414 ♣ COWBOYS FULL

guarantee "secure, safe and regulated" places to play. The alliance works with Congress to "establish new laws that clarify the legal status of poker and establish licensed and regulated Internet poker in the U.S.," providing links for sending letters and e-mail to congressmen, mainly in support of three bills in the House. It calls HR 6870, the Payments System Protection Act, "a reasonable compromise bill that passed the House Financial Services Committee with broad bipartisan support. It provides clarity to the vague and misguided requirements of UIGEA." The PPA also supports HR 2610, the Skill Game Protection Act, because it "clarifies federal law by expressly exempting games of skill like poker from UIGEA." It also encourages yes votes on HR 2046, the Internet Gambling Regulation and Enforcement Act, which would regulate online poker via licensing of site operators.

While the PPA and GPSTS lead the lobbying effort, the World Poker Association promotes the game "as a sport by advocating professionalism and uniform rules and standards of conduct, and by helping to create increased economic opportunities for players." It was founded in 2005 by Jesse Jones, a retired real estate investor who lives in Las Vegas and Hawaii. A soft-spoken cancer survivor, Jones was convinced that poker needed a better image than had often been projected by promoters and players, especially now that the game was on television. He designed the WPA to do what the PGA had done for golf, promoting professionalism and supporting the adoption of standardized tournament rules. "Can you imagine going to an NFL football game," he asks, "and they play four quarters a game, and then you go next week and they play five quarters? That's what we have in tournament poker now; standards that are not uniform." Above all, Jones hopes to establish a broad Code of Ethics accepted by tournament players worldwide. WPA members would "support professionalism in all aspects of poker competition, recognizing that the play of each person's poker hand is strictly an individual undertaking, and that any form of 'team cooperation' with respect to the play of any poker hand is strictly prohibited." They would attempt to "serve as role models for professionalism," treating all dealers, floormen, and fellow players with respect.

Speaking for the WPA, Jones publicly criticized Scotty Nguyen for his "most egregious" taunting of opponents at the final table of the 2008 H.O.R.S.E. championship, broadcast in prime time on ESPN and widely viewed on youtube.com. *Card Player* reported that Nguyen "repeatedly harassed, badgered, and taunted his opponents, breaking several of the

WSOP's own rules on his way to victory." Implying that he wasn't penalized by WSOP officials because he was a former main-event champion, Jones said the incident underscored the need for "uniform standards with clearcut rulings that are enforced in all circumstances."

Etiquette guidelines not covered by the WPA include the responsibility to play quickly, since the more hands dealt per hour, the more skill will determine the outcome. Unless your entire stack is on the line and you have mind-bending pot odds to calculate, you shouldn't take two minutes to act on your hand. Eventually a fellow player will call for a floorperson to put you on a sixty-second clock; if it ticks down before you act, your hand will be dead. For most decisions, one to ten seconds should be plenty of time. In order to mix up your tempos, occasionally pretending to think for a moment when you have a no-brainer is fine, but you shouldn't make a habit of this.

You should also keep your water bottle, iPod, BlackBerry, sunglasses case, family snapshots, or other good-luck charms out of your neighbors' space on the felt. Don't get drunk. Don't whine when you lose a big hand. Don't slow-roll the nuts for dramatic effect. A whooping war dance or thunderous hand clap to celebrate winning a pot, especially when you had the second-best hand until the river and insufficient odds to call all the previous bets, reveals that you don't have much class.

If the cards are running against you, don't call for a deck change. Better to accept that this happens all the time. It's no sin, however, to occasionally ask the dealer to give the cards an extrabig scramble before he starts to reshuffle. You can also try changing your luck by turning your cap upside down, inside out, backward, or tilting it at a 47.9-degree angle.

Even more crucial is behavior affecting the outcome of a hand. Always make sure to act in strict clockwise order. "Accidentally" acting out of turn in order to get a read on opponents is called "shooting an angle" and is rightly despised by honest and serious players. If a player to your right says, "Raise," and one or more other players have yet to act, don't fold your cards until the raiser has completed his bet, because knowing you will fold might affect how much he raises. Nor should you ever say or do anything that implies what your hole cards were after you folded them. If you folded 7-3 before the flop and the flop comes 3-7-7, slap neither the felt nor your forehead. Why not? Because your "D'oh!" routine would unduly signal to players still in the hand that one or both of the remaining sevens were dead.

It's also important to avoid making a string raise—that is, moving your chip-laden hand forward, releasing some or all of the chips, then illegally going back for more, in effect stringing together a raise while possibly gauging your opponent's reaction. If you want to raise five hundred, say, put the original bet plus five black chips in your hand, and lay them all out there at once. You can also say, "Raise five hundred." Once you've said that, you can move your hand back and forth as many times as necessary. Also note that if the original bet was two hundred, saying "Raise five hundred" requires you to put in seven hundred. If you want to raise only three hundred, say "Raise three hundred" or "Raise to five hundred" or "Make it five hundred all day." Or just put five hundred chip units together and push them all forward. How far? About halfway between your stack and the pot. "Splashing" them directly into the pot makes it impossible for others to see what the bet is. After the round of betting is complete, the dealer will pull all the chips to the middle.

Any form of collusion is illegal and unethical. This obviously includes teaming with partners to raise and reraise other players, but it also includes soft-playing each other—not betting strong hands, for example. Even if a friend is short-stacked a few places out of the money, not raising his blind with raiseworthy hole cards is cheating. Many such rules must be self-enforced, in much the same way that a PGA player uses the honor system to add a stroke for grounding his wedge in a sand trap, even if he's the only person who could see or feel that it happened.

Another note about deals: Second place in a tournament usually pays about twice what third pays but only half what the winner receives. Thus, making a deal with fellow finalists often makes sense, especially when three or four players have similar stacks and the blinds are disproportionately high, in which case luck more than skill will determine the finishing order. A typical deal would involve dividing 90 percent of third- through first-place money equally among the last three players, then playing on for the bracelet (or trophy) and the remaining 10 percent of the money. But if you offer your opponents a deal, or vice versa, negotiate with the understanding that all deals are voluntary.

Despite the fact that bluffing is very much like lying, there is a natural honesty to poker, something along the lines of honor among thieves. You would never steal your opponents' money away from the table, yet taking it by misrepresenting the strength of your hand with a bluff is well within both the letter and spirit of poker law. There is also a democratic fairness to the game. All players remaining in the hand make equal contributions to the pot. Each betting decision is made freely and openly (though the reasons for them remain private), and strictly in turn. Except for their hole cards, all players have the same information available to them, though some notice things more acutely. In tournaments, everyone starts with the same number of chips. Noble birth, ivied education, or an elite athlete's body confer no advantage, though acting talent and a vigorous brain always help.

In her memoir, *Poker Face*, the poet Katy Lederer (the younger sister of Annie Duke and Howard Lederer) compares the ruthlessly analytical minds of her siblings to her own way of playing. "I was able to 'read' people, but it proved problematic. I would sit at my table, look around at my opponents, and try my best to assess them by their postures and expressions, but it would be strangely painful. Or, not painful. It would make me feel *dirty*," she writes. "We would sit there, growing filthy together, handling our cards and the dirty plastic chips, trying not to bite our nails for fear of what had lodged itself beneath them."

Poker's "dirty" intimacy and fiduciary hazards aren't for everyone, certainly. Yet its grittiness and peril might help to explain why its outlaw cachet continues to linger, even when today's live games are played mostly by well-scrubbed folks sipping mineral water in state-sanctioned card rooms. Liquor up Front, Poker in the Rear? "Crooked Nose" McCall gunning down Bill Hickok from behind? An ornery Marlboro Man raising you the ranch from behind mirrored shades? Mirrored shades maybe, but smoking is now banned (thanks largely to the efforts of Casey Castle and Wendeen Eolis) in virtually every card room and all major tournaments. So is spewing "the F-bomb" and other loutish behavior.

The game's image has also improved because of civic-minded players like Jones; Don Cheadle, who brings out his fellow movie stars for charitable tournaments to benefit African causes; Jennifer Harman and Lee Watkinson, who do the same for animal rights and the National Kidney Foundation, as Phil Gordon and many others do for cancer research; Phil Ivey, whose Budding Ivey Foundation helps at-risk children in Nevada and New Jersey; tournament stars like J. C. Tran, Kathy Liebert, and Allen Cunningham, who nearly always play brilliantly but who wouldn't be caught dead bragging about it; and of course Barry Greenstein.

In the chapter of his *Ace on the River* called "How to Behave in the Poker Society," Greenstein wonders to what extent character is exposed at the table. "Many players who act appropriately in most social situations behave badly when they are losing," he writes. "Maybe we don't see a person's true character at the poker table, but rather, we see him at his worst." Others would argue that it's when the chips are down that character is most clearly revealed.

Greenstein admits that at least one ulterior motive for behaving decently is to keep the game "good"—that is, profitable. "A player who wins the pot should let his opponent win the argument," he suggests. "It is bad business to destroy people," even though "crybabies deserve something to cry about." He goes on to identify twenty-five traits of successful players, including manipulative, insensitive, and greedy. Yet it is much more important, he says, to be trustworthy, intelligent, honest (with yourself), and psychologically tough.

Greenstein's glossy, oversize paperback has hundreds of color photos of contemporary stars and illuminating chapters on brain chemistry, chaos theory, integrity, the hazards of sports betting, and how playing poker affects your family and sexuality—and vice versa. "Casinos hire good-looking employees to attract and distract customers," he writes. "If you are sexually frustrated, you may have trouble concentrating on poker." Even winning can lead to problems, he says, because chips "of large denomination can have an aphrodisiac effect." In exactly what sense might having lots of them not be a good thing? "Becoming a sugar daddy can have a devastating effect on one's gambling bankroll." Better, he says, to contribute some of your profits to charity, a suggestion that his friend Ivey and others have taken him up on.

The book's most enlightening passage for non–sugar daddies comes right up front in the dedication: to "the children of gamblers [who] were told everything was done so they could have toys and clothes and a nice place to live, but all they wanted was a little more of their parent's time. I apologize to my children"—Greenstein lists their names—"for when I have failed as a parent."

THE WORLD'S GAME

Let's put our chips in the middle of the table and see how
we do.

— BARACK OBAMA

As millions more live and virtual hands are dealt every day, poker
seems poised to become the world's card game. This is happening, in
part, because globalization—the convergence of the Internet and cable
television with vast economic events—has leveled the international
playing field, not only for political ideas and business innovations but
for previously local games such as baseball, soccer, basketball, Scrabble,
and poker. That such games are intrinsically beautiful is no small part
of it, either.

Scandinavians, Canadians, Australians, and East Asians have been
doing especially well at poker of late, though it's the Vietnamese in particular who dominate tournaments more than any other ethnic group.
A variety of cultural factors help to explain the disparity. Being clever
and lucky are highly esteemed in Vietnamese culture. Gambling carries
little stigma and is often lionized. The heavy stigma against it in Japan
and India, on the other hand, makes it unsurprising that relatively few
Japanese or Indian Americans play poker at all. The Vietnamese who

managed to emigrate after the Communists took over in 1975 were an ambitious and tough-minded lot. A report in the *Los Angeles Times* found that they tended to be "risk-takers willing to leave the familiarity of their homelands" and to "develop more aggressive gambling strategies than their U.S.-born counterparts."

Buddhists in general seem to embrace randomness more readily than those brought up in the Christian tradition, and many Vietnamese also believe that "guts" and "dare" are essential to gaming success, which helps them to play more aggressively at the poker table. Most of those who immigrated to the United States after the war, the so-called boat people, settled in California just as poker was becoming legal throughout the state. Men "the Master" Nguyen and others who had early success at the poker table tutored members of their extended families and gave their best students a stake in tournaments, often in exchange for half of their winnings—for life, in some cases. By the late 1990s, a stunning percentage of tournament champions were named Nguyen, Pham, Phan, or Tran. Many considered themselves to be "Men the Master's soldiers" and treated him "like God." Yet the Master seems happy to spread around some of the credit. "Americans made me who I am today," he has said. "I love America. Without America, I would probably be dead."

There were persistent rumors, however, that the soldiers colluded to help the Master in tournaments. Did jealousy of his success trigger at least a few of these rumors? Perhaps. One WSOP champion interviewed by Michael Kaplan said, "Some of Men's tournament wins were tainted because people dumped [chips] to him. We've been unable to prove this, but it's public knowledge in poker circles. There's collusion in which he plays partners and has his guys squeeze players out of key hands. They work out signals and do all kinds of dishonest things." In the face of some early allegations, Benny Binion admiringly called Nguyen "the Vietnamese Godfather," which could be taken in a number of ways. Nguyen himself told Kaplan in 2003 that cheating "goes against my Buddha. It's against my religion. I cheat you once and it comes back to me. I have a family, I have a nice thing going, you think I'd cheat you to make my life better? No! God punishes people like that." Looking Kaplan straight in the eye, he declared, "People say things, but nobody can prove anything. If they caught me with chips, I'd never be allowed to play anywhere, not ever again. I travel all over the world, I play poker, I win. That is what I do."

Whatever went on in the 1980s and '90s, these days few people doubt that Vietnamese players, perhaps more than any other ethnic group, are perfectly capable of dominating tournaments fair and square. Perhaps the best evidence is that *Card Player*'s 2007 Player of the Year title was awarded to David "the Dragon" Pham, who also won it seven years earlier. Pham is the cousin and former student of Men the Master, the only four-time winner (1997, 2001, 2003, 2005) of this widely respected award. The runner-up was J. C. Tran, who was born in South Vietnam and now has a business degree from Cal State Sacramento. The title is respected so highly because any good player can get lucky for a few days and win a big tournament, but the Player of the Year needs to be successful over fifty-two weeks. Whoever wins has a far more valid claim on the year-end laurels than whoever won the WSOP main event. The only misleading aspect of the POY system is that it doesn't factor in a per-start success rate, so it favors tournament grinders who buy into hundreds of events over players like Juanda, Ivey, Harman, Seidel, Harrington, Goehring, and Chau Giang, who tend to enter only the majors. This is not to say that playing every day (which more or less requires living in L.A. or Las Vegas) should be penalized, only that on-average excellence against the toughest competition should be a more important criterion in the POY standings.

The 2008 Player of the Year was John "the Razor" Phan, one of the very toughest players around. Phan lives in Long Beach, but he was born in Da Nang in 1974 and is considered the first Vietnamese hip-hop poker star. The more buttoned-down Dragon finished second in the standings, Men the Master sixteenth—of the 6,157 tournament players the computer kept track of worldwide. We should also recall that Johnny Chan, the first Asian-born WSOP champion and a man who came within a couple of hands of winning the main event three consecutive times, hails from Guangzhou, a Chinese city not far from Vietnam.

The Indonesian-born master John Juanda, who was twice runner-up for Player of the Year and won his fourth WSOP bracelet at the main event in London in 2008, is ethnically Chinese. When he first came to America in 1990, he spoke almost no English. He learned it well enough to sell Bibles door-to-door and earn an MBA while gradually picking up the American card game. Since he couldn't always follow the mumbled conversations taking place across the felt, he concentrated more on the action and the players' body language. When he couldn't understand what opponents were saying, he studied their facial expressions to make educated guesses. "You learn a lot more by listening than you do by talking," he says, advice any player could profit from, whatever language he speaks, or doesn't speak, at the table.

It's hard to predict the future of poker in Asia, but the enormous integrated resorts featuring megacasinos on the Chinese island of Macau earned more money in the first three quarters of 2008 than they did in 2007, which was more than all the casinos on the Las Vegas Strip put together. Large casinos are also being built in Singapore, Vietnam, and Australia. Because poker celebrities are among the most appealing lures for new customers, all these new casinos virtually guarantee that more poker tournaments will be hosted in these countries. Similar resorts are being considered in Korea, Japan, Taiwan, Hong Kong, and Thailand. People already play poker in those places, both online and in private games, but as gaming-law expert Nelson Rose points out, the impetus for building casinos "is usually the legalization of a more attractive form of gambling in a nearby jurisdiction. The sight of all that disposable income, some from a state's own citizens, going across the border to another state, does more than anything else to weaken even antigambling lawmakers." The tipping point for East Asian poker was reached around 2005, and more growth appears likely.

While the number of events on the Asian poker circuit grew to six in 2009 and the boom in Australia continued, the European Poker Tour, sponsored by PokerStars, held multimillion-euro events in London, Deauville, Dortmund, Copenhagen, Prague, Barcelona, Budapest, San Remo, and Monte Carlo. Other online sites hosted major live events in Dublin, Paris, Helsinki, and Moscow. More than a few Scandinavians have suggested that poker has become the second-most popular pastime in their part of the world, especially after twenty-two-year-old Peter Eastgate won the WSOP main event in November 2008—the first Dane and the youngest player ever to do so. Relatively new to Latin America, tournament participation has been spurred by stars like Humberto Brenes and Carlos Mortensen, and the circuit now stops in Costa Rica, Colombia, Ecuador, Chile, Brazil, Uruguay, and Argentina. Sizable events are also being hosted in Swaziland and South Africa, while the All Africa Poker Channel, launched in 2005, continues to build audience share.

The global boom has made it increasingly necessary that some international body be set up to govern the game—and defend it. With the Bush administration in the United States and politicians in other countries branding poker as just another game of chance, there was a pressing need for an authoritative voice to assert that poker is primarily a game of skill, or as Anthony Holden put it, a "mind-sport."

In early 2009, a consortium of European players and businessmen asked Holden to become the founding president of a not-for-profit body seeking to demonstrate that poker is just as respectable as chess or bridge, to encourage government recognition of this throughout the world, to exempt poker from laws regulating games of pure chance, and to establish a framework for self-regulation within the game itself. By May, Holden had formally established the International Federation of Poker in Lausanne, Switzerland. His first move was to enlist as many member nations as possible, as well as representatives of both the online and on-land poker communities. He also sought formal recognition from the International Olympic Committee, the International Mind-Sports Association, and other such governing bodies. With the 2012 Summer Olympics set to take place in his hometown of London, his goal was to make poker a part of it.

Two decades ago, with the cold war ending in America's favor, David Parlett wrote that poker was "the national vying game of the United States, and its international prominence is as much due to the prominence and influence of American culture as to its own individual merits." Lately, however, even with American prestige on the wane during the Bush administration, the game has flourished on its own merits in just about every Western-style democracy. Its global popularity today can be traced to many of the same reasons it developed in America two hundred years ago. The more an economic system encourages optimism, self-reliance, math skill, and entrepreneurial spirit, the more poker players it breeds.

Who makes long money from poker these days? Mainly the owners of card rooms, casinos, and online sites. Among the players, it seems to be mostly young "ballas," a studly term borrowed from basketball. Many of these risk-loving, hyperaggressive young men cut their teeth online long before turning twenty-one, the minimum age for playing live tournaments in American casinos. After steady success on PokerStars since the age of seventeen, Peter Eastgate earned $9,152,416 for winning the main event at the Rio; Moscow resident Ivan Demidov, an old-timer at twenty-seven, took home $5,809,595 for finishing second. Tom Dwan, an online intimidator born the same year as Eastgate, has already won many millions in cash games, though he is also famous for losing a \$723,938 pot on October 26, 2008. In that month alone, the five biggest winners online netted some startling sums in the six-handed no-limit hold'em and pot-limit Omaha games on Full Tilt.

Gus Hansen	\$2,873,376
Phil Ivey	1,932,807
Tom "durrr" Dwan	1,031,368
Ilari "Ziigmund" Sahamies	862,750
John Juanda	830,997

The stakes these men play for, the adrenalized intensity and spiky variance of their games, and the talent of the competition all make it inevitable that on bad nights they will "get stuck" seven-figure amounts. In spite or because of this, they and a few dozen others have quickly achieved pro athlete status, which in turn produces thousands of wannabes determined to play for similar stakes. The biggest games on Full Tilt have as many as five hundred railbirds watching and criticizing every last call, bet, and raise.

As the essayist Charles Lamb noted in the early nineteenth century, "Cards are war, in disguise of sport." In sports as in war as in poker, testosterone gooses competitive fury. Helen Fisher and the University of Pittsburgh study (among many others) remind us that evolution favors men with a taste for risking everything for a shot at becoming top dog. For them, it's all about the ring or the bracelet, though the millions that come with it don't hurt. To clinch the athletic connection, the promotional clothing of PokerStars, Full Tilt, UltimateBet, and other sites mimics football, hockey, and basketball jerseys, to go with their ubiquitous baseball caps. That the World Series is broadcast on ESPN makes the connection even more unavoidable. All the money in the world could never buy a chance to play in the Super Bowl, NBA Finals, or baseball's World Series, but \$10,000 guarantees a seat in the other one, or in any number of lucrative televised tournaments. And the more hopeful novices are tempted to buy in to them, the juicier they get for the pros. That said, the all-time leading money winner at the WSOP, Jamie Gold, is a member of the former contingent.

Another big factor determining who profits from poker is the income tax U.S. citizens must pay on tournament winnings, while many foreign players pay nothing. Such taxes make it impossible for all but a tiny number of American tournament players to stay in the black. It has always been much easier to hide income from cash games. While the

winners of more than $600 in a tournament must fill out W2G paper-
work, tax evaders may pocket some of their profits from cash games under the IRS radar.

What do the moist-eared ballas and hairy-eared grinders do after the
fish have been gutted? They wait for more fish to arrive. And they seldom have to wait very long. "Stakes have doubled in terms of what the
out-of-towners will play for," Daniel Negreanu told one reporter.
"Random recreational guys who used to be $80/$160 players at the
Mirage have moved up to $300/$600. And now the $10/$20 no-limit
games attract novices who would have once sat down in $5/$10 limit
games. But they're playing no-limit and losing $20,000 or $30,000 in a
sitting." Negreanu recalled that a few years earlier no-limit cash games
were "dead because good players get the money so quickly in that
game. These days, though, people lose their money and we see a never-
ending supply of fresh meat. It never seems to stop. Suckers come and
leave and more suckers replace them. But people are willing to gamble.
They see it on TV and think it's easy."

"Unlike backgammon and chess, poker is a wonderful game because
it has enough of a luck component that bad players sometimes beat
good players, which keeps the bad players interested," Steve Zolotow
added. "But on the other side of it, poker requires enough skill that you
can keep growing and keep learning more about the game." He was
also quite happy to note, "During the last few years, I've traveled
around the world playing" tournaments.

After winning another eight Olympic gold medals in Beijing (for a
total of fourteen and counting), Michael Phelps said, "I think it would
be cool to play in the World Series of Poker. My game is a little off
right now, so I'll have to start improving it a little bit. But I think that
would be cool. . . . It would be cool to meet some of those poker guys."
By September 2008, he was competing in Las Vegas tournaments, honing his game for the WPT circuit and the WSOP the following summer. On October 18, he made the final table of the third event he had
entered. As his hero Young Jeezy might put it, "Nothin like ya man, he
aint grindin like this." Or maybe that should be, "I'm so paid."

Phelps is continuing the tradition of successful competitors in other
fields turning to professional poker on a part- or full-time basis. Today
this faction includes magician Antonio Esfandiari, Cirque du Soleil
founder Guy Laliberté, French pop star Patrick Bruel, PGA pro Rocco
Mediate, mixed martial arts fighters Mike Swick and Matt Hughes, six-

time grand slam tennis champion Boris Becker, and Cy Young Award winner and World Series MVP Orel Hershiser. The hundreds of actors who play major events include Ben Affleck, Gabe Kaplan, Tobey Maguire, Jennifer Tilly, James Woods, Don Cheadle, Chad Brown, Mimi Rogers, Matt Damon, Jack Black, and Leonardo DiCaprio. Their numbers are swelled by the facts that Los Angeles is a hotbed of hold'em and most stars have plenty of money and leisure time, and by the importance of acting when competing against live opponents. There are plenty of home games in Hollywood, played for stakes both titanic and minuscule. The cast of *Ocean's 12* held a nightly hold'em tournament while filming in Rome but kept the buy-in to fifty euros. Johnny Carson, too, liked his poker longer on camaraderie than cutthroat one-upsmanship. He and other well-paid entertainers—Steve Martin, Neil Simon, Carl Reiner, Martin Short—shared a monthly meal in their informal Gourmet Poker Club before playing low-stakes dealer's-choice while shooting the Malibu breeze.

The man who has won more poker tournaments than anyone, T. J. Cloutier, used to make his living as a tight end and linebacker in the Canadian Football League. Another tight end, Shannon Sharpe, a likely NFL Hall of Famer, represented Absolute Poker on the circuit in 2005, a relationship that Jeffrey Pollack would surely understand. Pro Bowl defensive tackle Chris Zorich plays in a variety of home games and charitable events in and around Chicago, where he starred as a Bear.

According to a *USA Today* cover story, "The World Series of Poker has nothing on the NFL draft. As the league's 32 teams have nitpicked hundreds of college players eligible for [the] draft in New York City, many of the teams also have jockeyed for an edge by trying to conceal their true intentions." The story notes that the weeks before the draft "are filled with misinformation campaigns, media leaks and smoke screens as teams play what amounts to a high-stakes game of bluffing." One way a football team executes a predraft bluff is by concocting or exaggerating drug-use or injury reports about a particular player. It can leak misleading information through the media or by word of mouth along the NFL grapevine. The bluffing team's goal is to downplay the value of a player they covet so that a team picking earlier doesn't draft him. The other teams' job is to suss out that player's actual market value. Several teams have flown a player they have no interest in drafting to their headquarters for predraft visits while ignoring the player they most want to draft. "Every head coach, every GM, everyone involved with any team right now is playing poker," according to Kansas City Chiefs coach Herm Edwards. "Whatever someone says, it's about half-true. That's the way the game is played."

Exactly which variants are played at actual poker tables is also evolving, of course. Even as H.O.R.S.E. has established itself as the gold standard of limit poker skill, exotic new variants like badugi are attracting more players. Badugi is a four-card game involving three draws, after which the lowest hand with four different suits takes the pot. While its modern form developed in Korea, it is also reminiscent of both Renaissance *mus* and primero.

New variants have always developed in opposition to the reigning game of choice, as well as a way to keep the bad players interested. The facedown cards of draw poker gave way to the exposed cards of stud, much as the original high-only games led to lowball, high-low, razz, and badugi. That a premium hand in pot-limit Omaha includes four high cards of two different suits is part of the reason badugi is catching on: If you keep catching terrible Omaha hands, goes the logic, why not try a game in which those hole cards will win you some money? The number of hands per hour and players per table are also in flux. Today, especially online, nine-handed action is giving way to much faster six-handed and heads-up play. Such trends are very much in keeping with pendulum swings in other parts of the culture, where crew cuts and narrow pants of one decade give way to long hair and bell-bottoms, or Anglo muscle cars jacked up on struts share the road with the lowriding coupes of pachucos.

Whatever the variant, what used to be mainly a cheating contest is now, for better or worse, at the heart of our on-again-off-again romance with market democracy. More than politics, warfare, business, or physical sports, poker has become the arena in which men and women of every race and background compete on the most equal footing. In a single generation, the World Series has crowned champions from the United States, China, Iran, Vietnam, Ireland, Spain, Australia, Laos, Norway, Indonesia, and Denmark. No other arena is nearly as inclusive. America has long been a melting pot, and its favorite card game—some say its national pastime—has become a sturdy crucible in which folks from all over the planet find themselves welcome contenders.

NOTES

1. Pokerticians

3 *Obama was asked by the Associated Press* Associated Press, "Questions for the Candidates," May 17, 2007.

4 *"When it turned out that I could sit down"* Rick Pearson and Ray Long, "Barack Obama: Careful Steps, Looking Ahead," *Chicago Tribune*, May 3, 2007.

4 *the Committee Meeting* Michael Scherer and Michael Weisskopf, "Candidates' Vices: Craps and Poker," *Time*, July 2, 2008, 30–31.

4 *"You hung up your guns at the door"* Terry Link, interview with the author, January 15, 2008.

4 *"We all became buddies in the card games"* Scherer and Weisskopf, "Candidates' Vices."

4 *Another regular was a lobbyist* Christopher Wills, "How Obama Plays Poker Could Be Telling," Associated Press, September 24, 2007.

4 *"a fun way for people to relax"* Ibid.

4 *his lanky table-mate played "calculated" poker* Terry Link, interview with the author.

4 *"When Barack stayed in"* Wills, "How Obama Plays Poker."

5 *"an inebriated woman companion"* David Mendell, *Obama: From Promise to Power* (New York: Harper, 2007), 123.

5 *"quickly whisked out of the place"* Terry Link, interview with the author.

5 *"Obama usually left a winner"* Scherer and Weisskopf, "Candidates' Vices."

5 *learned the game from his maternal grandfather* Johnny Brannon, "Hawai'i's Imperfect Melting Pot a Big Influence on Young Obama," *Honolulu Advertiser*, February 10, 2007.

5 *whose black friends played poker as well* Barack Obama, *Dreams from My Father* (New York: Crown, 1996), 76.

5 *played with classmates at Punahou High School* Wills, "How Obama Plays Poker."

5 *"When he'd shoot an 11 on a hole"* Larry Dorman, "Make Room for Golf Clubs in the Oval Office," *New York Times*, December 31, 2008, B9.

6 *"He understands how you network"* Ryan Lizza, "Making It: How Chicago Shaped Obama," *New Yorker*, July 21, 2008, 52.

6 *"the first significant campaign reform law"* Janny Scott, "In Illinois, Obama Proved Pragmatic and Shrewd," *New York Times*, July 30, 2007.

6 *other bills mandating tax credits* Lizza, "Making It," 57.

6 *After being "spanked"* Mendell, *Obama*, 143.

6 *"Even as I hope for some measure of peace"* Lizza, "Making It," 58.

6 *"The Republicans, like the perpetual raiser"* David Mamet, "Poker Party," *Los Angeles Times*, September 16, 2005.

7 *"Life is run by poker players"* Jon Meacham, "Hidden Depths," *Newsweek*, September 8, 2008.

7 *"We don't throw the first punch"* Lauren Appelbaum, MSNBC.com, October 6, 2008.

7 *"Let's put our chips in the middle of the table"* Roger Simon, "Audacity Wins," Politico.com, November 5, 2008.

7 *"the national game is not base-ball"* New York Times, February 12, 1875, 4.

8 *Contrasting Obama with his predecessor* Tim Shipman, "Poker Players Deal Obama a Full House," *London Sunday Telegraph*, July 7, 2008.

8 *"personality identification playing cards"* Tom Zucco, "Troops Dealt an Old Tool," *St. Petersburg Times*, April 12, 2003.

9 *Washington received a rebuke* James Thomas Flexner, *Washington: The Indispensible Man* (Boston: Little, Brown, 1974), 52.

9 *"Your question reminds me of an incident"* Carl Sandburg, *Abraham Lincoln: The Prairie Years and the War Years* (New York: Harcourt, 1954), 269.

9 *"Poker was not the national game for nothing"* Shelby Foote, *The Civil War: A Narrative—Fort Sumter to Perryville* (New York: Random House, 1958), 162.

9 *a "mornin' glory,"* Edmund Morris, *The Rise of Theodore Roosevelt* (New York: Random House, 1979), 123.

10 *"to get inside the machine"* David McCullough, *Mornings on Horseback: The Story of an Extraordinary Family, a Vanished Way of Life, and the Unique Child Who Became Theodore Roosevelt* (New York: Simon & Schuster, 1981), 254.

10 *a set of silver scales* Edmund Morris, *Theodore Rex* (New York: Random House, 2001), 233.

10 *"When I say I believe in a square deal"* *The Wisdom of Theodore Roosevelt* (New York: Citadel Press, 2003), 76.

10 *"We drew to a pair of deuces"* James David Barber, *The Pulse of Politics: Electing Presidents in the Media Age* (Edison, NJ: Transaction Books, 1992), 229.

10 *"Forget that I'm President of the United States"* Francis Russell, "The Four Mysteries of Warren Harding," *American Heritage*, April 1963.

11 *His friends gathered around their boxy wooden radios* Tom and Betsy Madden, interviews with the author (their grandson), ca. 1962.

11 *"He never learned to play golf or tennis"* David McCullough, *Truman* (New York: Simon & Schuster, 1992), 191.

11 *chips embossed with the presidential seal* www.archives.gov/publications/prologue/2003/spring/truman-poker.html.

11 *attended cadet dances "only now and then"* Dwight D. Eisenhower, *At Ease: Stories I Tell My Friends* (Garden City, NY: Doubleday, 1967).

12 *play with Truman a couple of times* Robert A. Caro, *Means of Ascent* (New York: Knopf, 1990), 126.

12 *ability to call Khrushchev's bluff* Michael Dobbs, *One Minute to Midnight: Kennedy, Khrushchev, and Castro on the Brink of Nuclear War* (New York: Knopf, 2008), 351.

12 *credits Khrushchev as "the one who made a wise fold"* Aaron Brown, interview with the author, August 25, 2008.

12 *"As in poker"* Oskar Morgenstern, "Cold War Is Cold Poker," *New York Times Magazine*, February 5, 1961, 21.

13 *"He played poker and Boston"* Stanley P. Hirshson, *The White Tecumseh: A Biography of General William T. Sherman* (New York: Wiley, 1998), 380.

14 *"A man who couldn't hold a hand in a first-class poker game"* A. Alvarez, *Poker: Bets, Bluffs, and Bad Beats* (San Francisco: Chronicle, 2001), 75.

14 *"cult of the common man"* Garry Wills, *Nixon Agonistes: The Crisis of the Self-Made Man* (Boston: Houghton Mifflin, 1970), 119.

14 *the Giants used a telescope and buzzer wire*   Joshua Prager, *The Echoing Green: The Untold Story of Bobby Thomson, Ralph Branca and the Shot Heard Round the World* (New York: Pantheon, 2006), 222.

15 *"I was naturally excited"*   Richard M. Nixon, *RN: The Memoirs of Richard Nixon* (New York: Simon & Schuster, 1990), 34.

15 *"iron butt"*   Wills, *Nixon Agonistes*, 20 and elsewhere.

15 *"got to know his fellows, not in foxholes"*   Ibid., 72.

15 *"Out there Nixon passed over the traditional Quaker objections"*   Quoted ibid., 73.

15 *"He found poker's local theoreticians"*   Ibid., 72.

16 *"eased his way into the military"*   Ibid., 160.

16 *"It helps, watching Nixon's 'ruthless' singlemindedness"*   Ibid., 72–73.

16 *"Like Nixon, he made large sums of money"*   Ibid., 119.

16 *"a hot political property"*   Nixon, *RN*, 28.

16 *"anathema"*   Ibid., 29.

17 *"the pressures of wartime"*   Ibid., 29.

17 *"as good a poker player"*   Donald Jackson, "Portrait of the Young Nixon," *Life*, November 6, 1970.

17 *"In the intense loneliness and boredom"*   *RN*, 29, 34.

17 *Nixon called her "the Pink Lady"*   Greg Mitchell, *Tricky Dick and the Pink Lady* (New York: Random House, 1998), 5.

19 *disproportionally inclined to take chances*   Peter D. Whybrow, *American Mania: When More Isn't Enough* (New York: Norton, 2005), 57.

19 *"It's not about where you come from"*   Emily Bazelon, "The Hypomanic American," *New York Times Magazine*, December 11, 2005, 76.

19 *traits called "hypomania"*   Whybrow, *American Mania*, 115.

20 *In America, "You have the genes"*   Quoted in Bazelon, "The Hypomanic American."

20 *"the game closest to the Western conception of life"*   John Lukacs, "Poker and the American Character," *Horizon* 5, no. 8, (1963).

20 *"Those living in the instability of a democracy"*   Alexis de Tocqueville, *Democracy in America*, trans. Gerald E. Bevan (New York: Penguin, 2003), 643.

2. Loaded Knucklebones to Donkeys in Cyberspace

24 *In* The Selfish Gene   Richard Dawkins, *The Selfish Gene* (New York: Oxford University Press, 2006), 77.

24 *the instinctual poker face*   Steven Pinker. "The Known World," *New York Times Book Review*, May 27, 2007, 12–13.

24 *Pleistocene hunters risked life and limb*   Dawkins, *Selfish Gene*, 56–57, 162.

25 *larger portions of protein and more opportunities to mate*   David M. Buss, *The Evolution of Desire* (New York: Basic Books, 2003), 86, 200.

25 *protection became even more vital*   Ibid., 28–41.

26 *"If the bones land short side up"*   David G. Schwartz, *Roll the Bones: The History of Gambling* (New York: Gotham, 2006), 7.

27 *By 3500 BCE, Sumerians and Egyptians*   Ibid., 9–11.

28 venus, *which meant charm or beauty*   Aaron Brown, interview with the author, August 27, 2008.

28 *the great Hindu epic* Mahabharata   Schwartz, *Roll the Bones*, 14–15.

28 *"These dice nuts, born of a lofty tree"*   Quoted in ibid., 14.

3. A Shivering Shaman and the Concubines of Invention

30 *The anthropologist Stewart Culin traced the lineage*   David G. Schwartz, *Roll the Bones: The History of Gambling* (New York: Gotham, 2006), 41–42; see also Roger Tilley, *The History of Playing Cards* (New York: Clarkson Potter, 1973), 10–11.

31 "htou-tjyen," *means "fighting tablets"*   Schwartz, *Roll the Bones*, 41–42.

31 *roughly three thousand members*   Ibid.

32 *As David Parlett notes*   David Parlett, *The Oxford Guide to Card Games* (New York: Oxford Univerity Press, 1990), 15.

33 *the Chinese fanned them from the top*   Schwartz, *Roll the Bones*, 42–43.

33 *"made possible when an Arab army"*   Jared Diamond, *Guns, Germs, and Steel: The Fate of Human Societies* (New York: W. W. Norton, 1997), 238.

34 *The highest cards were the* malik *(sultan)*   Schwartz, *Roll the Bones*, 44–47.

34 *cards were called* kridapatram   Ibid.

4. Jeanne d'Arc and La Hire to the Naked Singularity of Spades

35 *In the earliest years of the Renaissance*   David G. Schwartz, *Roll the Bones: The History of Gambling* (New York: Gotham, 2006), 46–56.

36 *On Florentine decks, the ladies and dancers*   A. Alvarez, *Poker: Bets, Bluffs, and Bad Beats* (San Francisco: Chronicle, 2001), 33.

36 *Mary, Queen of Scots, had gambled*   Antonia Fraser, *Mary, Queen of Scots* (New York: Delta, 1993), 7, 180.

37 *Henry VIII played cards "compulsively"*   Antonia Fraser, *The Wives of Henry VIII* (New York: Vintage, 1993), 13, 132, 153, 279, 291.

37 *Elizabeth played with the men of her court*   Alison Weir, *The Life of Elizabeth I* (New York: Ballantine, 1998), 29, 230, 242.

37 *player of* giochi proibiti   Margaret F. Rosenthal, *The Honest Courtesan: Veronica Franco, Citizen and Writer in Sixteenth-Century Venice* (Chicago: University of Chicago Press, 1992), 166.

37 *Giacomo Casanova, loved to play whist*   J. Rives Childs, *Casanova: A New Perspective* (New York: Paragon House, 1988), 263.

39 *"Power belonged to kings by divine right"*   Edward O. Wilson, *Sociobiology: The New Synthesis* (Cambridge, MA: Harvard University Press, 1975), 560.

40 *Wilson goes on to suggest*   Ibid.

5. Dr. Jerome Cardplayer and the Vying Games That Gave Rise to Poker

42 *"became a craze of scandalous proportions"*   David Parlett, *The Oxford Guide to Card Games* (New York: Oxford University Press, 1990), 77.

42 *basset was "the most courtly"*   Ibid. (Parlett is the primary source for my descriptions of games in this chapter.)

43 *defined by Seymour in 1720*   Richard Seymour, *The Court Gamester* (London: E. Curll, 1720), 163.

44 *"Primiera is often described as 'the' ancestor of Poker"*   Parlett, *Oxford Guide to Card Games*, 91.

45 Capitolo del gioco della Primiera   Francesco Berni, "Commento al capitolo della primiera," www.nuovorinascimento.org.

45 Liber de Ludo Aleae (Book on Games of Chance)   Girolamo Cardano, trans.

Sydney Henry Gould, reprinted in Oystein Øre, *Cardano: The Gambling Scholar* (Princeton, NJ: Princeton University Press, 1953), 182–241.

45 *deemed* primiero *"the noblest"* Ibid., 206.

46 *"Even if gambling were an evil"* Ibid., 189.

46 *cast the horoscope of fifteen-year-old King Edward VI* Girolamo Cardano, *The Book of My Life*, trans. Jean Stoner (New York: NYRB Classics, 2002), 58.

46 *"When I observed that the cards were marked"* Ibid., 92–93.

47 *"The latter is open"* Cardano, *Book on Games of Chance*, 206.

47 *at least a century before the work of Blaise Pascal* Øre, *Cardano: The Gambling Scholar*, viii.

48 *"a beachhead"* Leonard Mlodinow, *The Drunkard's Walk: How Randomness Rules Our Lives* (New York: Pantheon, 2008), 49.

48 *"The greatest advantage in gambling"* Cardano, *Book on Games of Chance*, 188.

6. *Poque* to Pokuh to Poker

49 *poque was limited to four players* David Parlett, *The Oxford Guide to Card Games* (New York: Oxford University Press, 1990), 96.

50 *1897 edition of* Foster's Complete Hoyle R. F. Foster, *Foster's Complete Hoyle* (New York: Frederick Stokes, 1897), 163.

50 *"Sailors from Persia"* Frank R. Wallace, *Poker: A Guaranteed Income for Life* (Wilmington: I & O Publishing, 1968), 179.

50 *the claim in 1950 by Louis Coffin* Cited in Parlett, *The Oxford Guide to Card Games*, 113.

50 *as isn't a card-related word* Ibid., 112.

50 *"When French colonists arrived"* Lynn Loomis and Mason Malmuth, *The Fundamentals of Poker* (Henderson, NV: Two Plus Two, 1992), 3.

50 *"adapted their own game of* poque*"* A. Alvarez, *Poker: Bets, Bluffs, and Bad Beats* (San Francisco: Chronicle, 2001), 32.

51 "Je poque de dix" Parlett, *Oxford Guide to Card Games*, 113.

51 *Fundamental Theorem of Poker* David Sklansky, *The Theory of Poker* (Henderson, NV: Two Plus Two, 1994), 16.

53 *5,308,483, including well over a million slaves* Henry Adams, *History of the United States of America During the Administrations of Thomas Jefferson* (1889; New York: Library of America, 1986), 5.

53 *"There is on the globe one single spot"* Quoted in Joseph J. Ellis, *American Sphinx: The Character of Thomas Jefferson* (New York: Knopf, 1996), 244.

54 *"speaking the same language"* Quoted in Stephen Ambrose, *Undaunted Courage: Meriwether Lewis, Thomas Jefferson, and the Opening of the American West* (New York: Simon & Schuster, 1997), 56.

54 *New Orleans soon became the second-wealthiest* www.neworleanscvb.com.

54 *"The mixture of chance"* John M. Findlay, *People of Chance: Gambling in American Society from Jamestown to Las Vegas* (New York: Oxford University Press, 1986), 51.

55 *(called "taking in" by brag players)* Henry G. Bohn, *The Hand-Book of Games* (London: H. G. Bohn, 1850), 384.

55 *According to Hoyle* *The American Hoyle* (New York: Dick & Fitzgerald, 1864), 190ff.

56 *A new wrinkle called the* jackpot Ibid., 203.

7. Mississippi Steamboats, the Internet Card Rooms of 1814

59 *"the beginning of a new era in America"* Henry Adams, *History of the United States of America During the Administrations of Thomas Jefferson* (1889; New York: Library of America, 1980), 1019.

59 The New Orleans, *Fulton's first craft* Kirkpatrick Sale, *The Fire of His Genius: Robert Fulton and the American Dream* (New York: Free Press, 2002), 155–71.

59 *Female passengers slept in a cabin belowdecks* Editors of Time-Life Books, *Gamblers of the Old West* (Richmond, VA: Time, Inc., 1996), 51–52.

59 *changed the nature of commerce* Sale, *The Fire of His Genius*, 127, 133.

59 *in the twenty years after the* New Orleans *first steamed* Ibid., 188.

60 *run the gauntlet of British guns* mvn.usace.army.mil/PAO/history/MISSR NAV/steamboat.asp.

60 *at least four hundred gaming dens* John M. Findlay, *People of Chance* (New York: Oxford University Press, 1988), 59.

60 *staked all he owned on a bet* Ibid., 38.

60 *intentionally shot Dickinson in the groin* www.academicamerican.com/jacksoniandemocracy.html.

60 *You must risque to win."* Findlay, *People of Chance*, 39.

60 *rose from twenty in 1818* Walter A. McDougall, *Freedom Just Around the Corner: A New American History, 1585–1828* (New York: Harper, 2004), 428.

61 *Truman's ancestors traveled by steamboat* David McCullough, *Truman* (New York: Simon & Schuster, 1992), 17.

61 *"glorious with expectancy"* Mark Twain, *Life on the Mississippi* (1883; New York: Viking Penguin, 1984), 65–66.

62 *Pilots were represented* Michael Gillespie, *Come Hell or High Water: A Lively History of Steamboating on the Mississippi and Ohio Rivers* (Stoddard, WI: Heritage Press, 2001), 117.

62 *About fourteen hundred people would be killed* McDougall, *Freedom Just Around the Corner*, 428.

63 *annual "contribution" of $5,000* David G. Schwartz, *Roll the Bones: The History of Gambling* (New York: Gotham, 2006), 248–53 (which also recounts the story of John Davis). Cf. Abbye A. Gorin and William E. Meneray, "Gambling in Louisiana, it's a tradition!" www.tulane.edu/~rivgate/appendix.

63 *"Davis had arrived at the popular American formula"* Findlay, *People of Chance*, 61.

64 *"the anonymity of the riverboat"* Schwartz, *Roll the Bones*, 253.

64 *the professional gambler among them* Time-Life, *Gamblers of the Old West*, 55.

64 *By the 1830s, at least six hundred sharps* Tyler Bridges, *Bad Bet on the Bayou: The Rise and Fall of Gambling in Louisiana and the Fate of Governor Edwin Edwards* (New York: Farrar, Straus and Giroux, 2001), 8.

64 *as high as fifteen hundred* Schwartz, *Roll the Bones*, 253.

64 *"portrayed as members of groups out of social favor"* Findlay, *People of Chance*, 74.

64 *so much a part of riverboat life* Bridges, *Bad Bet on the Bayou*, 8; Schwartz, *Roll the Bones*, 253.

65 *As the gambler Tom Ellison recalled* Time-Life, *Gamblers of the Old West*, 61.

65 *Henry Hill recalled a game* Ibid., 54.

65 *In Melville's* The Confidence-Man Herman Melville, *The Confidence-Man* (1857; New York: Modern Library, 2003), 8–9.

65 *Thomas Thorpe, a reporter for* Harper's Thomas B. Thorpe, "Remembrances of the Mississippi," *Harper's New Monthly Magazine*, December 1855–May 1856.

65 *"an old black trunk"* Quoted in Gillespie, *Come Hell or High Water*, 137.
66 *"Steamboat Playing Cards"* James N. Anno, *An Encyclopedia of Draw Poker* (Jericho, NY: Exposition Press, 1973), 10; Leonard Schneir, *Gambling Collectibles* (Atglen, PA: Schiffer Publishing, 1993), 152.

8. The Cheating Game

68 *"Few people were literate enough"* Aaron Brown, *The Poker Face of Wall Street* (Hoboken: John Wiley, 2006), 325.
68 *a riverboat captain holding quad kings* Editors of Time-Life Books, *Gamblers of the Old West* (Richmond, VA: Time, Inc., 1996), 75.
68 *On a "foggy, wretched night"* Joe Cowell, *Thirty Years Passed Among the Players in England and America Interspersed with Anecdotes and Reminiscences . . . During the Theatrical Life of Joe Cowell, Comedian* (New York: Harper, 1844), quoted in James N. Anno, *An Encyclopedia of Draw Poker* (Jericho, NY: Exposition Press, 1973), 10–13.
70 *"The modern game of Draw-Poker"* *The American Hoyle* (New York: Dick & Fitzgerald, 1864), iii–iv.
70 *The* Hoyle *of 1845 spelled it "Poke"* 1845 *Hoyle* quoted at www.4gamesters .com/history-poker.htm.
70 *"one of the most dangerous pitfalls"* 1857 *Hoyle* quoted ibid.
70 *The 1864 Hoyle stated flatly* *The American Hoyle*, 172.
71 *compare the eleven pages spent on poker* Ibid., v–viii.
71 *George Washington kept detailed records* Willard Stern Randall, *George Washington: A Life* (New York: Henry Holt, 1997), 44–52.
71 *that whist was played "not for money"* Byron Liggett, "Benjamin Franklin: Printer, Patriot, Player," *Poker Player*, September 5, 2005.
72 *Robert Bailey, a lowborn Virginia rake* Jackson Lears, *Something for Nothing: Luck in America* (New York: Viking, 2003), 103–106.
73 *methods for "ringing in" a marked deck* Leonard Schneir, *Gambling Collectibles* (Atglen, PA: Schiffer Publishing, 1993), 74.
73 *George Devol, even hired black men* George H. Devol, *Forty Years a Gambler on the Mississippi* (1887; Bedford, MA: Applewood Books, 1996), 45.

9. Styles and Technologies of Cheating

75 *"It was dead easy money"* Editors of Time-Life Books, *Gamblers of the Old West* (Richmond, VA: Time, Inc., 1996), 48–49.
75 *enormous diamond pins known as "headlights"* Ibid., 54.
75 *The notorious James Ashby* Ibid.
75 *the biggest dandy of all* Ibid.
77 *Teammates also made a habit* Henry Chafetz, *Play the Devil: A History of Gambling in the United States from 1492 to 1950* (New York: Bonanza Books, 1960), 70.
77 *"Holding out one card"* Gary R. Brown, "The Science of Cheating at Cards," *American Heritage*, Summer 1998.
78 *"take all the chumps"* Ibid.
78 *P. J. Kepplinger, a San Francisco sharp* Ibid.
78 *Evans customers were encouraged* Leonard Schneir, *Gambling Collectibles* (Atglen, PA: Schiffer Publishing, 1993), 73.
78 *Cards marked with phosphorescent ink* Time-Life, *Gamblers of the Old West*, 120.

80 *As one sharp put it, "I knew that if [my victim]"* Ibid., 112.

80 *In Vicksburg in 1835* John A. Findlay, *People of Chance* (New York: Oxford University Press, 1980), 47.

80 *The theory behind these "club cards"* Brown, "The Science of Cheating at Cards."

80 *"smudgy movers"* Ibid.

81 *a thick dark paste called "gook"* Ibid.

81 *transfer a tiny smear of moisture* Ibid.

81 *a line of unglazed "Steamboat" decks* Ibid.

81 *Openly advertised in catalogs* Schneir, *Gambling Collectibles*, 66–82.

81 *Some sharps even worked as middlemen* Time-Life, *Gamblers of the Old West*, 117–27.

82 *"That's what went as gambling"* Ibid., 61.

10. Sharps Reformed and Unreconstructed

83 *tempered in the early '50s* John M. Findlay, *People of Chance* (New York: Oxford University Press, 1986), 95.

84 *"with prospecting for gold such a big gamble"* Daniel Walker Howe, *What Hath God Wrought: The Transformation of America, 1815–1848* (New York: Oxford University Press), 819.

84 *The lynching of five blacklegs in Vicksburg* David G. Schwartz, *Roll the Bones: The History of Gambling* (New York: Gotham, 2006), 252–53.

84 *learned to read a marked deck* Henry Chafetz, *Play the Devil: A History of Gambling in the United States from 1492 to 1950* (New York: Bonanza Books, 1960), 87.

84 *"the Cheating Game"* Ibid.

84 *a by-product of his conversion to Christianity* Ibid., 88–89.

85 Gambling Unmasked, The Gambler's Mirror Leonard Schneir, *Gambling Collectibles* (Atglen, PA: Schiffer Publishing, 1993), 157.

85 *Abridged editions were sold at his lectures* Chafetz, *Play the Devil*, 88.

85 *Green proclaimed from the podium* Ibid.

85 *"a wide-spread organization"* Ibid., 89.

86 *"men of wealth and influence"* Ibid., 90.

86 *"I am approached with the most opposite opinions"* Quoted in Susan Jacoby, *Freethinkers: A History of American Secularism* (New York: Metropolitan Books, 2004), 118.

86 *"not less than five millions"* Chafetz, *Play the Devil*, 91.

86 *the influential Whig broadsheet* Laurence Admiral Glasco, *Ethnicity and Social Structure: Irish, Germans, and Native-born of Buffalo, NY, 1850–1860* (Manchester, NH: Ayer Publishing, 1980), 288.

87 *remained behind in camp and cheated* Editors of Time-Life Books, *Gamblers of the Old West* (Richmond, VA: Time, Inc., 1996), 68–71.

87 *Grant indulged his tastes for alcohol and brag* Charles Bracelen Flood, *Grant and Sherman: The Friendship That Won the Civil War* (New York: Farrar, Straus and Giroux, 2005), 10.

87 *"Paymasters in the army were among the best suckers"* George H. Devol, *Forty Years a Gambler on the Mississippi* (Bedford, MA: Applewood Books, 1996), 211.

88 *bilking another paymaster out of $19,000* Ibid., 158.

88 *"After cheating all the soldiers I could"* Ibid., 20.

88 *I was on board the* Sultana   Ibid., 35–40.

89 *"The first lick he hit me"*   Ibid., 97.

89 *"Gentlemen, at last I have found my papa"*   Ibid., 98.

89 *Devol's guise as a planter was clinched*   Ibid., 45.

89 *cashed them in for $1,000 apiece*   Byron Liggett, "George Devol, King of the Riverboat Gamblers," *Poker Player*, May 29, 2006.

89 *"It is said of me that I have won more money"*   Time-Life, *Gamblers of the Old West*, 68.

89 *adhered to a code of "honor among thieves"*   Devol, *Forty Years a Gambler*, 355.

89 *"A gambler's word is as good as his bond"*   Ibid., 365–66.

90 *a "hook-nosed son of Abraham"*   Ibid., 267.

90 *"Simon! Simon!"*   Quoted in Time-Life, *Gamblers of the Old West*, 68.

11. Decks Cold and Colder

91 *Twain was mighty particular*   *New York Times*, September 9, 1912.

91 *scores of nineteenth-century books*   Leonard Schneir, *Gambling Collectibles* (Atglen, PA: Schiffer Publishing, 1993), 63–70; Rich McComas, *The Evolution of Poker: A Bibliography of 600+ Poker Books*, www.holdemsecrets.com/books.htm.

91 *Twain's "The Professor's Yarn"*   Mark Twain, *Life on the Mississippi* (1883; New York: Penguin, 1984), 268–73.

94 *"It was on a trip from Memphis to Natchez"*   *New York Sun* story reprinted in David A. Curtis, *Queer Luck: Poker Stories* (New York: Brentanos, 1899), 131–57.

94 *Twain was a truth teller*   Everett Emerson, *Mark Twain: A Literary Life* (Philadelphia: University of Pennsylvania Press, 2000), 41.

94 *Flash Kate enters the card room*   Curtis, *Queer Luck*, 137.

97 American Buffalo, *David Mamet's 1976 play*   David Mamet, *American Buffalo* (New York: Grove Press, 1977), 81–83.

12. The Mary Situation

99 *story published in the* New York Sun   David A. Curtis, *Queer Luck: Poker Stories* (New York: Brentanos, 1899), 99–108.

99 *Morton Smith Wilkinson*   bioguide.congress.gov/scripts/biodisplay.pl?index=W000476.

13. Look Away, Dixie Land

104 *Perhaps the best player in the district*   Aaron Brown, interview with the author, August 1, 2008.

104 *"practically all of the congressmen"*   Eugene Edwards, *Jackpots: Stories of the Great American Game* (New York: Jamieson-Higgins, 1900), 38.

105 *"nothing to do with their salaries"*   Ibid., 36–37.

105 *parents on opposite sides of the slavery question*   David McCullough, *Mornings on Horseback* (New York: Simon & Schuster, 2001), chaps. 1–2.

105 *"There is some of the onerest men here"*   www.civilwarhome.com.

106 *"between supper at 6:30 and lights out at 9:00"*   Neil Kagan and Stephen G. Hyslop, eds., *Eyewitness to the Civil War: The Complete History from Secession to Reconstruction* (Washington, DC: National Geographic Society, 2007), 180.

106 *usually featured patriotic imagery*   Leonard Schneir, *Gambling Collectibles* (At-
glan, PA: Schiffer Publishing, 1993), 138–43.

107 *Highlander decks produced by the L. I. Cohn Company*   Ibid.

107 *"To Commemorate the Greatest Event in Naval History"*   Henry Chafetz, *Play
the Devil: A History of Gambling in the United States from 1492 to 1950* (New
York: Bonanza Books, 1960), 256.

107 *agree that all four deuces were wild*   R. F. Foster, *Foster's Complete Hoyle* (New
York: Frederick Stokes, 1897), 222.

107 *Other variations in hand rank*   Ibid., 189–90.

107 *arrested by Union detective Lafayette Baker*   Chafetz, *Play the Devil*, 246.

108 *a monthlong stay in the capital of poker*   Carl Sandburg, *Abraham Lincoln: The
Prairie Years and the War Years* (New York: Harcourt, 1954), 22–25.

109 *an army of eleven thousand regulars*   Geoffrey C. Ward et al., *The Civil War: An
Illustrated History* (New York: Knopf, 1990), 81.

109 *the Royal Navy began fitting out its fleet*   Shelby Foote, *The Civil War, vol. 1, Fort
Sumter to Perryville* (New York: Random House, 1958), 157.

109 *Lincoln had a yarn*   Doris Kearns Goodwin, *Team of Rivals: The Political Genius
of Abraham Lincoln* (New York: Simon & Schuster, 2005), 398.

109 *"loaded to the muzzle"*   Ward, *The Civil War*, 81.

109 *Edward Bates confided in his diary*   Goodwin, *Team of Rivals*, 398–99.

109 *"One war at a time"*   Ibid., 399.

109 *"We must stick to American principles"*   Foote, *The Civil War*, 1:160.

110 *Lincoln responded with the yarn*   Sandburg, *Abraham Lincoln*, 269.

110 *"downright gall and wormwood"*   Foote, *The Civil War*, 1:162.

110 *"a pretty bitter pill to swallow"*   Goodwin, *Team of Rivals*, 711.

14. The Wizard

111 *black-bearded colonel*   www.statelib.lib.in.us.

111 *"So fierce did his passion become"*   William J. Stier, "Nathan Bedford Forrest,"
Civil War Times, December 1999.

112 *"No damned man kills me and lives"*   Geoffrey G. Ward et al., *The Civil War:
An Illustrated History* (New York: Knopf, 1990), 346.

112 *"Should my demand be refused"*   Shelby Foote, *The Civil War, vol. 3, Red River
to Appomattox* (New York: Random House, 1974), 109.

112 *"Keepin' the skeer on 'em"*   Ibid., 371.

112 *he was often compared to the devil*   Ibid., 374.

112 *At a prebattle parley*   Shelby Foote, *The Civil War, vol. 2, Fredericksburg to
Meridian* (New York: Random House, 1963), 185.

113 *the size of Forrest's regiment*   Ibid., 186.

113 *"Cheer up, Colonel"*   Randall Bedwell, *May I Quote You, General Forrest: Obser-
vations and Utterances of the South's Great Generals* (Nashville: Cumberland
House, 1997), 9.

113 *"hunted down and killed"*   Ward, *The Civil War*, 346.

113 *"He was the only Confederate cavalryman"*   Foote, *The Civil War*, 2:65.

113 *Forrest fought "by ear"*   Ward, *The Civil War*, 346.

113 *"gittin' thar fust with the most men"*   Bruce Catton, *The Civil War* (New York:
Mariner, 2004), 146.

113 *While Forrest went off on his next raid*   James M. McPherson, *The Battle Cry
of Freedom: The Civil War Era* (New York: Oxford University Press, 1988),
513.

113 *"We were all lying in camp"*   Stier, "Nathan Bedford Forrest."

114 *Forrest found himself in the midst of the enemy*   Ward, *The Civil War*, 121; Foote, *The Civil War*, 1:349–50.

114 *he "barely glanced up"*   Chambersburg, PA, *Valley Spirit*, June 8, 1864.

114 *"I'm really glad to see you"*   Ibid.

115 *Cushman was rescued by bluecoats*   Stewart Sifakis, *Who Was Who in the Civil War* (New York: Facts on File, 1988), 161.

115 *the nickname "Little Major"*   Michael Fitzpatrick, "Pauline Cushman, Union Spy," *Military Images*, May/June 2000, 4.

115 *Bragg had made "several grave mistakes"*   Ulysses S. Grant, *Memoirs and Selected Letters: Personal Memoirs of U.S. Grant/Selected Letters, 1839–1865* (New York: Library of America, 1990), 449.

115 *both imperious and incompetent*   McPherson, *The Battle Cry of Freedom*, 516–19.

115 *written dispute with* himself   Grant, *Memoirs*, 450.

115 *"You have threatened to arrest me"*   Foote, *The Civil War*, 2:813.

116 *"not the first sign of surrender was ever given"*   John Cimprich, *Fort Pillow: A Civil War Massacre, and Public Memory* (Baton Rouge: Louisiana State University Press, 2005), 102.

116 *"The slaughter was awful"*   Ibid., 81.

116 *"The river was dyed with the blood"*   Ward, *The Civil War*, 335.

116 *"You have been good soldiers"*   Foote, *The Civil War*, 3:1002.

117 *"Mary, in spite of her objections"*   W. J. Florence, *The Handbook of Poker* (London, 1892), 169.

117 *five German generals*   Frank Stroupe, "Nathan Bedford Forrest Biography," freeinfosociety.com.

117 *"That's a good thing"*   Jack Hurst, *Nathan Bedford Forrest: A Biography* (New York: Vintage, 1994), 284.

118 *"We have but one flag"*   Ibid., 367.

118 *Mahone ran a troop transport train*   Sifakis, *Who Was Who in the Civil War*, 428–29.

119 *"Bedlam in flames"*   Foote, *The Civil War*, 3:537.

119 *"When General Mahone held Virginia in his vest pocket"*   Charles William Calhoun, *Gilded Age Cato: The Life of Walter Q. Gresham* (Lexington: University Press of Kentucky, 1988), 67.

119 *In one session, Mahone had already anted*   Eugene Edwards, *Jackpots: Stories of the Great American Game* (New York: Jamieson-Higgins, 1900), 42–44.

120 *"Well, General," replied the man*   Ibid., 44.

15. Nary a Pair

121 *lost nearly all of the family's considerable fortune*   C. Stuart Chapman, *Shelby Foote: A Writer's Life* (Oxford: University of Mississippi Press, 2003), 20–21.

121 *"had every reason to expect"*   Ibid., 21.

122 *"He could play the best game of poker"*   Shelby Foote, *The Civil War*, vol. 2, *Fredericksburg to Meridian* (New York: Random House, 1963), 233.

122 *"All was* coleur de rose!*"*   Gene Smith, "The Destruction of Fighting Joe Hooker," *American Heritage*, October 1993.

122 *"a damned liar!"*   Ibid.

123 *"played Joseph Hooker like a fiddle"*   John Steele Gordon, *American Heritage* blog, January 19, 2007, www.americanheritage.com/blog/20071_17_24.shtml.

123 *probably been "a lot shorter"* Ibid.
123 *Lincoln shocked him by calling his bluff* Doris Kearns Goodwin, *Team of Rivals: The Political Genius of Abraham Lincoln* (New York: Simon & Schuster, 2005), 631–35.
124 *"Then, sir," replied Pemberton* Foote, *The Civil War*, 2:609–10.
124 *Foote declared that Pemberton "won"* Ibid., 610.
124 *As he wrote in his* Memoirs Ulysses S. Grant, *Memoirs and Selected Letters* (New York: Library of America, 1990), 129.
125 *"I have known a few men"* Ibid., 65.
125 *"an exalted opinion of his own military genius"* Ibid., 450.
125 *"all lion, none of the fox"* James M. McPherson, *The Battle Cry of Freedom: The Civil War Era* (New York: Oxford University Press, 1998), 753.
126 *"I seed Hood bet $2500"* Shelby Foote, *The Civil War, vol. 3, Red River to Appomattox* (New York: Random House, 1974), 424.
126 *"We must have peace"* www.rjgeib.com/thoughts/sherman/sherman-to-burn-atlanta.html.
126 *November 8, the* New York Times *declared* Goodwin, *Team of Rivals*, 664.
126 *including 70 percent* Ibid., 666.
127 *bushels of $1,000 CSA war bonds* Stanley P. Hirshson, *The White Tecumseh: A Biography of William Tecumseh Sherman* (New York: Wiley, 1997), 258.
127 *"until they were as crooked as a ram's horn"* Burke Davis, *Sherman's March: General William T. Sherman's Devastating March Through Georgia and the Carolinas* (New York: Vintage, 1988), 127.
127 *"Each of the two Presidents"* Foote, *The Civil War*, 772.
128 *At a meeting with Lincoln* Goodwin, *Team of Rivals*, 710–11.
128 *"I have always thought 'Dixie' one of the best tunes"* Foote, *The Civil War*, 3:958.

16. Aces and Eights

129 *Two-thirds of the value of Confederate assets* Heather Cox Richardson, *West from Appomattox: The Reconstruction of America After the Civil War* (New Haven: Yale University Press, 2007), 44–48.
129 *"spirit of lawlessness seems to pervade the town"* Ibid., 17–18.
130 *bestowed the nickname "Wolverines"* Robert M. Utley, *Cavalier in Buckskin: George Armstrong Custer and the Western Military Frontier* (Norman: University of Oklahoma Press, 1988), 15.
130 *Custer reported that "paying quantities"* Doane Robinson, *A History of the Dakota or Sioux Indians* (Pierre: South Dakota State Historical Society, 1904), 413.
130 *"THE NATIONAL DEBT TO BE PAID WHEN CUSTER RETURNS"* Byron Liggett, "Gambling in the U.S. Military," *Gambling Times*, Winter 2002.
130 *a long-haired gunman* James Bankes, "Wild Bill Hickok," *Wild West*, August 1996.
131 *bodyguard of a St. Louis abolitionist* www.nps.gov/archive/peri/hickock.htm.
131 *"I never let on that I was good shot"* George Ward Nichols, "Wild Bill," *Harper's New Monthly Magazine*, February 1867, 281.
131 *"before a heap of generals"* Ibid., 282.
131 *"Whether on foot or on horseback"* Joseph G. Rosa, *They Called Him Wild Bill: The Life and Adventures of James Butler Hickok* (Norman: University of Oklahoma Press, 1979), 111.
131 *"He was a delight to look upon"* Bankes, "Wild Bill Hickok."

131 *Hickok stood "six foot and an inch"* Nichols, "Wild Bill," 274.

132 *a game at the Old Southern Hotel* Rosa, *They Called Him Wild Bill*, 74.

132 *"I think you are wrong, Dave"* Ibid., 121.

132 "Fine, I'll just keep your watch" William E. Connelley, *Wild Bill and His Era: The Life and Adventures of James Butler Hickok* (1933; Whitefish, MT: Kessinger Publishing, 2008), 84–85. From "Old Southern Hotel" to "he acted in self-defense" is a summary of published accounts by Richard O'Connor, William E. Connelley, and Joseph G. Rosa gathered by Wikipedia under "Wild Bill Hickok–Davis Tutt shootout."

132 *"Do you not regret"* Rosa, *They Called Him Wild Bill*, 280.

132 *salary came to $150 a month* Ibid., 182.

133 *"Leave town on the eastbound train"* Ibid., 181.

133 *On June 8, the* Abilene Chronicle Ibid., 185.

133 *his headquarters was a well-lighted poker table* Margaret Odrowaz-Sypniewska, "James Butler Hickok," www.angelfire.com/mi4/polcrt/WBHickok.html.

133 *"The Marshal has, with his assistants"* Rosa, *They Called Him Wild Bill*, 199.

133 *gonorrheal ophthalmalia from one of the prostitutes* Ibid., 269.

133 *"put in most of his time playing poker"* Ibid., 219.

134 *Agnes was famous in her own right* Ibid., 236.

134 *it was "the middle of July"* Bankes, "Wild Bill Hickok."

134 *at a place called the Senate* Rosa, *They Called Him Wild Bill*, 322 (quoting the *Black Hills Pioneer*, November 11, 1876).

134 *Hickok had killed his loudmouth brother Lew* Ibid., 325.

134 *McCall had lost $110* Ibid., 296.

135 *"His head, which is covered by a thick crop"* *Chicago Inter-Ocean*, August 17, 1876.

135 *On July 17, he wrote* Rosa, *They Called Him Wild Bill*, 296.

135 *Rich "only laughed"* Ibid., 297.

135 *Massie was indulging his habit* Ibid., 298.

135 *encouraging him to knock it off* Bankes, "Wild Bill Hickok."

135 *Part of the bullet lodged in Massie's left wrist* Rosa, *They Called Him Wild Bill*, 298–99.

136 *"his fingers were still crimped up"* Frank J. Wilstach, *Wild Bill Hickok: The Prince of Pistoleers* (New York: Doubleday, 1926), 284–85.

136 *the August 3* Deadwood Traveler Rosa, *They Called Him Wild Bill*, 299.

136 *death by hanging on March 1, 1877* Kathy Weiser, "Jack McCall: Cowardly Killer of Wild Bill Hickok," www.legendsofamerica.com/WE-JackMcCall.html.

17. Early Draw Primers

138 *"Poker, unfortunately, is one of the few games"* Henry T. Winterblossom, *The Game of Draw Poker* (New York: W. H. Murphy, 1875), vi.

138 *"If they have never indulged in the game"* Ibid., 11.

139 *"Those who have winked"* Ibid., 72.

139 *"You discard the odd suit"* Ibid., v–vii.

139 *"It may then be set down as an axiom"* Ibid., viii.

140 *poker is "not only a selfish game"* Ibid., 10.

140 *"It is perfectly clear"* Ibid., 71.

141 *"So many cultivated men"* Quoted in John Stravinsky, ed., *Read 'Em and Weep: A Bedside Poker Companion* (New York: Harper, 2004), 46.

141 *"undetected roguery"* Ibid., 50.

141 *When holding a pair and drawing three new cards* Blackbridge's poker math is summarized and quoted in *The American Hoyle* (New York: Dick & Fitzgerald, 1864), 194–95.

141 *"Nearly all Poker-players"* Quoted in Stravinsky, *Read 'Em and Weep*, 52.

141 *along with such titles as* Poker Principles and Chance Laws List of titles from Rich McComas, *The Evolution of Poker: A Bibliography of 600+ Poker Books*, www.holdemsecrets.com/books.htm.

142 *"This young, wild-looking and crazy-acting hippie"* Doyle Brunson, *Doyle Brunson's Super System: A Course in Power Poker* (New York: Cardoza, 2002), 51.

142 *"Of course," Caro said* Ibid., 52.

142 *"High draw has not been solved"* Steve Zolotow, interview with the author, April 2, 2007.

18. Stud Poker

143 *"Five Card Stud—one down, four up"* Bruce Olds, *Bucking the Tiger* (New York: Farrar, Straus and Giroux, 2001), 104.

143 *began his professional life* Gary L. Roberts, *Doc Holliday: The Life and Legend* (New York: Wiley, 2007), 48–49.

143 *he had a few months to live* Karen Holliday Tanner, *Doc Holliday: A Family Portrait* (Norman: University of Oklahoma Press, 2001), 5.

143 *career in dentistry was cut short* John Myers, "Doc Holliday," www.kansasheritage.org/families/holliday.html.

144 *His weapons of choice* Roberts, *Doc Holliday*, 197, 323, 67.

144 *"the most skillful gambler"* Tanner, *Doc Holliday*, 232.

144 *won $40,000* Ben T. Traywick, "'Doc' Holliday," www.americanwest.com/pages/docholid.htm, 1996.

144 *the Budapest-born madam "Big Nose" Kate Horony* Roberts, *Doc Holliday*, 380, 392.

144 *two of the Earps were wounded* Ibid., 183–95.

144 *Five-card stud first cropped up* *The American Hoyle* (New York: Dick & Fitzgerald, 1864), 205.

144 *"that reckless period"* George Henry Fisher, *Stud Poker Blue Book: The Only Standard Authority* (1934; Las Vegas: Gambler's Book Club Press, 1983), 9.

145 *"a cowboy invention"* David Parlett, *The Oxford Guide to Card Games* (New York: Oxford University Press, 1990), 113.

145 *"specifically prohibited it"* Herbert Asbury, *Sucker's Progress* (1938; New York: Thunder's Mouth, 2003), 32–33.

146 *echo of "sold down the river"* Tom and Betsy Madden, interviews with the author, ca. 1962.

146 *"a philosophical side"* James Wickstead, *How to Win at Stud Poker* (1938; New York: Casino Press, 1976), 98.

147 *"Unless your hole card"* Ibid., 101.

147 *"presumption of the cards' mercy"* Ibid., 102.

147 *"It certainly is no particularly pleasant satisfaction"* Ibid., 103.

147 *"Play to win, or don't bother"* Olds, *Bucking the Tiger*, 108.

148 *"the simplest and, by general consent, dullest variety"* Parlett, *The Oxford Guide to Card Games*, 108.

19. High Plains Drifters

149 *a "petite 5'4" beauty"*   Byron Liggett, "Poker Alice: The Most Famous Female Frontier Gambler," *Poker Player,* July 10, 2006.

149 *the love of her life*   Mildred Fielder, *Poker Alice* (Deadwood, SD: Centennial Distributors, 1978), 11.

150 *Frank taught Alice to play poker*   "Poker Alice," sangres.com.

150 *"the most lawless"*   Herbert Asbury, *Sucker's Progress* (1938; New York: Thunder's Mouth, 2007), 342.

150 *Oscar Wilde's lecture tour of the West*   Richard Ellmann, *Oscar Wilde* (New York: Knopf, 1988), 204.

150 *netted about $225,000*   Liggett, "Poker Alice."

150 *a taste for fat stogies*   "Poker Alice," sangres.com; photograph, www.sd4history .com/Unit4/images/PokerAlice.jpg.

151 *pawned her wedding ring*   Liggett, "Poker Alice."

151 *Called Poker's Palace*   Ibid.

151 *"I went to the bank for a $2,000 loan"*   "Poker Alice," sangres.com.

152 *"well preserved and remarkable"*   Bill Bulow, unpublished autobiography, courtesy of his grandson, Skip Plotnicki.

152 *"At my age I suppose I should be knitting"*   "Poker Alice," sangres.com.

152 *Pettigrew acquired his reputation*   W. J. Florence, *The Handbook of Poker* (London, 1892), 148–50.

153 *"What in thunder did you draw to?"*   Ibid.

153 *known as the Statesmen's Game*   Ibid.

153 *an outlaw and a gentleman*   Leonard Lund, "Poker Jim Dropped In," *Minot Daily News,* February 24, 1973, 11.

153 *"It was almost impossible to drag him away"*   Kim Fundingsland, "The Legend of Poker Jim," *Minot Daily News,* December 16, 2006.

153 *W Bar was a highly profitable operation*   Lund, "Poker Jim Dropped In."

154 *"the chance to find a poker game in Glendive"*   Fundingsland, "The Legend of Poker Jim."

154 *found Jim's body nine miles from camp*   Lund, "Poker Jim Dropped In."

154 *crashed onto the rickety table below*   Ibid.

20. Cowboys Play Poker

155 *beneath a portrait of Colonel Theodore Roosevelt*   en.wikipedia.org/wiki/ Image:GWBrooseveltWHSSA.jpg.

155 *"extraordinarily attractive, slender, graceful"*   David McCullough, *Mornings on Horseback* (New York: Simon & Schuster, 2001), 220.

156 *"It was a grim and evil fate"*   www.theodoreroosevelt.org/life/timeline.

156 *leading inspection tours*   McCullough, *Mornings on Horseback,* 293.

156 *recommended "the strenuous life"*   Theodore Roosevelt, "The Strenuous Life," speech before the Hamilton Club, Chicago, April 10, 1899, www.bartleby .com/58/1.html.

156 *"undergo the monotonous drudgery"*   Theodore Roosevelt, *Ranch Life and the Hunting Trail,* illus. Frederic Remington (New York: Century Co., 1918), 26.

156 *needed time for reading and writing*   Ibid., 36.

156 *Frederic Remington, for making sketches*   McCullough, *Mornings on Horseback,* 337.

157 *"quiet, rather self-contained men"* Roosevelt, *Ranch Life and the Hunting Trail*, 10.

157 *went on their "sprees"* Ibid.

157 *played too much poker, drank too much whiskey* Ibid., 90–91; McCullough, *Mornings on Horseback*, 319.

157 *"If a man is built like that Prince boy"* Owen Wister, *The Virginian* (New York: Macmillan, 1904), 124.

157 *the First U.S. Volunteer Cavalry* Edmund Morris, *The Rise of Theodore Roosevelt* (New York: Coward, McCann, 1979), 643–49.

157 *"an American mosaic of cowboys"* John Allen Gable, "Theodore Roosevelt," www.trthegreatnewyorker.com/writer/theodore_roosevelt.htm.

157 *"quite a number of professional gamblers"* Theodore Roosevelt, *The Rough Riders* (New York: Scribner, 1899), 45.

158 *"a splendid little war"* G.J.A. O'Toole, *The Spanish War: An American Epic* (New York: Norton, 1986), 17.

158 *a Square Deal, promising that all Americans* Edmund Morris, *Theodore Rex* (New York: Random House, 2001), 233.

158 *the "value of empire"* Jackson Lears, *Something for Nothing: Luck in America* (New York: Viking, 2003), 218.

158 *Roosevelt's 1901 interview with Pat Garrett* Morris, *Theodore Rex*, 66–67.

159 *"A charge of gambling"* "Mr. Davis Loses at Draw Poker," *New York Times*, September 30, 1880.

160 *"It is not to play faro"* "Where Cards Are Played," *New York Times*, May 9, 1886.

160 *"Poker-playing is found to be a source of trouble"* "Gossip of the Clubs," *New York Times*, November 20, 1887.

161 *"Nothing that the Americans"* "Ravages of Poker in Vienna," reprinted in *New York Times*, August 18, 1898.

161 *to be banned—unsuccessfully* David M. Hayano, *Poker Faces: The Life and Work of Professional Card Players* (Berkeley: University of California Press, 1982), 168.

161 *"permitted the prisoners, criminal and civil"* *New York Times*, July 31, 1895.

161 *"play was resumed and it continued"* *New York Times*, March 18, 1900.

161 *"The Hyphen," as the hotel was known* Tom and Betsy Madden, interviews with the author.

162 *"I liked being with them"* Michael Munn, *John Wayne: The Man Behind the Myth* (New York: NAL, 2004), 42.

162 *the Young Men's Purity, Abstinence and Snooker Pool Association* Randy Roberts and James S. Olson, *John Wayne: American* (Lincoln: University of Nebraska Press, 1997), 113.

162 *"the westerns were especially fun"* Byron Liggett, "John Wayne: Gambler, Gunslinger, Great American," *Poker Player*, July 1, 2005.

162 *the dogs that played Lassie* Matthew Valencia, "A Big Deal," *The Economist*, December 19, 2007, 38.

162 *Wayne returned the dogs* Liggett, "John Wayne: Gambler, Gunslinger, Great American."

162 *a screening room, wet bar, and poker table* Roberts and Olson, *John Wayne: American*, 506.

21. Dogs Playing Poker

164 *born in upstate New York in 1844* www.dogsplayingpoker.org/bio/coolidge/bio1.html.

164 *invented what he called "comic foregrounds"* Ibid.

165 *also bought work from Charles Russell* www.brownandbigelow.com/BBCorp Website/history.htm.

165 *humanized dogs weren't unusual* Moira Harris, "It's a Dog's World, According to Coolidge," in Jake Austen, ed., *A Friendly Game of Poker* (Chicago: Chicago Review Press, 2003), 166–67.

165 The Poker Night, *in fact* Donald Spoto, *The Kindness of Strangers: The Life of Tennessee Williams* (New York: Da Capo, 1997), 118.

166 *"poker literature is assuming formidable proportions"* New York Times, February 12, 1875, 4.

166 *"Poker, yachting, hunting"* Reprinted in *The New York Times*, December 10, 1882, 12.

167 *"an almost continuous poker game"* David McCullough, *Truman* (New York: Simon & Schuster, 1972), 136.

168 *Critics have ranked them as icons* Annette Ferrara, "Lucky Dog! The Art History of C. M. Coolidge's Dogs Playing Poker," *TENbyTEN*, no. 10: Luck; Harris, "It's a Dog's World."

168 *When the gavel came down* money.cnn.com/2005/02/16/poker_dogs.

168 Dogs Playing Polka payplay.fm/blpc.

22. The Mirror, the Riffle, the Shift, and the Shark

169 *"Card sharping has been reduced to a science"* Quoted in Gary R. Brown, "The Science of Cheating at Cards," *American Heritage*, Summer 1998.

171 *Secretary of State Elihu Root* Edmund Morris, *Theodore Rex* (New York: Random House, 2001), 431.

172 *"it is the inclination of most all poker players"* Theodore Hardison, *Poker* (St. Louis: Hardison Publishing, 1914), 4.

172 *"solely for the protection of lovers of card games"* Ibid., 5–6.

173 *"The performer generally makes some pretense"* Ibid., 24.

173 *"when quite a young boy"* Ibid., 8–9.

173 *"envy rather than of founded suspicion"* Ibid., 22.

23. The Education of a Poker Player, Part 1

176 *its 1,450 residents* David Kahn, *The Reader of Gentlemen's Mail: Herbert O. Yardley and the Birth of American Codebreaking* (New Haven, CT: Yale University Press, 2004), 1.

176 *his mother suddenly died of* Ibid., 2.

176 *a game he had learned from his grandfather* Herbert O. Yardley, *The Education of a Poker Player* (New York: Simon & Schuster, 1957), 90.

176 *"It is one thing to face eleven football opponents"* Ibid., 5.

176 *"I figure the odds for every card I draw"* Ibid., 52.

177 *"about twenty feet square"* Ibid., 3–4.

177 The walls of Monty's office were hung Ibid., 11.

177 *"My own uncle, a giant of a man"* Ibid., vi.

178 the *"seventy-five percent"* Monty deems Ibid., 15–17.

178 *allowed to play "open"* Ibid., 5.

178 *When One-Eye Jones, a stud player from Indy* Ibid., 46–50.

179 *"essentially we are no different"* Ibid., 22.

179 *they'd never known him to lie or cheat* Kahn, *The Reader of Gentlemen's Mail*, 5.

179 *"went back to subduing the Indians"* Ibid., 16.

180 *"worth four divisions to the British Army"* Ibid., 46.

180 *"helped push the United States into war"* Ibid., 20.

180 *"By lifting my eyes"* Ibid., 9.

181 *"the rare gift of originality of mind"* Ibid., 29.

181 *"Overnight," writes Kahn, "cryptology outgrew"* Ibid., 45.

181 *bet hands of draw in his sleep* Frank E. Vandiver, *Black Jack: The Life and Times of John J. Pershing* (College Station: Texas A & M University Press, 1977), 64.

181 *photograph shows four French and British soldiers* John Ellis, *Eye-Deep in Hell: Trench Warfare in World War I* (New York: Pantheon, 1976), 194.

182 *"To keep from going crazy"* David McCullough, *Truman* (New York: Simon & Schuster, 1992), 136.

182 *returned to his grandsons Lloyd and Bill* "Watch Lost in WWI Returned to Grandsons," Associated Press, June 8, 2007.

182 *his opposite numbers at the Ritz and the Crillon* Kahn, *The Reader of Gentlemen's Mail*, 45, 48.

182 *an unfortunate tendency to drop names* Ibid., 46.

182 *beautiful black-haired dancer named Jacqueline* Ibid., 47–48.

182 *ambulances to take overserved guests* Ibid.

182 *left a briefcase full of highly confidential documents* Ibid., 48–49.

182 *"the large and constant stream of information"* Ibid., 50.

183 *"As the doughboy said when his grandmother"* George Henry Fisher, *Stud Poker Blue Book: The Only Standard Authority* (1934; Las Vegas: Gambler's Book Club Press, 1983), 3.

183 *"hot dogs, beer, and women"* J. Kossuth, "How Cobb Played the Game," wso.williams.edu/~jkossuth/cobb/index.html.

183 *"I was young and rather innocent"* Jonathan Eig, *Luckiest Man: The Life and Death of Lou Gehrig* (New York: Simon & Schuster, 2005), 165.

184 *"Koshi, Washington URGENT 0073"* Kahn, *The Reader of Gentlemen's Mail*, 77–79.

184 *"Stud poker is not a very difficult game"* Ibid., 79.

185 *"out of a practically unknown field"* Ibid., 82.

185 *"exceptionally meritorious and distinguished services"* Ibid., 81.

185 *"Gentlemen do not read each other's mail"* Ibid., 98.

24. Hump Guns Down Brain over Stud Debt!

186 *have Jackson posthumously inducted* www.thepetitionsite.com/takeaction/100066978.

186 *inducted ten years later into the Poker Hall of Fame* www.thepokerforum.com/pokerhalloffame.htm.

187 *four Louisville Grays had been expelled* Daniel A. Nathan, *Saying It's So: A Cultural History of the Black Sox Scandal* (Champaign: University of Illinois Press, 2002), 16.

187 *"The men who ran professional baseball"* Daniel A. Nathan, "The Big Fix: Arnold Rothstein Rigged the 1919 World Series. Or Did He?" *Legal Affairs*, March/April 2004.

187 *"Abe Attell did the fixing"* Eliot Asinof, *Eight Men Out* (New York: Henry Holt, 1963), 219.

187 *"If nine guys go to bed with a girl"* Ibid., 30.

188 *"This is America, not Jerusalem"* Leo Katcher, *The Big Bankroll: The Life and Times of Arnold Rothstein* (New York: Da Capo, 1994), 20.
188 *Rothstein's nicknames* David Pietrusza, *Rothstein: The Life, Times, and Murder of the Criminal Genius Who Fixed the 1919 World Series* (New York: Carroll & Graf, 2003), 17ff.
188 *conducted business standing on the corner* Ibid., 3–7.
188 *played in the biggest poker games* Ibid., 8, 21, 136.
188 *George "Hump" McManus* Katcher, *The Big Bankroll*, 320.
188 *"Titanic" Thompson, up from Arkansas* Pietrusza, *Rothstein*, 9–14.
189 *By dawn on Monday, A.R. owed Thompson* Ibid., 10.
189 *"I think, my friends"* Ibid., 11.
189 *"That's A.R.," he said.* Katcher, *The Big Bankroll*, 321.
189 *Bernstein's Hall of Fame bio* www.thepokerforum.com/pokerhalloffame.htm.
190 *"Arnold, rigged or not, you have to pay"* Pietrusza, *Rothstein*, 11.
190 *"I'm not going to give them a cent"* Ibid., 12.
190 *Rothstein was worth several million dollars* Katcher, *The Big Bankroll*, 319.
190 *"They'll get their money"* Ibid., 329.
190 *"Keep this for me"* Ibid., 3.
191 *Colt .38 Detective Special* Pietrusza, *Rothstein*, 284.
191 *taken to Polyclinic Hospital* Katcher, *The Big Bankroll*, 330.
191 *Irish detective Patrick Flood* Ibid., 6.
191 *"Me Mudder did it"* Laura Ward, *Famous Last Words* (New York: Sterling, 2004), 64.
191 *bet heavily on Herbert Hoover* Pietrusza, *Rothstein*, 5.

25. The Education of a Poker Player, Part 2

193 *"I felt very small in my rags"* David Kahn, *The Reader of Gentlemen's Mail: Herbert O. Yardley and the Birth of American Codebreaking* (New Haven, CT: Yale University Press, 2004), xviii.
193 *"I could do no more than stare"* Ibid., xix.
194 *"intelligence into a significant instrument of war"* Kahn, *The Reader of Gentlemen's Mail*, 20.
194 *Yardley "never sold information"* Ibid., 24.
194 *Yardley "sold his soul"* Ibid., x.
195 *Enigma-type machine code-named "Red"* Frank J. Rafalko, ed., *A Counterintelligence Reader* (Washington, DC: National Counterintelligence Center, 2004), vol. 2, chapter 2.
195 *Major Yardley's Secret Ink, Inc.* Kahn, *The Reader of Gentlemen's Mail*, 163.
195 *"Three-Fingered HOY"* Ibid.
195 *"In view of the state of excitement"* Ibid., 159.
195 *"as bad as it could be"* Ibid., 161.
195 *HR 4220, "For the Protection of Government Records"* Ibid.
196 *"I think everybody is pretty well convinced"* Ibid., 171.
196 *"MGM offered me ten thousand dollars"* Ibid., 174.
196 *"one of the numerous intimate expensive dancing joints"* Ibid., 193.
197 *reviewer for* The New York Times *was impressed* Andre Sennwald, *New York Times*, October 26, 1935.
197 *"Movies were seldom written"* Kahn, *The Reader of Gentlemen's Mail*, 178–79.
197 *his desire to help avenge* Ibid., 187–88.
198 *"While studying a series of kana"* Ibid., 193.

198 *"an extremely witty man"* Yardley, *The Education of a Poker Player*, 95.
199 *"everyone knew his real name"* Ibid., 128.
199 *"I'll play with you no more!"* Ibid., 93–94.
199 *"I became a marked man in the Orient"* Ibid., 71.
199 *"a proto–James Bond"* Anthony Holden, *Big Deal: One Year as a Professional Poker Player* (New York: Viking, 1990), 97.

26. The Secretary, the President, His Wife, and Her Lover

200 *"How about another sippy?"* Jon Meacham, *Franklin and Winston: An Intimate Portrait of an Epic Friendship* (New York: Random House, 2003), 145.
200 *a game of low-stakes poker* Doris Kearns Goodwin, *No Ordinary Time: Franklin and Eleanor Roosevelt—The Home Front in World War II* (New York: Simon & Schuster, 1994), 33.
200 *Eleanor Roosevelt adamantly refused* Ibid., 21.
200 *his love affair with Lucy Mercer* Joseph Persico, *Franklin and Lucy: President Roosevelt, Mrs. Rutherford, and the Other Remarkable Women in His Life* (New York: Random House, 2008), 11, 122–30.
200 *presidential secretary Marguerite "Missy" LeHand* Goodwin, *No Ordinary Time*, 119.
201 *"Missy was in love with her boss"* Ibid., 20–21.
201 *"no symptoms of impotentia coeundi"* Persico, *Franklin and Lucy*, 165.
201 *"Everyone in the closely knit inner circle"* Goodwin, *No Ordinary Time*, 121.
201 *Regulars in the poker games* Ibid., 119, 159–60; Robert H. Jackson, *That Man: An Insider's Portrait of Franklin D. Roosevelt* (New York: Oxford University Press, 2003), 75–77, 153–62; Jean Edward Smith, *FDR* (New York: Random House, 2007), 439.
201 *a cigar-smoking AP reporter* Doris Kearns Goodwin, 109th Landon Lecture, Kansas State University, April 22, 1997.
201 *"I wish I could lie down"* Persico, *Franklin and Lucy*, 204.
201 *"I remember your eyes"* Goodwin, *No Ordinary Time*, 221.
201 *the president usually chose either seven-card stud* Jonathan Alter, *The Defining Moment: FDR's Hundred Days and the Triumph of Hope* (New York: Simon & Schuster, 2006), 241.
201 *Woolworth's* Smith, *FDR*, 439.
201 *Jackson lost only $2.30* Jackson, *That Man*, 146.
201 *"the worst I've ever eaten"* Quoted in Smith, *FDR*, 336.
202 *$1-limit affair* Ibid., 439.
202 *"an exchange of much conversation but little money"* Jackson, *That Man*, 141.
202 *"the Powder River rules"* Ibid., 143.
202 *"studied the players as much as he did the cards"* Ibid.
202 *poker winnings exceeded his congressional salary* John S. Cooper, "Cactus Jack Garner: Not Worth a Bucket of Warm . . . ," www.suite101.com.
202 *"just for conversation"* Smith, *FDR*, 338.
202 *"the worst damn fool mistake I ever made"* Cooper, "Cactus Jack Garner."
203 *"America of the Civil War and America of the Nuclear Age"* Alistair Cooke, quoted in George F. Will, "In Cactus Jack's Footsteps," *Jewish World Review*, January 6, 2000.
203 *"forgotten man at the bottom of the economic pyramid"* Franklin Roosevelt, radio address, April 7, 1932.

203 *"Establish a strict limit"* James M. Wickstead, *How to Win at Stud Poker* (New York: Casino Press, 1984), 99.

203 *"loses his ability to diagnose"* Ibid., 98.

203 *"It was the president's custom"* Goodwin, *No Ordinary Time*, 159–60.

204 *"matters in Europe"* Jackson, *That Man*, 76.

204 *"While Roosevelt continually renewed his energies"* Goodwin, *No Ordinary Time*, 419.

204 *"The Fuhrer seems to have aged 15 years"* Ibid., 420.

204 the fuhrer had developed *"severe stomach cramps"* John Toland, *Adolf Hitler: The Definitive Biography* (New York: Doubleday, 1976), 402.

204 *"I have to relax before [bed]"* Ibid., 815–16.

205 sections of a map indicating escape routes www.loc.gov/preserv/bachbase/images/203.2.jpg

205 *Hitler, as the joker* Byron Liggett, "Gambling in the U.S. Military," *Gambling Times*, Winter 2002–2003.

205 *Davis made young "Ike" memorize poker odds* Carlo D'Este, *Eisenhower: A Soldier's Life* (New York: Henry Holt, 2002), 25.

205 *"He dinned percentages into my head night after night"* Quoted in Matthew F. Holland, *Eisenhower Between the Wars: The Making of a Gentleman and Statesman* (Westport, CT: Greenwood Publishing Group, 2001), 61.

205 attended *"cadet dances only now and then"* Dwight D. Eisenhower, *At Ease: Stories I Tell My Friends* (Garden City, NY: Doubleday, 1967), www.eisenhower.archives.gov; Dwight D. Eisenhower with Edwin Corbin, *In Review: Pictures I've Kept* (New York: Doubleday, 1969), 15.

205 *courted the hard-to-get Mamie Doud* Stephen Ambrose, *Eisenhower: Soldier and President* (New York: Simon & Schuster, 1991), 30.

205 *Sitting down in one game* D'Este, *Eisenhower*, 98.

205 *replica of his West Point class ring* Ibid., 101.

206 *Eisenhower had stood his ground* Ibid., 129.

206 *"This was not achieved easily"* Eisenhower, *At Ease*; "Presidential Poker: Dwight D. Eisenhower," *Poker News*, April 27, 2005.

206 *dummy paratroopers dropped by the SAS* Stephen Ambrose, *D-Day: June 6, 1944: The Climactic Battle of World War II* (New York: Simon & Schuster, 1994), 302.

206 *"the favorite boredom killer"* Ibid., 155.

206 *Hemingway, Irwin Shaw, the photographer Robert Capa* Ibid., 172.

206 *"it was considered very bad form"* Quoted in Alex Kershaw, *Blood and Champagne: The Life and Times of Robert Capa* (New York: Macmillan, 2002), 117.

206 *"like nothing I'd ever seen before"* Ambrose, *D-Day*, 533.

207 *"Fellas, some of us are never getting out of this"* Ibid., 171.

207 *"I don't know that anybody has ever invented a word"* Robert Morgan and Ron Powers, *The Man Who Flew the* Memphis Belle: *Memoir of a WWII Bomber Pilot* (New York: Dutton, 2001), 13.

27. The Education of a Poker Player, Part 3

209 *fine organizer who had "perhaps suffered unduly"* David Kahn, *The Reader of Gentlemen's Mail: Herbert O. Yardley and the Birth of American Codebreaking* (New Haven, CT: Yale University Press, 2004), 203.

209 *"the attack might never have occurred"* "Herbert Yardley, Cryptographer, Dies; Broke Japan's Diplomatic Code in 1921," *New York Times*, August 8, 1958.

209 *"Canada recovered. Yardley did not"* Kahn, *The Reader of Gentlemen's Mail*, 215.

209 *broke its newsstand record* Ibid., 233.

209 *"like one big-assed bird"* Ibid., 234.

209 *"What Goren and Vanderbilt have done"* www.highstakespublishing.co.uk/titles.php/itemcode/5.

210 *dim-witted boss, who is known as "the Donkey"* Herbert O. Yardley, *The Education of a Poker Player* (New York: Simon & Schuster, 1957), 78.

210 *Monty and sixteen-year-old Herb watch* Ibid., 59–61.

210 *"was disinherited because of his poker debts"* Ibid., 18.

210 *"The Gold-Bug"* Kahn, *The Reader of Gentlemen's Mail*, 10.

211 *"Most persons successful in cryptology"* Yardley, *The Education of a Poker Player*, 87–89.

211 *"Because of his insolence I dragged the money in"* Ibid., 89.

211 *came to be known as Old Adhesive* Kahn, *The Reader of Gentlemen's Mail*, 232.

211 *"A good player develops the patience to wait"* David Sklansky, *The Theory of Poker* (Henderson, NV: Two Plus Two, 1994), 6.

212 *its "smoke-filled pages"* Yardley, *The Education of a Poker Player*, foreword by Ian Fleming (London: High Stakes Publishing, 2005), 4–6.

212 *"I had a marriage I could not handle"* Quoted in Anthony Holden, *Big Deal: One Year as a Professional Poker Player* (New York: Viking, 1990), 97.

28. The Buck Stops with Vinson—or Winston

214 *the president had less than a year to live* Doris Kearns Goodwin, *No Ordinary Time: Franklin and Eleanor Roosevelt* (New York: Simon & Schuster, 1994), 495.

214 *"I hardly know Truman"* David McCullough, *Truman* (New York: Simon & Schuster, 1992), 304.

215 *seeing both Missy LeHand* Goodwin, *No Ordinary Time*, 286–87, 600–602; Joseph Persico, *Franklin and Lucy* (New York: Random House, 2008), 163–66, 312–40.

215 *"Bring out our best champagne!"* William L. Shirer, *The Rise and Fall of the Third Reich* (New York: Simon & Schuster, 1960), 1110.

216 *Truman had learned to play cards* McCullough, *Truman*, 40.

216 *"I like to play cards and dance"* Raymond H. Geselbracht, "Harry Truman, Poker Player," *Prologue*, 35, no. 1 (Spring 2003), www.archives.gov/publications/prologue/2003/spring/truman-poker.html.

216 *artillery training in Montigny-sur-Aube* McCullough, *Truman*, 114.

216 *a cascade of creatively violent profanity* Ibid., 123.

217 *chase Vaughan "out of a hand"* Robert G. Nixon, oral history interview with Harry Vaughan, Truman Library, www.trumanlibrary.org/oralhist/nixon.htm.

217 *Bruce Lambert called him a "chump"* Robert G. Nixon, oral history interview with Bruce Lambert, Truman Library, www.trumanlibrary.org/oralhist/nixon.htm.

217 *"Anything, you know, like women"* McCullough, *Truman*, 435.

218 *"running a straight stud filibuster"* Anthony Holden, *Big Deal: One Year as a Professional Poker Player* (New York: Viking, 1990), 194.

218 *"You know I'm almost like a kid"* Geselbracht, "Harry Truman, Poker Player."

218 *Clifford was charged with organizing the games* Ibid.

218 *Ten percent of each pot went into a "poverty bowl"* Ibid.

218 *Truman "loved wild games"* Nixon, oral history interviews.

219 *"lean over and look at my cards"* Geselbracht, "Harry Truman, Poker Player."
219 *"Truman just couldn't bear to fold"* Robert G. Nixon, oral history interview with Randall Jessee, Truman Library, www.trumanlibrary.org/oralhist/nixon .htm.
219 *"Well, we're going to play Vinson now"* Ibid.
219 *loved the "vitality in the game"* Geselbracht, "Harry Truman, Poker Player."
219 *when Churchill joined Truman's game* McCullough, *Truman*, 488.
220 *Churchill was down $250* Jack Kelly, "Poker," *American Heritage*, November/ December 2006, www.americanheritage.com/articles/web/20061219-poker -gambling.shtml.
220 *"do nothing but good"* McCullough, *Truman*, 488.

29. Cold War Poker

221 *mathematician who had fled Nazi persecution in Germany* Nathan Myhrvold, "John von Neumann," *Time*, March 21, 1999.
222 *"On the Theory of Parlor Games"* Adam Brandenburger and Elizabeth Stein, "The Work of John von Neumann (1903–1957)," mayet.som.yale.edu/ coopetition/vN.html.
222 *"la théorie du jeu"* Ibid.
222 *Morgenstern and von Neumann decided to cowrite* Maria Joao Cardoso De Pina Cabral, "John von Neumann's Contribution to Economic Science," *International Social Science Review*, Fall–Winter 2003, findarticles.com/p/articles/ mi_moIMR/is_/ai_113139424?tag=artBody;col1., 4.
223 *analyze business models, poker hands* Robert J. Leonard, "From Parlor Games to Social Science: von Neumann, Morgenstern, and the Creation of Game Theory, 1928–1944," *Journal of Economic Literature* 33 (June 1995): 730–61.
223 *Kistiakowsky said their play was so weak at first* Richard Rhodes, *The Making of the Atomic Bomb* (New York: Simon & Schuster, 1986), 566.
223 *especially the poker players among them* John von Neumann, Letter to Lt. Col. Wade M. Jackson, March 26, 1953, courtesy of George Dyson.
223 *"the bombing of which"* Rhodes, *The Making of the Atomic Bomb*, 626–30.
223 *we needed to make Japan* Henry Stimson, "The Decision to Use the Atomic Bomb," *Harper's*, February 1947.
224 *called the bomb the "master card"* Henry Stimson, "Hiroshima diary," May 15, 1945, Henry Lewis Stimson Papers, Manuscripts and Archives, Yale University Library.
224 *"a royal straight flush"* Ibid., May 14, 1945.
224 *"Anything that's based on the theory of games"* Quoted in Fred I. Greenstein, *The Hidden Hand Presidency: Eisenhower as Leader* (Baltimore: Johns Hopkins University Press, 1994), 26.
225 *"The Cold War is sometimes compared"* Oskar Morgenstern, "Cold War Is Cold Poker," *New York Times Magazine*, February 5, 1961, 14, 21–22.
226 *"Unquestionably the most successful bluff"* Ibid.
226 *"destroy Red China's military potential"* Ibid.
227 *"can be analysed in almost uncanny detail"* Anthony Holden, *Big Deal: One Year as a Professional Poker Player* (New York: Viking, 1990), 195.
227 *"In no sense did Khrushchev"* John Lewis Gaddis, *We Now Know: Rethinking Cold War History* (New York: Oxford University Press, 1998), 223.
227 *"folded his hand and conceded the pot"* Holden, Big Deal, 195.

227 *remove our fifteen medium-range Jupiter missiles* Michael Dobbs, *One Minute to Midnight: Kennedy, Khrushchev, and Castro on the Brink of Nuclear War* (New York: Knopf, 2008), 233–34, 270.

227 *"As in poker," writes Morgenstern* Morgenstern, "Cold War Is Cold Poker."

30. Dowling and Kriegel, Blotzsky and Witherspoon

229 *In the press room of Baton Rouge City Hall* Allen Dowling, *The Great American Pastime* (South Brunswick, NJ: A. S. Barnes, 1970), 45–55.

230 *"Poker's too deadly an exercise"* Ibid., 53.

230 *Perhaps the grimmest game* Ibid., 168–70.

231 *When Dowling "had recovered what I'd lost"* Ibid., 159.

231 *"reluctant to put greenbacks into circulation"* Ibid., 162–63.

231 *As for his fellow ink-stained wretches* Ibid., 173.

231 *"resolved that when my judgment"* Ibid., 50.

232 *"Witherspoon may have you classed as a tough hombre"* Ibid., 52.

232 *"they figured it was their duty"* Ibid., 167.

233 *Downsides include "silly" games* Ibid., 178.

233 *"poverty" or "Depression" poker* Tom and Betsy Madden, interviews with the author.

233 *"I don't believe there is anything equal to the rattle"* Dowling, *The Great American Pastime*, 160–61.

234 *a Louisiana state senator* Ibid., 164.

234 *describes the rites of passage* Leonard Kriegel, "Poker's Promise," *New York Times Magazine*, July 5, 1992, reprinted in John Stravinsky, ed., *Read 'Em and Weep* (New York: Harper, 2004), 136–38.

234 *"opportunity may knock, but it seldom nags"* David Mamet, "Things I Have Learned Playing Poker on the Hill," *Writing in Restaurants* (New York: Viking, 1986), 96.

31. The Legend of Johnny and the Greek

237 *saying it was 1949 and another saying 1951* 1949: Don Jenkins, *Johnny Moss: Poker's Finest Champion of Champions* (Las Vegas: JM Press, 1981), 1; 1951: Jon Bradshaw, *Fast Company* (New York: Vintage, 1987), 17.

237 *Regulars at his casino included H. L. Hunt* Sally Denton and Roger Morris, *The Money and the Power: The Making of Las Vegas and Its Hold on America, 1947–2000* (New York: Knopf, 2001), 32.

237 *Benny's reputation as a "square craps fader"* Ibid., 31.

237 *"I was never a real good poker player"* Mary Ellen Glass, *Lester Ben "Benny" Binion—Some Recollections of a Texas and Las Vegas Gaming Operator* (Reno: University of Nevada Oral History Program, 1976), 13.

237 *"There's no way in the world I'd harm anybody"* Ibid., 30–31.

238 *Benny was targeted for hits* Denton and Morris, *The Money and the Power*, 31–33.

238 *the eleven times he'd survived attempts* Ibid., 35.

238 *"the art of civilized bushwhacking"* David M. Hayano, *Poker Faces: The Life and Work of Professional Card Players* (Berkeley: University of California Press, 1982), 147.

238 *poker in Vegas took place in ring games* A. Alvarez, *The Biggest Game in Town* (New York: Houghton Mifflin, 1983), 28.

239 *"He recited poetry"* Jonathan Grotenstein and Storms Reback, *All-In: The (Almost) Entirely True Story of the World Series of Poker* (New York: St. Martin's, 2005), 14–15.

239 *"Dealin' from the bottom of the pack"* Alvarez, *The Biggest Game in Town*, 28.

240 *"What are you going to do, Johnny, sleep your life away?"* Ibid., 29–30.

240 *only once "every four or five days"* Ibid., 29.

240 *factual status* www.snopes.com/luck/einstein.asp.

240 *"I guess I have to call you"* Alvarez, *The Biggest Game in Town*, 31.

240 *"Mr. Moss, I have to let you go"* Ibid., 32.

241 *"Back then there was lots of cheating"* Justin Marchand, "Doyle Brunson: Poker's Living Legend," *Card Player*, July 11, 2006.

241 *Moss had promptly lost the entire Dandalos bundle* "Michael Craig's Journal," PokerWorks.com, August 8, 2006.

241 *several discrepancies in accounts* Ibid.

241 *"the whole thing wasn't made up"* Michael Craig, interview with the author, October 29, 2007.

32. Hold Me, Darlin'

245 *civil penalties of up to $50,000* Chuck Humphrey, "Texas Statutes," www.gambling-law-us.com/State-Laws/Texas/, § 45.004. CIVIL PENALTY.

245 *limit hold'em at the Elks Club* Don Jenkins, *Johnny Moss: Poker's Finest Champion of Champions* (Las Vegas: JM Press, 1981), 50.

246 *"Outlined against a blue-gray October sky"* Grantland Rice, *New York Herald Tribune*, October 18, 1924.

246 *In Super System 2, Crandell Addington recalls* Doyle Brunson, *Doyle Brunson's Super System 2* (New York: Cardoza, 2005), 69–84.

246 *California Club downtown* Ibid., 77.

247 *"Where in the heck is this place Vietnam?"* Anthony Holden, *Bigger Deal: A Year Inside the Poker Boom* (New York: Simon & Schuster, 2007), 16.

248 *"Nicknamed the 'Red Menace'"* Anthony Holden, *Holden on Hold'em: How to Play and Win at the Biggest Deal in Town* (New York: Little, Brown, 2008), 11.

248 *"You couldn't see the hole cards!"* Holden, *Bigger Deal*, 110.

249 *"The resulting explosion of poker on cable television"* Holden, *Holden on Hold'em*, 13.

249 *"The best poker variations strike the right balance"* Dan Harrington and Bill Robertie, *Harrington on Hold'em*, Vol. 1, *Strategic Play* (Henderson NV: Two Plus Two, 2004), 13.

250 *publication of Kill Phil* Blair Rodman and Lee Nelson, *Kill Phil: The Fast Track to Success in No-Limit Hold'em Poker Tournaments* (Las Vegas: Huntington Press, 2005).

250 *Addington scoffs, "This style of play"* Doyle Brunson's Super System 2, 83–84.

33. The Opposite of a Peace Sign

251 *jungle hooches* John Kildea, *No Names, No Faces, No Pain* (Westminster, MD: Heritage Books, 2006), 21.

251 *Hanoi prison cells* John McCain, *Faith of My Fathers* (New York: Random House, 1999), 333.

251 *air-conditioned offices* Frederic L. Borch III, *Judge Advocates in Vietnam: Army Lawyers in Southeast Asia, 1959–75* (Fort Leavenworth, KS: U.S. Army Com-

mand and General Staff College Press, 2003), 68; photo on www.allanfurtado
.com/jimschlegel.htm.

251 *"Serving the 'Tri-State Area' of South Vietnam"* Jeffrey Tillman, caption to his
photograph on www.vhpamuseum.org/Places/places.shtml.

252 *"intensified and expanded psychological activities"* McGeorge Bundy, National
Security Action Memorandum No. 330, April 9, 1965, Johnson Library, National Security File. Secret (declassified), www.fas.org/irp/offdocs/nsam-lbj/
nsam-330.htm.

252 *John F. Kennedy Special Warfare Center* Herbert Friedman, "The 24th
PSYOP Detachment in Vietnam," www.psywarrior.com/24thPsyopDet.html.

252 *dropping primitive leaflets* Herbert Friedman, "The Death Card," www
.psywarrior.com/DeathCard; and Friedman, "The 24th PSYOP Detachment
in Vietnam."

252 *"sprinkled enemy territory with playing cards"* Ian Urbina, "Forked-Tongue
Warriors," *Village Voice*, October 9–15, 2002.

253 *"couldn't afford to part with that ace"* Charles W. Brown, "ACE HIGH—This
Card Was No Joker," *Cacti Times Magazine*, 1966, quoted in Friedman, "The
Death Card."

253 *"one of the platoon leaders"* Brown, "ACE HIGH."

253 *the company hired the J. Walter Thompson agency* Friedman, "The Death
Card."

253 *Follow-up stories were soon published* Ibid.

253 *"The story we heard was that the Vietnamese"* Ibid.

254 *We understood the card to be a double whammy* Ibid.

254 *"I understand that my job means killing"* Ibid.

254 *"a case [of] transposed symbolism"* Friedman, "The 24th PSYOP Detachment
in Vietnam."

254 *"just another example of cultural ignorance"* Ibid.

254 *"Did it work? I'm not sure"* Friedman, "The Death Card."

255 *"Thus," writes the military historian Robert Chandler* Quoted in Friedman, "The
24th PSYOP Detachment in Vietnam."

255 *The bottom line on the ach bich?* Friedman, "The Death Card."

256 *2,355 days as "Uncle Ho's guest"* Spike Nasmyth, *2355 Days: A POW's Story*
(New York: Three Rivers Press, 2001), 162.

256 *"Dick could convince Zorba the Gook"* Ibid, 192–93.

256 *"perfectly round, perfectly decorated"* John Derrell Sherwood, *Afterburner:
Naval Aviators and the Vietnam War* (New York: NYU Press, 2004), 141.

256 *"secret ingredient" to add to his chip recipe* Nasmyth, *2355 Days*, 193.

256 *Nasmyth was one of the "poker czars"* Ibid.

256 *"When we got home, I mailed IOU letters"* Ralph Wetterhahn, "Ante Up," *Military Officer Magazine*, January 2005, www.moaa.org.

256 *even if his own winnings didn't come to $3,740.25* Nasmyth, *2355 Days*, 193.

256 *"an IOU for another $250 in imaginary chips"* McCain, *Faith of My Fathers*,
333.

256 *"It even had ash trays"* Ted Ballard, "Christmases in the Dungeons of North
Vietnam," www.pownetwork.org/bios/s/s123.htm, December 29, 1996.

34. Two Burn Holes in a Blanket

258 *O'Neill "moved that all of us at the briefing"* Tip O'Neill with William Novak, *Man of the House: The Life and Political Memoirs of Speaker Tip O'Neill* (New York: Random House, 1987), 191.

259 *"That's a lot of briefings"* Ibid., 192.

259 *"a good look at the other side of the issue"* Ibid.

259 *"squat, red-faced man with a bull neck"* Quoted in Joseph H. Alexander, "Across the Reef: The Marine Assault of Tarawa," www.nps.gov/archive/wapa/indepth/extContent/usmc.

259 *"a Marine's Marine"* Ibid.

259 *"the most formidable poker player in his division"* Ibid.

260 *"The commonest mistake in history"* A. D. Livingston, *Poker Wit and Wisdom* (Guilford, CT: Lyons Press, 2006), 109.

260 *"strong enough to prevent a war and wise enough"* "Navy to Christen New Guided-Missile Destroyer *Shoup*," U.S. Department of Defense, February 23, 2001, www.defenselink.mil/releases/release.aspx?releaseid=2837.

260 *"Every senior officer"* Ibid.

260 *"It curdles my blood"* O'Neill, *Man of the House*, 193.

260 *Nguyen Cao Ky, who played poker with reporters* Jason McManus, "The New Realism," *Time*, February 18, 1966.

260 *"the Vietnam conflict was a civil war"* O'Neill, *Man of the House*, 195.

261 *Jensen "had been losing more than he could afford"* Ibid., 196–97.

261 *Johnson "always liked to talk in poker terms"* David Halberstam, *The Best and the Brightest* (New York: Random House, 1972), 700.

261 *"the Johnson boys loved poker"* Robert A. Caro, *The Years of Lyndon Johnson: The Path to Power* (New York: Knopf, 1982), 28.

261 *"more than held his own"* Ibid., 71.

261 *did play with Truman "two or three times"* Robert A. Caro, *The Years of Lyndon Johnson: Means of Ascent* (New York: Knopf, 1990), 126.

261 *"If we allow Vietnam to fall"* McManus, "The New Realism."

262 *"Tip, what kind of a son of a bitch are you?"* O'Neill, *Man of the House*, 198.

263 *"China was more likely to enter the war"* Aaron Brown, interview with the author, August 28, 2008.

263 *"If it hadn't been for Vietnam"* O'Neill, *Man of the House*, 206.

263 *"too deep into the war"* Halberstam, *The Best and the Brightest*, 752.

35. The World Series of Poker, Part 1

264 *including one of the Manson family* Becky Binion Behnen, interview with the author, May 11, 2000.

265 *Second Annual Texas Gamblers Reunion* *Doyle Brunson's Super System 2* (New York: Cardoza, 2005), 79.

265 *Moore's wife, LaFayne, had the idea* Ibid.

265 *the Holiday "had a couple of old poker tables"* Dana Smith, Tom McEvoy, and Ralph Wheeler, *The Championship Table at the World Series of Poker 1970–2002* (Las Vegas: Cardsmith, 2003), 10.

265 *Texas road gamblers who showed up* *Doyle Brunson's Super System 2*, 79.

265 *either voted or named "King of Cards"* Jonathan Grotenstein and Storms Reback, *All-In: The (Almost) Entirely True Story of the World Series of Poker* (New York: St Martin's, 2005), 16–20.

265 *the engraving on Addington's reads*   Crandell Addington, interview with the author, June 27, 2008.

266 *Vickrey's $3,000 sweetener, he said, "didn't happen"*   Ibid.

266 *"That was a good thing up there in Reno"*   Grotenstein and Reback, *All-In*, 20.

266 *fewer than fifty poker tables in all of Las Vegas*   Nolan Dalla, "A Brief History of the World Series of Poker," www.worldseriesofpoker.com/wsop/history.asp.

267 *"I know you're a young man who thinks he's tough"*   Grotenstein and Reback, *All-In*, 23.

267 *"I couldn't understand why the fuck"*   Ibid.

267 *"In those days it warn't no one game"*   A. Alvarez, *The Biggest Game in Town* (New York: Houghton Mifflin, 1983), 32.

267 *"If you want to get the press involved"*   Grotenstein and Reback, *All-In*, 24.

268 *Tom Snyder gave him, Binion, and Bernstein*   Ibid., 33.

268 *"like he's between acts as a circus clown"*   Al Reinert, "Inside the World Series of Poker," *Texas Monthly*, August 1973.

268 *began hawking autographed copies*   Grotenstein and Reback, *All-In*, 29–30.

268 *"This poker game here gets us a lot of advertisement"*   Mary Ellen Glass, *Lester Ben "Benny" Binion—Some Recollections of a Texas and Las Vegas Gaming Operator* (Reno: University of Nevada Oral History Program, 1976), 81.

269 *"We had seven players last year"*   Ibid.

269 *"My kitchens get dirty," he threatened*   Ibid., 54.

269 *Benny "always had some oddball item"*   T. J. Cloutier, interview with the author, May 8, 2000.

36. Gardena, That Seventies Poker Capital

272 *The clubs' gaming licenses*   David N. Hayano, *Poker Faces: The Life and Work of Professional Card Players* (Berkeley: University of California Press, 1982), 30.

272 *"a no-nonsense, speedy affair"*   Ibid., 30–31.

273 *"Chipgirls" in large, bulging aprons*   Ibid., 35.

273 *hired proposition players*   Ibid., 36.

273 *Hayano reports that 90 percent*   Ibid., 40–41.

273 *stand pat "with absolutely nothing at all"*   Ibid., 147.

274 *Gardena's "more heterogeneous modern class"*   Ibid., 18.

274 *"I thought it would be fun doing this"*   Ibid., 20.

274 *"career professionals"*   Ibid., 27.

274 *few pros in Gardena have more than two years of college*   Ibid.

274 *"I see these guys down here more than my wife"*   Ibid., 28.

274 *Hayano calls poker "the existential game"*   Ibid., 138, 140.

275 *"the ambiance of airport gate waiting areas"*   Aaron Brown, *The Poker Face of Wall Street* (Hoboken, NJ: John Wiley, 2006), 145.

275 *"anxious to preserve a friendly image"*   Ibid., 115.

275 *"as if they were star athletes"*   Ibid., 116–17.

276 *If Caro's nickname "makes you think"*   Ibid., 105.

276 *"two players against me can play"*   Ibid., 147–48.

276 *winners comprised barely 2 percent*   Ibid., 108–10.

276 *Brown reckons that during the '70s*   Ibid.

277 *The bottom line*   Ibid., 112.

277 *"almost all" the pros worked as props*   Mason Malmuth, interview with the author, December 31, 2007.

277 *"If I play one thousand hours a year and win"*   Ibid.

278 *"At the old Rainbow Club"* Joe Bob Briggs, "Larry Flynt Takes on the Indians," UPI, March 1, 2001.
278 *"but I swear I'm straight now"* Ibid.
278 *"I intuitively suspected I was better off"* Sklansky, *The Theory of Poker*, 191.

37. The World Series of Poker, Part 2

280 *World Series revenue multiplied a hundredfold* While Horseshoe revenues from tournament juice and other sources are unknown, I arrived at "a hundredfold" by comparing total WSOP buy-ins in 1971 (under $70,000) to those in 1998 ($7 million plus), www.cardplayer.com/tournaments/wsop.
280 *"Jack is the boss," said their father* Mary Ellen Glass, *Lester Ben "Benny" Binion—Some Recollections of a Texas and Las Vegas Gaming Operator* (Reno: University of Nevada Oral History Program, 1976), 88.
280 *a $1.45 billion string of casinos* Osamu Tsukimori and William Spain, "Harrah's to Buy Binion's Horseshoe," *Dow-Jones Market Watch*, January 13, 2004.
281 *Moss, Dandalos, Felton McCorquodale, and Wild Bill Hickok* www.pokerpages.com/pokerinfo/halloffame/.
281 *hitting inside straight draws, backdooring flushes* Dana Smith, Tom McEvoy, and Ralph Wheeler, *The Championship Table at the World Series of Poker 1970–2002* (Las Vegas: Cardsmith, 2003), 67.
282 *"I won all of the little pots"* Ibid.
282 *"With one card to come, I had two queens"* Ibid.
282 *"In poker the thickness of a card"* Ibid., back cover.
282 *"You could've played as good as God"* Jonathan Grotenstein and Storms Reback, *All-In: The (Almost) Entirely True Story of the World Series of Poker* (New York: St. Martin's, 2005), 78.
283 *the classic novice's rationale: "I had a feeling"* Ibid.
283 *the Binions had struck a deal with a start-up cable outfit* Ibid., 80–81.
283 *out-of-control sports bettor* Nolan Dalla and Peter Alson, *One of a Kind: The Rise and Fall of Stuey "the Kid" Ungar, the World's Greatest Poker Player* (New York: Atria, 2005), 77–86.
284 *phenomenal card sense and IQ of 185* Ibid., 82.
284 *"I just have to make myself hate my opponents"* Alex Williams, "The Boy King Has Left the Table," *New York Times*, June 26, 2005.
284 *"Many players who bought in for $10,000"* Dalla and Alson, *One of a Kind*, 110.
285 *What Kaplan called "the last straw"* Gabe Kaplan, interview with the author, May 7, 2007.
285 *"Moss thought for a few seconds"* Ibid.
285 *"If you'd had a Rolex"* Ibid.
285 *"In all the years I've played poker"* Dalla and Alson, *One of a Kind*, 113.
285 *"I made two mistakes in the same hand"* Smith, McEvoy, and Wheeler, *The Championship Table*, 69.
286 *"Perry had more chips than Stuey"* Ibid., 71.
287 *Green, with an open-end straight draw* A. Alvarez, *The Biggest Game in Town* (New York: Houghton Mifflin, 1983), 182.

38. The World Series of Poker, Part 3

289 *they had "made the final casino"* Dana Smith, Tom McEvoy, and Ralph Wheeler, *The Championship Table at the World Series of Poker, 1990–2002* (Las Vegas: Cardsmith, 2003), 80–81.

289 *Shandel had dealt earlier rounds* Pamela Shandel, interview with the author, July 2, 2005.

290 *"I did it! I did it!"* Tom McEvoy, interview with the author, June 30, 2005.

290 *Chan netted more than either of them* Ibid.

290 *Standing on a chair above Peate's left shoulder* Pamela Shandel, interview with the author.

290 *Other Shandel photos capture Bobbi* Ibid.

291 *He recommended constant aggression* *Doyle Brunson's Super System: A Course in Power Poker* (New York: Cardoza, 2002), 417–513.

291 *"changed my life overnight"* Tom McEvoy, interview with the author, September 6, 2007.

292 *"I didn't have any feel as to how I should be playing"* Smith, McEvoy, and Wheeler, *The Championship Table*, 111.

293 *originally played with backgammon checkers* Erik Seidel, interview with the author, August 9, 2008.

293 *In 1989, the WSOP comprised fourteen events* www.cardplayer.com/tournaments/event_list/243.

293 *more than $6.2 million in prize money* Ibid.

293 *Eric Drache had left to run poker operations* Eric Drache, interview with the author, March 24, 2008.

293 *new wrinkles doubled satellite participation* Jack McClelland, interview with the author, June 2006.

293 *"If you don't know the rules"* Steve Marzolf, "Interview with Jack McClelland," www.texasholdem-poker.com/interviews/jack_mcclelland.

294 *efforts to compensate for low self-esteem* Phil Hellmuth, interview with the author, September 2004.

294 *"In ten years," he would gloat* Jonathan Grotenstein and Storms Reback, *All-In: The (Almost) Entirely True Story of the World Series of Poker* (New York: St. Martin's, 2005), 156–57.

295 *"a diminutive stick-insect of thirty-four-going-on-twelve"* Anthony Holden, *Big Deal: One Year as a Professional Poker Player* (New York: Viking, 1990), 32–33.

295 *"Although I often reached the final table"* A. Alvarez, *Poker: Bets, Bluffs, and Bad Beats* (San Francisco: Chronicle, 2001), 105.

296 *"I had been preparing for this day"* Ibid., 116.

39. The World Series of Poker, Part 4

297 *key heads-up hand of the 1990 main event* Dana Smith, Tom McEvoy, and Ralph Wheeler, *The Championship Table at the World Series of Poker 1970–2002* (Las Vegas: Cardsmith, 2003), 115–117; Jonathan Grotenstein and Storms Reback, *All-In: The (Almost) Entirely True Story of the World Series of Poker* (New York: St. Martin's, 2005), 161–71.

298 *"without question the most incredible hand"* Grotenstein and Reback, *All-In*, 164.

298 *"I entered hoping to get a piece of the pie"* Smith, McEvoy, and Wheeler, *The Championship Table*, 115–117.

298 *"I called him in a heartbeat"* Nolan Dalla and Peter Alson, *One of a Kind: The Rise and Fall of Stuey "the Kid" Ungar, the World's Greatest Poker Player* (New York: Atria, 2005), 206–207.

299 *"How could he not be there?"* Ibid., 205–10.

299 *enough chips remained for him to finish ninth* Ibid., 210.

299 *Other bracelets were awarded that year* www.cardplayer.com/tournaments/event_list/242.

301 *Alan Goehring won $768,625* www.cardplayer.com/tournaments/results/1709.

301 *Vahedi enlisted in the army* Amir Vahedi, interviews with the author, 2004–2008.

302 *"the new Stuey Ungar"* Dalla and Alson, *One of a Kind*, 211.

302 *after a seesaw sparring match* Ibid., 211–13.

302 *"When a guy makes a call like that"* Ibid., 212.

303 *"I knew Stuey was having problems"* Ibid., 246.

303 *"Stu's very good at looking at a player"* Ibid., 250.

303 *"I'm going to kill your ass"* Ibid., 251–52.

304 *a cardboard Chiffon toilet paper box* Ibid., 258.

304 *found dead in Room 16 of the Oasis Motel* Ibid., 293.

304 *"At least three of those tournaments"* Doyle Brunson, interview with the author, July 2007.

305 *"The same neural circuitry involved in the highs"* Sandra Blakeslee, "Hijacking the Brain Circuits with a Nickel Slot Machine," *New York Times*, February 19, 2002.

305 *"may also have been dealt a genetic hand"* Steven Pinker, *How the Mind Works* (New York: Norton, 1997), 361.

40. The World Series of Poker, Part 5

306 *at least twelve of the twenty-one bracelets* www.cardplayer.com/tournaments/event_list/235.

306 *escaped in a small boat from Communist Vietnam* en.wikipedia.org/wiki/Scotty_Nguyen.

307 *Scotty Nguyen $1,000,000* www.cardplayer.com/tournaments/results/118.

307 *nickname referred to his birth on December 25* J. J. Furlong, interview with the author, May 2000.

307 *J. J. Furlong $1,000,000* www.cardplayer.com/tournaments/results/1709.

307 *determined "to win the damn t'ing"* Padraig Parkinson, interview with the author, May 2000.

308 *Hieu "Tony" Ma $367,040* www.cardplayer.com/tournaments/results/2595.

308 *sister Mel and twelve-year-old son, Mark* Jerri and Harry Thomas, interview with the author, May 2000.

309 *Thomases credited Danny Robison* Ibid.

309 *"This has been a dream for a long time"* Andrew Glazer, "Mom Defeats the Seven Studs," Casino.com, April 27, 2000.

309 *earned while protecting a friend's child* Jennifer Harman, interview with the author, May 2000.

309 *took a ten-minute lesson from Lederer* Ibid.

309 *Jennifer Harman $146,250* www.cardplayer.com/tournaments/results/2604.

310 *Jerri Thomas $135,975* www.cardplayer.com/tournaments/results/2596.

310 *Jay Heimowitz $284,000* www.cardplayer.com/tournaments/results/2616.

311 *listed his occupation as "student"*   Chris Ferguson, interview with the author, May 2000.

311 *Chris Ferguson $151,000*   www.cardplayer.com/tournaments/results/2602.

312 *"somehow the magic was gone"*   Ivo Donev, interview with the author, May 2000.

312 *practicing on Wilson Turbo software*   Ibid.

312 *Ivo Donev $85,800*   www.cardplayer.com/tournaments/results/2597.

313 *Phil Ivey $195,000*   www.cardplayer.com/tournaments/results/2607.

313 *"Poker doesn't belong to white American males"*   Andrew Glazer, *Card Player*, November 10, 2000.

314 *In May 2000, there was also a jury*   James McManus, *Positively Fifth Street* (New York: Farrar, Straus and Giroux, 2003), 339–53.

314 *"Some crowd here this mornin'"*   Ibid., 194.

315 *promised Linda Johnson to control it*   Linda Johnson, interview with the author, April 2000.

316 *Glazer cited the NASDAQ*   Andrew Glazer, interview with the author, May 2000.

318 *Henry Orenstein's under-the-table cameras*   Anthony Holden, *Bigger Deal: A Year Inside the Poker Boom* (New York: Simon & Schuster, 2007), 111.

318 *John Duthie £1,000,000*   www.msoworld.com/mindzine/news/card/poker million.html.

319 *broadcast live to three hundred million households*   Promoter Barry Hearn, interview with the author, November 2000.

41. Small Ball, the Bluff, and the Boom

320 *averaged 1.1 million viewers*   Steven Lipscomb, interview with the author, July 2004.

321 *definitive hand of their heads-up endgame*   Jonathan Grotenstein and Storms Reback, *All-In: The (Almost) Entirely True Story of the World Series of Poker* (New York: St. Martin's, 2005), 261; Matt Lessinger, *The Book of Bluffs* (New York: Warner Books, 2005), 220–29; www.youtube.com/watch?v=IgdnUlIdvxE.

322 *concentrating on his trip home*   Lessinger, *The Book of Bluffs*, 226.

323 *compared it to moving the British Open*   Anthony Holden, interview with the author, July 2006.

324 *politics, publishing, sports, and new media*   Jeffrey Pollack, interviews with the author, 2006–2008.

325 *"a thirty-five-year-old start-up"*   Ibid.

325 *Players Advisory Committee*   www.worldseriesofpoker.com, media kit, 29.

325 *"Players measure themselves against each"*   Jeffrey Pollack, interview with the author, June 29, 2008.

325 *risen by 46 percent*   Stephen A. Murphy, "2008 WSOP Final Table Ratings Up 46 Percent," Card Player.com, www.cardplayer.com/poker-news/article/5525/2008-wsop-final-table-ratings-up-46-percent.

325 *"fifty-six hundred players"*   Steve Marzolf, "Interview with Jack McClelland," www.texasholdem-poker.com/interviews/jack_mcclelland.

326 *the interactive media company Reactrix*   Jon Friedberg, interview with the author, September 8, 2006.

326 *Classic semibluff reraise*   Ibid.

327 *"an amount that appears as if I want John to call"*   Ibid.

327 *"She had called me out and both of us knew it"*   Shawnee Barton, interview with the author, July 15, 2006.

327 *"I like your game, girl"* Ibid.

328 *Leyser filed suit in Las Vegas District Court* Lisa Wheeler, "The Facts in Leyser vs. Gold WSOP $6M Lawsuit," *Card Player*, August 24, 2006, www.cardplayer .com/poker-news/article/1307/the-facts-in-leyser-vs-gold-wsop-6m-lawsuit.

328 *the case was settled out of court* "Jamie Gold Agrees to Settle WSOP Prize Money Dispute," Associated Press, February 7, 2007.

329 Decade-by-decade table based on payout results available on www.cardplayer .com/tournaments/wsop.

42. Drawing Red Lines in the Desert, or How (Not) to Bluff a Martyr

330 *"Iran has joined the club of nuclear nations"* "Iran's Nuclear Progress," *Washington Post* editorial, April 13, 2006, A20.

330 *"We want to solve this issue diplomatically"* Jennifer Loven, "Bush Declines to Take Military Action off the Table in Dealing with Iran," Associated Press, April 18, 2006.

331 *"cut off the hands of any aggressor"* David Fickling, "Iran 'Will Cut off Hands of Aggressors,'" *Guardian*, April 18, 2006.

331 *"simpletons and traitors"* John Burns, "Rally in Tehran Pays Lip Service to the Revolutionary Zeal of '79," *New York Times*, November 5, 1999.

331 *uranium-enrichment program "is our red line"* David E. Sanger and Elaine Sciolino, "Iran Strategy: Cold War Echo," *New York Times*, April 30, 2006.

331 *"We say, be angry at us and die of this anger"* "Iran's President to World: Get Used to It," Associated Press, April 14, 2006.

331 *"Ahmadinejad and the Iranian regime are bluffing"* Gerald Steinberg, *Toronto Globe and Mail*, April 20, 2006.

331 *"Is there any art more beautiful"* S. Enders Wimbush, "Understanding the Iran Crisis," House Committee on Foreign Affairs, January 31, 2007.

331 *had formed a human chain* Matthias Kuntzel, "Ahmadinejad's Demons," *New Republic*, April 24, 2006, 123 (Kuntzel is quoting a report in *Kayan*, which he calls "a publication loyal to Khameini").

332 *"a screwdriver's turn away"* Howard LaFranchi, "Iran's Oil Gambit—A Potential Affront to the U.S.," *Christian Science Monitor*, August 30, 2005.

332 *"It's time," he said, "for people to show their cards"* www.whitehouse.gov/news/ releases/2003/03/20030306-8.html.

333 *"Limit poker is a science, but no-limit is an art"* A. Alvarez, *The Biggest Game in Town* (New York: Houghton Mifflin, 1983), 35.

333 *"a single atomic bomb has the power"* Aluf Benn, "Israel Turns up the Heat on Iran," Salon.com, January 28, 2002, dir.salon.com/story/news/feature/2002/ 01/28/mullahs/.

333 *a national humiliation* Michael Slackman, "Iranians Dismiss U.S. Terms for Beginning Direct Talks," *New York Times*, June 2, 2006.

334 *publicly beaten for participating in a card game* "Female Gamblers Caned in Indonesia," August 19, 2005, www.corpun.com/idj00508.htm.

335 *"The Israelis seem to mean it"* Jeremy Bernstein, "The Secrets of the Bomb," *New York Review of Books*, May 25, 2006.

335 *"bazaar behavior"* Warren Christopher, "Welcome to the Bazaar," *New York Times*, June 13, 2006.

336 *"We hope America has learned a lesson"* Nazila Fathi, "Iran Launches 10 Missiles in Exercise: War Games Precede Nuclear Deadline," *International Herald Tribune*, August 21, 2006.

43. Fooled by Randomness

337 *"In philosophy there is no such thing as 'luck'"* James M. Wickstead, *How to Win at Stud Poker* (New York: Casino Press, 1984), 140.

338 *"People think mastering the skill is the hard part"* Jesse May, *Shut Up and Deal* (New York: Anchor, 1998), 8.

340 *"A black swan is an outlier"* Nassim Nicholas Taleb, "Learning to Expect the Unexpected," www.edge.org/3rd_culture/taleb04/taleb_index.html.

341 *"Lucky fools do not bear the slightest suspicion"* Nassim Nicholas Taleb, *Fooled by Randomness* (New York: Random House, 2005), 18.

341 *"try to create excitement by emphasizing luck"* Mike D'Angelo, "The Real Suckers at the Table?" *Esquire*, May 2007.

341 *the phoniest hand ever filmed* Ibid.

341 Card Player *columnists* Roy Cooke, "A Famous Movie Poker Hand," *Card Player*, October 4, 2005, 12–16; Michael Wiesenberg, "Implausible Play in *The Cincinnati Kid*?" *Card Player*, August 23, 2005, 72–74.

342 *"Change ten river cards"* Stephen J. Dubner, "Phil Gordon Answers Your Poker Questions," Freakonomics blog, nytimes.com, April 18, 2008.

342 *"Those hands in particular have been the difference"* Daniel Negreanu, FullContactPoker.com, July 14, 2005.

343 *"You can set up all the plays in the world"* T. J. Cloutier with Tom McEvoy, *Championship Pot-Limit and No-Limit Hold'em: On the Road to the World Series of Poker* (Las Vegas: Cardsmith, 1997), 126.

343 *"The volatility in tournaments is out of sight"* Dan Harrington, interview with Justin Marchand, *Card Player*, December 11, 2007, 65–70.

44. Bunches of Luck

345 *fifty-two cards can be shuffled into 52! sequences* precisioncalc.com/Tutorial.html.

346 *"People said it was a pity to see him"* Mark Twain, "Science vs. Luck," *The Galaxy*, October 1870, www.twainquotes.com/Galaxy/18701od.html.

347 *"I do not believe in luck"* Herbert O. Yardley, *The Education of a Poker Player* (New York: Simon & Schuster, 1957), vii.

347 *"I don't believe in luck"* Brian Townsend, *Card Player*, September 4, 2007.

348 *"if you include cash games in the generalizations"* Crandell Addington, interview with the author, August 29, 2007.

348 *"Tournaments are more luck-dependent"* Peter Alson, interview with the author, September 4, 2007.

348 *Barney Boatman: "I think you'll find"* Barney Boatman, interview with the author, March 27, 2008.

348 *Mason Malmuth: "The right way to answer this"* Mason Malmuth, interview with the author, September 1, 2007.

349 *Aaron Brown broke down the odds* Aaron Brown with Brandon Adams, "Luck and Skill in Poker," *Bluff*, July 2007.

349 *"pretty close to fifty–fifty"* Chris Ferguson, interview with the author, May 10, 2000.

349 *Chau Giang, on the other hand* Dana Smith, *Card Player*, July 1994.
349 *"Poker is a hundred percent skill and a hundred percent luck"* Tom McEvoy, interview with the author, December 2006.
350 *"The luck factor influences"* Andy Beal, interview with the author, July 20, 2006.
350 *Doyle Brunson admits he's "got no idea"* Doyle Brunson, interview with the author, September 10, 2007.
350 *"The mystery of poker, and so its infinite fascination"* Anthony Holden, *Bigger Deal: A Year Inside the Poker Boom* (New York: Simon & Schuster, 2007), 53.
350 *"If one really wishes to be a master"* Howard Lederer, "Poker and Zen," www.howardlederer.com/howard-lederer-poker-article9.html.
351 *"experienced card players believe"* Larry W. Phillips, *Zen and the Art of Poker* (New York: Plume, 1999), 76.
351 *"At least on some level, I attempt to gauge"* Jim Karamanis, interview with the author, February 7, 2008.
351 *R. L. Wing's commentary on the Tao* R. L. Wing, *The Tao of Power* (New York: Broadway, 1986), 98.

45. The Biology and Eros of No-Limit Hold'em Tournaments

352 *"No girl I have ever seen at a poker table"* David Spanier, *Total Poker* (New York: Simon & Schuster, 1979), 148.
353 *"Women are no longer considered as accessories"* David Spanier, *The Little Book of Poker* (Las Vegas: Huntington Press, 2000), 24–26.
353 *count grew steadily through 2004* www.cardplayer.com/tournaments.
353 *2005 University of Pittsburgh study* John Tierney, "What Women Want," *New York Times*, May 24, 2005.
354 *"Evolution has selected for men"* Ibid.
354 *Women already comprise roughly a third* Sandra Witzel, "Online Poker a Women's Game?" *Earth Times*, February 6, 2007.
355 *"This is not to say that sex cannot enter poker"* Spanier, *The Little Book of Poker*, 24–26.
355 *"Poker is fun, tense and exciting"* www.mayerlabs.com/images/pdf/Kimono _Ad_PR.pdf.
355 *ad for Interpoker.com* *Woman Poker Player*, June 2006, 17.
356 *"Lucky at Cards, Lucky in Love"* Toby Leah Bochan, *The Badass Girl's Guide to Poker* (Avon, MA: Adams Media, 2005), 145.
356 *"The mood is energized—there's money at stake"* Ibid., 147.
356 *"PMS anyone?"* Ibid., 94.
356 *"the more intelligent and social the species"* Edward O. Wilson, *Sociobiology: The New Synthesis* (Cambridge, MA: Harvard University Press, 1975), 164, 188, 189.
357 *"There is a rhythm of tension-discharge"* Spanier, *Total Poker*, 136.
357 *"Playing with poker chips"* Ibid., 141.
357 *"At this rate it'll be a couple hundred years"* Jennifer Harman, interview with the author, May 2006.

46. The Andy Game, Part 1

359 *He recently lost thirty pounds* Andy Beal, interview with the author, July 20–21, 2005, with follow-ups by e-mail and telephone.
359 *Andy bought in for $10 million* Ibid.

360 *He can't get his mind off the death a few days ago*   Todd Brunson, interview with the author, December 2005.

360 *"Once I get rolling and draw a bead"*   Ibid.

360 *his opponent's poker day usually began*   Andy Beal, interview with the author.

362 *Pierre Fermat's famous Last Theorem*   Ibid.; www.bealconjecture.com/.

362 *he launched Beal Aerospace*   www.bealaerospace.com/.

363 *"You have a million dollars in tournament winnings"*   Quoted in Michael Kaplan, "Poker: Raising the Stakes," *Cigar Aficionado*, March/April 2006.

364 *"As a group, tournament players"*   Barry Greenstein, interview with the author, June 10, 2006.

365 *Enter Ted Forrest*   Michael Craig, *The Professor, the Banker, and the Suicide King: Inside the Richest Poker Game of All Time* (New York: Warner, 2005), 13–21.

365 *"I didn't fly all the way out here"*   Andy Beal, interview with the author.

365 *Half went to Children Inc.*   www.barrygreenstein.com/charities/.

365 *"I didn't want to throw my whole life away"*   Barry Greenstein, interview with the author.

366 *"If she showed up with me, some of them would assume"*   Ibid.

367 *"So, Lyle, did you have fun?"*   Craig, *The Professor, the Banker, and the Suicide King*, 160.

367 *"they almost killed me," he said*   Todd Brunson, interview with the author.

368 *Howard, for his part, said he "felt honored"*   Howard Lederer, interview with the author, May 24, 2008.

369 *"Neither of my folks wanted me to play poker"*   Todd Brunson, interview with the author.

371 *the 2002 WSOP heads-up championship*   www.cardplayer.com/tournaments/results/1939.

371 *"accidentally on purpose"*   Andy Beal, interview with the author.

371 *"got in Andy's head"*   Howard Lederer, interview with the author.

372 *"Andy couldn't help but feel a little flattered"*   Craig, *The Professor, the Banker, and the Suicide King*, 232.

372 *Chip was "playing way too tight"*   Ibid., 232–38.

372 *stuck $8 million, having lost forty big bets*   Ibid.

372 *"One said he played exactly right"*   Ibid.

373 *"Who the fuck negotiated these circumstances?"*   Ibid., 227.

373 *"If I lose two million," he told them*   Ibid., 236.

374 *"I had a campout with my twin eight-year-old daughters"*   Andy Beal, interview with the author.

374 *"It's good, you know, that he wins"*   Jennifer Harman, interview with the author, May 2006.

374 *"I gotta say," he said, "that was the tits"*   Andy Beal, interview with the author.

47. The Andy Game, Part 2

376 *"If not, then God bless 'em"*   Andy Beal, interview with the author, July 20–21, 2005.

376 *"I feel great," she said*   Jennifer Harman, interview with the author, May 2006.

376 *"Wiring twenty million dollars to Dallas"*   Todd Brunson, interview with the author, July 2006.

377 *"at least once, for Chrissake"*   Andy Beal, interview with the author.

377 *published an open letter in* Card Player "From the Desk of Andy Beal," www.cardplayer.com/magazine/article/14268.

378 *"The problem that the pros have is not bankroll"* archives2.twoplustwo.com/ showthreaded.php?Cat=0&Number=1077522&page=&fpart=&vc=.

379 *"poorly disguised attempt to bust the Corporation"* extempore.livejournal.com, October 2, 2004.

379 *"I'm very surprised at the hostile tone"* "From the Desk of Doyle Brunson," www.cardplayer.com/magazine/article/14293.

380 *devolved into "an essay-writing contest"* Gabe Kaplan, interview with the author, December 2004.

380 *"the luck has probably broken in our favor"* Michael Craig, *The Professor, the Banker, and the Suicide King: Inside the Richest Poker Game of All Time* (New York: Warner, 2005), 241.

380 *"Playing forty or fifty hours"* Andy Beal, interview with the author.

380 *"We normally don't interfere with someone's private life"* George Anders, "Maverick Banker in Texas Chases Distressed Assets," *Wall Street Journal,* January 13, 2005, online.wsj.com/article/SB110556884311724524-search.html.

381 *"All right, Doyle," Andy wrote in another open letter* Barry Shulman, "Beal Accepts Brunson's Counter (Almost)," *Card Player,* April 19, 2005, www .cardplayer.com/magazine/article/14637.

381 "Andy is back, *and he has given ground on all fronts"* Ibid.

382 *"Andy is done with poker for good"* Lisa Wheeler, "Andy Beal Versus the Corporation," CardPlayer.com, www.cardplayer.com/magazine/article/15345.

382 *"He is very eccentric and he may be back"* Ibid.

382 *On February 12, he won $4.9 million* Ibid.

382 *Craig reported that, beginning with limits of $30,000* Michael Craig, "The Banker & the Ice Man," *Bluff,* May 2006, www.bluffmagazine.com/magazine/ 2006_05_86.asp.

383 *"The river card was the jack of clubs"* Ibid.

383 *"If I lose today," said Phil* Ibid.

384 *"I really feel like I snatched defeat from the jaws of victory"* Ibid.

384 *"our Andy Beal tournament"* Jack McClelland, interview with the author, April 9, 2005.

385 *"Isn't there a much better use for the time and money?"* Quoted in Shulman, "Beal Accepts Brunson's Counter (Almost)."

385 *"It was a thrill to be a part of those matches"* Howard Lederer, interview with the author, May 24, 2008.

385 *"You just don't keep climbing Mount Everest"* Andy Beal, interview with the author, May 2, 2008.

48. LH and AI

386 *Billings was a poker pro who went back to grad school* Darse Billings, interview with the author, April 2001, with supplementary information at www.cs .ualberta.ca/~darse/.

386 *Strategically, it followed Sklansky's* Theory Ibid.

387 *no person or institution had volunteered* Ibid.

387 *"Computers are very dumb," he admitted* Marta Gold, "No Bluffing— Computer Poker Is in the Works," *Edmonton Journal,* July 6, 1998, B1.

387 *"A computer could play fair-to-middling poker"* *Doyle Brunson's Super System: A Course in Power Poker* (New York: Cardoza, 2002), 18.

387 *IBM's Deep Blue* Charles Krauthammer and William Dowell, "Deep Blue Funk," *Time*, February 26, 1996.

388 *"When it comes to imperfect information"* Darse Billings, interview with the author, June 2002.

388 *"chess-playing computers don't do that"* Ivars Peterson, "Playing Your Cards Right: Poker Comes out of the Back Room and into the Computer Science Lab," *Science News Online*, July 18, 1998.

388 *She called her program Gala* Daphne Koller and A. J. Pfeffer, "Representations and Solutions for Game-Theoretic Problems," *Artificial Intelligence*, July 1997, robotics.stanford.edu/~koller/papers/galapaper.html.

389 *"re-expressed as the product of the realization weights"* Ibid., 1190.

389 *"a recipe,"* as well as *"an ambidextrous artifact"* David Berlinski, "Iterations of Immortality," *Harper's*, January 2000, 15–16.

389 *"this is more of an exercise"* Peterson, "Playing Your Cards Right."

389 *"an automated game-theoretic analysis"* Koller and Pfeffer, abstract of "Representations and Solutions for Game-Theoretic Problems."

389 *Ferguson had learned to play no-limit hold'em online* Chris Ferguson, interview with the author, November 11, 2008.

390 *the payouts were in "ether bucks" only* Ibid.

390 *The IRC experience also motivated him* Ibid.

391 *"Polaris was beating me like a drum"* John Markoff, "In Poker Match Against a Machine, Humans Are Better Bluffers," *New York Times*, July 7, 2007.

391 *"to bob and weave like a real player"* CardPlayer.com, September 29, 2007.

392 *"The bots are closing in"* Ian Ayres, "Poker Bots on the Rise: A Guest Blog," Freakonomics column, nytimes.com, November 12, 2007.

392 *"poker is harder than chess for computers"* Markoff, "In Poker Match Against a Machine."

392 *Polaris 2.0 chalked up three wins* Clara Ho, "U of A Computer Scores Major Poker Victory," edmontonjournal.com, July 6, 2008.

392 *"My navigation system could have played that hand better"* Live blog of the event, www.cs.ualberta.ca/~games/poker/man-machine/Live/Day4/.

392 *"There are two really big changes"* Undated interview on technovelgy.com.

393 *"one Darwinian struggle"* Ayres, "Poker Bots on the Rise."

393 *"at confounding the expectations"* Ibid.

394 *Phoenix Biotechnology has developed a drug* Curezone.com, October 20, 2008, curezone.com/forums/fm.asp?i=1281213.

394 *Koller's work with molecular biologists* John Markoff, "Pursuing the Next Level of Artificial Intelligence," *New York Times*, May 3, 2008.

49. The Poker World Is Flat (In Spite of the UIGEA)

395 *Friedman calls Globalization 3.0* Thomas L. Friedman, *The World Is Flat* (New York: Farrar, Straus and Giroux, 2005), 10.

396 *Gates "played poker until six"* Jeanne M. Lesinky, *Bill Gates* (Minneapolis: Lerner, 2005), 23.

396 *"basically an extension of the all-night poker games"* Nate Orenstam interview with Ballmer, February 13, 2002, valleyofthegeeks.com.

397 *"In poker, a player collects different pieces"* Bill Gates, *The Road Ahead*, rev. ed. (New York: Penguin, 1995), 43.

397 *$500,000 on PokerStars, $200,000 on UltimateBet* James Hipwell, "An-

nette_15 Tops the PokerStars TLB," February 5, 2007, www.pokerverdict
.com/Online-Poker-News/1674/annette_15_tops_the_pokerstars_tlb.html.

399 *Senator Frank Lautenberg (D-NJ) stated* Nelson I. Rose, "The Unlawful
Internet Gambling Enforcement Act of 2006 Analyzed," www.gamblingand
thelaw.com/columns/2006_act.htm.

399 *"did not make it impossible or illegal for Americans"* Gary Rivlin and Matt Rich-
tel, "D'Amato Never Folds," *New York Times*, March 5, 2007.

399 *"Frist's last-minute addition of this amendment"* Lianna Elias, "Pros Voice
Opinions About UIGEA," PokerListings.com, October 13, 2006.

399 *"As a lifelong poker player," said Doyle Brunson* Sarah Polson, "Bush Signs
Port Security, Internet Gambling Bill," www.pokerlistings.com, October 13,
2006.

399 *"Internet poker is a great source of enjoyment"* Ibid.

400 *"This last-minute deal reeks of political gamesmanship"* Earl Burton, "Reaction
to Online Gaming Bill Vehement and Outraged," PokerNews.com, October 2, 2006.

400 *Allyn Jaffrey Shulman wasn't alone in pointing out* Allyn Jaffrey Shulman,
"A Comprehensive Analysis of the Internet Gambling Prohibition Act,"
CardPlayer.com, May 2, 2006.

401 *"By creating carve-outs"* www.caribbeannetnews.com/cgi-script/csArticles/
articles/000005/000585.htm.

401 *"There has never been legislation"* Shulman, "A Comprehensive Analysis of the
Internet Gambling Prohibition Act."

401 *Shulman also reminds us that the Supreme Court* Ibid.

402 *why the federal government should expend resources* Ibid., Section 2. Financial
Institutions and Section 4. Exclusions.

402 *"You might remember a failed experiment"* www.igcouncil.org/content/view/
112/99/.

403 *Shulman agreed with Conyers* Shulman, "A Comprehensive Analysis of the
Internet Gambling Prohibition Act," section headed "A Voice of Reason."

403 *Wayne Abernathy of the American Bankers Association* "Testimony of Wayne
Abernathy on Behalf of the American Bankers Association Before the Sub-
committee on Domestic and International Monetary Policy Committee on Financial Services, United States House of Representatives," April 2, 2008.

403 *Representative Barney Frank (D-MA) introduced a bill* www.govtrack.us/
congress/bill.xpd?bill=h110–2046.

403 *75 percent of Americans oppose* Letter from Steven J. Yeager, PPA Arizona state
director, to Representative Ed Pastor, March 24, 2008, Re: Support Online
Poker and HR 2610.

50. Cheating 2.0

405 *"Today, in a regulated casino"* Anthony Holden, *Bigger Deal: A Year Inside the
Poker Boom* (New York: Simon & Schuster, 2007), 10.

405 *"use a certified and independently tested"* Justin Marchard, interview with the
author, April 10, 2008.

406 *"Any of them would be crazy"* Lou Krieger and Sharee Bykofsky, *Secrets the
Pros Won't Tell You About Winning Hold'em Poker* (New York: Kensington,
2006), 250.

406 *the $100 million or so they wager* Justin Marchand, interview with the author.

406 *"quite convinced—but can't prove"*   Michael Wiesenberg, interview with the author, May 11, 2008.

407 *"worked for the previous ownership of UltimateBet"*   Bob Pajich, "Owner of UltimateBet Confirms Security Breach," CardPlayer.com, May 29, 2008.

408 *brilliantly creative statistical analysis by David Paredes*   Michael Kaplan, "Gunning for Cheats," *Cigar Aficionado*, December 2008, 126.

408 *Subsequent posts on TwoPlusTwo*   Summarized by "Kevmath" on forumserver .twoplustwo.com/29/news-views-gossip/ub-scandal-sticky-251207/, July 15, 2008.

408 *Catania alleged that it was Russ Hamilton*   Dan Cypra, PokerNewsDaily.com, September 30, 2008.

408 *nineteen different player accounts*   Kaplan, "Gunning for Cheats," 126.

409 *UltimateBet quietly began to refund money*   Dan Cypra, "KGC Appoints Frank Catania to Lead Ultimate Bet Investigation," PokerNewsDaily.com, July 30, 2008.

409 *filed a $75 million lawsuit*   Mike Brunker, "Poker Site Cheating Plot a High-Stakes Whodunit," msnbc.com, September 18, 2008.

409 *online gaming sites had established their headquarters*   A. Emmanuel, Internet Poker.Co.UK, August 29, 2007.

409 *"What did Phil Hellmuth and Annie Duke know"*   "Russ Hamilton Cheats Online Poker of Its Good Name," OnlinePokerInsider.com, October 15, 2008.

409 *"WOW!! Thanx for setting poker back 25 years"*   Seamarfan269, CardPlayer .com, September 29, 2008.

410 *"Huge sums of money were transferred"*   Kaplan, "Gunning for Cheats," 129.

410 *"We do not have super-user accounts"*   Ibid., 130.

410 *Jessica Simpson's asking price of $2 million*   Bob Pajich, "NakedPoker.com Drives Poker's Erotica Push," CardPlayer.com, September 13, 2006.

410 *"34C-24–34 brunette beauty from Fort Wayne"*   Ibid.

411 *TropicalPoker.com didn't last much longer*   Ibid.

411 *BombshellPoker.com resembled a site to troll*   Ibid.

411 *"Jamie truly epitomizes the Bodog spirit"*   "Jamie Gold Sued," pokerworks .com/poker-articles/poker-pulse/various/2006–08–24-jamie-gold-sued.html.

411 *Ayre terminated his relationship with Gold*   "All That Glitters Is Not Gold for Poker Champ," www.poker.co.uk/poker-news-detail.html?story=5237.

51. Poker School, Poker Law, Poker Ethics

413 *Antigua's victory over the UIGEA*   dev.gpsts.org/panelists-at-european-think -tank-take-aim-at-us-policy-on-gaming-trade-dispute.

413 *The Poker Players' Alliance is a like-minded lobbying group*   pokerplayersalliance .org.

414 *"Can you imagine going to an NFL football game"*   Bob Pajich, "World Poker Association Pushes for Universal Rules," *Card Player*, August 28, 2008.

414 *establish a broad Code of Ethics*   www.wpapoker.org/?sect=rules&pg=code -of-ethics.

414 *Jones publicly criticized Scotty Nguyen*   Jesse Jones, "Scotty Nguyen's WSOP HORSE Final Table Conduct," WPAPoker.org.

414 *"repeatedly harassed, badgered, and taunted"*   Pajich, "World Poker Association Pushes for Universal Rules."

417 *"I was able to 'read' people, but it proved problematic"*   Katy Lederer, *Poker Face* (New York: Crown, 2003), 153.

417 *"Many players who act appropriately"* Barry Greenstein, *Ace on the River: An Advanced Poker Guide* (Fort Collins, CO: Last Knight Publishing, 2005), 42.

418 *"A player who wins the pot"* Ibid., 43.

418 *"It is bad business to destroy people"* Ibid., 45.

418 *trustworthy, intelligent, honest (with yourself)* Ibid., 64–69.

52. The World's Game

420 *"risk-takers willing to leave the familiarity of their homelands"* John M. Glionna, "Gambling Seen as No-Win Situation for Some Asians," *Los Angeles Times*, January 16, 2006, B1.

420 *Buddhists in general seem to embrace randomness* Keis Ohtsuka and Thai Duong, "Vietnamese Australian Gamblers' Views on Luck and Winning: A Preliminary Report," Victoria University, Melbourne, www.staff.vu.edu.au/Keis, 2000, 6.

420 *in exchange for half of their winnings* Michael Kaplan, "Dealing with the Master," *LA Weekly*, May 22, 2003.

420 *"Men the Master's soldiers"* Ibid.

420 *"the Vietnamese Godfather"* Ibid.

420 *cheating "goes against my Buddha"* Ibid.

421 *couldn't always follow the mumbled conversations* Daniel Negreanu, "Asian Poker Players," *Card Player*, January 14, 2005.

422 *enormous integrated resorts* I. Nelson Rose, "Which Way Asia?" www.GamblingAndTheLaw.com, #150, October 25, 2008.

422 *impetus for building casinos* Ibid.

423 *David Parlett wrote that poker* David Parlett, *The Oxford Guide to Card Games* (New York: Oxford University Press, 1990), 86.

423 *steady success on PokerStars since the age of seventeen* www.pokerstars.com/wsop/novembernine/peter-eastgate/.

424 *losing a $723,938 pot* www.gambling911.com/poker/new-world-record-online-poker-pot-102708.html.

424 *five biggest winners online* www.highstakesdb.com/reports.aspx.

425 *"Stakes have doubled"* Michael Kaplan, "Poker Raising the Stakes," *Cigar Aficionado*, March/April 2006.

425 *"Unlike backgammon and chess"* Ibid.

425 *"it would be cool to play in the World Series of Poker"* Kevin Van Valkenburg, *Baltimore Sun* blog, August 18, 2008.

425 *made the final table of the third event he had entered* www.pokerpages.com/tournament/result23027.htm.

425 *"Nothin like ya man, he aint grindin like this"* Young Jeezy, "Hustlaz Ambition."

426 *The cast of* Ocean's 12 The Matt Damon Column, www.fortunecity.com/lavendar/fullmonty/282/may2004.html.

426 *Johnny Carson, too, liked his poker* Kimberly Cutter, "The Players," *W*, February 2004.

426 *"The World Series of Poker has nothing on the NFL draft"* Jarrett Bell, "The Draft: It's Where Football Meets Poker," *USA Today*, April 15, 2008, 1–2.

SELECTED BIBLIOGRAPHY

Alson, Peter. *Take Me to the River: A Wayward and Perilous Journey to the World Series of Poker.* New York: Atria, 2006.

Alvarez, A. *The Biggest Game in Town.* New York: Houghton Mifflin, 1983.

———. *Poker: Bets, Bluffs, and Bad Beats.* San Francisco: Chronicle, 2001.

Apostolico, David. *Machiavellian Poker Strategy: How to Play Like a Prince and Rule the Poker Table.* New York: Lyle Stuart, 2005.

Austen, Jake, ed. *A Friendly Game of Poker: 52 Takes on the Neighborhood Game.* Chicago: Chicago Review Press, 2003.

Auster, Paul. *The Music of Chance.* New York: Viking, 1990.

Bennet, Rick. *King of a Small World.* New York: Arcade, 1995.

Brown, Aaron. *The Poker Face of Wall Street.* Hoboken, NJ: John Wiley, 2006.

Brunson, Doyle. *Doyle Brunson's Super System: A Course in Power Poker.* 3rd ed. New York: Cardoza, 2002.

———. *Doyle Brunson's Super System 2.* New York: Cardoza, 2005.

Cardano, Girolamo. *The Book of My Life.* Trans. Jean Stoner. New York: NYRB Classics, 2002.

———. *The Book on Games of Chance.* Trans. Sydney Henry Gould. New York: Holt, 1961.

Cloutier, T. J., with Tom McEvoy. *Championship Pot-Limit and No-Limit Hold'em: On the Road to the World Series of Poker.* Las Vegas: Cardsmith, 1997.

Craig, Michael. *The Professor, the Banker, and the Suicide King: Inside the Richest Poker Game of All Time.* New York: Warner, 2005.

———, ed. *Full Tilt Poker Strategy Guide: Tournament Edition.* New York: Warner, 2007.

Dalla, Nolan, and Peter Alson. *One of a Kind: The Rise and Fall of Stuey "the Kid" Ungar, the World's Greatest Poker Player.* New York: Atria, 2005.

Devol, George H. *Forty Years a Gambler on the Mississippi.* 1887; Bedford, MA: Applewood Books, 1996.

Findlay, John M. *People of Chance: Gambling in American Society from Jamestown to Las Vegas.* New York: Oxford University Press, 1986.

Foote, Shelby. *The Civil War: A Narrative.* 3 vols. New York: Random House, 1958, 1963, 1974.

Frankel, Martha. *Hats & Eyeglasses: A Memoir.* New York: Tarcher, 2008.

Gilbert, Kenneth. *Alaskan Poker Stories.* Seattle: Robert D. Seal, 1958.

Gordon, Phil. *Phil Gordon's Little Green Book: Lessons and Teachings in No Limit Texas Hold'em.* New York: Simon & Schuster, 2005.

Grotenstein, Jonathan, and Storms Reback. *All-In: The (Almost) Entirely True Story of the World Series of Poker.* New York: St. Martin's, 2005.

Hansen, Gus. *Every Hand Revealed.* New York: Lyle Stuart, 2008.

Harrington, Dan, and Bill Robertie. *Harrington on Hold'em.* 6 vols. Henderson NV: Two Plus Two, 2004–2008.

Hayano, David M. *Poker Faces: The Life and Work of Professional Card Players.* Berkeley: University of California Press, 1982.

Holden, Anthony. *Big Deal: One Year as a Professional Poker Player.* New York: Viking, 1990.

———. *Bigger Deal: A Year Inside the Poker Boom.* New York: Simon & Schuster, 2007.

———. *Holden on Hold'em: How to Play and Win at the Biggest Deal in Town.* New York: Little, Brown, 2008.

Jessup, Richard. *The Cincinnati Kid.* Boston: Little, Brown, 1963.

Kahn, David. *The Reader of Gentlemen's Mail: Herbert O. Yardley and the Birth of American Codebreaking.* New Haven, CT: Yale University Press, 2004.

Konik, Michael. *Telling Lies and Getting Paid.* Las Vegas: Huntington Press, 2001.

Krieger, Lou, and Sheree Bykofsky. *Secrets the Pros Won't Tell You About Winning Hold'em Poker.* New York: Kensington, 2006.

Lears, Jackson. *Something for Nothing: Luck in America.* New York: Viking, 2003.

Lederer, Katy. *Poker Face: A Girlhood Among Gamblers.* New York: Crown, 2003.

Lessinger, Matt. *The Book of Bluffs.* New York: Warner, 2005.

Lubet, Steven. *Lawyers' Poker.* New York: Oxford University Press, 2006.

Malmuth, Mason. *Poker Essays.* Henderson, NV: Two Plus Two, 1996.

———. *Gambling Theory.* 6th ed. Henderson, NV: Two Plus Two, 2004.

Mamet, David. *American Buffalo.* New York: Grove Press, 1977.

———. *Writing in Restaurants.* New York: Penguin, 1987.

———. "Poker Party." *Los Angeles Times*, September 16, 2005.

Matros, Matt. *The Making of a Poker Player.* New York: Lyle Stuart, 2005.

May, Jesse. *Shut Up and Deal.* New York: Anchor, 1998.

McCullough, David. *Truman.* New York: Simon & Schuster, 1992.

McEvoy, Tom. *Tournament Poker.* Las Vegas: Cardsmith, 1995.

McPherson, Conor. *The Seafarer.* New York: Theatre Communications Group, 2007.

Mlodinow, Leonard. *The Drunkard's Walk: How Randomness Rules Our Lives.* New York: Pantheon, 2008.

Morgenstern, Oskar. "Cold War Is Cold Poker," *New York Times Magazine*, February 5, 1961, 14, 21–22.

Negreanu, Daniel. *Daniel Negreanu's Power Hold'em Strategy.* Las Vegas: Cardoza, 2008.

Øre, Oystein. *Cardano: The Gambling Scholar.* Princeton, NJ: Princeton University Press, 1953.

Parlett, David. *The Oxford Guide to Card Games.* New York: Oxford University Press, 1990.

Phillips, Larry W. *Zen and the Art of Poker.* New York: Plume, 1999.

Schwartz, David G. *Roll the Bones: The History of Gambling.* New York: Gotham, 2006.

Sklansky, David. *The Theory of Poker.* Henderson, NV: Two Plus Two, 1994.

———, and Mason Malmuth. *Hold'em Poker for Advanced Players.* Henderson, NV: Two Plus Two, 1999.

Spanier, David. *Total Poker.* New York: Simon & Schuster, 1979.

Stravinsky, John, ed. *Read 'Em and Weep: A Bedside Poker Companion.* New York: Harper, 2004.

Taleb, Nassim Nicholas. *Fooled by Randomness.* 2d ed. New York: Random House, 2005.

———. *The Black Swan.* New York: Random House, 2007.

Twain, Mark. *Life on the Mississippi*. 1883; New York: Penguin, 1984.

Williams, Tennessee. *A Streetcar Named Desire*. New York: Signet, 1951.

Wills, Garry. *Nixon Agonistes: The Crisis of the Self-Made Man*. Boston: Houghton Mifflin, 1970.

Yardley, Herbert O. *The Education of a Poker Player*. New York: Simon & Schuster, 1957.

ABC player. One who plays by the book or wagers in predictable patterns.

Ace-high. Five-card hand with no pair, straight, or flush; beats only a king-high hand or lower.

Aces up. Pair of aces plus any other pair. Similarly, kings up, queens up, and so on.

Action. The betting sequence; whose turn it is to check, bet, or fold. "The action's on you, sir." May also refer to the level of stakes or betting aggression. "He dominates the black-chip action at the Commerce."

Action game. One in which several players are happy to put money in the pot with drawing hands; one dominated by gamblers, as opposed to rocks who wait for big pocket pairs.

Advance action checkbox. Online box that allows you to check, fold, or bet before the action gets to you.

Advertise. Enter pots with, and eventually turn over, hole cards to show how loose or tight you are playing, ideally to be used to your advantage later on, when you'll play in the opposite fashion.

Age, or eldest hand. Early poker term for player immediately to the left of the dealer; the first to act; in modern terms, under the gun.

Aggressive. Style of play that favors betting and raising with less than premium hands.

Ajax. Ace-jack as hole cards.

AK47. Ace-king as hole cards, after the deadly Soviet submachine gun.

All blue. A club flush.

All-in. Having all your chips in the pot. "He went all-in holding ace-queen."

American Airlines. A-A as hole cards.

Angle shooter. Player attempting to win extra money with tactics of dubious legitimacy, e.g., pretending to mistakenly play out of turn. In earlier decades called a cardsharp, sharp, or sharper.

Anna Kournikova. Ace-king as hole cards, after the Russian tennis player and model who looked great but usually didn't play very well.

Ante. Small compulsory bet that all stud players must post before the hand starts. In hold'em, antes come into effect during the later stages of a tournament.

Around front. Early position.

As nas. Five-card pokerlike game played in Persia.

ATM. Automatic Teller Machine. A veritable cash station who spits out money to opponents. Such weak but well-funded players are also maligned as donkeys, fish, live ones, deadwood, yum-yums, pigeons, contributors, johns, ahi, and producers.

Avatar. Icon or caricature representing an online player.

Baby. Small card, 8 or lower.

Backdoor. Make a big hand you weren't expecting by hitting two lucky cards in a row. "Drawing to a straight, he backdoored a flush."

Backer. Someone who covers some or all of the costs of a tournament for a strong player in exchange for an agreed-upon cut of the winnings; the stronger the player, the lower the percentage he must return to his backer.

Bad beat. Have a big hand overcome on the last card by someone playing a long-shot draw. To take one is to have been sucked out on, to have lost to a lucky maniac.

Bad game. One with too many good players; one in which you are an underdog.

Badugi. Four-card version of lowball in which the best hand is A-2-3-4 of different suits.

Bellybuster. Straight draw that lacks one inside card, such as 7-8-10-J. Also called a gutshot draw, or a gutter.

Best of it. Having the odds in your favor.

Bet. Put money in the pot, hoping to either increase its size (called a value bet) or win it right there (often with a weak hand, as a bluff).

Bet into. Aggressively wager first against a player who has represented a very strong hand by her earlier action.

Bet on the come. Bet and raise before your hand is made. Also called a semi-bluff.

Bicycle. Lowest possible straight, also known as a wheel. Also, a brand of playing cards.

Big-bet poker. All games with no-limit or pot-limit structure, usually hold'em and Omaha.

Big blind. Mandatory bet posted before the flop by the player two seats to the left of the dealer. (The small blind sits one to the left of the dealer and is forced to post half the big blind.)

Big slick. Ace-king in the hole. Also called "Walking Back to Houston" (because so many players got broke with it in the big games in Dallas or Shreveport), Anna Kournikova and other names.

Big tiger. Mid-twentieth-century term for a high straight with one gap, e.g., 8-9-10-jack-king, which in some home games was accorded higher value than an actual straight.

Blackleg. Nineteenth-century term for a professional cardsharp or cheater.

Blank. Card that improves no one's hand.

Blaze. Any five picture cards; a hand recognized in parts of the nineteenth-century South; beats two pairs but loses to three of a kind.

Blind out. Lose most of your chips by posting antes and blinds, not by playing hands. A weak-passive way to exit a tournament.

Blinds. In hold'em and Omaha (also known as the flop games), the mandatory bets posted by the player one to the left of the dealer (the small blind) and two to the left (the big blind, usually twice the size of the small).

Bluff. Bet aggressively with a weak hand, thereby representing a strong one. The signature tactic of poker, though successfully deployed less often than romantics would like to believe.

Board. In hold'em or Omaha, the community cards dealt faceup in the middle of the table: first three simultaneously (called the flop), then a fourth (called the turn), then a fifth (called the river).

Board lock. The nuts. The best possible hand given the cards on the board. Also known as the boss hand, mortal nuts, absolute nuts, and (in high-low games) locka-locka.

Boat, or full boat. Full house. Three cards of one rank, two of another.

Boss trips. Highest possible three of a kind, which you hope becomes the boss full, the highest possible full house.

Bot. A computer program designed to play poker online.

Brag. Early term for bet or bluff.

Brick. Worthless card that helps, or appears to help, none of the players. Also called a rag or a blank.

Bring it in. Make the first optional bet.

Broadway. Ace-high straight.

Bubble. Cutoff point just before prize money begins to be paid in a tournament. As a verb, to finish one or two places out of the money, the worst of all possible outcomes.

Buck. Nickname for the rotating dealer's button, from the days when a buckhorn-handled knife was often used; indicates who is dealt the last card and acts last.

Buckwheat. Weak but well-funded player. According to Allen Dowling, a golden brown wheaten delicacy that causes drooling.

Bullet. Ace. Chips are also called bullets, in the sense that they are ammunition in a tabletop war.

Bully. Use a big stack of chips (instead of strong cards) to intimidate opponents.

Bump. Raise.

Burn and turn. What the dealer does before revealing the flop, turn, and river.

Burn card. Card from the top of the deck discarded by the dealer before he turns over the board cards.

Bust. Go broke, or break another player. Lose all your chips or win all of another player's. "With cowboys full, I busted his ass."

Busted hand. Four-card straight or flush that fails to "get there."

Button. Disc that rotates clockwise and indicates which player is the dealer; in games with nonplaying dealers, the button indicates which player acts last. In Harry Truman's day, it was called the buck.

Buy-in. Amount of money required to sit in a game or enter a tournament; literally, the chips you buy to put into action.

California Bible or prayer book. Poker deck.

Call. Match an opponent's bet but not raise.

Calling station. Weak player who calls far too often and is therefore almost impossible to bluff.

Cap. Make the final raise in a limit game. The number of allowable raises per round of betting varies from venue to venue, but is usually four.

Cappuccino. Cap the betting.

Card dead. Having gone a long, frustrating period without being dealt a playable hand.

Card rack. Player receiving far more than his fair share of strong hands.

Cards speak. Rule according to which a hand turned over at the showdown may be determined as the winner (or not), even if the player didn't realize it.

Case card. Last card of that rank in the deck, often the one that miraculously doubles you up or ushers you, tail between legs, to the rail.

Cash. Make the money in a tournament.

Cash game. Any nontournament poker action.

Cash in. Exchange chips for money.

Catch. Receive a card you need to make your hand.

Catch perfect. Receive exactly the card you need, such as the 4 of diamonds to complete a straight flush.

Catch up. Receive a card that gives you a better hand than the one you were drawing against.

CDU. Courtesy double up. Provided by an opponent with a bigger stack who stupidly but generously calls your all-in bet with a weak hand.

Change gears. Suddenly play much less, or much more, aggressively.

Chase. Call bets with draws instead of made hands, an especially dangerous tactic in no-limit hold'em. Chasing makes more sense in limit games, though whether it is correct always depends on the pot odds.

Check. Decline to bet when the action gets to you. Can be done only when no bets have been made by players acting before you in that round. Requires the player to either say "check" or tap the table with his hand.

Check-raise. Check when it's your turn to bet, then raise when your opponent(s) have bet. A tactic often thwarted when its intended victims also check.

Checks. Chips, usually the higher denominations.

Cheese (a piece of). Weak hand.

Chips. Clay or composite discs representing different amounts of money. Usually, red chips are worth $5, greens $25, blacks $100, purples $500.

Cinch. Unbeatable hand.

Coffee-housing. Table talk, often designed to distract opponents or to coax information from them. "Slim coffee-housed his way through the final table, until he got heads-up with Ivey."

Coin flip. Two hold'em hands all-in before the flop with a roughly equal chance of winning. A-K v. QQ is the classic example. See also *race*.

Cold. Unlucky. A run of bad cards. Not to be confused with a cold deck.

Cold-call. Call a raise without having made a bet (only possible when more than two players are in the hand).

Cold deck. Presequenced deck snuck into the game by a cheat that gives his victim the second-best hand. In *The Sting*, a cold deck allows Paul Newman to show down four jacks against Robert Shaw's four 9s. Also called a Double Duke.

Collusion. Two or more cheats using cold decks, marked cards, or under-the-table signals, or playing online from, for example, the same college dorm room and sharing information about their hole cards.

Come over the top. Reraise, usually with a dramatic number of chips. Also called playing back or, simply, coming. Not to be confused with betting on the come.

Connectors. Two or more hole cards in sequence, such as 9-10 in hold'em or 10-J-Q-K in Omaha.

Coordinated board. Community cards that make straights or flushes possible.

Court cards. Jacks, queens, and kings.

Cover. Have more chips than your opponent in a hand.

Cowboy. King.

Cranberry. A $25,000 Bellagio chip, named for its dominant color.

Crying call. Call with a hand you think has a small chance of winning, or when long pot odds mathematically "force" you to call, especially if you complain while doing so.

CTC. Call to crack. Call a preflop bet with the intention of making a hand that beats, for example, pocket aces, hoping to bust the rock who waited for them so darn patiently and very well might overplay them.

Cutoff seat. Last to act before the dealer or button.

Dance. Fight for the chips in the pot. "Anyone else wanna dance?"

Dead card. One no longer in play because of a misdeal or other irregularity.

Dead hand. One no longer in play because a player folded it, or exposed it too soon, often by accident.

Dead man's hand. Aces and eights, after Wild Bill Hickok, who was gunned down from behind in August 1876 (in Deadwood) while holding it.

Dead money. Buy-ins of players supposed to have no chance of winning prize money; chips put into the pot by a player who later folded.

Deadwood. Town in Dakota where Wild Bill Hickok was gunned down while playing poker. Also, the pile of discards and folded hands in the center of the table.

Dealer. Person who shuffles the deck, deals the cards, and pushes the pots to those holding the winning hands. In most home games, the players take turns dealing; in casinos, nonplaying professionals deal. According to Barry Greenstein, dealers "are just the messengers of poker hands, but are often blamed for the message."

Dealer's choice. Game in which each player, in turn, chooses the variant to be played while he deals.

Deuce. A 2; the lowest card, after a nickname for the devil.

Dime or dime ball. $1,000. A big dime could refer to $10,000, $100,000, or any $100 followed by zeros.

Dog. Underdog.

Dominate. Have a heavily favored hand, such as kings against queens. When two hold'em hands share a common card, such as A-K and A-Q, the former hand dominates.

Donkey or donk. Very bad poker player; a dumb ass.

Double bellybuster. Sequence of five cards, such as 4-6-7-8-10, with two gaps, either of which can be filled to make a straight. Gives you the same eight outs as an open-ended straight draw but is more easily disguised.

Double Duke. Nineteenth-century term for a cold deck.

Down cards. Hole cards, kept face-down until the showdown.

Doyle Brunson. 10-2 as hole cards. Also, the author of *Super System* and two-time world champion, who won in 1975 and '76 while holding those cards.

Draw. Four cards to a straight or a flush, with one or two cards still to be revealed. As a verb: remain in a hand hoping to complete a straight or flush.

Draw dead. Have no chance to make the best hand, even with cards still to come; draw to a straight, for example, when another player already has a flush or full house.

Draw fat. Have numerous outs; that is, have many cards still in the deck that would win you the pot; to have, for example, top pair and both a straight draw and a flush draw, when all you need to beat is two pairs.

Draw out on. Make a big hand on the river, defeating a hand that was leading until that point. See also *bad beat*.

Draw poker. Variant in which players are dealt five cards facedown and have the option of replacing up to four of them to make a stronger hand.

Draw thin. Have a very small number of outs.

Ducks. Deuces; 2s. "With ducks on the pond, and two in my hand, I checked."

Dutch or Skipping straight. Such as 2-4-6-8-10, which beats two pairs but loses to three of a kind and a Blaze; recognized mainly in the nineteenth-century South.

Early position. The first three or four players to act in a nine- or ten-handed game.

El Paso. Fold, as in, "I pass." Pasadena and Pasolini mean the same thing.

EPT. European Poker Tour.

EV. Expected value. What a hand would be expected to win if it were played out thousands of times. All-in before the flop, K-K will win 80 percent of the time against 9-9. Three-handed, K-K has 65.28 percent EV, 10-10 has 19.21 percent, and 7-7 has 15.28 percent.

Eyes of Texas. Aces in the hole.

Family pot. One with several players, sometimes everyone at the table, seeing the flop. Also called multiway action. Much more common in limit than in no-limit hold'em.

Fast. A loose game with a lot of action. To play fast is to bet aggressively with a wide variety of hands; to go for broke.

Favorite. Hand likeliest to win at a showdown.

Fifth Street. Fifth and final community card in hold'em, usually called the river. In stud, the fifth card dealt to each player, after which the size of the bets doubles.

Fill, or Fill up. Complete a full house.

Fish. Weak but well-funded player; a sucker; a donkey. If you look around the table and don't know who it is . . .

Flag. Red, white, and blue Bellagio chip worth $5,000.

Flat-call. Call when a raise is expected. See also *slowplay* and *smooth call*.

Float. Call a bet on the flop with a weak hand, with the intention of bluffing on the turn or river.

Floorman or -person. Card room official who enforces rules and settles disputes.

Flop. First three community cards, exposed simultaneously. As a verb, to make a strong hand by combining these cards with your hole cards. "He flopped a set of jacks but just checked."

Flop lag. Hitting your hand but only after you folded before the flop; or having the current flop improve your hole cards from the previous hand.

Flush. Five cards of one suit. Beats a straight and three of a kind, loses to a full house. Originally called a flux by brag players.

Fold. Decline to call a bet. Requires that you push your cards into the muck, thereby relinquishing any chance to win the pot.

Four of a kind. Extremely strong hand that loses only to a straight flush or a higher four of a kind. Also called quads.

Fourth Street. Fourth community card. Also known as the turn.

Four tits. Queen-queen as hole cards.

Free card. A new card you didn't have to call a bet to see. "We'd all checked the flop, so he turned that third seven for free."

Freeroll. Compete with other people's money. "After winning a supersatellite, she was freerolling in the Big One." Also, when two players have tied hands, such as K-K v. K-K, but a flush draw on the board gives the player with the king of that suit a chance to win the pot.

Freezeout. Tournament without rebuys played until one contestant has all the chips.

Full. Full house.

Full house. Three cards of one rank, two of another. Called a "full hand" until the middle of the twentieth century.

Game selection. Choosing a game or table you're likely to win at.

Game theory. Branch of mathematics designed to evaluate decision-making when two or more parties have competing interests, have incomplete information, and are able to employ deception.

Get there. Make your hand. "I needed a club that didn't pair the board, and I got there."

Give action. Call bets against an aggressive player when your own hand is not yet very strong.

Gone goose. Someone about to lose a big pot, often big enough to contain all his chips.

Good game. One that features bad players.

GPSTS. Global Poker Strategic Thinking Society.

Grinder. Subsistence pro who grinds out a meager living at lower-stakes games.

Gutshot. Inside straight draw, such as 5-6-8-9. With only four outs to complete it (the four 7s), a gutshot draw is half as likely to get there as an open-ended or up-and-down straight draw, such as 4-5-6-7.

Heads-up. Action between only two players.

Hero call. Call of a large bet with a mediocre hand.

High draw. Five-card draw poker in which the highest hand wins; the most popular variant for most of the nineteenth and much of the twentieth century.

High-low. Variant in which the highest and lowest hand split the pot.

Highway 5. Fifth street, or the river. The final community card in hold'em or Omaha, or the fifth card in stud.

Hold'em. Variant, thought to have originated in Texas, in which each player receives two hole cards, to be combined with five community cards (revealed in a 3-1-1 pattern) to make the best five-card hand.

Hold out. Illegally hide cards, up your sleeve for example, to be inserted later on in your poker hand to make it stronger.

Hole cards. Pocket cards dealt facedown.

Hollywood. Make a big production of thinking long and hard, staring down your opponent, and behaving like you don't want to call, especially when preparing to make a huge raise.

Hooks. Jacks.

H.O.R.S.E. Acronym for a mixed game of hold'em, Omaha eight-or-better, razz, stud, and stud eight-or-better.

Horseshoe. Shortened name of Binion's Horseshoe, a hotel-casino in downtown Las Vegas founded by Benny Binion in 1951 and home of the World Series of Poker from 1970 to 2004. Also, a heavy, clangorous, U-shaped, forged-metal item of equine hoofware that a dumb-lucky poker player may be fairly accused of having lodged up his ass.

Ignorant end. Low end of a straight. Not a bad hand, but one that is often beaten by a higher straight.

Implied pot odds. Ratio of the amount of money you expect to win (on later streets if you make your hand) to the size of the bet you must call to continue drawing to it. Can be much higher in no-limit than in limit action.

Inside straight draw. Sequence of four connecting cards with a gap in it, such as 8-9-J-Q, which requires a 10 to make a straight. Also called a gutshot draw or bellybuster draw.

Internet player. Often derogatory term for a novice who won an online satellite but is deemed unworthy of competing in a high-stakes on-land event against seasoned professionals. Sophisticated moves are thought to be lost on these players: they chase foolish long shots and cannot be bluffed. The term is used less often as more and more experts play for high stakes on the Internet.

In the tank. Where you go (in your head) for a minute or two while weighing a tough decision, as in a think tank.

Isolate. Raise with the intention of reducing the number of players in the hand to a single opponent.

Jesse James. 4-5 as hole cards, after the outlaw's Colt .45 sidearm.

Johnnies. Jacks.

Kibitz. Talk while, or instead of, playing.

Kick. Raise.

Kicker. Side card accompanying a pair, two pairs, or three of a kind; the higher kicker often determines who wins the pot.

Knave. Jack.

Knee action. Signals given under the table by players involved in illegal collusion.

Lammer. Chip used only to buy into or to play in a tournament.

Late position. The last two or three players to act.

Lay down. Fold a strong hand. "With a four hearts on the board, she decided to lay down her straight." As a noun: "His tough laydown saved him the rest of his stack."

Leak. Bad poker habit that causes you to lose money.

Level. Interval in a tournament during which the blinds (and, in the latter stages, the antes) are a fixed amount, before being raised to the next level. Usually, the higher a tournament's buy-in, the longer its levels.

Limit poker. Variants in which the betting amounts are fixed.

Limp. Enter a pot by calling the big blind instead of raising. "Four limpers got to see the flop." More common in limit than in no-limit poker, wherein "loose limps sink chips."

Little slick: A-Q or K-Q suited as hole cards in hold'em.

Live action. Game at a single table played without escalating blinds, as opposed to tournament action. Also called side action, especially when a tournament is under way in the same casino.

Live one. Weak but well-funded opponent. A fish.

Lock. Unbeatable hand.

Locka-locka. The nut high and nut low in high-low variants.

Loose. Raising and calling bets with a wide range of weak hole cards; calling bets when the pot odds fail to justify it.

Loose-passive. Calling with a wide range of hands; failing to raise with anything less than the nuts.

Lowball. Variants in which the lowest hand wins.

M. Ratio of a tournament player's chip stack to the total of antes and blinds per round, after Paul Magriel, its coiner, as described in Dan Harrington's *Harrington on Hold'em* series. The lower your M, the more strongly you should consider going all-in, instead of making a standard bet.

Made hand. Strong hand, such as three of a kind or a flush, no longer requiring a card to complete it. Also called a real hand.

Make the deck. Shuffle.

Maniac. Loose, reckless player.

Mark. Sucker; fish.

Mechanic. Dealer who cheats by dexterously manipulating the sequence of cards in the deck to his own or a partner's advantage.

Middle position. In a nine-handed game, the fourth and fifth players to the right of the button.

Min-raise. The smallest raise possible. A raise to $800 when the blinds are $200 and $400.

Monster. Extremely strong hand, very often the nuts.

Motorhead. The spade ace, after the British metal band and their sulfurous classic "The Ace of Spades."

Move. Large bet without a strong hand. "I sensed she was putting a move on me, so I reraised all-in. I was wrong."

Move in. Bet all your chips, usually as a raise or a reraise.

Muck. Scattered pile of previously folded cards facedown in front of the dealer. Cards touching any part of this pile are dead. As a verb: push your hole cards into this pile. "As soon as I reraised, he mucked."

Multiway pot. Involves three or more players. Called a family pot when seven or eight are involved.

Nit. Neurotically conservative or unsociable player; someone who wins a few dollars early and immediately gets up from the table, or who insists that niggling aspects of the rules or etiquette be enforced.

NLH or NLHE. No-limit hold'em.

No-limit. Betting structure in which a player can wager all the chips he has in front of him.

Nut, or the nuts. Highest possible hand given the community cards. If neither a pair nor three of a suit appear on the board, the highest possible straight is the nuts. Also called a lock, a cinch, the mortal nuts, the stone cold nuts.

Nut-nut. To hold, in Omaha or stud high-low, the best possible high and low hands.

Off-suit. Pocket cards of different suits. Also called unsuited.

Omaha. Variant in which players receive four cards facedown, any two of which must be combined with three of the five community cards. Often played high-low eight-or-better, in which the high and low hands split the pot and all five low cards must be smaller than 9. The most popular form is pot-limit Omaha played for high only.

On the bubble. Low on chips in one of the last few places before prize money is awarded. The Bubble Boy (or Girl) is the last player eliminated without getting paid.

On the come. Betting or calling before your drawing hand is made.

On tilt. Play poorly because you're upset about previous hands. Also called steaming.

Open. Make the first bet.

Open stakes. Outmoded rule permitting players to bet more money than they have on the table; to bet their ranch or plantation, for example, by placing the deed in the pot. In extreme cases, such as in *A Big Hand for the Little Lady*, to take your cards across the street for a bank loan in the middle of a hand.

OTF. Out there flappin'. Play in a wild, undisciplined manner.

Outflop. Make a better hand on the flop than your opponent, especially when the opponent's hand was stronger preflop.

Outkicked. Lose a pot while holding the same highest pair as another player because your second card, your kicker, is lower than your opponent's.

Out of position. Forced to act before your opponent(s).

Outs. Unseen cards that could complete a winning hand. If you hold four diamonds, the nine other diamonds give you nine outs to a flush. But if your opponent has a set or two pairs, you may in fact have only six or seven "real" or "good" outs.

Overbet. Bet more than the size of the pot.

Overcall. Call made after another player has already called a bet.

Overcard. Any card in your hand higher than the highest card on the board; or any card on the board higher than the pair in your hand.

Overpair. Pocket pair higher than any card on the board.

Over the top. Reraise.

Over-under. Dividing line for bettors who choose whether the outcome will exceed or fall short of it. "The over-under for the winner's age is 49."

Paint. Any jack, queen, or king.

Pair. Two cards of the same rank.

Pass. Fold.

Passive. Rarely bet or raise without a big hand.

Perfect-perfect. Two miracle cards in a row that give a player exactly what he needs to win a pot, e.g., two cards that complete a straight flush when an opponent has the ace-high flush, a full house, or quads.

Pip. Icon or mark on a card indicating its rank. The 5 of hearts has five red heart-shaped pips, for example. Also 3-3 in the hole, after Scottie Pippen, number 33 for the Chicago Bulls, who retired his number in 2005.

Play back. Raise or, especially, reraise.

Player of the Year. *Card Player*'s computerized ranking system for tournament success, based on finishes at or near the top of events, weighted in favor of larger buy-ins and fields.

Play it as it lays. A declaration that the full value of, say, a $5,000 chip has been wagered, not some smaller fraction of its value.

Play the board. Show down a hold'em hand that doesn't improve on the five community cards.

Pocket cards. Hole cards.

Pocket rockets. Aces in the hole. Also known as asses, bullets, Fric and Frac, steeples, sticks, and other affectionate monikers.

Position. Your place in the clockwise rotation with respect to the dealer. Those first to act are in early position; those who act later have the advantage of knowing whether and how much you've bet. "He had position on me, so I folded my suited connectors."

Post. Put the small or large blind (and/or the ante) into the pot before any cards are dealt.

Pot. Chips at stake in the center of the table. Also, the maximum bet in a pot-limit game.

Pot-committed. Having such a high percentage of your chips already in the pot that it would be incorrect to fold no matter what cards appeared or what the next bet was.

Pot-limit. Structure that prohibits bets larger than the current size of the pot but makes possible very large bets on the later streets.

Pot odds. Ratio of the money in the pot to the amount you must put in to remain in the hand.

P.O.Y. Player of the Year.

Presto. 5-5 in the hole.

Prop. Proposition player hired by the house to help games get started and fill seats at short tables to keep those games from breaking up.

Put on. Make an educated guess about an opponent's hand, based on his betting patterns or physical tells. "I'd put him on ace-king, so when the flop came with babies, I bet."

Quads. Four of a kind.

Quartered. Split half the pot in a high-low game. It is also possible to be sixthed or even eighthed.

Race. When a no-limit hold'em player is all-in before the flop against a single opponent with a hand roughly equal in value to his, such as Q-Q v. A-K or Q-10

v. 6-6. Once the two hands are turned faceup, it is the dealer—or the random order of the shuffled deck, or Lady Luck—who decides which player wins the pot. Note that Q-Q v. J-J is *not* a race, because the overpair is about an 80 percent favorite. Only when neither hand is more than a 55 percent favorite is the matchup considered a race. Also called a coin flip.

Rag. Small card not helpful to your hand. Also called a blank.

Railbird. Spectator.

Rainbow. Flop with three different suits, or a five-card board without three of one suit.

Raise. Not only match an opponent's bet but increase it by at least 100 percent.

Rake. Percentage of each pot or tournament buy-in removed by the house to cover its expenses and turn a profit.

Razz. Form of seven-card stud in which the lowest hand wins.

Read. Study body language, eyes, or betting patterns for a tell, to help determine the strength of an opponent's hand.

Rebuy. Purchase another set of chips, assuming the tournament's format permits it. In 2009, the WSOP eliminated all rebuy tournaments from its schedule. In cash games, of course, rebuying remains common practice.

Represent. Pretend, via bet size and body language, to have a particular hand: a flush with three or four hearts on the board, for example.

Reraise. Raise a player who has already raised on that round of betting.

Reverse implied pot odds. Ratio of the amount of money you might lose if you don't make your hand to the size of the bet you must call to continue drawing to it.

Ring game. Nontournament poker played at one table, in which the chips are worth real money and can be cashed in at any time. Also called a side game, a cash game, or live action.

River. Fifth and final community card, also known as Fifth Street in hold'em. As a verb, to make your hand on that card. "She rivered a little flush to beat my set of queens." A river rat is vermin who does this too often, or a bad card that jumps up and bites you.

Rock. Solid, conservative player who seldom enters pots without a strong starting hand.

Rotation. Nineteenth-century term for a straight.

Rounder. Professional who plays for high stakes, often traveling far and wide to find the best games.

Round-the-corner straight. Nonstandard hand such as Q-K-A-2-3, which beats three of a kind but loses to a regular straight; recognized mainly in the nineteenth-century South.

Royal. Ace-high straight flush, the highest possible hand.

Runner-runner. Two consecutive lucky cards on the final two streets that make someone's hand.

Running (good or bad). On a winning or losing streak.

Saddam. The ace of spades, after Saddam Hussein's card in the Iraqi Most Wanted decks issued to U.S. armed forces in 2003 to help them track down fifty-two senior members of the Ba'ath Party.

Sandbag. Slowplay; play timidly in the early rounds of betting while holding a very strong hand, to avoid scaring other players out of the pot.

Satellite. Small tournament, usually one table, that awards a seat in a larger tournament to a single winner.

Scare card. A third jack or fourth club on the board, for example, making it much more likely that someone has a very big hand. Often used by bluffers to represent a big hand.

Scared money. Player with a too-small bankroll who plays too cautiously as a result.

See. Call a bet.

Semibluff. Bet or raise with a hand you don't think is the best one at the moment but which has a reasonable chance of improving to the best hand. Also called bluffing with outs.

Set. Pocket pair that combines with the board to make three of a kind. Note that a pair on the board matching a card in your hand is called trips. Because only one card of the three appears on the board, a set is more easily disguised and cannot be duplicated, and is therefore more valuable.

Set in. Bet as much as your opponent has left in front of him; put him all-in, should he call.

Set over set. When a set beats a lower set.

Short stack. Stack of chips much smaller than the average stack at the table, or in the tournament.

Show down. Turn over your pocket cards to compare the strength of your hand with the hands of other players still in the pot. At the *showdown*, after all bets are completed, the best five-card poker hand wins.

Shut down. Stop betting when a scare card comes, or when you think you are behind.

Shut out. Force an opponent out of a pot (or "off his hand") with a large bet.

Side action. Cash game when a tournament is in progress. Also called live action or a ring game.

Side pot. In a multiway pot, when one player is all-in and others have enough chips to keep betting, the new bets go into a side pot, which can be won only by a player who has contributed chips to it.

Simpleton. Early term for a weak, stupid player; a donkey.

Sit-and-go (SNG). A very small tournament, usually online and involving one table, though sometimes as many as five.

Skipper. Straight with every other card in a sequence, such as 6-8-10-Q-A, which nineteenth-century house rules sometimes declared was the second-best possible hand, losing only to a skipper flush (or to five of a kind when the joker was played as a wild card).

Slowplay. Check or only call an opponent's bet while holding a strong hand, in hopes of winning more money from him on later betting rounds. Also called trapping or sandbagging.

Slowroll. Pause for a moment or two before turning over the nuts; a taunting maneuver practiced by players without any class.

Small blind. Sits one to the left of the dealer in flop games; forced to post (or bet "blind") half of the big blind; forced to act first on all subsequent betting rounds.

Smooth call. Call when a raise is expected. See also *slowplay*.

Snap off. Reraise a bluffer.

Sockalay. Mid-twentieth-century term for a player who commands respect.

Softplay. Play very passively against a friend. Because this is unfair to the other players, it is illegal in casinos and public card rooms.

Spike. Appear unexpectedly on the board, making a big hand for one of the players. "She spiked a deuce to run down my jacks."

Splash around. Play loose, unfocused poker, tossing lots of chips into pots you have a small chance of winning.

Splash the pot. Carelessly throw your bet forward, causing some of the chips to enter the pot, making the size of your bet impossible to count.

Squeeze. Slowly and minutely fan your hole cards, one at a time, scanning only the far left edge of the letter or number.

Steal. Bet enough chips to cause all opponents to fold, especially when your own hand is weak. "She's been stealing blinds all afternoon."

Steam. Play too aggressively because you are angry. See also *tilt*.

Steel wheel. 5-high straight flush.

Straddle. Make a blind bet on the button or under the gun of twice the big blind; the straddler then has the option to raise when the action gets back around to him. Not legal in tournaments.

String bet. Illegal action that involves going back to your stack midbet for additional chips. Can be easily avoided by verbally declaring the size of your bet before your hand first moves forward.

Stub. The undealt portion of the deck.

Stuck. Losing money.

Stud. Form of poker played without community cards. In seven-card stud, the commonest version today, each player receives two cards facedown, four cards faceup, and the final card facedown. Allows for fewer players than hold'em, and requires a better short-term memory. In five-card stud, each player receives one card facedown, four cards faceup.

Suck out. Complete a lucky draw on the river, especially with a hand a smart player would have folded earlier.

Suited. Having pocket cards of the same suit. Weak players tend to overestimate the added value of a suited hand, especially in no-limit hold'em.

Suited connectors. Suited and consecutive pocket cards; the jack and queen of clubs, for example.

Super-satellite. Multitable tournament that awards seats in a later event with a buy-in roughly ten times as large.

Sweat. Watch a friend play, from a seat as close behind him as possible.

Table stakes. The near-universal rule that allows only the chips or money on the table before a hand began to be bet during that hand.

Take a card off. Call a bet with a drawing hand, hoping to improve.

Tap city. Busted, broke, down to the felt.

Tell. Nervous tic, mannerism, or habit that helps opponents read the strength of your hand. "He had tells from here to Las Vegas."

Throw a party. Lose a lot of money, often because of a tell.

Tiger. Seven-high hand without any pair, straight, or flush, which beats a straight but loses to a flush; recognized mainly in the nineteenth-century South.

Tight. Conservative, unimaginative play. A player who waits patiently for strong hole cards before entering a pot.

Tight-aggressive. Combines conservative starting-hand requirements with vigorous betting on the few hands actually played.

Tilt, or on tilt. Play badly because angry or frustrated. Also called steaming.

Timing. Having the best hand when it counts, often in a huge pot against two or more opponents. Or the opposite: having a weak hand in the clutch, or having pockets aces in the big blind and watching everyone fold to you.

T. J. Cloutier. The 9-J (not 10-J) of clubs in the hole, after the former Cal and CFL tight end and linebacker and the man with the most poker tournament wins.

Toke. Tip for the dealer.

Torture. Make big bets against an opponent whose hand is clearly beaten, even if it's not clear to the victim.

Trap. Check, or smooth call, to disguise a strong hand.

Trash hand. Bad cards.

Trey. 3.

Trips. Three of a kind, usually with one in your hand, two on the board; not to be confused with a set. Called triplets, or triplettes, in poker's early decades.

Trouble hand. Fairly strong hole cards that are often second-best when the pot becomes large. K-J suited, for example.

Turn. Fourth community card; also called Fourth Street. As a verb, to make one's hand with that card. "She turned a set of treys to beat his two pairs."

Uday and Qusay. Pocket aces, after the former Hussein heirs apparent depicted (as the ace of hearts and ace of clubs, respectively) in the Iraqi Most Wanted decks.

Underdog. Hand not a favorite to win at a showdown.

Underpair. Any pair smaller than at least one card on the board; assumes that another player has (or may have) paired that card.

Under the gun (UTG). Position of the player forced to act first. In flop games, the player sitting to the left of the big blind before the flop, to the left of the dealer thereafter; in stud, the one to the left of the bring-in.

Unsuited. Hole cards of different suits.

Up. Word following the larger of two pairs when declaring your hand. A player with two kings and a smaller pair has "kings up."

Value bet. Wager made while holding a strong hand, in hopes of increasing the size of the pot to be won. While a bluffer needs his opponent to fold, a value bettor hopes to be called.

Weapons of mass destruction. A-A as hole cards.

Whale. Big fish; bad player with plenty of money to lose.

Wheel. 5-high straight, called a steel wheel when all five cards are of the same suit.

Whipsaw. A series of bets, raises, and sometimes reraises, usually made by two players with a caller trapped between them.

Wild card. The joker or some other card that can be designated as any other card in the deck. If deuces are wild, J-J-J-2-2 becomes five jacks. Serious poker players never use wild cards anymore. No tournaments sanction them, either.

Wired. Hole cards of matching rank. "With wired cowboys, I came back over the top of him."

Worst of it. Having the odds against you. "With only eight outs, I was taking the worst of it."

WPT. World Poker Tour.

WSOP. World Series of Poker.

ACKNOWLEDGMENTS

Sine quibus non: Jonathan "the Translator" Galassi, Gena "the Greek" Hamshaw, Sloan "Honcho" Harris.

Those without whom little good would have come of all this: Jeff Seroy, Kathy Daneman, Spenser Lee, Jesse Coleman, Cynthia Merman, Lisa Silverman, Debbie Glasserman, Ben White, Lorin Stein, and Susan Mitchell at Farrar, Straus and Giroux. Kristyn Keene and Ron Bernstein at ICM.

For poker insight, I thank Crandell Addington, Eric Adelstein, Ulvis Alberts, Peter Alson, Al Alvarez, Jay Barasch, Amarillo Shawnee Barton, Ali Binazir, Aaron Brown, Doyle and Todd Brunson, Avery Cardoza, Action Allen Cherry, T. J. Cloutier, Jeff Cohen, Michael Craig, Nolan Dalla, Troy Denkinger, Raj Desai, Eric Drache, Art Duncan, Bob and Maureen Feduniak, Chris Ferguson, Jennifer Harman, Anthony Holden, Gabe Kaplan, Jim Karamanis, Curt Kohlberg, Steve Krex, Howard Lederer, Justin Marchand, Mansour Matloubi, Jack McClelland, Tom McEvoy, Terry McManus, Minneapolis Jim Meahan, Dan Michalski, Rock Solid Mike, Charles Nesson, Brett Nichols, Bob Pajich, Chiro Steve Paul, Erik Seidel, Mike Sexton, Pamela Shandel, Norm Silverman, Allyn and Barry Shulman, Jeff Shulman, Michael Wiesenberg, Pilot Dave Williamson, Bob Wilson, Des Wilson, Ken Wolfe, Andrew Woods, and Steve Zolotow.

For help and encouragement, I'm grateful to June Arra, Paul Ashley, John and Sheri Calarco, Chris Calhoun, Wendy Chang, Frances Coady, Billy Collins, Christopher Dickey, Sam Douglas, Tanya Farrell, Gary Feinerman, Shawn Gillen, Bob Harris, Colin Harrison, Jeanine Jiganti, Geoff Johnson, Darin Keesler, David Kerns, Beth Kohl, Jonathan Landman, Jay Lovinger, Trixie McGillicuddy, Brian McManus, Bridget McManus, Ellen McManus, Grace McManus, Mary McManus, James Meader, Jeff Miller, Susan Morrison, Bob Newman, Fred Novy, Steve Radulovich, David Remnick, George Roeder, David Schwartz, Michelle and Steve Schragel, Master Steven Smith, Fisher Stevens, Glenn Stout, Jeffrey Toobin, Scott Turow, David Ulin, Brendan Vaughan, Scott Veale, David and Keegan Yaccino.

INDEX